Introduction
to Old English

Introduction
to Old English

Peter S. Baker

Blackwell
Publishing

350 Main Street, Malden, MA 02148-5018, USA
108 Cowley Road, Oxford OX4 1JF, UK
550 Swanston Street, Carlton South, Melbourne, Victoria 3053, Australia
Kurfürstendamm 57, 10707 Berlin, Germany

First published 2003 by Blackwell Publishing Ltd

Library of Congress Cataloging-in-Publication Data has been applied for

ISBN 0-631-23453-5 (hardback); ISBN 0-631-23454-3 (paperback)

A catalogue record for this title is available from the British Library.

Set in 10/12^1/$_2$pt Minion
by Graphicraft Limited, Hong Kong
Printed and bound in the United Kingdom
by MPG Books Ltd, Bodmin, Cornwall

For further information on
Blackwell Publishing, visit our website:
http://www.blackwellpublishing.com

Contents

Further Reading

Index

Preface

This *Introduction to Old English* is for students whose interests are primarily literary or historical rather than linguistic. It aims to provide such students with a guide to the language that is detailed enough to enable them to read with facility, but it omits a great deal of the historical linguistic material that has traditionally been included even in beginning grammars. The linguistic material that the student needs in order to read Old English well is presented here as morphological feature rather than as historical 'sound change'. For example, *i*-mutation is understood as one of several ways of inflecting nouns, verbs, adjectives and adverbs. Its origin as a phonological change is treated briefly, as a sidelight rather than as an essential fact. Students who are interested in learning more about the history of the English language than is presented here may consult one of the grammars or linguistics texts listed in the References (pp. 318–19) and discussed under Further Reading (pp. 324–7).

This book assumes as little as possible about the student's knowledge of traditional grammar and experience of learning languages. Technical terminology is avoided where possible, and, where unavoidable, it is defined in simple terms. A brief grammar review is provided for those who need help with grammatical terminology.

The contents of this book are accessible via the Internet. The grammar may be consulted at the website of the Richard Rawlinson Center for Anglo-Saxon Studies at Western Michigan University (http://www.wmich.edu/medieval/rawl/index.html) or at that of Blackwell Publishing (http://www.blackwellpublishing.com/), and the texts in the anthology are available on-line at the *Old English Aerobics* website (http://www.engl.virginia.edu/OE/

OEA/). Additional texts will be added to the *Old English Aerobics* website from time to time; these will be presented in such a way that they can either be used on-line or printed as a supplement to this book. The author and his publishers expect that students will find it a convenience to have this material available via the Internet as well as in printed form.

I would like to thank both the Rawlinson Center and Blackwell Publishing for agreeing to an innovative publishing venture. I would also like to thank James R. Hall of the University of Mississippi, Dan Wiley of Hastings College, and an anonymous reader for the Rawlinson Center for a number of valuable suggestions. Most of all I am indebted to my students at the University of Virginia who for the past two years have used this book and helped me to refine it. Among these students I am especially grateful to Samara Landers and John Bugbee for specific suggestions.

P. S. B.

How to use this book

This book can be read in any of several ways. If you have a great deal of experience learning languages, you may wish to read through from beginning to end, possibly skipping chapter 3. If you are like most students, though, reading about grammar is not your favourite activity, and you'd like to get started reading Old English texts as quickly as possible. In that case, you should first read the 'Quick Start' sections that begin most chapters. Then you may begin to read easy texts such as the 'minitexts' scattered through the book and 'The Fall of Adam and Eve' (reading 1 in the Anthology). As you read these Old English texts, go back and read the rest of chapters 2 and 5–12.

Once you have finished reading chapters 2–12, you are ready for the more advanced texts in the Anthology. Remember, as you read, that it is important to make liberal use of the glossary. Look up not only words you do not know, but also words you do know that seem to be used awkwardly, for these may not mean what you think they do. If you are not sure you have identified the words correctly, check the list of references in the glossary entry to see if the word is there. The glossary lists the grammatical forms of words that can be inflected; you may check the number, person and other characteristics of words by locating forms in these lists, but remember that the glossary's 'parsing' is no substitute for learning inflections.

This book contains over 200 short passages illustrating grammatical and other points. As you encounter these passages, you may find it profitable to look up words exactly as if you were reading a minitext or one of the texts in the anthology – all words in even the shortest passages are registered in the glossary. Consult the accompanying translations to check your understanding of the grammar and sense of the Old English; if you find you have mis-understood a passage, use the translation to help you puzzle it out. Following this procedure will speed your acquisition of the language and improve your comprehension.

As you read, you will notice that some paragraphs are boxed with an exclamation mark in the margin. These paragraphs contain valuable tips and sometimes also alert you to possible pitfalls. You will also notice that some paragraphs are set in small type and marked with an *i* in a circle. These communicate useful or interesting information that you may not need to know right away. If one of these paragraphs looks confusing, skip it now and return to it later.

No one book on Old English has everything you need. Consult the list of references and the 'Further Reading' section in the back of this book to start reading in areas that interest you.

Chapter 1

The Anglo-Saxons and Their Language

1.1 Who were they?

'Anglo-Saxon' is the term applied to the English-speaking inhabitants of Britain up to the time of the Norman Conquest, when the Anglo-Saxon line of English kings came to an end. The people who were conquered in 1066 had themselves arrived as conquerors more than six centuries earlier.

According to the Venerable Bede, whose *Historia Ecclesiastica Gentis Anglorum* (Ecclesiastical History of the English People), completed in the year 735, is the most important source for the early history of England, the Anglo-Saxons arrived in the island of Britain during the reign of Martian, who in 449 became co-emperor of the Roman Empire with Valentinian III and ruled for seven years.

Before that time, Britain had been inhabited by Celtic peoples: the Scots and Picts in the north, and in the south various groups which had been united under Roman rule since their conquest by the emperor Claudius in AD 43. By the beginning of the fifth century the Roman Empire was under increasing pressure from advancing barbarians, and the Roman garrisons in Britain were being depleted as troops were withdrawn to face threats closer to home. In AD 410, the same year in which the Visigoths entered and sacked Rome, the last of the Roman troops were withdrawn and the Britons had to defend themselves. Facing hostile Picts and Scots in the north and Germanic raiders in the east, the Britons decided to hire one enemy to fight the other: they engaged Germanic mercenaries to fight the Picts and Scots.

It was during the reign of Martian that the newly hired mercenaries arrived. These were from three Germanic nations situated near the northern coasts of Europe: the Angles, the Saxons and the Jutes. According to Bede, the mercenaries succeeded quickly in defeating the Picts and Scots and then sent word to their homes of the fertility of the island and the cowardice of the Britons. They soon found a pretext to break with their employers, made an alliance with the Picts, and began to conquer the territory that would eventually be known as England – a slow-moving conquest that would take more than a century.

It is now difficult to measure the accuracy of Bede's account of the coming of the Anglo-Saxons. But Bede's story gives us essential information about how these people looked at themselves: they considered themselves a warrior people, and they were proud to have been conquerors of the territory they inhabited. Indeed, the warrior ethic that pervades Anglo-Saxon culture is among the first things that students notice on approaching the field.

But Europe had no shortage of warrior cultures in the last half of the first millennium. What makes Anglo-Saxon England especially worthy of study is the remarkable literature that flourished there. The Anglo-Saxon kingdoms converted to Christianity in the late sixth and seventh centuries, and by the late seventh and early eighth centuries had already produced two major authors: Aldhelm, who composed his most important work, *De Virginitate* (On Virginity), twice, in prose and in verse; and the Venerable Bede, whose vast output includes biblical commentaries, homilies, textbooks on orthography, metre, rhetoric, nature and time, and of course the *Historia Ecclesiastica*, mentioned above. A small army of authors, Bede's contemporaries and successors, produced saints' lives and a variety of other works in prose and verse, largely on Christian themes.

These seventh- and eighth-century authors wrote in Latin, as did a great many Anglo-Saxon authors of later periods. But the Anglo-Saxons also created an extensive body of vernacular literature at a time when relatively little was being written in most of the other languages of Western Europe. In addition to such well-known classic poems as *Beowulf*, *The Dream of the Rood*, *The Wanderer*, *The Seafarer* and *The Battle of Maldon*, they left us the translations associated with King Alfred's educational programme, a large body of devotional works by such writers as Ælfric and Wulfstan, biblical translations and adaptations, *The Anglo-Saxon Chronicle* and other historical writings, law codes, handbooks of medicine and magic, and much more. While most of the manuscripts that preserve vernacular works date from the late ninth, tenth and eleventh centuries, the Anglo-Saxons were producing written work in their own language by the early seventh century, and many scholars believe that *Beowulf* and several other important poems date from the eighth century. Thus we are in possession of five centuries of Anglo-Saxon vernacular literature.

To learn more about the Anglo-Saxons, consult the 'Further Reading' section at the back of this book and choose from the works listed there: they will give you access to a wealth of knowledge from a variety of disciplines. This book will give you another kind of access, equipping you with the skills you need to encounter the Anglo-Saxons in their own language.

1.2 Where did their language come from?

Bede tells us that the Anglo-Saxons came from *Germania*. Presumably he was using that term as the Romans had used it, to refer to a vast and ill-defined territory east of the Rhine and north of the Danube, extending as far east as the Vistula in present-day Poland and as far north as present-day Sweden and Norway. This territory was nothing like a nation, but rather was inhabited by numerous tribes which were closely related culturally and linguistically.[1]

The languages spoken by the inhabitants of *Germania* were a branch of the Indo-European family of languages, which linguists believe developed from a single language spoken some five thousand years ago in an area that has never been identified – perhaps, some say, the Caucasus. From this ancient language come most of the language groups of present-day Europe and some important languages of South Asia: the Celtic languages (such as Irish, Welsh and Scottish Gaelic), the Italic languages (such as French, Italian, Spanish and Romanian, descended from dialects of Latin), the Germanic languages, the Slavic languages (such as Russian and Polish), the Baltic languages (Lithuanian and Latvian), the Indo-Iranian languages (such as Persian and Hindi), and individual languages that do not belong to these groups: Albanian, Greek and Armenian. The biblical Hittites spoke an Indo-European language, or a language closely related to the Indo-European family, and a number of other extinct languages (some of them poorly attested) were probably or certainly Indo-European: Phrygian, Lycian, Thracian, Illyrian, Macedonian, Tocharian and others.

The Germanic branch of the Indo-European family is usually divided into three groups:

North Germanic, that is, the Scandinavian languages, Swedish, Danish, Norwegian, Icelandic and Faroese;

East Germanic, that is, Gothic, now extinct but preserved in a fragmentary biblical translation from the fourth century;

West Germanic, which includes High German, English, Dutch, Flemish and Frisian.

---

[1] For an early account of the Germanic tribes, see *Germania*, a work by the late first- and early second-century Roman historian Tacitus.

Within the West Germanic group, the High German dialects (which include Modern German) form a subgroup distinct from English and the other languages, which together are called 'Low German' because they were originally spoken in the low country near the North Sea.[2]

Surely the language spoken by the Germanic peoples who migrated to Britain was precisely the same as that spoken by the people they left behind on the Continent. But between the time of the migration and the appearance of the earliest written records in the first years of the eighth century, the language of the Anglo-Saxons came to differ from that of the people they had left behind. We call this distinct language Old English to emphasize its continuity with Modern English, which is directly descended from it.

1.3   What was Old English like?

We often hear people delivering opinions about different languages: French is 'romantic', Italian 'musical'. For the student of language, such impressionistic judgements are not very useful. Rather, to describe a language we need to explain how it goes about doing the work that all languages must do; and it is helpful to compare it with other languages – especially members of the language groups it belongs to.

Languages may be compared in a number of ways. Every language has its own repertory of sounds, as known by all students who have had to struggle to learn to pronounce a foreign language. Every language also has its own rules for accentuating words and its own patterns of intonation – the rising and falling pitch of our voices as we speak. Every language has its own vocabulary, of course, though when we're lucky we find a good bit of overlap between the vocabulary of our native language and that of the language we're learning. And every language has its own way of signalling how words function in utterances – of expressing who performed an action, what the action was, when it took place, whether it is now finished or still going on, what or who was acted upon, for whose benefit the action was performed, and so on.

The following sections attempt to hit the high points, showing what makes Old English an Indo-European language, a Germanic language, a West Germanic and a Low German language; and also how Old and Modern English are related.

---

[2]   The Low German languages are often called 'Ingvaeonic' after the *Ingvaeones*, a nation that, according to Tacitus, was located by the sea.

1.3.1 The Indo-European languages

The Indo-European languages do certain things in much the same way. For example, they share some basic vocabulary. Consider these words for 'father':

Old English	*fæder*	
Latin	*pater*	} *Father*
Greek	*patếr*	
Sanskrit	*pitṛ*	

You can easily see the resemblance among the Latin, Greek and Sanskrit words. You may begin to understand why the Old English word looks different from the others when you compare these words for 'foot':

Old English	*fōt*	
Latin	*pedem*	} *Foot*
Greek	*póda*	
Sanskrit	*pā́dam*	

If you suspect that Latin *p* will always correspond to Old English *f*, you are right, more or less.[3] For now, it's enough for you to recognize that the Indo-European languages do share a good bit of vocabulary, though the changes that all languages go through often bring it about that the same word looks quite different in different languages.[4]

All of the Indo-European languages handle the job of signalling the functions of words in similar ways. For example, all add endings to words. The plural form of the noun meaning 'foot' was *pódes* in Greek, *pedēs* in Latin, and *pā́das* in Sanskrit – and English *feet* once ended with -*s* as well, though that ending had already disappeared by the Old English period. Most Indo-European languages signal the function of a noun in a sentence or clause by inflecting it for case[5] (though some languages no longer do, and the only remaining trace of the case system in Modern English nouns is the possessive *'s*). And most also classify their nouns by gender – masculine, feminine or neuter (though some have reduced the number of genders to two).

---

[3] There is a complication, called 'grammatical alternation'; see §7.4.2.
[4] For example, it's not at all obvious that Modern English *four* and Latin *quattuor*, or Modern English *quick* and Latin *vivus* 'alive', come from the same Indo-European word – but they do.
[5] Inflection is the addition of an ending or a change in the form of a word (for example, the alteration of a vowel) to reflect its grammatical characteristics. See chapter 4 for a definition and explanation of case.

Indo-European languages have ways to inflect words other than by adding endings. In the verb system, for example, words could be inflected by changing their root vowels, and this ancient system of 'gradation' persists even now in such Modern English verbs as *swim* (past-tense *swam*, past participle *swum*). Words could also be inflected by shifting the stress from one syllable to another, but only indirect traces of this system remain in Old and Modern English.

1.3.2 *The Germanic languages*

Perhaps the most important development that distinguishes the Germanic languages from others in the Indo-European family is the one that produced the difference, illustrated above, between the *p* of Latin *pater* and the *f* of Old English *fæder*. This change, called 'Grimm's Law' after Jakob Grimm, the great linguist and folklorist who discovered it, affected all of the consonants called 'stops' – that is, those consonants produced by momentarily stopping the breath and then releasing it (for example, [p], [b], [t], [d]):[6]

Unvoiced stops ([p], [t], [k]) became unvoiced spirants ([f], [θ], [x]), so that Old English *fæder* corresponds to Latin *pater*, Old English *þrēo* 'three' to Latin *tres*, and Old English *habban* 'have' to Latin *capere* 'take'.
Voiced stops ([b],[7] [d], [g]) became unvoiced stops ([p], [t], [k]), so that Old English *dēop* 'deep' corresponds to Lithuanian *dubùs*, *twā* 'two' corresponds to Latin *duo* and Old English *æcer* 'field' to Latin *ager*.
Voiced aspirated stops ([bʰ] [dʰ], [gʰ])[8] became voiced stops ([b] [d], [g]) or spirants ([β], [ð], [ɣ]), so that Old English *brōðor* corresponds to Sanskrit *bhrátar-* and Latin *frater*, Old English *duru* 'door' to Latin *fores* and Greek *thúra*, and Old English *ġiest* 'stranger' to Latin *hostis* 'enemy' and Old Slavic *gosti* 'guest'.

Almost as important as these changes in the Indo-European consonant system was a change in the way words were stressed. You read in §1.3.1 that the Indo-European language sometimes stressed one form of a word on one

---

[6] For the meanings of these International Phonetic Alphabet (IPA) symbols and of terms such as 'stop', 'spirant', 'voiced' and 'unvoiced', see Appendix B. IPA symbols in this book are enclosed in square brackets.
[7] The consonant [b] for some reason was exceedingly rare in Indo-European, as a glance at the *b* entries in a Latin dictionary or the *p* entries in an Old English dictionary will show. Indo-European antecedents for Germanic words containing [p] are difficult to find.
[8] An aspirated stop is a consonant that is accompanied by an *h*-like breathing sound. Most Indo-European languages altered the voiced aspirated stops in some way; for example, in Latin [bʰ] and [dʰ] became *f*, and [gʰ] became *h*.

syllable and another form on another syllable. For example, in Greek the nominative singular of the word for 'giant' was *gígās* while the genitive plural was *gigóntōn*. But in Germanic, some time after the operation of Grimm's Law, stress shifted to the first syllable. Even prefixes were stressed, except the prefixes of verbs and the one that came to Old English as *ġe-* (these were probably perceived as separate words rather than prefixes). The fact that words in Germanic were almost always stressed on the first syllable had many consequences, not least of which is that it made Old English much easier than ancient Greek for modern students to pronounce.

Along with these sound changes came a radical simplification of the inflectional system of the Germanic languages. For example, while linguists believe that the original Indo-European language had seven cases, the Germanic languages have four, and sometimes traces of a fifth. And while students of Latin and Greek must learn a quite complex verb system, the Germanic verb had just two tenses, present and past. Germanic did introduce one or two complications of its own, but in general its inflectional system is much simpler than those of the more ancient Indo-European languages, and the Germanic languages were beginning to rely on a relatively fixed ordering of sentence elements to do some of the work that inflections formerly had done.

1.3.3 West Germanic and Low German

The West Germanic languages differ from North and East Germanic in a number of features which are not very striking in themselves, but quite numerous. For example, the consonant [z] became [r] in North and West Germanic. So while Gothic has *hazjan* 'to praise', Old English has *herian*. In West Germanic, this [r] disappeared at the ends of unstressed syllables, with the result that entire inflectional endings were lost. For example, the nominative singular of the word for 'day' is *dagr* in Old Icelandic and *dags* in Gothic (where the final [z] was unvoiced to [s]), but *dæġ* in Old English, *dag* in Old Saxon, and *tac* in Old High German.

Low German is defined in part by something that *did not* happen to it. This non-event is the 'High German consonant shift', which altered the sounds of the High German dialects as radically as Grimm's Law had altered the sounds of Germanic. Students of Modern German will recognize the effects of the High German consonant shift in such pairs as English *eat* and German *essen*, English *sleep* and German *schlafen*, English *make* and German *machen*, English *daughter* and German *Tochter*, English *death* and German *Tod*, English *thing* and German *Ding*. Another important difference between High German and Low German is that the Low German languages did not distinguish person in plural verbs. For example, in Old High German one would say *wir nemumēs* 'we take', *ir nemet* 'you (plural) take', *sie nemant* 'they take', but in Old English one said *wē nimað* 'we take', *ġē nimað* 'you (plural) take', *hīe nimað* 'they take', using the same verb form for the first, second and third persons.

The most significant differences between Old English (with Old Frisian) and the other Low German languages have to do with their treatment of vowels. Old English and Old Frisian both changed the vowel that in other Germanic languages is represented as *a*, pronouncing it with the tongue farther forward in the mouth: so Old English has *dæg* 'day' and Old Frisian *dei*, but Old Saxon (the language spoken by the Saxons who didn't migrate to Britain) has *dag*, Old High German *tac*, Gothic *dags*, and Old Icelandic *dagr*. Also, in both Old English and Old Frisian, the pronunciation of a number of vowels was changed (for example, [o] to [e]) when [i] or [j] followed in the next syllable. This development, called *i*-mutation (§2.2.2), has implications for Old English grammar and so is important for students to understand.

Old English dramatically reduced the number of vowels that could appear in inflectional endings. In the earliest texts, any vowel except *y* could appear in an inflectional ending: *a, e, i, o, u, æ*. But by the time of King Alfred *i* and *æ* could no longer appear, and *o* and *u* were variant spellings of more or less the same sound; so in effect only three vowels could appear in inflectional endings: *a, e* and *o/u*. This development of course reduced the number of distinct endings that could be added to Old English words. In fact, a number of changes took place in unaccented syllables, all tending to eliminate distinctions between endings and simplify the inflectional system.

1.3.4   Old and Modern English

The foregoing sections have given a somewhat technical, if rather sketchy, picture of how Old English is like and unlike the languages it is related to. Modern English is also 'related' to Old English, though in a different way; for Old and Modern English are really different stages in the development of a single language. The changes that turned Old English into Middle English and Middle English into Modern English took place gradually, over the centuries, and there never was a time when people perceived their language as having broken radically with the language spoken a generation before. It is worth mentioning in this connection that the terms 'Old English', 'Middle English' and 'Modern English' are themselves modern: speakers of these languages all would have said, if asked, that the language they spoke was English.

There is no point, on the other hand, in playing down the differences between Old and Modern English, for they are obvious at a glance. The rules for spelling Old English were different from the rules for spelling Modern English, and that accounts for some of the difference. But there are more substantial changes as well. The three vowels that appeared in the inflectional endings of Old English words were reduced to one in Middle English, and then most inflectional endings disappeared entirely. Most case distinctions were lost; so were most of the endings added to verbs, even while the verb system became more complex, adding such features as a future tense, a perfect and a pluperfect. While the number of endings was reduced, the order of elements within clauses and sentences became more fixed, so that (for example) it came to sound archaic and awkward to place an object before the verb, as Old English had frequently done.

The vocabulary of Old English was of course Germanic, more closely related to the vocabulary of such languages as Dutch and German than to French or Latin. The Viking age, which culminated in the reign of the Danish king Cnut in England, introduced a great many Danish words into English – but these were Germanic words as well. The conquest of England by a French-speaking people in the year 1066 eventually brought about immense changes in the vocabulary of English. During the Middle English period (and especially in the years 1250–1400) English borrowed some ten thousand words from French, and at the same time it was friendly to borrowings from Latin, Dutch and Flemish. Now relatively few Modern English words come from Old English; but the words that do survive are some of the most common in the language, including almost all the 'grammar words' (articles, pronouns, prepositions) and a great many words for everyday concepts. For example, the words in this paragraph that come to us from Old English (or are derived from Old English words) include those in table 1.1.

Table 1.1 Some Modern English words from Old English

about	by	from	now	these
all	come	great	of	this
almost	Danish	in	old	thousand
and	do	into	or	time
are	England	it	some	to
as	English	king	speaking	was
at	everyday	many	such	were
borrowings	for	middle	ten	which
brought	French	more	than	word
but	friendly	most	the	year

1.4 Old English dialects

The language spoken by the Anglo-Saxons at the time of their migration to Britain was probably more or less uniform. Over time, however, Old English developed into four major dialects: Northumbrian, spoken north of the river Humber; Mercian, spoken in the midlands; Kentish, spoken in Kent; and West Saxon, spoken in the southwest.

All of these dialects have direct descendants in modern England, and American regional dialects also have their roots in the dialects of Old English. 'Standard' Modern English (if there is such a thing), or at least Modern English spelling, owes most to the Mercian dialect, since that was the dialect of London.

Most Old English literature is not in the Mercian dialect, however, but in West Saxon, for from the time of King Alfred (reigned 871–99) until the Conquest Wessex dominated the rest of Anglo-Saxon England politically and culturally. Nearly all Old English poetry is in West Saxon, though it often contains spellings and vocabulary more typical of Mercian and Northumbrian – a fact that has led some scholars to speculate that much of the poetry was first composed in Mercian or Northumbrian and later 'translated' into West Saxon. Whatever the truth of the matter, West Saxon was the dominant language during the period in which most of our surviving literature was recorded. It is therefore the dialect that this book will teach you.

Chapter 2

Pronunciation

2.1 Quick start

No one knows exactly how Old English sounded, for no native speakers survive to inform us. Rather, linguists have painstakingly reconstructed the pronunciation of the language from various kinds of evidence: what we know of Latin pronunciation (since the Anglo-Saxons adapted the Latin alphabet to write their own language), comparisons with other Germanic languages and with later stages of English, and the accentuation and quantity of syllables in Old English poetry. We believe that our reconstruction of Old English pronunciation is reasonably accurate; but some aspects of the subject remain controversial, and it is likely that we will never attain certainty about them. The greatest Old English scholar in the world today might very well have difficulty being understood on the streets of King Alfred's Winchester.

Despite the uncertainties, you should learn Old English pronunciation and get into the habit of reading texts aloud to yourself. Doing so will give you a clearer idea of the relationship between Old and Modern English and a more accurate understanding of Old English metre, and will also enhance the pleasure of learning the language.

2.1.1 Vowels and diphthongs

Old English had six simple vowels, spelled *a, æ, i, o, u* and *y,* and probably a seventh, spelled *ie.* It also had two diphthongs (two-part vowels), *ea* and *eo.*

Each of these sounds came in short and long versions. Long vowels are always marked with macrons (e.g. *ā*) in modern editions for students, and also in some scholarly editions. However, vowels are never so marked in Old English manuscripts.

When we speak of vowel length in Old English, we are speaking of *duration*, that is, how long it takes to pronounce a vowel. This fact can trip up the modern student, for when we speak of 'length' in Modern English, we are actually speaking of differences in the *quality* of a vowel. If you listen carefully when you say *sit* (with 'short' *i*) and *site* (with 'long' *ī*), you'll notice that the vowels are quite different: the 'short' version has a simple vowel [ɪ],[1] while the 'long' version is a diphthong, starting with a sound like the *u* in *but* and ending with a sound like the *i* in *sit* [ʌɪ]. The same is true of other long/short pairs in Modern English: they are always qualitatively different. We do give some vowels a longer duration than others (listen to yourself as you pronounce *beat* and *bead*), but this difference in duration is never significant: that is, it does not make a difference in the meaning of a word. Rather, we pronounce some vowels long and others short because of the influence of nearby sounds.

> **!** Vowel length (that is, duration) is significant in Old English because it does make a difference in the meanings of words. For example, Old English *is* means 'is' while *īs* means 'ice', *ac* means 'but' while *āc* means 'oak', and *ġe* means 'and' while *ġē* means 'you' (plural). The significance of length means that the macrons that appear in the texts you will be reading are not there only as guides to pronunciation, but also to help you decide what words mean. If you absent-mindedly read *mǣġ* 'kinsman' as *mæġ* 'may', you will never figure out the meaning of the sentence you are reading.

Simple vowels
The following list of vowels deals with quality only; you may assume that the short and long vowels sound alike except for a difference in duration. The list cites a number of Modern English words for comparison: these are from the Mid-Atlantic dialect of American English and may not be valid for speakers of British English or other American dialects.

> *a* is pronounced [ɑ], as in Modern English *father*. Examples: *macian* 'make', *bāt* 'boat'.

---

[1]   This book frequently uses symbols from the International Phonetic Alphabet (IPA) for convenience of reference, though it also gives examples wherever possible. For a table of the IPA symbols relevant to the study of Old English, see Appendix B.

æ is pronounced [æ], as in Modern English *cat*. *Bæc* 'back', *rǣdan* 'read'.

e is pronounced [e], as in Modern English *fate*; that is, it is like the *e* of a continental European language, not like the 'long' or 'short' *e* of Modern English (actually [i] or [ɛ]). *Helpan* 'help', *fēdan* 'feed'.

i is pronounced [i], as in Modern English *feet*; that is, it is like the *i* of a continental European language, not like the 'long' or 'short' *i* of Modern English (actually [ʌɪ] or [ɪ]). *Sittan* 'sit', *līf* 'life'.

o is pronounced [o], as in Modern English *boat*. *God* 'God', *gōd* 'good'.

u is pronounced [u], as in Modern English *tool*; it is never pronounced [ʌ] as in Modern English *but*. *Full* 'full', *fūl* 'foul'.

y is pronounced [y], like the *ü* in German *über* or *Füße*, or like the *u* in French *tu* or *dur*. Make it by positioning the tongue as you do to say *feet* while rounding the lips as you do to say *tool*. *Cyning* 'king', *brȳd* 'bride'.

ie which appears mainly in early West Saxon, is difficult to interpret. It was probably approximately [ɪ], like the *i* of Modern English *sit*. In late West Saxon, words that contained this vowel are rarely spelled with *ie*, but rather with *i* or *y*. *Ieldesta* 'eldest', *hīeran* 'hear'.

ℹ️ Many grammars tell you to pronounce short *e* as [ɛ], like the *e* in Modern English *set*, short *i* as [ɪ], like the *i* of Modern English *sit*, and short *u* as [ʊ], like the *u* of Modern English *pull*. You can get away with these pronunciations, though they probably do not represent the Old English vowels accurately.

In unaccented syllables, where few vowel sounds were distinguished (see §1.3.3), vowels were probably pronounced less distinctly than in accented syllables. In late Old English (*c*.1000 and later), frequent spelling confusion shows that by then the language was beginning to approach the Middle English situation in which all vowels in unaccented syllables were pronounced [ə] (a neutral schwa, like the *a* in *China*). But unaccented vowels *were* distinguished in Old English, and it is important to pronounce them, for vowel quality often is the only thing that distinguishes one ending from another. For example, dative singular *cyninge* and genitive plural *cyninga*, genitive singular *cyninges* and nominative plural *cyningas* are distinguished only by vowel quality.

Diphthongs
Old English has two digraphs (pairs of letters) that are commonly interpreted as diphthongs: *ea* and *eo*.[2]

---

[2]   A digraph *io* appears primarily in early texts, and for the student's purposes is best taken as a variant of *eo*.

Both *ea* and *eo* can represent short or long sounds, equivalent in length to the short and long vowels. Beyond this generally agreed fact, there is controversy about what sound these digraphs represent. Here we present the most widely accepted view.

> *eo* represents [eo] or [eʊ], a diphthong that started with [e] and glided to a rounded sound, [o] or [ʊ]. Examples: *ċeorl* 'freeman' (Modern English *churl*), *dēop* 'deep'.
>
> *ea* represents [æɑ], a diphthong that started with [æ] and glided to [ɑ] (as in *father*). *Feallan* 'fall', *rēad* 'red'.

Some grammar books say that the spelling *ie* also represents a diphthong, but this book interprets it as a simple vowel.

Perhaps the most common error students make when trying to pronounce Old English diphthongs is to break them into two syllables – for example, to pronounce *Bēowulf* as a three-syllable word when in fact it has only two syllables. Remember that there is a *smooth* transition between the two vowels of a diphthong, and this is as true of the unfamiliar diphthongs of Old English as it is of the familiar ones of Modern English (like those of *site* and *sound*).

2.1.2   Consonants

Most Old English consonants are pronounced as in Modern English, and most of the differences from Modern English are straightforward:

1   Old English scribes wrote the letters þ ('thorn') and ð ('eth') interchangeably to represent [θ] and [ð], the sounds spelled *th* in Modern English. Examples: *þing* 'thing', *brōðor* 'brother'.

2   There are no silent consonants. Old English *cniht* (which comes to Modern English as *knight*) actually begins with [k]. Similarly *hlāf* (Modern English *loaf*) and *hring* (*ring*) begin with [h], *gnæt* (*gnat*) with [g], and *wrīðan* (*writhe*) with [w]. Some Old English consonant combinations may be difficult to pronounce because they are not in Modern English. If you find this to be so, just do your best.

3   The consonants spelled *f*, *s* and *þ/ð* are pronounced as voiced [v], [z] and [ð] (as in *then*) when they fall between vowels or other voiced sounds. For example, the *f* of *heofon* 'heaven', *hæfde* 'had' and *wulfas* 'wolves' is voiced. So are the *s* of *ċēosan* 'choose' and the *ð* of *feðer* 'feather'.

4   These same consonants were pronounced as unvoiced [f], [s] and [θ] (as in *thin*) when they came at the beginning or end of a word or adjacent to

at least one unvoiced sound. So *f* is unvoiced in *ful* 'full', *cræft* 'craft' and *wulf* 'wolf'. Similarly *s* is unvoiced in *settan* 'set', *frost* 'frost', and *wulfas* 'wolves', and *þ/ð* is unvoiced in *þæt* 'that' and *strengð* 'strength'.

5 When written double, consonants must be pronounced double, or held longer. We pronounce consonants long in Modern English phrases like 'big gun' and 'hat trick', though never within words. In Old English, *wile* 'he will' must be distinguished from *wille* 'I will', and *freme* 'do' (imperative) from *fremme* 'I do'.

6 This book sometimes prints *c* with a dot (*ċ*) and sometimes without. Undotted *c* is pronounced [k]; dotted *ċ* is pronounced [tʃ], like the *ch* in Modern English *chin*. This letter is never pronounced [s] in Old English. It has a special function in the combination *sc* (see item 10 below).

7 The letter *g*, like *c*, is sometimes printed with a dot and sometimes without. Dotless *g* is pronounced [g], as in *good*, when it comes at the beginning of a word or syllable. Between voiced sounds dotless *g* is pronounced [ɣ], a voiced velar spirant.[3] This sound became [w] in Middle English, so English no longer has it. Dotted *ġ* is usually pronounced [j], as in Modern English *yes*, but when it follows an *n* it is pronounced [dʒ], as in Modern English *angel*.

8 The combination *cg* is pronounced [dʒ], like the *dge* of Modern English *sedge*. Examples: *hrycg* 'ridge, back', *brycg* 'bridge', *ecg* 'edge'.

9 Old English *h* is pronounced [h], as in Modern English, at the beginnings of syllables, but elsewhere it is pronounced approximately like German *ch* in *Nacht* or *ich* – that is, as a velar [x] or palatal [ç] unvoiced spirant (pronounced with the tongue against the velum [soft palate] or, after front vowels, against the hard palate). Examples: *nēah* 'near', *niht* 'night', *þēah* 'though', *dweorh* 'dwarf'.

10 The combination *sc* is usually pronounced [ʃ], like Modern English *sh*: *scip* 'ship', *æsc* 'ash (wood)', *wȳscan* 'wish'. But within a word, if *sc* occurs before a back vowel (*a, o, u*), or if it occurs after a back vowel at the end of a word, it is pronounced [sk]: *ascian* 'ask' (where *sc* was formerly followed by a back vowel), *tūsc* 'tusk'. When *sc* was pronounced [sk] it sometimes underwent metathesis (the sounds got reversed to [ks]) and was written *x*: *axian* for *ascian*, *tux* for *tusc*. Sometimes *sc* is pronounced [ʃ] in one form of a word and [sk] or [ks] in another: *fisc* 'fish', *fiscas/fixas* 'fishes'.

---

[3] Practise making this sound: raise the back of your tongue to the velum (the soft palate) as you do when pronouncing a *k*. Instead of a stop, though, pronounce a spirant, somewhat like the *ch* of German *Nacht*, but *voiced*. If you are sure you cannot pronounce the [ɣ], pronounce it [w] instead.

2.1.3 Sermonette

When students of Old English go wrong in translating, it is often because they have done a sloppy job of looking up words in a dictionary or glossary. Remember, when you look up words, that vowel length is significant, and so is the doubling of consonants. *Biddan* 'ask, pray' and *bīdan* 'await, experience' are completely different words, but some students mess up their translations because they look at them as equivalent. Don't fall into this trap!

On a related point, you will notice as you go along that the spelling of Old English is somewhat variable. Scribes at that time lacked our modern obsession with consistency. Rather than insisting that a word always be spelled the same way, they applied a set of rules for rendering the sounds of their language in writing, and these rules sometimes allowed them to get the job done in more than one way. Further, scribes sometimes mixed up the dialects of Old English, writing (for example) Mercian *þēostru* 'darkness' instead of West Saxon *þīestru*. These minor inconsistencies sometimes lead students to believe that *anything goes* in Old English spelling, and this belief leads them into error.

It is not true that anything goes in Old English spelling. Though you will have to get used to frequent variations, such as *ie/i/y* and *iung* for *ġeong* 'young', you *won't* often see confusion of *æ* and *ea*, or indeed of most vowels, or of single and double consonants, or of one consonant with another. For a list of spelling variants that you *will* frequently see, consult Appendix A.

Get into the habit of recognizing the distinctions that are important in Old English and doing an accurate job of looking up words, and you will avoid a lot of frustration.

2.2 More about vowels

2.2.1 Short a, æ *and* ea

The short sounds spelled *a, æ* and *ea* are all derived from the same vowel (spelled *a* in most other Germanic languages). The split of one vowel into two vowels and a diphthong, which occurred before the period of our written texts, was conditioned by the sounds that surrounded it in the word (the details are complex and controversial: see Lass [64], pp. 41–53). The effects of this split were not long-lasting; by the Middle English period *a, æ* and *ea* had coalesced into one vowel, spelled *a*.

The reason it is important for you to know about the relationship of *a, æ* and *ea* is that these sounds vary within paradigms. If *æ* or *ea* occurs in a short syllable (see §2.4) and a back vowel (*a, o, u*) follows, the *æ* or *ea* becomes *a*. Add the plural ending *-as* to *dæġ* 'day' and you get *dagas*; add plural *-u* to *ġeat* 'gate' and you get *gatu*.

2.2.2   I-*mutation*

I-mutation[4] is a shift in the quality of a vowel so that it is pronounced with the tongue higher and farther forward than usual – closer to its position when you pronounce the vowel [i] (as in *feet*). The correspondences between normal and mutated vowels are shown in table 2.1. Notice that the *i*-mutation of *a* produces a different result depending on whether a nasal consonant (*m* or *n*) follows.

Table 2.1   *i*-mutation

	short		long	
unmutated	*mutated*	*unmutated*	*mutated*
a	æ	ā	ǣ
an/am	en/em		
æ	e		
e	i		
ea	ie (i, y)	ēa	īe (ī, ȳ)
eo	ie (i, y)	ēo	īe (ī, ȳ)
o	e	ō	ē
u	y	ū	ȳ

🛈 I-mutation arose in prehistoric Old English when [i] or [j] followed in the next syllable. It is a subspecies of a common type of sound change called 'vowel harmony', in which one of a pair of neighbouring vowels becomes more like the other.

The vowels ǣ, ē and (long and short) ĭ are not subject to *i*-mutation.

The ĭe that arose by *i*-mutation of ĕa and ĕo occurs mainly in early West Saxon texts; *i* and *y* occur in later texts (see §2.1.1).

The results of *i*-mutation are sometimes different in dialects other than West Saxon. In these dialects, the *i*-mutation of ĕa was normally ĕ, and *i*-mutation did not affect ĕo; in Kentish, the *i*-mutation of ŭ was ĕ. You will sometimes meet with these spellings in West Saxon texts (see Appendix A).

The effects of *i*-mutation are still evident in Modern English. The vowels of such plurals as *men* (singular *man*), *lice* (*louse*) and *teeth* (*tooth*) exhibit *i*-mutation, as does the comparative adjective *elder* (*old*); and *i*-mutation

---

[4]   German linguists call it *Umlaut*. Because of the great influence of German linguistics at the time when the historical evolution of the Germanic languages was being worked out, you will occasionally see this term even in grammars written in English.

accounts for most of the verbs that both change their vowels and add a past-tense ending (e.g. *sell/sold*, *buy/bought*, in which the present has *i*-mutation but the past does not).

All of these categories of Modern English words exhibiting *i*-mutation were already present in Old English. *I*-mutation also appears in some forms of certain nouns of relationship, some comparative adverbs, and many verb forms.[5] Examples: the nominative plural of *mann* 'man' is *menn*; the nominative plural of *lūs* 'louse' is *lȳs*; the comparative of *eald* 'old' is *ieldra*; the comparative of the adverb *feor* is *fier*; the third-person singular of the strong verb *ċēosan* 'choose' is *ċīest*.

ⓘ Some Modern English words which we still perceive as being derived from other words have mutated vowels: for example, *length* from *long*, *feed* from *food*, *heal* from *whole*. These words and many more were present in Old English: *lengðu* from *lang*, *fēdan* from *fōda*, *hǣlan* from *hāl*.

2.2.3   Silent e; o *for* u

When *ċ*, *ġ* or *sc* (pronounced [ʃ]) occurs before a back vowel, it is sometimes followed by an *e*, which probably should not be pronounced, but merely indicates that the *ċ* should be pronounced [ʧ], the *ġ* [j] or [ʤ], and the *sc* [ʃ]. For example, you will see *sēċean* 'seek' as well as *sēċan*, *ġeþinġea* 'of agreements' as well as *ġeþinġa*, and *sceolon* 'must' (plural) as well as *sculon*.

Notice that *sceolon* has *o* in the first syllable while *sculon* has *u*. These two spellings do not indicate different pronunciations; rather, the Old English spelling system appears (for unknown reasons) to have prohibited the letter-sequence *eu*, and scribes sometimes wrote *eo* instead to avoid it. Other words that are spelled with *o* but pronounced [u] are *ġeō* 'formerly', *ġeong* 'young', *ġeoguð* 'youth' and *Ġeōl* 'Yule'. For these you may also encounter the spellings *iu*, *iung*, *iuguð*, *Ġiul* and *Iul*.

2.3   More about *c* and *g*

The dots that we print over *c* and *g* are not in the manuscripts that preserve the Old English language for us; rather, modern scholars have supplied them. Further, the relationship between Old English pronunciation and Modern English outcome is not always straightforward, as you can see from Modern

---

[5]   For the effects of *i*-mutation in these paradigms, see §§6.1.3, 6.3.2, 7.1.1, 7.3.2, 7.4, 8.4 and 10.2.1.

English *seek*, which comes from Old English *sēċan*. So what are the rules for the pronunciation of Old English *c* and *g*? We print dots over *c* and *g* when they come in these environments:

- Before the front vowels *i* and *ie* and the diphthongs *ea* and *eo*.
- Before *y* in late West Saxon, but only in words where it was spelled *ie* in early West Saxon.
- At the end of a syllable, we print *ġ* following any front vowel (*æ, e, i*), unless a back vowel (*a, o, u*) immediately follows. The same is true of *ċ*, but only after *i*.
- In a few words where *g* is not descended from an older [g] or [ɣ], as is usually the case, but rather from [j]: *ġeāra* 'of yore', *ġeoc* 'yoke', *ġeoguð* 'youth', *Ġeōl* 'Yule', *ġeōmor* 'unhappy', *ġeong* 'young'; internally, in *smēaġan* 'ponder', *frēoġan* 'set free' and a few other words.

Otherwise, we generally print plain *c* and *g*.

C was pronounced [k] in *camb* 'comb', *cǣġ* 'key', *cēne* 'keen, brave', *bacan* 'bake', *bōc* 'book'. It was pronounced [ʧ] in *ċeaf* 'chaff', *ċīdan* 'chide', *ċierran* (late West Saxon *ċyrran*) 'turn', *iċ* 'I'.

G was pronounced [g] in *gōd* 'good', *glæd* 'glad'. It was pronounced [ɣ] (the voiced velar spirant) in *dagas* 'days', *sorga* 'sorrows', *sigan* 'descend'. It was pronounced [j] in *ġiestrandæġ* 'yesterday', *sleġen* 'slain', *mæġ* 'may', *seġl* 'sail' (noun), *seġlode* 'sailed'. It was pronounced [ʤ] in *enġel* 'angel', *senġe* 'I singe'.

As soon as you start to read Old English texts you will notice that these rules apply well enough at the beginnings of syllables, but don't always seem to work elsewhere. For example, the *c* in *sēċan* 'seek' has a dot even though it comes before a back vowel, and the *c* in *macian* 'make' lacks a dot even though it comes before a front vowel. Such anomalies arise from the fact that the changes that produced the sounds spelled *ċ* and *ġ* took place long before the time of our written texts, and the sounds that produced those changes often disappeared later as a result of the simplification of unaccented syllables that is characteristic of Old English (see §1.3.3).[6] This fact is inconvenient for students of Old English, for it means that you cannot be certain how to pronounce some words unless you know their prehistory.

Often it is enough to know about the grammar of a word to decide how to pronounce it. In class 1 weak verbs (§7.3), the root syllable had formerly been followed by [i], which either disappeared or came to be spelled *e*, or [j], which usually disappeared; so *c* and *g* should generally be dotted at the ends of those

---

[6]   We can tell what these sounds were because they are often preserved unchanged in related languages. For example, in Old Saxon the word that appears in Old English as *sēċan* is *sōkian*, and in Gothic it is *sokjan* – the sound that produced *i*-mutation and changed [sk] to [ʧ] is still present in those languages.

syllables. Examples: *senġan* 'singe', *senċan* 'cause to sink', *sēċan* 'seek', *īeċan* 'increase', *bīeġan* 'bend'. In class 2 weak verbs, the root syllable had formerly been followed by a back vowel, even though that vowel often disappeared; so *c* and *g* at the ends of those root syllables should not be dotted. Examples: *macian* 'make', *bōgian* 'dwell', *swīgian* 'fall silent'.

When the vowel of any syllable has undergone *i*-mutation (§2.2.2), that is a sign that [i] or [j] once followed, and so *c* or *g* at the end of such a syllable should be dotted. Athematic nouns like *man/men*, which change their vowels (§6.1.3), do so as a result of *i*-mutation; so the plural of *bōc* 'book' is *bēċ*, and the plural of *burg* 'stronghold' is *byrġ*.

2.4 Syllable length

The *length* of a syllable (sometimes called its weight) is important in both Old English grammar and metre. A long syllable has a long vowel or diphthong or ends with at least one consonant. These one-syllable words are long: *sǣ* 'sea', *fæt* 'container', *blind* 'blind', *dǣd* 'deed', *hēng* 'hung'. A short syllable must have a short vowel or diphthong and must not end with a consonant. The demonstrative pronoun *se* (§5.1.3) is a short syllable.

When a single consonant falls between two syllables, it belongs to the second. Add an ending to *fæt* 'container', for example *fæte*, and the -*t*- no longer belongs to the first syllable, but rather to the second: *fæ-te*, in which the first syllable is now short rather than long. Add an ending to *dǣd* 'deed' (*dǣ-de*), and the first syllable is still long because it contains a long vowel.

Two short syllables may count as one long one, so a two-syllable word like *reċed* 'hall' behaves like a word with one long syllable. But when a two-syllable word begins with a long syllable – for example, *hēafod* 'head' – the second syllable counts as short, even if a consonant ends it. If you ponder this long enough, it may start to make some sense.

2.5 Accentuation

All Old English words are accented on the first syllable, except that words beginning with the prefix *ge*- are accented on the second syllable, and verbs beginning with prefixes are accented on the next syllable after the prefix. It may seem odd, but it is a fact that nouns and adjectives with prefixes (except *ġe*-) are accented on the prefixes. The verb *forwéorðan* 'perish' is accented on the second syllable; a noun derived from it, *fórwyrd* 'destruction', is accented on the prefix.

Words borrowed from Latin are accented on the first syllable, despite Latin rules of accentuation. So *paradīsus* 'paradise' is accented on the first syllable (*páradīsus*) instead of on the penultimate (*paradísus*), as in Latin.

2.6   On-line pronunciation practice

You will find pronunciation exercises at www.engl.virginia.edu/OE. Audio also accompanies the *Old English Aerobics* text 'The Fall of Adam and Eve' and several exercises.

2.7   Summary

The table below presents the Old English pronunciation rules in summary form. Make a copy of it and keep it by your side as you practise reading aloud.

Spelling	Pronunciation
a	[ɑ] as in Modern English *father*
æ	[æ] as in Modern English *cat*
e	[e] as in Modern English *fate*
ea	[æɑ] a diphthong, starting with [æ] and ending with [ɑ]
eo	[eo] or [eʊ] a diphthong, starting with [e] and ending with [o] or [u]
i	[i] as in Modern English *feet*
ie	[ɪ] as in Modern English *sit*
o	[o] as in Modern English *boat*
u	[u] as in Modern English *fool*
y	[y] as in German *über* or *Füße*, French *tu* or *dur*
c	[k] as in Modern English *cow*
ċ	[tʃ] as in Modern English *chew*
cg	[dʒ] like the *dge* in Modern English *edge*
f	[f] as in Modern English *fox*; between voiced sounds [v]
g	[g] as in Modern English *good*; between voiced sounds [ɣ], a voiced velar spirant
ġ	[j] as in Modern English *yes*; after *n* [dʒ] as in *angel*
h	within words or finally, [x] or [ç] like German *ch*
s	[s] as in Modern English *sin*; between voiced sounds [z]
sc	[ʃ] usually as in Modern English *show*; occasionally [sk]
þ/ð	[θ] as in Modern English *thin*; between voiced sounds, [ð] as in *then*

Chapter 3

Basic Grammar: A Review

The remaining chapters of this book will often employ grammatical terminology. If you are not familiar with (or need to be reminded about) such terms as the names of the parts of speech and the elements of the sentence, or such concepts as the phrase and the clause, read this chapter.

3.1 Parts of speech

The traditional parts of speech are functional categories (a noun names a thing, a verb expresses an action), but they are also grammatical categories: a verb, for example, is a word that takes a particular set of endings and comes at a particular place in a sentence or clause. The functional and grammatical categories do not always match neatly. In Modern English, as we know well, nouns can quite often be used as verbs, adjectives as nouns, and prepositions as adverbs: the parts of speech can overlap quite a bit. You will find that the same is true in Old English.

3.1.1 Nouns

A noun is the name of a person, place or thing. The 'thing' need not be concrete: for example, it can be a thought, an activity or a principle.

The noun may be *inflected* (endings supplied or its form altered) to mark its number (singular or plural) or case (in Modern English, subjective/ objective or possessive – but there are more cases in Old English).

3.1.2   *Pronouns*

According to the classic definition, a pronoun is a word used in place of a noun. However, some pronouns work like adjectives, modifying the meaning of a noun rather than replacing it. While the more familiar kind of adjective may modify or limit the meaning of a noun in a novel way, creating, just possibly, a concept that has never been spoken of before ('a transcendental cow', 'a nuclear teapot'), the adjectival pronoun modifies the sense of the noun by narrowing its reference in a very limited and stereotyped way: '*this* cow' (the one here with me), '*each* teapot' (all of them, but considered one by one). The adjectival pronoun can quite generally be used as a 'classic' pronoun, standing in for a noun rather than modifying one ('Have you seen *this*?' 'I have heard the mermaids singing, *each* to *each*').

Pronouns are of seven types: personal, demonstrative, interrogative, indefinite, relative, reflexive and reciprocal. Here is a rundown of these types:

Personal. The personal pronouns (Modern English *I*, *you*, *she*, *he*, *it*, etc.) refer to specific objects and are inflected for person – the first person referring to the speaker, the second person to someone or something the speaker is addressing, and the third person to any other thing.

Demonstrative. These pronouns point out specific things (Modern English *this*, *that*). The Modern English definite article *the* is in origin a demonstrative pronoun, and Old English used a demonstrative where we now use the definite article.

Interrogative. Interrogative pronouns introduce questions, either direct (e.g. '*Who* are you?') or indirect (e.g. 'He asked *who* you were').

Indefinite. This is a relatively large group of pronouns that indicate that we are speaking about one or more members of some category of things but do not specify exactly which. Modern English examples are *all*, *any*, *anyone*, *each*, *few*, *many*, *none*, *one* and *something*.

Relative. A relative pronoun introduces an adjective clause (also called a relative clause). In Modern English the most common relatives are *that* and *who*.

Reflexive. A reflexive pronoun is used as a direct object, indirect object, or object of a preposition to refer to the same thing as the subject. Examples:

Direct object: The cat grooms *himself*.
Indirect object: The president gave *himself* a raise.
Object of a preposition: Look within *yourself*.

Reciprocal. These pronouns refer individually to the things that make up a plural antecedent and indicate that each of those things is in the position of object of the other as subject. That sounds complicated, and it is; but the idea is well known to speakers of Modern English, who use the phrases *each other* and *one another* to express it.

When a pronoun has an antecedent (a noun it refers back to), it must agree with that antecedent in gender and number. This rule holds in both Old and Modern English (see further §11.3).

3.1.3   Verbs

A verb describes an action or a state of being. Examples of Modern English verbs describing action: *run, jump, think*. Verbs describing a state of being: *lack, abound, be*.

There are several ways to divide up the paradigm (the list of inflectional forms) for any verb; the following scheme seems likely to be useful to students of Old English.

Infinitive. In both Old and Modern English, the infinitive is the form that dictionaries use as the headword for verb entries. In Modern English it is the same as the present form, sometimes preceded by *to* ('ride', 'to ride'), but in Old English it has its own endings that distinguish it from the present forms. It is in origin a noun built on the verbal root. In Modern English we can still see the noun-like quality of the infinitive in constructions where it functions as a subject, object or complement:

To marry is better than *to burn*.
Louis loves *to run*.
The best course is usually *to ignore* insults.

These usages are also present in Old English. And both Old and Modern English use the infinitive to complete the sense of an auxiliary verb:

We must *go*.
He ought *to stay*.
You may *do* as you like.

Finite verb. This verb form makes a statement about a subject: the subject *is* something, or *does* something:

> Larry *has* brains.
> Larry *is* a fool.
> Larry *thinks* clearly.

The finite verb can be inflected for person (first, second, third), number (singular, plural), tense (past, present, and in Modern English future) and mood (indicative, subjunctive, imperative). The other verb forms cannot be so marked.

Every clause requires a finite verb; even a clause whose subject is unstated will rarely omit the verb. In general, finding and understanding the finite verb is the key to decoding complex clauses and sentences in Old English, and so it is essential that you get familiar with the finite verb paradigms.

In Modern English, finite verbs are inflected for tense, but only minimally for person, number and mood: only the third person present singular is so inflected.[1] The Old English finite verb has only two tenses, past and present, but it is much more fully inflected than in Modern English for person, number and mood.

Present participle. This is an adjective-like verb form that generally expresses ongoing, repeated or habitual action. It is sometimes used as an adjective, sometimes as a noun and sometimes as part of a periphrastic verb:

> the *flowing* water
> *bowling* is fun
> the Lord was *speaking*

Past participle. This verb form is so called because of the resemblance between it and the past-tense form of the verb. It is descended from an Indo-European verbal adjective.

In Old English and all the Germanic languages, the past participle retained its adjectival function; indeed, it is still easy to think of Modern English examples, e.g. 'I'll have my eggs poached'. The past participle is also used to form a periphrastic passive:

[1]   The Modern English verb *to be* differs from most others in distinguishing all three persons: *I am, you are, he is.* The modal auxiliaries, on the other hand, do not distinguish person at all: *I may, you may, she may.*

The king was *slain*.
Mistakes were *made*.

It may also be used to make periphrastic perfect and pluperfect forms (indicating that the action they describe has been completed), though in Old English there are other ways to do so as well:

We have *begun* this work
When God had *made* all things

These usages all arise from the perfective sense of the past participle: it expresses the state that is consequent upon an action having been completed.

Infinitives, past participles and present participles are collectively called *verbals.* They have in common that they are often used with auxiliaries (as you have seen) to make periphrastic constructions in which the auxiliary expresses person, number, tense and mood while the verbal conveys lexical information.

3.1.4   Adjectives

An adjective modifies or limits the meaning of a noun. If I speak of 'a car', I could be referring to any car in the world. But if I speak of 'a *green* car', I have modified the meaning of 'car' and limited the set of objects to which I am referring.

In Indo-European languages generally, the adjective is inflected to agree with the grammatical characteristics (gender, case and number) of the noun it is modifying. In Modern English we have almost entirely stopped inflecting our adjectives: the only endings that remain are *-er* to make a comparative and *-est* to make a superlative. But in Old English the adjective has different endings depending on the gender, case and number of the noun it is modifying.

3.1.5   Adverbs

Adverbs are traditionally defined as words that modify adjectives, verbs and other adverbs. Adverbs like *finally, wonderfully* and *very* are easy to understand in both Old and Modern English. Conjunctive adverbs, which provide logical transitions between clauses, can be a little trickier. Examples of conjunctive adverbs in Modern English are *however, nevertheless, therefore, then* and *thus*. These are related to conjunctions in meaning and function, and in consequence are often confused with them by both speakers of Modern English and students of Old English.

3.1.6   Prepositions

A preposition introduces a prepositional phrase – that is, a word-group that functions (usually) as an adverb or adjective and consists of a preposition together with a noun, noun phrase or pronoun (the 'object of the preposition'). In such phrases, the preposition defines the relationship between the sentence-element the phrase is modifying and the object of the preposition.

In a sentence like this one

Fishes swim *in the water*.

the prepositional phrase 'in the water' acts as an adverb modifying 'swim'. The preposition 'in' tells us that the phrase has to do with space and, more precisely, location relative to 'the water'. Other prepositions work similarly, modifying nouns and verbs by defining the relationships between them and other things.

3.1.7   Conjunctions

Conjunctions are usually defined as words that link sentence elements. This definition can be a little misleading, since conjunctions often come at the beginnings of sentences where they do not appear to link anything.

Coordinating conjunctions are true linking words: they join together words and clauses that are grammatically parallel. Modern English examples are *and*, *or* and *but*. *Subordinating conjunctions* introduce subordinate clauses: they are 'linking words' in the sense that they signal the relationship between the subordinate and the principal clause. Modern English examples are *when*, *where*, *although* and *as*. *Correlative conjunctions* come in pairs, for example, *either . . . or*, *both . . . and*.

3.1.8   Interjections

An interjection is an exclamation, usually expressing emotion or surprise or establishing a rhetorical level. Modern English examples are *Oh!* and *Gosh!* A justly famous interjection in Old English is *Hwæt*, which begins many poems (including *Beowulf*); it is sometimes interpreted as a call for attention and sometimes as a signal that what follows is in an elevated style.

3.2   Phrases

The function of a word in a sentence may be performed by a *phrase*, a group of words that forms a cohesive unit but lacks a subject and verb. The most important kinds of phrase to know about are these:

Noun phrases consist of a noun or pronoun with modifiers, including pronouns, adjectives, other phrases and clauses:

> *The archbishop of York* sent to the king.
> *He who laughs last* laughs best.
> So much depends upon *a red wheelbarrow*.

Participial phrases function as adjectives or nouns and include present participles or past participles:

> *Giving alms* may help you get to heaven.
> It is a tale *told by an idiot*.

Prepositional phrases consist of prepositions and their objects. They function as adjectives or adverbs:

> Variety is the spice *of life*.
> We live *in Scottsville*.
> Never judge a book *by its cover*.

A phrase can contain any number of words and can also contain clauses and other phrases, which can in turn contain other clauses and phrases.

3.3   Clauses

A clause is a group of words that contains a subject and a finite verb. It is rather like a sentence in this respect, and in fact a simple declarative sentence (such as 'I like ice cream') is nothing more than an independent clause standing by itself – it is indeed the defining characteristic of an independent clause that it can stand by itself.

But a sentence of any complexity also contains one or more *subordinate clauses*. A subordinate clause is a sentence-like group of words (containing a subject and a verb) that functions as a word in another grammatical structure – in a sentence, clause or phrase. Subordinate clauses are classified according to the kinds of words they can stand in for: nouns, adjectives and adverbs.

Noun clauses in Modern English begin with such words as *that, which, what* and *whoever*. A noun clause may function as the subject or object of a verb, as a complement, or as the object of a preposition; in fact, a noun clause can come pretty much anywhere a noun can come. Examples:

> You said *that you would be here today.*
> *What you thought you saw* was an illusion.
> *Whoever wins* will be a wealthy man.

Adjective clauses are also called 'relative clauses'; but 'adjective clause' is a better term since these clauses always function as adjectives, modifying a noun or pronoun. In Modern English adjective clauses commonly begin with *that* or *who* (*whom*).

> We do eat from all the trees *that are in paradise.*
> Those *who cannot remember the past* are condemned to repeat it.

Adverb clauses are extremely various and very common. They function as adverbs, modifying verbs, adjectives and adverbs, and they answer such questions as 'when?' 'where?' 'why?' and 'with what intention?' The types of adverb clauses that you should know about (with some – not all – of the Modern English words that can introduce them) are conditional (*if*), concessive (*although*), temporal (*when, before, after*), causal (*because*), place (*where, whence, whither*), purpose (*in order that, so that*), result (*so that*), comparison (*as*). Just a few examples:

> *When it rains,* it pours.
> We will be sorry *if you leave.*
> *As I write* I keep looking for casualties.
> In countries *where associations are free,* secret societies are unknown.

Like phrases, clauses can contain phrases and other clauses. We call a style that features much subordination *hypotactic;* we call a style that features the concatenation of clauses (either with or without *and*) *paratactic.* Some say that Old English literature generally is characterized by parataxis, but this is not true. Rather, some Old English works (such as the *Anglo-Saxon Chronicle*) tend to be paratactic, while others (such as King Alfred's Preface to his translation of Gregory's *Pastoral Care*) are rather more hypotactic. In poetry it can be difficult to tell independent clauses from subordinate clauses, and for that reason it is a matter of some controversy how paratactic or hypotactic Old English poetry is (see further §15.2.5).

3.4   Elements of the sentence or clause

Sentences and clauses are made up of elements such as subjects, verbs and objects. Such an element may be a single word, but a clause or phrase can also function as an element of a sentence or clause.

3.4.1   Subject

The subject names what the sentence or clause is about. It may be a noun, pronoun, noun phrase or a list (a compound subject):

Noun: *Warriors* should keep their swords sharp.
Pronoun: *They* won't do you any good if they're dull.
Noun phrase: *My sword* is razor sharp.
Noun phrase: *He who has a good sword* has a good friend.
List: *My sword and my shield* are friends in battle.

In the first sentence the subject is a single noun, and in the second it's a single pronoun. More often than not, though, the subject will be a noun phrase – and noun phrases come in many shapes and sizes. In the third sentence the subject consists of a possessive pronoun and a noun, and in the fourth it consists of a pronoun and a relative clause. The fifth shows a very simple example of a compound subject.

In Old English, as in Modern English, subjects can be simple or complex. Old English differs somewhat from Modern English in that a compound subject can be split. In Old English, a sentence structured like this one

My shield protects me and my sword.

could be interpreted as having a compound subject, 'my shield and my sword'. But in Modern English, 'and my sword' must be taken as part of a compound object, 'me and my sword'. Old English also differs from Modern English in that it often omits the subject when the context makes it obvious what it is.

3.4.2   Verb

The verb is a part of speech, but it is also an element of the sentence. Grammarians classify Modern English verbs as *transitive, intransitive or linking*. We will use the first two of those terms, but we'll call the 'linking verb' a *copula.*

A **transitive verb** has a direct object (§3.4.3). For example, the verbs in these sentences are transitive:

> In this year the Viking army *broke* the peace.
> Sigebryht *slew* the nobleman who had stood by him longest.

In the first sentence, the object is 'the peace'; in the second it is a noun phrase, 'the nobleman who had stood by him longest'.

An intransitive verb does not have a direct object, though it may be followed by an adverbial element (an adverb, a phrase or an adverb clause). Some examples:

> In this year archbishop Wulfstan *died*.
> This Cynewulf *reigned* for thirty-one years.

In the second sentence the verb is followed by an adverbial element (a prepositional phrase), but this is not a direct object.

A copula links the subject of a sentence to a *complement*, which characterizes the subject in some way. The verbs in these sentences are copulas:

> Hrothgar *was* a good king.
> They *were* the first ships of Danish men who sought the land of the English.

The copula is usually a form of the verb *to be*; the complement can be a noun, pronoun, adjective or noun phrase. In the first sentence the complement is a short noun phrase, 'a good king'; in the second sentence the complement is a long noun phrase containing several nested elements.

In both Old and Modern English the verb may consist of an auxiliary ('helping') verb and an infinitive (e.g. 'may contribute', 'must pay') or, to make the passive, a form of the verb *to be* and a past participle (e.g. 'was arrested'). And of course these two constructions can be combined (e.g. 'must be excused').

3.4.3   *Object*

The 'direct object' is usually defined as the noun, pronoun or noun phrase that directly receives the action of a verb. Such definitions are usually followed by examples like these:

> Rob painted *the house*.
> Let us break *bread* together.

Here the verbs are 'action verbs', and the direct objects ('the house', 'bread') are actually affected by the actions that the verbs specify.

But it is always dangerous to bind grammatical concepts too closely to the logical relationships expressed by language. Here is another example of a direct object:

Newton pondered *the nature of the universe.*

Few persons would claim that Newton affected 'the nature of the universe' by pondering it; the direct object in this sentence does not 'receive the action of the verb' in anything like the sense in which 'the house' and 'bread' received the actions of the verbs 'painted' and 'break'. Further, the sentence about Newton might easily be rewritten thus, with little change of sense:

Newton thought deeply about the nature of the universe.

Here the verb 'thought' is followed by a prepositional phrase, 'about the nature of the universe' – not a direct object. And yet it says the same thing about Newton that the other sentence says.

What all our examples of direct objects have in common is their *grammatical* relationships to their verbs: in Modern English, the direct object follows the verb and does not have a preposition in front of it.

In Old English, the direct object *may* follow the verb, but may also precede it (especially when the object is a pronoun). It is generally in the accusative case, though some verbs have their direct objects (or what we translate as direct objects) in the dative or genitive case.

An 'indirect object' is a thing that has some indirect relationship to the action of a verb. Such relationships are extremely various: one may, for example, benefit from or be disadvantaged by some action, witness some action, or be the destination of some movement.

3.4.4   Complement

The complement was defined above in §3.4.2; here we will expand on that definition a little. The complement restates the subject of a sentence or clause, characterizing it in some way, for example defining, categorizing, describing or renaming. It usually follows the verb *to be*, but it may follow other verbs as well:

Æthelflæd was *the ruler of the Mercians.*
Beowulf was *brave.*
Greek is considered *a difficult language.*
This plant is called *cinquefoil.*

Notice that the complement may be a noun, pronoun, adjective or noun phrase.

3.4.5   Predicate

The *predicate* is the finite verb together with the direct object or complement, any other elements (such as indirect objects) that are governed by the verb, and any elements (such as adverbs or prepositional phrases) that modify the verb. In short, it includes everything in the clause except the subject. Predicates may be compounded:

Suzy *grabbed her bag, threw a kiss to her mother,* and *ran out the door.*

3.5   On-line exercises

Old English Aerobics has an exercise on the elements of the sentence using Modern English and very simple Old English examples. Try it now; if you don't do well, reread this chapter and try again.

Chapter 4

Case

4.1   What is case?

Case is the inflection of nouns, pronouns and adjectives to signal their functions in sentences and clauses. Those who have studied Latin or German know the concept of case well, for it is important in those languages.

In Modern English, however, case has nearly disappeared. Adjectives have no case endings at all. Nouns are generally inflected for case only when singular, and then only by adding 's to form the possessive.[1] In these sentences, the difference in form between the two italicized words is one of case:

> The *king* is in the hall.
> The *king's* bodyguard is in the tavern.

We make more case distinctions with pronouns than we do with nouns. We use one form for subjects:

> *We* will learn this language.
> *She* sold lemon platt.

We use another form for direct objects, indirect objects and objects of prepositions:

---

[1]   The plural possessive, *s*', is for the most part merely a graphical convention, though we do occasionally make an *audible* possessive plural by adding 's to an anomalous plural form like *men*.

They beat *us* at bridge.
Don't lie to *me*.
Reader, I married *him*.

And we use still another form for possessives:

Our swords are better than *your* swords.
My mother warned me about *their* wiles.

Modern English distinctions such as *king/king's*, *I/me/my*, *he/him/his* and
we/us/our have descended to us directly from Old English, though over the
centuries the number of distinct case forms, and even the number of cases,
has declined. Modern English pronouns have at most three cases, which grammarians call *subjective*, *objective* and *possessive*. Old English, on the other hand,
had five: *nominative*, *accusative*, *genitive*, *dative* and *instrumental*.

> The Modern English subjective case is descended from the Old English nomin-
> ative, and the Modern English possessive is from the Old English genitive. The
> Modern English objective has taken over the functions of the Old English accusat-
> ive, dative and instrumental; it has distinct forms only in pronouns, and these
> forms are from the Old English dative.

4.2   Uses of the cases

Case, as mentioned above, tells us something about the function of a noun,
adjective or pronoun in a sentence or clause. You will find that quite often
you must recognize the case of a word before you can decide whether it is a
subject, object or something else, just as you may have to recognize the distinction between *king* and *king's* to understand a Modern English sentence.

But it is worth pointing out as well that you will not always be able to
recognize the case of a word by its ending. For example, the nominative
singular form of the Old English word for 'name' is *nama*, but the other
singular forms are all *naman*, and the nominative and accusative plural forms
are also *naman*. That there are five cases in Old English and that any noun can
be either singular or plural might lead you to expect ten distinct forms of
every noun. But there are only *four* distinct forms of the word *nama* 'name',
and no Old English noun has more than *six* distinct forms.

Obviously, Old English must have had some feature other than case to help
speakers and listeners decide what a noun, adjective or pronoun was doing in
a sentence. In Modern English, word-order tells us most of what we need to
know. In the sentence 'Rover bit Fido', we understand that the subject of the

sentence is *Rover*, the verb is *bit*, and the object is *Fido* because the standard word-order in a declarative English sentence is Subject–Verb–Object. There are more permissible word-orders in Old English than in Modern English, but Old English word-order is not at all 'free', as some sources may tell you. In fact there are just a few common word-orders. If you learn what to expect, you will find that word-order is a help in Old English, just as it is in Modern English.

Word-order will be discussed more fully in chapter 12. The point we are making here is that case is only one of the signals, along with word-order and your feeling for what makes sense in a particular context, that tell you how a word is functioning in a sentence.

Before we throw a lot of case forms at you (in the next chapter), we will discuss the functions of each case.

4.2.1 Nominative

The nominative case has few functions, and since there are few complications in its use, it is very easy to understand.

Subject. The subject of any sentence or clause will be in the nominative case.
Complement. The complement (the word on the other side of a copula or 'linking verb', usually 'to be') is always in the nominative. In this sentence:

Sēo sunne is swīðe *brād*
[The sun is very *broad*]

both *sunne* (the subject) and *brād* (the complement) are in the nominative case.
Address. When the speaker addresses someone directly, the name or title by which he calls the person he is speaking to is nominative. In this sentence

Ġeseoh þū, *cyning*, hwelċ þēos lār sīe
[See, *king*, what kind of teaching this is]

cyning 'king' is nominative.

4.2.2 Accusative

Direct objects of transitive verbs are usually in the accusative case. Thus in this sentence:

His āgen swustor bebyrġde his *līċ*
[His own sister buried his *corpse*]

līċ 'corpse' is accusative. Objects of certain prepositions are sometimes or always accusative, and the accusative can be used adverbially in certain expressions of time.

In Old English the accusative has partly fallen together with the nominative. For example, nominative and accusative are never distinguished in the plural or in any neuter noun, pronoun or adjective, and they have also fallen together in the singular of strong masculine nouns.

4.2.3   Genitive

To put it very broadly indeed, the genitive modifies or limits a word (usually a noun) by associating it with something. For example, in the phrase *þæs cyninges* sweord 'the king's sword', the sense of *sweord* is modified by our saying that it belongs to the king: we're not speaking of just any sword. In this respect, a word in the genitive case is like an adjective, limiting the reference of the word it is associated with.

Most genitives fall into one of three categories:

Possessive. This is the ancestor of the Modern English 'possessive case'. It does not always indicate actual possession, but often some other kind of association. For example, **sanctes Ēadmundes** *mæssedæġ* 'the feast *of* St Edmund' does not mean that the day actually belongs to St Edmund, but rather that he is venerated on that day.

Partitive. The partitive genitive represents the whole collection of things to which a particular thing or subset of things belongs, for example, *ǣlċ* **þāra manna** 'each of *the men*', **ealra cyninga** *betst* 'best *of all kings*'. As the translations with 'of' suggest, Modern English has a roughly similar construction made with the preposition *of*; but Old English used the partitive genitive much more extensively than we use this partitive construction, for example, *maniġ* **manna** 'many *men*', *twelf* **mīla** *lang* 'twelve *miles* long'. Expect to find the partitive genitive used with any word that expresses number, quantity or partition.

Descriptive. This genitive attributes a quality to a thing, for example,

> þæt lamb sceal bēon *hwītes hīwes*
> [the lamb must be *of a white colour*]

Here the translation with *of* echoes the genitive construction and shows that similar constructions are still possible in Modern English, but it is now more idiomatic to say 'white in colour'.

A few prepositions sometimes have objects in the genitive case (see §10.5), and some verbs have genitive direct objects. Genitive constructions may also be used adverbially, especially in expressions of time (see §10.2).

4.2.4   Dative

In all of the Germanic languages the dative case is an amalgam of several older cases that have fallen together: dative, locative, ablative and instrumental. Old English retains traces of the instrumental case (see §4.2.5), but for the most part that too has fallen together with the dative.

In view of its diverse origins, it should be no surprise that the dative case has a variety of functions. Of these, the easiest for the speaker of Modern English to understand is that of object of a preposition. The objects of certain prepositions (*æfter, æt, be, fram, mid, of, tō*) are usually or always in the dative case. With other prepositions the case may be either dative or accusative, depending on the writer's dialect or the meaning of the preposition.

But the dative can be used without prepositions, and then the modern reader must be aware of its possible meanings:

Interest. Here the dative signifies that one is in some way interested in the outcome of an action. This category includes the 'indirect object':

Ġif *him* his sweord
[Give *him* his sword]

But the dative of interest also covers situations in which something has been taken away:

Benam hē *him* his bisceopscīre
[He took his bishopric away *from him*]

Direct object. Some verbs have their direct objects in the dative case. It is not always easy to tell the difference between a direct and an indirect object: for example, should we translate *him* hīerde as 'obeyed him' or 'was obedient to him'? But in this matter it is sufficient for the student to be guided by modern usage and leave the technical aspects to the linguists.

Possession. The dative often indicates possession, for example:

Him wæs ġeōmor sefa
[*Theirs* was a sad mind (i.e. Their minds were sad)]

Often the dative of possession may also be interpreted as a dative of interest.

Comparison. The dative may express likeness or equality:

> and ġē bēoð þonne *englum* gelīċe
> [and you will then be like *the angels*]

The dative that expresses unlikeness is rare enough that beginners probably should not worry about it.

Instrument, means, manner. These senses of the dative overlap, and so are grouped together here. In Modern English we generally express them with prepositions like 'with' and 'by', for example, 'Ecgferth struck Æthelbryht with his sword'; 'He was wounded by a spear'; 'We sing the mass with joy'. In Old English, too, instrument, means and manner can be expressed with prepositions, especially *mid* and *fram*. But they are very commonly expressed by the dative alone, for example,

> for þan iċ hine *sweorde*   swebban nelle[2]
> [therefore I will not kill him *with a sword*]
>
> þū scealt *yfelum dēaðe* sweltan
> [you must die by *a wretched death*]

This usage is especially common in poetry (see §15.2.2). To express the instrument, Old English may use the instrumental case (which exists only in the masculine and neuter singular), but it may equally well use the dative.

When translating the dative, it is often necessary to supply a preposition, because in Modern English prepositions very commonly express what used to be expressed by the dative alone.

4.2.5   Instrumental

The instrumental case was disappearing during the centuries when Old English was being written. It has a distinct form only in masculine and neuter singular adjectives and pronouns; everywhere else the dative is used.

Instrument, means, manner. These uses occur mainly in early texts, for example:

---

[2] *Beowulf*, l. 679.

hē forðon *fǣġre ænde* his lif betȳnde
[he therefore concluded his life *with a beautiful end*].

Accompaniment. This usage is not common, but it does occur in the *Chronicle* entry for 755, which students often read:

Ond þā ġeascode hē þone cyning *lȳtle werode*
[And then he learned of the king (being) *with a little force*]

Expressions of time. Such expressions are largely formulaic, for example, *ǣlċe dæġe* 'each day', *þȳ ilcan ġēare* 'in the same year'. They occur frequently in both early and late texts.

4.3   On-line exercises

Old English Aerobics has an elementary exercise on case using Modern English and simple Old English sentences. Try this exercise now. *Old English Aerobics* also has exercises on the nominative, accusative, genitive and dative cases, using easy to intermediate sentences. Try these exercises after you have read the next three chapters and started to read your first Old English text.

Chapter 5

Pronouns

5.1 Quick start

Before you read any farther, download the 'Magic Sheet' (a one-page summary of Old English inflections, http://www.engl.virginia.edu/OE/courses/handouts/magic.html) and print it out on the best colour printer you can find. Keep this sheet by your side as you read Old English.

The pronouns[1] you will meet with most often are the personal pronouns (with the closely related possessive adjectives) and the demonstratives.

5.1.1 Personal pronouns

You will find the personal pronouns easy to learn because of their resemblance in both form and usage to those of Modern English. The first-person pronouns (table 5.1) are quite similar to those of Modern English, especially in prose, where you will generally see accusative singular *mē* rather than *mec*.

The second-person pronouns, on the other hand, have changed radically since the Old English period (table 5.2). Modern English does not distinguish number or any case but the possessive; in fact there are now only two forms of the pronoun, *you* and *your*. By contrast, the second-person pronouns of Old English look a lot like the first-person pronouns, distinguishing number

---

[1] For a general discussion of pronouns, see §3.1.2.

Table 5.1 First-person pronouns

	singular	*plural*
nominative	iċ 'I'	wē 'we'
accusative	mē, mec 'me'	ūs 'us'
genitive	mīn 'my'	ūre 'our'
dative	mē 'me'	ūs 'us'

and at least three of the cases. Old English does not use the second-person singular as a 'familiar' form, the way Middle English sometimes does: þū is simply singular. Like *mec*, accusative singular *þec* is mainly poetic.

Table 5.2 Second-person pronouns

	singular	*plural*
nominative	þū 'you'	ġē 'you'
accusative	þē, þec 'you'	ēow 'you'
genitive	þīn 'your'	ēower 'your'
dative	þē 'you'	ēow 'you'

The third-person pronouns, unlike the first- and second-person pronouns, are inflected for gender, but only in the singular (table 5.3).

Table 5.3 Third-person singular pronouns

	masculine	*neuter*	*feminine*	*plural*
nominative	hē 'he'	hit 'it'	hēo 'she'	hīe 'they'
accusative	hine 'him'	hit 'it'	hīe 'her'	hīe 'them'
genitive	his 'his'	his 'its'	hire 'her'	hira 'their'
dative	him 'him'	him 'it'	hire 'her'	him 'them'

! Notice that several singular forms are repeated in table 5.3. As you study the pronouns, nouns and adjectives, you will find that forms repeat themselves in the same pattern:

- Neuter nominative and accusative singular forms are the same
- Neuter and masculine genitive singular forms are the same

- Neuter and masculine dative singular forms are the same
- Feminine genitive and dative singular forms are the same

If you learn these patterns you will save yourself some of the labour of memorizing paradigms.

The third-person plural pronouns may cause some difficulty at first, because they don't start with *th-* the way their Modern English counterparts do. Also confusing is that dative plural *him* is exactly the same as the masculine/neuter dative singular pronoun. You will need to take extra care in memorizing these plural pronouns.

5.1.2   Possessive adjectives

Possessive adjectives are the pronoun-like forms we use with nouns to signal possession:

my sword
the sword is *mine*
your shield
the shield is *yours*
her spear
the spear is *hers*

These are closely related to the genitive personal pronouns, but we call them adjectives because they modify nouns. In Old English the third-person genitive pronouns are used as possessive adjectives:

his hring [*his* ring]
hire healsbēag [*her* necklace]
hira fatu [*their* cups]

These work like Modern English possessives in that they agree in gender and number with their antecedents, not with the nouns they modify. To make first- and second-person possessive adjectives, strong adjective endings (§8.2) are added to the genitive pronoun forms; these agree with the nouns they modify, not with their antecedents:

mīnum scipe [*my* ship (dative)]
þīnne wæġn [*your* wagon (accusative)]
ēowru hors [*your* horses (nominative plural)]

5.1.3 Demonstrative pronouns

There are two demonstrative pronouns, *se/þæt/sēo* (table 5.4) and *þes/þis/þēos* (table 5.5). The first does the job of Modern English *that/those* and also that of the definite article *the*. The second does the same job as Modern English *this/these*. As with the third-person pronouns, gender is distinguished only in the singular.

Table 5.4   Demonstrative pronoun 'the', 'that', 'those'

	masculine	*neuter*	*feminine*	*plural*
nominative	se	þæt	sēo	þā
accusative	þone	þæt	þā	þā
genitive	þæs	þæs	þǣre	þāra, þǣra
dative	þām	þām	þǣre	þām
instrumental	þȳ, þon	þȳ, þon		

Table 5.5   Demonstrative pronoun 'this', 'these'

	masculine	*neuter*	*feminine*	*plural*
nominative	þes	þis	þēos	þās
accusative	þisne	þis	þās	þās
genitive	þisses	þisses	þisse, þisre	þisra
dative	þissum	þissum	þisse, þisre	þissum
instrumental	þȳs	þȳs		

Modern English *that* comes from the neuter nominative/accusative form. Notice that the same patterns occur here as in the third-person pronouns: neuter nominative and accusative forms are the same, masculine and neuter forms are the same in the genitive and dative cases, and feminine genitive and dative forms are the same.

The instrumental case is distinguished only in the masculine and neuter singular; elsewhere you will see the dative instead.

5.2   More about personal and demonstrative pronouns

5.2.1   The dual number

The first- and second-person pronouns have dual as well as singular and plural forms (table 5.6). Dual pronouns are used to refer to two things:

'we two', 'you two'. Use of the dual is optional: the plural will do just as well. It is used to emphasize that two persons or things are being discussed, as in Riddle 85:

Ġif wit unc ġedǣlað,   mē bið dēað witod
[If the two of us part from each other, death is ordained for me]

There is no dual verb form; dual pronouns agree with plural verbs.

Table 5.6   Dual pronouns

	first person	*second person*
nominative	wit 'we two'	ġit 'you two'
accusative	unc 'us two'	inc 'you two'
genitive	uncer 'of us two'	incer 'of you two'
dative	unc 'us two'	inc 'you two'

5.2.2   Common spelling variants

Personal and demonstrative pronouns receive relatively little stress in most sentences, and as a result they may be pronounced somewhat indistinctly. Long vowels are frequently shortened (though this book always marks them with their etymologically correct lengths), and *i*, *ie* and *y* are frequently confused. Thus you will see not only *hine* (for example), but also *hyne* and *hiene*, and not only *hīe*, but also *hī* and *hȳ*. For *hīe* you will also see occasional *hiġ* and *hēo*. For *him* you will see not only *hym*, but also, in the plural, *heom*.

In *þām*, *ǣ* varies with *ā*. In late Old English you will also see *þane* for *þone*. You may expect to see occasional *y* or *eo* for *i* in forms of *þes* (e.g. *þysne*, *þeossa*), and also occasional variation between *-s-* and *-ss-*.

5.3   Interrogative pronouns

There are three common interrogative pronouns: *hwā* (table 5.7), the ancestor of Modern English *who*/*what*; *hwelċ*/*hwilċ*/*hwylċ*, which gives Modern English *which*; and *hwæþer* 'which of two'. *Hwā* has only a singular form; there is no distinction between masculine and feminine. The instrumental form is the ancestor of Modern English *why*, and is used to mean 'why'.

Minitext A. Psalm I

King Alfred reportedly translated the first fifty psalms into Old English; this version of Psalm I may be his. For the rest of this prose translation, see Bright and Ramsay [15].

[1] Ēadiġ bið se wer þe ne gǣð on ġeþeaht unrihtwīsra,[a] ne on þām weġe ne stent synfulra, ne on heora wōlbǣrendum[b] setle ne sitt; [2] ac his willa bið on Godes ǣ, and ymb his ǣ hē bið smēaġende dæġes and nihtes. [3] Hē bið swā þām trēowe þe bið āplantod nēah wætera rynum, þæt selð his wæstmas tō rihtre tīde, and his lēaf and his bladu ne fealwiað ne ne sēariað;[c] eall him cymð tō gōde þæt þæt hē dēð. [4] Ac þā unrihtwīsan ne bēoð nā swelċe, ne him ēac swā ne limpð;[d] ac hīe bēoð dūste ġelīcran, þonne hit wind tōblǣwð. [5] Þȳ ne ārīsað þā unrihtwīsan on dōmes dæġ, ne þā synfullan ne bēoð on ġeþeahte þǣra rihtwīsena; [6] for þām God wāt hwelċne weġ þā rihtwīsan ġeearnedon, ac þā unrihtwīsan cumað tō wītum.

[a]   unrihtwīsra: of the unrighteous.
[b]   Wōlbǣrendum translates pestilentiae, the reading of most Anglo-Saxon psalters; the reading of the 'Hebrew' version, derisorum 'of the scornful ones', is closer to that of most modern translations.
[c]   The translator here adds a note: swā byð þām men þe wē ǣr ymb sprǣcon 'so it is for the man whom we spoke of before'.
[d]   ne him ēac swā ne limpð: nor does it happen to them thus.

Table 5.7   Interrogative pronoun

	masculine and feminine	*neuter*
nominative	hwā 'who'	hwæt 'what'
accusative	hwone, hwæne	hwæt
genitive	hwæs	hwæs
dative	hwām, hwǣm	hwām, hwǣm
instrumental	hwȳ, hwon	hwȳ, hwon

The other two interrogative pronouns mentioned above are inflected as strong adjectives (§8.2).

5.4   Indefinite pronouns

The interrogative pronouns can also be used as indefinite pronouns: you must judge which is intended from the context. The addition of the prefix ġe- to these pronouns alters the meaning somewhat:

hwā 'anyone'	*ġehwā* 'each, everyone, someone'
hwelċ 'any, anyone'	*ġehwelċ* 'each'
hwæþer 'either, both'	*ġehwæþer* 'both'

These pronouns can also be modified by placing them in the phrases *swā hwā swā* 'whoever', *swā hwēlċ swā*, *swā hwæþer swā* 'whichever'. Yet another indefinite pronoun may be made by prefixing *nāt-*, a negative form of the verb 'to know': *nāthwelċ* 'someone or other', 'something or other' (literally 'I don't know who', 'I don't know which'). Here are a few examples:

wite *ġehwā* þæt þā yfelan ġeþōhtas ne magon ūs derian
[let *everyone* know that those evil thoughts may not harm us]

Swā hwylċe swā ne woldon hlāfordas habban
[*Whoever* did not wish to have lords]

þāra banena byre *nāthwylċes*[2]
[the son *of one or another* of those killers]

Other indefinite pronouns are inflected like adjectives.

5.5   Relative pronouns

There are several ways to make a relative pronoun. One is simply with the indeclinable particle *þe*:

Þā bēoð ēadiġe *þe* ġehȳrað Godes word
[They are blessed *who* obey God's word]

Another is to use a form of the demonstrative *se* with *þe*:

Hē lifode mid þām Gode *þām þe* hē ǣr þēowode
[He lived with that God *whom* he earlier had served]

A third way is to use a form of the demonstrative pronoun alone, without *þe*:

Danai þǣre ēa, *sēo* is irnende of norþdæle
[the river Don, *which* flows from the north]

---

[2]   *Beowulf*, l. 2053.

When a demonstrative is used, its case and number will usually be appropriate to the following adjective clause. That is the case with both of the examples above, since *þēowian* takes the dative and nominative *sēo* is the subject of the clause that it introduces. Sometimes, though, the demonstrative will agree with the word that the adjective clause modifies:

> Uton wē hine ēac biddan þæt hē ūs ġescylde wið grimnysse *myssenlicra yfela and wīta þāra þe* hē on middanġeard sendeð for manna synnum.
> [Let us also entreat him that he shield us from the severity *of various evils and punishments that* he sends to the earth because of men's sins.]

The relative pronoun *þāra þe* agrees with the genitive plural noun phrase *myssenlicra yfela and wīta*, which lies outside the adjective clause (*þāra þe ... synnum*).

5.6   Reflexive pronouns

The personal pronoun can be used by itself as a reflexive, and *self/sylf* can be added for emphasis. Examples:

> Iċ ondrēd *mē*
> [I was afraid]

> Iċ ðā sōna eft *mē selfum* andwyrde
> [I then immediately afterwards answered *myself*]

Old English sometimes uses a reflexive pronoun where it would make no sense to use one in Modern English: when this happens the translator may simply ignore it.

5.7   Reciprocal pronouns

There are several ways to express what Modern English usually expresses with the phrase *each other*. One may simply use a plural personal pronoun where we say *each other*, optionally adding *self* to the pronoun for emphasis. Or one can use a construction such as *ǣġðer ... ōðer* or *ǣġhwylċ ... ōðer* 'each ... other'. An example of each style:[3]

---

[3]   From *Beowulf*, l. 2592, and *The Battle of Maldon*, l. 133.

þæt ðā āglǣcan   *hȳ* eft ġemētton
[that the contenders met *each other* again]

ǣġðer hyra *ōðrum*   yfeles hogode
[*each* of them intended harm *to the other*]

In the first sentence you must rely on context to tell you that the pronoun is reciprocal.

5.8   On-line exercise

Old English Aerobics has a session on the pronoun, using easy to intermediate Old English sentences. Read the sentences carefully and work the exercises. If *Old English Aerobics* doesn't tell you you've done a good job, try the exercises again after you've read more. *Old English Aerobics* also has an on-line version of Minitext A, accompanied by exercises on the pronoun.

Chapter 6

Nouns

6.1 Quick start

In Modern English almost all nouns[1] are declined[2] in pretty much the same way: we add -s to make plurals and -'s to make possessives. There are notable exceptions, however. The plural of *ox* is not *oxes*, but *oxen*, and the plural of *child* has the same ending, but preceded by -r-. And of course several very common nouns make plurals by changing their vowels: for example, *tooth/teeth* and *mouse/mice*.

Our nouns with -s plurals, nouns with -en plurals, the noun with -r-, and the nouns that change their vowels belong to different *declensions* – classes of nouns that are declined in similar ways. Though we have just one major declension in Modern English and a few minor ones, in Old English there were several major declensions and several more minor ones. You must learn the forms for each of the major declensions, and you should acquire enough knowledge of the minor ones to enable you to be on the lookout for them.

In Modern English we do not think of nouns as having gender; rather, the things they refer to have gender (or they do not, in which case they are 'neuter'). But gender is an attribute of every Old English noun, and the *grammatical gender* of a noun does not necessarily correspond to the *natural*

---

[1] For a general discussion of nouns, see §3.1.1.
[2] To decline a noun is to list all of its possible forms.

gender of the thing it refers to. For example, *wīf* 'woman' is neuter and *wīfman* 'woman' is masculine; and nouns that refer to inanimate objects are very often masculine or feminine (for example, masculine *stān* 'stone', feminine *benċ* 'bench'). Further, different endings are added to nouns of different gender (for example, the nominative plural of masculine *wer* 'man' is *weras*, of neuter *scip* 'ship' *scipu*, and of feminine *cwēn* 'queen' *cwēna*).

! You can make the job of learning the nouns easier by looking for patterns within the paradigms. Take particular note of these:

- Neuter and masculine genitive singular forms are the same within each major declension
- All dative singular forms are the same within each major declension
- All genitive plural forms end in *-a*
- All dative plural forms end in *-um*

You should also look for resemblances between the noun and pronoun paradigms. The more patterns and resemblances you find, the less you'll have to memorize.

Most nouns fall into one of two major declensions, conventionally called 'strong' and 'weak'. There are also several minor declensions; we'll look at one of these (the 'athematic' nouns) in the Quick Start section and save the others for later.

6.1.1 Strong nouns

Table 6.1 shows the basic endings of the strong nouns. Notice how much duplication there is in this table. Often one cannot tell the gender of a noun from its ending: strong masculines and neuters differ only in the nominative/ accusative plural, and gender is never distinguished in the dative singular or in the genitive and dative plural. Further, one cannot always tell the case: nominative and accusative singular are not distinguished in masculine and neuter nouns, accusative, genitive and dative singular are not distinguished in feminine nouns, and nominative and accusative plural are never distinguished at all.

Table 6.2 adds these endings to several common masculine and neuter nouns. It also shows that the neuter nominative/accusative plural ending *-u* appears only after short syllables (see §2.4); neuters with long syllables have no ending.

Table 6.1 Strong masculines and neuters

		masculine	neuter	feminine
singular	nominative	–	–	-u/–
	accusative	–	–	-e
	genitive	-es	-es	-e
	dative	-e	-e	-e
plural	nominative/accusative	-as	-u/–	-a
	genitive	-a	-a	-a
	dative	-um	-um	-um

Table 6.2 Strong masculines and neuters

		masculine	short neuter	long neuter
singular	nominative/accusative	stān 'stone'	scip 'ship'	þing 'thing'
	genitive	stānes	scipes	þinges
	dative	stāne	scipe	þinge
plural	nominative/accusative	stānas	scipu	þing
	genitive	stāna	scipa	þinga
	dative	stānum	scipum	þingum

! An endless plural may seem a great inconvenience at first – how will you be able to tell a plural when you see it? In practice, you'll find that one of three things will be true when you come across an endingless neuter: (1) a nearby pronoun will tell you what you need to know (*þæt þing* singular, *þā þing* plural); (2) the context will make clear whether the noun is singular or plural; or (3) it won't matter. If you stay alert to the likelihood that some plural nouns will lack endings, you won't get into trouble.

Although the nominative and accusative are always the same for strong masculines and neuters, you may often find the case of a masculine singular noun by looking at the pronoun in front of it (if there is one): *se stān* or *þes stān* is nominative, while *þone stān* or *þisne stān* is accusative. Since the nominative and accusative are the same for *all* neuter words – nouns, pronouns and adjectives – you must rely on context to tell whether a neuter is nominative or accusative.

The nominative/accusative singular of masculine and neuter nouns often ends in *-e*: *ende* 'end', *wine* 'friend', *spere* 'spear', etc. These forms look the same as the dative singular; do not be confused by the resemblance.

Feminine nouns (table 6.3) look much less familiar than masculines or even neuters. The feminines do not have the masculine/neuter genitive *-es* or the masculine plural *-as*, which give us the dominant Modern English noun endings, and so the strong feminine declension seems to be furnished with none of the comforts of home. The good news, on the other hand, is that the strong feminines have relatively few endings, so you have less to memorize.

Table 6.3 Strong feminines

		short stem	long stem
singular	nominative	ġiefu 'gift'	sorg 'sorrow'
	accusative	ġiefe	sorge
	genitive/dative	ġiefe	sorge
plural	nominative/accusative	ġiefa	sorga
	genitive	ġiefa	sorga
	dative	ġiefum	sorgum

Like the strong neuters, the strong feminines come in short and long varieties. The ending *-u* appears in the nominative singular after short syllables, but is dropped after long ones. Sometimes, however, the ending gets restored, for example, in *lenġu* 'length', *iermðu* beside *iermð* 'misery', and *brædu* beside *bræd* 'breadth'.

Among the strong feminine nouns are a great many that represent abstract concepts, made from adjectives and other nouns. These include nouns ending in *-þ* such as *strengþ* 'strength' and *hælþ* 'health', those ending in *-ness* such as *clænness* 'cleanness' and *ġīferness* 'greed', and those ending in *-ung* such as *leornung* 'learning' and *ġeōmrung* 'groaning'.

6.1.2   Weak nouns

Table 6.4 shows the endings of the weak declension, ancestor of the Modern English nouns with anomalous plural *-en*. These nouns make even fewer distinctions of gender and case than the strong nouns do: the rule that neuter words do not distinguish between nominative and accusative (mentioned in §5.1.1) accounts for its having accusative singular *-e* where the masculine and feminine have *-an*;[3] otherwise, the only difference among the genders is that

---

[3]   Weak neuters are actually quite rare: only *ēage* 'eye' and *ēare* 'ear' are attested.

Table 6.4   Weak noun endings

		masculine	neuter	feminine
singular	nominative	-a	-e	-e
	accusative	-an	-e	-an
	genitive	-an	-an	-an
	dative	-an	-an	-an
plural	nominative/accusative	-an	-an	-an
	genitive	-ena	-ena	-ena
	dative	-um	-um	-um

Table 6.5   Weak nouns

		masculine	neuter	feminine
singular	nominative	nama 'name'	ēage 'eye'	tunge 'tongue'
	accusative	naman	ēage	tungan
	genitive	naman	ēagan	tungan
	dative	naman	ēagan	tungan
plural	nominative/accusative	naman	ēagan	tungan
	genitive	namena	ēagena	tungena
	dative	namum	ēagum	tungum

the masculine nominative singular ends in *-a* while the neuter and feminine end in *-e*. Most case endings are simply *-an*. Table 6.5 adds these endings to three common nouns.

> **!**   The fact that most forms end in *-an* can cause problems for the student who expects to be able to find out the case and number of a noun from its inflection. When in doubt about a weak noun ending in *-an*, look first for a pronoun or adjective that agrees with it. The noun in *þæs guman* can only be genitive singular, and the phrase should thus be translated 'the man's'; in *godfyrhte guman*, the strong nominative/accusative plural adjective tells us that the phrase must be translated 'God-fearing men'.
>
>   But what about a noun that lacks modifiers, as in the phrase *eorðan bearnum*?[4] A noun that, like *eorðan*, comes just before another noun

---

[4]   *Cædmon's Hymn*, l. 5.

has a good chance of being a genitive, and in fact this phrase should be translated 'the children of earth'. But ultimately the context will help you decide. If you haven't yet found the subject of the clause you're reading and the verb is plural, consider the possibility that the noun in -*an* is a plural subject:

þæs ne wēndon ǣr   witan Scyldinga[5]
[the wise men of the Scyldings had not expected that]

Similarly, if the verb wants an object, consider that as a possibility. In short, find out what's missing in the clause and try the noun in that function. Don't lose heart: remember that writers of Old English, when they wanted to be understood, did not write clauses containing unresolvable ambiguities. After you've puzzled out a few difficult instances of weak nouns, you should start to get the hang of them.

6.1.3   Athematic nouns

The athematic nouns[6] are those that sometimes have *i*-mutation (§2.2.2) of the root vowel instead of an ending; they are the ancestors of Modern English nouns like *man/men* and *tooth/teeth* (see table 6.6).

Table 6.6   Athematic nouns

		masculine	*short feminine*	*long feminine*
singular	nominative/accusative	mann 'man'	hnutu 'nut'	bōc 'book'
	genitive	mannes	hnyte	bēċ
	dative	menn	hnyte	bēċ
plural	nominative/accusative	menn	hnyte	bēċ
	genitive	manna	hnuta	bōca
	dative	mannum	hnutum	bōcum

[5] *Beowulf*, l. 778.
[6] The inflections of Indo-European nouns were generally added to a 'stem' built from a 'root' syllable and a 'thematic element' (a sort of suffix). The athematic nouns are so called because they are descended from a class of Indo-European nouns that lacked thematic elements.

> ! The distribution of mutated forms differs in Old and Modern English: some mutated forms appear in the singular, while some plurals are unmutated. Also, as you might guess from the presence in the table of *hnutu* and *bōc*, which are no longer athematic, this declension once contained more nouns than it does now. In fact, in the Old English period some of the athematic nouns were already beginning to move into the strong declensions: feminine *āc* 'oak', for example, has for the dative singular both *ǣċ* and strong *āce*.

Several nouns that end in -nd, especially frbond 'friend', fbond 'enemy', are declined like the athematic nouns, though they are not, technically speaking, members of this declension. Several of these have partly or entirely gone over to the strong declension; for example, you are about as likely to encounter the plural frbondas as frcend.

6.2   More about strong nouns

6.2.1   *Two-syllable nouns*

Two-syllable nouns have syncopation (loss of a vowel) in the second syllable when the first syllable is long and an ending follows, as table 6.7 shows. The syncopated vowel often gets restored, so you should not be surprised to see *enġeles* or *hēafodes*.

Table 6.7   Two-syllable strong nouns

		masculine	*neuter*	*feminine*
singular	nominative/accusative	enġel 'angel'	hēafod 'head'	sāwol 'soul'
	genitive	enġles	hēafdes	sāwle
	dative	enġle	hēafde	sāwle
plural	nominative/accusative	enġlas	hēafdu	sāwla
	genitive	enġla	hēafda	sāwla
	dative	enġlum	hēafdum	sāwlum

> ⓘ Notice that the nominative/accusative plural of *hēafod* ends in -*u* even though the first syllable is long. Two-syllable neuters follow the rule in §2.4: if the first syllable is short, the ending -*u* is dropped; if it is long, the ending remains

(syncopation in the second syllable does not affect this rule). Thus you will see the plurals *hēafdu* 'heads' and *reċed* 'halls'. But two-syllable feminines generally lack *-u* in the nominative singular, whatever the length of the first syllable.

6.2.2 Nouns with changes in the stem syllable

The consonant that ends a noun may change if an ending follows. A simple example of this kind of change is Modern English *wolf*, plural *wolves*. The same change, from an unvoiced to voiced spirant ([f] to [v], [s] to [z], [θ] to [ð]), takes place in Old English whenever a voiced sound precedes and an ending follows, though this change is rarely reflected in the spelling (see §2.1.2, item 3).

In addition, as you read in §2.3, *c* alternates with *ċ* and *g* with *ġ* depending on whether the inflectional syllable contains a back vowel, and the *sc* pronounced [ʃ] (like Modern English *sh*) alternates with the *sc* pronounced [sk].

When an ending begins with a back vowel (*a*, *o*, *u*), *æ* or *ea* in a short root syllable becomes *a* (§2.2.1). That is why *dæġ* 'day' alternates with *dagas* 'days' and *ġeat* 'gate' with *gatu* 'gates' in table 6.8. The *a* of the plural is sometimes changed back to *æ* or *ea* by analogy with the singular, so you will see *æscas* as well as *ascas* and *hwælas* 'whales' as well as *hwalas*.

Feminines like *sacu* 'strife' should have *-æ-* rather than *-a-* in the root syllable before the ending *-e*: accusative singular *sæce*, etc. Such forms do occur, but one frequently finds *-a-* before *-e* as well.

Table 6.8 Masculines and neuters with changed stems

		masculine	masculine	neuter
singular	nominative/accusative	dæġ 'day'	æsc 'ash tree'	ġeat 'gate'
	genitive	dæġes	æsces	ġeates
	dative	dæġe	æsce	ġeate
plural	nominative/accusative	dagas	ascas	gatu
	genitive	daga	asca	gata
	dative	dagum	ascum	gatum

Old English does not permit *h* to fall between voiced sounds; it is always dropped in that environment, and the preceding vowel is lengthened. The loss of *h* produces nouns like those in table 6.9. A vowel at the beginning of an ending is always dropped when no consonant remains after the loss of *h*; so you'll see forms like dative singular *fēo*. We expect the genitive plural to look exactly like the dative singular, but Old English resolves the ambiguity by borrowing the ending *-ena* from the weak declension (§6.1.2).

Table 6.9   Masculines ending in *h*

singular	nominative/accusative	wealh 'foreigner'	feoh 'money'
	genitive	wēales	fēos
	dative	wēale	fēo
plural	nominative/accusative	wēalas	–
	genitive	wēala	fēona
	dative	wēalum	–

6.2.3   Nouns with -w- or -ġ- before the ending

Some nouns add -*w*- or -*ġ*- before the ending; but when there is no ending the *w* appears as -*u* or -*o* (lost after a long syllable – see §6.1.1) and the *ġ* as -*e*. These nouns are illustrated in table 6.10. Words like *here* are quite rare, and nouns with -*w*- are usually neuter or feminine. These nouns will cause you little trouble if you remember that the headword form in your glossary or dictionary lacks the -*w*-.

ⓘ   Sometimes what is rather unattractively called a 'parasite vowel' gets inserted before *ġ* or *w*, and we then end up with forms like *heriġas* and *beaduwa*.

Table 6.10   Nouns with -*ġ*- and -*w*-

		masculine	*neuter*	*feminine*
singular	nominative	here 'army'	searu 'skill'	beadu 'battle'
	accusative	here	searu	beadwe
	genitive	herġes	searwes	beadwe
	dative	herġe	searwe	beadwe
plural	nominative/accusative	herġas	searu	beadwa
	genitive	herġa	searwa	beadwa
	dative	herġum	searwum	beadwum

6.3   Minor declensions

The minor declensions contain relatively few nouns, but the ones they contain tend to be common. As a declension is disappearing from a language, the nouns it contains move into the major declensions. The last nouns to leave these minor declensions are usually the ones in daily use, like Modern English *man/men*, *tooth/teeth* and *child/children*, for the familiarity of the words keeps their inflections from coming to seem strange. So although the minor declensions contain few nouns, you are likely to encounter most of them in the course of your reading.

6.3.1   u-*stem nouns*

This declension contains only masculines and feminines, and they are declined alike. There is, on the other hand, a distinction between short stems and long stems in the nominative singular (see §6.1.1), so table 6.11 illustrates one short stem and one long stem without regard to gender.

Table 6.11   *u*-stem nouns

		short stem	*long stem*
singular	nominative/accusative	sunu	hand
	genitive/dative	suna	handa
plural	nominative/accusative	suna	handa
	genitive	suna	handa
	dative	sunum	handum

Often *u*-stem nouns use a mix of forms, some of them being from the strong declensions. For example, *winter* was originally a *u*-stem, but one frequently sees strong genitive singular *wintres*.

6.3.2   *Nouns of relationship*

The nouns of relationship that end in -*r* belong here: *fæder* 'father', *mōdor* 'mother', *brōðor* 'brother', *sweostor* 'sister', *dohtor* 'daughter'. These have endless genitive singulars and usually *i*-mutation (§2.2.2) in the dative singular (table 6.12). The feminines here are exceptions to the rule that the genitive and dative singular must always be the same in feminine words.

Fæder and *mōdor* have partly gone over to the strong declensions, in that the nominative/accusative plurals are *fæderas* and *mōdra*. *Fæder* and *sweostor* lack mutated vowels in the dative singular.

Table 6.12   Nouns of relationship

		masculine	*feminine*
singular	nominative/accusative	brōðor	dohtor
	genitive	brōðor	dohtor
	dative	brēðer	dehter
plural	nominative/accusative	brōðor	dohtor
	genitive	brōðra	dohtra
	dative	brōðrum	dohtrum

6.3.3   Nouns with -r- plurals

The *-r-* of Modern English *children* shows that it once belonged to this declension, and in fact we find a plural *cilderu* or *cildra* in early West Saxon and similar forms in some other dialects. But in late West Saxon the word *cild* has gone over to the strong neuters. Several neuter nouns remain in this declension, though, even in late West Saxon (table 6.13). Like *lamb* are *cealf* 'calf' and *æġ* 'egg'. Scattered instances of other words (including *cild* in early texts) show that this declension was once somewhat larger.

Table 6.13   Nouns with -r- plurals

	singular	*plural*
nominative/accusative	lamb 'lamb'	lambru
genitive	lambes	lambra
dative	lambe	lambrum

6.3.4   Nouns with -þ- endings

The genitive/dative singular and all plural forms of these nouns contain the element *-þ-*, as you can see in table 6.14, which shows poetic words for 'man, warrior' and 'maiden'. In these nouns the *-þ-* element is in the process of being re-analysed as part of the word's stem rather than as part of the inflectional

Minitext B. A Miracle of St Benedict

From Bishop Wærferth of Worcester's Old English translation of the *Dialogues* of Pope Gregory the Great. See Hecht [47], pp. 122–3.

[1] Ēac hit ġelamp sume dæġe þæt þā ġebrōðru timbredon þæs mynstres hūs. [2] And þā læġ þǣr ān stān tōmiddes, þone hīe mynton hebban ūp on þæs hūses timbrunge, ac hine ne mihton twēġen men ne þrīe onstyrian. [3] Þā ēodon þǣr mā manna tō, ac hē swā þēah wunode fæst and unwendedlīċ, efne swelċe hē wǣre hæfd be wyrtwalan in þǣre eorðan. [4] And ēac hit openlīċe mihte bēon onġieten þæt se ealda fēond sæt ofer þām stāne, þone ne mihton swā maniġra wera handa onstyrian. [5] Þā for þǣre earfoþnesse wæs sended tō þām Godes were, and þā brōðru bǣdon þæt hē cōme and mid his ġebedum þone fēond onweġ ādrife, þæt hīe mihten þone stān ūp āhebban. [6] Þā sōna swā se Godes wer þider cōm, hē dyde þǣr his ġebed and his bletsunge. [7] And þā wearð se stān mid swā miċelre hrǣdnesse ūp āhafen, swelċe hē ǣr nǣniġe hefiġnesse on him næfde.

ending; that is why we find -þ- in the nominative singular (often for *hæle*, always for *mæġþ*). Other nouns belonging to this declension are *ealu* 'ale' (genitive/dative singular *ealoþ*) and *mōnaþ* 'month', which has entirely gone over to the strong nouns except in the nominative/accusative plural, where we find *mōnaþ* as well as *mōnþas*.

Table 6.14 Nouns with -þ- endings

		'man, warrior'	'maiden'
singular	nominative/accusative	hæle, hæleþ	mæġþ
	genitive	hæleþes	mæġþ
	dative	hæleþe	mæġþ
plural	nominative/accusative	hæleþ	mæġþ
	genitive	hæleþa	mæġþa
	dative	hæleþum	mæġþum

6.4 On-line exercises

Old English Aerobics has a session on the noun, using easy to intermediate Old English sentences. Read the sentences carefully and work the exercises. Minitext B is also on-line, accompanied by exercises on the nouns it contains.

Chapter 7

Verbs

7.1 Quick start

Old English verbs[1] can be daunting, for a typical verb appears in more forms than a typical pronoun, noun or adjective. While no noun has more than six distinct forms, most verbs have fourteen. (Modern English verbs, by contrast, normally have four or five forms.) Further, while some nouns, like *mann* 'man', have two different vowels in the root syllable, some verbs have as many as five. (The Modern English maximum, leaving aside the verb *to be*, is three.)

This multiplicity of forms may cause you difficulty when looking up verbs in the dictionary or figuring out their grammatical characteristics. But you can see from the 'Magic Sheet' that, despite its inevitable complications, the Old English verb system is really quite orderly. If you keep that orderliness in view as you work through the 'Quick start' section and the rest of this chapter, you will find the verbs to be much easier than they look.

7.1.1 Strong and weak verbs

Table 7.1 shows all the forms of two common verbs. *Fremman*[2] 'do' belongs to the so-called 'weak' class of Old English verbs, those that make the past

---

[1] For a general discussion of verbs, see §3.1.3.
[2] By convention, glossaries and dictionaries use the infinitive as the headword for verb entries, and when citing verbs we cite the infinitive.

Table 7.1 Basic verb paradigms *Ignore for now*

	weak	*strong*
infinitives	fremman 'do'	helpan 'help'
	tō fremmanne	tō helpanne
present indicative	iċ fremme	iċ helpe
	þū fremest	þū hilpst
	hēo fremeþ	hē hilpþ
	wē fremmaþ	wē helpaþ
past indicative	iċ fremede	iċ healp
	þū fremedest	þū hulpe
	hēo fremede	hē healp
	ġē fremedon	ġē hulpon
present subjunctive	hē fremme	iċ helpe
	hīe fremmen	hīe helpen
past subjunctive	iċ fremede	þū hulpe
	wē fremeden	wē hulpen
imperative	freme	help
	fremmaþ	helpaþ
participles	fremmende	helpende
	fremed	holpen

tense by adding a dental consonant (*-d-* or *-t-*) as a suffix. The Old English weak verbs correspond roughly to the Modern English 'regular' verbs. *Helpan* 'help' is a 'strong' verb, one that does not add a dental suffix to make its past tense, but rather changes the vowel of its root syllable. The Old English strong verbs correspond to Modern English 'irregular' verbs such as *sing* (past *sang*, past participle *sung*).

Take note of these points about the paradigms for *fremman* and *helpan* (further details will come later in the chapter):

1   There are just two tenses, past and present. Old English has various strategies for referring to future time: it uses auxiliary verbs (including *willan*), explicit references to time (e.g. *tōmorgen* 'tomorrow'), and the simple present, relying on context to express futurity.

2   Similarly, Old English has no settled way of expressing what Modern English expresses with the perfect and pluperfect – that is, that an action is now complete or was complete at some time in the past. It can use forms of the verb *habban* 'to have' with the past participle, as Modern English does (*hæfð onfunden* 'has discovered', *hæfde onfunden* 'had discovered'), it can use the adverb *ǣr* 'before' with the simple past (*ǣr onfand* 'had

Table 7.2 Personal endings

present indicative	singular	plural
first person	-e	
second person	-st	-aþ
third person	-þ	
past indicative		
first person	-e / –	
second person	-st / -e	-on
third person	-e / –	
all subjectives		
all persons	-e	-en

discovered'), or it can use the past tense alone, in which case you must infer the correct translation from the context.

3   While the Modern English verb has only one personal ending (-s for the third-person singular), most Old English verb forms have such endings. These are mostly the same for both weak *fremman* and strong *helpan*, but notice that in the singular past indicative the endings are different. The personal endings are shown separately in table 7.2.

4   Person is distinguished only in the indicative singular, never in the plural or subjunctive. For example, table 7.1 gives the present first-person plural indicative form *wē fremmaþ*, but the second person is *ġē fremmaþ* and the third person *hīe fremmaþ*, with the same verb forms. Further, only the second person is distinguished in the singular past indicative: the first- and third-person forms are the same.

5   The root vowels of strong verbs undergo *i*-mutation (§2.2.2) in the present second- and third-person singular indicative: thus the second-person singular of *helpan* is *hilpst*, that of *faran* 'travel' is *færst*, and that of *ċēosan* 'choose' is *ċīest*. The same does not occur in the weak paradigms or in those of strong verbs whose vowels are not subject to *i*-mutation (e.g. *wrītan* 'write', second-person singular *wrītst*).

6   While a Modern English verb descended from the strong verbs never has more than one vowel in the past tense, most Old English strong verbs have *two* past forms with different vowels, distributed as in table 7.1. The form used for the first- and third-person singular past indicative (e.g. *healp*) is called the 'first past', and the form used everywhere else in the past tense (e.g. *hulpon*) is called the 'second past'.

7   The present participle ending in *-ende* is used where Modern English uses the present participle in *-ing*: in constructions that express continuing action (for example, 'was living') and as adjectives ('the living God').

7.1.2   Preterite-present verbs *ignore for now*

Most of the Old English auxiliaries (also called 'helping verbs') belong to a class of verbs called 'preterite-presents', whose present tenses look like strong past tenses ('preterites') and whose past tenses look like weak pasts. Modern English still has several of these verbs, whose forms we here classify as 'present' and 'past' according to their origins, even though we no longer think of the past forms as past:

present	past	present	past
can	could	shall	should
may	might	——	ought[3]
——	must[4]		

The Modern English 'present' forms betray their affiliation with the strong past by a peculiarity of their inflection: like a past tense, they lack the ending *-s* in the third-person singular.

The class of preterite-present verbs is larger in Old English than in Modern English and includes several verbs that are not auxiliaries. Table 7.3 (p. 66) shows the inflection of a few common ones.[5] The present forms of these verbs match the past forms of strong verbs almost precisely: the main differences are that the second-person singular forms have the first past rather than the second past vowel and the ending *-st* or *-t*, and the present subjunctive forms sometimes have *i*-mutation (§2.2.2).

7.1.3   Bēon 'to be'

The verb *bēon* 'to be' in Old English is a mess, but so is 'to be' in Modern English. To the extent that the Old and Modern English verbs look alike, *bēon* will be easy to learn for students who are native speakers of English.

The forms in table 7.4 (p. 67) are an amalgam of three different verbs: one that accounts for the present forms in the first column, one that accounts for

---

[3]   The present form of *ought* is *owe*, which has, however, become a regular verb with its own past tense.

[4]   The original present tense of *must* has been lost.

[5]   Most of the verb paradigms in the remainder of this chapter are abbreviated. You can easily complete them by supplying the correct personal endings.

Table 7.3 Preterite-present verbs

'know how to'	'be able to'		'be obliged to'	'know'
		infinitive		
cunnan	*magan		sculan	witan
		present indicative		
iċ cann	iċ mæġ		iċ sceal	iċ wāt
þū canst	þū meaht		þū scealt	þū wāst
hēo cann	hē mæġ		hit sceal	hēo wāt
wē cunnon	ġē magon		hīe sculon	ġē witon
		past indicative		
iċ cūðe	hēo meahte, mihte		hit sceolde	hē wisse, wiste
þū cūðest	þū meahtest, mihtest		þū sceoldest	þū wistest
wē cūðon	ġē meahton, mihton		hīe sceoldon	wē wisson, wiston
		present subjunctive		
iċ cunne	hēo mæġe		þū scyle, scule	hē wite
		past subjunctive		
iċ cūðe	hēo meahte, mihte		þū sceolde	hē wisse, wiste
		participles		
——	——		——	witende
-cunnen, cūð	——		——	witen

all the *b-* forms, and one that accounts for all the *w-* forms. Paradigms derived from these three verbs overlap, so that there are two complete sets of present forms,[6] two sets of imperatives, two infinitives and two present participles.

The *b-* forms are often used with reference to future time, as in this sentence on the Day of Judgement:

On þām dæġe ūs *bið* ætēowed se opena heofon and enġla þrym.
[On that day *will be* revealed to us the open heaven and the host of angels.]

But the *b-* forms sometimes are simple presents, as here:

Ðēos wyrt þe man betonican nemneð, hēo *biþ* cenned on mædum and on clǣnum dūnlandum.
[This herb that one calls betony *is* produced in meadows and in open hilly lands.]

---

[6] Present forms of the verb *wesan* (*weseð*, *wesað*) are also attested, but they are rare.

You'll have to look to the context to tell you whether to translate a *b*- form of *bēon* as a future.

Table 7.4   *bēon*

infinitives	bēon, wesan			
present indicative	iċ eom	iċ bēo	past indicative	iċ wæs
	þū eart	þū bist		þū wǣre
	hē is	hēo bi∂		hit wæs
	hīe sind, sindon	wē bēo∂		ġē wǣron
present subjunctive	hē sīe	þū bēo	past subjunctive	iċ wǣre
	wē sīen	ġē bēon		hīe wǣren
imperative	bēo, wes			
	bēo∂, wesa∂			
participles	bēonde, wesende			
	ġebēon			

7.2 More about endings

7.2.1 Assimilation

When the personal ending -*st* or -*þ* or the -*d*- of the weak past immediately follows a consonant, the result may be a sequence of consonants that is difficult to pronounce. In such cases, one or both consonants are altered so that they are more similar to each other, an effect called assimilation:

1 The ending -*d*- becomes -*t*- when it immediately follows an unvoiced consonant. The singular past of *slǣpan* 'sleep' is *slǣpte*, and that of *mētan* 'meet' is *mētte*. The same change occurs in Modern English, though it is not always reflected in the spelling (say *reached* aloud: what is the final consonant?).
2 The ending -*∂* becomes -*t* when it immediately follows *d*, *s* or *t*. For example, the third-person singular of *rǣdan* 'read' is *rǣtt* (see also item 3), of *rǣsan* 'rush' *rǣst*, and of *grētan* 'greet' *grētt*.
3 When a *d* or *g/ġ* at the end of a root syllable comes in contact with the ending -*st* or -*∂*, it is changed to *t* or *h*: for example, the second-person singular of *fēdan* 'feed' is *fētst*, and the third-person singular of *bīeġan* 'bend' is *bīeh∂*.

4   Whenever one of these rules has produced a double consonant at the end
of a word, or when the ending -ð follows a root ending in ð, the double
consonant may be simplified. For example, the third-person singular of
cīdan 'chide' can be cītt or cīt, and that of cȳðan 'make known' may be
cȳðð or cȳð. A double consonant will always be simplified when preceded
by another consonant: so the past singular of sendan 'send' is sende, not
*sendde.

7.2.2   Plurals ending in -e

Before the pronouns wē 'we' and ġē 'you', any plural ending may appear as
-e. For example:

> Nū bidde wē þē, lēof, þæt ðū ġebidde for hȳ, and hȳ eft āwende tō ðām þe
> hēo ǣr wæs.
> [Now we ask you, sir, that you pray for her, and turn her back into what
> she was before.]

Here the verb in the main clause would be biddaþ if it did not immediately
precede the pronourn wē.

7.2.3   Subjunctive plural endings

In Old English of the tenth century you will frequently see subjunctive plural
-on (sometimes -an) as well as -en, and in Old English of the eleventh century
subjunctives in -en are quite rare. Thus an early text will normally have present
subjunctive plural bidden 'ask', but a later one will have biddon. In the past
tense, where the indicative plural personal ending is already -on, the distinction between indicative and subjunctive plural is lost: for biddan 'ask', both
forms are bǣdon in late Old English.

7.3   More about weak verbs

Germanic weak verbs fall into three classes: the first two of these are well
represented in Old English and the third has almost disappeared (the few
remaining class 3 verbs are discussed below, §7.3.4). Of the four weak verbs
in table 7.5, sceþþan, herian and hǣlan belong to class 1, and lufian belongs
to class 2.

Table 7.5   Weak verbs

	1A 'injure'	1B 'praise'	1C 'heal'	2 'love'
infinitives	sceþþan	herian	hǣlan	lufian
	tō sceþþanne	tō herianne	tō hǣlanne	tō lufianne
present indicative Sg 1	ić sceþþe	ić herie	ić hǣle	ić lufie
2	þū sceþest	þū herest	þū hǣlst	þū lufast
3	hēo sceþeþ	hē hereþ	hit hǣlþ	hē lufað
Pl	wē sceþþaþ	ġē heriaþ	hīe hǣlaþ	wē lufiað
past indicative Sg 1	ić sceþede	ić herede	ić hǣlde	ić lufode
2	þū sceþedest	þū heredest	þū hǣldest	þū lufodest
3	hit sceþede	hē herede	hēo hǣlde	hēo lufode
Pl	ġē sceþedon	hīe heredon	wē hǣldon	hīe lufodon
present subjunctive Sg	hē sceþþe	ić herie	þū hǣle	hēo lufie
Pl	hīe sceþþen	ġē herien	wē hǣlen	ġē lufien
past subjunctive Sg	ić sceþede	þū herede	hē hǣlde	hēo lufode
Pl	hīe sceþeden	wē hereden	ġē hǣlden	ġē lufoden
imperative Sg	sceþe	here	hǣl	lufa
Pl	sceþþaþ	heriaþ	hǣlaþ	lufiað
participles	sceþende	heriende	hǣlende	lufiende
	sceþed	hered	hǣled	lufod

7.3.1   Classes 1 and 2

Class 1 is marked by *i*-mutation (§2.2.2) in the root syllable. If the root is short (§2.4), gemination (the doubling of the consonant at the end of the root syllable) occurs in certain forms, including the infinitive; but if the consonant is *r*, you will find -*ri*- or -*rġ*- instead of -*rr*-. The -*i*- or -*ġ*- represents a consonant [j], so *herian* is a two-syllable word: [her-jɑn].

ⓘ The geminated form of *f* is *bb* (*swebban* 'put to sleep', third-person singular *swefeþ*); that of *g* is *cg* (*bycgan* 'buy', third-person singular *byġeð*).

Class 2 lacks *i*-mutation. Wherever you find gemination in class 1 verbs with short root syllables, you will find an element spelled -*i*- or -*iġ*- after the root syllable of the class 2 verb.[7] This -i- is a syllable all by itself – weighty enough, in fact, to be capable of bearing metrical stress, as we see in this line:

```
×   × /   / ×     × ×   / \ ×
Him þā secg hraðe       ġewāt sīðian⁸
```
[The man then quickly departed journeying]

where stress falls on both the first and second syllables of *sīðian*.

! The present third-person singular of the class 2 weak verb looks like the present plural of the other major verb classes (for example, *hē lufað* 'he loves', *wē sceþþað* 'we injure'). To avoid being confused by this resemblance, you should learn to recognize a class 2 weak verb when you see one. If your glossary (unlike the one in this book) doesn't tell you the class of the verb, then look at the headword. If the root syllable ends with any consonant but *r* and is followed by -i-, chances are it is a class 2 weak verb, and the present third-person singular will end with -að.

In some verbs, a vowel is inserted before the endings that do not begin with vowels (-st, -ð, -d-). In verbs like *sceþþan* and *herian* this vowel is -e-, in verbs like *hælan* the vowel is absent, and in all class 2 weak verbs it is -a- or -o-. Often the vowel is omitted in class 1 verbs with short root syllables, so you can expect to see (for example) *fremst* and *fremþ* as well as *fremest* and *fremeþ*. This is the rule rather than the exception when the root syllable ends with *d* or *t*: so the past tense of *āhreddan* 'rescue' is *āhredde* and that of *hwettan* 'urge' is *hwette*.

7.3.2 Weak verbs that change their vowels

Verbs like Modern English *buy/bought*, which both change their vowels in the past tense and add the dental consonant characteristic of the weak past, should not be confused with verbs like *swim/swam*, which are descended from the Old English strong verbs. *Buy/bought* belongs to a group of class 1 weak verbs in which the vowels of the present tense are subject to *i*-mutation (§2.2.2) while the vowels of the past tense are not. Table 7.6 illustrates with *cwellan* 'kill', *sēċan* 'seek' and *þenċan* 'think'.

---

[7] This element did not cause *i*-mutation because it did not begin with *i* at the time that *i*-mutation took place. Rather, it was a long syllable [oːj], which later became the syllable spelled -i-.

[8] *Genesis A*, l. 2018. For the metrical notation, see chapter 13.

Table 7.6 Weak verbs that change their vowels

	'kill'	*'seek'*	*'think'*
infinitive	cwellan	sēċan	þenċan
present indicative	iċ cwelle	iċ sēċe	iċ þenċe
	þū cwelest	þū sēċst	þū þenċst
	hēo cweleþ	hē sēċþ	hit þenċþ
	wē cwellaþ	ġē sēċaþ	hīe þenċaþ
past indicative	iċ cwealde	hēo sōhte	hē þōhte
present subjunctive	hē cwelle	iċ sēċe	þū þenċe
past subjunctive	iċ cwealde	hēo sōhte	hē þōhte
imperative	cwele	sēċ	þenċ
	cwellaþ	sēċaþ	þenċaþ
participles	cwellende	sēċende	þenċende
	cweald	sōht	þōht

A *ċ*, *cg* or *ġ* at the end of the root syllable of one of these weak verbs is always changed to *h* before the past-tense ending *-t-*. Old English also has a rule that when *n* precedes *h*, it is dropped and the preceding vowel is lengthened. Thus the past tense of *þenċan* is *þōhte* and that of *brenġan* 'bring' is *brōhte*.

ⓘ The vowels of *cwellan* are not as predicted in table 2.1 (p. 17) because the unmutated vowel in the forms with *e* was actually *æ*, not *ea*. Similar verbs include *cweċċan* 'shake' (past *cweahte*), *reċċan* 'narrate' (*reahte*), *sellan* 'give' (*sealde*) and *tellan* 'count, relate' (*tealde*).

7.3.3 Contracted verbs

The rule that *h* is always dropped between vowels (already mentioned in connection with nouns, §6.2.2) introduces some complications in the verb paradigm. Table 7.7 illustrates with the class 2 weak verb *smēaġan* 'ponder'.

The underlying (and unattested) verb is **smēahian* or **smēahiġan*, but the *h* has been lost in all forms, since it always comes between vowels. Notice the *-ġ-* that comes before the ending in certain forms: it is a remnant of the syllable spelled *-i-* or *-iġ-* in normal class 2 weak verbs. Like *smēaġan* are *þrēaġan* 'chastise', *twēoġan* 'doubt' and *frēoġan* 'set free'.

Table 7.7　Contracted weak verbs

'ponder'	*singular*	*plural*
infinitive	smēaġan	
present indicative	iċ smēaġe	
	þū smēast	wē smēaġað
	hēo smēað	
past indicative	iċ smēade	ġē smēadon
present subjunctive	hēo smēaġe	hīe smēaġen
past subjunctive	hē smēade	wē smēaden
imperative	smēa	smēaġað
present participle	smēaġende	
past participle	smēad	

7.3.4　Class 3 weak verbs

Obeying the rule that the most common words are the last to leave a dying class (§6.3), class 3 contains only *habban* 'have', *libban* 'live', *secgan* 'say' and *hycgan* 'think' (table 7.8), together with a few odd remnants. Each of these verbs has partly gone over to other classes, and the resulting confusion makes it impractical to describe the characteristics of the class. The best course is to study the paradigms and be prepared to encounter these anomalous verbs in your reading.

7.4　More about strong verbs

Most strong verbs are inflected in pretty much the same way as *helpan* (table 7.1, p. 63). You will be able to predict the present paradigm of almost any strong verb if you know how *i*-mutation affects the vowels of root syllables (§2.2.2) and how the endings -*st* and -*ð* interact with consonants at the ends of root syllables (the rules for weak verbs outlined at §7.3.1 also apply to strong verbs). Once you have learned the gradation patterns for the strong verbs, you will easily master the past paradigms as well.

7.4.1　The strong verb classes

The Germanic languages have seven classes of strong verbs, each characterized by its own gradation pattern. Gradation is an Indo-European grammatical

Table 7.8 Class 3 weak verbs

		infinitive		
habban	libban, lifġan	secgan		hycgan

		present indicative		
iċ hæbbe	iċ libbe, lifġe	iċ secge		iċ hycge
þū hæfst, hafast	þū lifast, leofast	þū seġst, sagast		þū hyġst, hogast
hēo hæfð, hafað	hē lifað, leofað	hēo seġð, sagað		hē hyġ(e)ð, hogað
wē habbaþ	ġē libbað	wē secgaþ		ġē hycgað

		past indicative		
iċ hæfde	hē lifde, leofode	hēo sæġde		iċ hog(o)de, hyġde

		present subjunctive		
hē hæbbe	iċ libbe, lifġe	þū secge		iċ hycge

		past subjunctive		
iċ hæfde	þū lifde, leofode	hēo sæġde		hē hog(o)de, hyġde

		imperative		
hafa	leofa	sæġe, saga		hyġe, hoga
habbaþ	libbaþ, lifġaþ	secgaþ		hycgaþ

		participles		
hæbbende	libbende, lifġende	secgende		hycgende
ġehæfd	ġelifd	ġesæġd		ġehogod

feature whereby the root vowels of words are altered to signal changes in grammatical function. For example, if the present tense of a Modern English verb contains 'short' *i* followed by *n* or *m*, the past-tense form will usually have *a* and the past participle *u*: *drink, drank, drunk*; *ring, rang, rung*; *swim, swam, swum*.

Old English has some variations within the Germanic classes, as table 7.9 shows. This table includes the present third-person singular indicative so that you can see how *i*-mutation affects each class. You should understand, however, that the vowel of this form is not part of the gradation pattern inherited from Indo-European, but rather a relatively recent phenomenon. Eventually the English language would discard the *i*-mutation of the second- and third-person singular, but the ancient gradation patterns of the strong verbs are still with us.

Table 7.9 Classes of strong verbs

	infinitive	3rd pers.	first past	second past	past participle
1	wrītan	wrītt	wrāt	writon	writen
2a	ċēosan	ċīesð	ċēas	curon	coren
2b	lūcan	lȳcð	lēac	lucon	locen
3a	singan	singð	sang	sungon	sungen
3b	helpan	hilpð	healp	hulpon	holpen
3c	hweorfan	hwierfð	hwearf	hwurfon	hworfen
4a	stelan	stilð	stæl	stǣlon	stolen
4b	niman	nimð	nam	nōmon	numen
5	sprecan	spricð	spræc	sprǣcon	sprecen
6	bacan	bæcð	bōc	bōcon	bacen
7a	hātan	hǣtt	hēt	hēton	hāten
7b	flōwan	flēwð	flēow	flēowon	flōwen

! Students often ask if they should memorize the strong verb classes. The answer is a qualified 'yes'. The qualification is that you should take note of patterns within these classes and use them as mnemonic devices. Most of the vowels of classes 1–5, especially, are derived from a single gradation pattern, and though these vowels have been altered by the influence of surrounding sounds, they still resemble each other:

1 The vowels of the present tense are mid or high vowels – that is, pronounced with the tongue at or near the roof of the mouth ([e,i]) – or diphthongs that begin with these vowels.

2 The vowels of the first past are low vowels – that is, pronounced with the tongue and jaw lowered ([ɑ,æ]) – or diphthongs that begin with these vowels.

3 The vowels of the second past, though their original resemblance to each other has been obscured, are mostly short; in classes 4–5 they are long and low.

4 The vowels of the past participle are mostly variations on the short vowels of the second past, but in class 5 the vowel is the same as the present.

The gradation patterns of classes 6–7 differ from those of 1–5 and must be memorized separately.

ⓘ Class 2 verbs like *lūcan* 'lock' do not conform to the standard gradation pattern; the *ū* of the present tense has never been satisfactorily explained.

A few class 3 verbs have *u* in the present tense. Of these, the one you will meet most frequently is *murnan* 'mourn' (first past *mearn*, second past *murnon*).

The *ō* of class 4b appears before nasal consonants. *Cuman* 'come' belongs to this subclass, but its present tense is anomalous.

The present tense of class 6 sometimes has *æ* or *ea*.

Class 7 has a variety of vowels in the present tense, not just *ā* and *ō*. The past-tense vowels *ē* and *ēo* are what distinguish this class.

You may observe the same gradation patterns you have seen here in families of words derived from the same root. For example, *lēof* 'beloved' has the same vowel as a class 2 present, *ġelēafa* 'belief' has the same vowel as the first past, *ġelīefan* 'believe' has the first past vowel with *i*-mutation, and *lufian* 'love' and *lof* 'praise' have the vowels of the second past and past participle.

7.4.2 Verbs affected by grammatical alternation

Grammatical alternation[9] is an alternation between one consonant and another to mark the grammar of a word. Only three pairs of consonants alternate in this way:

þ : *d*   *h* : *g*/*ġ*   *s* : *r*

Grammatical alternation affects the paradigms of most strong verbs whose roots end with the consonants *þ*, *h* and *s*: three such verbs are shown in table 7.10.

At the end of the root syllable *h* is often dropped, in verbs like *tēon* 'accuse' (see next section), but enough forms with *h* remain to show the alternation clearly.

ⓘ Although the Modern English strong verbs no longer show the effects of grammatical alternation, it remains in some fossilized past participles such as *forlorn* (from *forlēosan*, past participle *forloren*) and *sodden* (from the past participle of *sēoðan*).

---

[9] A translation of the German phrase 'der grammatische Wechsel'. In grammars written in English you will usually see it referred to as 'Verner's Law' after the Danish linguist Karl Verner, who described its origin. Here we prefer the German term as more descriptive of its function in the recorded language.

Table 7.10 Grammatical alternation

	'seethe'	*'accuse'*	*'choose'*
infinitive	sēoðan	tēon	cēosan
present indicative	ić sēoðe	ić tēo	ić ćēose
	þū sīeðst	þū tīehst	þū ćīest
past indicative	ić sēað	ić tāh	ić cēas
	þū sude	þū tige	þū cure
	ġē sudon	hīe tigon	wē curon
present subjunctive	hē sēoðe	ić tēo	þū cēose
past subjunctive	ić sude	þū tige	hē cure
past participle	soden	tigen	coren

You will notice this alternation not only in verb paradigms, but also in families of words derived from the same root; for example, *hliehhan* 'laugh' and *hlagol* 'inclined to laugh', *nēah* 'near' and *nǣġan* 'approach', *lēosan* 'lose' and *lor* 'loss', *cweðan* 'say' and *cwide* 'saying'.

7.4.3 Contracted verbs

As you have just seen, some strong verbs are subject to contraction as a result of the loss of *h* between voiced sounds – the same rule that produces contracted weak verbs (§7.3.3). Table 7.11 illustrates with three very common verbs, *sēon* 'see', *slēan* 'slay' and *fōn* 'take'. The contraction affects only some present-tense forms, the infinitives and the present participle; past-tense forms that might have been affected have *g* (by grammatical alternation) instead of *h*. Verbs of classes 1, 2 and 5 have *ēo* in contracted forms; those of class 6 have *ēa*; those of class 7 have *ō*.

🛈 The alternation *h/w* in *sēon* is the result of a rare anomaly in the rule of grammatical alternation, the result of which is that *ġ* varies with *w* in the second past and past participle. For example, the usual past participle is *sewen*, but you may sometimes see *seġen* instead.

The *-n-* that appears in some forms of *fōn* (and also *hōn* 'hang') was at one time distributed throughout the paradigm. But the rule that *n* cannot appear before *h* (§7.3.2) caused it to be dropped in all forms but those with *g*. *Fōn* is also unusual in that the form with *g* has been extended to the first past (whose vowel is also the same as that of the second past).

Table 7.11 Contracted strong verbs

	'see'	'slay'	'take'
infinitive	sēon	slēan	fōn
present indicative	iċ sēo	iċ slēa	iċ fō
	þū siehst	þū sliehst	þū fēhst
	hēo siehþ	hē sliehð	hit fēhþ
	wē sēoð	ġē slēað	hīe fōð
past indicative	iċ seah	hēo slōh	hē fēng
	hīe sāwon	wē slōgon	ġē fēngon
present subjunctive	hē sēo	iċ slēa	þū fō
past subjunctive	iċ sāwe	þū slōge	hē fēnge
imperative	seoh	sleah	fōh
	sēoþ	slēað	fōð
participles	sēonde	slēande	fōnde
	sewen, seġen	slagen	fangen

7.4.4 Tips on strong verbs

! This would be a good time to go over all the verb paradigms you have seen so far, noting basic similarities. Notice particularly that in the present tense the second- and third-person singular forms are usually different from all the others. These are the forms in which the personal ending does not begin with a vowel.

Present-tense strong verbs cause few difficulties, since the endings make them easy to identify; past plurals are easy as well, for the same reason. But past singulars, which either lack an ending or end only in -e, are easy to confuse with nouns and adjectives. As you gain experience with the language, this kind of confusion will become less likely. But in the meantime, here are some tips to help you get it right.

- Look up words carefully. Learn what kind of spelling variations you can expect in Old English (see §2.1.3 and Appendix A); when two words look alike but their spelling differences are not what you'd expect, you may conclude that they are different words. *Wearð* 'became' looks like *weorð* 'value, price', but *ea* normally does not vary with *eo*; *nam* 'took' looks like *nama* 'name', but endings are rarely lost in Old English. If the glossary you're using has a great many references to the texts you're reading, check to see if the glossary entry you're looking at has a reference to the word you're trying to figure out. If it doesn't, look for an entry that does.

- Examine the grammatical context of the sentence or clause you're reading. Have you located a subject? a verb? an object? If the word you're looking at is *bēag* and you need a verb, try it as the first past of *būgan* 'bow'; if you need a noun, try it as 'ring'.
- Examine the word-order (see chapter 12). Is the word in a place where you'd normally expect to find a subject, an object or a verb?
- Once you've got a tentative translation, apply a sanity test: does it make sense? If it seems ungrammatical, or grammatical but absurd, try something else.

If you're using the on-line texts in *Old English Aerobics*, you won't have any difficulty distinguishing nouns and verbs because every word is clearly marked with its part of speech and a good bit of other grammatical information. *Don't let this feature make you complacent!* Pay attention to the form of the words you're looking up and ask yourself how the editor knew this word was a verb or that word plural. Remember that very few Old English texts are marked up the way the ones in *Old English Aerobics* are. The transition from on-line to printed texts will be very difficult if you have abused the convenience of *Old English Aerobics*.

7.5   Verbs with weak presents and strong pasts

A few verbs have the characteristics of the first weak class in the present tense and of strong class 5 or 6 in the past tense. For example, *hebban* 'lift' has a present tense like that of *fremman* 'do' or *sceþþan* 'harm' (tables 7.1, 7.5): *iċ hebbe, hē hefeð*, etc. But the past third-person singular indicative of this verb is *hōf*, the plural is *hōfon*, and the past participle is *hafen* (the vowel is the same as that of the present, but without *i*-mutation).

Some common verbs behave in this way, for example, *biddan* 'ask', *licgan* 'lie', *scieppan* 'make, create', *sittan* 'sit'. The dual nature of these verbs (which most glossaries, including the one in this book, classify as strong) is a curiosity, but it will cause you little difficulty.

7.6 More about preterite-present verbs

Here we list each preterite-present verb with its principal present and past forms. Infinitives preceded by asterisks are not attested.

āgan. *possess.* iċ **āh,** þū **āhst,** hīe **āgon;** past **āhte.**

cunnan. *know (how to).* iċ **can,** hīe **cunnon;** past **cūðe.**

dugan. *be good (for something).* iċ **dēag,** hīe **dugon;** subjunctive **duge, dyġe;** past **dohte.**

*durran. *dare.* iċ **dearr,** hīe **durron;** subjunctive **durre, dyrre;** past **dorste.**

magan. *may.* iċ **mæġ,** þū **meaht,** hīe **magon;** past **meahte, mihte.**

*mōtan. *must, be allowed.* iċ **mōt,** þū **mōst,** hīe **mōton;** past **mōste.**

ġemunan. *remember.* iċ **ġeman,** hīe **ġemunon;** subjunctive **ġemune, ġemyne;** past **ġemunde.**

*ġe-, *benugan. *be enough.* hit **ġeneah,** hīe **ġenugon;** past **benohte.**

sculan. *must.* iċ **sceal,** þū **scealt,** hīe **sculon;** subjunctive **scyle, scule;** past **sceolde.**

þurfan. *need.* iċ **þearf,** þū **þearft,** hīe **þurfon;** subjunctive **þurfe, þyrfe;** past **þorfte.**

unnan. *grant, give, allow.* iċ **ann,** hīe **unnon;** past **ūðe.**

witan. *know.* iċ **wāt,** þū **wāst,** hīe **witon;** past **wisse, wiste.**

In addition to what you learned in §7.1.2, keep these points in mind:

1　The past tense is usually built on the second past root, with -d- or -t- added. In fact, it often looks like the past tense of the weak verbs that change their vowels (§7.3.2), though sometimes the forms have been subject to phonological changes that can produce surprising results.

2　When the root syllable ends in *g* (*āgan, dugan, magan*), past -d- becomes -t-; *g* becomes *h* before that ending and before second-person singular present indicative -t (compare §7.3, items 1 and 3).

7.7　*Dōn, gān, willan*

The verbs *do, go* and *will* (table 7.12) are still anomalous in Modern English, and in much the same way as in Old English: *dōn* 'do' has a past form that is paralleled in no other verb; *gān* 'go' lacks a past form of its own and has apparently borrowed the past of another verb, now disappeared; and *willan* 'desire' has distinctive inflections in the present tense.

Table 7.12 dōn, gān, willan

	'do'	'go'	'will'
infinitive	dōn	gān	willan
present indicative	iċ dō	iċ gā	iċ wille
	þū dēst	þū gǣst	þū wilt
	hēo dēð	hit gǣð	hē wile
	wē dōð	ġē gāð	hīe willað
past indicative	iċ dyde	hit ēode	hēo wolde
	þū dydest	þū ēodest	þū woldest
	wē dydon	ġē ēodon	hīe woldon
present subjunctive	iċ dō	hēo gā	þū wille
past subjunctive	iċ dyde	hēo ēode	þū wolde
participles	dōnde	——	willende
	ġedōn	ġegān	——

The present forms of *dōn* and *gān* look like those of normal strong verbs (see §7.4). But the past tense of *dōn* is built on a syllable that looks somewhat like a weak past (though its origin is a mystery), and *gān* has a past tense that also looks weak and in any case does not belong to the same root that gives us the present forms. *Willan* looks a bit like a preterite-present verb, but it is not; and its first- and third-person singular present and plural present are quite different from the preterite-present forms.

7.8 Negation

Most verbs are negated very simply by placing the adverb *ne* 'not' directly in front of them. In independent clauses, the word-order that follows will normally be Verb–Subject (see §12.3):

Se þe mē *ne lufað*, *ne hylt* hē mīne sprǣċe.
[He who *does not love* me *does not keep* my sayings.]

Ne is contracted with certain verbs, for example, *nis* 'is not', *næs* 'was not' (from *bēon*), *næfð* 'does not have', *næfde* 'did not have' (*habban*), *nyllað* 'will not', *noldon* 'would not' (*willan*), *nāh* 'does not have', *nāhte* 'did not have' (*āgan*), *nāt* 'does not know' (*witan*). Notice that all of the verbs so contracted begin with a vowel, *h* or *w*. Not all verbs beginning with those sounds are contracted, but only the more common ones; and those common verbs need not be contracted. You will also see *ne wæs*, *ne hæfð* and so on.

The Modern English rule that two negatives make a positive does not apply in Old English; rather, the addition of more negative adverbs to a sentence adds emphasis to its negativity:

Ne bēo ġē *nāteshwōn* dēade, ðēah ðe ġē of ðām trēowe eton.
[You will *certainly not* be dead, though you eat from the tree.]

Here the additional negative adverb *nāteshwōn* makes the sentence more emphatic than it would be with *ne* alone; since we cannot use double negatives the same way in Modern English, we must resort to a different strategy to represent this emphasis in our translations. Common negative adverbs are *nā*, *nales*, *nāteshwōn* and *nātōþæshwōn*.

7.9 The verbals

Old English forms periphrastic verbs much as Modern English does, with auxiliary verbs and verbals (infinitives or participles – see §3.1.3):

auxiliary + infinitive (will find, may find, etc.)
auxiliary + past participle (has found, had found, was found)
to be + present participle (is finding)

This section lists a few ways in which the infinitives and participles of Old English differ from those of Modern English.

7.9.1 Infinitives

The inflected infinitive is often used with *bēon* to express obligation, necessity or propriety. It can usually be translated with *should* or *must* and an infinitive:

hyt ys ġȳt ġeornlīċe tō āsmēaġeanne
[it should further be diligently investigated]

Verbs of knowing, seeing, hearing and commanding may be followed by an accusative object and an infinitive expressing what that object is doing or should do. The construction remains in sentences like 'I saw him dance', but in Old English it is more frequent and it comes where we no longer use it. Examples:

Ġewīt fram mē, forþon þe iċ *ġesēo þē* on forhæfdnesse þurhwunian.
[Depart from me, for I *see you are persevering* in abstinence.]

Hǣlend fērde þǣr forþ and þā *ġehȳrde þone blindan cleopian.*
[The Savior went forth there and then *heard the blind man call out.*]

Drihten, ġyf þū hyt eart, *hāt mē cuman* tō þē ofer þās wæteru.
[Lord, if it is you, *command me to come* to you over these waters.]

The object is often unexpressed, especially after verbs of commanding:

And se cyng þā *hēt niman* Sīferðes lāfe and ġebringan hī binnan Mealdelmesbyriġ.
[And then the king *commanded* [*someone*] *to take* Siferth's widow and bring her into Malmesbury.]

It is sometimes appropriate to translate such sentences with a passive construction ('commanded her to be brought') even though the Old English construction is not passive.

7.9.2 *Participles*

The Old English present participle is often used as a noun denoting the performer of an action, e.g. *rodora Rǣdend* 'Ruler of the heavens' (*Rǣdend* being the present participle of *rǣdan* 'rule'). You will often find such forms listed separately as nouns in glossaries and dictionaries.

🛈 The Modern English participle in -*ing* can also be used as a noun denoting the action of a verb (e.g. 'living well is the best revenge'), but for this purpose Old English uses the infinitive.

A construction consisting of a noun or pronoun and participle, both in the dative case, is occasionally used where one would expect an adverb clause or another construction expressing time or cause. This noun phrase may sometimes be introduced by a preposition.

And Offa ġefēng Myrċena rīċe, *ġeflȳmdum Beornrede.*
[And Offa seized the kingdom of the Mercians *after Beornred had been driven out.*]

Æfter Agustini fyliġde in biscophāde Laurentius, þone hē forðon *bi him lifiġendum* ġehālgode, þȳ lǣs *him forðfērendum* se steall ǣniġe hwīle būton heorde taltriġan ongunne.

[After Augustine, Lawrence followed in the bishopric, whom he consecrated *while he was still alive* for this reason: lest *by his passing away* the position should for any time, being without a guide, begin to be unstable.]

ⓘ Those who know Latin will recognize the similarity between this construction and the ablative absolute, of which it is generally thought to be an imitation.

7.10   The subjunctive

Because speakers of Modern English seldom use the subjunctive mood, the Old English subjunctive is difficult for us to get used to. We do still use it when stating conditions contrary to fact, as in

> If I *were* a carpenter,
> and you were a lady,
> would you marry me anyway?

Here the subjunctive *were* (the indicative would be *was*) suggests that the speaker is not in fact a carpenter. We also use the subjunctive in noun clauses following verbs of desiring and commanding. For example:

The king desired that the knight *go* on a quest.
The king commanded that the knight *go* on a quest.
I suggest that you *be* a little quieter.
I move that the bypass *be* routed east of town.
I wish that I *were* wiser.

Here the subjunctives tell us that the condition described in the noun clause is not a present reality or a future certainty, but a possibility mediated by someone's desire. Some of these usages are disappearing: the first two examples above sound a little archaic, and it would now be more idiomatic to say 'The king wanted the knight to go on a quest' and 'The king commanded the knight to go on a quest', using infinitive constructions rather than subjunctives.

Aside from these common uses, the subjunctive now appears mainly in fixed or formulaic expressions, for example, 'come what may', 'thanks be to God'.

The subjunctive is far more common in Old English than in Modern English, and you must get used to seeing it in environments where you do not expect it. As in Modern English, the subjunctive is used for conditions contrary to fact. A made-up example:

Ġif iċ *wǣre* trēowwyrhta . . .
[If I *were* a carpenter . . .]

It is also used in noun clauses following verbs of desiring and commanding:

Iċ wȳsce þæt iċ wīsra *wǣre*.
[I wish that I *were* wiser.]

But the subjunctive is also used in noun clauses where we would not now use it:

Hīe cwǣdon þæt hē *wǣre* wīs.

Here the subjunctive in the noun clause following *Hīe cwǣdon* 'They said' does not signal a condition contrary to fact, and *cwǣdon* 'said' is hardly a verb of desiring or commanding. In fact, the fairest translation of this sentence would be

They said that he *was* wise.

making no attempt at all to reproduce the subjunctive. What then does the subjunctive express?

Think of it as implying a point of view towards the action of the verb. In clauses following verbs of desire, the point of view is obvious. In *Hīe cwǣdon þæt hē wǣre wīs*, it is merely that the speaker is reporting an opinion. He is not necessarily taking a position on the rightness or wrongness of that opinion. It may indeed be obvious that he is in complete agreement:

Þæt folc ðā ðe þis tācen ġeseah cwæð þæt Crist *wǣre* sōð wītega.
[Then the people who saw this sign said that Christ *was* a true prophet.]

The following sentence is similar, but it uses the indicative:

Be him āwrāt se wītega Isaias þæt hē *is* stefn clipiendes on wēstene.
[Concerning him (John the Baptist) the prophet Isaiah wrote that he *is* the voice of one crying in the wilderness.]

The choice between subjunctive and indicative may often be a matter of individual preference or rhetorical emphasis.

Another common environment in which the subjunctive does not necessarily indicate doubt or unreality is the concessive clause introduced by *þēah* or *þēah þe* 'though', which always takes the subjunctive whether or not the statement it contains is known to be true. For example:

Minitext c. Wulfstan's Translation of the Apostles' Creed

From the sermon 'To Eallum Folke' by Wulfstan, Bishop of Worcester and Archbishop of York. See Bethurum [9], pp. 166–8.

[1] Wē ġelȳfað on ænne God ælmihtiġne þe ealle þing ġesceōp and ġeworhte. [2] And wē ġelȳfað and ġeorne witon þæt Crist Godes sunu tō mannum cōm for ealles mancynnes ðearfe. [3] And wē ġelȳfað þæt hine clæne mæden ġebære, Sancta Maria, þe næfre nāhte weres ġemānan. [4] And wē ġelȳfað þæt hē miċel ġeðolode and stīðlīċe þrōwode for ūre ealra nēode. [5] And wē ġelȳfað þæt hine man on rōde āhēnge and hine tō dēaðe ācwealde and hine siðð̄an on eorðan bebyriġde. [6] And wē ġelȳfað þæt hē tō helle fērde and ðærof ġehergode eal þæt hē wolde. [7] And wē ġelȳfað þæt hē siðð̄an of dēaðe ārise. [8] And wē ġelȳfað þæt hē æfter þām tō heofonum āstige. [9] And wē ġelȳfað and ġeorne witon þæt hē on dōmes dæġ tō ðām miċlan dōme cymð. [10] And wē ġelȳfað þæt ealle dēade men sculon þonne ārīsan of dēaðe and þone miċlan dōm ealle ġesēċan. [11] And wē ġelȳfað þæt ðā synfullan sculon þanon on ān tō helle faran and ðær ā siðð̄an mid dēoflum wunian on byrnendum fȳre and on ēċan forwyrde, and ðæs æniġ ende ne cymð æfre tō worulde. [12] And wē ġelȳfað þæt ðā gōdan and wel Cristenan þe hēr on worulde Gode wel ġecwēmdon þonne on ān sculon intō heofonum faran and ðær siðð̄an wununge habban mid Gode selfum and mid his enġlum ā on ēċnesse. Amen.

Ne sceal nān man swā þēah, þēah hē synful *sīe*, ġeortrūwian.
[Nevertheless, no man must despair, though he *be* sinful.]

Here *þēah* has a sense something like 'even if', implying that the man may or may not be sinful; the subjunctive is appropriate (if a little archaic) even in Modern English. But compare:

God is mildheort, þēah ðe ūre yfelnes him oft *ābelge*.
[God is merciful, though our wickedness often *angers* him.]

Here the writer can have no doubt that we do often anger God, but the verb *ābelge* is still in the subjunctive mood.

In general, you can expect relative clauses, clauses of place, and 'when' and 'while' clauses to take the indicative. Concessive clauses and 'before' and 'until' clauses more often take the subjunctive. But the mood in many kinds of clause varies as it does in noun clauses, and linguists argue ceaselessly about the meaning of the subjunctive and the indicative in several common constructions.

> **!** Beginners (and scholars too!) sometimes feel that they must always translate the Old English subjunctive with a Modern English subjunctive or with a subjunctive-like construction such as the conditional ('would anger'). But it is often best, as the discussion above shows, to translate the subjunctive with a plain indicative. You must determine as nearly as you can what the subjunctive is doing in each instance and decide what Modern English construction best renders that sense.

The Old English subjunctive is often used to make a first- or third-person imperative, and then the best translation usually converts the subject of the verb into an object of 'let'. In plural constructions, the -*n* of the ending is generally dropped.

Sīe hē āmānsumod.
[Let him be excommunicated.]

Ete hīe hrædlīce.
[Let them eat quickly.]

Lufie wē ūre nēxtan.
[Let us love our neighbours.]

This usage survives in some formulaic phrases such as 'God be thanked'.

7.11   On-line exercises

Old English Aerobics has a session on the verb, using easy to intermediate Old English sentences. Minitext c is also on-line, accompanied by exercises on the verbs it contains.

Chapter 8

Adjectives

8.1 Quick start

Surely the oddest grammatical feature belonging to the Germanic languages is that they can inflect almost any adjective in either of two very different ways. If the adjective follows a demonstrative pronoun (§5.1.3), possessive adjective (§5.1.2), or genitive noun or noun phrase, one of the so-called 'weak' endings is added to it; otherwise it is given a 'strong' ending. This distinction is widespread (all the early Germanic languages have it) and surprisingly durable: strong and weak adjectives were still distinguished in Chaucer's English, and they are distinguished even now in German.

At this point you may be grumbling that we have arbitrarily doubled the amount of memorization required to learn the adjectives. If so, calm down: adjectives are really quite easy. The weak adjectives are almost exactly the same as the weak nouns (§6.1.2). Most of the strong adjective endings resemble those of either the strong nouns (§6.1.1) or the demonstrative pronouns. In this chapter you will see almost no endings that you have not seen before.

Indeed (though some Old English teachers may not approve of our telling you so), you may find it possible to read Old English prose pretty well without having put in a lot of work on adjectives. In a noun phrase like *þæs æðelan bōceres* 'the noble scholar's', you can get the information that the phrase is genitive singular from either the demonstrative pronoun or the noun. The weak adjective *æðelan* doesn't tell you much. In a phrase like *ġeonge prēostas* 'young priests', the strong ending of the adjective *ġeonge* is less ambiguous, but it is also redundant: you can get all the information you need from the noun. It becomes important to recognize the adjective's ending when it gets separated from its noun:

> hē lēt him þā of handon   *lēofne* flēogan
> *hafoc* wið þæs holtes[1]
> [he then let his *beloved hawk* fly from his
> hands towards the woods]

Here *hafoc* 'hawk' is the accusative direct object of *lēt* 'let'. The adjective *lēofne* 'beloved' is separated from this noun by the infinitive *flēogan* 'fly', and so it is helpful that *lēofne* has the masculine accusative singular ending *-ne* so that you can associate it correctly with its noun. You will run into this kind of situation more often in poetry than in prose.

Table 8.1 summarizes the adjective endings.

Table 8.1   Adjective endings

		masculine	*neuter*	*feminine*
			Strong	
singular	nominative	–	–	-u / –
	accusative	-ne	–	-e
	genitive	-es	-es	-re
	dative	-um	-um	-re
plural	nominative/accusative	-e	-u / – / -e	-a / -e
	genitive	-ra	-ra	-ra
	dative	-um	-um	-um
			Weak	
singular	nominative	-a	-e	-e
	accusative	-an	-e	-an
	genitive	-an	-an	-an
	dative	-an	-an	-an
plural	nominative/accusative	-an	-an	-an
	genitive	-ra / -ena	-ra / -ena	-ra / -ena
	dative	-um	-um	-um

---

[1]   *The Battle of Maldon*, ll. 7–8.

8.2 Strong adjectives

Table 8.2 shows the strong endings attached to an adjective with a long stem. (Forms in **bold** type should be compared with the demonstrative pronouns (§5.1.3), others with the strong nouns (§6.1.1).) The adjectives are subject to the same kinds of transformations that affect the nouns. Those with long stems differ from those with short stems (table 8.3) in that the feminine nominative singular and the neuter nominative/accusative plural end in *-u* (see §6.1.1 for an explanation). Table 8.3 also shows that when the vowel of an adjective with a short stem is *æ* or *ea*, it alternates with *a* (§§2.2.1, 6.2.2). In some other adjectives, *h* is dropped between voiced sounds (§6.2.2), so, for example, the masculine accusative singular of *hēah* 'high' is *hēane* and the feminine nominative singular is *hēa*.

Table 8.2 Strong adjectives (long stems)

'good'		*masculine*	*neuter*	*feminine*
singular	nominative	gōd	gōd	gōd
	accusative	**gōdne**	gōd	gōde
	genitive	gōdes	gōdes	**gōdre**
	dative	**gōdum**	**gōdum**	**gōdre**
	instrumental	gōde	gōde	
plural	nominative/accusative	**gōde**	gōd, **gōde**	gōda, -e
	genitive		**gōdra**	
	dative		gōdum	

Table 8.3 Strong adjectives (short stems)

'vigorous'		*masculine*	*neuter*	*feminine*
singular	nominative	hwæt	hwæt	hwatu
	accusative	**hwætne**	hwæt	hwate
	genitive	hwætes	hwætes	**hwætre**
	dative	**hwatum**	**hwatum**	**hwætre**
	instrumental	hwate	hwate	
plural	nominative/accusative	**hwate**	hwatu, **-e**	hwata, -e
	genitive		**hwatra**	
	dative		hwatum	

! The masculine/neuter dative singular ending -*um* may cause confusion, for this is also the ending of the dative plural nouns and adjectives, and you may already have come to think of it as plural. Remember it this way: -*um* is always dative, and in nouns it is always plural.

The second syllable of a two-syllable adjective, like that of a two-syllable noun (§6.2.1), may be syncopated, so the dative plural of *hāliġ* 'holy' is *hālgum* but the masculine accusative singular is *hāliġne*.

The nominative and accusative plural ending -*e* is very frequent for both feminines and neuters in late Old English, when -*e* becomes the dominant ending for all genders. You will also see occasional -*a* in nominative and accusative plural neuters.

Possessive adjectives (§5.1.2) are always declined strong, and so is *ōðer* 'other, second', regardless of context.

8.3   Weak adjectives

The weak adjectives (table 8.4) are almost exactly like the weak nouns (§6.1.2). The difference is that the ending of the genitive plural of a weak adjective is usually the same as that of a strong adjective.

Table 8.4   Weak adjectives

'*good*'		*masculine*	*neuter*	*feminine*
singular	nominative	gōda	gōde	gōde
	accusative	gōdan	gōde	gōdan
	genitive	gōdan	gōdan	gōdan
	dative	gōdan	gōdan	gōdan
plural	nominative/accusative	gōdan	gōdan	gōdan
	genitive		gōdra, -ena	
	dative		gōdum	

There is no distinction between long and short stems, except that *æ* or *ea* in a short root syllable always becomes *a* (§2.2.1), so the weak masculine nominative singular of *hwæt* 'vigorous' is *hwata*. Because all weak endings begin with vowels, *h* is always dropped at the end of a root syllable (§6.2.2), so the weak nominative/accusative plural of *hēah* 'high' is *hēan*. As with nouns and

Minitext D. On Danish Customs

From a letter by Ælfric, Abbot of Eynsham, to an unidentified 'Brother Edward'. For the full text, see Kluge [59].

[1] Ić secge ēac ðē, brōðor Ēadweard, nū ðū mē þisses bæde, þæt ġē dōð unrihtlīċe þæt ġē ðā Engliscan þēawas forlætað þe ēowre fæderas hēoldon, and hæðenra manna þēawas lufiað þe ēow ðæs līfes ne unnon,[a] [2] and mid ðām ġeswuteliað þæt ġē forsēoð ēower cynn and ēowre yldran mid þām unþēawum, þonne ġē him on tēonan[b] tysliað ēow on Denisc,[c] āblēredum hneccan and āblendum ēagum. [3] Ne secge ić nā māre embe ðā sceandlican tyslunge, būton þæt ūs secgað bēċ þæt se bēo āmānsumod þe hæðenra manna þēawas hylt on his līfe and his āgen cynn unwurþað mid þām.

[a] *þe ēow ðæs līfes ne unnon*: who do not allow you life; who wish you ill.
[b] *him on tēonan*: as an injury to them.
[c] *on Denisc*: in Danish fashion.

strong adjectives (§§6.2.1, 8.2), the second syllable of a two-syllable adjective can be syncopated, so the weak nominative/accusative plural of *hāliġ* 'holy' is *hālgan*.

Comparative adjectives and ordinal numbers (except for *ōðer* 'second') are always declined weak.

8.4 Comparison of adjectives

The comparative adjective is made by adding *-r-* between the root syllable and the inflectional ending, which is always weak regardless of context. The superlative is made by adding *-ost*, which may be followed by either a weak or a strong inflection. Examples:

heard 'hard, fierce'	heardra	heardost
milde 'kind'	mildra	mildost
hāliġ 'holy'	hāliġra	hālgost
sweotol 'clear'	sweotolra	sweotolost

Some adjectives have *i*-mutation (§2.2.2) in the comparative and superlative forms, and in these cases the superlative element is usually *-est*. For example:

eald 'old'	ieldra	ieldest
ġeong 'young'	ġinġra	ġinġest
hēah 'high'	hīera	hīehst
lang 'long'	lenġra	lenġest
strang 'strong'	strenġra	strenġest

You may occasionally encounter unmutated forms, e.g. *strangost* 'strongest'.

A few adjectives have anomalous comparative and superlative forms; these are still anomalous in Modern English, though sometimes in different ways:

gōd 'good'	betera	betst
	sēlra	sēlest
lȳtel 'small'	lǣssa	lǣst
miċel 'large'	māra	mǣst
yfel 'bad'	wiersa	wierrest, wierst

Modern English has lost the alternative comparative and superlative *sēlra* 'better' and *sēlest* 'best'.

> **!** Comparative adjectives sometimes cause problems for students who are not on the lookout for them, or who confuse comparative -*r*- with the -*r*- of the feminine genitive/dative singular ending -*re* or the genitive plural -*ra*. The Old English comparative -*r*- may not look enough like the Modern English comparative -*er* to be easy for you to detect. The only solution to the problem is to be alert when you read.

8.5 On-line exercises

Old English Aerobics has a session on the adjective, using easy to intermediate Old English sentences. Minitext D is also on-line, accompanied by exercises on the adjectives it contains.

Chapter 9

Numerals

9.1 Quick start

Numbers are of two kinds, *cardinal* and *ordinal*. Cardinal numbers (such as Modern English *one*, *two* . . .) may function either as nouns or as adjectives:

As noun:
Fēower sīðon *seofon* bēoð *eahta and twentiġ*
[*Four* times *seven* are *twenty-eight*]

As adjective:
On *ānum* dæġe bēoð *fēower and twentiġ* tīda
[In *one* day there are *twenty-four* hours]

Ordinal numbers (such as Modern English *first*, *second* . . .) are always adjectives, and all of them are declined weak (§8.3) except for *ōðer* 'second', which is always strong (§8.2):

Þone *forman* dæġ hīe hēton Sunnandæġ
[They called the *first* day Sunday]

Þone *ōðerne* dæġ hīe hēton Mōnandæġ
[They called the *second* day Monday]

Minitext E. Weeks of the Year

From the *Enchiridion* by Byrhtferth, a monk of Ramsey. See Baker and Lapidge [5], pp. 30–3.

[1] Efne seofon bēoð seofon; twīa seofon bēoð fēowertȳne; þrīwa seofon bēoð ān and twēntiġ; fēower sīðon seofon bēoð eahta and twēntiġ; fīf sīðon seofon bēoð fīf and þrīttiġ; syx sīðon seofon bēoð twā and fēowertiġ; seofon sīðon seofon bēoð nigon and fēowertiġ; eahta sīðon seofon bēoð syx and fīftiġ; nigon sīðon seofon bēoð þrēo and syxtiġ; tȳn sīðon seofon bēoð hundseofontiġ. [2] Twēntiġ sīðon seofon bēoð ān hund and fēowertiġ; þrīttiġ sīðon seofon bēoð twā hundred and tȳn; fēowertiġ sīðon seofon bēoð twā hundred and hundeahtatiġ; fīftiġ sīðon seofon bēoð þrēo hundred and fīftiġ. [3] Ġīt þǣr sind fīftȳne tō lāfe; tōdǣlað þā eall swā þā ōðre. [4] Twīa seofon bēoð fēowertȳne; nū þǣr is ān tō lāfe.

9.2 Cardinal numbers

Here are the cardinal numbers one–twelve:

ān	fēower	seofon	tīen
twēġen, twā	fīf	eahta	endleofan
þrīe, þrēo	siex	nigon	twelf

The cardinal *ān* is usually declined as a strong adjective; when it is declined weak (*āna*) it means 'alone': *hē āna læġ* 'he lay alone'. The cardinals *two* and *three* have their own peculiar inflectional system, shown in table 9.1. If you substitute a *b-* for the *tw-* of *twēġen*, you will get *bēġen* (*bā*, *bū*, etc.) 'both'.

Table 9.1   The numerals *twēġen* and *þrīe*

		masculine	*neuter*	*feminine*
'two'	nominative/accusative	twēġen	twā, tū	twā
	genitive		twēġa, twēġra	
	dative		twǣm, twām	
'three'	nominative/accusative	þrīe	þrēo	þrēo
	genitive		þrēora	
	dative		þrim	

Cardinals above three occasionally have grammatical endings, but generally are not declined at all. The numbers thirteen–nineteen are made by adding *-tīene* to the numbers *þrēo–nigon*: *þrēotīene*, *fēowertīene*, etc. From twenty through to the sixties, numbers are in the form *ān and twentiġ* 'twenty-one'.

Starting with seventy, Old English prefixes *hund-* to the expected forms: *hundseofontiġ* 'seventy', *hundeahtatiġ* 'eighty', *hundnigontiġ* 'ninety', *hundtēontiġ* or *ān hund* 'one hundred', *hundtwelftiġ* or *hundtwentiġ* 'one hundred and twenty'. These curious forms seem to reflect a number system, common to all the earliest Germanic languages, in which counting proceeded by twelves and sixty was a significant number in much the same way that one hundred is now.

9.3 Ordinal numbers

Here are the ordinal numbers first–twelfth:

forma, fyrmest	fēorða	seofoða	tēoða
ōðer	fifta	eahtoða	endlyfta
þridda	siexta	nigoða	twelfta

For 'first' you may also find *ǣrest*, but *fyrst* is not common.

For 'thirteenth' to 'nineteenth', add the element *-tēoða* in place of ordinal *-tīene*: for example, *þrēotēoða* 'thirteen'. For 'twentieth' and higher, add *-tigoða*, *-tegoða* or *-teogoða*: *fifteogoða* 'fiftieth', *fīf and hundeahtatigoða* 'eighty-fifth'.

9.4 On-line exercise

Old English Aerobics contains an on-line version of Minitext E, accompanied by exercises on the numbers it contains.

Chapter 10

Adverbs, Conjunctions and Prepositions

10.1   Quick start

Adverbs, conjunctions and prepositions[1] are relatively easy because they are not inflected. Many of them, however, have changed their meanings since the end of the Old English period; further, some have been lost and others have taken their places, so many of these exceedingly common words will be unfamiliar to you at first. You should memorize the most common of them early on, especially the adverbs *ǣr* 'before', *ēac* 'also', *siððan* 'afterwards' and *þā* 'then'; the conjunctions *ac* 'but', *for þām þe* 'because', *oð þæt* 'until' and *þā* 'when'; and the prepositions *be* 'by, near', *mid* 'with', *of* 'from', *wið* 'opposite, against' and *ymb(e)* 'near, by'.

10.2   Adverbs

An adverb may be made from an adjective by adding *-e*; since many adject-ives are made by adding *-lić* to nouns or other adjectives, you will often see adverbs ending in *-līċe*.[2] Examples: *wearme* 'warmly' from *wearm* 'warm',

---

[1]   For general discussions of these parts of speech, see §§3.1.5, 3.1.6, 3.1.7.
[2]   The suffix *-lić* is generally thought to have had a long vowel when an ending followed, but otherwise a short vowel.

sārlīċe 'painfully' from *sār, sārliċ* 'painful'. The adverb corresponding to *gōd* 'good', however, is *wel*.

Adverbs may also be made by adding case endings to nouns, for example, genitive *dæġes* 'by day', *unþances* 'unwillingly'; dative *nēode* 'necessarily', *hwīlum* 'at times'. Some of the most common adverbs are conjunctive or prepositional: that is, they are related (and sometimes identical) to certain conjunctions and prepositions. Such adverbs often relate to place, time, extent, degree, negation or affirmation.

Some of the most common adverbs are listed in table 10.1.[3] Adverbs marked with ☆ have corresponding conjunctions that are identical in form and related in meaning; for these, see further §§10.3 and 10.4.

Table 10.1 Common adverbs

ā 'always'	heonan 'hence'	sōna 'immediately'
ādūn(e) 'down'	hēr 'here'	☆ swā 'so'
æfre 'ever'	hider 'hither'	☆ swelċe 'likewise'
æfter 'after'	hūru 'indeed'	swīðe 'very'
☆ ǣr 'before'	hwæðre 'nevertheless'	tō 'too'
ætgædere 'together'	hwīlum 'at times'	☆ þā 'then'
ēac 'also'	in 'in'	☆ þanon 'thence'
eall 'entirely'	innan 'from within'	☆ þǣr 'there'
eft 'afterwards'	nā 'not at all'	þæs 'afterwards'
fela 'much'	næfre 'never'	☆ þēah 'nevertheless'
feor 'far'	ne 'not'	☆ þenden 'while'
forð 'forwards'	neoðan 'from below'	☆ þider 'thither'
☆ for þām 'therefore'	nese 'no'	☆ þonne 'then'
ful 'very'	niðer 'down'	þus 'thus'
furðum 'even'	☆ nū 'now'	ufan 'from above'
ġēa 'yes'	ofdūne 'down'	ūp 'up'
ġeāra 'formerly'	oft 'often'	ūt 'out'
ġīese 'yes'	on 'on, forward'	ūtan 'from outside'
ġīet 'yet'	☆ siððan 'afterwards'	wel 'well'

Interrogative adverbs, used (of course) in asking questions, are listed in table 10.2. The Modern English interrogatives (*where, when*, etc.) can be used as subordinating conjunctions (e.g. 'I know *where* you live') or to introduce adjective clauses (e.g. 'on the street *where* you live'), but the same is rarely true for Old English, which instead will use one of the conjunctions listed in §10.3 or the relative particle *þe*.

---

3 The word-lists in this chapter do not display all definitions of the words they contain. For complete collections of definitions, you must consult a dictionary.

Table 10.2   Interrogative adverbs

hū 'how'	hwǣr 'where'
hwider 'whither'	hwonne 'when'
hwanon 'whence'	hwȳ 'why'

10.2.1   Comparison of adverbs

Adverbs made from adjectives normally add -*or* to make the comparative and -*ost* to make the superlative: *ġearwor* and *ġearwost* from *ġearwe* 'readily' (adjective *ġearo* 'ready'), *lēoflīcor, lēoflīcost* from *lēoflīċe* 'lovingly' (adjective *lēof, lēoflīċ* 'beloved').

Other adverbs may add -*rra* or -*ra* for the comparative and -*mest* for the superlative (e.g. *norþerra, norþmest* from *norþ* 'northwards').

A few common adverbs make their comparatives by applying *i*-mutation to the root vowel (omitting the ending); the superlatives may or may not have *i*-mutation:

ēaðe 'easily'	īeð	ēaðost
feorr 'far'	fierr	fierrest
lange 'long'	lenġ	lenġest
sōfte 'softly'	sēft	sōftost

Others are anomalous:

lȳtle, lȳt 'a little'	lǣs	lǣst, lǣsest
miċle 'much'	mā	mǣst
nēah 'near'	nīer	nīehst, nēxt
wel 'well'	bet, sēl	betst, sēlest
yfle 'badly'	wiers(e)	wierrest, wierst

10.3   Conjunctions

The coordinating conjunctions *and/ond* 'and', *ac* 'but' and *oððe* 'or' will cause you no difficulty. The subordinating conjunctions are more difficult, for they do not always resemble the Modern English words to which they correspond in function. The most common subordinating conjunctions are listed in table 10.3. Here, as in table 10.1, conjunctions with matching adverbs are marked ☆.

> **!** The ambiguity of some of the conjunctions with matching adverbs may optionally be resolved by adding the particle *þe*, which marks the word as a conjunction: these are indicated in the table. A few others may be doubled to mark them as conjunctions: *swā* may mean 'so' or 'as', but *swā swā* always means 'as'; similarly *þā þā* means 'when' and *þǣr þǣr* means 'where'.

Table 10.3 Subordinating conjunctions

æfter þām (þe) 'after'	☆ nū 'now that'	☆ þǣr 'where'
☆ ǣr 'before'	oð þæt 'until'	þæs þe 'after'
ǣr þām (þe) 'before'	☆ siððan 'after'	þæt 'that, so that'
būtan 'unless'	☆ swā 'as'	☆ þēah (þe) 'though'
☆ for þām (þe) 'because'	☆ swelċe 'as if'	☆ þenden 'while'
ġif 'if'	☆ þā 'when'	☆ þider (þe) 'whither'
hwæðer 'whether'	þā hwīle þe 'while'	☆ þonne 'when'
nemþe 'unless'	☆ þanon 'whence'	wið þām þe 'provided that'

The correlative conjunctions (like Modern English *both . . . and*) are as follows:

ǣġðer . . . ġe 'both . . . and'
hwæðer . . . oððe 'whether . . . or'
nā þæt ān . . . ac ēac swilċe 'not only . . . but also'
nāðor . . . ne 'neither . . . nor'
ne . . . ne 'neither . . . nor'
þȳ . . . þȳ 'the . . . the' (as in 'the more, the merrier')

10.4 Correlation

Correlation is a construction in which an adverb at the beginning of an independent clause recapitulates or anticipates an adverb clause. The conjunction that begins the adverb clause is related in sense to the adverb in the independent clause (e.g. 'when . . . then'); these two words are said to be correlative.

Correlation is much rarer in Modern English than in Old English, but it is still fairly common with conditional clauses:

If you were in Philadelphia, *then* you must have seen Independence Hall.

Minitext F. A Vision of Hell

The resemblance between this passage from a homily on Michaelmass and *Beowulf* ll. 1357–66 has often been remarked. For the complete text of the homily, see Morris [72], pp. 196–211.

[1] Swā Sanctus Paulus wæs ġesēonde on norðanweardne þisne middanġeard, þǣr ealle wæteru niðer ġewītað, and hē þǣr ġeseah ofer ðām wætere sumne hārne stān. [2] And wǣron norð of ðām stāne āweaxene swīðe hrīmiġe bearwas, and ðǣr wǣron þȳstru ġenipu, and under þām stāne wæs nicra eardung and wearga. [3] And hē ġeseah þæt on ðām clife hangodon on ðām īsiġean bearwum maniġe swearte sāwla be heora handum ġebundne, and þā fȳnd þāra on nicra onlīċnesse heora grīpende wǣron, swā swā grǣdiġ wulf. [4] And þæt wæter wæs sweart under þām clife nēoðan, and betweox þām clife on ðām wætere wǣron swelċe twelf mīla. [5] And ðonne ðā twigu forburston þonne ġewiton þā sāwla niðer þā þe on ðām twigum hangodan, and him onfēngon ðā nicras. [6] Ðis ðonne wǣron ðā sāwla þā ðe hēr on worulde mid unrihte ġefirenode wǣron, and ðæs noldon ġeswīcan ǣr heora līfes ende. [7] Ac uton nū biddan Sanctus Michael ġeornlīċe þæt hē ūre sāwla ġelǣde on ġefēan, þǣr hīe mōton blissian ā būton ende on ēċnesse.

Other correlations can be used in Modern English for emphasis or rhetorical effect. The King James Bible (1611) has

For *where* your treasure is, *there* will your heart be also.

We understand this perfectly well, though it sounds a bit archaic.

Most instances of correlation in Old English will cause you no difficulty. Here are some examples:

And *ðēah* ðe hē ġehēran ne wolde, *hwæðre* hē ġeðyldelīċe wæs from him eallum āræfned.
[And *though* he would not obey, *nevertheless* he was patiently tolerated by all of them.]

þider þe hē sylfa tōweard wæs æfter dēaþe, *þider* hē his ēagan sende ǣr his dēaðe, þæt hē þȳ blīþelīcor þrōwade.
[*where* he himself was headed after death, *there* he directed his eyes before his death, so that he could suffer more happily.]

Correlation can cause difficulties when the conjunction and adverb have the same form, as they often do (see tables 10.1 and 10.3):

þā . . . þā 'when . . . then'
þonne . . . þonne 'when . . . then'
þǣr . . . þǣr 'where . . . there'
swā . . . swā 'as . . . so'

In such cases you must sometimes allow context to guide you to the correct reading. But with certain conjunction/adverb pairs, word-order can help you decide which is the conjunction and which the adverb: see further §§12.5 and 15.2.5.

10.5 Prepositions

Here we will briefly list the most common prepositions and offer notes on their usage. The information you will need about each preposition, in addition to its meanings, is what case the object of the preposition may take and whether the case of that object influences the meaning of the preposition. This information is usually, but not always, supplied by glossaries and dictionaries.

æfter, *after, according to,* usually with dative, sometimes with accusative.
ǣr, *before* (in time), usually with dative, sometimes with accusative.
æt, with dative, *at, from*; with accusative, *until, up to.*
be, *by, near, along, about, in relation to,* with dative.
beforan, *before, in front of, in the presence of, ahead of,* with dative or (usually with an added sense of motion) accusative.
betweox, *between, among,* with dative or accusative.
binnan, with dative, *within*; with accusative, *to within.*
bufan, with dative, *above*; with accusative, *upwards.*
būtan, *outside, except, without,* with dative or accusative.
ēac, *besides, in addition to,* with dative.
for, *before, in front of, because of, in place of, for the sake of,* usually with dative, sometimes with accusative.
fram, *from, by,* with dative.
ġeond, *throughout, through,* usually with accusative, sometimes with dative.
in, with dative, *in*; with accusative, *into.*
innan, with dative, *in, within, from within*; with accusative, *into.*
mid, *with, and, by means of,* usually with dative, sometimes with accusative.
of, *from, of,* with dative.
ofer, with dative, *over, upon, throughout*; with accusative (usually with an added sense of motion), *over, across, throughout, more than.*
on, with dative, *in, on*; with accusative, *into, onto.* In West Saxon, *on* is usual where you would expect *in.*

onġēan, *opposite,* *towards,* *in opposition to,* with dative or (usually with an added sense of motion) accusative.

oð, *up to,* *as far as,* *until,* usually with accusative, sometimes with dative.

tō, with dative, *to,* *towards,* *at,* *for;* with genitive, *at.* With dative, *tō* often forms an idiom to be translated with 'as': *tō ġefēran* 'as a companion'.

tōġēanes, *towards,* *in preparation for,* *in opposition to,* with dative.

þurh, *through,* *by means of,* usually with accusative, sometimes with dative or genitive.

under, *under,* with dative or (usually with an added sense of motion) accusative.

wið, *towards,* *opposite,* *against,* *in exchange for,* with accusative, dative or genitive.

ymb(e), *near,* *by,* *about,* *after,* usually with accusative, sometimes with dative.

Some prepositions have the same meaning whatever the case of the object: for, these, some authors favour the dative while others favour the accusative. But several prepositions have different meanings depending on the case of the object. For these, the dative is generally associated with location while the accusative is associated with movement towards.

Study this list of prepositions carefully, for you will meet with a number of these words in every text you read.

10.6   On-line exercises

Old English Aerobics has sessions on adverbs and conjunctions and on prepositions, using easy to intermediate-level texts. There you will also find an on-line version of Minitext F, with exercises on the adverbs, conjunctions and prepositions it contains.

Chapter 11

Concord

11.1 Quick start

Concord is agreement in gender, case, number or person between different words that share a reference. For example, if a sentence contains a proper noun 'Paul' and somewhat later a pronoun 'he', and they refer to the same person, we say that they agree in number (for both are singular) and gender (for both are masculine).

As speakers or writers of a language we experience concord as a set of rules to learn and follow (and sometimes complain about). As listeners or readers we recognize that concord helps us decode sentences.

> Elizabeth Bennet had been obliged, by the scarcity of gentlemen, to sit down for two dances; and during part of that time, Mr Darcy had been standing near enough for *her* to overhear a conversation between *him* and Mr Bingley, who came from the dance for a few minutes, to press *his* friend to join it.

In this passage two grammatical rules help us to determine the reference of the pronouns 'her', 'him' and 'his'. The first of these is that a pronoun must agree with its antecedent in gender and number; this rule associates 'her' with Elizabeth Bennet (rather than Darcy, who would otherwise be a possible antecedent) and prevents our associating 'him' or 'his' with Elizabeth Bennet. The second is that a pronoun must be associated with the most recent possible antecedent; by this rule we understand 'his friend' to mean 'Bingley's friend' rather than 'Darcy's friend'.

We work out the reference of the pronouns in a passage like the one above without conscious effort. Indeed the Modern English rules of concord are few and relatively simple:

- The subject must agree with its verb in person and number. For most Modern English verbs this simply means that we must remember that a third-person singular subject generally takes a special verb form ending in -s. The verb *to be*, however, distinguishes all three persons in the present singular (*I am, you are, she is*) and the second person in the past singular (*I was, you were, he was*).
- The pronoun must agree with its antecedent in gender and number. If you speak of a woman named Ruth in one clause and then in the next clause want to refer to her with a pronoun, the pronoun must be both feminine and singular.
- The pronouns *that* and *this*, when used adjectivally, must agree in number with the nouns they modify: *that wolf, those wolves; this horse, these horses.* These pronominal adjectives are not inflected for gender.

The first two Modern English rules of concord are largely the same as in Old English. The third Modern English rule is a remnant of an Old English rule that a noun and all its modifiers (adjectives and pronouns used adjectivally) must agree in gender, case and number. All three of these rules are a little more complex in Old English than in Modern English, so you will have to pay careful attention to the rules of concord – at first, anyway.

11.2   Subject and verb

The Old English verb must agree with its subject in person and number. The Old English finite verb always distinguished number and often distinguished person, and this relatively great degree of expressiveness can help you locate hard-to-find subjects, as here:

> Þæt wæs yldum cūþ,
> þæt hīe ne mōste, þā Metod nolde,
> se scynscaþa   under sceadu breġdan.[1]
> [It was known to men
> that the demonic foe could not, if God did not wish it,
> drag them under the shadows.]

---

[1]   *Beowulf,* ll. 705–7.

In the noun clause that begins in the second line of this passage, the nominative/accusative third-person plural pronoun *hīe* comes before the verb *mōste* 'could', where Modern English grammar leads us to expect the subject. But the verb is plainly singular, so plural *hīe* cannot be the subject. Looking further, we find the nominative singular noun phrase *se scynscaþa* 'the demonic foe'; this is the subject.

A verb's personal ending is actually a statement or restatement of the subject, conveying much of the information that a personal pronoun can convey. In fact, in situations where Modern English uses a pronoun subject, the Old English finite verb can sometimes express the subject all by itself:[2]

Hēt þā bord beran,   beornas gangan
[(He) then commanded the men to bear their shields (and) to go]

Ġewiton him þā fēran
[Then (they) departed travelling]

Nū sculon heriġean   heofonrīċes Weard
[Now (we) must praise the Guardian of the kingdom of heaven]

In these fragments, the subjects of the verbs *hēt* 'commanded', *ġewiton* 'departed' and *sculon* 'must' are unexpressed, but context and the form of the verb together give us enough information to figure them out for ourselves.

Compound subjects may be split in Old English, one part divided from the others by the verb or some other sentence element. When this happens, the verb will typically agree with the first part of the subject. Consider these sentences:

Hēr Henġest ond Horsa fuhton wiþ Wyrtgeorne þām cyninge
[Here Hengest and Horsa fought with King Vortigern]

Hēr cuōm Ælle on Bretenlond ond his þrīe suna, Cymen ond Wlenċing ond Ċissa
[Here Ælle and his three sons, Cymen and Wlencing and Cissa, came to Britain]

In the first, the compound subject is arranged as in Modern English and the verb (*fuhton*) is plural. In the second, however, the first part of the compound subject, *Ælle*, is divided from the other parts by a prepositional phrase (*on Bretenlond* 'to Britain'), and the verb (*cuōm*, an archaic form of *cōm* 'came') is singular. A spectacular example of this sort of construction is at the beginning of Riddle 46:

---

[2] Passages from *The Battle of Maldon*, l. 62, *Beowulf*, l. 301, and *Cædmon's Hymn*, l. 1.

> Wer sæt æt wīne   mid his wīfum twām
> ond his twēġen suno   ond his twā dohtor,
> swāse ġesweostor,   ond hyra suno twēġen,
> frēolicu frumbearn.

To the Modern English eye it looks as if *Wer* 'A man' is the sole subject of the singular verb *sæt* 'sat', and that everything following *mid* 'with' is part of a long prepositional phrase ('with his two wives and his two sons . . .'). But in fact the whole of the prepositional phrase is *mid his wīfum twām*; everything that follows is nominative and therefore part of a compound subject. The correct translation (rearranging the sentence so that the parts of the subject come together) is as follows: 'A man, his two sons, his two daughters (beloved sisters), and their two sons (noble first-borns) sat at wine with his two wives'.

11.2.1   *Impersonal verbs*

Impersonal verbs are those that lack a subject, or that have only *hit* 'it' as a 'placeholder' subject. We still have such verbs in Modern English:

> *It rained* yesterday.
> *It seems* to me that the world has grown smaller.
> *It is fitting* that children obey their parents.

Old English has many more such verbs than Modern English, and they often lack the subject *hit*:

> Nāp nihtscūa,   norþan *snīwde*[3]
> [The night-shadow darkened, *(it) snowed* from the north]

> *Hit gedafenað* þæt hē wel ġelǣred sȳ mid godcundre lāre.
> [*It is fitting* that he be well taught in divine doctrine.]

Frequently what looks to us like the *logical* subject of the impersonal verb is in the dative or the accusative case:

> *Mē hingrode* and ġē mē sealdon etan; *mē þyrste* and ġē me sealdon drincan.
> [*I was hungry* and you gave me something to eat; *I was thirsty* and you gave me something to drink.]

> Ġehȳrað mīn swefn, ðe *mē mǣtte*.
> [Hear my dream, which *I dreamed*.]

---

³   *The Seafarer*, l. 31.

Þā ongan *hine* eft *langian* on his cȳþþe.
[Then *he* began *to long* for his homeland again.]

In such cases it makes no sense to translate with an impersonal construction; you may translate the dative or accusative as the subject of the verb.

11.3   Pronoun and antecedent

A pronoun typically restates a noun, called its *antecedent*; it must agree with this antecedent in gender and number.[4] Modern English pronouns obey the same rule, but the Old English rule behaves a little differently because of the way the language handles gender. Consider this passage:

Sēo sunne gǣð betwux heofenan and eorðan. On ðā healfe ðe *hēo* scīnð þǣr bið dæġ, and on ðā healfe ðe *hēo* ne scīnð þǣr bið niht.
[The sun goes between heaven and earth. On the side where *it* shines there is day, and on the side where *it* does not shine there is night.]

Students sometimes ask whether the use of the feminine pronoun *hēo* to refer to the sun means that it is being personified. It doesn't mean that at all; rather, the pronoun is simply agreeing with the feminine noun *sunne* 'sun' and must be translated 'it', not 'she'.

On the other hand, when the pronoun refers to a human being, it will very likely take on the 'natural gender' of its antecedent rather than its grammatical gender:

Abrames wīf wæs ðā ġȳt wuniġende būtan ċildum, and *hēo* hæfde āne þīnene, ðā Eġyptiscan Agar.
[Abraham's wife continued still to be without children, and *she* had a maid-servant, the Egyptian Agar.]

The grammatical gender of *wīf* is neuter, but the pronoun *hēo*, which refers to it, is feminine.

When a pronoun anticipates the noun it refers to, it may appear as neuter singular, regardless of the gender and number of the noun. We do something like this in Modern English:

Who's there? It's Bob.

---

[4]   When a pronoun is used as an adjective, it obeys the rule for modifiers (§11.4) rather than the rule for pronouns.

A famous Old English example comes near the beginning of *Beowulf* (l. 11):

> þæt wæs gōd cyning!
> [*that* was a good king!]

where we get neuter singular *þæt* instead of masculine singular *se*. A stranger example is in a passage quoted below (p. 110), *Þæt synt fēower sweras* 'They are four columns', where the same pronoun refers to a masculine plural noun.

11.4 Noun and modifiers

A noun and all its modifiers must agree in gender, case and number. Though this rule has all but disappeared in Modern English, it is very important in Old English. Every time a demonstrative pronoun is used as an 'article', for example, it agrees with its noun:

> Þā þæs on merġen *se* mæsseprēost ābēad *þæs* mædenes word *þām* mæran bisceope . . .
> [When, the morning after, *the* priest reported *the* virgin's words to *the* famous bishop . . .]

Here the demonstrative is used three times to modify a noun:

> se mæsseprēost: masculine nominative singular
> þæs mædenes: neuter genitive singular
> þām mæran bisceope: masculine dative singular

and each time, it matches its noun exactly in gender, case and number. What is true of pronouns is equally true of adjectives:

> Ðā ārison sōna of þām *sweartan* flocce *twēġen eġesliċe* dēoflu mid *īsenum* tōlum.
> [Then from that *dark* company *two terrifying* devils instantly arose with *iron* tools.]

Here the adjectives agree with their nouns as follows:

> þām sweartan flocce: masculine dative singular
> twēġen eġesliċe dēoflu: masculine[5] nominative plural
> īsenum tōlum: neuter dative plural

---

[5]   In a rare anomaly, the plural of *dēofol* 'devil' is neuter in form, but may agree with either masculine or neuter pronouns and adjectives.

The adjective is frequently separated from its noun, especially in poetry. When this happens, the rules of concord will help you to match up the adjective with its noun:

> Slōh ðā wundenlocc
> þone fēondsceaðan   fāgum mēċe,
> *heteþoncolne*,   þæt hēo *healfne* forċearf
> þone swūran him.[6]
>
> > [Then the wavy-haired one struck
> > the *hostile-minded* enemy with a decorated sword,
> > so that she cut through *half*
> > of his neck.]

In the main clause of this sentence, *þone fēondsceaðan* 'the enemy' is the direct object of the verb *slōh* 'struck'. We can tell by its ending that the adjective *heteþoncolne* 'hostile-minded', in the next line, agrees with accusative *fēondsceaðan*; since an adjective normally comes before its noun in Modern English, we must move it in our translation, making a noun phrase 'the hostile-minded enemy'. In the clause of result that follows (*þæt hēo . . . swūran him*), the adjective *healfne* 'half' agrees with *þone swūran* 'the neck', though it is separated from it by the verb *forċearf* 'cut through'. Once again we must gather the fragments of a noun phrase in our translation: 'half of his neck'.

Past and present participles are often inflected as adjectives, even when they form periphrastic verb forms:

> ēowre ġefēran þe mid þām cyninge *ofslæġene* wǣrun
> [your companions who were *slain* with the king]
>
> Dryhten, hwænne ġesāwe wē þē *hingriġendne* oððe *þyrstendne*?
> [Lord, when did we see you *hungering* or *thirsting*?]

Here the participles *ofslæġene*, *hingriġendne* and *þyrstendne* all have adjective endings.

🛈 When participles are inflected, the ending *-e* is added to the nominative/ accusative plural of all genders and may occasionally be omitted. Feminine nominative singular *-u* also may be omitted.

11.5   Bad grammar?

It is probably fair to say that the schools of Anglo-Saxon England offered little or no instruction in Old English grammar and that vernacular texts generally

---

[6]   *Judith*, ll. 103–6.

Minitext G. From *Solomon and Saturn*

Solomon and Saturn is a dialogue between the biblical king Solomon and the pagan god Saturn, in which Solomon answers questions posed by Saturn concerning God and the nature of creation. For the complete text, see Cross and Hill [28].

[1] Hēr cȳð hū Saturnus and Saloman fettode ymbe heora wīsdōm.

[2] Þā cwæð Saturnus tō Salomane: Saga mē hwær God sæte þā hē ġeworhte heofonas and eorðan. Iċ þē secge, hē sætt ofer winda feðerum.

[3] Saga mē, hwelċ wyrt ys betst and sēlost? Iċ þē secge, liliġe hātte sēo wyrt, for þām þe hēo ġetācnað Crist.

[4] Saga mē, hwelċ fugel ys sēlost? Iċ ðē secge, culfre ys sēlost; hēo ġetācnað þone hālgan gāst.

[5] Saga mē, hwanon cymð līġetu? Iċ secge, hēo cymð fram winde and fram wætere.

[6] Saga mē, hwelċ man ǣrost wǣre wið hund sprecende? Iċ þē secge, Sanctus Petrus.

[7] Saga mē, hwæt ys hefegost tō berenne on eorðan? Iċ þē secge, mannes synna and hys hlāfordes yrre.

[8] Saga mē, for hwan bið sēo sunne rēad on ǣfen? Iċ þē secge, for ðām hēo lōcað on helle.

[9] Saga mē, hwȳ scīnð hēo swā rēade on morgene? Iċ þē secge, for ðām hire twēonað hwæðer hēo mæġ oþþe ne mæġ þisne middaneard ġeondscīnan swā hire beboden is.

did not pass through the hands of copy-editors on their way to 'publication'. Old English was an unpoliced language for which 'correct' grammar was governed by usage rather than by the authority of experts. Under these circumstances we should expect to find what look to the rigorously trained modern grammarian rather like errors. Consider this passage, for example, by a learned author:

> Þæt synt fēower sweras, þā synd þus ġeċīġed on Lȳden: iustitia, þæt ys rihtwīsnys; and ōðer hātte prudentia, þæt ys snoternys; *þridde* ys temperantia, þæt ys ġemetgung; *fēorðe* ys fortitudo, þæt ys strengð.
>
> [They (the cardinal virtues) are four columns, which are called thus in Latin: *iustitia*, or righteousness; and the *second* is called *prudentia*, or prudence; the *third* is *temperantia*, or temperance; the *fourth* is called *fortitudo*, or strength.]

Notice the sequence of ordinal numbers here: *ōðer*, *þridde*, *fēorðe*. The first of these could be any gender, but *þridde* and *fēorðe* have the neuter/feminine weak nominative singular ending -*e* (§8.3). They do not agree in gender with masculine *sweras*, their grammatical antecedent, but rather with feminine nouns such as *rihtwīsnys* and *snoternys*. Editors of an earlier age tended to 'fix' such 'errors'; modern editors, on the other hand, are more likely to conclude that what looks like 'bad grammar' to us did not necessarily look so to the Anglo-Saxons. If the text is readable, there is little reason to emend.

Another example of what we are talking about comes at *Beowulf*, ll. 67–70, where Hrothgar decides to build his great hall Heorot:

> Him on mōd bearn
> þæt healreċed   hātan wolde,
> medoærn miċel   men ġewyrċean
> *þone* yldo bearn   æfre ġefrūnon
> [It came into his mind
> that he would command men to build
> a hall – a great mead-hall
> *which* the children of men would always hear about]

Here the problem is with *þone* in the last line, which looks as if it should be a masculine relative pronoun 'which', but does not agree in gender with the nearest antecedent, neuter *medoærn* 'mead-hall'. Early editors emended *þone* to *þon*[*n*]*e* 'than', creating yet another problem by positing an 'unexpressed comparative'. The better solution is to recognize that writers of Old English were less punctilious than we are about concord. Further, masculine nouns are more common in Old English than either feminines or neuters; when you find an otherwise unmotivated disagreement of gender, it is likely to involve a shift from feminine or neuter to masculine.

Do not get carried away with finding 'errors' in the Old English texts you read. Violations of the rules of concord are relatively rare, and generally you will be able to see why they happened, as in the examples above.

11.6   On-line exercises

In *Old English Aerobics* you will find two sessions on concord: the first deals with pronouns and adjectives and the second with subjects and verbs. Both are accompanied by intermediate-level sentences. Minitext G is also available on-line, where it is accompanied by exercises on concord.

Chapter 12

Word-order

12.1   Quick start

You may read in some sources, especially older ones, that Old English word-order is 'free' compared to that of Modern English, and you may conclude that writers of Old English could mix up their words in any order at all. But though word-order was freer then than now, there are just a few common word-orders in Old English clauses. Learn these and the job of learning the language will become much easier. The main Old English word-orders are these:

Subject–Verb. This, of course, is how most Modern English sentences are arranged.

Verb–Subject. This word-order still occurs in Modern English sentences like 'There are plenty of fish in the sea', and often in questions, such as 'Are you sleeping?'

Subject . . . Verb. The finite verb is delayed until the end of the clause.

Each of these can occur in several different environments, but, as you will see, each is also typical of particular kinds of clause.

12.2   Subject–Verb

Since this is the standard word-order of the Modern English clause, you'll be glad to know that it is very common in Old English. It is typical of independent clauses, though it also occurs frequently in subordinate clauses. Sometimes you'll be able to translate a sentence that uses this word-order almost word-for-word:

> Ēac swylċe *ðā nȳtenu* of eallum cynne and eallum fugolcynne *cōmon* tō Noe, intō ðām arce, swā swā *God bebēad.*
> [Also *the beasts* of each species and (of) each species of bird *came* to Noah, into the ark, as *God commanded.*]

The direct object, when it is a noun or noun phrase, will generally follow the verb:

> *God bletsode* ðā *Noe and his suna* and cwæð him tō: 'Weaxað and bēoð ġemenifylde and āfyllað ðā eorðan.'
> [*God* then *blessed Noah and his sons* and said to them: 'Increase and be multiplied and fill the earth.']

Old English has a tendency to place pronoun objects – direct and indirect – early in the clause. A pronoun object will usually come between the subject and the verb:

> And iċ *hine ġesēo* and bēo ġemyndiġ ðæs ēċean weddes ðe ġeset is betwux Gode and eallum libbendum flæsce.
> [And I *will see it* and be mindful of the eternal covenant that is established between God and all living flesh.]

If the clause has both a direct and an indirect object, and one of them is a pronoun, the pronoun will come first:

> Hēr ġē magon ġehȳran þæt hē ġyfð *ūs anweald*, ġif wē on hine ġelȳfað, Godes bearn tō bēonne.
> [Here you may hear that he gives *us the power*, if we believe in him, to be God's children.]

If the indirect object had been a noun and the direct object a pronoun, the direct object would have come first.

Though you will most frequently find a noun object after the verb and a pronoun before, there is no hard-and-fast rule for the placement of objects. Sometimes you will find a pronoun object after the verb, and sometimes the object will come before the subject:

> and iċ *fordō hī* mid ðǣre eorðan samod.
> [I *will destroy them* together with the earth.]

Ðone cyning hī brōhton cucene tō Iosue.
[They brought *the king* alive to Joshua.]

Since the location of the direct object in Modern English is fixed after the verb, its mobility in Old English may occasionally cause problems. Keep an eye on the inflections and, when they don't help you, let the context guide you to the correct reading.

Adverbial elements, including prepositional phrases and adverb clauses, occur in various places in the sentence. Though such elements are also mobile in Modern English, you will often find them where we cannot now put them, as in *God bletsode **ðā** Noe*, quoted above, which we can translate 'God *then* blessed Noah', '*then* God blessed Noah' or 'God blessed Noah *then*', but not 'God blessed *then* Noah'. Similarly, *ġif wē **on hine** ġelȳfað*, also quoted above, must be translated 'if we believe *in him*', not 'if we *in him* believe'.

12.3   Verb–Subject

This word-order is common in independent clauses introduced by the adverbs *þā* 'then', *þonne* 'then', *þǣr* 'there', *þanon* 'thence', *þider* 'thither', the negative adverb *ne*, and the conjunctions *and/ond* and *ac* 'but'.

Since Old English narrative often advances in a series of *þā*-clauses, you'll find the Verb–Subject word-order quite frequent in narrative:

Ðā *cwæð Drihten* tō Caine: 'Hwǣr is Abel ðīn brōðor?'
Ðā *andswarode hē* and cwæð: 'Iċ nāt; seġst ðū, sceolde iċ mīnne brōðor healdan?'
Ðā *cwæð Drihten* tō Caine: 'Hwæt dydest ðū? Þīnes brōðor blōd clypað tō mē of eorðan'.
[Then *the Lord said* to Cain: 'Where is Abel, your brother?'
Then *he answered* and said: 'I don't know: do you say I must look after my brother?'
Then *the Lord said* to Cain: 'What have you done? Your brother's blood cries to me from the earth.']

This word-order also occurs in independent clauses not introduced by an adverb or adverbial element:

Wǣron hī ēac swȳþe druncene, for ðām þǣr wæs brōht wīn sūðan.
[They were also very drunk, for wine had been brought from the south.]

When the clause contains a direct object, it will usually follow the subject, but it may also come first in the clause, as in §12.2.

The Verb–Subject word-order is also characteristic of questions, whether or not introduced by an interrogative word:

Him cwæð Nicodemus tō: 'Hū *mæġ se ealda mann* eft bēon ācenned? *Mæġ hē*, lā, inn faran tō his mōdor innoðe eft, and swā bēon ġeedcenned?'
[Nicodemus said to him, 'How *can the old man* be born again? *May he*, indeed, go into his mother's womb again, and thus be reborn?']

In Modern English this word-order is used mostly in questions, but, as you have seen, in Old English it is also used in declarative sentences. You must therefore be careful not to make assumptions about the kind of clause you are reading based on this word-order. When Unferth makes fun of a youthful exploit that Beowulf undertook with Breca, he begins his speech thus:

Eart þū se Bēowulf,   se þe wið Brecan wunne[1]

The Verb–Subject word-order has suggested to most editors that the line is a question, to be translated 'Are you the Beowulf who contended with Breca?' But it has been plausibly suggested that it is instead a statement, to be translated 'You're *that* Beowulf, the one who contended with Breca!'

Commands also generally have the Verb–Subject word-order unless the subject is omitted, as happens more often than not when the command is positive:

Ne *wyrċ ðū* ðē āgrafene godas.
[Do not *make* graven gods for yourself.]

Ārwurða fæder and mōdor.
[*Honour* (your) father and mother.]

12.4 Subject . . . Verb

The Subject . . . Verb word-order is commonly found in subordinate clauses and clauses introduced by *and/ond* or *ac* 'but', though it does sometimes occur in independent clauses. The subject comes at the beginning of the clause and the finite verb is delayed until the end (though it may be followed by an adverbial element such as a prepositional phrase).

Gode ofðūhte ðā ðæt *hē* mann ġeworhte ofer eorðan.
[Then it was a matter of regret to God that *he had made* man upon the earth.]

[1]   *Beowulf*, l. 506.

In the noun clause (ðæt . . . eorðan), the direct object of ġeworhte comes between the subject and the verb. You may also find indirect objects, complements, adverbial elements and various combinations of these in the same position:

Adverbial element:

Se Iouis wæs swā swīðe gāl þæt hē on hys swustor ġewīfode.
[This Jove was so very lustful that he married his sister.]

and þā bēċ ne magon bēon āwæġede, þe þā ealdan hǣðenan be him āwriton þuss.
[and the books that the old heathens wrote thus about them may not be nullified.]

Complement:

Nū secgað þā Deniscan þæt se Iouis wǣre, þe hī Þōr hātað, Mercuries sunu.
[Now the Danes say that this Jove, whom they call Thor, was Mercury's son.]

Indirect object and object:

and Adam him eallum naman ġesceōp
[and Adam made names for them all]

> **!** If you find you are having difficulty locating the end of a clause and the word-order appears to be Subject . . . Verb, consider the possibility that the finite verb marks the end of the clause.

12.5   Correlation

When a subordinate clause and an independent clause are correlated (§10.4), and are introduced by an ambiguous conjunction/adverb pair (especially þā 'when, then', þonne 'when, then' and þǣr 'where, there'), you can usually tell the subordinate clause from the independent clause by looking at the word-order. In this situation, the tendency of the independent clause introduced by an adverb to have the word-order Verb–Subject and that of the subordinate clause to have the order Subject–Verb or Subject . . . Verb will usually tell you which clause is which.

Minitext H. Orosius on the Reign of Caligula

From the Old English translation of the *History in Reply to the Pagans* by Paulus Orosius (see Bately [6]).

[1] Æfter ðām þe Rōmeburg ġetimbred wæs seofon hunde wintra ond hundnigontiġ, wearþ Gaius Gallica*[a]* cāsere fēower ġēar. [2] Hē wæs swīþe ġefylled mid unþēawum ond mid firenlustum, ond ealle hē wæs swelċe Rōmāne þā wyrþe wǣron, for þām þe hīe Cristes bebod hyspton ond hit forsāwon. [3] Ac hē hit on him swīþe wræc, ond hīe him swā lāðe wǣron þæt hē oft wȳscte þæt ealle Rōmane hæfden ǣnne swēoran, þæt hē hine raþost forċeorfan meahte. [4] Ond mid unġemete mǣnde*[b]* þæt þǣr þā næs swelċ sacu swelċ þǣr oft ǣr wæs; ond hē self fōr oft on ōþra lond ond wolde ġewin findan, ac hē ne meahte būton*[c]* sibbe.

[a] An error for Caligula, the nickname of the infamous emperor Gaius Julius Caesar (AD 12–41).
[b] The subject *hē* is omitted; see §11.2.
[c] *ne mehte būton*: could not [find anything] but.

! Simply put, the rule is this: when two clauses are correlated, the subordinate clause will have the subject before the verb, while the independent clause will have the verb before the subject. Examples:

Ðonne *sēo sunne ūp ārīst*, þonne *wyrċð hēo* dæġ.
[When *the sun rises*, then *it brings about* day.]

Ðǣr *ēower goldhord is*, ðǣr *bið ēower* heorte.
[Wherever *your treasure is*, there *is your heart*.]

Þā hē þā *se cyning þās word ġehȳrde*, þā *hēt hē* hī bīdan on þǣm ēalonde þe hī ūp cōmon.
[When *the king heard* these words, then *he commanded* them to wait on the island where they had come ashore.]

In each of these examples, the subordinate clause has the word-order Subject–Verb while the independent clause has Verb–Subject.

Unfortunately, this rule does not work in poetry. In prose it will work most of the time, but you cannot count on it absolutely.

12.6   Periphrastic verbs

In Modern English auxiliary and verbal may be separated by an adverbial element, but usually we keep them together. In Old English, on the other hand, they may come together or be widely separated. Here are some typical patterns:

Subject–Verb:

ond ēac se miċla here *wæs* þā þǣrtō *cumen*
[and also the great (Viking) army *had* then *come* to that place]

Þǣr man *meahte* þā *ġesēon* ermðe þǣr man oft ǣr ġeseah blisse[2]
[There one *might* then *see* misery where before one had often seen bliss]

Verb–Subject:

Hæfde se cyning his fierd on tū *tōnumen*
[The king *had divided* his army in two]

Ðǣr *mihton ġesēon* Winċeasterlēode rancne here and uneargne
[There the people of Winchester *could see* the bold and uncowardly (Viking) army]

Subject . . . Verb:

Ac sōna swā hīe tō Bēamflēote cōmon, ond þæt ġeweorc *ġeworht wæs*
[But as soon as they came to Benfleet, and the fortification *had been constructed*]

The splitting of periphrastic verb forms and the placement of verbals and finite verbs at the ends of clauses can give Old English a 'foreign' look. But there are sources of comfort here: when finite verb and verbal are separated, the last one will usually mark the end of a clause, helping you with the problem of finding clause boundaries. When they are not separated, your Modern English sense of how clauses are constructed will generally serve you well.

12.7   On-line exercise

Minitext H is available in *Old English Aerobics*, where it is accompanied by exercises on word-order.

---

[2]   This sentence illustrates the point made in §12.5 that you cannot always count on word-order to tell you which clause is independent and which subordinate.

Chapter 13

Metre

The Anglo-Saxons wrote what we call *alliterative poetry* after its most salient feature, the system of alliteration that binds its verses together and is largely responsible for its distinctive sound. Similar metrical systems are found in Old Icelandic, Old Saxon and Old High German: all of these cultures inherited a common Germanic metre, which they adapted as their languages and cultures changed. English poets continued to write alliterative poetry as late as the fifteenth century, and the metre has often been revived – most notably by the twentieth-century poet Ezra Pound.

There is more to Old English metre than alliteration. The poetry also employed a strict rhythmic scheme, which you will find to be markedly different from the rhythms employed by later poets such as Chaucer and Shakespeare. These later rhythms are based on the regularly timed recurrence of stressed syllables in the line. In Old English metre, the line consists of two *verses* (also called *half-lines*) divided by a syntactical boundary called a *caesura*. Each verse must conform to one of five rhythmic patterns (or *types*, as they are generally called), which we designate with the letters A–E. Verses of all types have in common that they always (well, *almost* always) contain two stressed syllables, called *lifts*, and two or more groups of unstressed syllables, called *drops*. The arrangement of lifts and drops depends on the type. The lifts do not necessarily come at regular intervals.

Why some rhythmic patterns were permissible in Old English poetry while others were forbidden is a subject of vigorous debate among scholars. The answer, if we had it, might tell us why the permissible rhythms sounded 'good', or sounded 'like poetry'. At present the most plausible theory is that the rhythms of poetry were based on those of ordinary speech, but with added rules that enabled listeners to recognize the boundaries between verses and lines. In much the same way, we can recognize the organization of Shakespearean blank verse when we hear actors recite it, even though there are no rhymes to tell us where the lines end.

Modern editions of Old English poetry print it as you have seen it in this book, in long lines with the caesura marked by a space. You should be aware, though, that in Old English manuscripts the poetry is not broken into lines, but rather written continuously, like prose. Like other editorial conventions (such as the use of modern capitalization and punctuation), the arrangement of poetic lines in printed editions is a compromise: it makes Old English texts more accessible to modern readers, but it conceals some interesting characteristics of Old English manuscript culture. You should track down a facsimile of the manuscript of a poem you are reading (follow the references in Further Reading, §8) and compare it with the printed edition.

❶ The term 'line' refers to the way poetry is broken into lines in modern books. Since Old English poetry is not broken into lines on the page, our speaking of 'lines' would probably seem strange to an Old English poet. We retain the term here, however, for want of a better one.

The first verse in a line is generally called the *on-verse* or *a-verse* and the second verse is called the *off-verse* or *b-verse*. When referring to specific verses, use the line number plus *a* for the on-verse and *b* for the off-verse: 'l. 11a', 'll. 234b–236a'. If you don't need that degree of precision in referring to passages of poetry, it is perfectly all right to use the line number alone.

13.1   Alliteration

Alliteration is the repetition of a consonant sound at the beginning of a syllable. In addition, any syllable that begins with a vowel alliterates with any other syllable that begins with a vowel. In Old English poetry, only the alliteration of lifts is significant. The combinations *sc*, *sp* and *st* may alliterate only with themselves. In most poems, however, *ġ* can alliterate with *g* and *ċ* with *c*. The italic letters in this list alliterate:

*c*lyppe	*c*ysse
ġe*þ*ōht	*þ*enċan
*ē*adiġ	*ġ*eendod
*f*oremihtiġ	*f*ēond
*ġ*ecunnod	*ċ*ēole
*g*ōd	*ġ*eogoð

These words, on the other hand, contain sounds that you might expect to alliterate, but do not:

ġehāten	ġēar
foremihtig	mǣre
forweorðan	fēond
stān	sāriġ
scōp	sǣ

In each poetic line, one or two lifts in the on-verse must alliterate with the first lift in the off-verse. The second lift in the off-verse normally does not alliterate with any of the three other stressed syllables in the line. These lines illustrate the three patterns:[1]

$$\times\ (/)\ \times\ /\ \times\ /\ \backslash\ \times\ /$$
xa|ay: þæt biþ in eorle   indryhten þēaw

$$\times\ \times\ \times\ /\ \backslash\ \times\ /\ \times\ /\ \times$$
ax|ay: þæt hē his ferðlocan   fæste binde.

$$\times\ \times\ /\ /\ \times\ /\ \times\ \times\ /\ \times$$
aa|ax: ne se hrēo hyġe   helpe ġefremman

🛈 It is customary to mark a lift with a stroke. A backward stroke (\) marks a half-lift, and × marks an unstressed syllable, part of a drop. In this book, a stroke in parentheses marks a syllable that one would expect to receive metrical stress even though the rules of Old English accentuation indicate that it should not be stressed (see §13.2.1).

The pattern xa|ay occurs mostly when the first lift in a verse is weak (as when it is a syllable of a finite verb). When the first lift is strong (as when it is a syllable of a noun, adjective or verbal), it normally *must* alliterate, so the pattern will be ax|ay or aa|ax. A competent poet would not write a line like this one:

$$\times\ \times\ /\ /\ \times\ /\ \times\ \times\ /\ \times$$
ne se wō hyġe   helpe ġefremman

Occasionally you will meet with *transverse alliteration* (the pattern ab|ab) and *crossed alliteration* (ab|ba). These probably were regarded as especially ornate:[2]

---

[1] *The Wanderer*, ll. 12–13, 16. Since the quotations in this chapter are intended only to illustrate metrical principles, translations are omitted.

[2] *Beowulf*, ll. 32, 2615.

Þǣr æt hȳðe stōd   hringedstefna
brūnfāgne helm,   hringde byrnan

Other unusual kinds of alliteration (such as syllables in the drop alliterating
with a lift) are probably incidental and without metrical significance.

13.2   Rhythm

13.2.1   Lifts, half-lifts and drops

We mentioned at the head of this chapter that a verse generally has two lifts,
or stressed syllables. A lift will normally be a long syllable (for the distinction
between long and short syllables, see §2.4). The italicized syllables in these
words are long:

> *hlēoð*rode   *heal*le
> *frēo*lic   *weġ*

But the italicized syllables in these words are short and so will not normally be
lifts, even though they are the stressed syllables of their words:

> *we*ra   *du*ru
> *da*gas   ā*bro*cen

Two short syllables can, however, add up to what is called a *resolved lift*, which
we mark with a tie between a stroke and an × ($\stackrel{\frown}{/\times}$). For example, in this line,

$$\stackrel{\frown}{/\times} \quad \times \quad / \quad \times \qquad \stackrel{\frown}{/\times} \quad \backslash \quad \times\times \quad /$$
monegum mǣġþum   meodosetla oftēah[3]

the first two syllables of *monegum* and *meodosetla* make resolved lifts. In
addition, a lift may consist of a single short syllable when it immediately
follows another lift.

There is a strong tendency in Old English poetry to group weakly stressed
words that are not proclitic[4] at the beginning of a clause or immediately after
the first lift in a clause. These weakly stressed words include conjunctions,

---

[3]   *Beowulf*, l. 5.
[4]   A proclitic word is normally found immediately before another word. Adjectives and adjectival pronouns ('*green* cheese', '*this* cow') are normally proclitic, and so are prepositions ('*in* the
scabbard').

finite verbs, adverbs and pronouns; you will often find them clustered right at the beginning of a verse, before the first lift, as here,

× × × × × / × × /

syþðan hē hire folmum æthrān[5]

where a conjunction and two pronouns (five syllables in all) constitute the drop that comes before the first lift. When a word that normally is weakly stressed occurs somewhere other than its accustomed position, it acquires stress. Thus a finite verb, adverb or pronoun will be stressed if it does not come before or immediately after the first lift, and a proclitic, such as a preposition, will be stressed if it follows the word it normally precedes:[6]

/× × × / ×

Hete wæs onhrēred

× × × / × /

ðā hē ġebolgen wæs

× × × × / / ×

for ðon iċ mē on hafu

/ \ / ×

grundwong þone

In the first of these examples, the finite verb *wæs*, coming right after the first lift (*hete*), remains unstressed, but in the second example *wæs* at the end of the clause is stressed. In the third example, a preposition (*on*) comes after its object (*mē*), and in the fourth example, a pronoun used as an adjectival 'article' follows the noun it modifies. Both the preposition and the pronoun are lifts. The preposition even participates in the alliterative pattern of the line.

The second element of a compound noun normally has a half-stressed syllable, or half-lift (this is still true: say 'the flashlight' aloud to yourself and listen to the relative stress levels of *the*, *flash* and *light*). In Old English metre, a half-stress may sometimes be treated as part of the drop and sometimes as the lift:[7]

/× \ / ×

medudrēam māran

/ × \ ×

bēodġenēatas

5   *Beowulf*, l. 722b.
6   *Beowulf*, ll. 2556a, 723b, 2523b, 2588a.
7   *Beowulf*, ll. 2016a, 1713b.

In the first example, the half-stress *-drēam* comes where you expect a drop, while in the second the half-stress *-nēa-* comes where you expect a lift.

13.2.2   Rhythmic types

Every correctly constructed verse belongs to one of the five rhythmic types. The rhythmic patterns of these types are not fixed, but rather flexible. Each type has a basic form and a range of variations on that form. The rhythmic patterns of modern verse also have variations. In this line, for example,

The whiskey on your breath

which we perceive as having three iambs (×/|×/|×/), we in fact pronounce the second iamb as two unstressed syllables (×/|××|×/). The phonetic realization of a poetic line can differ quite a bit from its basic form; in fact, any poem in which the two do not differ is certain to strike us as monotonous. The differences between basic form and phonetic realization are themselves governed by rules that ensure that the verse retains its integrity so that we can still recognize it as poetry.

A. Basic form: lift, drop, lift, drop. This is the most common type of verse. Examples:[8]

/   ×   /   ×
ēower lēode

/   ×   ×   /̣×   ×
sorge ġefremede

Notice that the drop may consist of more than one unstressed syllable. Either or both of the drops may also be replaced by a half-lift. The second lift may also be replaced by a half-lift, but half-lifts cannot replace both drops and lifts in the same verse.

❶ Many metrists believe that verses were subdivided into feet. If so, the first line above would be divided /×|/× and the second would be divided /×|/̣×. Not all scholars agree that verses were so divided. This book takes no position on that question, but omits the division into feet as unlikely to be of much use to students beginning to read poetry.

---

[8]   *Beowulf*, ll. 596b, 2004b.

An extra syllable may precede the first lift in an A-type verse; this phenomenon, called *anacrusis*, occurs only in on-verses. This line exhibits
anacrusis:

```
×   /   ×  ×   /  ×
```
in mǣġþa ġehwǣre[9]

You will frequently encounter A-type verses in which the first lift is so
weak that you may have difficulty locating it at all. These 'light' A-type
verses typically occur at the beginnings of clauses. They are always
on-verses. Examples:[10]

```
(/)   × ×   ×   × /   ×
```
hī hyne þā ætbǣron

```
(/)   ×   ×   /  ×
```
Ðā cōm of mōre

B. Basic form: drop, lift, drop, lift. B-type verses are especially common as
off-verses, though they also occur as on-verses:[11]

```
×   ×  / ×     /
```
Ne scel ānes hwæt

```
×   × /   × /
```
þæt se sīð ne ðāh

The first drop may have as many as five syllables, but the second can
have no more than two.

C. Basic form: drop, lift, lift, drop. Verses of this type, in which the clash-
ing stresses are rather startling to the modern ear, are more often than
not off-verses. Examples:[12]

```
×     /     / ×
```
Oft Scyld Scēfing

```
×    × ×   /    / ×
```
þēah hē him lēof wǣre

---

9   *Beowulf,* l. 25a.
10 *Beowulf,* ll. 28, 118a.
11 *Beowulf,* ll. 3010b, 3058b.
12 *Beowulf,* ll. 4a, 203b.

Though the first drop may have as many as five syllables, the second drop may have only one. The second lift is often a short syllable, since it immediately follows the first (see §13.2.1):

×   × /   / ×
þæt hīe ǣr drugon[13]

D. Basic forms: lift, lift, half-lift, drop; lift, lift, drop, half-lift. D-type verses often consist of a word of one long or two short syllables followed by a word of three syllables; alternatively, a D-type verse may be a compound whose second element has three syllables. The drop at or near the end of the verse never has more than one syllable. Examples:[14]

/×   /   \ ×
sunu Ecglāfes

/ / \   ×
fletsittendum

/   / × \
hār hilderinc

Some D-type verses are 'extended', with a one- or two-syllable drop after the first lift:[15]

/   ×   /   \ ×
wēoldon wælstōwe

/×   / × \
hwīlum hildedēor

E. Basic form: lift, half-lift, drop, lift. The E-type verse is the inverse of the D-type, frequently consisting of a three-syllable word followed by a word of one long syllable or two short ones:[16]

/   \ ×   /
edwenden cwōm

/   \   × /
stefn in becōm

---

[13] *Beowulf*, l. 15a.
[14] *Beowulf*, ll. 590b, 1788a, 1307a.
[15] *Beowulf*, ll. 2051a, 2107a.
[16] *Beowulf*, ll. 1774b, 2552b.

Minitext I. Riddle 80

This is one of ninety-five riddles preserved in the Exeter Book (see textual note for reading 8 in the anthology). For an edition of the Riddles, see Williamson [93]. This source (and others as well) will give you the solution to this riddle, but try to figure it out for yourself before looking it up.

Ić eom æþelinges   eaxlġestealla,
fyrdrinces ġefara,   frēan mīnum lēof,
cyninges ġeselda.   Cwēn mec hwīlum
hwītloccedu   hond on leġeð,
5   eorles dohtor,   þēah hīo æþelu sȳ.
Hæbbe mē on bōsme   þæt on bearwe ġewēox.[a]
Hwīlum ić on wloncum   wicge rīde
herġes on ende;   heard is mīn tunge.
Oft ić wōðboran   wordlēana sum
10   āġyfe æfter ġiedde.   Good is mīn wīse
ond ić sylfa salo.   Saga hwæt ić hātte.

[a] This line probably refers to mead, made of honey from beehives kept in the woods.

The drop may consist of two short syllables (never more):

/   \   × ×/
feorhsweng ne oftēah[17]

13.2.3   Hypermetric verses

Occasionally you will encounter clusters of lines in which the verses appear to be exceptionally long. These extended verses, which we call *hypermetric*, occur rarely in *Beowulf*, but frequently in *The Dream of the Rood* and *Judith*. Here is a sample:

Þurhdrifan hī mē mid deorcum næġlum.   On mē syndon þā dolg ġesīene,
opene inwidhlemmas.   Ne dorste ić hira nænigum sceððan.
Bysmeredon hīe unc būtū ætgædere.   Eall ić wæs mid blōde bestēmed,
begoten of þæs guman sīdan,   siððan hē hæfde his gāst onsended.[18]
[They drove dark nails through me. The wounds, open wicked wounds,
are visible on me. I did not dare to harm any of them.
They reviled both of us together. I was entirely drenched with blood,
poured from the man's side after he had sent forth his spirit.]

[17]   *Beowulf*, l. 2489b.
[18]   *The Dream of the Rood*, ll. 46–9.

Exactly what is going on in this kind of verse is a matter of some disagreement. The traditional view is that hypermetric on-verses are normal verses with a prefix that usually takes the form /×× or /× (but is sometimes longer), while hypermetric off-verses have an extra-long drop before the first lift, thus:

> /x̠ × /   \   /   ×
> opene inwidhlemmas

> × ×   ×   ×   / × × / ×
> Eall iċ wæs mid blōde bestēmed

We may interpret the first of these verses as an A-type with /x̠× prefixed and the second as another A-type with ×××× prefixed.

Some scholars have argued that this traditional view provides an inadequate explanation of the hypermetric verses. It is beyond the scope of a grammar book to discuss in detail the competing theories regarding these verses. You may take the traditional view as a starting point, read further, and decide for yourself what stylistic effect these verses may have had.

Chapter 14

Poetic Style

Reading poetry is always more challenging than reading prose. Poets employ figurative language more intensively than most prose writers do, they leave much for readers to infer, and in many poetic traditions (including those of England and America in the relatively recent past) their language is deliberately archaic. Here, for example, are the first two stanzas of Thomas Gray's *Elegy Written in a Country Churchyard*:

> The curfew tolls the knell of parting day,
>   The lowing herd wind slowly o'er the lea,
> The ploughman homeward plods his weary way,
>   And leaves the world to darkness and to me.
>
> Now fades the glimmering landscape on the sight,
>   And all the air a solemn stillness holds,
> Save where the beetle wheels his droning flight,
>   And drowsy tinklings lull the distant folds.

Gray's eighteenth-century masterpiece has stylistic features rarely found in prose of that time. The contraction *o'er* 'over', dialectal in origin, is rare outside of poetry, and *lea*, from Old English *lēah* 'pasture, meadow', had been an almost exclusively poetic word for centuries.

Further, the word-order of this passage makes it look strange to the modern eye. In line 3 an adverbial element (*homeward*) comes where it does not normally occur, line 5 has the word-order Verb–Subject, and line 6 has Subject . . . Verb. These three divergences from Modern English word-order would make good Old English, as you remember from chapter 12. Gray's use of such archaisms is typical of the poetic idiom of his time, and although that idiom is now out of favour, we still recognize it with no difficulty.

Old English poetry employs a number of words that are rarely or never found in prose, and its syntax differs from that of prose in several respects. The result of these differences is that there is a distinctively poetic Old English idiom, which probably was as easily recognizable to English people of that time as Gray's poetic idiom is to us.

14.1 Vocabulary

A large number of words are found exclusively, or almost exclusively, in poetry. Some of these are dialectal in origin (much Old English poetry, whether written in the north or the south, displays northern dialect features), while others are presumably archaisms. You might expect most poetic words to represent unusual concepts, but frequently they appear in place of quite common words, as these examples show:[1]

āwa, adv. *always* (for usual *ā*).
æfnan, wk. 1. *perform, do* (for *fremman*).
benn, fem. *wound* (for *wund*).
ellor, adv. *elsewhere* (for *elles ġehwǣr*).
elra, pron. adj. *another* (for *ōðer*).
fricgan, st. 5. *ask* (for *ascian, axian*).
gamol, adj. *old* (for *eald*).
ġeador, adv. *together* (for *ætgædere* or *tōgædere*).
grēotan, st. 2. *weep* (for *wēpan*).
holm, masc. *sea* (for *sǣ*).

mearh, masc. *horse* (for *hors*).
ōr, neut. *beginning, origin* (for *fruma* or *anġinn*).
sǣlan, wk. 1. *fasten, moor* (for *fæstnian*).
siġel, masc. or neut. *sun* (for *sunne*).
sīn, possessive adj. *his* (for *his*).
swefan, st. 5. *sleep* (for *slǣpan*).
til, adj. *good* (for *gōd*).
welhwylċ, indefinite pron. *every* (for *ġehwylċ*).
wītiġ, adj. *wise* (for *wīs*).

Poetic vocabulary has an especially large number of words for human beings, and most of the words within this group mean 'man', 'warrior' or both:

---

[1] This and other lists of poetic words in this chapter are largely based on the glossary in Klaeber [57], which indicates which words occur only or mostly in poetry and which are unique to *Beowulf*. These lists present words found in *Beowulf* and at least one other poem. The abbreviations are those used in this book's glossary (p. 229).

beorn, masc. *man, noble, warrior.*
byre, masc. *son, young man.*
eafora, masc. *son, heir.*
freca, masc. *warrior.*
guma, masc. *man, warrior.*
hæle, hæleð, masc. *man, warrior.*
hyse, masc. *young man.*
ides, fem. *woman, lady.*

mago, masc. *son, young man.*
mæġð, fem. *maiden, woman.*
niþðas, masc. *men.*
rinc, masc. *man, warrior.*
secg, masc. *man, warrior.*
wiga, masc. *warrior.*
ylde, masc. *men.*

Old English is a compounding language, frequently making new words by forming compounds from old ones. Most of the words in the list above can appear as elements of compounds, greatly expanding the group of words for human beings. Here, for example, are the compounds of *rinc*:

beadorinc, masc. *battle-warrior.*
fyrdrinc, masc. *army-warrior.*
gumrinc, masc. *man-warrior.*
gūþrinc, masc. *war-warrior.*
heaðorinc, masc. *war-warrior.*

hererinc, masc. *army-warrior.*
hilderinc, masc. *war-warrior.*
magurinc, masc. *son-warrior, young warrior.*
sǣrinc, masc. *sea-warrior.*

Most of these compounds are redundant, or they state the obvious: that a warrior goes to war, or is a man, or someone's son. Normally we expect a compound noun to consist of a base word (the second element) with a modifier (the first element); but the only compound in the list that fits this pattern is *sǣrinc* 'warrior who goes to sea'. Compounds in which the first element does not modify the second are common enough in Old English poetry that we have a specialized term to describe them: *poetic compounds*. In these the first element fills out the rhythm of a line and supplies alliteration. The poetic compounds you are most likely to meet have first elements meaning 'war', 'battle', 'slaughter' or 'army': *beadu-, gūð-, here-, hild(e)-, wæl-, wīġ-*. For example, here are the compounds in *Beowulf* with the first element *beadu-*:

beadufolm, fem. *battle-hand,* i.e. a hand used in battle.
beadogrīma, adj. *battle-mask,* i.e. helmet with mask.
beadohræġl, neut. *battle-garment,* i.e. coat of mail.
beadulāċ, neut. *war-play,* i.e. battle.
beadolēoma, masc. *battle-light,* i.e. sword (which gleams in battle).

beadomēċe, masc. *battle-sword.*
beadorinc, masc. *battle-warrior.*
beadurōf, adj. *battle-bold.*
beadurūn, fem. *battle-speech, hostile speech.*
beaduscearp, adj. *battle-sharp* (describing a weapon).
beaduscrūd, neut. *battle-garment.*
beaduserce, fem. *battle-corslet.*

Some of these (*beadomēċe, beadorinc, beaduserce*) are true poetic compounds, while in others the first element does modify the second: a *beadohrægl* is not just any garment, but one worn to battle, i.e. a coat of mail. But more striking than this compound is *beadolēoma* 'battle-light', in which the first element provides a clue to the riddle of the second, a metonymic reference to a gleaming sword. This kind of compound is called a *kenning*, and it is one of the most striking features of Old English poetic style. A good poet may coin his own kennings (*Beowulf* has many unique ones), but a number of them appear to belong to a common stock of poetic terms. Here are some kennings that appear in *Beowulf* and at least one other poem:

bāncofa, masc. *bone-chamber*, i.e. body.

bānfæt, neut. *bone-container*, i.e. body.

bānhūs, neut. *bone-house*, i.e. body.

bānloca, masc. *locked bone-enclosure*, i.e. body.

brēosthord, neut. *breast-hoard*, i.e. feeling, thought, character.

frumgār, masc. *first spear*, i.e. chieftain.

hronrād, fem. *whale-road*, i.e. sea.

merestræt, fem. *sea-street*, i.e. the way over the sea.

nihthelm, masc. *night-helmet*, i.e. cover of night.

sāwoldrēor, masc. or neut. *soul-blood*, i.e. life-blood.

sundwudu, masc. *sea-wood*, i.e. ship.

swanrād, fem. *swan-road*, i.e. sea.

wordhord, neut. *word-hoard*, i.e. capacity for speech.

Sāwoldrēor and *sundwudu* are like *beadolēoma* in being metonymic; others (like the *bān-* compounds) are metaphorical, while some are even more complex: a *hronrād* is metaphorically a road over the sea, and metonymically for use by whales (and other sea-creatures, but especially ships). Kennings are not always compounds: they can be compound-like phrases consisting, generally, of two nouns, the first in the genitive case, as in *hwæles ēþel* 'the whale's home' or *bēaga brytta* 'giver of rings'.

The best glossaries will give you both a literal translation of a kenning and an interpretation of it:

flæschoma, masc. *flesh-covering*, i.e. the body.

But you must be on your guard, for some glossaries may supply only an interpretation. To do so, of course, is to rob poetry of much of what makes it poetry. If you suspect that the definition of a compound is not literal but rather an interpretation, go to a dictionary and look up its elements separately.

To give you an idea of how many poetic words may be available for a single concept, we end this section with a list of poetic words meaning 'king, lord' used in *Beowulf* and at least one other poem:

bēagġyfa, masc. *ring-giver*.
bealdor, masc. *lord*.
brego, masc. *lord, ruler*.
folcāgend, masc. *possessor of the people*.
folccyning, masc. *king of the people*.
folctoga, masc. *leader of the people*.
frēa, masc. *lord*.
frēadrihten, masc. *lord-lord*.
frumgār, masc. *first spear*.
goldġyfa, masc. *gold-giver*.
goldwine, masc. *gold-friend*.
gūðcyning, masc. *war-king*.
herewīsa, masc. *leader of an army*.
hildfruma, masc. *battle-first*.
hlēo, masc. *cover, shelter*.

lēodfruma, masc. *first of a people*.
lēodġebyrġea, masc. *protector of a people*.
mondryhten, masc. *lord of men*.
rǣswa, masc. *counselor*.
siġedryhten, masc. *lord of victory*.
sincġifa, masc. *treasure-giver*.
sinfrēa, masc. *great lord*.
þenġel, masc. *prince*.
þēodcyning, masc. *people-king*.
þēoden, masc. *chief, lord*.
wilġeofa, masc. *joy-giver*.
wine, masc. *friend*.
winedryhten, masc. *friend-lord*.
wīsa, masc. *guide*.
woroldcyning, masc. *worldly king*.

14.2 Variation

Variation is the repetition in different words of an element of a sentence, clause or phrase. In Old English poetry you should expect to meet frequently with sentences whose subjects, objects or other elements are repeated one or more times. In the simplest case an element may appear twice, perhaps on either side of another element:[2]

> þǣr hē *dōme* forlēas
> *ellenmǣrðum.*
> > [There he lost *glory*,
> > *the reputation for valour.*]

> Hæfde ðā forsīðod   *sunu Ecgþēowes*
> under ġynne grund   *Ġēata cempa*
> nemne him heaðobyrne   helpe ġefremede
> [Then *the son of Ecgtheow, the champion of the Geats,*
> would have fared badly under the spacious earth
> if (his) battle-corslet had not given him help]

> Ðā se ġist onfand
> þæt se beadolēoma   *bītan* nolde,
> aldre *sceþðan*
> > [Then the stranger found
> > that the battle-light would not *bite*,
> > *injure* (her) life]

---

[2]   *Beowulf*, ll. 1471–2, 1550–2, 1522–4.

In the first passage, two dative objects of *forlēas* appear on either side of that verb; in the second two subjects appear on either side of a prepositional phrase. In the third, two infinitives governed by *nolde* are separated by that verb; the second infinitive, used transitively, is accompanied by its object.

! Take note of these points about variation:

- The elements in variation, when they are nouns, are different from compound noun phrases, which are sometimes split (§11.2), because here each element has the same referent. 'Glory' and 'the reputation for valour' both name the thing that Unferth lost, and 'the son of Ecgtheow' and 'the champion of the Geats' are the same person. In a compound subject like *Henġest ond Horsa*, the two nouns refer to two different persons.
- We say that variation is 'the repetition of a sentence element' rather than 'the repetition of an idea' to emphasize that variation is a grammatical as well as a stylistic phenomenon. The grammatical construction in which a sentence element gets repeated is called *apposition*.
- In Modern English, appositive elements are normally grouped together, as in the translations above. In Old English poetry, though appositive elements *may* be grouped together, they are more likely to be separated. Because of this difference you must often rearrange sentence elements when translating passages of poetry that contain variation.

Variation can be much more complicated – and interesting – than in the examples quoted above. Study this passage, in which Beowulf describes how he once survived an attack by a school of sea-monsters:

> Næs hīe ðǣre fylle   ġefēan hæfde,
> mānfordǣdlan,   þæt hīe mē þēgon,
> symbel ymbsǣton   sǣgrunde nēah.[3]
> [They did not, the evil destroyers,
> have joy of that meal, that they devoured me,
> sat around the feast near the sea-bottom.]

Let's count the variations in these three lines. First, the subject of the sentence, *hīe* 'they', is repeated in the next line with *mānfordǣdlan* 'evildoers'. Next, the verb *hæfde* 'had' has two objects, the first a noun, *ġefēan* 'joy', and the

---

[3]   *Beowulf*, ll. 562–4.

second a noun clause, *þæt . . . nēah*. (Did anyone say that elements in variation all had to be the same part of speech, or even that they all had to be words?) Within that noun clause there are two predicates: first, *mē þēgon* 'devoured me' states the matter plainly; then *symbel . . . nēah* 'sat around the feast near the sea-bottom' restates the same action, but more elaborately.

So far you have seen variations consisting of just two elements. But variations can have more elements than that. A poet may easily line up five of them:

> hlehhan ne þorftun
> þæt hēo *beaduweorca* beteran wurdun
> on campstede *cumbolġehnastes,*
> *gārmittinge, gumena ġemōtes,*
> *wǣpenġewrixles . . .*[4]
>   [they had no need to laugh
> that they were better *at battle-works*
> on the battlefield, *at the clash of banners,*
> *at the meeting of spears, at the gathering of men,*
> *at the exchange of weapons . . .*]

Clearly this poet has allowed his enthusiasm for variation to get the better of his sense of proportion. Further, his piling up of conventional terms for battle adds nothing to our sense of what this battle was about. Let's see what a better poet can do with variation:

> Calde ġeþrungen
> wǣron mīne fēt, forste ġebunden
> caldum clommum, þǣr þā ċeare seofedun
> hāt ymb heortan . . .[5]
>   [My feet were
> oppressed by cold, bound with frost,
> with cold fetters, where cares sighed,
> heat around my heart . . .]

In this passage a seafarer describes conditions at sea. There are three variations here: the past participles *ġeþrungen* 'pressed, pinched' and *ġebunden* 'bound', both modifying *fēt* 'feet', the datives *calde* 'cold', *forste* 'frost' and *caldum clommum* 'cold fetters', which go with them, and the nominatives *ċeare* 'cares' and *hāt* 'heat'. Through these variations, the speaker incrementally introduces the metaphor of cold and frost as shackles which constrain him; we are unprepared for the sudden introduction of his 'cares', whose

---

[4] *The Battle of Brunanburh*, ll. 47–51.
[5] *The Seafarer*, ll. 8–11.

temperature contrasts sharply with what has gone before, and which tell us in the most dramatic way that the cold is not so much a physical as an emotional hardship. Here, as often happens, careful attention to the variations you meet will be repaid with greater appreciation of the poet's artistry.

14.3 Formulas

If you were to search for 'o'er the lea' (from Gray's *Elegy*, quoted above, p. 129) in a reasonably complete database of English poetry, you would find that it occurs frequently in poems of the eighteenth and nineteenth centuries.[6] It is a *formula*, a set phrase used in a conventional way. When a poem – or a poetic tradition – uses formulas frequently, we say it is *formulaic*. Homeric poetry, as is well known, is formulaic: every student who has ever read the *Iliad* remembers the 'rosy-fingered dawn'.

It has long been recognized that Old English poetry is also formulaic. We will discuss Old English formulas under two headings: phrases and themes.

14.3.1 Phrases

Look at these lines from *Beowulf*, all of which introduce speeches:[7]

Hrōðgār maþelode,   helm Scyldinga
[Hrothgar, helmet of the Scyldings, spoke]

Unferð maþelode,   Ecglāfes bearn
[Unferth, the son of Ecglaf, spoke]

Bēowulf maþelode,   bearn Ecgþēowes
[Beowulf, the son of Ecgtheow, spoke]

Such lines are common in *Beowulf*: clearly we are dealing with a formula here, but it differs from 'o'er the lea' in being variable, not fixed. From the examples above, we might hazard a guess at the principles by which it was constructed: it consisted of the name of the person who was about to speak, the verb *maþelode* 'spoke, made a speech' and, in the second half-line, a noun phrase consisting of a noun and a genitive modifier, in variation with the proper name.

---

[6] For example, a search of the Chadwyck-Healey database of English poetry, 600–1900 (http://www.chadwyck.com) yields 118 instances of the phrase.
[7] Lines 456, 499, 529.

So far so good; and it is easy to find additional examples of formulas on exactly that pattern:

Wīġlāf maðelode, Wēohstānes sunu[8]
[Wiglaf, the son of Weohstan, spoke]

But it is not hard to find formulas that belong to the same *formulaic system* but diverge from the pattern:[9]

Weard maþelode ðǣr on wicge sæt
ombeht unforht
[The guard spoke where he sat on his horse,
a fearless officer]

Wulfgār maþelode (þæt wæs Wendla lēod;
wæs his mōdsefa manegum ġecȳðed,
wīġ ond wīsdōm)
[Wulfgar spoke (he was a man of the Wendels;
his character, his warfare and wisdom
were known to many)]

Now we know that the first word in the formula does not have to be a name, and that the verb can be followed not only by a noun phrase, but also by a clause or even a parenthetical statement. There is a good bit of flexibility in this formulaic system. You will find it to be generally true that the Old English poetic formula is not a set phrase, but rather a syntactical pattern built around a word or short phrase.

An analysis of the first fifty half-lines of *Beowulf*, in a classic article by Francis P. Magoun [66], showed that about three quarters of them were paralleled in other Old English poems. Although a parallel in another poem does not guarantee that a phrase is a formula, it is nevertheless clear that *Beowulf* is heavily formulaic. So, it should be added, is most Old English poetry.

Magoun's article has often been reprinted, and so you are very likely to encounter it in your study of Old English poetry. Magoun made some rather sweeping claims in that article, of which the most influential was that the formulaic character of Old English poetry showed that it had been composed orally. His argument is simple, logical and compelling; but you should be aware that a central claim on which Magoun's 'oral-formulaic theory' rests, that 'the recurrence in a given poem of an appreciable number of formulas

---

[8] *Beowulf*, l. 2862.
[9] *Beowulf*, ll. 286–7, 348–50.

or formulaic phrases brands the latter as oral, just as a lack of such repetitions marks a poem as composed in a lettered tradition', has long since been shown to be false. It turns out that a number of Old English poems that are unlikely to have been composed orally, such as translations of Latin poems, are every bit as formulaic as *Beowulf*. Many scholars still hold that *Beowulf* and other important poems were composed orally, but few now rest their arguments to that effect entirely on the formulaic character of these poems.

14.3.2   Themes

One of the better Old English poems is a paraphrase of that part of Exodus which narrates the escape of the Hebrews from Egypt. As the Hebrews race towards the Red Sea, pursued by the doomed Egyptians, we find these lines:

> Hrēopon herefugolas,   hilde grǣdiġe,
> dēawiġfeðere,   ofer drihtnēum,
> wonn wælċēasega.   Wulfas sungon
> atol ǣfenlēoð   ǣtes on wēnan,
> carlēasan dēor,   cwyldrōf beodan
> on lāðra lāst   lēodmæġnes fyl;
> hrēopon mearcweardas   middum nihtum.[10]
> [The dewy-feathered war-birds, greedy
> for battle, and the dark corpse-picker
> screamed over the corpses. Wolves, careless
> wild animals, expecting a meal, sang
> a terrible evening song; the slaughter-bold awaited
> the fall of the army on the path of the hated ones;
> the border-wardens screamed in the middle of the nights.]

This grisly passage, which depicts carrion-eating birds and wolves hungrily awaiting the outcome of a battle, has no parallel in the poem's biblical source. It may, however, remind readers of *The Battle of Maldon* of this passage, which occurs just as the battle is getting underway:

> Þǣr wearð hrēam āhafen,   hremmas wundon,
> earn ǣses ġeorn;   wæs on eorþan ċyrm.[11]
> [There an outcry was raised up, ravens circled
> and the eagle eager for carrion; there was an uproar upon the earth.]

---

[10]   *Exodus*, ll. 162–8.
[11]   Lines 106–7.

And those who have read *The Battle of Finnsburg* may be reminded of these two half-lines:

> Hræfen wandrode,
> sweart and sealobrūn.[12]
> [The dark and deep brown
> raven wandered]

In fact, whenever men gather to do battle in Old English poetry, it is customary for some combination of ravens, eagles and wolves to gather as well, in expectation of a feast of human flesh. Their doing so is a formulaic *theme*, a motif or narrative element that occurs, generally at predictable moments, in various poems.

Readers of Old English elegies such as *The Wanderer*, *The Seafarer* and *The Wife's Lament* will recognize such a theme in the storms and frost that symbolize the speakers' emotional state. Readers of *Beowulf* should know that the Unferth episode (ll. 499–607) is a formulaic narrative element called a *flyting* with parallels in several poetic traditions, especially the Norse. Indeed, formulaic themes are pervasive in Old English poetry, though they tend to be harder to spot than formulaic phrases.

The formulaic theme, like the formulaic phrase, is a flexible form, allowing expanded, leisurely treatments like the one in the Old English *Exodus* or extremely compressed treatments like the one in *The Battle of Finnsburg*. The choices these poets made were consonant with their other stylistic choices: *Exodus* is an ornate and much-elaborated treatment of the biblical story while *The Battle of Finnsburg* is spare and fast-paced.

14.3.3   Originality and quality

Naive readers of Old English poetry sometimes worry that, if poets were required by the tradition in which they worked to use formulaic diction, motifs and narrative elements, they must have had difficulty saying anything new. And if they could say nothing new, how could they say anything good? Keep the following points in mind when thinking about the implications of formulaic diction and themes.

First, although Old English poetry is formulaic, few scholars, if any, now believe Magoun's assertion that a poem such as *Beowulf* must have been made up entirely of formulas. On the contrary, it is probable that the *Beowulf* poet not only composed a great many lines that conformed to no formulaic

---

[12]   Lines 34–5.

Minitext J. Extract from *Maxims I*

The poem from which this extract is taken is a collection of proverbs and gnomes preserved in the Exeter Book. The present excerpt, ll. 81–92, addresses the duties and proper behaviour of a queen.

        Cyning sceal mid ċēape   cwēne ġebicgan,
        bunum ond bēagum;   bū sceolon ǣrest
        ġeofum gōd wesan.   Gūð sceal in eorle,
        wīġ ġeweaxan,   ond wīf ġeþēon

85   lēof mid hyre lēodum,   leohtmōd wesan,
        rūne healdan,   rūmheort bēon
        mēarum ond māþmum,   meodorǣdenne,[a]
        for ġesīðmæġen   symle ǣghwǣr
        eodor æþelinga   ǣrest ġegrētan,

90   forman fulle   tō frēan hond
        ricene ġerǣcan,   ond him rǣd witan[b]
        boldāgendum   bǣm ætsomne.

[a] *meodorǣdenne*: in the assembly. The dative here expresses location, a relatively rare usage.
[b] *ond him rǣd witan*: know what is good advice for them. The pronoun *him* is dative plural.

pattern, but also coined a great many of his own kennings. The same is no doubt true of other poets as well.

Second, as we have seen, both the formulaic phrase and the formulaic theme were flexible: the materials that Old English poets worked with were not building blocks of fixed shape, size and colour, but rather a generous set of malleable shapes and flexible rules for the construction of poetry, rather like the vocabulary and grammar of a language.

Third, it is clear that Anglo-Saxon audiences valued originality in poetry less than we do – or at least they evaluated the 'originality' of poetry differently from the way we do now. The formulas of *Beowulf* and other poems, together with such features as frequent use of the phrase *iċ ġefræġn* 'I have heard', seem to have assured the audience that both the matter and manner of these poems were traditional, and the poet was not presuming to try anything new. Old English poets avoided the appearance of originality.

But if an entertainer must offer some kind of novelty to keep an audience engaged, the best poets certainly did so – sometimes by playing with the formulaic elements of style. Here is what becomes of the 'Beasts of Battle' theme in the hands of the *Beowulf* poet, as a messenger, having announced Beowulf's death to the waiting Geats, predicts that a time of strife is nearly upon them:

> Forðon sceall gār wesan
> moniġ morgenċeald   mundum bewunden,
> hæfen on handa,   nalles hearpan swēġ
> wīġend weċċean,   ac se wonna hrefn
> fūs ofer fǣġum   fela reordian,
> earne secgan   hū him æt ǣte spēow,
> þenden hē wið wulf   wæl rēafode.[13]
> [Therefore must many a
> morning-cold spear be grasped in fists,
> raised in the hand, not the sound of the harp
> wake the warriors, but the dark raven,
> greedy over the doomed, talking away,
> saying to the eagle how it went for him at his meal,
> while, with the wolf, he plundered the slain.]

We imagine a morning scene, announced to us by an attribute applied to the chill of the spears that warriors must grasp. Then we are told what will awaken the warriors that morning: not the sound of the harp, as in peacetime, but the excited 'talking' of the raven as he describes to the eagle how he and the wolf 'plundered' (that is, ate) the corpses on the battlefield. We have traded direct statement ('the raven wheeled above') for indirection: we do not see the raven eat, but rather enter the warriors' minds as they hear him croak and imagine what he is saying. Their terror makes this passage by far the darkest of all the 'Beasts of Battle' passages in Old English poetry.

These lines are untraditional in a way, but an audience could hardly fail to respond to them.

---

[13]   Lines 3021–7.

Chapter 15

The Grammar of Poetry

You are already aware of some of the grammatical differences between prose and poetry. You know, for example, that Old English poetry has some rules of its own for the ordering of sentence elements (§13.2.1), and you know that poetry makes heavy use of apposition (§14.2). Here we will discuss the grammar of poetry in greater detail.

15.1   Inflections

15.1.1   Pronouns

You will frequently see accusative singular *þec* 'you' and *mec* 'me' where prose has *þē* and *mē* (see §5.1.1).

Instead of the genitive singular pronoun *his*, you will sometimes see *sīn* 'his' used as a possessive adjective. It takes strong adjective endings.

15.1.2   Verbs

You may (rarely) see a present first-person singular verb with the archaic ending *-o* or *-u*: for example *fullǣstu* 'assist' in *Beowulf*, l. 2668, but more often *hafo, hafu* 'I have' instead of West Saxon *habbe*.

The present second-person singular and third-person singular endings are -*st* and -*ð* in West Saxon (see table 7.2, p. 64). But in poetry, which frequently displays northern dialect features, you will often see -*est* and -*eð* instead. And where West Saxon has *i*-mutation of the root vowel (§7.4), these longer forms generally lack it. For example, the West Saxon present third-person singular of *healdan* 'hold' is *hielt* (for the -*t*, see §7.2.1, item 2), but you will see *healdeð* in poetry; and the West Saxon present third-person singular of *brūcan* 'make use of' is *brȳcð*, but you will see *brūceð* in poetry.

Certain archaic and dialectal verb forms occur in both prose and poetry, but more often in poetry. These include *cwōm* (past tense of *cuman* 'come'), *sǣgon*, *sēgon* (past plural of *sēon* 'see'), *ġēong* (past tense of *gangan* 'to go'), and alternate forms of third-class weak verbs (see §7.3.4), especially *hafast*, *hafað* beside *hæfst*, *hæfð*.

15.1.3 Adjectives

In poetry, weak adjectives are frequently found where you would normally find strong adjectives in prose – that is, where no demonstrative pronoun or possessive adjective precedes (for the usual rule, see the beginning of chapter 8). Example:

> wolde blondenfeax   beddes nēosan
> *gamela* Scylding.[1]
> [the grey-haired one, the *old* Scylding, wished
> to seek his bed.]

The strong form corresponding to *gamela* 'old' would be *gamol*.

The reverse does not happen: strong adjectives are not used with preceding pronouns or possessive adjectives. You will never see such phrases as **þone gōdne cyning*.

15.2 Syntax

15.2.1 Omission of subjects and objects

You learned in §11.2 that a pronoun subject may be omitted in Old English. In fact, when reading poetry you will frequently encounter clauses with

---

[1] *Beowulf*, ll. 1791–2.

unexpressed subjects. Often it is no more than a matter of one subject belonging with two predicates:

> Ðā ārās mæniġ goldhladen ðeġn,   ġyrde hine his swurde.[2]
> [Then many a gold-laden thegn arose (and) girded his sword on himself.]

As the translation suggests, we can do much the same thing in Modern English, though we usually say *and* between the two predicates. But sometimes it is not so easy to figure out the reference of an unexpressed subject:

> Sceolde lǣndaga
> æþeling ǣrgōd   ende ġebīdan,
> worulde līfes,   ond se wyrm somod,
> þēah ðe hordwelan   hēolde lange.[3]
> [The good old prince
> had to experience the end of his transitory days,
> of his life in the world, and the worm along with him,
> though (he) had held the hoard-wealth for a long time.]

The subject of the clause in the last line is evidently the dragon (which has been guarding the only treasure that interests us in the last third of *Beowulf*), but the subject of the preceding clause, being compound, does not match it precisely.

In the examples above, the reference of the unexpressed subject is someone or something that has recently been mentioned. But the unexpressed subject need not have an antecedent:

> Þǣr mæġ nihta ġehwǣm   nīðwundor sēon
> fȳr on flōde.[4]
> [There every night (one) may see an evil wonder,
> fire in the water.]

Here it is a simple matter to supply a pronoun subject.

Direct objects may also be omitted. Usually the object will be expressed in a nearby clause (though not always *as* an object):

> Ðā ġȳt hīe him āsetton   seġen gyldenne
> hēah ofer hēafod,   lēton holm beran,
> ġēafon on gārsecg.[5]

[2]   *The Battle of Finnsburh*, l. 13.
[3]   *Beowulf*, ll. 2341–4.
[4]   *Beowulf*, ll. 1365–6.
[5]   *Beowulf*, ll. 47–9.

[Then further they set up for him a golden standard,
high over head, let the sea bear (him),
gave (him) unto the sea.]

There can be no doubt as to whom they are sending out onto the sea; it is the one for whom they set up the standard.

15.2.2   Omission of prepositions

You will remember from an earlier chapter (§4.2.4) that words in the dative case are often used by themselves where Modern English would use a preposition. This tendency is even more pronounced in poetry than in prose. Examples:

Weorða ðē selfne
gōdum dǣdum   ðenden ðīn God reċċe.[6]
[Honour yourself
with good deeds for as long as God cares for you.]

þonne hand wereð
feorhhord *fēondum.*[7]
[when my hand defends
my life-hoard *from enemies.*]

seġe *þīnum lēodum*   miċċle lāþre spell[8]
[say *to your people* a much more hateful message]

As you can see, you will frequently have to supply a preposition when you encounter a word in the dative that lacks one. But there is no one Modern English preposition that is always appropriate. You will have to judge from the context what the dative is doing and how best to translate it.

In the first passage above, notice also the clause *ðenden ðīn God reċċe* 'for as long as God cares for you'. Here the verb *reċċan* takes the genitive of what one cares for, and we supplied a preposition in translating it. Verbs that govern words in the genitive case are common in both verse and prose. For example, *ġielpan* 'boast' takes the genitive of what one is boasting of (you must supply the preposition *of* or *about*) and *þancian* 'thank' takes the genitive of what one is grateful for (you must supply the preposition *for*). A good glossary or dictionary will tell you about the cases that verbs govern.

---

6   *Waldere*, I, ll. 22–3.
7   *Waldere*, II, ll. 21–2.
8   *The Battle of Maldon*, l. 50.

15.2.3 *Adjectives used as nouns*

In Modern English, when we wish to name a thing by mentioning one of its attributes, we use an adjective with a placeholder noun: 'the wise one', 'the big one'. In Old English poetry it is more common to use a demonstrative pronoun with a weak adjective:

> Þā wæs Nerġendes
> þēowen þrymful, þearle ġemyndiġ
> hū hēo *þone atolan* ēaðost mihte
> ealdre benǣman ǣr *se unsȳfra*,
> *womfull* onwōce.[9]
>   [Then the Saviour's handmaiden
> was filled with glory, vigorously thoughtful
> how she could most easily deprive
> *the terrible one* of life before *the unclean one*,
> *the impure one* awoke.]

Here Holofernus (about to be beheaded by Judith) is *þone atolan* 'the terrible one', *se unsȳfra* 'the unclean one', and finally *womfull* 'the impure one'. The last of these is a strong adjective unaccompanied by either a demonstrative or a noun. Strong adjectives are used as nouns less often than weak adjectives are, but it happens often enough that you should be prepared for it.

15.2.4 *Word-order*

The basic patterns of Old English word-order that you learned in chapter 12 apply as well for poetry as they do for prose. To illustrate, here is a short passage with the word-order of each clause indicated:

1 **Verb–Subject:**
Ðā *wearð breahtm* hæfen.
2 **Verb–Subject:**
                         Beorg *ymbstōdan*
hwearfum *wrǣcmæcgas.*
3 **Subject–Verb:**
                         Wōð ūp *āstāg*
ċearfulra ċirm.
4 **Verb–Subject:**
                         Cleopedon moniġe
fēonda foresprecan, firenum gulpon:

---

[9] *Judith*, ll. 73–7.

Minitext κ. Grendel's *mere*

The punctuation and capitalization of this extract from *Beowulf* (ll. 1357b–72) are those of the manuscript. See if you can find the boundaries of the clauses and their types without benefit of modern punctuation.

Hīe dȳgel lond
wariġeað wulfhleoþu   windiġe næssas
frēcne fenġelād   ðǣr fyrġenstrēam

1360	under næssa ġenipu niþer ġewīteð
	flōd under foldan nis þæt feor heonon
	mīlġemearces þæt se mere standeð
	ofer þǣm hongiað hrinde bearwas
	wudu wyrtum fæst wæter oferhelmað
1365	þǣr mæġ[a] nihta ġehwǣm nīðwundor sēon
	fȳr on flōde nō þæs frōd leofað
	gumena bearna þæt[b] þone grund wite
	ðēah þe hǣðstapa hundum ġeswenċed
	heorot hornum trum holtwudu sēċe
1370	feorran ġeflȳmed ǣr hē feorh seleð
	aldor on ōfre ǣr[c] hē in wille
	hafelan beorgan nis þæt hēoru stōw.

[a] The subject of this verb is unexpressed; see §15.2.1.
[b] *þæs frōd ... þæt*: so wise ... that.
[c] *ǣr ... ǣr*: first ... before (correlated).

5 **Subject–Verb:**
'Oft *wē ofersēgon*   bi sǣm twēonum
þēoda þēawas,   þrǣce mōdiġra
6 **Subject ... Verb:**
þāra *þe* in ġelimpe   līfe *wēoldon*'.[10]
[*1* Then a cry was raised. *2* The devils stood
around the mound in crowds. *3* The noise, the uproar
of the miserable ones rose up. *4* Many advocates
for the enemies called out, boasted criminally:
5 'Often we have observed, between the two seas,
the customs of the nations, the power of those proud ones
6 who lived their lives in prosperity'.]

---

[10] *Guthlac*, ll. 262–8.

Each clause in this passage (chosen nearly at random) uses a standard word order. If the passage seems difficult, that is because the poet is vigorously taking advantage of the flexibility of these standard word orders. For example, in (1) the finite verb is an auxiliary, and the verbal (a past participle) is delayed to the end of the clause (§12.6), and in (2) the direct object comes before the verb instead of after the subject (§12.3).

Variation (§14.2) or, to use the grammatical term, apposition, would seem likely to violate the norms of Old English word order. In (3) the subject *Wōð* is varied by *ċearfulra ċirm*, and thus a subject follows as well as precedes the verb: the word-order is really Subject–Verb–Subject. But you will often find that it is possible to look at such clauses as hybrids of two standard word-orders: in this case Subject–Verb and Verb–Subject. Clause (4), where the word-order is Verb–Subject–Verb, can also be seen as a hybrid. It is as if poets saw the clause as containing several positions where a subject, verb or other element would be permissible and set out to fill up those positions.

It would be nice if you could always count on elements in variation coming in 'normal' positions, but sometimes they do not:

> Hē ǣrest sceōp   eorðan bearnum
> heofon tō hrōfe,   hāliġ Scyppend.[11]
> [he, the holy Creator, first created
> heaven as a roof for the children of men.]

The beginning of this sentence, with its order Subject–Verb . . . Object, looks normal enough, but the variation *hāliġ Scyppend* comes where a subject normally does not come (as part of a sequence Verb . . . Object–Subject). This example should serve as a reminder that you must be especially attentive to grammatical form and context when reading poetry. We can tell that *hāliġ Scyppend* is a subject, in variation with *Hē*, because it is nominative in form and because the poem has been talking about God.

15.2.5   Independent and subordinate clauses

In §§10.2–10.4 you learned that some adverbs have the same form as con-junctions and that the two occur together in correlative constructions. In §12.5 you learned further that word-order will often tell you which clause of a correlative construction is independent and which is subordinate. We also warned you there, however, that the word-order rule does not work in poetry. So how can you tell, in a sentence like the one that follows, whether we have a correlative construction, and if we do, which clause is independent? (We omit editorial punctuation to discourage you from prejudging the case.)

[11]   *Cædmon's Hymn*, ll. 5–6.

Ðā wæs on ūhtan   mid ǣrdæġe
Grendles gūðcræft   gumum undyrne
þā wæs æfter wiste   wōp up āhafen
miċel morgenswēġ[12]
[When/Then Grendel's warcraft was manifest
to men at dawn, early in the day,
when/then after the feasting weeping, a great morning-sound,
was raised up.]

Even where we don't have ambiguous adverb/conjunction pairs, it can be difficult to distinguish independent and subordinate clauses:

Nū ēow is ġerȳmed   gāð ricene tō ūs
guman tō gūþe[13]

If *Nū* is an adverb, the translation should go like this:

Now the way is open to you; go quickly to us,
men to battle.

But if *Nū* is a conjunction, it should go like this instead:

Now that the way is open to you, go quickly to us,
men to battle.

How to read such sentences as these is a matter of controversy. Until around the middle of the twentieth century, editors more often than not interpreted ambiguous clauses as independent and supplied punctuation to match that interpretation. In any case, editors showed an aversion to sentences in which subordinate clauses preceded independent clauses. In a passage like the following, we have a choice of translating *Þā* as 'then' and punctuating the first clause with a semicolon or translating *Þā* as 'when' and punctuating with a comma:

Þā of wealle ġeseah   weard Scildinga
se þe holmclifu   healdan scolde
beran ofer bolcan   beorhte randas
fyrdsearu fūslicu   hine fyrwyt bræc
mōdġehygdum   hwæt þā men wǣron.[14]

---

[12] *Beowulf*, ll. 126–9.
[13] *The Battle of Maldon*, ll. 93–4.
[14] *Beowulf*, ll. 229–33.

[Then/when the guardian of the Scyldings, he who
had to hold the sea-cliffs, saw from the wall
(them) bearing their bright shields, their ready army-trappings,
over the gangway;/, curiosity tormented him
in his mind-thoughts (to know) what those men were.]

Early editors and translators would almost invariably choose 'then' and the
semicolon. Recent editors are more likely to interpret the first clause as subordinate and punctuate with a comma.

Our decision whether to interpret a clause as independent or subordinate
rarely makes much difference in the sense of a passage, but it does make a
significant difference in the way we perceive its style. A paratactic style (one
with relatively few subordinate clauses – see §3.3) was once thought to be
'primitive', especially by scholars who were interested in recovering, in Old
English poetry, a genuine experience of English or Germanic cultural origins.
Now, on the other hand, scholars are more likely to deny the possibility (and
perhaps also the value) of recovering the origins of a culture, and further to
deny that parataxis is in any way 'primitive'. Such modern scholars have been
open to arguments that Old English poetry is less paratactic than formerly
believed.

But how can you decide, in a particular passage, whether a clause is independent or subordinate? The following rule seems to work for clauses that
contain an auxiliary and a verbal: if the auxiliary precedes the verbal and is
unstressed, the clause is independent, but if the auxiliary follows the verbal
and is stressed, the clause is subordinate. So this clause, in which the auxiliary
wearð precedes the verbal *ġeġearewod* and is unstressed, is independent:

Þā wearð snelra werod   snūde ġeġearewod,
cēnra tō campe.[15]
[Then the host of the bold and the brave was quickly
prepared for battle.]

This clause, on the other hand, in which a stressed auxiliary (*hafað*) follows
the verbal (*ġetācnod*), is subordinate:

                swā ēow ġetācnod hafað
mihtiġ Dryhten   þurh mīne hand.[16]
                [as the mighty Lord
has signalled to you through my hand.]

---

[15]   *Judith*, ll. 199–200.
[16]   *Judith*, ll. 197–8.

It may be uncertain whether clauses in which stressed auxiliaries precede verbals, or which do not contain auxiliaries, are independent or subordinate – unless, of course, the context tells us, as it often does.

The existence of clauses that may be either independent or subordinate has occasioned debate, some holding that Old English had a type of clause that fell somewhere between independent and subordinate while others believe that Old English clauses were always one or the other, even if we do not always know how to distinguish them. In this connection it is worth noting that the rule for distinguishing independent and subordinate clauses that contain auxiliaries was not discovered until relatively recently (see Donoghue [31]). It is not inconceivable that a rule for distinguishing other clauses has yet to be discovered.

Chapter 16

Reading Old English Manuscripts

If you continue long enough in your study of Old English, you will sooner or later want to consult one or more of the roughly four hundred manuscripts (complete books and fragments) in which the language is recorded. Some 65 per cent of these manuscripts are owned by just three libraries: the British Library in London, the Bodleian Library in Oxford, and the Parker Library in Corpus Christi College, Cambridge. These and most other libraries will grant you access to their collections if you come with the proper credentials and have a legitimate research interest in Old English manuscripts. A great many manuscripts have been published in facsimile editions: these include all of the poetic manuscripts along with some of the most important of the prose ones. Eventually the series Anglo-Saxon Manuscripts in Microfiche Facsimile will include every manuscript that contains even a word of Old English (see Further Reading §8 for references). The availability of so many facsimiles means that you can work with Old English manuscripts even if your circumstances do not allow you to consult the real thing.

16.1 Construction of the manuscript

Most Anglo-Saxon manuscripts were written on vellum (Old English *fell*) made of calf skin. This was stretched, scraped smooth, whitened with chalk, cut into sheets, ruled with a stylus, and folded into quires of eight leaves (four sheets), or sixteen pages. After the scribes had done their work, the quires were sewn together and bound.

16.2   The Old English alphabet

The Anglo-Saxons adopted the styles of script employed by the Irish missionaries who had been instrumental in the conversion of the northern kingdoms. These styles included Insular half-uncial, used for fine books in Latin, and the less formal minuscule, used for both Latin and the vernacular. Beginning in the tenth century Anglo-Saxon scribes began to use caroline minuscule (developed in Francia during the reign of Charlemagne) for Latin while continuing to write Old English in Insular minuscule. Thereafter Old English script was increasingly influenced by caroline minuscule even as it retained certain distinctively Insular letter-forms. Once you have learned these letter-forms you will be able to read Old English manuscripts of all periods without difficulty.

Here are the basic letter-forms of Old English script, illustrated in a late Old English style:

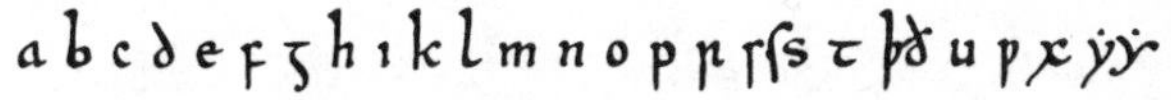

a b c ꝺ e ꝼ ᵹ h ı k l m n o p � ꞃ ſs ꞇ þ ð u ƿ x ẏ

Take particular note of these features:

- the rounded shape of ꝺ (**d**);
- the ꝼ (**f**) that extends below the baseline instead of sitting on top of it;
- the distinctive Insular ᵹ (**g**);
- the dotless ı (**i**);
- the ꞃ (**r**) that extends below the baseline;
- the three shapes of **s**, of which the first two (the Insular long ſ and the high ſ) are most common;
- the ꞇ (**t**) that does not extend above the cross-stroke;
- the ƿ ('wynn'), usually transliterated as **w** but sometimes printed as ƿ, derived from the runic letter ᚹ;
- the ẏ (**y**), usually dotted, which comes in several different shapes.

Old English has no use for **q** or **z**. **J** and **v** do not have the status of separate letters but are occasional variant shapes of **i** and **u** (more common in roman numbers than elsewhere). Old English scribes used **k** rarely, and only to represent the [k] sound, never the [tʃ] (*ċ*).

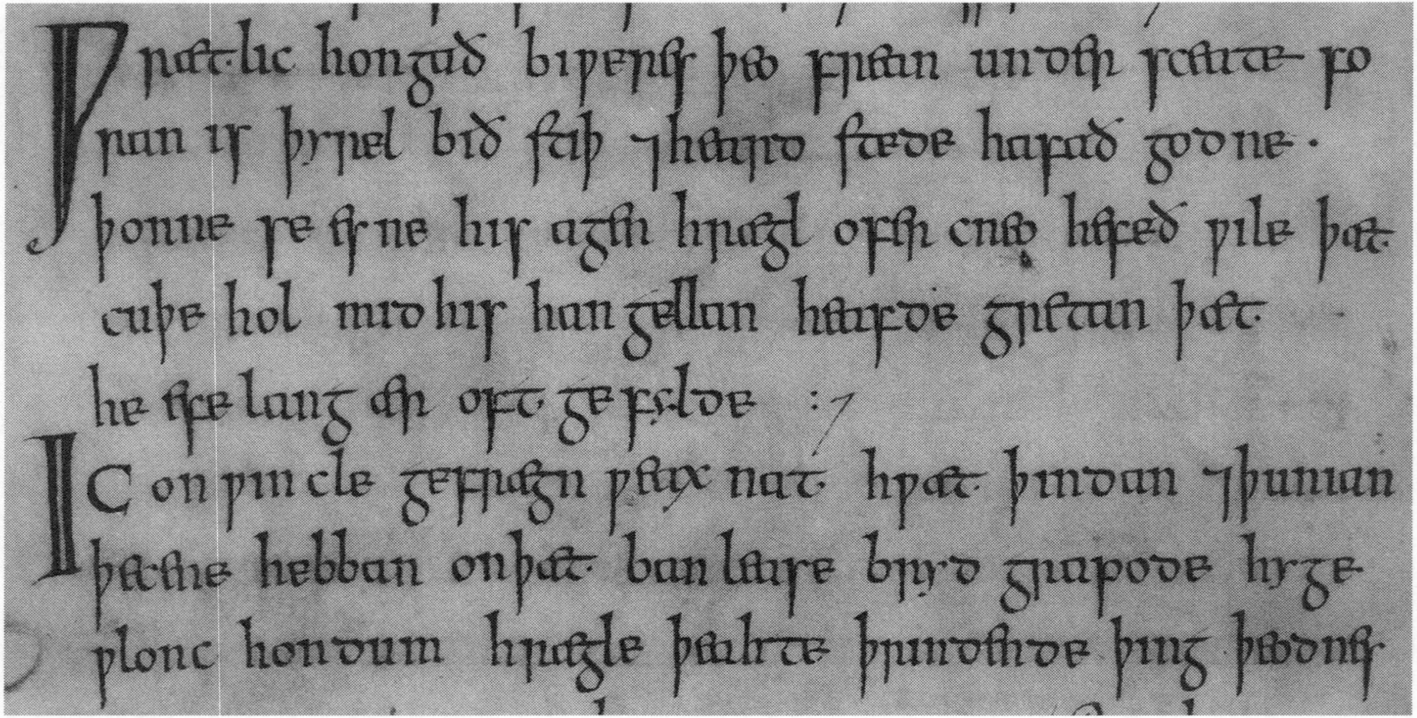

Wrætlic hongað bi weres þeo frean under sceate fo
ran is þyrel bið stiþ ⁊ heard hafað stede godne·
þonne se esne his agen hrægl ofer cneo hefeð wile þæt
cuþe hol mid his hangellan heafde gretan þæt
he efe lang ær oft gefylde :7
IC on wincle gefrægn weax nat· hwæt· þindan ⁊ þunian
þecene hebban on þæt· banlease bryd grapode hyge
wlonc hondum hrægle þeahte þrindende þing þeodnes

Plate I A portion of fol. 112v of the Exeter Book. Reprinted with kind permission of the Dean and Chapter of Exeter Cathedral

Minitext L. Two Riddles

Plate 1 shows a portion of fol. 112v of the Exeter Book, containing Riddles 44 and 45. Read and transcribe these, normalizing punctuation and capitalization and arranging them in poetic lines.

Minitext M. Two Laws of Ine

Plate 2 shows two sections of the Laws of Ine, king of Wessex (688–728), preserved in Cambridge, Corpus Christi College, MS 173, the Parker Chronicle and Laws (for a complete facsimile see Flower and Smith [34]). The part of the manuscript containing these laws was written around the middle of the tenth century.

16.3   Abbreviations

Old English scribes used only a few abbreviations, of which the most common is ꞇ (= *and, ond*), a sign (Latin *nota*) from the shorthand system developed by Cicero's assistant M. Tullius Tiro, and hence called the Tironian *nota*. Another common abbreviation is ꝥ for *þæt*. A stroke over a letter often signals that an *m* or *n* has been omitted; thus **bocū** stands for *bocum* and **ᵹumā** for *guman*. The *ġe-* prefix can also be abbreviated with a stroke (ᵹ̅), as can *þonne* (**þoñ**).

16.4   Punctuation and capitalization

Writers of Modern English follow a rather strict set of rules for punctuation – for example, placing a semicolon between independent clauses that are not coordinated with *and* and a comma between independent clauses that are so coordinated. Such punctuation guides the reader through the syntax of the sentence. Where the rules give us a choice, say, among comma, semicolon and dash, we use punctuation as a rhetorical device, marking the intensity of a pause or the formality of a clause boundary.

   Old English scribes did not have so strict a set of rules to follow, and usage varies widely even among books produced at the same time and place. Some scribes used punctuation with fair reliability to mark clause- and sentence-boundaries, while others punctuated so lightly that their work is, for practical purposes, unpunctuated. To meet the expectations of readers accustomed to modern rules of punctuation, it has long been the practice of editors to

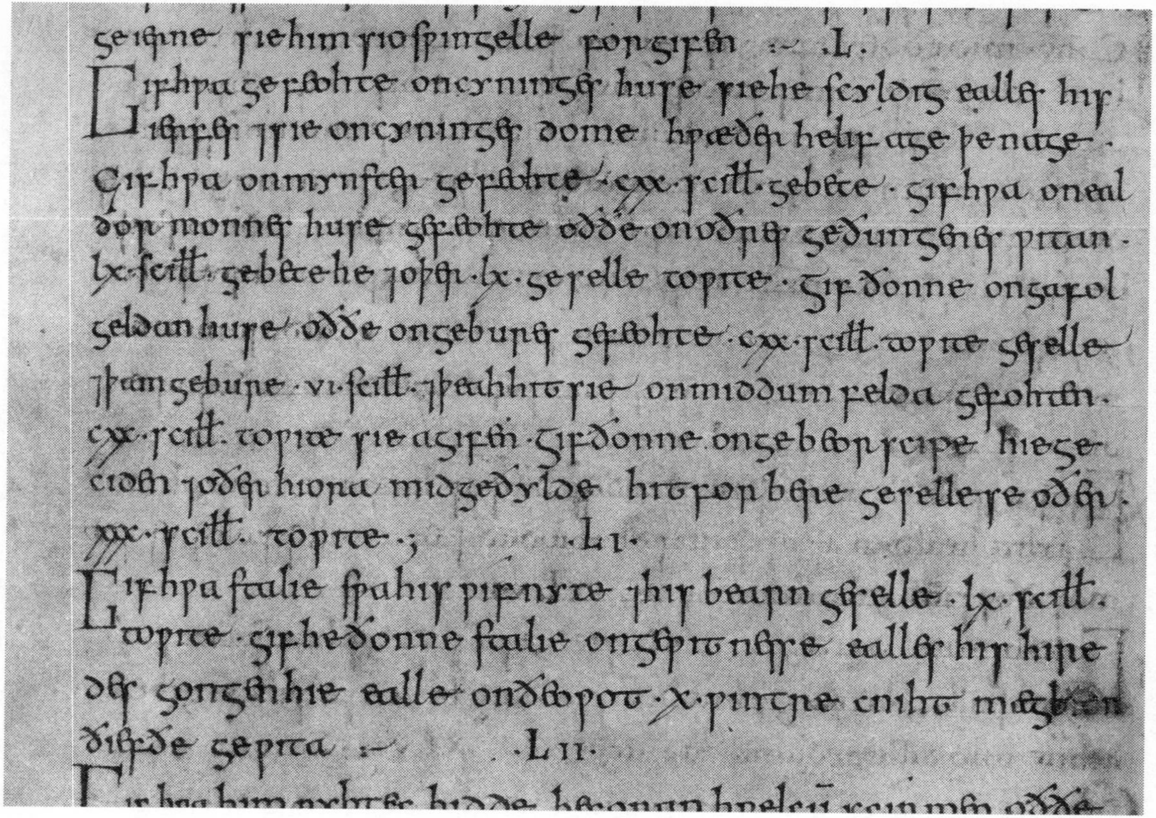

Plate II Two sections of the Laws of Ine, king of Wessex (688–728). Reprinted with kind permission of the Master and Fellows of Corpus Christi College, Cambridge.

modernize the punctuation of Old English works. Editors have debated how heavy this editorial punctuation should be, how much it should be influenced by the punctuation of the manuscript, and whether modern punctuation is adequate for representing Old English syntax.

Here is a passage from a manuscript of Ælfric's homilies, illustrating the punctuation used by one good scribe.[1]

Ic ðancɩᵹe þā ælmɩhtɩᵹū Scẏppende mɩð ealɲe heoɲtan · þ hé me ɽẏnɲullū þæɽ ᵹeuðe · þ ɩc ðaɽ tɽá beᴄ hɩm to loɲe ꝺ to puɲꝺmẏnte anᵹelcẏnne onɲɲeah ðam unᵹelæɲeðū · ða ᵹelæɲeðan ne beðuɲɲon þẏɽɽeɲa boca · ꝼoɽ ðan þe hɩm mæᵹ heoɲa aᵹen láɲ ᵹenɩhtɽumɩan;

[I thank the almighty Creator with all my heart that he has granted to me, a sinful one, that I have, in praise and worship of him, revealed these two books to the unlearned English nation; the learned have no need of these books because their own learning can suffice for them.]

The most common mark of punctuation is the point, which sometimes is placed on the baseline (as in Modern English) and sometimes, as here, somewhat above the line. The semicolon is used where a heavier syntactical or rhetorical break is indicated (here at the end of a pair of related sentences, which the translation coordinates with a semicolon). You may also occasionally see ⁏ (the *punctus elevatus*, marking a lighter pause than the semicolon but a heavier one than the point), and sometimes the ꝫ (the *punctus interrogativus* or question mark – but marking the end of a question is optional). At the ends of sections you may see some combination of punctuation marks used as an ornament.

The function of acute accents, such as those in the preceding and following quotations, is uncertain. They are more often than not found over long vowels, but they also appear over short ones. They are especially common on one-syllable words.

In some poetic manuscripts punctuation is used to separate verses and lines – a convenience to modern readers, since scribes always wrote poetry from margin to margin, as if it were prose. Here are the first lines of *The Battle of*

---

[1] Cambridge, University Library, MS. Gg. 3. 28, fol. 255r. A facsimile of this page is printed as the frontispiece to Henel [48]. The passage is printed as in the manuscript, except that word- and line-division have been normalized (see §16.5 below). In this and the other quotations in this chapter, the style of script is not intended to reproduce that of the manuscripts being quoted.

Brunanburh from the oldest manuscript of that poem[2] (the original line-breaks have been retained here):

> Añ dccc.xxxvii her æþelſtan cyning · eorla dryhten · beorna
> beahgifa · ⁊ his broþor eác · eadmund æþeling · ealdorlangne tir ·
> geſlogon æt ſæcce · ſþeorda ecgum · ymbe brunanburh ·

[Anno 937. Here King Æthelstan, lord of warriors, ring-giver of men, and also his brother, Prince Edmund, struck life-long glory in battle with the edges of swords near Brunanburh.]

As you can see from these passages, proper names are not capitalized. Some scribes capitalized words for God and the beginnings of sentences, but most did not do so with any consistency. Those editors who modernize punctuation usually do the same with capitalization.

16.5   Word- and line-division

Word-division is far less consistent in Old English than in Modern English; it is, in fact, less consistent in Old English manuscripts than in Latin written by Anglo-Saxon scribes. You may expect to see the following peculiarities:[3]

* spaces between the elements of compounds, e.g. *aldor mon*;
* spaces between words and their prefixes and suffixes, e.g. *be æftan, gewit nesse*;
* spaces at syllable divisions, e.g. *lon gert*;
* prepositions, adverbs and pronouns attached to the following words, e.g. *uuiþþra palū, hehæþde*;
* many words, especially short ones, run together, e.g. *þær þehequce hæfde*.

The width of the spaces between words and word-elements is quite variable in most Old English manuscripts, and it is often difficult to decide whether a scribe intended a space. 'Diplomatic' editions, which sometimes attempt to reproduce the word-division of manuscripts, cannot represent in print the variability of the spacing on a hand-written page.

---

[2]   Cambridge, Corpus Christi College, MS. 173, fol. 26r. This is the Parker manuscript of the *Anglo-Saxon Chronicle* (see reading 3), in which the poem is the entry for the year 937. For a facsimile of this manuscript see Flower and Smith [34].

[3]   Most of the examples in the following list are from reading 3.

Most scribes broke words freely at the ends of lines. Usually the break takes place at a syllable boundary, e.g. ꝋ[lᵹᵉᵑ] (= *ofslægen*), [ꝼū-ne] (= *sumne*), [heo-fenum]. Occasionally, however, a scribe broke a word elsewhere, e.g. [foþhæf-ðnerre]. Some scribes marked word-breaks with a hyphen, but many did not mark them in any way.

16.6   Errors and corrections

Everyone who writes makes mistakes, and it is probably safe to say that every Old English text of any length at all contains errors. Most manuscripts also contain corrections, either by the scribe himself or by a later corrector. But the correction of texts was often inconsistently carried out, and may not have taken into account errors already present in the copy from which corrections were being entered. In general you should not assume that a corrected text retains no uncorrected errors.

When a corrector added words to a text, he usually placed a comma below the line at the insertion point and wrote the addition above the line; longer additions might be written in the margin, very long ones on an added leaf. To delete a letter, the scribe would place a point under it; to delete a word or phrase he would underline it. Some correctors erased text, but erasure roughened the vellum, making it difficult to write on; so erasure was most suitable when no substitute text was to be supplied.

Appendix A

Common Spelling Variants

A.1 Vowels of accented syllables

Sounds	Environments	Examples
a ~ ea	When back vowel follows (or once followed) in next syllable.	*gatu ~ ġeatu* 'gates'; *gladian ~ gleadian* 'gladden'.
a ~ o	Before *m* and *n*.	*maniġ ~ moniġ* 'many'.
e ~ eo	When back vowel follows (or once followed) in next syllable.	*medo ~ meodo* 'mead'; *werod ~ weorod* 'troop'.
e ~ y	Late; between *s* and *l*.	*self ~ sylf* 'self'; *sellan ~ syllan* 'give'.
ea ~ a	Mercian and Northumbrian; before *l* + consonant.	*ealdor ~ aldor* 'life'; *healdan ~ haldan* 'hold'.
ĕa ~ ĕ	Late; before *c, g* and *h* or after *ċ, sc* and *ġ*.	*sceal ~ scel* 'must'; *seah ~ seh* 'saw'.
ĕo ~ ĭo	Frequent in a variety of texts.	*Bēowulf ~ Bīowulf*.
eo ~ u/o	Late; between *w* and *r*.	*weorðan ~ wurðan* 'become'; *weorold ~ woruld* 'world'.
eo/i ~ u	Late; after *w* when next syllable contains a back vowel; *w* may be lost.	*sweostor ~ swustor* 'sister'; *cwicu ~ cucu* 'alive'.

Sounds	Environments	Examples
i ~ eo/io	When back vowel follows (or once followed) in next syllable.	*clipian* ~ *cleopian* 'call'; *ġewritu* ~ *ġewriotu* 'writings'.
i ~ y	Late; near labial consonants (*b*, *m*, *p*, *w*) and *r*.	*clipian* ~ *clypian* 'call'; *miċel* ~ *myċel* 'large'.
ĭe ~ ĭ/ȳ	Late and widespread.	*nīed* ~ *nȳd/nīd* 'necessity'; *iernan* ~ *irnan/yrnan* 'run'.
ĭe/ĭ/ȳ ~ ĕo/ĭo	Non-West Saxon; when *ĭe/ĭ/ȳ* is from *i*-mutation of *ĕo/ĭo*.	*þīestru* ~ *þēostru* 'darkness'; *āfierran* ~ *āfeorran* 'remove'.
ĭe/ĭ/ȳ ~ ĕ	Kentish; when *ĭe/ĭ/ȳ* is from *i*-mutation of *ĕa*.	*hliehhan* ~ *hlehhan* 'laugh'; *hīeran* ~ *hēran* 'hear'.

A.2   Unaccented syllables

Sounds	Environments	Examples
-an ~ -a	Late; weak noun and adjective ending.	*mōnan* ~ *mōna* genitive singular 'of the moon'.
-iġ ~ -ī	Adjective ending.	*maniġ* ~ *manī* 'many'.
-ness ~ -niss/-nyss	Feminine suffix.	*ēadiġness* ~ *ēadiġniss* ~ *ēadiġnyss* 'prosperity'.
-od- ~ -ad-	Past and past participle of second-class weak verbs.	*wunode* ~ *wunade* 'dwelled, remained with'.
-on ~ -an/-un	Late; plural verb ending.	*writon* ~ *writan* 'wrote'; *wǣron* ~ *wǣrun* 'were'.
-u ~ -o	Feminine nominative singular and neuter nominative plural.	*scipu* ~ *scipo* 'ships'.
-um ~ -on/-un	Late; dative ending.	*sīðum* ~ *sīðon* 'times'; *ārum* ~ *ārun* 'oars'.

A.3   Consonants

Sounds	Environments	Examples
doubling	Before *l* or *r*.	*miċle ~ miċċle* 'large'; *nǣdre ~ nǣddre* 'serpent'.
undoubling	At the ends of words; after consonants; in unaccented syllables.	*mann ~ man* 'man'; *ġeornness ~ ġeorness* 'zeal'; *gyldenne ~ gyldene* 'golden'.
fn ~ mn/mm	Late.	*stefn ~ stemn* 'voice'; *hrefnas ~ hremmas* 'ravens'.
g ~ h	At the ends of words.	*sorg ~ sorh* 'sorrow'; *burg ~ burh* 'city'.
ġ ~ i/iġ	Late; after front vowels.	*dæġ ~ dæi* 'day'; *þeġn ~ þeiġn* 'thegn'.
ġeo ~ iu	At the beginnings of words.	*ġeong ~ iung* 'young'; *ġeogoð ~ iugoð* 'youth'.
r	Undergoes metathesis in syllables ending in *n* or *s*.	*irnan ~ rinnan* 'run'; *forst ~ frost* 'frost'.
sc ~ x	When *sc* is pronounced [sk] (see §2.1.2, item 10).	*ascian ~ axian* 'ask'; *fiscas ~ fixas* 'fishes'.
sco/scu ~ sceo	At the beginnings of words.	*sculan ~ sceolan* 'must'; *scort ~ sceort* 'short'.

Appendix B

Phonetic Symbols and Terms

B.1 International Phonetic Alphabet symbols

Symbol	Description	Example
ɑ	open back unrounded vowel	mann 'man'
ɑː	long open back unrounded vowel	ān 'one'
æ	open-mid to open front unrounded vowel	bæc 'back'
æː	long open-mid to open front unrounded vowel	rǣdan 'read'
ʌ	open-mid back unrounded vowel	Modern English *but*
b	voiced bilabial stop	bōc 'book'
β	voiced bilabial spirant	
ç	voiceless palatal spirant	niht 'night'
d	voiced dental/alveolar stop	dēofol 'devil'
ʤ	voiced postalveolar affricate	enġel 'angel'
ð	voiced dental spirant	feðer 'wing'
e	close-mid front unrounded vowel	etan 'eat'
eː	long close-mid front unrounded vowel	hēr 'here'
ə	mid central unrounded vowel	Modern English *China*
ɛ	open-mid front unrounded vowel	Modern English *set*
f	voiceless labiodental spirant	feorr 'far'
g	voiced velar stop	gōd 'good'
ɣ	voiced velar spirant	āgan 'own'

Symbol	Description	Example
h	voiceless glottal spirant	hand 'hand'
i	close front unrounded vowel	sittan 'sit'
iː	long close front unrounded vowel	bītan 'bite'
ɪ	close to close-mid front unrounded vowel	iernan 'run'
ɪː	long close to close-mid front unrounded vowel	hīeran 'hear'
j	voiced palatal approximant	ġē 'you'
k	voiceless velar stop	camb 'comb'
l	alveolar lateral approximant	lamb 'lamb'
m	bilabial nasal	mann 'man'
n	dental/alveolar nasal	nū 'now'
ŋ	velar nasal	singan 'sing'
o	close-mid back rounded vowel	open 'open'
oː	long close-mid back rounded vowel	ōr 'origin'
p	voiceless bilabial stop	prēost 'priest'
r	alveolar trill	rǣdan 'read'
s	voiceless alveolar spirant	sittan 'sit'
ʃ	voiceless postalveolar spirant	scip 'ship'
t	voiceless dental/alveolar stop	twēġen 'two'
ʧ	voiceless postalveolar affricate	ċild 'child'
θ	voiceless dental spirant	þēaw 'custom'
u	close back rounded vowel	burg 'stronghold'
uː	long close back rounded vowel	būgan 'bow'
ʊ	close to close-mid back rounded vowel	Modern English *put*
v	voiced labiodental spirant	heofon 'heaven'
w	voiced labio-velar approximant	weall 'wall'
x	voiceless velar spirant	beorht 'bright'
y	close front rounded vowel	yfel 'evil'
yː	long close front rounded vowel	brȳd 'bride'
z	voiced alveolar spirant	rīsan 'rise'

B.2   Phonetic terms

back vowel. A vowel pronounced toward the back of the mouth, e.g. [ɑou].

front vowel. A vowel pronounced toward the front of the mouth, e.g. [ieæ].

high vowel. A vowel pronounced with the tongue raised, e.g. [iuy].

liquid. A term applied to the consonants [l] and [r].

low vowel. A vowel pronounced with the tongue and jaw lowered, e.g. [æɑ].

nasal. A consonant pronounced by passing air through the nose: [m] and [n].

rounded vowel. A vowel pronounced with the lips rounded, e.g. [uoy].

spirant. A consonant produced by passing air through a narrow opening in the mouth, e.g. [fsθvz]; also called a fricative.

stop. A consonant produced by momentarily stopping the breath, e.g. [bgkp]; also called a plosive.

unvoiced. Pronounced while the vocal chords are not vibrating, e.g. [fhkpst].

voiced. Pronounced while the vocal chords are vibrating. A vowel is always voiced; so are the consonants [bdgvz].

Anthology

1   The Fall of Adam and Eve

This reading is from a translation of the first several books of the Old Testament by two writers – one anonymous, the other Ælfric, pupil of St Æthelwold, monk of Cerne, and later Abbot of Eynsham. The present extract is from Ælfric's section of the work. For a facsimile of the magnificently illustrated manuscript, see Dodwell and Clemoes [30], and for a complete text see Crawford [27].

If your class is using the *Guide to Old English*, compare the text in that book (printed from a different manuscript) with this one. Can you spot the substantive differences?

[1] Ēac swylċe[1] sēo nǣddre wæs ġēapre ðonne ealle ðā ōðre nȳtenu ðe God ġeworhte ofer eorðan. And sēo nǣddre cwæð tō ðām wīfe: 'Hwī forbēad God ēow ðæt ġē ne ǣton of ǣlcum trēowe binnan Paradīsum?'

[2] Þæt wīf andwyrde: 'Of ðǣra trēowa wæstme ðe synd on Paradīsum wē etað:

[3] and of ðæs trēowes wæstme þe is onmiddan neorxnawange, God bebēad ūs ðæt wē ne ǣton, ne wē ðæt trēow ne hrepodon, ðī lǣs ðe wē swelton.'[2]

[4] Ðā cwæð sēo nǣdre eft tō ðām wīfe: 'Ne bēo[3] ġē nāteshwōn dēade, ðēah ðe ġē of ðām trēowe eton.

---

[1] *Ēac swylċe*: likewise, moreover.
[2] A subjunctive. In this late text the plural subjunctive ending is *-on* rather than *-en* (see §7.2.3).
[3] *Ne bēo*: will not be. Before *wē* or *ġē* a plural verb sometimes ends in *-e* (see §7.2.2). Here the *-e* has disappeared because the root syllable ends in a vowel.

[5] Ac God wāt sōðlīċe ðæt ēowre ēagan bēoð ġeopenode on swā hwylċum dæġe swā⁴ ġē etað of ðām trēowe; and ġē bēoð ðonne englum ġelīċe, witende æġðer ġe gōd ġe yfel.'

[6] Ðā ġeseah ðæt wīf ðæt ðæt trēow wæs gōd tō etenne, be ðām ðe hyre ðūhte, and wlitiġ on ēagum and lustbǣre on ġesyhðe; and ġenam ðā of ðæs trēowes wæstme and ġeæt, and sealde hyre were: hē æt ðā.

[7] And heora bēġra ēagan wurdon ġeopenode: hī oncnēowon ðā ðæt hī nacode wǣron, and sȳwodon him fīclēaf and worhton him wǣdbrēċ.

[8] Eft ðā ðā God cōm and hī ġehȳrdon his stemne ðǣr hē ēode on neorxnawange ofer midne dæġ, ðā behȳdde Adam hine, and his wīf ēac swā dyde, fram Godes ġesihðe onmiddan ðām trēowe neorxnawonges.

[9] God clypode ðā Adam, and cwæð: 'Adam, hwǣr eart ðū?'

[10] Hē cwæð: 'Ðīne stemne iċ ġehīre, lēof, on neorxnawange, and iċ ondrǣde mē, for ðām ðe iċ eom nacod, and iċ behȳde mē.'

[11] God cwæð: 'Hwā sǣde ðē ðæt ðū nacod wǣre, ġyf ðū ne ǣte of ðām trēowe ðe iċ ðē bebēad ðæt ðū ne ǣte?'

[12] Adam cwæð: 'Ðæt wīf ðe ðū mē forġēafe tō ġefēran sealde mē of ðām trēowe, and iċ ætt.'

[13] God cwæð tō ðām wīfe: 'Hwī dydestū⁵ ðæt?' Hēo cwæð: 'Sēo nǣdre bepǣhte mē and iċ ætt.'

[14] God cwæð tō ðǣre nǣddran: 'For ðan ðe ðū ðis dydest, ðū bist⁶ āwyrġed betweox eallum nȳtenum and wildēorum. Ðū gǣst on ðīnum brēoste and ytst ðā eorðan eallum dagum ðīnes līfes.⁷

[15] Iċ sette fēondrǣdenne betwux ðē and ðām wīfe and ðīnum ofspringe and hire ofspringe; hēo tōbrȳtt ðīn hēafod and ðū syrwst onġēan hire hō.'

[16] Tō ðām wīfe cwæð God ēac swylċe: 'Iċ ġemǣnifylde ðīne yrmða and ðīne ġeēacnunga; on sārnysse ðū ācenst ċild, and ðū bist under weres anwealde and hē ġewylt ðē.'

[17] Tō Adame hē cwæð: 'For ðān ðe ðū ġehȳrdest ðīnes wīfes stemne and ðū ǣte of ðǣm trēowe ðe iċ ðē bebēad ðæt ðū ne ǣte, is sēo eorðe āwyrġed on ðīnum weorce. On ġeswyncum ðū ytst of ðǣre eorðan eallum dagum ðīnes līfes.

[18] Ðornas and brēmelas hēo āsprȳt ðē, and ðū ytst ðǣre eorðan wyrta.

[19] On swāte ðīnes andwlitan⁸ ðū brȳċst ðīnes hlāfes oð ðæt ðū ġewende tō eorðan, of ðǣre ðe ðū ġenumen wǣre, for ðān ðe ðū eart dūst and tō dūste ġewyrst.'

---

⁴ *swā hwylċum dæġe swā*: whatever day. For this construction, see §5.4.
⁵ A contraction of *dydest þū*.
⁶ *ðū bist*: you will be. All of the following present tense verbs should be translated as futures.
⁷ *ðīnes līfes*: of your life.
⁸ *ðīnes andwlitan*: of your face.

2   The Life of St Æthelthryth

St Æthelthryth, the seventh-century Abbess of Ely, was one of Anglo-Saxon England's most widely venerated saints. This life of her by Ælfric (see headnote to reading 1) was written in the last years of the tenth century. Ælfric's collection of saints' lives is edited in Skeat [86].

VIIII KALENDAS IULII. NATALE SANCTE ÆÐELDRYÐE VIRGINIS.
[1] Wē wyllað nū āwrītan, þēah ðe hit wundorlić sȳ, be ðǣre hālgan sancte Æðeldrȳðe[1] þām Engliscan mǣdene, þe wæs mid twām werum and swā ðēah wunode mǣden, swā swā þā wundra ġeswuteliað þe hēo wyrċð ġelōme. [2] Anna[2] hātte hyre fæder, Ēastengla cynincg, swȳðe Cristen man, swā swā hē cȳdde mid weorcum, and eall his tēam wearð ġewurðod þurh God. [3] Æðeldrȳð wearð þā forġifen ānum ealdormenn[3] tō wīfe. [4] Ac hit nolde se ælmihtiga God þæt hire mæġðhād wurde mid hǣmede ādylegod, ac hēold hī on clǣnnysse, for ðan þe hē is ælmihtiġ God and mæġ dōn eall þæt hē wile, and on manegum wīsum his mihte ġeswutelað.

[5] Se ealdorman ġewāt þā ðā hit wolde God, and hēo wearð forġifen Ecfride cynincge,[4] and twelf ġēar wunode unġewemmed mǣden on þæs cynincges synscype, swā swā swutele wundra hyre mǣrða cȳðaþ and hire mæġðhād ġelōme. [6] Hēo lufode þone Hǣlend þe hī hēold unwemme, and Godes ðēowas wurðode. [7] Ān þǣra wæs Wilfrid bisceop,[5] þe hēo swȳðost lufode, and hē sǣde Bēdan þæt se cyning Ecfrid him oft behēte myċel on lande and on fēo, ġif hē lǣran mihte Æðeldrȳðe his ġebeddan þæt hēo bruce his synscipes. [8] Nū cwæð se hālga Beda, þe þās bōc ġesette, þæt se ælmihtiga

---

[1]   Æthelthryth (d. 679), founder of the monastery at Ely, was daughter of King Anna of the East Angles. She is one of the royal and noble women who played an important role in the development of the Church in Anglo-Saxon England and whose numbers include Æthelthryth's sister Seaxburh, Eafe and Mildrith of Minster-in-Thanet, Hild of Whitby, and others. Bede's account of Æthelthryth in his *Ecclesiastical History*, Bk. IV ch. 19, is the source of the present life of her.
[2]   Anna was king of the East Angles from *c*.636 to *c*.654; he was killed in battle with Penda, the pagan king of Mercia.
[3]   According to Bede, one Tondberct of the South Gyrwas. According to the Life of St Æthelthryth in the *Liber Eliensis*, Tondberct gave her Ely as part of her 'dowry' (i.e. bride-price or morning-gift).
[4]   Ecgfrith, king of the Northumbrians (670–85), who plays a major role in Bede's *Ecclesiastical History*. Ecgfrith later married one Eormenburg, who after his death took orders and became an abbess herself.
[5]   Wilfrid (634–709), the willful and controversial Bishop of York (664–709), whose conflicts with King Ecgfrith of Northumbria are told both by Bede and by Wilfrid's biographer, Eddius Stephanus (see Colgrave [29]).

God mihte ēaðe ġedōn nū on ūrum dagum þæt Æðeldrȳð þurhwunode unġewemmed mǣden, þēah ðe hēo wer hæfde, swā swā on ealdum dagum hwīlon ǣr ġetīmode þurh þone ylcan God þe ǣfre þurhwunað mid his ġecorenum hālgum, swā swā hē sylf behēt.

[9] Æðeldrȳð wolde ðā ealle woruldþincg forlǣtan, and bæd ġeorne þone cynincg þæt hēo Criste mōste þēowian on mynsterliċre drohtnunge, swā hire mōd hire tō spēon. [10] Þā lȳfde hire se cynincg, þēah þe hit embe lang wǣre, þæs þe hēo ġewilnode, and Wilfrid bisceop þā hī ġehādode tō myneċene, and hēo syððan on mynstre wunode sume twelf mōnað swā, and hēo syððan wearð ġehādod eft tō abudissan on Eliġmynstre, ofer manega myneċena, and hēo hī mōdorlīċe hēold mid gōdum ġebysnungum tō þām gāstlican līfe.

[11] Be hire is āwryten þæt hēo wel drohtnode tō ānum mǣle fæstende, būtan hit frēolsdæġ wǣre, and hēo syndriġe ġebedu swȳðe lufode[6] and wyllen weorode, and wolde seldhwænne hire līċ baðian būtan tō hēahtīdum, and ðonne hēo wolde ǣrest ealle ðā baðian þe on ðām mynstre wǣron, and wolde him ðēnian mid hire þīnenum, and þonne hī sylfe baðian.

[12] Þā on þām eahteoðan ġēare siððan hēo abbudisse wæs, hēo wearð ġeuntrumod, swā swā hēo ǣr wītegode, swā þæt ān ġeswel wēox on hire swūran myċel under þām ċynnbāne, and hēo swīðe þancode Gode þæt hēo on þām swūran sum ġeswinc þolode. [13] Hēo cwæð: 'iċ wāt ġeare þæt iċ wel wyrðe eom þæt mīn swūra bēo ġeswenċt mid swylċere untrumnysse, for ðan þe iċ on iugoðe frætwode mīnne swūran mid mæniġfealdum swūrbēagum, and mē is nū ġeþūht þæt Godes ārfæstnyss þone gylt āclǣnsiġe, þonne mē nū þis ġeswel scȳnð for golde, and þes hāta bryne for hēalicum ġymstānum.'

[14] Þā wæs þǣr sum lǣċe on ðām ġelēaffullum hēape, Cynefryð ġehāten, and hī cwǣdon þā sume þæt se lǣċe sceolde āscēotan þæt ġeswell. [15] Þā dyde hē sōna swā, and þǣr sāh ūt wyrms. [16] Wearð him þā ġeðūht swilċe hēo ġewurpan mihte, ac hēo ġewāt of worulde mid wuldre tō Gode on þām ðriddan dæġe syððan se dolh wæs ġeopenod, and wearð bebyrġed swā swā hēo bæd sylf and hēt, betwux hire ġeswustrum, on trēowenre ċyste.

[17] Þā wearð hire swustor Sexburh[7] ġehādod tō abbudissan æfter hire ġeendunge, sēo ðe ǣr wæs cwēn on Cantwarebyriġ. [18] Þā wolde sēo Sexburh æfter syxtȳne ġēarum dōn hire swustor bān of ðǣre byrġene ūp and beran intō þǣre ċyrċan; and sende þā ġebrōðra tō sēċenne sumne stān tō swilċere nēode, for ðan þe on þām fenlande synd fēawa weorcstāna. [19] Hī rēowan þā tō Grantanċeastre, and God hī sōna ġehradode, swā þæt hī þǣr ġemētton āne

---

[6]   That is, she prayed by herself as well as communally at the canonical hours. According to Bede, she prayed each day from the hour of matins (between midnight and 3 a.m.) until dawn unless prevented by illness.

[7]   Seaxburg, Anna's eldest daughter, was married to Erconberht, king of Kent (640–64) before joining her sister at Ely. She was the mother of St Ercongota, celebrated by Bede in his *Ecclesiastical History*, Bk. III ch. 8.

mǣre þrūh wið þone weall standende, ġeworht of marmstāne eall hwītes blēos bufan þǣre eorðan, and þæt hlyd ðǣrtō ġelimplīċe ġefēġed, ēac of hwītum marmstāne, swā swā hit macode God.

[20] Þā nāman ðā ġebrōðra blȳðelīċe þā ðrūh and ġebrōhton tō mynstre, myċċlum ðanciġende Gode; and Sexburh sēo abbudisse hēt slēan ān ġeteld bufan ðā byrġene, wolde þā bān gaderian. [21] Hī sungon ðā ealle sealmas and līċsang þā hwīle þe man ðā byrġene bufan ġeopenode. [22] Þā læġ hēo on ðǣre ċyste swilċe hēo lǣġe on slǣpe, hāl eallum limum, and se lǣċe wæs ðǣr ðe þæt ġeswell ġeopenode, and hī sċēawode ġeorne. [23] Þā wæs sēo wund ġehǣled þe se lǣċe worhte ǣr; ēac swilċe þā ġewǣda þe hēo bewunden wæs mid wǣron swā ansunde swylċe hī eall nīwe wǣron.[8]

[24] Sexburh þā hyre swuster swīðe þæs fæġnode, and hī þwōgon ðā syððan þone sāwllēasan līċhaman, and mid nīwum ġewǣdum bewundon ārwurðlīċe, and bǣron into ðǣre ċyrċan, blyssiġende mid sangum, and lēdon hī on ðǣre þrȳh, þǣr ðǣr hēo līð oð þis on myċelre ārwurðnysse, mannum tō wundrunge. [25] Wæs ēac wundorliċ þæt sēo ðrūh wæs ġeworht þurh Godes foresċēawunge hire swā ġemǣte, swylċe hēo hyre sylfre swā ġesċeapen wǣre, and æt hire hēafde wæs āhēawen se stān ġemǣte þām hēafde þæs hālgan mǣdenes.

[26] Hit is swutol þæt hēo wæs unġewemmed mǣden, þonne hire līċhama ne mihte formolsnian on eorðan, and Godes miht is ġeswutelod sōðlīċe þurh hī, þæt hē mæġ ārǣran ðā formolsnodan līċhaman, se ðe hire līċ hēold hāl on ðǣre byrġene ġīt oð þisne dæġ; sȳ him ðæs ā wuldor. [27] Þǣr wǣron ġehǣlede þurh ðā hālgan fēmnan fela ādliġe menn, swā swā wē ġefyrn ġehȳrdon; and ēac ðā þe hrepodon þæs rēafes ǣniġne dǣl þe hēo mid bewunden wæs wurdon sōna hāle; and manegum ēac fremode sēo ċyst miċċlum þe hēo ǣrest on læġ, swā swā se lārēow Bēda on ðǣre bēċ sǣde þe hē ġesette be ðysum.

[28] Oft woruldmenn ēac hēoldon, swā swā ūs bēċ secgað, heora clǣnnysse on synscipe for Cristes lufe, swā swā wē mihton reċċan ġif ġē rohton hit tō ġehȳrenne. [29] Wē secgað swā ðēah be sumum ðeġne, se wæs þrȳttiġ ġēara mid his wīfe on clǣnnysse. [30] Þrȳ suna hē ġestrȳnde, and hī siððan būta ðrīttiġ ġēara wǣron wuniġende būtan hǣmede and fela ælmyssan worhton oð þæt se wer fērde tō munuclīċere drohtnunge; and Drihtnes englas cōmon eft on his forðsīðe and feredon his sāwle mid sange tō heofonum, swā swā ūs secgað bēċ. [31] Manega bysna synd on bōcum be swylċum, hū oft weras and wīf wundorlīċe drohtnodon and on clǣnnysse wunodon tō wuldre þām Hǣlende þe þā clǣnnysse āstealde, Crist ūre Hǣlend, þām is ā wurðmynt and wuldor on ēċnysse. Amen.

---

[8]   It is a frequent motif in hagiographical literature for the saint's body to be discovered undecayed after years, or even decades. It was included in the lives to provide evidence of the saint's sanctity.

3   Cynewulf and Cyneheard

This selection, the entry for the year 755 (an error for 757) in the *Anglo-Saxon Chronicle*, offers a detailed account of the deaths of two feuding members of the West-Saxon royal family. The wealth of detail here is remarkable for such an early *Chronicle* entry (the final paragraph, on the Mercian succession, is much more typical of the eighth-century entries). Presumably the chronicler thought this exemplary tale of loyalty in extreme circumstances compelling enough to justify a radical departure from his usual style.

For a complete text of the earliest manuscript of the *Chronicle*, see Bately [7].

Anno .dcc.lv. [1] Hēr Cynewulf benam Siġebryht his rīċes ond Westseaxna wiotan[1] for unryhtum dǣdum, būton Hamtūnscīre, ond hē hæfde þā oþ hē ofslōg þone aldormon þe him lenġest wunode. [2] Ond hiene þā Cynewulf on Andred[2] ādrǣfde, ond hē þǣr wunade oþ þæt hiene ān swān ofstang æt Pryfetesflōdan; ond hē wræc þone aldormon Cumbran.[3] [3] Ond se Cynewulf oft miċlum ġefeohtum feaht uuiþ Bretwālum, ond ymb .xxxi. wintra þæs þe hē rīċe hæfde hē wolde ādrǣfan ānne æþeling se was Cyneheard hāten, ond se Cyneheard wæs þæs Siġebryhtes brōþur. [4] Ond þā ġeascode hē[4] þone cyning lȳtle werode on wīfcȳþþe on Merantūne,[5] ond hine þǣr berād ond þone būr[6] ūtan beēode ǣr hine þā men onfunden þe mid þām kyninge wǣrun. [5] Ond þā onġeat se cyning þæt, ond hē on þā duru ēode ond þā unhēanlīċe hine werede oþ hē on þone æþeling lōcude, ond þā ūt rǣsde on hine[7] ond hine miċlum ġewundode. [6] Ond hīe[8] alle on þone cyning wǣrun feohtende oþ þæt hīe hine ofslæġenne hæfdon. [7] Ond þā on þæs wīfes ġebǣrum onfundon þæs cyninges þeġnas þā unstilnesse, ond þā þider urnon swā hwelċ

---

[1]   *Ond Westseaxna wiotan* is the remainder of a compound subject. See also sentence [10].

[2]   Also called *Andredesweald*, this is the area of Sussex now known as The Weald. According to the *Anglo-Saxon Chronicle* for 893, Andred was a great forest, 120 miles long and 30 miles broad.

[3]   Cumbra is the name of the loyal *ealdorman* whom Sigebryht had slain.

[4]   I.e. Cyneheard.

[5]   Suggested identifications of this place include Merton, Surrey, and Marten, Wiltshire. But this *Merantūn* has never been identified with certainty.

[6]   A *būr* is usually an interior chamber, especially a bed-chamber. It could be a cottage, however, and that seems to be the sense here, as it is difficult to imagine how Cyneheard's men could surround an interior chamber. The action suggests that Cynewulf is in a cottage with his mistress while his men are together in a hall some distance away.

[7]   The doorway was easy for Cynewulf to defend because none of his attackers could get behind him. His rushing out at Cyneheard, while understandable, was a strategic error.

[8]   I.e. Cyneheard and his men.

swā þonne ġearo wearþ ond radost. [8] Ond hiera se æþeling ġehwelċum feoh ond feorh ġebēad, ond hiera næniġ hit ġeþicgean nolde, ac hīe simle feohtende wǣran oþ hīe[9] alle lǣgon būtan ānum Bryttiscum ġīsle,[10] ond se swīþe ġewundad wæs.

[9] Ðā on morgenne ġehīerdun þæt þæs cyninges þeġnas þe him beæftan wǣrun þæt se cyning ofslæġen wæs. [10] Þā ridon hīe þider ond his aldormon Ōsriċ ond Wīferþ his þeġn ond þā men þe hē beæftan him lǣfde ǣr, ond þone æþeling on þǣre byriġ mētton þǣr se cyning ofslæġen læġ (ond þā gatu him tō belocen hæfdon),[11] ond þā þǣrtō ēodon.[12] [11] Ond þā ġebēad hē[13] him hiera āgenne dōm fēos ond londes ġif hīe him þæs rīċes ūþon, ond him cȳþdon þæt hiera mǣgas him mid wǣron þā þe him from noldon.[14] [12] Ond þā cuǣdon hīe þæt him nǣniġ mǣġ lēofra nǣre þonne hiera hlāford, ond hīe nǣfre his banan folgian noldon. [13] Ond þā budon hīe[15] hiera mǣgum þæt hīe ġesunde from ēodon, ond hīe[16] cuǣdon þæt tæt[17] ilce hiera ġefērum ġeboden wǣre þe ǣr mid þām cyninge wǣrun. [14] Þā cuǣdon hīe þæt hīe hīe þæs ne onmunden[18] 'þon mā þe ēowre ġefēran þe mid þām cyninge ofslæġene wǣrun.'[19] [15] Ond hīe þā ymb þā gatu feohtende wǣron oþ þæt hīe þǣrinne fulgon ond þone æþeling ofslōgon ond þā men þe him mid wǣrun, alle būtan ānum, se wæs þæs aldormonnes godsunu,[20] ond hē his feorh ġenerede, ond þēah hē wæs oft ġewundad. [16] Ond se Cynewulf rīcsode .xxxi. wintra, ond his līċ līþ æt Wintanċeastre ond þæs æþelinges æt Ascanmynster, ond hiera ryhtfæderencyn gǣþ tō Ċerdiċe.[21]

---

[9] I.e. Cynewulf's men.

[10] A *ġīsl* (a hostage, exchanged between warring groups as a pledge of peace) also aids his captors in *The Battle of Maldon*, ll. 265–72.

[11] The unexpressed subject of this parenthetical clause is 'Cyneheard and his men'.

[12] That is, Cynewulf's men proceeded to the *byriġ* at *Merantūn*.

[13] I.e. Cyneheard.

[14] *him from noldon*: did not wish to leave him.

[15] I.e. Cynewulf's men, who are offering their kinsmen the opportunity to leave.

[16] I.e. Cyneheard's men, who will refuse the offer to allow them to leave unharmed. Presumably it is clear to all present that Cynewulf's men now have the upper hand.

[17] I.e. *þæt*. The initial *þ* has become assimilated to the *t* at the end of the preceding word. This presumably happened more often in speech than is represented in writing.

[18] *hīe þæs ne onmunden*: did not consider themselves worthy of that (offer).

[19] The sudden shift into direct discourse seems awkward to the modern reader, and presumably seemed so to some medieval scribes as well: three of the five manuscripts of this entry in the *Anglo-Saxon Chronicle* read *heora* for *ēowre*, converting the passage to indirect discourse.

[20] The sole survivor among Cyneheard's men was saved by his godfather, the *ealdorman* Osric. The chronicler is careful to establish that special circumstances attended the survival of Osric's godson and the British hostage in the earlier battle: neither could be accused of cowardice.

[21] Cerdic is the legendary founder of the kingdom of Wessex. His arrival (with his son Cynric) is recorded in the *Anglo-Saxon Chronicle* for 495.

[17] Ond þȳ ilcan ġēare mon ofslōg Æþelbald Mierċna cyning[22] on Seccandūne, ond his līċ līþ on Hrēopadūne; ond Beornrǣd fēng tō rīċe ond lȳtle hwīle hēold ond unġefēalīċe. [18] Ond þȳ ilcan ġēare Offa[23] fēng tō rīċe ond hēold .xxxviiii. wintra, ond his sunu Ecgferþ[24] hēold .xli. daga ond .c. daga. [19] Se Offa wæs Þincgferþing,[25] Þincgferþ Ēanwulfing, Ēanwulf Ōsmōding, Ōsmōd Ēawing, Ēawa Pybing, Pybba Crēoding, Crēoda Cynewalding, Cynewald Cnebing, Cnebba Iceling, Icel Ēomǣring, Ēomǣr Angelþowing, Angelþēow Offing, Offa Wǣrmunding, Wǣrmund Wyhtlǣġing, Wihtlǣġ Wōdening.[26]

4 The Martyrdom of Ælfheah

This extract from the *Anglo-Saxon Chronicle* recounts events of the years 1011 and 1012, when a Viking war-band besieged and entered Canterbury, sacked the city and captured many of its inhabitants, including monks and nuns. Among their captives was Ælfheah, Archbishop of Canterbury, whom they seem to have expected the Church to ransom. When Ælfheah refused to allow ransom to be paid for him (perhaps because the Church's finances were straitened at the time), the Vikings brutally killed him. The present chronicler (probably a monk of St Augustine's, Canterbury) saw the attack on Canterbury as a blow aimed at the very heart of the kingdom. The English responded to the murder by proclaiming the archbishop a martyr and saint; his day (19 April) was widely observed during the eleventh century.

For an edition of the manuscript from which this reading is taken, see O'Keeffe [75].

---

[22] Æthelbald was king of Mercia for a remarkably long time, 716–57 (this entry incorrectly dates his death to 755).

[23] Offa was the greatest of the Mercian kings, ruling not only his own kingdom, but also Sussex, Kent and East Anglia. He was responsible for the construction of Offa's dike, an earthen fortification that runs almost 150 miles along the Welsh border.

[24] The entry is looking far ahead: Ecgferþ didn't get his chance to rule until 794, according to the *Anglo-Saxon Chronicle* (actually 796).

[25] The words *Se Offa wæs Þincgferþing* begin a genealogy of the kind often found in the *Anglo-Saxon Chronicle*. The suffix *-ing* is a patronymic: thus this phrase should be translated 'this Offa was the son of Þincgferþ'.

[26] Woden was one of the chief gods in the pre-Christian pantheon of Anglo-Saxon England and also, according to legend, the founder of several Anglo-Saxon royal lines, including those of Kent, Wessex, Northumbria and Mercia. His name appeared in genealogies long after the Anglo-Saxons had embraced Christianity.

Mille .xi. [1] Hēr on þissum ġēare sende se cyning[1] and his witan tō ðām here[2] and ġyrndon friðes, and him gafol and metsunge behēton wið þām ðe hī hiora herġunge ġeswicon. [2] Hī hæfdon þā ofergān (.i.) Ēastengle and (.ii.) Ēastsexe and (.iii.) Middelsexe and (.iiii.) Oxenafordscīre and (.v.) Grantabricscīre and (.vi.) Heortfordscīre and (.vii.) Buccingahāmscīre and (.viii.) Bedefordscīre and (.ix.) healfe Huntadūnscīre and miċel (.x.) on Hamtūnscīre, and be sūþan Temese ealle Kentingas and Sūðsexe and Hæstingas and Sūðrīġe and Bearrocscīre and Hamtūnscīre and miċel on Wiltūnscīre. [3] Ealle þas unġesǣlða ūs ġelumpon þuruh unrǣdas, þæt man nolde him a tīman gafol bēodon oþþe wið ġefeohtan. [4] Ac þonne hī mǣst tō yfele[3] ġedōn hæfdon, þonne nam mon frið and grið wið hī, and naþelǣs, for eallum þissum griðe and gafole, hī fērdon ǣghweder flocmǣlum and heregodon ūre earme folc and hī rȳpton and slōgon. [5] And þā on ðissum ġēare betweox Natiuitas Sancte Marie[4] and Sancte Michaeles mæssan[5] hī ymbsǣton Cantwareburuh, and hī intō cōmon þuruh syruwrenċas, for ðan Ælmǣr[6] hī beċyrde, þe se arcebisceop Ælfēah[7] ǣr ġenerede æt his līfe.[8] [6] And hī þǣr ðā ġenāman þone arcebisceop Ælfēah and Ælfweard cynges ġerēfan and Lēofrūne abbatissan and Godwine bisceop;[9] and Ælfmǣr abbud[10] hī lēton āweġ. [7] And hī ðǣr ġenāmon inne ealle þā ġehādodan men and weras and wīf, þæt wæs unāsecgendliċ ænigum men hū miċel þæs folces wæs,[11] and on þǣre byriġ syþþan wǣron

---

[1]   Æthelred, whose reign began in 978 after the murder of his half-brother Edward, would be driven from the country in 1013 by the Viking army led by Swein Forkbeard. Æthelred returned to England after Swein's death the following year and died in 1015; he was succeeded by Swein's son Cnut. Æthelred is often called 'the Unready' ('Unready' rendering Old English *unrǣd* 'folly') on account of his supposed incompetence as king. His bad reputation may not be fully deserved, but his reign was marked by increasingly severe Viking incursions and infighting among his nobles. His reign was also one of the most productive periods of Old English literature, for Ælfric and Wulfstan were his contemporaries, and a great many vernacular manuscripts (including, probably, the one that contains *Beowulf*) were produced during his time.

[2]   In the *Anglo-Saxon Chronicle* the word *here* is usually used of a Viking army. This one was under the command of Thorkell the Tall, who is reputed to have tried to save Ælfheah's life and was among those who joined Æthelred in 1012.

[3]   *mǣst tō yfele*: the greatest harm.

[4]   The feast of the birth of St Mary (8 Sept.).

[5]   Michaelmass (29 Sept.).

[6]   Not the abbot Ælfmǣr mentioned later (though the names are equivalent), but rather, according to another source, an archdeacon. Nothing more is known of him.

[7]   Ælfheah had been Bishop of Winchester before being appointed Archbishop of Canterbury in 1006. As far as we know, his short tenure as archbishop was distinguished only by the spectacular nature of its end.

[8]   *ġenerede æt his līfe*: saved his life.

[9]   Godwine was Bishop of Rochester.

[10]   Ælfmǣr was abbot of St Augustine's monastery in Canterbury. The identities of the other persons mentioned here are uncertain.

[11]   *hū miċel þæs folces wæs*: how much of the population it was.

swā lange swā hī woldon. [8] And ðā hī hæfdon þā buruh ealle āsmēade, wendon him þā tō scypan and lǣddon þone arcebisceop mid him. [9] Wæs ðā rǣpling, se ðe ǣr wæs hēafod Angelkynnes and Cristendōmes. [10] Þǣr man mihte ðā ġesēon yrmðe þǣr man oft ǣr ġeseah blisse on þǣre earman byriġ þanon cōm ǣrest Cristendōm and blis for Gode and for worulde.[12] [11] And hī hæfdon þone arcebisceop mid him swā lange oð þǣne tīman þe hī hine ġemartiredon.

Mille .xii. [12] Hēr on þissum ġēare cōm Ēadriċ ealdorman[13] and ealle þā yldestan witan, ġehādode and lǣwede, Angelcynnes tō Lundenbyriġ tōforan þām Ēastron. [13] Þā wæs Ēasterdæġ on þām datarum Idus Aprilis.[14] [14] And hī ðǣr þā swā lange wǣron oþ þæt gafol eal ġelǣst wæs ofer ðā Ēastron, þæt wæs ehta and fēowertiġ þūsend punda. [15] Ðā on þǣne Sæternesdæġ wearð þā se here swȳðe āstyred anġēan þone bisceop, for þām ðe hē nolde him nān feoh behātan, ac hē forbēad þæt man nān þing wið him syllan ne mōste. [16] Wǣron hī ēac swȳþe druncene, for ðām þǣr wæs brōht wīn sūðan. [17] Ġenāmon þā ðone bisceop, lǣddon hine tō hiora hūstinge on ðone Sunnanǣfen octabas Pasce,[15] þā wæs .xiii. kalendas Mai,[16] and hine þǣr ðā bysmorlīċe ācwylmdon, oftorfedon mid bānum and mid hrȳþera hēafdum. [18] And slōh hine ðā ān hiora mid ānre æxe ȳre[17] on þæt hēafod, þæt mid þām dynte hē nyþer āsāh, and his hāliġe blōd on þā eorðan fēol, and his hāligan sāwle tō Godes rīċe āsende.[18] [19] And mon þone līċhaman on merġen ferode tō Lundene, and þā bisceopas Ēadnōþ and Ælfūn[19] and sēo buruhwaru hine underfēngon mid ealre ārwurðnysse and hine bebyriġdon on Sancte Paules mynstre, and þǣr nū God sutelað þæs hālgan martires mihta. [20] Ðā þæt gafol ġelǣst wæs and friðāþas āsworene wǣron, þā tōfērde se here wīde swā hē ǣr ġegaderod wæs. [21] Ðā bugon tō þām cynge of ðām here fīf and fēowertiġ scypa, and him behēton þæt hī woldon þysne eard healdan, and hē hī fēdan sceolde and scrȳdan.

---

[12] *for Gode and for worulde*: both religious and secular.

[13] Eadric Streona, the powerful and treacherous *ealdorman* of Mercia, was now suspected of sympathy for the Danes and would in fact join Cnut in 1016. He was murdered in London in 1017 ('very justly', according to one chronicler).

[14] 13 April.

[15] The octave of Easter, i.e. a week after Easter.

[16] 19 April.

[17] Possibly 'the back of an axe'; but the meaning of *ȳre* is uncertain.

[18] The unexpressed subject of *āsende* is *hē* (i.e. Ælfheah).

[19] Eadnoth (d. 1016) was Bishop of Dorchester. Ælfun was Bishop of London; in 1013 Æthelræd sent him to Normandy with his sons Edward and Alfred a short time before he fled there himself.

5   *Sermo Lupi ad Anglos*

Wulfstan (d. 1023) was Bishop of London until 1002 and then Bishop of Worcester and Archbishop of York (the two titles had been held by the same person since 972 because York under the Viking kings was barely a functional see). He was an adviser to Æthelræd during the later years of his reign and wrote several of that king's law codes; he also wrote law codes for Cnut. Wulfstan was not primarily a writer of homilies; he wrote many fewer than his contemporary and correspondent Ælfric (see Bethurum [9]). The *Sermo Lupi ad Anglos*, however, reveals him as a writer of extraordinary power. As you read, notice the strong binary rhythms, the many rhymes and alliterations, and the chains of grammatically parallel words and phrases.

For editions of this homily, see Bethurum [9], pp. 255–75 (which presents three different versions), Whitelock [92] (especially valuable for its very full annotations), and Melissa J. Bernstein, ed., The Electronic *Sermo Lupi ad Anglos* (http://www.cif. rochester.edu/˜mjbernst/wulfstan/). In this text, *-an* is often written for *-um* and *-on*, and the *-o-* of class 2 weak verbs often appears as *-e-*.

Sermo Lupi ad Anglos, quando Dani maxime persecuti sunt eos, quod fuit anno millesimo .xiiii. ab incarnatione Domini nostri Iesu Cristi[1]
[1] Lēofan men, ġecnāwað þæt sōð is. [2] Ðēos worold is on ofste, and hit nēalǣċð þām ende, and þȳ hit is on worolde aa swā lenġ swā wyrse.[2] [3] And swā hit sceal nȳde for folces synnan ǣr antecristes tōcyme yfelian swȳþe, and hūru hit wyrð þænne eġesliċ and grimliċ wīde on worolde. [4] Understandað ēac ġeorne þæt dēofol þās þēode nū fela ġēara dwelode tō swȳþe, and þæt lȳtle ġetrēowþa wǣran mid mannum, þēah hȳ wel spǣcan, and unrihta tō fela rīcsode on lande. [5] And næs ā fela manna þe smēade ymbe þā bōte swā ġeorne swā man scolde, ac dæġhwāmlīċe man īhte yfel æfter ōðrum[3] and unriht rǣrde and unlaga maneġe ealles tō wīde ġynd ealle þās þēode. [6] And wē ēac for þām habbað fela byrsta and bysmara ġebiden, and ġif wē æniġe bōte ġebīdan scylan, þonne mōte wē þæs tō Gode earnian bet þonne wē ǣr þysan dydan, [7] for þām mid miċlan earnungan wē ġeearnedan þā yrmða þe ūs onsittað, and mid swȳþe miċelan earnungan wē þā bōte mōtan æt Gode ġerǣċan ġif hit sceal heonanforð gōdiende weorðan. [8] Lā hwæt, wē witan ful ġeorne þæt tō miċlan bryċe sceal miċel bōt nȳde, and tō miċlan bryne wæter

---

[1] 'The Sermon of *Lupus* to the English, when the Danes were persecuting them most, which was in the year 1014 from the incarnation of our Lord Jesus Christ.' Latin *Lupus* 'wolf' is Wulfstan's *nom de plume*. In 1013 Æthelræd had been driven from his throne by the Danish king Swein; after Swein's death in 1014 Æthelræd was restored to his throne, but Swein's son Cnut remained a threat.

[2] *swā lenġ swā wyrse*: worse and worse.

[3] *yfel æfter ōðrum*: one evil after another.

unlȳtel, ġif man þæt fȳr sceal tō āhte[4] ācwenċan. [9] And miċel is nȳdþearf manna ġehwilċum þæt hē Godes lage ġȳme heonanforð ġeorne and Godes ġerihta[5] mid rihte ġelæste. [10] On hæþenum þēodum ne dear man forhealdan lȳtel ne miċel þæs þe ġelagod is tō ġedwolgoda weorðunge, and wē forhealdað æġhwær Godes ġerihta ealles tō ġelōme. [11] And ne dear man ġewanian on hæþenum þēodum inne ne ūte æniġ þæra þinga þe ġedwolgodan brōht bið and tō lācum betæht bið, and wē habbað Godes hūs inne and ūte clæne berȳpte, and Godes þēowas syndan mæþe and munde ġewelhwær bedælde. [12] And ġedwolgoda þēnan ne dear man misbēodan on æniġe wīsan mid hæþenum lēodum, swā swā man Godes þēowum nū dēð tō wīde þær Cristene scoldan Godes lage healdan and Godes þēowas griðian.

[13] Ac sōð is þæt iċ secge: þearf is þære bōte, for þām Godes ġerihta wanedan tō lange innan þysse þēode on æġhwylċan ende,[6] and folclaga wyrsedan ealles tō swȳþe, and hāliġnessa syndan tō griðlēase wīde, and Godes hūs syndan tō clæne berȳpte ealdra ġerihta and innan bestrȳpte ælċra ġerisena. [14] And wydewan syndan fornȳdde on unriht[7] tō ċeorle, and tō mæneġe foryrmde and ġehȳnede swȳþe, and earme men syndan sāre beswicene and hrēowlīċe besyrwde and ūt of þysan earde wīde ġesealde, swȳþe unforworhte,[8] fremdum tō ġewealde, [15] and cradolċild ġeþēowede þurh wælhrēowe unlaga for lȳtelre þȳfþe[9] wīde ġynd þās þēode, and frēoriht fornumene and þrælriht[10] ġenyrwde and ælmæsriht ġewanode; and, hrædest is tō cweþenne,[11] Godes laga lāðe and lāra forsāwene. [16] And þæs[12] wē habbað ealle þurh Godes yrre bysmor ġelōme, ġecnāwe se ðe cunne; and se byrst wyrð ġemæne, þēh man swā ne wēne, eallre þysse þēode, būtan God beorge.

[17] For þām hit is on ūs eallum swutol and ġesēne þæt wē ær þysan oftor bræcan þonne wē bēttan, and þȳ is þysse þēode fela onsæġe. [18] Ne dohte hit nū lange inne ne ūte, ac wæs here and hunger, bryne and blōdgȳte on ġewelhwylċan ende oft and ġelōme. [19] And ūs stalu and cwalu, strīċ and steorfa, orfcwealm and uncoþu, hōl and hete and rȳpera rēaflāc derede swȳþe

---

[4] *tō āhte*: in any way.

[5] These *gerihta* are compulsory payments to the Church such as tithes and Peter's Pence.

[6] *on æġhwylċan ende*: in every part.

[7] *on unriht*: unjustly.

[8] Those who were guilty of certain crimes could be enslaved. Here Wulfstan condemns the selling of persons who have committed no crimes; he is thought also to have opposed all selling of persons to foreigners. For a useful commentary on Wulfstan's views on slavery as represented in the *Sermo Lupi*, see Pelteret [77].

[9] Under Anglo-Saxon law, any member of a family found to be complicit in a crime could be enslaved along with the actual perpetrator. Here Wulfstan condemns the enslavement of children so young they could not be complicit, and adds that the crime is sometimes petty theft. The laws of Cnut would forbid the penal enslavement of children under the age of twelve.

[10] Slaves had the right to earn money for themselves on various religious holidays during the year. Some slaves were able by this means to purchase their own freedom.

[11] *hrædest is tō cweþenne*: to put it briefly; in short.

[12] *þæs*: because of that.

þearle, and ūs ungylda[13] swȳþe ġedrehtan, and ūs unwedera foroft wēoldan unwæstma. [20] For þām on þysan earde wæs, swā hit þincan mæġ, nū fela ġeara unriht fela and tealte ġetrȳwða æġhwær mid mannum. [21] Ne bearh nū foroft ġesib ġesibban þe mā þe fremdan, ne fæder his bearne, ne hwīlum bearn his āgenum fæder, ne brōþor ōþrum; ne ūre æniġ his līf ne fadóde swā swā hē scólde, ne ġehādode regollīċe, ne læwede lahlīċe.[14] [22] Ac worhtan[15] lust ūs tō lage ealles tō ġelōme, and nāþor ne hēoldan ne lāre ne lage Godes ne manna swā swā wē scoldan. [23] Ne æniġ wið ōþerne ġetrȳwlīċe þōhte swā rihte swā hē scolde, ac mæst ælċ swicode and ōþrum derede wordes and dæde,[16] and hūru unrihtlīċe mæst ælċ ōþerne æftan hēaweþ sceandlican onscytan, dō māre ġif hē mæġe.[17]

[24] For þām hēr syn[18] on lande ungetrȳwþa miċle for Gode and for worolde,[19] and eac hēr syn on earde on mistliċe wīsan hlāfordswican maneġe. [25] And ealra mæst hlāfordswice se bið on worolde þæt man his hlāfordes sāule beswīce, and ful miċel hlāfordswice ēac bið on worolde þæt man his hlāford of līfe forræde oððon of lande lifiendne drīfe; and æġþer is geworden on þysan earde: [26] Ēadweard man forrædde and syððan ācwealde and æfter þām forbærnde.[20] [27] And godsibbas and godbearn tō fela man forspilde wīde ġynd þās þēode tōēacan ōðran ealles tō manegan þe man unscyldiġe forfōr ealles tō wīde. [28] And ealles tō maneġe hāliġe stōwa wīde forwurdan þurh þæt þe[21] man sume men ær þām ġelōgode, swā man nā ne scolde ġif man on Godes grīðe mæþe witan wolde.[22] [29] And Cristenes folces tō fela

[13] The reference is probably to the Danegeld, a tax levied so that tribute could be paid to marauding Vikings. Beginning in 991 this tax was collected as needed, and in the reign of Cnut it became a regular tax for the support of the king's army. It was discontinued in the reign of Edward the Confessor.

[14] It is a commonplace in Wulfstan's works that those in religious orders should obey the rule of their order and those in secular life should obey the law.

[15] The unexpressed subject of this verb is wē.

[16] wordes and dæde: in word and in deed.

[17] dō māre ġif hē mæġe: [and] would do more if he could.

[18] This text occasionally has syn for synd, the indicative present plural of the verb bēon.

[19] for Gode and for worolde: both religious and secular.

[20] In 978, King Edward, whom the chronicles described as ċild unweaxen on his accession in 975, was murdered by members of the household of his half-brother Æthelræd, who succeeded him as king. No other source claims that Edward's body was burned; rather, he was buried without ceremony and later translated to the nunnery at Shaftesbury, where miracles were reported at his tomb. He is known to history as Edward the Martyr. An earlier version of this sermon adds after the sentence on Edward's murder: and Æþelræd man dræfde ūt of his earde 'and Æthelræd was driven out of his land'. Perhaps the circumstances surrounding the later revisions made it impolitic to allude to Æthelræd's exile.

[21] þurh þæt þe: because.

[22] on Godes grīðe mæþe witan wolde: were willing to honour God's sanctuary. The circumspect wording of this passage tells us little about the unsuitable admissions that had caused harm to monasteries.

man ġesealde ūt of þysan earde nū ealle hwīle;[23] and eal þæt is Gode lāð, ġelȳfe
se þe wille. [30] And scandliċ is tō specenne þæt ġeworden is tō wīde, and
eġesliċ is tō witanne þæt oft dōð tō maneġe þe drēogað þā yrmþe, þæt scēotað
tōgædere and āne cwenan ġemænum ċēape[24] bicgað ġemæne, and wið þā āne
fȳlþe ādrēogað, ān æfter ānum[25] and ælċ æfter ōðrum, hundum ġelīccast þe
for fȳlþe ne scrīfað, [31] and syððan wið weorðe syllað of lande fēondum tō
ġewealde Godes ġesceafte and his āgenne ċēap þe hē dēore ġebōhte.

[32] Ēac wē witan ġeorne hwær sēo yrmð ġewearð þæt fæder ġesealde bearn
wið weorþe and bearn his mōdor, and brōþor sealde ōþerne fremdum tō
ġewealde;[26] and eal þæt syndan miċle and eġeslīċe dæda, understande se þe
wille. [33] And ġit hit is māre and ēac mæniġfealdre þæt dereð þysse þēode.
[34] Mæniġe synd forsworene and swȳþe forlogene, and wed synd tōbrocene
oft and ġelōme, and þæt is ġesȳne on þysse þēode þæt ūs Godes yrre heteliċe
onsit, ġecnāwe se þe cunne.

[35] And lā, hū mæġ māre scamu þurh Godes yrre mannum ġelimpan
þonne ūs dēð ġelōme for āgenum ġewyrhtum? [36] Ðēh þræla hwylċ hlāforde
ætlēape and of Cristendōme tō wīċinge weorþe, and hit æfter þām eft ġeweorþe
þæt wæpnġewrixl weorðe ġemæne þeġene and þræle,[27] ġif þræl þæne þeġen
fulliċe āfylle,[28] licge æġylde ealre his mæġðe.[29] [37] And ġif se þeġen þæne þræl
þe hē ær āhte fulliċe āfylle, ġylde þeġenġylde.[30] [38] Ful earhlīċe laga and
scandlīċe nȳdġyld þurh Godes yrre ūs syn ġemæne, understande se þe cunne,
and fela unġelimpa ġelimpð þysse þēode oft and ġelōme. [39] Ne dohte hit nū
lange inne ne ūte, ac wæs here and hete on ġewelhwilċan ende oft and ġelōme,
and Engle nū lange eal siġelēase and tō swȳþe ġeyriġde þurh Godes yrre, and
flotmen swā strange þurh Godes þafunge þæt oft on ġefeohte ān fēseð tȳne
and hwīlum læs, hwīlum mā, eal for ūrum synnum. [40] And oft tȳne oððe
twelfe, ælċ æfter ōþrum, scendað tō bysmore þæs þeġenes cwenan and hwīlum
his dohtor oððe nȳdmāgan þær hē on lōcað þe læt hine sylfne rancne and
rīċne and ġenōh gōdne ær þæt ġewurde. [41] And oft þræl þæne þeġen þe ær
wæs his hlāford cnyt swȳþe fæste and wyrċð him[31] tō þræle þurh Godes yrre.
[42] Wā lā þære yrmðe and wā lā þære woroldscame þe nū habbað Engle, eal
þurh Godes yrre. [43] Oft twēġen sæmen oððe þrȳ hwīlum drīfað þā drāfe
Cristenra manna fram sæ tō sæ ūt þurh þās þēode ġewelede tōgædre, ūs
eallum tō woroldscame, ġif wē on eornost æniġe cūþon āriht understandan.

[44] Ac ealne þæne bysmor þe wē oft þoliað wē ġyldað mid weorðscipe þām þe ūs scendað. [45] Wē him ġyldað singallīċe, and hȳ ūs hȳnað dæġhwāmlīċe. [46] Hȳ hergiað and hȳ bærnað, rȳpaþ and rēafiað and tō scipe lædað; and lā, hwæt is æniġ ōðer on eallum þām ġelimpum būtan Godes yrre ofer þās þēode, swutol and ġesæne?

[47] Nis ēac nān wundor þēah ūs mislimpe, for þām wē witan ful ġeorne þæt nū fela ġēara menn nā ne rōhtan foroft hwæt hȳ worhtan wordes oððe dæde,[32] ac wearð þes þēodscipe, swā hit þinċan mæġ, swȳþe forsyngod þurh mæniġfealde synna and þurh fela misdæda: [48] þurh morðdæda and þurh māndæda, þurh ġitsunga and þurh ġīfernessa, þurh stala and þurh strūdunga, þurh mannsylena and þurh hæþene unsida, þurh swicdōmas and þurh searacræftas, þurh lahbryċas and þurh æswicas, þurh mæġræsas and þurh manslyhtas, þurh hādbryċas and þurh æwbryċas, þurh sibleġeru and þurh mistliċe forliġru. [49] And ēac syndan wīde, swā wē ær cwædan, þurh āðbriċas and þurh wedbryċas and þurh mistliċe lēasunga forloren and forlogen mā þonne scolde, and frēolsbriċas and fæstenbryċas wīde ġeworhte oft and ġelōme. [50] And ēac hēr syn on earde apostatan ābroþene and ċyriċhatan hetole and lēodhatan grimme ealles tō maneġe, and oferhogan wīde godcundra rihtlaga and Cristenra þēawa, and hocorwyrde dysiġe[33] æġhwær on þēode – oftost on þā þing þe Godes bodan bēodaþ and swȳþost on þā þing þe æfre tō Godes lage ġebyriað mid rihte. [51] And þȳ is nū ġeworden wīde and sīde tō ful yfelan ġewunan, þæt menn swȳþor scamað nū for[34] gōddædan þonne for misdædan, for þām tō oft man mid hocere gōddæda hyrweð and godfyrhte lehtreð ealles tō swȳþe; [52] and swȳþost man tæleð and mid olle ġegrēteð ealles tō ġelōme þā þe riht lufiað and Godes eġe habbað be æniġum dæle.[35] [53] And þurh þæt þe[36] man swā dēð þæt man eal hyrweð þæt man scolde herian and tō forð lāðet þæt man scolde lufian, þurh þæt man ġebringeð ealles tō maneġe on yfelan ġeþance and on undæde, swā þæt hȳ ne scamað nā þēh hȳ syngian swȳðe and wið God sylfne forwyrċan hȳ mid ealle,[37] [54] ac for īdelan onscytan hȳ scamað þæt hȳ bētan heora misdæda, swā swā bēċ[38] tæċan, ġelīċe þām dwæsan þe for heora prȳtan lēwe nellað beorgan[39] ær hȳ nā ne magan, þēh hȳ eal willan.[40]

[55] Hēr syndan þurh synlēawa, swā hit þinċan mæġ, sāre ġelēwede tō maneġe on earde. [56] Hēr syndan mannslagan and mæġslagan and mæsserbanan and

---

32 *wordes oððe dæde*: in word or deed.
33 *hocorwyrde dysiġe*: derisive foolish [people].
34 *menn swȳþor scamað nū for*: one is now more ashamed of.
35 *be ænigum dæle*: in any part; at all.
36 *þurh þæt þe*: because.
37 *mid ealle*: entirely.
38 More specifically, penitential manuals, which assigned penances for various sins.
39 *lēwe nellað beorgan*: will not guard against an injury.
40 People who are not ashamed of their sins but are ashamed of empty calumnies directed against them are, according to Wulfstan, like those foolish persons who will not protect themselves from injury until it is too late to do so even if they want to.

mynsterhatan; and hēr syndan mānsworan and morþorwyrhtan; and hēr syndan myltestran and bearnmyrðran and fūle forleġene hōringas maneġe; and hēr syndan wiċċan and wælcyrian; and hēr syndan rȳperas and rēaferas and woroldstrūderas and, hrædest is tō cweþenne, māna and misdǣda unġerīm ealra. [57] And þæs ūs ne scamað nā, ac þæs ūs scamað swȳþe þæt wē bōte āġinnan swā swā bēċ tǣċan, and þæt is ġesȳne on þysse earman forsyngodon þēode. [58] Ēalā, miċel magan maneġe ġȳt hērtōēacan ēaþe beþenċan[41] þæs þe ān man ne mehte on hrædinge[42] āsmēaġan, hū earmlīċe hit ġefaren is nū ealle hwīle wīde ġynd þās þēode. [59] And smēaġe hūru ġeorne ġehwā hine sylfne and þæs nā ne latiġe ealles tō lange. [60] Ac lā, on Godes naman wutan dōn swā ūs nēod is, beorgan ūs sylfum[43] swā wē ġeornost magan þe lǣs wē ætgædere ealle forweorðan.

[61] Ān þēodwita wæs on Brytta tīdum, Gildas hātte.[44] [62] Se āwrāt be heora misdǣdum hū hȳ mid heora synnum swā oferlīċe swȳþe God ġegrǣmedan þæt hē lēt æt nȳhstan Engla here heora eard ġewinnan and Brytta dugeþe fordōn mid ealle. [63] And þæt wæs ġeworden, þæs þe hē sǣde, þurh rīċra rēaflāc and þurh ġītsunge wōhgestrēona, ðurh lēode unlaga and þurh wōhdōmas, ðurh biscopa āsolcennesse and þurh lȳðre yrhðe Godes bydela þe sōþes ġeswugedan ealles tō ġelōme and clumedan mid ċeaflum þǣr hȳ scoldan clypian. [64] Þurh fūlne ēac folces gǣlsan and þurh oferfylla and mæniġfealde synna heora eard hȳ forworhtan and selfe hȳ forwurdan. [65] Ac utan dōn swā ūs þearf is, warnian ūs be swilċan; and sōþ is þæt iċ secge, wyrsan dǣda wē witan mid Englum þonne wē mid Bryttan āhwǣr ġehȳrdan. [66] And þȳ ūs is þearf miċel þæt wē ūs beþenċan and wið God sylfne þingian ġeorne. [67] And utan dōn swā ūs þearf is, ġebūgan tō rihte and be suman dǣle[45] unriht forlǣtan and bētan swȳþe ġeorne þæt wē ǣr brǣcan. [68] And utan God lufian and Godes lagum fylġean, and ġelǣstan swȳþe ġeorne þæt þæt wē behētan þā wē fulluht underfēngan, oððon þā þe æt fulluhte ūre forespecan wǣran. [69] And utan word and weorc rihtlīċe fadian and ūre inġeþanc clǣnsian ġeorne and āð and wed wǣrlīċe healdan and sume ġetrȳwða habban ūs betwēonan būtan uncræftan. [70] And utan ġelōme understandan þone miċlan dōm þe wē ealle tō sculon, and beorgan ūs ġeorne wið þone weallendan bryne hellewītes, and ġeearnian ūs þā mǣrða and þā myrhða þe God hæfð ġeġearwod þām þe his willan on worolde ġewyrċað. [71] God ūre helpe.[46] Amen.

---

[41] *miċel magan maneġe ġȳt hērtōēacan ēaþe beþenċan*: in addition, many could call to mind much . . . The *þæs þe* that begins the next clause is a partitive genitive with *miċel*; translate it 'that'.

[42] *on hrædinge*: briefly.

[43] *ūs sylfum*: ourselves.

[44] Gildas is the sixth-century author of *De Excidio Britanniae* 'On the Ruin of Britain', which, as Wulfstan reports, views the coming of the Angles, Saxons and Jutes to Britain as divine punishment for the sins of the Britons.

[45] *be suman dǣle*: to some degree.

[46] *God ūre helpe*: God help us. *Helpan* takes a genitive object.

6 The Story of Cædmon

The story of Cædmon, the illiterate cowherd who received the gift of song from God, is told in Book Four, Chapter 25 of Bede's *Ecclesiastical History of the English People*. It was translated into Old English, probably during the reign of King Alfred the Great, by an anonymous Mercian scholar.

For a complete edition of the Old English Bede, see Miller [67]. For an edition of *Cædmon's Hymn* in West Saxon and Northumbrian versions, see Krapp and Dobbie [60], vol. 6, pp. 105–6.

[1] In ðeosse abbudissan[1] mynstre wæs sum brōðor syndriġlīċe mid godcundre ġife ġemǣred ond ġeweorðad, for þon hē ġewunade ġerisenliċe lēoð wyrċan þā ðe tō ǣfestnisse ond tō ārfæstnisse belumpen, swā ðætte swā hwæt swā hē of godcundum stafum þurh bōceras ġeleornode, þæt hē æfter medmiċlum fæce in scopġereorde mid þā mǣstan swētnisse ond inbryrdnisse ġeglænġde ond in Engliscġereorde wel ġeworht forþbrōhte. [2] Ond for his lēoþsongum moniġra monna mōd oft tō worulde forhogdnisse ond tō ġeþēodnisse þæs heofonlican līfes[2] onbærnde wǣron. [3] Ond ēac swelċe[3] moniġe ōðre æfter him in Ongelþēode ongunnon ǣfeste lēoð wyrċan; ac nǣniġ hwæðre him þæt ġelīċe dōn meahte, for þon hē nales from monnum ne þurh mon ġelǣred wæs, þæt hē þone lēoðcræft leornade, ac hē wæs godcundlīċe ġefultumed ond þurh Godes ġife þone songcræft onfēng. [4] Ond hē for ðon nǣfre nōht lēasunge ne īdles lēoþes wyrċan meahte, ac efne þā ān þā ðe tō ǣfestnisse belumpon, ond his þā ǣfestan tungan ġedeofanade singan.

[5] Wæs hē se mon in weoruldhāde ġeseted oð þā tīde þe hē wæs ġelȳfdre ylde,[4] ond nǣfre nǣniġ lēoð ġeleornade. [6] Ond hē for þon oft in ġebēorscipe, þonne þǣr wæs blisse intinga ġedēmed,[5] þæt hēo ealle sceoldon þurh endebyrdnesse[6] be hearpan singan, þonne hē ġeseah þā hearpan him nēalēċan, þonne ārās hē for forscome[7] from þǣm symble ond hām ēode tō his hūse. [7] Þā hē

---

[1] Hild (d. 680), daughter of Hereric, a nephew of Edwin, the first Christian king of Northumbria, and his wife Breguswith. She was baptized with Edwin in 627 and entered the religious life in 647, very likely after being widowed. In 657 she became abbess of the double monastery of Whitby, where she hosted the famous Synod of Whitby, at which the English Church decided to follow Roman practice in calculating the date of Easter.

[2] *ġeþēodnisse þæs heofonlican līfes*: membership in the heavenly life.

[3] *ēac swelċe*: likewise; moreover.

[4] *ġelȳfdre ylde*: of an advanced age.

[5] *blisse intinga ġedēmed*: judged to be cause for merriment.

[6] *þurh endebyrdnesse*: in order.

[7] It is tempting to emend *forscome* to *scome*, as the word *forscome* is not attested elsewhere and the other, later manuscripts have *for scome* (in various spellings) where this one has *for forscome*. But the related word *forscamung* is attested as a gloss to the Latin word *pudor* 'modesty', and the sense 'modesty' works well here.

þæt þā sumre tīde dyde, þæt hē forlēt þæt hūs þæs ġebēorscipes ond ūt wæs gongende tō nēata scipene, þāra heord him wæs þǣre neahte beboden, þā hē ðā þǣr in ġelimpliċe tīde his leomu on reste ġesette ond onslēpte, þā stōd him sum mon æt þurh swefn ond hine hālette ond grētte ond hine be his noman nemnde: 'Cedmon, sing mē hwæthwugu.' [8] Þā ondswarede hē ond cwæð: 'Ne con iċ nōht singan; ond iċ for þon of þeossum ġebēorscipe ūt ēode ond hider ġewāt, for þon iċ nāht singan ne cūðe.' [9] Eft hē cwæð, se ðe wið hine sprecende wæs: 'Hwæðre þū meaht singan.' [10] Þā cwæð hē: 'Hwæt sceal iċ singan?' Cwæð hē: 'Sing mē frumsceaft.'

[11] Þā hē ðā þās andsware onfēng, þā ongon hē sōna singan in herenesse Godes Scyppendes þā fers ond þā word þe hē nǣfre ġehȳrde, þāra endebyrdnes[8] þis is:

[12] Nū sculon[9] heriġean   heofonrīċes weard,
Meotodes meahte   ond his mōdġeþanc,
weorc wuldorfæder,   swā hē wundra ġehwæs,
ēċe Drihten,   ōr onstealde.
[13] Hē ǣrest sceōp   eorðan bearnum[10]
heofon tō hrōfe,   hāliġ Scyppend;
þā middanġeard   monncynnes weard,
ēċe Drihten,   æfter tēode
fīrum foldan,[11]   Frēa ælmihtiġ.

[14] Þā ārās hē from þǣm slǣpe, ond eal þā þe hē slǣpende song fæste in ġemynde hæfde, ond þǣm wordum sōna moniġ word in þæt ilce ġemet Gode wyrðes[12] songes tōġeþēodde. [15] Þā cōm hē on morgenne tō þǣm tūnġerēfan þe his ealdormon wæs; sæġde him hwylċe ġife hē onfēng; ond hē hine sōna tō

---

[8]   The word *endebyrdnes* 'order' suggests that the text is quoting Cædmon's poem exactly; Bede's original Latin here says *quorum iste est sensus* (of which this is the sense). After his Latin paraphrase of the hymn, Bede adds, 'This is the sense, but not the very order [*ordo*] of the words which he sang while sleeping; for songs may not, however well composed they are, be translated literally from one language to another without harm to their beauty and dignity.' The Old English translator has omitted this sentence, for an obvious reason. In two eighth-century copies of the Latin text of Bede's *Ecclesiastical History* a version of *Cædmon's Hymn* in the Northumbrian dialect is written in the margin; it is not impossible that it was Bede's intention that the Old English poem should be transmitted with his text.

[9]   The unexpressed subject of *sculon* is *wē*. The omission of first-person subjects is not unusual in Old English (see §15.2.1). Both of the eighth-century copies and two of the earliest of the West-Saxon copies that accompany the Old English Bede omit the pronoun; a number of copies dating from the tenth century and later insert *we*, presumably because the text as originally recorded was by then beginning to look a little cryptic.

[10]   *eorðan bearnum*: for the children of earth.

[11]   *fīrum foldan*: the earth for the people.

[12]   *Gode wyrðes*: worthy of God.

þǣre abbudissan ġelǣdde ond hire þā cȳðde ond sǣġde. [16] Þā hēht hēo ġesomnian ealle þā ġelǣredestan men ond þā leorneras, ond him ondweardum hēt secgan þæt swefn ond þæt lēoð singan, þæt ealra heora dōme¹³ ġecoren wǣre, hwæt oððe hwonon þæt cumen wǣre.

[17] Þā wæs him eallum ġeseġen, swā swā hit wæs, þæt him wǣre from Drihtne sylfum heofonliċ ġifu forġifen. [18] Þā rehton hēo him ond sǣġdon sum hāliġ spell ond godcundre lāre word; bebudon him þā, ġif hē meahte, þæt hē in swinsunge lēoþsonges þæt ġehwyrfde. [19] Þā hē ðā hæfde þā wīsan onfongne, þā ēode hē hām tō his hūse, ond cwōm eft on morgenne,¹⁴ ond þȳ betstan lēoðe ġeglenġed him āsong ond āġeaf þæt him beboden wæs.

[20] Ðā ongan sēo abbudisse clyppan ond lufiġean þā Godes ġife in þǣm men; ond hēo hine þā monade ond lǣrde þæt hē woruldhād ānforlēte ond munuchād onfēnge, ond hē þæt wel þāfode. [21] Ond hēo hine in þæt mynster onfēng mid his gōdum ond hine ġeþēodde tō ġesomnunge þāra Godes þēowa; ond hēht hine lǣran¹⁵ þæt ġetæl þæs hālgan stǣres ond spelles. [22] Ond hē eal þā hē in ġehȳrnesse ġeleornian meahte mid hine ġemyndgade, ond swā swā clǣne nēten eodorcende in þæt swēteste lēoð ġehwerfde. [23] Ond his song ond his lēoð wǣron swā wynsumu tō ġehȳranne þætte þā seolfan his lārēowas¹⁶ æt his mūðe wreoton ond leornodon. [24] Song hē ǣrest be middanġeardes ġesceape ond bi fruman moncynnes ond eal þæt stǣr Genesis (þæt is sēo ǣreste Moyses bōoc), ond eft bi ūtgonge Israhēla folces of Ægypta londe ond bi ingonge þæs ġehātlandes, ond bi ōðrum monegum spellum þæs hālgan ġewrites canōnes bōca,¹⁷ ond bi Crīstes menniscnesse ond bi his þrōwunge ond bi his ūpāstīġnesse in heofonas, ond bi þæs Hālgan Gāstes cyme ond þāra apostola lāre, ond eft bi þǣm dæġe þæs tōweardan dōmes ond bi fyrhtu þæs tintreġlican wiites, ond bi swētnesse þæs heofonlecan rīċes hē moniġ lēoð ġeworhte. [25] Ond swelċe ēac ōðer moniġ be þǣm godcundan fremsumnessum ond dōmum hē ġeworhte. [26] In eallum þǣm hē ġeornlīċe ġēmde þæt hē men ātuge from synna lufan ond māndǣda, ond tō lufan ond tō ġeornfulnesse āwehte gōdra dǣda, for þon hē wæs se mon swīþe ǣfest ond regollecum þēodscipum ēaðmōdlīċe underþēoded. [27] Ond wið þǣm þā ðe

---

¹³ *ealra heora dōme*: by the judgement of them all.

¹⁴ The text does not say whether Cædmon dreamed another song or composed it while waking. The later metaphor of a ruminating animal suggests silent meditation. The Icelandic *Egil's Saga* depicts the poet Egil composing his 'Head-Ransom' poem to placate the Viking king Eirik of York, who intended to put him to death. He stayed up all night to do it, and so important was concentration to the process of composition and memorization that his friend Arinbjorn had to sit up with him to keep away a sparrow that had been distracting him with its singing.

¹⁵ *hēht hine lǣran*: commanded (one) to teach him.

¹⁶ *þā seolfan his lārēowas*: his teachers themselves.

¹⁷ *þæs hālgan ġewrites canōnes bōca*: of the books of the canon of holy scripture.

in ōðre wīsan dōn woldon hē wæs mid welme miċelre ellenwōdnisse onbærned, ond hē for ðon fæġre ænde[18] his līf betŷnde ond ġeendade.[19]

[28] For þon þā ðǣre tīde nēalǣċte his ġewītenesse ond forðfōre, þā wæs hē fēowertŷnum dagum ǣr þæt hē wæs līċhomlicre untrymnesse þryċċed ond hefgad, hwæðre tō þon[20] ġemetlīċe þæt hē ealle þā tīd meahte ġe sprecan ġe gongan. [29] Wæs þǣr in nēaweste untrumra monna hūs, in þǣm heora þēaw wæs þæt hēo þā untrumran ond þā ðe æt forðfōre wǣron inlǣdon sceoldon ond him þǣr ætsomne þeġnian. [30] Þā bæd hē his þeġn on æfenne þǣre neahte þe hē of worulde gongende wæs þæt hē in þǣm hūse him stōwe ġeġearwode, þæt hē ġerestan meahte. [31] Þā wundrode se þeġn for hwon[21] hē ðæs bǣde, for þon him þūhte þæt his forðfōr swā nēah ne wǣre; dyde hwæðre swā swā hē cwæð ond bibēad.

[32] Ond mid þŷ[22] hē ðā þǣr on reste ēode ond hē ġefēonde mōde sumu þing mid him sprecende ætgædere ond glēowiende wæs þe þǣr ǣr inne wǣron, þā wæs ofer midde neaht þæt hē fræġn hwæðer hēo æniġ hūsl inne hæfdon. [33] Þā ondswarodon hēo ond cwǣdon: 'Hwylċ þearf is ðē hūsles? Ne þīnre forþfōre swā nēah is, nū þū þus rōtlīċe ond þus glædlīċe tō ūs sprecende eart.' [34] Cwæð hē eft: 'Berað mē hūsl tō.' [35] Þā hē hit þā on honda hæfde, þā fræġn hē hwæþer hēo ealle smolt mōd ond, būton eallum incan, blīðe tō him hæfdon. [36] Þā ondswaredon hȳ ealle ond cwǣdon þæt hēo nǣniġne incan tō him wiston, ac hēo ealle him swīðe blīðemōde wǣron; ond hēo wrixendlīċe hine bǣdon þæt hē him eallum blīðe wǣre. [37] Þā ondswarade hē ond cwæð: 'Mīne broðor, mīne þā lēofan, iċ eom swīðe blīðemōd tō ēow ond tō eallum Godes monnum.' [38] Ond swā wæs hine ġetrymmende mid þȳ heofonlecan weġneste ond him ōðres līfes ingong ġeġearwode.

[39] Þā ġȳt hē fræġn hū nēah þǣre tīde wǣre þætte þā brōðor ārīsan scolden ond Godes lof rǣran ond heora ūhtsong[23] singan. [40] Þā ondswaredon hēo: 'Nis hit feor tō þon.'[24] [41] Cwæð hē: 'Teala: wuton wē wel þǣre tīde bīdan.' [42] Ond þā him ġebæd ond hine ġeseġnode mid Crīstes rōdetācne ond his hēafod onhylde tō þām bolstre ond medmiċel fæc onslēpte, ond swā mid stilnesse his līf ġeendade.

---

[18] *fæġre ænde*: with a beautiful end.

[19] Here Bede's account of Cædmon starts to take on some of the characteristics of a saint's life. As in many saints' lives, his equanimity and confidence in the face of death was a sign of unusual faith, and his ability to foresee the time of his death was taken as a sign of divine favour.

[20] *tō þon*: to that extent.

[21] *for hwon*: for what reason; why.

[22] *mid þŷ*: when.

[23] *Ūhta* is dawn. *Ūhtsong* corresponds to Bede's *laudes nocturnas*, 'lauds' or 'nocturns', one of the canonical hours, or eight daily services, observed by monks living under the Benedictine Rule. *Ūhtsang* was ordinarily timed to end at dawn; Cædmon would have participated in this service every day since becoming a monk.

[24] *tō þon*: until then.

[43] Ond swā wæs ġeworden þætte swā swā hlūttre mōde ond bilwitre ond smyltre wilsumnesse Drihtne þēode, þæt hē ēac swylċe swā smylte dēaðe middanġeard wæs forlǣtende ond tō his ġesihðe becwōm. [44] Ond sēo tunge þe swā moniġ hālwende word in þæs Scyppendes lof ġesette, hē[25] ðā swelċe ēac þā ȳtmæstan word in his herenisse, hine seolfne seġniende ond his gāst in his honda bebēodende, betȳnde. [45] Ēac swelċe þæt is ġeseġen þæt hē wǣre ġewis his seolfes forðfōre of þǣm we nū secgan hȳrdon.

7 Boethius on Fame

King Alfred, who ruled the West Saxons from 870 to 899, is chiefly remembered for two accomplishments, either of which would have been sufficient to earn him his epithet 'the Great': he stopped the advance of the Vikings in England, inaugurating a century of relative peace and stability, and he instituted and led a programme of educational reform, initiating a tradition of vernacular literary prose that lasted until the Conquest. As part of this reform, Alfred himself translated several works: the *Pastoral Care* of Pope Gregory the Great (in the preface to which, edited in Mitchell and Robinson [66], he outlines his educational programme), *The Consolation of Philosophy* by the sixth-century philosopher Boethius, the *Soliloquies* of St Augustine, and the first fifty psalms.

Alfred generally treated his source quite freely; you may wish to consult either the Latin text or one of the numerous available translations to spot the passages that he added or altered. He renders the allegorical figure *Philosophia* as *Wīsdōm* 'Wisdom' or *Ġesceādwīsnes* 'Reason'; the figure which in the source is understood to be Boethius himself is here allegorized as *Mōd* 'Mind'. The present selection, corresponding to Book II, Prose vii and Metre vii of the source, follows the discourse of *Philosophia/Wīsdōm* on temporal power, which closes with a metre on the disastrous reign of Nero.

The standard edition of King Alfred's Boethius is Sedgefield [83]; the metres have been edited separately in Krapp and Dobbie [60], vol. 5, and, with commentary and glossary, in Griffiths [44].

[1] Ðā se Wīsdōm ðā þis lēoð āsungen hæfde, ðā ġesūgode hē, ond þā andswarode þæt Mōd ond þus cwæð: [2] 'Ēalā, Ġesceādwīsnes, hwæt, þū wāst þæt mē næfre sēo ġītsung ond sēo ġemǣġð þisses eorðlican anwealdes forwel

---

[25] Clearly the Old English translator has lost track of his sentence here. The noun phrase with included adjective clause, *Ond seo tunge . . . lof ġesette* should function as the subject of the whole sentence; but the subject awkwardly changes from 'the tongue' to 'he' (i.e. Cædmon) at this point.

ne līcode, ne iċ ealles forswīðe ne ġirnde þisses eorðlican rīċes,[1] būton tōla iċ wilnode þēah ond andweorces tō þām weorce þe mē beboden was tō wyrċanne, þæt was þæt iċ unfracoðlīċe ond ġerisenlīċe meahte stēoran ond reċċan þone anwald þe mē befæst wæs. [3] Hwæt, þū wāst þæt nān mon ne mæġ nænne cræft cȳðan ne nænne anweald reċċan ne stīoran būtan tōlum ond andweorce; þæt bið ælċes cræftes andweorc þæt mon þone cræft būton wyrċan ne mæġ. [4] Þæt bið þonne cyninges andweorc ond his tōl mid tō rīcsianne þæt hē hæbbe his lond full monnad: hē sceal habban ġebedmen ond ferdmen[2] ond weorcmen.[3] [5] Hwæt, þū wāst þætte būtan þissum tōlum nān cyning his cræft ne mæġ cȳðan. [6] Þæt is ēac his ondweorc þæt hē habban sceal tō ðæm tōlum, þām þrim ġefērscipum, bīwiste. [7] Þæt is þonne heora bīwist: land tō būgianne ond ġifa ond wæpnu ond mete ond ealu ond clāþas ond ġehwæt þæs ðe þā þrē ġefērscipas behofiġen.[4] [8] Ne mæġ hē būtan þisum þās tōl ġehealdan ne būton þisum tōlum nān þāra þinga wyrċan þe him beboden is tō wyrċenne.

[9] 'For þȳ iċ wilnode andweorces þone anweald mid tō reċċenne, þæt mīne cræftas ond anweald ne wurden forġitene ond forholene, for þām[5] ælċ cræft ond ælċ anweald bið sōna forealdod ond forsugod ġif hē bið būton wīsdōme. [10] For ðæm ne mæġ nōn[6] mon nænne cræft bringan būton wīsdōme, for ðæm þe swā hwæt swā[7] þurh dysiġ ġedōn bið, ne mæġ hit mon næfre tō cræfte ġerēċċan. [11] Þæt is nū hraðost tō secganne[8] þæt iċ wilnode weorðfullīċe tō libbanne þā hwīle þe[9] iċ lifde ond æfter mīnum līfe þæm monnum tō læfanne þe æfter mē wæren mīn ġemyndiġ[10] on gōdum weorcum.'

[12] Ðā ðis þā ġesprecen was, þā ġesūgode þæt Mōd, ond sēo Ġesceādwīsnes ongon sprecan ond þus cwæþ: [13] 'Ēalā, Mōd, ēalā, ān yfel is swīðe swīðe tō

---

[1]   From this point most of *Mōd*'s speech has been added by Alfred to his source.

[2]   The first element of *ferdmen* is a word for 'army', usually spelled *fierd* (in early West Saxon) or *fyrd* (in late West Saxon). The vowel of this word, which arises from the *i*-mutation of *ea* (see §2.2.2), is often spelled *e* in this text, e.g. *onġetan* 16 (spelled *ongietan*, *ongitan* and *ongytan* elsewhere in this anthology) and *nēten* 18 (spelled *nīeten* in early West Saxon and *nȳten* in the later texts in this anthology). This spelling is characteristic of non-West Saxon dialects; if you keep it in mind as you read this text you may save yourself some trips to the glossary.

[3]   It is a commonplace in medieval literature that society is composed of three 'estates': those who pray (the clergy and those in monastic orders), those who fight (the nobility) and those who work (the commoners).

[4]   *ġehwæt ... behofiġen*: literally 'everything of that which the three fellowships require'; but translate 'everything that the ...'.

[5]   The adverb *for þȳ* at the beginning of this sentence is correlated with the conjunction *for þām* here (see §10.4).

[6]   A peculiarity of this text is its occasional spelling of *ō* for *ā* before *n*.

[7]   *swā hwæt swā*: whatever (see §5.4).

[8]   *Þæt is nū hraðost tō secganne*: to put it briefly.

[9]   *þā hwīle þe*: for as long as.

[10]   *wæren mīn ġemyndiġ*: remembered me.

anscunianne: þæt is þæt þætte swīðe singallīċe ond swīðe hefiġlīċe beswīċð
ealra þāra monna mōd þe bēoð on heora ġecynde ġecorene, ond þēah ne bēoð
tō þām hrōfe þonne ġīt cumen fulfremedra mæġena; þæt is þonne wilnung
lēases ġilpes ond unryhtes anwealdes ond unġemetlīċes hlīsan gōdra weorca[11]
ofer eall folc. [14] For þon wilnigað moniġe woruldmen anwealdes þe[12] hīe
woldon habban gōdne hlīsan, þēah hī his unwyrðe sīen; ġe furðum se ealra
forcūþesta wilnað þæs ilcan. [15] Ac se þe wile wīslīċe ond ġeornlīċe æfter
þām hlīsan spyrian, þonne onġit hē swīðe hræðe hū lȳtel hē bið, ond hū læne,
ond hū tēdre, ond hū bedæled ælċes gōdes.

[16] 'Ġif þū nū ġeornlīċe smēaġan wilt ond witan wilt ymb ealre þisse
eorðan ymbhwyrft from ēasteweardum ðisses middanġeardes oð westeweardne,
ond from sūðeweardum oð norðeweardne, swā swā þū liornodest on þǣre
bēċ þe Astralogium hātte,[13] ðonne meaht þū onġetan þæt hē is eal wið þone
heofon tō metanne swilċe ān lȳtlu price on brādum brede, oðþe rondbēag on
scelde, æfter wīsra monna dōme. [17] Hū ne wāst þū[14] þæt ðū leornodest on
Ptolomeus bōcum, se tōwrāt ealles þises middanġeardes ġemet on ānre bēċ?[15]
[18] Þǣr þū meaht on ġesēon þæt eall moncynn ond ealle nētenu ne notiġað
furðum nāwer nēah fēorðan dǣles þisse eorðan, ðæs þe[16] men ġefaran magan,
for þǣm þe hȳ hit ne magon eall ġebūgian, sum for hǣte, sum for ċile; ond
þone mǣstan dǣl his hæfð sǣ oferseten. [19] Dō nū of ðām fēorðan dǣle an
þīnum mōde eall þæt sēo sǣ his ofseten hæfð, ond eal þā sceard þe hīo him[17]
on ġenumen hæfð, ond eall þæt his fennas ond mōras ġenumen habbað, ond
eall þæt on eallum þīodum wēstes[18] liġeð. [20] Þonne meaht þū onġitan þætte
þæs ealles nis monnum þonne māre lǣfed tō būgianne, būton swelċe ōn lȳtel
cafertūn. [21] Is þæt þonne fordyslic ġeswinc þæt ġē winnað ēowre worulde[19]
tō ðon[20] þæt ġē wilniað ēowerne hlīsan unġemetlīċe tō brǣdanne ofer swelċne
cafertūn swelċe þæt is ðætte men būgiað þisse worulde[21] – ful nēah swilċe

[11]   hlīsan gōdra weorca: fame (or approbation) for good deeds.
[12]   The adverb for þon at the beginning of this sentence is correlated with the conjunction þē
(more often spelled þȳ) here.
[13]   The Latin text does not allude to a specific work, but rather in a general way to 'astrological
[that is, astronomical] accounts'.
[14]   Questions beginning Hū ne are generally to be translated 'Do not . . . ?' In this sentence Hū ne
wāst þū means 'Do you not know . . . ?'
[15]   Ptolemy (fl. first half of second century) is best known for his Almagest, which summarized
Greek astronomy; however, the allusion here is to his Geography. The Anglo-Saxons had no
first-hand knowledge of Ptolemy's works.
[16]   Genitive ðæs þe agrees with dǣles.
[17]   The antecedent of hīo is sǣ; that of him (and the other masculine pronouns in this sentence)
is dǣle. The gender of the pronouns prevents their being ambiguous.
[18]   The genitive wēstes is adverbial: translate 'lies waste'.
[19]   winnað ēowre worulde: struggle all your lives.
[20]   tō ðon: for the purpose.
[21]   Take the genitive phrase þisse worulde with cafertūn: 'a little courtyard (or vestibule) of this
world'.

ān price for þæt ōðer. [22] Ac hwæt rūmedliċes oððe miċelliċes oððe weorðfulliċes[22] hæfð se ēower ġilp[23] þe ġē þær būgiað on þām fīftan dǣle healfum[24] londes ond unlondes, mid sǣ, mid fænne, mid ealle,[25] swā hit is ġenerwed. [23] Tō hwon[26] wilniġe ġē þonne tō unġemetlīċe þæt ġē ēowerne naman tōbrǣden ofer þone tēoðan dǣl, nū his māre nis mid sǣ, mid fænne, mid ealle?

[24] 'Ġeðenċað ēac þæt on ðisum lȳtlan pearroce þe wē ǣr ymb sprǣcon būgiað swīðe manega þēoda ond swīðe mislica ond swīðe unġelica, ǣġþer ġe on sprǣċe ġe on þēawum ġe on eallum sidum ealra þāra þēoda þe ġē nū wilniað swīðe unġemetlīċe þæt ġē scylen ēowerne naman ofer tōbrǣdan. [25] Þæt ġē nǣfre ġedōn ne magon, for ðon hiora sprǣċ is tōdǣled on twā ond on hundseofontiġ, ond ǣlċ þāra sprǣċa is tōdǣled on manega þīoda, ond þā sint tōleġena ond tōdǣlda mid sǣ ond mid wudum ond mid muntum ond mid fennum ond mid manegum ond mid mislicum wēstenum ond unġefērum londum, þæt hit furðum ċēpemen ne ġefarað. [26] Ac hū mag ðǣr þonne synderlīċe ānes rīċes monnes nama cuman, þonne þǣr mon furðum þǣre burge naman ne ġehērð ne þǣre þēode þe hē on hāmfæst bið? [27] Þȳ iċ nāt hwelċe dysiġe[27] ġē ġirnað þæt ġē woldon ēowerne naman tōbrǣdan ġeond ealle eorþan; þæt ġē nǣfre ġedōn ne magon, ne furðum nāwer nēah.

[28] 'Hwæt, þū wāst hū miċel Rōmāna rīċe wæs on Marcuses dagum þæs heretogan, se wæs ōðre naman hāten Tullius ond þriddan Cicero. [29] Hwæt, hē cȳðde on sumre his bōca[28] ðætte þā ġēt Rōmāna nama ne cōme ofer þā muntas þā wē hātað Caucaseas, ne ðā Sciððeas þe on ōðre healfe þāra munta būgiað furðum þǣre burge naman ne þæs folces ne ġehērdon, ac þā hē cōm ǣrest tō Parðum, ond wæs þǣr swīðe nīwe; ac hē[29] wæs þēah þǣrymbūtan manegum folce swīðe eġeful. [30] Hū ne onġite ġē nū hū nearo se ēower hlīsa bīon wile þe ġē þǣr ymb swincað ond unrihtlīċe tioliað tō ġebrǣdanne? [31] Hwæt wēnstū hū miċelne hlīsan[30] ond hū miċelne weorðscipe ān Rōmānisc man mæġe habban on þām lande þǣr mon furðum ðǣre burge naman ne ġehērde, ne ealles ðæs folces hlīsa ne cōm?

[32] 'Þēah nū hwelċ mon unġemetlīċe ond unġedafenlīċe wilniġe þæt hē scyle his hlīsan tōbrǣdan ofer ealle eorþan, hē ne mæġ þæt forðbringan, for

---

[22] The genitives are partitive with *hwæt*. A literal translation would be 'what of that which is generous . . .'.

[23] *se ēower ġilp*: that fame of yours.

[24] *on þām fīftan dǣle healfum*: on half of the fifth part.

[25] *mid ealle*: and so forth.

[26] *Tō hwon*: for what purpose (*hwon* being an alternate instrumental form of *hwā* – see §5.3).

[27] *hwelċe dysiġe*: an instrumental phrase, 'for what folly'.

[28] Cicero's *De Republica*, known even to Boethius mainly through the commentary on a part of it in Macrobius, *In Somnium Scipionis*, which was very likely known to the Anglo-Saxons in Alfred's time.

[29] The antecedent of *hē* is *nama*.

[30] *Hwæt wēnstū hū miċelne hlīsan*: how much fame do you think.

þām þe þāra ðēoda þēawas sint swīðe unġelīċe ond hiora ġesetenessa swīðe mislica, swā ðætte þæt on ōðrum lande betst līcode, þætte þæt bið hwīlum on ðǣm ōðrum tǣlwyrðlicosð,[31] ond ēac miċles wītes wyrðe. [33] For ðǣm ne mæġ nān mon habban ġeliċ lof on ǣlċum londe, for þon ðe on ǣlċum londe ne līcað þæt on ōðrum līcað. [34] For ðȳ sceolde ǣlċ mon bīon on ðǣm wel ġehealden þæt hē on his āgnum earde līcode. [35] Þēah hē nū māran wilniġe, hē ne mæġ furðum þæt forðbringan, for þǣm þe seldhwonne bið þætte āuht monegum monnum ānes hwæt[32] liciġe. [36] For þȳ wyrð oft gōdes monnes lof āleġen inne in þǣre ilcan þēode þe hē on hāmfæst bið, ond ēac for þām þe hit oft swīðe sārlīċe ġebyrede þurh þā heardsǣlþa þāra wrītera ðæt hī for heora slǣwðe ond for ġīmelēste ond ēac for reċċelēste forlēton unwriten þāra monna ðēawas ond hiora dǣda, þe on hiora dagum formǣroste ond weorðġeornuste wǣron. [37] Ond þēah hī nū eall hiora līf ond hira dǣda āwriten hæfden, swā swā hī sceoldon ġif hī dohten, hū ne[33] forealdodon þā ġewritu þēah ond losodon þonēcan þe hit wǣre,[34] swā some swā þā wrīteras dydon, ond ēac þā ðe hī ymb writon? [38] Ond ēow þinċð þēah þæt ġē hæbben ēċe āre ġif ġē mæġen on ealre ēowerre worulde[35] ġeearniġan þæt ġē hæbben gōdne hlīsan æfter ēowrum dagum.

[39] 'Ġif þū nū ġetelest þā hwīla þisses andweardan līfes ond þisses hwīlendlican wið þæs unġeendodan līfes hwīla, hwæt bið hit þonne? [40] Tele nū þā lenġe þǣre hwīle þe þū þīn ēage on beprēwan mæġe wið tēn ðūsend wintra; þonne habbað þā hwīla hwæthwugu onlīċes,[36] þēah hit lȳtel sīe, þæt is þonne þæt heora ǣġþer hæfð ende. [41] Tele nū þonne þæt tēn þūsend ġēara, ġe ēac mā ġif þū wille,[37] wið þæt ēċe ond þæt unġeendode līf. [42] Þonne ne findst þū þǣr nāuht anlīċes, forðām þæt tēn ðūsend ġēara, þēah hit lang ðinċe, āscortaþ, ond þæs ōðres nǣfre ne cymð nān ende.[38] [43] For þǣm hit nis nō tō metanne[39] þæt ġeendodlīċe wið ðæt unġeendodlīċe. [44] Þēah þū nū telle from þises middanġeardes fruman oð ðone ende, ond mete þonne þā ġēar wið þæt ðe nænne ende næfð, þonne ne bið þǣr nāuht anlīċes. [45] Swā bið ēac se hlīsa þāra formǣrra monna; þēah hē hwīlum lang sīe, ond fela ġēara þurhwuniġe, hē bið þēah swīðe scort tō metanne wið ðone þe nǣfre ne ġeendað.

---

[31] The letter-sequence *sð* sometimes appears instead of *st* in early manuscripts.

[32] *ānes hwæt*: any one thing.

[33] *hū ne*: would not . . . ?

[34] *þonēcan þe hit wǣre*: as soon as it was done.

[35] *on ealre ēowerre worulde*: for you whole lives.

[36] *hwæthwugu onlīċes*: literally 'something of what is similar'; translate 'some similarity'.

[37] For *ġe ēac mā ġif þū wille* the Bodley text (Cotton is unavailable here and Junius is no help) has *ge þeah þu ma wille* 'and although you want more' or 'and nevertheless you want more', neither of which makes sense in this context. There is no equivalent phrase in the Latin source.

[38] *Nān ende* governs the partitive genitive *þæs ōðres* at the beginning of this clause.

[39] For *þǣm hit nis nō tō metanne*: 'Therefore one ought not to compare'. For this use of the inflected infinitive, see §7.9.1.

[46] Ond ġē ne reċċað ðēah hweðer ġē āuht tō gōde dōn wið ænegum ōþrum þingum būton wið þām lȳtlan lofe þæs folces, ond wið þǣm scortan hlīsan þe wē ǣr ymb sprǣcon. [47] Earniað⁴⁰ þæs ond forsīoð þā cræftas ēoweres inġeðonces ond ēowres andġietes ond ēowre⁴¹ ġesceādwīsnesse, ond woldon habban ēowerra gōdena weorca mēde æt fremdra monna cwiddunge. [48] Wilniað þærtō þǣre mēde þe ġē tō Gode sceolden.⁴²

[49] 'Hwæt, þū ġehērdest þætte ġiōdagum ġelomp þæt ān swīðe wīs mon ond swīðe rīċe ongan fandian ānes ūðwitan ond hine bismrode for ðǣm hē hine swā orgellīċe ūp āhōf ond bodode þæs þæt hē ūðwita wǣre. [50] Ne cȳðde hē hit mid nǣnum cræftum, ac mid lēasum ond ofermōdlicum ġelpe. [51] Þā wolde se wīsa mon his fandian hwæðer hē swā wīs wǣre swā hē self wēnde þæt hē wǣre. [52] Ongon hine þā hyspan ond hearmcwidian. [53] Þā ġehērde se ūðwita swīðe ġeþyldelīċe þæs wīsan monnes word sume hwīle, ac siððan hē his hispinge ġehēred hæfde, þā scylde hē onġēan swīðe unġeþyldelīċe, þēah hē ǣr līċette þæt hē ūðwita wǣre; ahsode⁴³ hine þā eft hwæðer him þūhte þæt hē ūþwita wǣre þe nǣre. [54] Ðā andswarode se wīsa mon him ond cwæð, "iċ wolde cweþan þæt þū ūðwita wǣre, gif þū ġeðyldiġ wǣre ond ġesūgian meahte".⁴⁴ [55] Hū langsum wæs him se hlīsa þe hē ǣr mid lēasungum wilnode? [56] Hū ne forbærst hē þā þǣrrihte for ðǣm ānum andwyrde? [57] Hwæt forstōd þonne þǣm betstum monnum þe ǣr ūs wǣron þæt hī swā swīðe wilnodon þæs īdelan ġelpes ond þæs hlīsan æfter heora dēaþe, oððe hwæt forstent hit þǣm þe nū sindon? [58] Þȳ wǣre ælċum men māre þearf þæt hē wilnode gōdra cræfta þonne lēases hlīsan. [59] Hwæt hæfð hē æt þām hlīsan æfter þæs līċhoman ġedāle ond þǣre sāwle? [60] Hū ne witon wē þæt ealle men līċhomlīċe sweltað, ond þēah sīo sāwl bið libbende? [61] Ac sīo sāwl færð swīðe frīolīċe tō hefonum siððan hīo ontīeġd bið ond of þǣm carcerne þæs līċhoman onlēsed bið. [62] Hēo forsihð þonne eall ðās eorðlican þing ond fæġnað þæs þæt hīo mōt brūcan þæs heofonlican⁴⁵ siððan hīo bið ābrogden from ðǣm eorðlican. [63] Þonne þæt mōd him selfum ġewita bið Godes willan.'

[64] Ðā se Wīsdōm þā þis spel āreaht hæfde, ðā ongan hē ġyddian ond ðus singende cwæð:

---

⁴⁰ The unexpressed subject of *earniað* (*not* an imperative), and of the other verbs in this and the following sentence, is *ġē*.

⁴¹ Feminine genitive singular; compare dative *ēowerre* 36. When the vowel of the second syllable of *ēowerre* is dropped, double *-rr-* gets simplified following another consonant (see §7.2.1, item 4).

⁴² *þærto*: from that source. *tō Gode*: from God. The infinitive that one expects to find with *sceolden* is unexpressed.

⁴³ The unexpressed subject of *ahsode* is the false philosopher.

⁴⁴ The translation alters the story somewhat. In Boethius's version the false philosopher sits patiently through the man's harangue and then says, 'can you see now that I'm a philosopher?' – thereby proving that he is not. Alfred's version, in which the false philosopher first defends himself and then asks the question, is less concise.

⁴⁵ Understand *þinges* with *heofonlican*.

[65] Ġif nū hæleða hwone   hlīsan lyste,
unnytne ġelp   āgan wille,
þonne iċ hine wolde   wordum biddan
þæt hē hine æġhwonon ūtan   ymbeþōhte,[46]
sweotole ymbsāwe   sūð, ēast and west,
hū wīdġil sint   wolcnum ymbūtan
heofones hwealfe.[47]   [66] Hiġesnotrum mæġ
ēaðe ðinċan   þæt þēos eorðe sīe
eall[48] for ðæt ōðer   uniġmet[49] lȳtel,
þēah hīo unwīsum   wīdġel þinċe,
on stede strongliċ   stēorlēasum men.
[67] Þēah[50] mæġ þone wīsan   on ġewitlocan
þǣre ġitsunge   ġelpes scamian[51]
ðonne hine þæs hlīsan   heardost lysteð,
and hē þēah ne mæġ   þone tōbrēdan
ofer ðās nearowan   nǣniġe ðinga[52]
eorðan scēatas: is ðæt unnet ġelp!
[68] Ēala, ofermōdan,   hwī ēow ā lyste
mid ēowrum swīran   selfra willum[53]
þæt swǣre ġioc   symle underlūtan?
[69] Hwȳ ġē ymb ðæt unnet   ealniġ swincen,
þæt ġē þone hlīsan   habban tiliað
ofer ðīoda mā   þonne ēow þearf sīe?
[70] Þēah ēow nū ġesǣle   þæt ēow sūð oððe norð
þā ȳtmestan   eorðbūende
on moniġ ðīodisc   miċlum herien,
ðēah hwā æðele sīe   eorlġebyrdum,
welum ġeweorðad,   and on wlencum ðīo,
duguðum dīore,   dēað þæs ne scrīfeð
þonne him rūm forlǣt   rodora Waldend,

---

[46]   *hine æġhwonon utan ymbeþōhte*: consider everywhere all around himself. *Utan* is often paired either with the preposition or the verb prefix *ymb(e)* to mean 'round about'. Here the combination has the force of a preposition with *hine* as its object.

[47]   The subject of this clause is *hwealfe*; *wolcnum* is the object of the preposition *ymbūtan*. The 'vaults' of the heavens are the heavenly spheres, which revolve around the earth and contain the moon, the sun, the planets and the fixed stars.

[48]   *Eall* here modifies *eorðe* in the preceding line.

[49]   For *unġemet*; *-iġ-* (probably pronounced [iː]) is a simplified version of the prefix *ġe-*, which appears in Middle English as *y-*.

[50]   *Þēah*: That is, despite their being wise enough to recognize the insignificance of the earth.

[51]   The genitive phrase *þǣre ġitsunge* is governed by *scamian*; the genitive *ġelpes* is governed by *ġitsunge*. Translate 'be ashamed of the greed for fame'.

[52]   *nǣniġe ðinga*: by no means; by any means.

[53]   *selfra willum*: by your own desires; of your own volition.

ac hē þone welegan   wǣdlum ġelīċe
efnmǣrne ġedēð   ælċes þinges.[54]
[71] Hwǣr sint nū þæs wīsan   Wēlandes[55] bān
þæs goldsmiðes,   þe wæs ġeō mǣrost?
[72] For þȳ iċ cwæð 'þæs wīsan   Wēlandes bān'
for ðȳ ængum ne mæġ   eorðbūendra
se cræft losian   þe him Crist onlǣnð.
[73] Ne mæġ mon æfre þȳ ēð   ænne wræċċan
his cræftes beniman   þe mon onċerran mæġ
sunnan onswīfan[56]   and ðisne swiftan rodor[57]
of his rihtryne   rinca æniġ.
[74] Hwā wāt nū þæs wīsan   Wēlandes bān,
on hwelċum hī hlǣwa   hrūsan þeċċen?
[75] Hwǣr is nū se rīċa   Rōmāna wita
and se aroda   þe wē ymb sprecað,
hiora heretoga,   se ġehāten wæs
mid þǣm burgwarum   Brūtus nemned?[58]
[76] Hwǣr is ēac se wīsa   and se weorðġeorna
and se fæstrǣda   folces hyrde,
se wæs ūðwita   ælċes þinges
cēne and cræftiġ,   ðǣm[59] wæs Cāton nama?[60]
[77] Hī wǣron ġefyrn   forðġewitene;
nāt nǣniġ mon   hwǣr hī nū sindon.
[78] Hwæt is hiora here[61]   būton se hlīsa ān?

---

[54]   *ælċes þinges*: in all respects.
[55]   In Germanic legend, Weland the goldsmith was captured and enslaved by Niðhad, but killed his captor's two sons, impregnated his daughter, and escaped by making a pair of wings for himself. Boethius's text here asks the whereabouts of the bones of Fabricius, a military hero; presumably Alfred thought Weland a good substitute because of the etymological connection between the name Fabricius and Latin *fabricor* 'make, build'.
[56]   The auxiliary verb *mæġ* governs two infinitives, *onċerran* and *onswīfan*; *sunnan* is the common object of both infinitives.
[57]   In ancient and medieval cosmology, the position of the earth is fixed and the heavens revolve around it once each day; that is why the *rodor* is here described as *swift*.
[58]   Either Lucius Junius Brutus, who expelled the Tarquins from Rome, or Marcus Junius Brutus, one of the assassins of Julius Caesar. The prose version of this metre shows that King Alfred thought this the latter Brutus and confused him with his inciter, Gaius Longinus Cassius. Notice that *nemned* is redundant, since this clause already contains a past participle *ġehāten*.
[59]   *Ðǣm* is a dative of possession (see §4.2.4).
[60]   Cato the Elder, whom Boethius here calls *rigidus Cato*; he was well known to the Anglo-Saxons as the supposed author of a collection of wise sayings, which circulated in both Latin and Old English.
[61]   *Here* 'army' does not normally have a sense that would be appropriate here; but 'glory' is a possibility, on the model of such words as *þrym* 'army, might, splendour'. However, since the line is unmetrical as well as difficult to understand, it is likely that the text is corrupt here.

[79] Se is ēac tō lȳtel   swelċra lārīowa,[62]
for ðǣm þā magorincas   māran wyrðe
wǣron on worulde.   [80] Ac hit is wyrse nū
þæt ġeond þās eorðan   ǣġhwǣr sindon
hiora ġelīcan   hwōn ymbsprǣċe,
sume openlīċe   ealle forġitene,
þæt hī se hlīsa   hīwcūðe ne mæġ
foremǣre weras   forð ġebrenġan.[63]
[81] Þēah ġē nū wēnen   and wilniġen
þæt ġē lange tīd   libban mōten,
hwæt īow ǣfre þȳ bet   bīo oððe þinċe?[64]
[82] For ðǣm þe nāne forlēt,   þēah hit[65] lang ðinċe,
dēað æfter dogorrīme,   þonne hē hæfð Drihtnes lēafe,
hwæt þonne hæbbe   hæleþa ǣniġ,
guma æt þǣm ġilpe,   ġif hine ġegrīpan mōt
se ēċa dēað   æfter þissum?[66]

8   A Lyric for Advent

This is the fifth in a collection of twelve Advent lyrics (the first a fragment), based on a group of antiphons sung at vespers during the Advent season. The antiphon that is the source of this lyric reads, *O Oriens, splendor lucis aeternae et Sol iustitiae, veni et illumina sedentes in tenebris et umbra mortis*: 'O Rising Sun, radiance of eternal light and Sun of righteousness, come and illuminate those who sit in darkness and the shadow of death.'

You may consult this poem in its context in one of the editions of the Exeter Book (see textual note, p. 226): Krapp and Dobbie [60] vol. 3 and Muir [73]. The lyrics were edited separately (with a translation) by Campbell [23].

Ēalā earendel,   enġla beorhtast,
ofer middanġeard   monnum sended,
ond sōðfæsta   sunnan lēoma,

---

[62] *swelċra lārīowa*: for such teachers.

[63] These two lines are difficult. With an assist from the Latin (*nec fama notos efficit*) and Alfred's prose translation (*þæt se hlīsa hīe furðum cūþe ne ġedēð*), translate 'that fame cannot bring forth very famous men as familiar', that is, make famous men familiar to us.

[64] 'What will ever be or seem better for you because of that?'

[65] That is, life.

[66] The Cotton text has *worulde* after the last word. It is presumably someone's gloss, which a scribe has incorporated, for it is unmetrical, ungrammatical and unnecessary.

torht ofer tunglas,   þū tīda ġehwane
5   of sylfum þē   symle inlīhtes.[1]
Swā þū, God of Gode   ġearo ācenned,
sunu sōþan fæder,   sweġles in wuldre
būtan anġinne   ǣfre wǣre,
swā þec nū for þearfum   þīn āgen ġeweorc
10   bideð þurh byldo   þæt þū þā beorhtan[2] ūs
sunnan onsende,   ond þē sylf[3] cyme
þæt ðū inlēohte   þā þe longe ǣr,
þrosme beþeahte   ond in þēostrum hēr,
sǣton sinneahtes,   synnum bifealdne,
15   deorc dēaþes sceadu   drēogan sceoldan.
Nū wē hyhtfulle   hǣlo ġelȳfað
þurh þæt word Godes   weorodum brungen,
þe on frymðe wæs   fæder ælmihtigum
efenēċe mid God,   ond nū eft ġewearð
20   flǣsc firena lēas   þæt sēo fǣmne ġebær
ġeōmrum tō ġēoce.   God wæs mid ūs
ġesewen būtan synnum;   somod eardedon
mihtiġ Meotudes bearn   ond se monnes sunu
ġeþwǣre on þēode.   Wē þæs þonc magon
25   secgan siġedryhtne   symle bi ġewyrhtum,[4]
þæs þe hē hine sylfne ūs   sendan wolde.

9   The Wanderer

This poem is one of the finest of the Old English 'elegies', laments for the transitory
nature of worldly goods. Most of the poem is in the voice of a man who, following the

[1]   The second-person singular ending -s is common in early texts and in some non-West Saxon
dialects. Although the language of the Exeter Book is predominantly West Saxon, the Advent
Lyrics may originally have been written in an Anglian dialect (Mercian or Northumbrian).

[2]   This adjective modifies *sunnan* in the next line (see §8.1).

[3]   *Þē* is a dative, apparently an unusual (and untranslatable) reflexive with *cuman*. *Sylf* is the
nominative subject of *cyme* and should be translated 'you yourself'. An alternative to this rather
awkward reading, suggested by an early editor, is to emend *þē* to *þū* and read the phrase *þū sylf* as
the subject: 'you yourself'.

[4]   *Bi ġewyrhtum* is often translated 'for his acts' or the like (i.e. we thank God for his acts): but
ġewyrht generally refers either to one's merits or deserts or to one's deeds as deserving of praise,
blame or recompense, and the phrase *be ġewyrhtum* elsewhere means 'according to one's deserts'.
The thought here seems to be that we are grateful to God in that his coming has enabled us to be
rewarded according to our deserts.

death of his lord, has been wandering the earth in search of another. He laments his own loss and the inevitability of loss with a poignancy that is not balanced by the brief introduction and conclusion in the voice of a Christian moralist.

The Wanderer is preserved in the Exeter Book (see textual note for reading 8). It has been edited separately by Dunning and Bliss [31]; see also Klinck [55].

　　　Oft him ānhaga　　āre ġebīdeð,
　　　Metudes miltse,　　þēah þe hē mōdċeariġ
　　　ġeond lagulāde　　longe sceolde
　　　hrēran mid hondum　　hrīmċealde sǣ,
5　　wadan wrǣclāstas.　Wyrd bið ful ārǣd.[1]
　　　Swā cwæð eardstapa,　earfeþa ġemyndiġ,
　　　wrāþra wælsleahta,　winemǣga hryre:[2]
　　　Oft[3] iċ sceolde āna　ūhtna ġehwylċe
　　　mīne ċeare cwīþan.　Nis nū cwicra nān
10　þe iċ him mōdsefan　mīnne durre
　　　sweotule āsecgan.　Iċ tō sōþe wāt
　　　þæt biþ in eorle　indryhten þēaw
　　　þæt hē his ferðlocan　fæste binde,
　　　healde his hordcofan,　hyċġe swā hē wille.[4]
15　Ne mæġ wēriġ mōd　wyrde wiðstondan,
　　　ne se hrēo hyġe　helpe ġefremman.
　　　For ðon dōmġeorne　drēoriġne[5] oft
　　　in hyra brēostcofan　bindað fæste;
　　　swā iċ mōdsefan　mīnne sceolde,
20　oft earmċeariġ,　ēðle bidǣled,
　　　frēomǣgum feor,　feterum sǣlan,

---

[1]　*Arǣd* is the past participle form of the verb *Arǣdan*, which has a range of meanings such as 'arrange', 'determine', 'decree', 'appraise', 'explain', 'interpret', 'read (aloud)', 'utter'. Though the meaning of the past participle is generally 'determined, resolute', in this line it is often glossed 'predetermined, foreordained, inexorable'. But that sense of the word is not otherwise attested in Old English, and the idea of 'fate' as 'inexorable' is not characteristic of Old English literature. The gloss 'resolute' offered here suggests that *wyrd* is a powerful force (or a strong tendency of events to turn out in certain ways), but not inexorable.

[2]　We expect the ending *hryra* for the genitive plural, but the vowels of unaccented syllables are often confused in late Old English.

[3]　It is generally agreed that a speech begins with this line. Most editors consider this the wanderer's first speech and place a quotation mark before *Oft*. Dunning and Bliss, however, consider lines 1–5 to be spoken by the wanderer as well. In view of the disagreements among scholars, and following the example of the Old English manuscript, this edition omits quotation marks altogether.

[4]　*hyċġe swā hē wille*: whatever he may think.

[5]　The adjectives *dōmġeorne* and *drēoriġne* are both used as nouns (see §15.2.3). Translate 'those who are *dōmġeorn*'; 'something *drēoriġ*'.

siþþan ġeāra iū   goldwine mīnne
hrūsan heolstre biwrāh,   ond iċ hēan þonan
wōd winterċeariġ   ofer waþema ġebind,
25 sōhte seledrēoriġ   sinces bryttan,
hwǣr iċ feor oþþe nēah   findan meahte
þone þe in meoduhealle   mīne⁶ wisse,
oþþe mec frēondlēasne   frēfran wolde,
wenian mid wynnum.   Wāt⁷ se þe cunnað
30 hū slīþen bið   sorg tō ġefēran
þām þe⁸ him lȳt hafað   lēofra ġeholena.
Warað hine wræclāst,   nales wunden gold,
ferðloca frēoriġ,   nalæs foldan blǣd.
Ġemon hē selesecgas   ond sincþeġe,
35 hū hine on ġeoguðe   his goldwine
wenede tō wiste.   Wyn eal ġedrēas.
For þon wāt se þe sceal   his winedryhtnes
lēofes lārcwidum   longe forþolian.
Ðonne sorg ond slǣp⁹   somod ætgædre
40 earmne ānhogan   oft ġebindað,
þinceð him on mōde   þæt hē his mondryhten
clyppe ond cysse   ond on cnēo lecge
honda ond hēafod,¹⁰   swā hē hwīlum ǣr
in ġeārdagum   ġiefstōlas brēac.¹¹
45 Ðonne onwæcneð eft   winelēas guma,
ġesihð him biforan   fealwe wēgas,
baþian brimfuglas,   brǣdan feþra,
hrēosan hrīm ond snāw,   hagle ġemenġed.
Ðonne bēoð þȳ hefiġran   heortan benne,
50 sāre æfter swǣsne.   Sorg bið ġenīwad
þonne māga ġemynd   mōd ġeondhweorfeð;

---

⁶ *mīne*: my people.

⁷ The verb *witan* 'to know' lacks an object here and in line 37. Read 'He understands (my situation) who . . .'.

⁸ *þām þe*: for him who.

⁹ The hypothetical person who has experienced loneliness and so 'knows' or 'understands' the speaker's state of mind is here imagined falling asleep and dreaming of happier days in the hall. The verb *þyncan* (line 41) is often used in Old and Middle English to introduce the contents of dreams.

¹⁰ These are generally interpreted as formal gestures of fealty rather than as informal gestures of affection. However, it must be admitted that we know almost nothing about the ceremony that would have accompanied a thegn's swearing fealty to his lord.

¹¹ For a thegn to 'use' or 'benefit from' the 'gift-seat' or 'throne' was presumably to receive gifts from his lord.

grēteð glīwstafum,[12]   ġeorne ġeondscēawað
secga ġeseldan.   Swimmað eft on weġ.[13]
Flēotendra[14] ferð   nō þǣr fela bringeð
55   cūðra cwideġiedda.   Ċearo bið ġenīwad
þām þe sendan sceal   swīþe ġeneahhe
ofer waþema ġebind   wēriġne sefan.
For þon iċ ġeþenċan ne mæġ   ġeond þās woruld
for hwan[15] mōdsefa   mīn ne ġesweorce,
60   þonne iċ eorla līf   eal ġeondþenċe,
hū hī fǣrlīċe   flet ofġēafon,
mōdġe maguþeġnas.   Swā þes middanġeard
ealra dōgra ġehwām   drēoseð ond fealleþ.
For þon ne mæġ weorþan wīs   wer, ǣr hē āge
65   wintra dǣl in woruldrīċe.   Wita sceal[16] ġeþyldiġ;
ne sceal nō tō hātheort   ne tō hrædwyrde
ne tō wāc wiga   ne tō wanhȳdiġ
ne tō forht ne tō fæġen   ne tō feohġīfre
ne nǣfre ġielpes tō ġeorn,   ǣr hē ġeare cunne.
70   Beorn sceal ġebīdan,   þonne hē bēot spriceð,
oþ þæt collenferð   cunne ġearwe
hwider hreþra ġehyġd   hweorfan wille.[17]

---

[12]   glīwstafum: with joy; joyfully.

[13]   Lines 51–3 are more difficult to interpret than to read. Having just awakened from a dream of the now-departed joys of the hall, the man thinks of his kinsmen, eagerly greets them and peers at them (secga ġeseldan) intently. But either they recede from his memory like the birds floating on the sea, or he has been imagining (in his half-awake state) that he actually sees them, and now perceives that they are only sea-birds floating on the water.

[14]   That is, of the sea-birds, which do not speak to him.

[15]   for hwan: for what reason; why.

[16]   sceal: should be. Forms of the verbs gān and bēon are often omitted after auxiliaries.

[17]   This passage reflects what appears to have been a common anxiety that one could make impressive vows before a battle and yet lose one's nerve at the hour of greatest need. Compare The Battle of Maldon, ll. 198–201:

Swa him Offa on dæg   ær asæde
on þam meþelstede,   þa he gemot hæfde,
þæt þær modiglice   manega spræcon
þe eft æt þearfe   þolian noldon.

So Offa had said the day before
in the meeting-place, when he held an assembly,
that many spoke bravely there
who afterwards would not hold out when danger threatened.

It is better not to boast at all, the speaker says, until one is thoroughly acquainted with oneself.

Onġietan sceal glēaw hæle   hū gæstliċ[18] bið,
þonne ealre þisse worulde wela   wēste stondeð,
75 swā nū missenlīċe   ġeond þisne middanġeard
winde biwāune   weallas stondaþ,
hrīme bihrorene,   hrȳðġe þā ederas.
Wōriað þā wīnsalo,   waldend licgað
drēame bidrorene,   duguþ eal ġecrong,
80 wlonc bī wealle.   Sume wīġ[19] fornom,
ferede in forðweġe: sumne fugel oþbær
ofer hēanne holm,   sumne se hāra wulf
dēaðe ġedælde,   sumne drēoriġhlēor
in eorðscræfe   eorl ġehȳdde.
85 Ȳþde swā þisne eardġeard   ælda Scyppend
oþ þæt burgwara   breahtma lēase
eald enta ġeweorc[20]   īdlu stōdon.
Se þonne þisne wealsteal   wīse ġeþōhte
ond þis deorce līf   dēope ġeondþenċeð,
90 frōd in ferðe,   feor oft ġemon
wælsleahta worn,   ond þās word ācwið:
Hwær cwōm[21] mearg? Hwær cwōm mago?   Hwær cwōm māþþumġyfa?

---

[18] This instance of *gæstlic* is almost universally glossed as 'terrifying' or the like, an extension of a presumed meaning 'ghastly' or 'spectral'. But although *Gæstlic, gástlic* is a common word, the meaning 'terrifying' is nowhere else attested for it; its usual meaning is 'spiritual'. The notion that it is 'terrifying' when the earth stands in ruins would be rather blandly predictable, if the poet were saying that; but it makes at least as much sense to take the common meaning 'spiritual' here: and indeed meditating on death and ruination does lead the speaker's mind to higher concerns.

[19] Notice that *wīg* is the subject and *sume* the object. What follows is one of the better variations on the common 'Beasts of Battle' formula, which imagines the raven, the eagle and the wulf feasting on the corpses of the slain (see §14.3.2). Here the bird bearing a corpse away over the sea recalls one's sending one's 'weary spirit' out over the sea.

[20] The formula *enta ġeweorc* is used of magnificent artifacts from the distant past. In *Beowulf* it is used of the giant sword with which Beowulf kills Grendel (1679) and the dragon's barrow and its contents (2717, 2774). In *The Ruin* 2 it is used of the Roman ruins at Bath, and similarly in *Andreas* 1495 it is used of an ancient edifice.

[21] This phrase, meaning 'what has become of', echoes the Latin formula *ubi sunt* 'where are', often used in sermons to convey the theme of the transitoriness of worldly goods. A similar echo of the *ubi sunt* formula occurs in Blickling Homily viii, speaking of the riches of past ages:

Ac hwyder gewiton þa welan and þa glengas and þa idlan blissa? Oþþe hwyder gewiton þa mycclan weorod þe him ymb ferdon and stodon? And hwær syndon þa þe hie heredan and him olyhtword sprecan? And hwær com seo frætwodnes heora husa and seo gesomnung þara deorwyrþra gimma oþþe þæt unmæte gestreon goldes and seolfres oþþe eal se wela þe him dæghwamlice gesamnodan ma and ma and nystan ne ne gemdon hwonne hie þæt eall anforlætan sceoldan? Oþþe hwær com heora snyttro and seo orþonce glaunes, and se þe þa gebregdnan domas demde, and seo wlitignes heora ræsta and setla, oþþe se

Hwǣr cwōm symbla ġesetu?   Hwǣr sindon seledrēamas?
Ēalā beorht bune!   Ēalā byrnwiga!
95   Ēalā þēodnes þrym!   Hū sēo þrāg ġewāt,
ġenāp under nihthelm,   swā hēo nō wǣre.
Stondeð nū on lāste   lēofre duguþe
weal wundrum hēah,   wyrmlīcum fāh.
Eorlas fornōman   asca þrýþe,
100   wǣpen wælġīfru,   wyrd sēo mǣre,
ond þās stānhleoþu   stormas cnyssað,
hrīð hrēosende   hrūsan bindeð,
wintres wōma,   þonne won cymeð,
nīpeð nihtscūa,   norþan onsendeð
105   hrēo hæġlfare   hæleþum on andan.
Eall is earfoðliċ   eorþan rīċe;
onwendeð wyrda ġesceaft   weoruld under heofonum.
Hēr bið feoh lǣne,   hēr bið frēond lǣne,
hēr bið mon lǣne,   hēr bið mǣġ lǣne,
110   eal þis eorþan ġesteal   īdel weorþeð.
Swā cwæð snottor on mōde;   ġesæt him sundor æt rūne.²²
Til biþ se þe his trēowe ġehealdeþ;   ne sceal nǣfre his torn tō ryċene
beorn of his brēostum ācýþan,   nemþe hē ǣr þā bōte cunne
eorl mid elne ġefremman.   Wel bið þām þe him āre sēċeð,
115 frōfre tō Fæder on heofonum,   þǣr ūs eal sēo fæstnung stondeð.

manigfealde licetung heora freonda and seo myccle menigo heora þeowa and seo scylfring
heora leohtfata þe him beforan burnon and ealle þa mycclan þreatas þe him mid ferdon
and embþrungon?

But where has the wealth gone, and the adornments and the idle pleasures? Or where
have the great armies gone, which travelled and stood about them? And where are those
who praised them and spoke flattering words to them? And what has become of the
ornamentation of their houses and the collection of valuable gems or the immense treasure of gold and silver or all the wealth of which they daily collected more and more
for themselves and neither knew nor cared when they would have to abandon it all? Or
what has become of their cleverness and their ingenious wisdom, or him who rendered
false judgements, and the beauty of their beds and seats, or the manifold hypocrisies of
their friends and the great company of their servants and the swinging of the lamps that
burned before them and all the great hosts that travelled with them and pressed about
them?

While the prevailing tone of the sermon is scorn for worthless riches, the speaker in *The Wanderer* seems to feel something more akin to regret for the loss of a good thing. One wonders
whether any of the sermon's scorn echoed in the minds of the audience of this poem.

²² Lines 111–15 are hypermetric – that is, they have an expanded rhythmic pattern (see §13.2.3).
Most editions print hypermetric lines as here, set into the left margin.

10   The Dream of the Rood

The Dream of the Rood is a dream-vision in which the cross tells the story of the crucifixion. Here Christ appears as a young hero-king, confident of victory as he rushes to mount the cross. By contrast, the cross itself (now stained with blood, now encrusted with gems in the manner of a reliquary) feels all the agony of crucifixion, and its physical pain is more than matched by the pain of its being forced to kill its young lord.

The text is from the tenth-century Vercelli Book (see textual note, p. 227); a portion of it is also carved in runes on an eighth-century stone cross in Ruthwell, Dumfriesshire. The earliness of the Ruthwell Cross guarantees the earliness of the poem, or at least the part of it that recounts the crucifixion (ll. 1–78).

For the poems of the Vercelli Book, see Krapp and Dobbie [60], vol. 2. Both the Vercelli and the Ruthwell texts have been edited separately, with full notes and glossary, in Swanton [88].

    Hwæt,[1] iċ swefna cyst   secgan wylle,
    hwæt mē ġemǣtte   tō midre nihte
    syðþan reordberend   reste wunedon.
    Þūhte mē þæt iċ ġesāwe   syllicre[2] trēow
5   on lyft lǣdan,[3]   lēohte bewunden,
    bēama beorhtost.   Eall þæt bēacen wæs
    begoten mid golde;   ġimmas stōdon
    fæġere æt foldan scēatum;[4]   swylċe þǣr fife wǣron[5]
    uppe on þām eaxleġespanne. Behēoldon þǣr enġel Dryhtnes ealle

[1]   The interjection *hwæt*, which begins many Old English poems, is often interpreted as a call for attention (and performed as a shout, followed by a long pause). But the word often comes within speeches (as at l. 90 below), where we suppose that the speaker already has the listener's attention. Rather than calling for attention, *hwæt* probably marks what follows as especially significant or signals an upward shift in rhetorical level.

[2]   *Syllicre* may be intensified by the comparative ending (as Modern English often does with the superlative, e.g. 'a most wonderful tree'), or an actual comparison may be implied ('more wonderful [than any other tree]').

[3]   The construction with accusative and infinitive following a verb of perceiving or commanding is discussed in §7.9.1. A strict translation would be 'It seemed to me that I saw [someone] lead a wonderful tree into the air'; a more idiomatic translation would employ the passive voice: 'It seemed to me that I saw a wonderful tree being led into the air.' See also ll. 51–2.

[4]   *Scēatum* has occasioned some difficulty, but there seems little doubt that the plural noun refers to a singular object, the earth's surface (compare l. 37, where the context is a greater help in interpreting the word).

[5]   This line begins the first of several groups of hypermetric verses (for which see §13.2.3). Others are at ll. 20–3, 30–4, 39–49, 59–69, 75 and 133.

10 fæġere þurh forðġesceaft.[6]   Ne wæs ðǣr hūru fracodes[7] ġealga,
    ac hine þǣr behēoldon   hāliġe gāstas,
    men ofer moldan,   ond eall þēos mǣre ġesceaft.
    Sylliċ wæs se siġebēam   ond iċ synnum fāh,
    forwunded mid wommum.   Ġeseah iċ wuldres trēow
15 wǣdum ġeweorðode,   wynnum scīnan,
    ġeġyred mid golde;   ġimmas hæfdon
    bewriġene weorðlīċe   Wealdendes trēow.
    Hwæðre iċ þurh þæt gold   onġytan meahte
    earmra[8] ǣrġewin,   þæt hit ǣrest ongan
20 swǣtan on þā swīðran healfe.[9]   Eall iċ wæs mid sorgum ġedrēfed;
    forht iċ wæs for þǣre fæġran ġesyhðe.   Ġeseah iċ þæt fūse bēacen
    wendan wǣdum ond blēom;   hwīlum hit wæs mid wǣtan bestēmed,
    beswyled mid swātes gange,   hwīlum mid since ġeġyrwed.
    Hwæðre iċ þǣr licgende   lange hwīle
25 behēold hrēowċeariġ   Hǣlendes trēow,
    oð ðæt iċ ġehȳrde   þæt hit hlēoðrode.
    Ongan þā word sprecan   wudu sēlesta:
    'Þæt wæs ġeāra iū   (iċ þæt ġȳta ġeman)
    þæt iċ wæs āhēawen   holtes on ende,
30 āstyred of stefne mīnum.   Ġenāman mē ðǣr strange fēondas,
    ġeworhton[10] him þǣr tō wǣfersȳne,   hēton mē heora wergas hebban.
    Bǣron mē ðǣr beornas on eaxlum   oð ðæt hīe mē on beorg āsetton;
    ġefæstnodon mē þǣr fēondas ġenōge.   Ġeseah iċ þā Frēan mancynnes
    efstan elne myċle   þæt hē mē wolde on ġestīgan.
35 Þǣr iċ þā ne dorste   ofer Dryhtnes word
    būgan oððe berstan,   þā iċ bifian ġeseah
    eorðan sċēatas.   Ealle iċ mihte[11]
    fēondas ġefyllan,   hwæðre iċ fæste stōd.
    Onġyrede hine þā ġeong hæleð   – þæt wæs God ælmihtiġ,
40 strang ond stīðmōd.   Ġestāh hē on ġealgan hēanne,
    mōdiġ on maniġra ġesyhðe,[12]   þā hē wolde mancyn lȳsan.

---

[6]   Lines 9b–10a are puzzling, since one expects the Lord's angels to observe the cross, rather than (as the grammar insists) 'all, fair through eternity' to observe an angel. But the cross may plausibly be described as an angel, especially as its role in this poem is the essentially angelic one of messenger. *Ealle* then refers to the heavenly host, who are observing the cross: 'All who are fair through eternity beheld the Lord's angel there.'

[7]   *fracodes*: of a criminal. The adjective is used as a noun: see §15.2.3.

[8]   *earmra*: of wretched ones. Compare l. 10.

[9]   According to legend, it was Christ's right side that the soldier of John 19:34 pierced with his spear. Notice that it is the cross, not Christ, who is imagined as having received the wound.

[10]   The unexpressed object of *geworhton* is *mē*.

[11]   *mihte*: might have.

[12]   *maniġra ġesyhðe*: the sight of many.

Bifode iċ þā mē se beorn ymbclypte.   Ne dorste iċ hwæðre būgan tō
  eorðan,
feallan tō foldan scēatum,   ac iċ sceolde fæste standan.
Rōd wæs iċ ārǣred.   Āhōf iċ rīcne Cyning,
45 heofona Hlāford,   hyldan mē ne dorste.
Þurhdrifan hī mē mid deorcan næġlum.   On mē syndon þā dolg ġesīene
opene inwidhlemmas.   Ne dorste iċ hira nǣnigum sceððan.
Bysmeredon hīe unc būtū ætgædere.   Eall iċ wæs mid blōde bestēmed,
begoten of þæs guman sīdan   siððan hē hæfde his gāst onsended.
50   Feala iċ on þām beorge   ġebiden hæbbe
wrāðra wyrda.   Ġeseah iċ weruda God
þearle þenian.[13]   Þȳstro hæfdon
bewriġen mid wolcnum   Wealdendes hrǣw,
scīrne scīman;   sceadu forðēode
55   wann under wolcnum.   Wēop eal ġesceaft,
cwīðdon Cyninges fyll.   Crist wæs on rōde.
Hwæðere þǣr fūse   feorran cwōman
tō þām æðelinge;   iċ þæt eall behēold.
Sāre iċ wæs mid sorgum ġedrēfed;   hnāg iċ hwæðre þām secgum tō
  handa,
60   ēaðmōd, elne myċle.   Ġenāmon hīe þǣr ælmihtiġne God,
āhōfon hine of ðām hefian wīte.   Forlēton mē þā hilderincas
standan stēame bedrifenne.   Eall iċ wæs mid strǣlum forwundod.
Ālēdon hīe ðǣr limwēriġne,   ġestōdon him æt his līċes hēafdum;
behēoldon hīe ðǣr heofenes Dryhten,   ond hē hine ðǣr hwīle reste,
65   mēðe æfter ðām miċlan ġewinne.   Ongunnon him[14] þā moldern wyrċan
beornas on banan[15] ġesyhðe.   Curfon hīe ðæt of beorhtan stāne;
ġesetton hīe ðǣron sigora Wealdend.   Ongunnon him þā sorhlēoð galan
earme on þā ǣfentīde.   Þā hīe woldon eft sīðian
mēðe fram þām mǣran þēodne;   reste hē ðǣr mǣte weorode.[16]
70   Hwæðere wē ðǣr grēotende   gōde hwīle
stōdon on staðole   syððan stefn ūp ġewāt
hilderinca.   Hrǣw cōlode
fæġer feorgbold.   Þā ūs man fyllan ongan
ealle tō eorðan.   Þæt wæs eġesliċ wyrd!

---

[13]   Translate 'I saw [someone] severely stretch out the God of hosts' or 'I saw the God of hosts
severely stretched out.' Compare ll. 4–5.
[14]   *Him* in ll. 65 and 67 is probably to be translated 'for him' (that is, for Christ). Some editors
read them as reflexives with *ongunnon*, but this usage is without precedent.
[15]   The killer of Christ is the cross itself.
[16]   'With a small troop', i.e. quite alone. The figure in which one understates the contrary is
called litotes. Here the poet states the contrary of the fact (Christ is not alone, but 'with a troop')
but understates it (Christ is 'with a *small* troop').

75 Bedealf ūs man on dēopan sēaþe;   hwæðre mē þǣr Dryhtnes þeǵnas,
frēondas ġefrūnon,[17]
ġyredon mē   golde ond seolfre.
Nū ðū miht ġehȳran,   hæleð mīn se lēofa,
þæt iċ bealuwara weorc   ġebiden hæbbe,
80   sārra sorga.[18]   Is nū sǣl cumen
þæt mē weorðiað   wīde ond sīde
menn ofer moldan   ond eall þēos mǣre ġesceaft,
ġebiddaþ him tō þyssum bēacne.   On mē bearn Godes
þrōwode hwīle;   for þan iċ þrymfæst nū
85   hlīfiġe under heofenum,   ond iċ hǣlan mæġ
ǣġhwylċne ānra   þāra þe him bið eġesa tō mē.[19]
Iū iċ wæs ġeworden   wīta heardost,
lēodum lāðost,   ǣr þan iċ him līfes weġ
rihtne ġerȳmde   reordberendum.
90   Hwæt, mē þā ġeweorðode   wuldres Ealdor
ofer holtwudu,   heofonrīċes Weard,
swylċe swā[20] hē his mōdor ēac,   Marian sylfe,
ælmihtiġ God   for ealle menn
ġeweorðode   ofer eall wīfa cynn.
95   Nū iċ þē hāte,   hæleð mīn se lēofa,
þæt ðū þās ġesyhðe   secge mannum,
onwrēoh wordum   þæt hit is wuldres bēam
se ðe ælmihtiġ God   on þrōwode
for mancynnes   manegum synnum
100   ond Adomes   ealdġewyrhtum.
Dēað hē þǣr byriġde;   hwæðere eft Dryhten ārās
mid his miċlan mihte   mannum tō helpe.
Hē ðā on heofenas āstāg,   hider eft fundaþ
on þysne middanġeard   mancynn sēċan
105   on dōmdæġe   Dryhten sylfa,
ælmihtiġ God   ond his enġlas mid,[21]
þæt hē þonne wile dēman,   se āh dōmes ġeweald,
ānra ġehwylcum   swā hē him ǣrur hēr
on þyssum lǣnum   līfe ġeearnaþ.

---

[17]   The line is metrically defective, but as the sense is complete it is difficult to guess what is
missing. Therefore most editors do not emend here.
[18]   The first object of *ġebiden* (which can take either an accusative or a genitive object) is accusative *weorc*, the second a genitive phrase, *sārra sorga*. This mixed construction was probably
introduced by a scribe, who perhaps altered accusative *sāra sorga* to a genitive.
[19]   *ǣġhwylċne . . . tō mē*: each of those for whom there is fear of me.
[20]   *swylċe swā*: in the same way as.
[21]   *mid*: with him.

110   Ne mæġ þær æniġ   unforht wesan
         for þām worde   þe se Wealdend cwyð.
         Frīneð hē for þære mæniġe   hwær se man sīe,
         se ðe for Dryhtnes naman   dēaðes wolde
         biteres onbyriġan,   swā hē ær on ðām bēame dyde.
115   Ac hīe þonne forhtiað,   ond fēa þenċaþ
         hwæt hīe tō Criste   cweðan onġinnen.
         Ne þearf ðær þonne æniġ   anforht wesan
         þe him ær in brēostum bereð   bēacna sēlest,
         ac ðurh ðā rōde sceal   rīċe ġesēċan
120   of eorðweġe   æġhwylċ sāwl
         sēo þe mid Wealdende   wunian þenċeð.'
         Ġebæd iċ mē þā tō þan bēame   blīðe mōde,
         elne myċle,   þær iċ āna wæs
         mǣte werede.   Wæs mōdsefa
125   āfȳsed on forðweġe;   feala ealra ġebād
         langunghwīla.²²   Is mē nū līfes hyht
         þæt iċ þone siġebēam   sēċan mōte
         āna oftor   þonne ealle men,
         well weorþian.   Mē is willa tō ðām
130   myċel on mōde,   ond mīn mundbyrd is
         ġeriht tō þære rōde.²³   Nāh iċ rīċra feala
         frēonda on foldan,   ac hīe forð heonon
      ġewiton of worulde drēamum,   sōhton him wuldres Cyning,
         lifiaþ nū on heofenum   mid hēahfædere,
135   wuniaþ on wuldre,   ond iċ wēne mē
         daga ġehwylċe   hwænne mē Dryhtnes rōd
         þe iċ hēr on eorðan   ær scēawode
         on þysson lǣnan   līfe ġefetiġe
         ond mē þonne ġebringe   þær is blis myċel,
140   drēam on heofonum,   þær is Dryhtnes folc
         ġeseted tō symle,   þær is singal blis,
         ond mē þonne āsette   þær iċ syþþan mōt
         wunian on wuldre,   well mid þām hālgum
         drēames brūcan.   Sī mē Dryhten frēond,
145   se ðe hēr on eorþan   ær þrōwode
         on þām ġealgtrēowe   for guman synnum.

---

²² *feala . . . langunghwīla*: I endured many of all times of longing.
²³ *Mundbyrd* is a legal term denoting the guardianship of a person (not just a minor, for nearly
everyone had a *mundbora* or protector), and also the compensation paid to the protector for an
offence committed against his ward. It is frequently used in religious contexts, where it implies a
comparison between the protection of a king or the head of a family and God's protection of the
faithful soul.

Hē ūs onlȳsde   ond ūs līf forġeaf
heofonlicne hām.   Hiht wæs ġenīwad[24]
mid blēdum ond mid blisse   þām þe þǣr bryne þolodan.
150   Se Sunu wæs sigorfæst   on þām sīðfate,
mihtiġ ond spēdiġ   þā hē mid maniġeo cōm,
gāsta weorode,   on Godes rīċe,
Anwealda ælmihtiġ,   enġlum tō blisse
ond eallum ðām hālgum   þām þe on heofonum ǣr
155   wunedon on wuldre   þā heora Wealdend cwōm,
ælmihtiġ God,   þǣr his ēðel wæs.

11   Wulf and Eadwacer

Wulf and Eadwacer is one of the most enigmatic Old English poems, since the story it alludes to is not known to us. It has given rise to many theories, of which perhaps the most widely credited is that the speaker (a woman, as *rēotugu* in l. 10 tells us) is being held prisoner on an island by Eadwacer, while Wulf (her lover or husband) is in exile, perhaps being hunted by the speaker's people. For accounts of the scholarship on the poem, see Klinck [58] and Muir [73].

Lēodum is mīnum[1]   swylċe him mon lāc ġife;
willað hȳ hine āþecgan[2]   ġif hē on þrēat[3] cymeð.
    Unġelīċ is ūs.[4]
Wulf is on īeġe,   iċ on ōþerre.
5   Fæst is þæt ēġlond,   fenne biworpen.
Sindon wælrēowe   weras þǣr on īġe;

---

[24]   The poem ends with a brief account of the Harrowing of Hell, Christ's release of the souls of the righteous from hell between the time of the crucifixion and that of the resurrection. The theme is a popular one in Old English homilies and religious poetry. Here the emphasis is on Christ's triumphal entrance into heaven with a host of souls.

[1]   The possessive adjective is divided from its noun here and in ll. 9 and 13 (see §8.1).

[2]   A weak first-class causative from *þicgan* 'to receive, take, eat, consume'. The literal meaning is 'to serve, feed' with accusative of the person served and dative of the things served, but a figurative meaning 'kill' is also attested.

[3]   The probable meaning of *on þrēat* here and in l. 7 is 'to (upon) a band of men'. A less likely (though still possible) reading would be to take *on þrēat* as an adverbial phrase meaning 'violently'.

[4]   'It is different with us.' There is little practical difference between the usages with adjective and adverb (in l. 8). Perhaps the adjective describes a static state, while the adverb describes a course of events.

willað hȳ hine āþecgan   ġif hē on þrēat cymeð.
Unġelīċe is ūs.
Wulfes iċ mīnes wīdlāstum   wēnum hogode,[5]
10   þonne hit wæs rēniġ weder   ond iċ rēotugu sæt,
þonne mec se beaducāfa[6]   bōgum bileġde,
wæs mē wyn tō þon,   wæs mē hwæþre ēac lāð.[7]
Wulf, mīn Wulf!   wēna mē þīne
sēoce ġedydon,   þīne seldcymas,
15   murnende mōd,   nales metelīste.
Ġehȳrest þū, Ēadwacer?   Uncerne eargne[8] hwelp
bireð wulf[9] tō wuda.
Þæt mon ēaþe tōslīteð   þætte næfre ġesomnad wæs,[10]
uncer ġiedd ġeador.

12   The Wife's Lament

This poem from the Exeter Book is spoken by a woman whose husband has been outlawed because of his involvement in a feud. She followed him into exile, but for unknown reasons her husband's kinsmen schemed to separate them, with the result that she now finds herself living in a remote and desolate place with dark, pagan associations. Here she laments her own emotional torment, but also that of her husband, whom she imagines suffering from cold and loneliness.

Such is the dominant interpretation of *The Wife's Lament*, but the text contains a number of ambiguities, and is in fact a good example of how an editor can steer a reader's interpretation by including or omitting a comma, or placing a sentence break here or there. The edition in Pope and Fulk [75] provides an excellent guide to the various ways in which the poem can be read.

---

[5]   MS. *dogode* is attested nowhere else in Old English; the best solution proposed has been to emend to *hogode*: 'I thought with hope of my Wulf's long journey'.

[6]   Probably Eadwacer, who will be mentioned by name in l. 16.

[7]   The syntax of ll. 9–12 is difficult. *Þonne* in l. 10 may mean 'when' and be subordinated to l. 9, and *þonne* in l. 11 may mean 'when' and be subordinated to l. 12. Or l. 9 may be a complete sentence, with ll. 10 and 11 coordinated, 'when . . . then'. Or ll. 10 and 11 may be 'when' clauses subordinated to l. 12.

[8]   MS. *earne* makes no sense. The only other plausible emendation is to *earmne* 'poor, pitiful'.

[9]   The common noun 'wolf' fits best with the image of a cub being carried off to the wood, but Old English manuscripts make no distinction between proper and common nouns, and it is probable that a pun is intended here. It is unfortunate that modern editorial procedures force us to make distinctions that the poet may not have intended.

[10]   The line echoes Matthew 19:6, *Quod ergo Deus coniunxit, homo non separet*: 'What therefore God hath joined together, let not man put asunder'.

Iċ þis ġiedd wrece   bi mē ful ġeōmorre,[1]
mīnre sylfre sīð.[2]   Iċ þæt secgan mæġ,
hwæt iċ yrmþa ġebād,   siþþan iċ ūp wēox,
nīwes oþþe ealdes,   nō mā þonne nū.

5   Ā iċ wīte wonn   mīnra wræcsīþa.
Ǣrest mīn hlāford ġewāt   heonan of lēodum
ofer ȳþa ġelāc;   hæfde iċ ūhtċeare
hwǣr mīn lēodfruma   londes[3] wǣre.
Ðā iċ mē fēran ġewāt[4]   folgað[5] sēċan,

10   winelēas wræcċa,   for mīnre wēaþearfe,
ongunnon þæt þæs monnes   māgas hycgan
þurh dyrne[6] ġeþōht   þæt hȳ tōdǣlden unc,
þæt wit ġewīdost   in woruldrīċe
lifdon lāðlicost,   ond mec longade.

15   Hēt mec hlāford mīn   herheard niman.[7]
Āhte iċ lēofra[8] lȳt   on þissum londstede,

---

[1]   The feminine dative singular ending of *ġeōmorre* announces unambiguously that the speaker in this poem is a woman.

[2]   Rather than make the possessive pronoun *mīn* agree with masculine accusative singular *sīð*, as one would expect, the poet makes it agree with the feminine genitive singular form of the pronoun *sylf*; so a literal translation of this verse would be 'the plight of my self'. The effect is to emphasize the feminine endings, in case any listener or reader had missed the ending of *ġeōmorre* in the preceding line.

[3]   *londes*: In the land. The genitive sometimes indicates the place where; see also l. 47.

[4]   *iċ mē fēran ġewāt*: I departed journeying; I departed on a journey.

[5]   Presumably the speaker was seeking to perform the 'office' of wife with her *hlāford*, or husband. The terminology used of this marriage is the same as what would be used of the relationship between a thegn and his lord.

[6]   For *dyrnne*, a strong masculine accusative singular. But a double consonant is frequently simplified when it follows another consonant (see Appendix A).

[7]   Editors do not agree on the interpretation of this line. *Herheard* is often glossed 'dwelling in the woods,' but a *herh* (the more standard spelling is *hearh* or *hearg*) is a pagan shrine or sanctuary. Once the word is used of a sacred grove, but the principal attribute of such a grove is not that it is wooded, but rather that it is a place of worship. Some have emended to *hēr eard niman* 'take up residence here'; Pope and Fulk [78] emends to *hēr hīred niman* 'set up a household here.'

This edition retains the manuscript reading *herheard* in its obvious sense; the verse should be translated 'take up residence in a pagan shrine'. That the resulting verse is difficult to interpret does not make the reading wrong, but only means that we do not know enough to interpret it. An arresting parallel is *Beowulf* 3072, where we read that a curse on the dragon's treasure specifies that whoever plunders the hoard should be *hergum ġeheaðerod, hellbendum fæst* 'confined in a pagan shrine, fast in hellish bonds'. Why being 'confined in a pagan shrine' should implicitly be compared to damnation is no longer clear; but what the hoard-robber of *Beowulf* is threatened with resembles the present reality of this poem's speaker.

[8]   This adjective is used as a noun. See §15.2.3 and compare ll. 26, 34 and 53.

holdra frēonda;   for þon is mīn hyġe ġeōmor.

Ðā iċ mē ful ġemæcne   monnan funde—[9]

heardsæliġne,   hyġeġeōmorne,

20   mōd mīþendne,   morþor hycgendne—

blīþe ġebæro   ful oft wit bēotedan

þæt unc ne ġedælde   nemne dēað āna

ōwiht elles.[10]   Eft is þæt onhworfen;

is nū ġeworden[11]   swā hit nō wære

25   frēondscipe uncer.   Sceal iċ feor ġe nēah

mīnes felalēofan   fæhðe drēogan.[12]

Heht mec mon wunian   on wuda bearwe,

under āctrēo   in þām eorðscræfe.

Eald is þes eorðsele;   eal iċ eom oflongad.

30   Sindon dena dimme,   dūna ūphēa,

bitre burgtūnas[13]   brērum beweaxne,

wīċ wynna lēas.   Ful oft mec hēr wrāþe beġeat

fromsīþ frēan.   Frȳnd sind on eorþan

lēofe lifġende,   leġer weardiað,

35   þonne iċ on ūhtan   āna gonge

under āctrēo   ġeond þās eorðscrafu.

Þær iċ sittan mōt   sumorlangne dæġ;

þær iċ wēpan mæġ   mīne wræcsīþas,

earfoþa fela,   for þon iċ æfre ne mæġ

40   þære mōdċeare   mīnre ġerestan,

ne ealles þæs longaþes   þe mec on þissum līfe beġeat.

---

[9]   The first and third person past indicative of *findan* is usually *funde* rather than expected *fand* (though the latter is attested).

[10]   The punctuation of ll. 18–23a is problematic, and editors' decisions about it influence the interpretation of the poem in important ways. At issue is whether the passage speaks of the man who has already been mentioned or introduces a new one, and whether the action described took place before or after the speaker was forced to take up residence in a pagan place. The punctuation adopted here is that of Pope and Fulk [78], the implication of which is that these lines refer to the time when the speaker first found her husband. Though he was already secretly plotting the crime that would bring about his outlawry, the two of them made happy and optimistic vows to each other.

[11]   *Ġeworden* is not in the manuscript. The line is metrically defective without some word in this place, and yet the sense is clear enough; in such a case an unobtrusive emendation like *ġeworden* seems best.

[12]   The speaker probably is forced to endure not her husband's enmity, but rather the consequences of his having become involved in a feud.

[13]   *Burgtūnas* refers figuratively to the surrounding hills. The imagery in this and the following lines dramatizes the speaker's confinement. Here the *burgtūnas* serve not to defend, but rather to imprison her; so too the briars that grow all around and her husband's departure, which 'seizes' her.

Ā scyle ġeong mon   wesan ġeōmormōd,[14]
heard heortan ġeþōht;   swylċe habban sceal
blīþe ġebǣro,   ēac þon[15] brēostċeare,
45   sinsorgna[16] ġedreag.   Sȳ[17] æt him sylfum ġelong[18]
eal his worulde wyn,   sȳ ful wīde fāh
feorres folclondes,[19]   þæt mīn frēond siteð
under stānhliþe   storme behrīmed,
wine wēriġmōd,   wætre beflōwen
50   on drēorsele,   drēogeð[20] se mīn wine[21]
miċle mōdċeare.   Hē ġemon tō oft
wynlicran wīċ.   Wā bið þām þe sceal
of langoþe   lēofes ābīdan.

13   The Husband's Message

This poem is found near the end of the Exeter Book, whose final folios have been badly damaged by fire. Despite the damage to the text, the situation it describes is clear: a husband has had to leave his country and his wife because of a feud; this poem is spoken by the rune staff he sends to his wife pledging his fidelity and asking her to join him. The poem seems to supply a happy ending to the darker narratives implied by *Wulf and Eadwacer* and *The Wife's Lament*.

Damaged places in the text are signalled with square brackets. These gaps are filled in where scholars have offered plausible reconstructions; however, a complete reconstruction of this poem is not possible.

---

[14]   Of the various interpretations offered of this and the following lines (to 45a), the most persuasive is that they are gnomic – a statement of a universal truth. Such gnomic statements are common in Old English poetry: see, for example, *The Wanderer*, ll. 65–77. Subjunctive *scyle* is frequent in such statements, though it should be translated as an indicative.

[15]   *ēac þon*: in addition to that.

[16]   Strong feminine nouns sometimes have weak endings in the genitive plural.

[17]   Translate the two clauses beginning with *sȳ* 'whether . . . or'. The construction survives in 'Jack and the Beanstalk':

> Be he live or be he dead,
> I'll grind his bones to make my bread.

[18]   *æt him sylfum ġelong*: dependent on himself. *Ġelong* agrees with *wyn* in the next line.

[19]   *feorres folclondes*: in a distant nation.

[20]   After the *sȳ* clauses, which speculate about the current condition of the speaker's husband (45b–47a), and a long clause of result (*þæt . . . drēorsele*, 47b–50a) that goes with the second *sȳ* clause, the main clause of this sentence begins here.

[21]   *se mīn wine*: that friend/love of mine.

For full editions of *The Husband's Message*, see Leslie [65] and Klinck [58]. The latter includes facsimiles of the manuscript pages, permitting the reader to visualize the damage to the text.

    Nū iċ onsundran þē   secgan wille
    [. . . . .] trēocyn   iċ tūdre āwēox
    in mec æld[a . . . . . .] sceal
    ellor londes¹ setta[n   . . . .]c
5   sealte strēamas [. . . . .]sse.
    Ful oft iċ on bātes [. . . . .] ġesōhte,
    þǣr mec mondryhten   mīn [onsende
    o]fer hēah hafu; eom nū hēr cumen
    on ċēolþele, ond nū cunnan scealt²
10   hū þū ymb mōdlufun   mīnes frēan
    on hyġe hycge. Iċ ġehātan dear
    þæt þū þǣr tīrfæste   trēowe findest.
    Hwæt, þec þonne biddan hēt³   se þisne bēam āgrōf
    þæt þū sinchroden   sylf ġemunde
15   on ġewitlocan   wordbēotunga
    þe ġit on ǣrdagum   oft ġesprǣcon,
    þenden ġit mōston   on meoduburgum
    eard weardiġan,   ān lond būgan,⁴
    frēondscype fremman. Hine fǣhþo ādrāf
20   of siġeþēode; heht⁵ nū sylfa þē
    lustum lǣran   þæt þū lagu drēfde
    siþþan þū ġehȳrde   on hliþes ōran
    galan ġeōmorne   ġēac on bearwe.
    Ne lǣt þū þec siþþan   sīþes ġetwǣfan,
25   lāde ġelettan   lifġendne monn.⁶
    Onġin mere sēċan,   mǣwes ēþel,
    onsite sǣnacan   þæt þū sūð heonan
    ofer merelāde   monnan findest
    þǣr se þēoden is   þīn on wēnum.⁷

---

¹ *ellor londes*: in another land.
² The unexpressed subject of *scealt* is *þū*.
³ The unexpressed object of *hēt* is *mec* (see §7.9.1).
⁴ *Būgan* is sometimes written for *būan* in late Old English, perhaps signalling that *g* between back vowels had already become [w], as in Middle English.
⁵ The subject of *heht* is *sylfa*; the unexpressed object is *mec*. *Þē* in this line goes with *lǣran* in the next.
⁶ The object of the imperative *lǣt* is *lifġendne monn* (notice the accusative ending of the participle). The object of *getwǣfan* is *þec*: 'hinder you from your journey'.
⁷ *þīn on wēnum*: waiting for you.

30   Ne mæġ him worulde   willa ġelimpan
        māra on ġemyndum,   þæs þe hē mē sæġde,
        þonne inc ġeunne   alwaldend God
        [þæt ġit] ætsomne   siþþan mōtan
        secgum ond ġesīþum   s[inc brytnian]
35   næġlede bēagas.   Hē ġenōh hafað
        fættan goldes,   [feohġestrēona
        þæt hē mi]d elþēode   ēþel healde,[8]
        fæġre foldan   [. . . . .
        . . .]ra hæleþa,   þēah þe hēr mīn wine[9]
40   [. . . . .]
        nȳde ġebæded,   nacan ūt āþrong
        ond on ȳþa ġelagu   [āna] sceolde
        faran on flotweġ,   forðsīþes ġeorn,
        menġan merestrēamas.   Nū se mon hafað
45   wēan oferwunnen;   nis him wilna gād,
        ne mēara ne māðma   ne meododrēama,
        ænġes ofer eorþan   eorlġestrēona,
        þēodnes dohtor,   ġif hē þīn beneah.
        Ofer eald ġebēot   incer twēġa[10]
50   ġehȳre[11] iċ ætsomne   ᚻ.ᚱ[12] ġeador,

---

[8]   The indicative is more frequent than the subjunctive in adjective clauses. The subjunctive *healde* here may indicate that we are to consider the present sentence as continuing the indirect discourse of ll. 30–5.

[9]   Though the text of the clause that begins here is too damaged to be recovered with any certainty, it evidently introduces an allusion to the time when the husband was forced to flee to the land that he now inhabits. We return to the present with *Nū* in l. 44.

[10]   *incer twēġa*: of the two of you.

[11]   The third letter of this word was erased, presumably as the first step in a correction that was never completed. *Gehȳre* is the most plausible of several suggestions that have been made as to the intended reading. This verb introduces a construction like the one discussed in §7.9.1, in which a verb of perceiving is followed by an accusative object and an infinitive expressing what that object is doing. In this case the speaker 'hears' the runes in ll. 50–1 taking a vow (*āþe benemnan*).

[12]   In the Old English runic alphabet (called the *fuþorc* after the first six runes in the sequence) each rune has a name that usually corresponds to an Old English word. In poetic manuscripts runes are sometimes used to represent these words. Here we are to understand that the husband's message to his wife consists of five runes cut on a staff:

ᚻ.   *siġel* 'sun' or *seġl* 'sail'
ᚱ.   *rād* 'road' or 'riding'
�.   usually *ēar* (of uncertain meaning), but here perhaps *eard* 'country', 'land'
ᚹ.   *wyn* 'joy'
ᛗ.   *man* 'man'

A plausible interpretation of these runes (and thus of the husband's message itself) might be 'take the sail-road [ᚻᚱ *seġlrād*] to the land [ᛏ *eard*] where you will find joy [ᚹ *wyn*] with your husband

ᛏ.ᚠ ond ᛗ   āþe benemnan
þæt hē þā wǣre   ond þā winetrēowe
be him lifġendum[13]   lǣstan wolde
þe ġit on ǣrdagum   oft ġesprǣconn.[14]

14   Judith

In this poem the biblical book of Judith (considered canonical by the Catholic Church but not by Protestants) has been recast in an unmistakably Anglo-Saxon mould, and with the characteristic theme that God rewards those who believe and trust in him with victory, glory and wealth.

The missing beginning of the poem presumably followed, in greater or lesser detail, the biblical account in telling how Holofernes, a general of the Assyrian army, has besieged the Judean city of Bethulia, whose leaders are preparing to surrender when Judith, a widow, ventures with a single maidservant to the Assyrian encampment. She pretends to defect and stays with the Assyrians for three days. By the fourth day, Holofernes is inflamed with desire for the beautiful widow, and here our fragment begins.

For an edition with in-depth commentary and glossary, see Griffith [43]. Interested students may wish to consult other treatments of the story by the Anglo-Saxon writers Aldhelm (in Latin, translated by Lapidge and Herren [62], pp. 126–7, and Lapidge and Rosier [63], p. 159) and Ælfric (ed. Assmann [3], pp. 102–16). All who read this poem should also read the biblical book, available in Bibles published under Catholic auspices and also in separate editions of the Old Testament Apocrypha.

twēode

ġifena in ðȳs ġinnan grunde.[1]   Hēo ðār ðā ġearwe funde[2]
mundbyrd æt ðām mǣran Þēodne   þā hēo āhte mǣste þearfe,
hyldo þæs hēhstan Dēman,   þæt hē hīe wið þæs hēhstan brōgan
5   ġefriðode, frymða Waldend.   Hyre ðæs Fæder on roderum

[ᛗ man].' These runes and the message they express constitute the vow of fidelity spoken of in the final lines of the poem: they may have been intended as a riddle for the audience to puzzle out.

[13]   be him lifġendum: while he is living (see §7.9.2).

[14]   A doubled consonant at the end of an inflectional syllable is highly unusual. At the end of the poem, this one (if not a simple error) may be a flourish of sorts.

[1]   The subject of twēode is almost certainly Judith; the verb probably was preceded by the negative adverb ne. Compare ll. 345–6, which echo this passage.

[2]   Notice the rhyme of grunde and funde. Rhyme is frequently used as an ornament in this poem (for example, in ll. 29, 63 and 113).

torhtmōd tīðe ġefremede,   þe³ hēo āhte trumne ġelēafan
ā tō ðām ælmihtigan.⁴   Ġefræġen iċ ðā Hōlofernus
wīnhātan wyrċean ġeorne   ond eallum wundrum þrymliċ
ġirwan ūp swǣsendo.   Tō ðām hēt se gumena baldor
10 ealle ðā yldestan ðeġnas.   Hīe ðæt ofstum miċlum
ræfndon rondwiġġende,   cōmon tō ðām rīcan þēodne
fēran, folces rǣswan.   Þæt wæs þȳ fēorðan dōgore
þæs ðe Iūdith hyne,   glēaw on ġeðonce
ides ælfscīnu,   ǣrest ġesōhte.

.X.

15 Hīe ðā tō ðām symle   sittan ēodon
wlance tō wīnġedrince   ealle his wēaġesīðas,
bealde byrnwiġġende.   Þǣr wǣron bollan stēape
boren æfter benċum ġelōme,   swylċe ēac būnan ond orcas
fulle fletsittendum.⁵   Hīe þæt fǣġe þēgon
20 rōfe rondwiġġende,   þēah ðæs se rīca ne wēnde
eġesful eorla dryhten.   Ðā wearð Hōlofernus,
goldwine gumena   on gytesālum,
hlōh ond hlȳdde,   hlynede ond dynede,
þæt mihten fīra bearn   feorran ġehȳran
25 hū se stīðmōda   styrmde ond ġylede
mōdiġ ond medugāl,   manode ġeneahhe
benċsittende   þæt hī ġebǣrdon wel.
Swā se inwidda   ofer ealne dæġ
dryhtguman sīne   drenċte mid wīne
30 swīðmōd sinces brytta,   oð þæt hīe on swīman lāgon,
oferdrenċte his duguðe ealle   swylċe hīe wǣron dēaðe ġesleġene,
āgotene gōda ġehwylċes.   Swā hēt se gumena aldor
fylġan fletsittendum   oð þæt fīra bearnum
nēalǣhte niht sēo þȳstre.   Hēt ðā nīða ġeblonden⁶
35 þā ēadigan mæġð⁷   ofstum fetiġan
tō his bedreste   bēagum ġehlǣste
hringum ġehrodene.   Hīe hraðe fremedon
anbyhtscealcas   swā him heora ealdor bebēad

³ ðæs . . . þe: for this reason . . . (namely) that. . . .
⁴ The use of adjectives as nouns (see §15.2.3) is especially frequent in this poem, for example
rīċa (l. 20), se stīðmōda (l. 25) and se bealofulla (l. 48).
⁵ The full (cups were borne) to the courtiers.
⁶ nīða ġeblonden: the one corrupted by evil.
⁷ The -þ or dental-stem noun mæġð (see §6.3.4) is attested here in the nominative, accusative
and genitive singular and in the nominative plural; in this poem it always lacks an ending.

byrnwiġena brego,   bearhtme[8] stōpon
40 tō ðām ġysterne   þǣr hīe Iūdithðe
fundon ferhðglēawe,   ond ðā fromlīċe
lindwiġġende   lǣdan ongunnon
þā torhtan mæġð   tō træfe þām hēan,
þǣr se rīca hyne   reste on symbel[9]
45 nihtes inne,[10]   Nerġende lāð
Hōlofernus.   Þǣr wæs eallgylden
flēohnet fæġer   ymbe þæs folctogan
bed āhongen   þæt se bealofulla
mihte wlītan þurh,   wiġena baldor
50 on ǣġhwylċne   þe ðǣrinne cōm
hæleða bearna,   ond on hyne nǣniġ
monna cynnes,   nymðe se mōdiga hwæne
nīðe rōfra[11]   him þe nēar hēte
rinca tō rūne ġegangan.   Hīe ðā on reste ġebrōhton
55 snūde ðā snoteran idese;   ēodon ðā stercedferhðe,
hæleð heora hēarran cȳðan   þæt wæs sēo hāliġe mēowle
ġebrōht on his būrġetelde.   Þā wearð se brēma on mōde
blīðe burga ealdor,   þōhte ðā beorhtan idese
mid wīdle ond mid womme besmītan.   Ne wolde þæt wuldres Dēma
60 ġeðafian þrymmes Hyrde,   ac hē him þæs ðinges ġestȳrde
Dryhten, dugeða Waldend.   Ġewāt ðā se dēofulcunda,
gālferhð gumena * * * ðrēate,[12]
bealofull his beddes nēosan,   þǣr hē sceolde his blǣd forlēosan
ǣdre binnan ānre nihte.   Hæfde ðā his ende ġebidenne
65 on eorðan unswǣslicne,   swylċne hē ǣr æfter worhte[13]
þearlmōd ðēoden gumena   þenden hē on ðysse worulde
wunode under wolcna hrōfe.   Ġefēol ðā wīne swā druncen
se rīċa on his reste middan   swā hē nyste rǣda nānne

---

[8] *bearhtme*: with noise; with revelry (see §4.2.4). This is the same word as *breahtma* in *The Wanderer*, l. 86. Metathesis, the shift of a consonant from one end of a syllable to the other, or the reversal of consonants (see §2.1.2, item 10), is responsible for the difference. Metathesis may cause a shift of *r* when a short vowel is followed by *d, n, s* or *ht*.

[9] *on symbel*: continuously.

[10] Take *inne* with *þǣr* in l. 44: 'wherein'.

[11] *nīðe rōfra*: of those renowned for enmity. This phrase and *rinca* in the next line go with *hwæne* in l. 52: 'any one of those . . .'.

[12] This line is defective in both metre and sense. Probably *gumena* is the beginning of a formula like those of ll. 9 and 32; the remainder of the line may have stated that Holofernes departed from his *ðrēat*.

[13] *swylċne hē ǣr æfter worhte*: such as he had worked for. This adjective clause modifies *ende* in l. 64.

on ġewitlocan.[14] Wiġġend stōpon
70 ūt of ðām inne   ofstum miċlum,
weras wīnsade   þe ðone wǣrlogan,
lāðne lēodhatan,   lǣddon tō bedde
nēhstan sīðe.   Þā wæs Nerġendes
þēowen þrymful,   þearle ġemyndiġ
75 hū hēo þone atolan   ēaðost mihte
ealdre benǣman   ǣr se unsȳfra,
womfull onwōce.   Ġenam ðā wundenlocc
Scyppendes mæġð   scearpne mēċe,
scūrum heardne   ond of sċēaðe ābrǣd
80 swīðran folme.   Ongan ðā sweġles Weard
be naman nemnan   Nerġend ealra
woruldbūendra,   ond þæt word ācwæð:
'Iċ ðē, frymða God   ond frōfre Gǣst,
Bearn Alwaldan,   biddan wylle
85 miltse þīnre   mē þearfendre,
Ðrȳnesse Ðrym.   Þearle ys mē nū ðā
heorte onhǣted   ond hiġe ġeōmor,
swȳðe mid sorgum ġedrēfed.   Forġif mē, sweġles Ealdor,
sigor ond sōðne ġelēafan,   þæt iċ mid þȳs sweorde mōte
90 ġehēawan þysne morðres bryttan.   Ġeunne mē mīnra ġesynta,
þearlmōd Þēoden gumena.   Nāhte iċ þīnre nǣfre
miltse þon māran þearfe.   Ġewrec nū, mihtiġ Dryhten,
torhtmōd tīres Brytta,   þæt mē ys þus torne on mōde
hāte[15] on hreðre mīnum.'   Hī ðā se hēhsta Dēma
95 ǣdre mid elne onbryrde,   swā hē dēð ānra ġehwylċne
hērbūendra   þe hyne him tō helpe sēċeð[16]
mid rǣde ond mid rihte ġelēafan.   Þā wearð hyre rūme on mōde
hāliġre hyht ġenīwod.[17]   Ġenam ðā þone hǣðenan mannan
fæste be feaxe sīnum,   tēah hyne folmum wið hyre weard
100 bysmerlīċe   ond þone bealofullan
listum ālēde   lāðne mannan,
swā hēo ðæs unlǣdan   ēaðost mihte
wel ġewealdan.   Slōh ðā wundenlocc
þone fēondsceaðan   fāgum mēċe,
105 heteþoncolne,   þæt hēo healfne forċearf
þone swēoran him,   þæt hē on swīman læġ,

---

[14] *hē nyste . . . ġewitlocan*: i.e. his senses (or reason) left him.
[15] In translating, the adverbs *torne* and *hāte* may be rendered as adjectives.
[16] *þe hyne him tō helpe sēċeð*: who seeks him as a help for himself.
[17] *hāliġre hyht ġenīwod*: hope renewed for the holy one.

druncen ond dolhwund.   Næs ðā dēad þā ġȳt,
ealles orsāwle;   slōh ðā eornoste
ides ellenrōf   ōðre sīðe
110 þone hǣðenan hund   þæt him þæt hēafod wand
forð on ðā flōre.   Læġ se fūla lēap[18]
gēsne beæftan;   gǣst ellor hwearf
under neowelne næs   ond ðǣr ġenyðerad wæs,
sūsle ġesǣled   syððan ǣfre
115 wyrmum bewunden,   wītum ġebunden,
hearde ġehæfted   in helle bryne
æfter hinsīðe.   Ne ðearf hē hopian nō,
þȳstrum forðylmed,   þæt hē ðonan mōte
of ðām wyrmsele,   ac ðǣr wunian sceal
120 āwa tō aldre[19]   būtan ende forð
in ðām heolstran hām,[20]   hyhtwynna lēas.

.XI.
Hæfde ðā ġefohten   foremǣrne blǣd
Iūdith æt gūðe,   swā hyre God ūðe
sweġles Ealdor,   þe hyre sigores onlēah.
125 Þā sēo snotere mæġð   snūde ġebrōhte
þæs herewǣðan   hēafod swā blōdiġ
on ðām fætelse   þe hyre foregenġa,
blāchlēor ides,   hyra bēġea nest,
ðēawum ġeðungen,   þyder on lǣdde,
130 ond hit þā swā heolfriġ   hyre on hond āġeaf
hiġeðoncolre   hām tō berenne,
Iūdith ġingran sīnre.   Ēodon ðā ġeġnum þanonne
þā idesa bā   ellenþrīste,
oð þæt hīe becōmon   collenferhðe,
135 ēadhrēðiġe mæġð,   ūt of ðām heriġe,
þæt hīe sweotollīċe   ġesēon mihten
þǣre wlitegan byriġ   weallas blīcan,
Bēthūliam.   Hīe ðā bēahhrodene
fēðelāste[21]   forð ōnettan

[18] Literally 'basket'; metaphorically 'the body', commonly thought of as a container for the soul.
[19] *āwa tō aldre*: forever and ever.
[20] The dative of *hām* sometimes lacks an ending. Some such instances are so-called 'endingless locatives' indicating location, as in the common phrase *æt hām* 'at home'. But some are not 'locative' in the usual sense, for example *siþþan hē from his āgnum hām fōr* 'after he journeyed from his own home' (Old English Orosius, ed. Bately [6], 14/21).
[21] *fēðelāste*: along the foot-path.

140   oð hīe glædmōde   ġegān hæfdon
       tō ðām wealgate.   Wiġġend sǣton
       weras wæċċende,   wearde hēoldon
       in ðām fæstenne,   swā ðām folce ǣr
       ġeōmormōdum   Iūdith bebēad
145   searoðoncol mæġð,   þā hēo on sīð ġewāt
       ides ellenrōf.   Wæs ðā eft cumen
       lēof tō lēodum,   ond ðā lungre hēt
       glēawhydiġ wīf   gumena sumne
       of ðǣre ġinnan byriġ   hyre tōġēanes gān
150   ond hī ofostlīċe   in forlǣtan
       þurh ðæs wealles ġeat,   ond þæt word ācwæð
       tō ðām siġefolce: 'Iċ ēow secgan mæġ
       þoncwyrðe þing,   þæt ġē ne þyrfen leng
       murnan on mōde.   Ēow ys Metod blīðe
155   cyninga Wuldor;   þæt ġecȳðed wearð
       ġeond woruld wīde   þæt ēow ys wuldorblǣd
       torhtliċ tōweard   ond tīr ġifeðe
       þāra lǣðða²²   þe ġē lange drugon.'
       Þā wurdon blīðe   burhsittende
160   syððan hī ġehȳrdon   hū sēo hāliġe spræc
       ofer hēanne weall.   Here wæs on lustum.²³
       Wið þæs fæstenġeates   folc ōnette,
       weras wīf somod,   wornum ond hēapum,
       ðrēatum ond ðrymmum   þrungon ond urnon
165   onġēan ðā Þēodnes mæġð   þūsendmǣlum,
       ealde ġe ġeonge.   Æghwylċum wearð
       men on ðǣre medobyriġ   mōd ārēted
       syððan hīe onġēaton   þæt wæs Iūdith cumen
       eft tō ēðle,   ond ðā ofostlīċe
170   hīe mid ēaðmēdum   in forlēton.
       Þā sēo glēawe hēt,   golde ġefrætewod,
       hyre ðīnenne   þancolmōde
       þæs herewǣðan   hēafod onwrīðan
       ond hyt tō bēhðe   blōdiġ ætȳwan
175   þām burhlēodum,   hū hyre æt beaduwe ġespēow.²⁴
       Sprǣc ðā sēo æðele   tō eallum þām folce:
       'Hēr ġē mágon sweotole,   siġerōfe hæleð,

---

²²   The genitive phrase *þāra lǣðða* is governed by *tīr* in l. 157. Read 'as recompense for the injuries'.
²³   *on lustum*: joyfull.
²⁴   Take the *hū* clause with *bēhðe*: 'as a token of how . . .'.

      lēoda rǣswan,   on ðæs lāðestan,
      hǣðenes heaðorinces[25] hēafod starian,
180   Hōlofernus[26] unlyfiġendes,
      þe ūs monna mǣst morðra ġefremede
      sārra sorga, ond þæt swȳðor ġȳt
      ȳċan wolde; ac him ne ūðe God
      lenġran līfes, þæt hē mid lǣððum ūs
185   eġlan mōste. Iċ him ealdor oðþrong
      þurh Godes fultum. Nū iċ gumena ġehwæne
      þyssa burglēoda biddan wylle
      randwiġġendra, þæt ġē recene ēow
      fȳsan tō ġefeohte syððan frymða God,
190   ārfæst Cyning, ēastan sende
      lēohtne lēoman. Berað linde forð,
      bord for brēostum ond byrnhomas,
      scīre helmas in sceaðena ġemong.[27]
      Fyllað folctogan fāgum sweordum
195   fǣġe frumgāras. Fȳnd syndon ēowere
      ġedēmed tō dēaðe, ond ġē dōm āgon
      tīr æt tohtan, swā ēow ġetācnod hafað
      mihtiġ Dryhten þurh mīne hand.'
      Þā wearð snelra werod snūde ġeġearewod
200   cēnra tō campe. Stōpon cynerōfe
      secgas ond ġesīðas, bǣron siġeþūfas,
      fōron tō ġefeohte forð on ġerihte[28]
      hæleð under helmum of ðǣre hāligan byriġ
      on ðæt dæġrēd sylf.[29] Dynedan scildas
205   hlūde hlummon. Þæs se hlanca ġefeah
      wulf in walde ond se wanna hrefn,
      wælġīfre fugel; wiston bēgen
      þæt him ðā þēodguman þōhton tilian
      fylle on fǣgum. Ac him flēah on lāst
210   earn ǣtes ġeorn, ūriġfeðera,
      salowiġpāda sang hildelēoð
      hyrnednebba. Stōpon heaðorincas,
      beornas tō beadowe, bordum beðeahte

---

[25] The mismatch of weak *lāðestan* and strong *hǣðenes* probably indicates that we should take *ðæs lāðestan* and *hǣðenes heaðorinces* as two genitive phrases in apposition.

[26] Latin nominatives ending in *-us* are often used as genitives in Old English, presumably owing to their resemblance to the Old English genitive ending *-es*.

[27] *in sceaðena ġemong*: into the assembly of enemies; among the enemy.

[28] *forð on ġerihte*: directly.

[29] *ðæt dæġrēd sylf*: that very dawn.

hwealfum lindum,   þā ðe hwīle ǣr
215   elðēodiġra   edwit þoledon
hǣðenra hosp.   Him þæt hearde wearð
æt ðām æscplegan   eallum forgolden
Assȳrium,   syððan Ebrēas
under gūðfanum   ġeġān hæfdon
220   tō ðām fyrdwīcum.   Hīe ðā fromlīċe
lēton forð flēogan   flāna scūras,
hildenǣdran   of hornbogan
strǣlas stedehearde.   Styrmdon hlūde
grame gūðfrecan,   gāras sendon
225   in heardra ġemang.³⁰   Hǣleð wǣron yrre,
landbūende   lāðum cynne,³¹
stōpon styrnmōde,   stercedferhðe,
wrehton unsōfte   ealdġenīðlan
medowēriġe.   Mundum brugdon
230   scealcas of sceaðum   scīrmǣled swyrd,
ecgum ġecoste,³²   slōgon eornoste
Assiria   ōretmǣcgas;
nīðhycgende   nānne ne sparedon
þæs herefolces,   hēanne ne rīċne,
235   cwicera manna   þe hīe ofercuman mihton.

.XII.
Swā ðā magoþeġnas   on ðā morgentīd
ēhton elðēoda   ealle þrāge
oð þæt onġēaton   ðā ðe grame wǣron,
ðæs herefolces   hēafodweardas
240   þæt him swyrdġeswing   swīðliċ ēowdon
weras Ebrisce.   Hīe wordum þæt
þām yldestan   ealdorþeġnum
cȳðan ēodon,   wrehton cumbolwigan
ond him forhtlīċe   fǣrspel bodedon,
245   medowērigum   morgencollan,
atolne ecgplegan.   Þā iċ ǣdre³³ ġefræġn
sleġefǣġe hǣleð   slǣpe tōbrēdan

---

³⁰ For the construction *in . . . ġemang*, see l. 193.
³¹ *lāðum cynne*: at the hateful people.
³² The dative *ecgum* vaguely indicates association: 'excellent with respect to their edges'.
³³ The adverb *ǣdre* goes with *tōbrēdan* in the next line rather than with *ġefræġn* here. This is a stylistic flourish that sometimes accompanies the *iċ ġefræġn* formula used by poets at narrative transitions (and already in this poem at l. 7). Compare *Beowulf* l. 2773, *Ðā iċ on hlǣwe ġefræġn hord rēafian* 'I heard that then the hoard in the mound was plundered'.

ond wið þæs bealofullan   būrġeteldes
wēriġferhðe   hwearfum þringan,
250   Hōlofernus.   Hogedon āninga
hyra hlāforde   hilde bodian
ǣr ðon ðe him se eġesa   onufan sǣte
mæġen Ebrēa.   Mynton ealle
þæt se beorna brego   ond sēo beorhte mæġð
255   in ðām wlitegan træfe   wǣron ætsomne,
Iūdith sēo æðele   ond se gālmōda,
eġesfull ond āfor.   Næs ðēah eorla nān
þe ðone wiġġend   āweċċan dorste
oððe ġecunnian   hū ðone cumbolwigan
260   wið ðā hālgan mæġð   hæfde ġeworden,[34]
Metodes mēowlan.   Mæġen nēalǣhte
folc Ebrēa,   fuhton þearle
heardum heoruwǣpnum,   hæfte[35] guldon
hyra fyrnġeflitu,   fāgum swyrdum
265   ealde æfðoncan;   Assȳria wearð
on ðām dæġeweorce   dōm ġeswiðrod,
bælċ forbīġed.   Beornas stōdon
ymbe hyra þēodnes træf   þearle ġebylde,
sweorcendferhðe.[36]   Hī ðā somod ealle
270   ongunnon cohhetan,   ċirman hlūde
ond gristbitian   (gōde orfeorme)
mid tōðon, torn þoliġende.   Þā wæs hyra tīres æt ende,[37]
ēades ond ellendǣda.   Hogedon þā eorlas āweċċan
hyra winedryhten;   him wiht ne spēow.
275   Þā wearð sīð ond late[38]   sum tō ðām arod[39]
þāra beadorinca   þæt hē in þæt būrġeteld
nīðheard nēðde   swā hyne nȳd fordrāf.
Funde ðā on bedde   blācne licgan
his goldġifan   gǣstes ġēsne,
280   līfes belidenne.   Hē þā lungre ġefēoll

---

[34]   hū ðone cumbolwigan . . . ġeworden: how it had turned out for the warrior with the holy maiden.

[35]   A synecdoche, the hilt standing for all the swords of the Hebrews.

[36]   The Assyrians are encouraged to think that Holofernes will awaken and lead them to victory – a false hope. The juxtaposition of ġebylde 'encouraged' and sweorcendferhðe 'gloomy' has troubled editors, some of whom have suggested emending the text. But the problem is more one for critics than for editors, since the sense is clear enough.

[37]   An impersonal construction: 'it was at the end of their glory'. The genitives in the next line are in variation with tīres.

[38]   sīð ond late: finally.

[39]   tō ðām arod: bold enough.

frēoriġ tō foldan,   ongan his feax teran
hrēoh on mōde,   ond his hræġl somod,
ond þæt word ācwæð   tō ðām wiġġendum
þe ðǣr unrōte   ūte wǣron:
285 'Hēr ys ġeswutelod   ūre sylfra[40] forwyrd,
tōweard ġetācnod,   þæt þǣre tīde ys
mid nīðum nēah ġeðrungen[41]   þe wē sculon nȳde losian,
somod æt sæċċe forweorðan.   Hēr lið sweorde ġehēawen,
behēafdod healdend ūre.'   Hī ðā hrēowiġmōde
290 wurpon hyra wǣpen ofdūne,   ġewitan him wēriġferhðe
on flēam sceacan.   Him mon feaht on lāst
mæġenēacen folc   oð se mǣsta dǣl
þæs heriġes læġ   hilde ġesǣġed
on ðām siġewonge,   sweordum ġehēawen
295 wulfum tō willan   ·ond ēac wælġīfrum
fuglum tō frōfre.   Flugon ðā ðe lyfdon,
lāðra lindwerod.   Him on lāste fōr
swēot Ebrēa   sigore ġeweorðod,
dōme ġedȳrsod;   him fēng Dryhten God
300 fæġre on fultum,[42]   Frēa ælmihtiġ.
Hī ðā fromlīċe   fāgum swyrdum
hæleð hiġerōfe   herpað worhton
þurh lāðra ġemong,   linde hēowon,
scildburh scǣron.[43]   Scēotend wǣron
305 gūðe ġegremede   guman Ebrisce;
þeġnas on ðā tīd   þearle ġelyste
gārġewinnes.   Þǣr on grēot ġefēoll
se hȳhsta dǣl   hēafodġerīmes
Assiria   ealdorduguðe,
310 lāðan cynnes.   Lȳthwōn becōm
cwicera tō cȳððe.   Ċirdon cynerōfe
wiġġend on wiðertrod,   wælscel oninnan
rēocende hrǣw.   Rūm wæs tō nimanne
londbūendum[44]   on ðām lāðestan,
315 hyra ealdfēondum   unlyfiġendum
heolfriġ hererēaf,   hyrsta scȳne,

---

[40] ūre sylfra: our very own.
[41] An impersonal construction: 'it has pressed near to the time'.
[42] him fēng . . . on fultum: the Lord God fairly undertook (to provide) help for them.
[43] This 'shield-fortification' is the shield-wall, a formation in which the men stand close enough together to present a wall of shields to the enemy. To 'cut' or 'break' the shield-wall is to create a gap in it so that warriors can attack from behind.
[44] londbūendum: that is, 'for the Hebrews'.

bord ond brādswyrd,   brūne helmas,
dȳre mādmas.   Hæfdon dōmlīċe
on ðām folcstede   fȳnd oferwunnen
320   ēðelweardas,[45]   ealdhettende
swyrdum āswefede.   Hīe on swaðe reston,[46]
þā ðe him tō līfe[47]   lāðost[48] wǣron
cwicera cynna.   Þā sēo cnēoris eall,
mǣġða mǣrost,   ānes mōnðes fyrst,[49]
325   wlanc, wundenlocc,   wǣgon ond lǣddon
tō ðǣre beorhtan byriġ,   Bēthūliam,[50]
helmas ond hupseax,   hāre byrnan,
gūðsceorp gumena   golde ġefrætewod,
mǣrra mādma[51]   þonne mon ǣniġ
330   āsecgan mǣġe   searoþoncelra.
Eal þæt ðā ðēodguman   þrymme ġeēodon,
cēne under cumblum   on compwīġe
þurh Iūdithe   glēawe lāre,
mǣġð mōdiġre.   Hī tō mēde hyre
335   of ðām sīðfate   sylfre brōhton,
eorlas æscrōfe,   Hōlofernes
sweord ond swātiġne helm,   swylċe ēac sīde byrnan
ġerēnode rēadum golde;[52]   ond eal þæt se rinca baldor
swīðmōd sinces āhte   oððe sundoryrfes,
340 bēaga ond beorhtra māðma,   hī þæt þǣre beorhtan idese
āġēafon ġearoþoncolre.   Ealles ðæs Iūdith sæġde
wuldor weroda Dryhtne,   þe hyre weorðmynde ġeaf
mǣrðe on moldan rīċe,   swylċe ēac mēde on heofonum,
sigorlēan in sweġles wuldre,   þæs þe hēo āhte sōðne ġelēafan
345 tō ðām ælmihtigan;   hūru æt þām ende ne twēode

---

[45] The subject in this clause is *ēðelweardas*, and the object is *fȳnd*.

[46] The literal sense of *āswefede* is 'put to sleep' and that of *reston* is 'rested'; the poet employs the common figure of death as a sleep (compare *The Dream of the Rood*, l. 64).

[47] *tō līfe*: while alive.

[48] Plural adjectives are occasionally uninflected in the predicate.

[49] *ānes mōnðes fyrst*: for one month.

[50] *Bēthūliam* with its Latin accusative singular ending is here used as a dative. This happens frequently, presumably because of the resemblance between the Latin accusative and some Old English dative endings.

[51] A partitive genitive is occasionally used without a governing word: read '(a quantity of) more excellent treasures than . . .'.

[52] Gold is frequently described as 'red' in medieval English texts. Many colour words have changed their meanings since Old English and Middle English times, their semantic boundaries moving on the colour spectrum. Probably 'red' then included some portion of what is now the 'yellow' section of the spectrum.

þæs lēanes þe hēo lange ġyrnde.   Ðæs sȳ ðām lēofan Drihtne
wuldor tō wīdan aldre,[53]   þe ġesceōp wind ond lyfte,
roderas ond rūme grundas,   swylċe ēac rēðe strēamas
ond sweġles drēamas,   ðurh his sylfes miltse.

Textual Notes

1   The Fall of Adam and Eve

Manuscript: London, British Library, MS Cotton Claudius B. iv (B). **Other
manuscript:** Oxford, Bodleian Library, MS Laud Misc. 509 (L). B's shelfmark,
'Cotton Claudius B. iv', indicates that it was once part of the library of Sir
Robert Cotton (1571–1631), a notable book collector, where it was the fourth
book on the second shelf of a case topped by a bust of the emperor Claudius.
All of Cotton's other manuscripts are similarly designated. In 1731 the
building that housed Cotton's collection was destroyed by a fire in which
some manuscripts were lost and many damaged. B escaped the fire with little
damage, but several other texts in this anthology, especially 7 and 14, are
from manuscripts that suffered greater damage.
  3 hrepodon] repodon.   15 and hire ofspringe] *from* L; *not in* B.

2   The Life of St Æthelthryth

Manuscript: London, British Library, MS Cotton Julius E. vii. This is the best
manuscript of Ælfric's collection of saints' lives.
  2 hatte] hatta.   11 awryten] awrytan.   26 formolsnodan] formolsnodon.

3   Cynewulf and Cyneheard

Manuscript: Cambridge, Corpus Christi College, MS 173. This is the earliest
manuscript of the *Chronicle*, probably written in the last decade of the ninth
century or at the beginning of the tenth and continued by various hands up to
the late eleventh century.
  16 ryhtfæderencyn] -en- *added in a later hand.*

---

[53]   *tō wīdan aldre*: forever.

4   The Martyrdom of Ælfheah

Manuscript: London, British Library, MS Cotton Tiberius B. i. The manuscript is generally thought to have been written at Abingdon around the middle of the eleventh century.

2 Hæstingas] hæsting.

5   *Sermo Lupi ad Anglos*

Manuscript: London, British Library, MS Cotton Nero A. i (I). **Other manuscript:** Oxford, Bodleian Library, MS Hatton 113 (E). The homily exists in three versions, apparently representing stages of revision by the author himself. Manuscripts I and E are copies of the latest version; I has close connections to Wulfstan himself and may contain notes in his own hand.

4 spæcan] swæcan.   ricsode] riosode.   5 dæghwamlice] dægliwamlice.   9 manna] mana.   13 ende] ænde.   16 bysmor] bysmora.   19 us ungylda] us *not in* I.   20 getrywða] getryða.   21 ne gehadode] ne *not in* I.   27 manegan] mænege I; manegan E.   31 syllað] sylleð.   34 gecnawe] gecnewe.   36 hwylc] wylc.   wæpngewrixl] wæþngewrixl.   43 sæmen] sæmæn.   47 menn] mænn.   49 þurh aðbricas] þur aðbricas.   50 on þa þing] of þa þing.   51 godfyrhte] godfyhte.   62 fordon] fordom.   70 miclan] miclam.

6   The Story of Cædmon

Manuscript: Oxford, Bodleian Library, MS Tanner 10 (T). **Other manuscripts:** Cambridge, Corpus Christi College, MS 41 (B); Oxford, Corpus Christi College, MS 279 (O); Cambridge, University Library, MS Kk. 3, 18 (Ca). T is the oldest manuscript of the Old English Bede, probably written in the first quarter of the tenth century. A manuscript of the later tenth century, London, British Library, MS Cotton Otho B. xi, was badly damaged in the Cotton Library fire of 1731. B, O and Ca all date from the eleventh century.

6 sceoldon] sealde T; sceoldon B.   11 þara endebyrdnes] þære endebyrdnesse T; þara endebyrdnes O.   14 Gode wyrðes] godes wordes T; gode wyrðes B, Ca; gode wyrþes O.   23 þa seolfan] seolfan þa T; ða sylfan his Ca; þa sylfan his O.   31 ne wære] wære T; ne wære B, O.   42 onhylde] ohylde T; onhylde B, O, Ca.

7   Boethius on Fame

Manuscripts: London, British Library, MS Cotton Otho A. vi (C); Oxford, Bodleian Library, MS Bodley 180 (B); Oxford, Bodleian Library, MS Junius 12 (J). C, written in the middle of the tenth century, contains a version that includes verse renderings of the metres. The version in B, written in the twelfth century, includes prose renderings of the metres. J, written in the seventeenth century by Franciscus Junius, contains a collation of C against B and a complete copy of the Old English metres in C.

C was badly damaged in the Cotton Library fire of 1731 (see reading 1); many pages were lost altogether, while most surviving pages suffered some degree of damage. Fortunately, all of the Old English metres had been transcribed in J by Junius, who had also collated the prose sections of C against those of B. Thus the Old English metres can be restored with confidence from Junius's transcript, while the prose can be partially restored from his collation.

The present text is based on C where it is legible. Where C is not available, readings are taken from J wherever possible. Otherwise, readings are from B, but the twelfth-century spellings of that manuscript have been altered to conform to the usage that prevails in C. Such normalizations of the spellings in B are not reported in the textual notes; readers interested in studying the text of the Old English Boethius in detail should consult Sedgefield [80].

5 þissum tolum] þissan tolan C; þissum tolum B.   16 ealre] ealræ C. ðisses] ....s C; þis B.   norðeweardne] norðeweardum C; norðeweardne B. 18 gefaran] geferan J; gefaran B.   hæte] hæto B.   20 cafertun] cauertun C; cafertun B.   21 worulde] woruld C.   cafertun] cauertun J; cafertun B. 25 þioda] þiod C; þeoda B.   40 lenge] lengu C; lenge B.   ge eac ma gif þu wille] ge þeah þu ma wille B.   45 formærra] formæra J; foremærena B. 55 þe] þa C.   61 of] for C; of B.   70 geweorðad] geweorðað J.   74 hi] in J. 82 þissum] þissum worulde C.

8   A Lyric for Advent

Manuscript: Exeter Cathedral MS 3501. This manuscript, generally called 'the Exeter Book', is a large collection of Old English poetry written in the late tenth century and donated to Exeter Cathedral (where it still resides) by Bishop Leofric in 1072. It contains such classics as *The Wanderer*, *The Seafarer* and the Riddles (see Minitext I).

9   The Wanderer

Manuscript: Exeter Cathedral MS 3501.
14 healde] healdne.   22 minne] mīne.   24 waþema] waþena.   28 freondleasne] freondlease.   29 wenian] weman.   53 eft] oft.   59 modsefa] modsefan.   64 weorþan] wearþan.   74 ealre] ealle.   89 deorce] deornce. 102 hrusan] hruse.

10   The Dream of the Rood

Manuscript: Vercelli, Biblioteca Capitolare cxvii. This manuscript, generally known as 'the Vercelli Book', is a late tenth-century manuscript of homilies and poems preserved in the library of Vercelli Cathedral, Italy, where it was perhaps left behind by an Anglo-Saxon on a pilgrimage to Rome.
2 hwæt] hæt.   17 Wealdendes] wealdes.   20 sorgum] surgum.   59 sorgum] *not in MS.*   70 greotende] reotende.   71 stefn] *not in MS.*   91 holtwudu] holmwudu.   117 anforht] unforht.   142 me] he.

11   Wulf and Eadwacer

Manuscript: Exeter Cathedral MS 3501.
9 hogode] dogode.   16 eargne] earne.

12   The Wife's Lament

Manuscript: Exeter Cathedral MS 3501.
20 hycgendne] hycgende.   24 geworden] *not in MS.*   25 Sceal] seal. 37 sittan] sittam.

13   The Husband's Message

Manuscript: Exeter Cathedral MS 3501. The folio containing this poem (123a–b) has sustained fire damage. To see the extent of the damage, consult the facsimile in Klinck [55].
21 læran] læram.   30 gelimpan] *not in MS.*

14 Judith

Manuscript: British Library, MS Cotton Vitellius A. xv. **Other manuscript:** Oxford, Bodleian Library, MS Junius 105. The Cotton manuscript (also known as the Nowell Codex) contains *Beowulf* and several prose tracts in addition to *Judith*. The text of *Judith* has suffered various kinds of damage. First, the beginning of the poem has been missing for as long as the manuscript has been known to modern scholarship. The extent of the missing part cannot now be determined (the section numbers are no guide, for scribes sometimes numbered the sections of several consecutive poems in a single series). Second, the last six lines of the poem were on a leaf that would have contained the beginning of another text. That leaf is now missing, probably removed by an early owner of the manuscript, Sir Robert Cotton (see headnote to reading 1), who disliked fragmentary texts and sometimes mutilated his books to remove them. The missing lines were copied onto the last extant leaf, probably by one of Cotton's ammanuenses. Third, this manuscript was damaged in the Cotton Library fire of 1731, with the result that many letters and words have been lost at the edges of pages. Fortunately, most of the missing matter can be supplied from a seventeenth-century transcript by Franciscus Junius, extant in MS Junius 105.

In the present text, gaps in the Cotton manuscript have been silently supplied from the Junius transcript. Readers who wish to discover how much of the text is missing should consult Krapp and Dobbie [60], vol. 5, in which letters taken from the Junius transcript are printed in italics.

47 ymbe] and ymbe.　85 þearfendre] þearf-fendre (*with line break between the two* fs).　87 heorte] heorte ys.　134 hie] hie hie.　142 heoldon] heoildon (*a botched correction*).　144 Iudith] iudithe.　150 forlætan] forlæton.　165 Þeodnes] þeoðnes.　179 starian] stariað.　194 Fyllað] fyllan.　201 sigeþufas] þufas.　207 wiston] westan.　234 ricne] rice.　247 tobredan] tobredon.　249 werigferhðe] weras ferhðe.　251 hilde] hyldo.　287 nyde] *not in MS.*　297 lindwerod] *only* lindw *visible at damaged edge of page.*　332 on] *abbreviation for* ond.

Glossary

This glossary contains all words that appear in the readings and in the minitexts; it also contains all words mentioned in the book, except those that appear only in glossary-like lists such as those in chapter 14, and all words that appear in the texts that accompany exercises in *Old English Aerobics*. For the sake of compactness, it uses these abbreviations:

acc.	accusative	masc.	masculine
adj.	adjective	neut.	neuter
adv.	adverb	nom.	nominative
anom.	anomalous	num.	number
card.	cardinal	ord.	ordinal
conj.	conjunction	pers.	personal
dat.	dative	pl.	plural
demonst.	demonstrative	poss.	possessive
fem.	feminine	prep.	preposition
gen.	genitive	pret. pres.	preterite-present verb
indef.	indefinite	pron.	pronoun
inst.	instrumental	sg.	singular
interj.	interjection	st. + number	strong verb of class *number*
interrog.	interrogative	wk. + number	weak verb of class *number*

In addition, the sign → is used for cross-references, of which a generous number are given. In alphabetizing, *æ* follows *a*, *þ/ð* follows *t*, and the prefix *ġe-* is ignored; so you must seek (for example) *ġefremman* under *f*.

a → on.

ā. adv. *always, forever.* ā, aa c/11, 12; f/7; 2/26, 31, etc.

abbatissan → abbudisse.

abbud. masc. *abbot.* acc. sg. 4/6.

abbudisse. fem. *abbess.* nom. sg. 2/12, 20; 6/20. acc. sg. abbatissan 4/6. gen. sg. abbudissan 6/1. dat. sg. abbudissan 2/10, 17; 6/15.

ābēad → ābēodan.

ābelgan. st. 3. *anger.* subj. sg. ābelge.

ābēodan. st. 2. *command, relate, present.* past 3sg. ābēad.

āberan. st. 4. *bear, carry.* 3sg. ābirð.

ābīdan. st. 1. *await* (with gen. object). inf. 12/53.

ābirð → āberan.

 āblend. adj. (past part. of āblendan 'blind'). *blind.* dat. pl. āblendum d/2.

āblered. adj. *bare.* masc. dat. sg. ābleredum d/2.

ābregdan. st. 3. *draw, withdraw, free from.* past 3sg. ābrǣd 14/79. past part. ābrogden 7/62.

ābroþen. adj. (past. part. of ābrēoþan). *degenerate, ignoble.* masc. nom. pl. ābroþene 5/50.

ac. conj. *but.* a/2, 4 (2x), 6; b/2, etc.

āc. fem. athematic. *oak.*

ācennan. wk. 1. *bring forth, give birth to, bear.* 1sg. ācenst 1/16. past part. ācenned, ācennede 8/6.

āclǣnsian. wk. 2. *cleanse.* subj. sg. āclǣnsige 2/13.

āctrēow. neut. *oak-tree.* dat. sg. āctrēo 12/28, 36.

ācwæð → ācweþan.

ācwellan. wk. 1. *kill.* past 3sg. ācwealde c/5; 5/26. past pl. ācwealdon.

ācwencan. wk. 1. *extinguish.* inf. 5/8.

ācweþan. st. 5. *say.* 3sg. ācwið 9/91. past 3sg. ācwæð 14/82, 151, 283.

ācwylman. wk. 1. *kill.* past pl. ācwylmdon 4/17.

ācȳþan. wk. 1. *reveal.* inf. 9/113.

ādlig. adj. *sick.* masc. nom. pl. ādlige 2/27.

ādrāf → ādrīfan.

ādrǣdan. st. 7. *be afraid.* past pl. ādrēdon.

ādrǣfan. wk. 1. *drive, exile.* past 3sg. ādrǣfde 3/2. inf. 3/3.

ādrēdon → ādrǣdan.

ādrencan. wk. 1. *flood, drown.* past 3sg. ādrencte.

ādrēogan. st. 2. *perform, commit, endure.* pl. ādrēogað 5/30.

ādrīfan. st. 1. *drive.* past 3sg. ādrāf 13/19. subj. past sg. ādrife b/5. past part. ādrifen.

ādrincan. st. 3. *drown.* past pl. ādruncon.

ādūne. adv. *down.*

ādylegian. wk. 2. *destroy.* past part. ādylegod 2/4.

geaf → gifan.

āfǣran. wk. 1. *frighten.* past part. āfǣred.

āfēdan. wk. 1. *feed.* 3sg. āfēt.

āflīeman. wk. 1. *drive out, expel.* past pl. āflīemdon.

āfor. adj. *bitter, sour, fierce.* masc. nom. sg. 14/257.

āfyllan. 1. wk. 1. *fill.* imp. pl. āfyllað. 2. wk. 1. *fell, kill.* subj. sg. āfylle 5/36, 37.

āfȳsan. wk. 1. *urge, impel.* past part. āfȳsed 10/125.

āgan. pret. pres. *have, possess, own.* 3sg. āh 10/107. pl. āgon 14/196. past 1sg. āhte 12/16. past 3sg. āhte 5/37; 14/3, 6, 339, 344, etc. subj. sg. āge m/2; 9/64. inf. 7/65.

negated. 1sg. nāh 10/131. past 1sg. nāhte 14/91. past 3sg. nāhte c/3. subj. sg. nāge m/2.

āgeaf → āgyfan.

āgēafon → āgyfan.

Agelesþrep. noun. *Agelesthrep.*

āgen. adj. *own.* neut. nom. sg. 8/9. masc. acc. sg. āgenne 3/11; 5/31. neut. acc. sg. d/3; la/4. masc. gen. sg. āgenes. masc. dat. sg. āgenum, āgnum 5/21; 7/34. fem. dat. sg. āgenre. dat. pl. āgenum 5/35.

āgēotan. st. 2. *pour out, spill, drain.* past part. āgoten, āgotene 14/32.

āgifen → āgyfan.

āginnan → onginnan.

āglǣcan. masc. *contender, formidable one.*

āgnum → āgen.

āgon → āgan.

āgoten- → āgēotan.

āgrafan. st. 6. *carve, inscribe.* past 3sg. āgrōf 13/13. past part. āgrafene.

āgyfan. st. 5. *give, deliver, give back.* 1sg. āgyfe ɪ/10. past 3sg. āgeaf 6/19; 14/130. past pl. āgēafon 14/341. past part. āgifen ᴍ/8.

āh → āgan.

āhafen → āhebban.

āhēawan. st. 7. *cut.* past part. āhēawen 2/25; 10/29.

āhebban. st. 6. *raise, lift, exalt.* past 1sg. āhōf 10/44. past 3sg. āhōf 7/49. past pl. āhōfon 10/61. inf. ʙ/5. past part. āhafen ʙ/7.

āhōn. st. 7. *hang.* subj. past sg. āhēnge ᴄ/5. past part. āhongen 14/48.

āhreddan. wk. 1. *rescue.*

ahsode → ascian.

āht. neut. *anything.* nom. sg. āuht 7/35, 46. dat. sg. āhte 5/8.

āhte → āgan.

āhwār. adv. *anywhere.* 5/65.

ālǣdan. wk. 1. *lead.* 1sg. ālǣde.

ālǣtan. st. 7. *give up, leave, allow.* 2sg. ālǣtst.

aldor → ealdor.

aldormon- → ealdorman.

aldre → ealdor.

ālecgan. wk. 1. *lay, put, place, give up, put down, conquer, inflict.* past 3sg. ālēde 14/101. past pl. ālēdon 10/63. past part. ālēd.

ālēfod. adj. *infirm.* masc. nom. pl. ālēfode.

ālicgan. st. 5. *end, diminish.* past part. ālegen 7/36.

alle → eall.

Alwalda. masc. nd-stem. *Almighty.* gen. sg. Alwaldan 14/84.

alwaldend. adj. *omnipotent.* masc. nom. sg. 13/32.

āmānsumian. wk. 2. *excommunicate, curse.* past part. āmānsumod ᴅ/3.

amen. interj. *amen.* 2/31.

an → on.

ān. A. card. num. as noun. *one.* nom. sg. ᴇ/1. gen. sg. ānes.

B. adj. and card. num. *one, a single, the same, a certain, alone.* masc. nom. sg. ān, ōn 5/58; 7/20, 31, 78. fem. nom. sg. 7/16, 21. neut. nom. sg. 7/13. masc. acc. sg. ǣnne ᴄ/1; ʜ/3. neut. acc. sg. 13/18. masc. gen. sg. ānes 14/324. masc. dat. sg. ānum 3/8, 15. fem. dat. sg. ānre 7/17; 14/64. neut. dat. sg. ānum 2/11; 7/56. wk. masc. nom. sg. āna 9/8; 10/123, 128; 12/22, 35, etc.

C. indef. pron. *a, a certain, one.* masc. nom. sg. ʙ/2; 2/7; 3/2; 4/18; 5/30, etc. masc. acc. sg. ānne, ǣnne 3/3; 7/73. masc. gen. sg. ānes 7/26, 49. masc. dat. sg. ānum 2/3; 5/30. fem. acc. sg. āne 2/19; 5/30 (2x). fem. gen. sg. ānre 4/18. neut. nom. sg. 2/12. neut. acc. sg. 2/20. neut. gen. sg. ānes 7/35. neut. dat. sg. ānum. gen. pl. ānra 10/86, 108; 14/95. neut. acc. pl. āne.

D. adv. *only.* 6/4.

anbidian. wk. 2. *await.* past pl. anbidodon.

anbyhtscealc. masc. *functionary, officer.* nom. pl. anbyhtscealcas 14/38.

geancsumod → geangsumian.

and. conj. *and.* and, ond ᴀ/2 (2x), 3 (2x); ʙ/2, etc.

anda. masc. *enmity, anger.* acc. sg. andan 9/105.

andettan. wk. 1. *confess, acknowledge.* subj. sg. andette.

andgiet. neut. *understanding, intellect.* gen. sg. andgietes 7/47.

Andred. noun. *The Weald, Wealden forest.* acc. sg. 3/2.

andswarode → ondswarian.

andswaru. fem. *answer.* acc. sg. andsware 6/11.

andweard. adj. *present.* masc. nom. sg. anweard. dat. pl. ondweardum 6/16. wk. neut. gen. sg. andweardan 7/39.

andweorc. neut. *material.* nom. sg. **and-weorc, ondweorc** 7/3, 4, 6. gen. sg. **and-weorces** 7/2, 9. dat. sg. **andweorce** 7/3.

andwlita. masc. *face.* gen. sg. **andwlitan** 1/19.

andwyrdan. wk. 1. *answer.* past 1sg. **andwyrde.** past 3sg. **andwyrde** 1/2. past pl. **andwyrdon.**

andwyrde. neut. *answer.* dat. sg. 7/56.

anforht. adj. *afraid.* masc. nom. sg. 10/117.

ānforlǣtan. st. 7. *let alone, relinquish.* subj. past sg. **ānforlēte** 6/20.

angēan → **ongēan.**

Angelcynn. neut. *the English.* gen. sg. **Angelcynnes, Angelkynnes** 4/9, 12.

anginn. neut. *beginning.* dat. sg. **anginne** 8/8.

geangsumian. wk. 2. *vex, afflict.* past part. **geancsumod.**

ānhaga. masc. *solitary one.* nom. sg. 9/1.

ānhoga. masc. *solitary thinker.* acc. sg. **ānhogan** 9/40.

āninga. adv. *immediately.* 14/250.

anlīces → **onlīc.**

anscunian. wk. 2. *avoid.* infl. inf. **tō anscunianne** 7/13.

ansund. adj. *whole.* fem. nom. pl. **ansunde** 2/23.

ansȳn. fem. *face, presence, sight.* dat. sg. **ansȳne.**

antecrist. masc. *antichrist.* gen. sg. **ante-cristes** 5/3.

anwald → **onweald.**

anweald- → **onweald.**

anwealda. masc. *ruler.* nom. sg. 10/153.

anweard → **andweard.**

āplantian. wk. 2. *plant.* past part. **āplantod** A/3.

apostata. masc. *apostate.* nom. pl. **apostatan** 5/50.

apostol. masc. *apostle.* gen. pl. **apostola** 6/24.

ār. fem. *honor, favor, grace, mercy, pros-perity.* acc. sg. **āre** 7/38; 9/114. gen. sg. **āre** 9/1.

ārās → **ārīsan.**

ārǣd. adj. (past part. of *ārǣdan*). *resolute.* fem. nom. sg. 9/5.

ārǣfnan. wk. 1. *tolerate.* past part. **ārǣfned.**

ārǣran. wk. 1. *raise.* inf. 2/26. past part. **ārǣred** 10/44.

arc. masc. *ark.* dat. sg. **arce.**

arcebiscop. masc. *archbishop.* nom. sg. **arcebisceop** 4/5. acc. sg. **arcebisceop** 4/6, 8, 11.

āreccan. wk. 1. *tell, expound.* past part. **āreaht** 7/64.

ārētan. wk. 1. *cheer.* past part. **ārēted** 14/167.

ārfæst. adj. *honourable, gracious.* masc. nom. sg. 14/190.

ārfæstness. fem. *honor, virtue, grace.* nom. sg. **ārfæstnyss** 2/13. dat. sg. **ārfæstnisse** 6/1.

āriht. adv. *rightly.* 5/43.

ārīsan. st. 1. *arise.* 3sg. **ārīst.** pl. **ārīsað** A/5. past 3sg. **ārās** 6/6, 14; 10/101. past pl. **ārison.** subj. past sg. **ārise** C/7. inf. C/10; 6/39.

ārlēas. adj. *dishonorable, base, impious.* gen. pl. **ārlēasra.** wk. masc. nom. sg. **ārlēasa.**

arod. adj. *bold.* masc. nom. sg. 14/275. wk. masc. nom. sg. **aroda** 7/75.

gearoþoncol. adj. *ready-witted.* fem. dat. sg. **gearoþoncolre** 14/341.

ārwurþian. wk. 2. *honor.* imp. sg. **ārwurða.**

ārwurþlīce. adv. *reverently.* 2/24.

ārwurþness. fem. *honor, reverence.* dat. sg. **ārwurðnysse** 2/24; 4/19.

āsāh → **āsīgan.**

asca → **æsc.**

Ascanmynster. neut. *Axminster, Devon.* acc. sg. 3/16.

āscēotan. st. 2. *shoot, lance.* inf. 2/14.

ascian. wk. 2. *ask.* past 3sg. **ahsode** 7/53.

geascian. wk. 2. *find out.* past 3sg. **geascode** 3/4.

āscortian. wk. 2. *grow short, elapse.* 3sg. **āscortaþ** 7/42.

āsecgan. wk. 3. *say, tell, express.* inf. 9/11; 14/330.

āsendan. wk. 1. *send.* past 3sg. **āsende** 4/18.

āsettan. wk. 1. *set, place.* past pl. **āsetton** 10/32. subj. sg. **āsette** 10/142.

āsīgan. st. 1. *sink, fall.* past 3sg. **āsāh** 4/18.

āsingan. st. 3. *sing, sing to.* past 3sg. **āsong** 6/19. past part. **āsungen** 7/1.

āsmēagan. wk. 2. *consider, investigate, search.* inf. 5/58. pres. part. **āsmēageanne.** past part. **āsmēade** 4/8.

āsolcenness. fem. *laziness.* acc. sg. **āsolcennesse** 5/63.

āsong → āsingan.

āspryttan. wk. 1. *sprout, bring forth.* 3sg. **āsprȳt** 1/18.

Assȳrias. masc. *Assyrians.* gen. pl. **Assiria, Assȳria** 14/232, 265, 309. dat. pl. **Assȳrium** 14/218.

āstāg → āstīgan.

āstāh → āstīgan.

āstellan. wk. 1. *supply, establish, institute.* past 3sg. **āstealde** 2/31.

āstīgan. st. 1. *climb, ascend.* past 3sg. **āstāg, āstāh** 10/103. subj. past sg. **āstige** c/8.

āstingan. st. 3. *put out.* past pl. **astungon.**

āstyrian. wk. 2. *stir, move, remove, excite, anger.* past part. **āstyred** 4/15; 10/30.

āsungen → āsingan.

āswebban. wk. 1. *put to sleep, kill.* past part. **āswefede** 14/321.

āswerian. st. 6. *swear.* past part. **āsworene** 4/20.

ātēon. st. 2. *draw away.* subj. past sg. **ātuge** 6/26.

ātēorian. wk. 2. *fail, become weary.* pl. **ātēoriað.**

atol. adj. *terrible, hideous, grisly.* masc. acc. sg. **atolne** 14/246. wk. masc. acc. sg. **atolan** 14/75.

ātuge → ātēon.

āþ. masc. *oath.* acc. sg. 5/69. dat. sg. **āþe** 13/51.

āþbryce. masc. *perjury.* acc. pl. **āðbricas** 5/49.

āþecgan. wk. 1. *serve, feed,* fig. *kill.* inf. 11/2, 7.

āþringan. st. 3. *crowd out, push out.* past 3sg. **āþrong** 13/41.

āuht → āht.

āwa. adv. *always, forever.* 14/120.

āwǣgan. wk. 1. *deceive, nullify.* past part. **āwǣgede.**

āweaxan. st. 7. *grow.* past 1sg. **āwēox** 13/2. past part. **āweaxene** F/2.

āweccan. wk. 1. *awaken.* past 3sg. **āwehte** 6/26. inf. 14/258, 273.

āweg → onweg.

āwendan. wk. 1. *change, transform.* subj. sg. **āwende.**

āwēox → āweaxan.

āwierged → āwyrgan.

āwrāt → āwrītan.

āwreccan. wk. 1. *awake.* past 3sg. **āwrehte.**

āwrēon. st. 1. *uncover.* past part. **āwrigene.**

āwrītan. st. 1. *write.* past 3sg. **āwrāt** 5/62. past pl. **āwriton.** inf. 2/1. past part. **āwriten, āwryten** 2/11; 7/37.

āwyrgan. wk. 1. *curse, damn.* past part. **āwierged, āwyrged** 1/14, 17.

ǣ. fem. *law.* acc. sg. A/2. dat. sg. A/2.

æcer. masc. *field.*

ǣdre. A. fem. *vein, artery.* nom. pl. **ǣdran.** B. adv. *forthwith.* 14/64, 95, 246.

ǣfen. neut. *evening.* acc. sg. G/8. dat. sg. **ǣfenne** 6/30.

ǣfenlēoþ. neut. *evening song.*

ǣfentīd. fem. *time of evening.* acc. sg. **ǣfentīde** 10/68.

ǣfest. adj. *pious.* masc. nom. sg. 6/26. neut. acc. pl. **ǣfeste** 6/3. wk. fem. acc. sg. **ǣfestan** 6/4.

ǣfestness. fem. *piety.* dat. sg. **ǣfestnesse, ǣfestnisse** 6/1, 4.

ǣfre. adv. *ever, always.* c/11; 2/8; 5/50; 7/73, 81, etc.

ǣftan. adv. *from behind.* 5/23.

æfter. A. adv. *afterwards, towards* (of purpose or intent). 6/13; 14/65.

B. prep. (usually with dat., sometimes with acc.). *after, on account of, for the sake of, according to, along* (of movement). c/8; I/10; 2/17, 18; 5/5, etc.

æfter þām þe. conj. *after.* H/1.

æfþonca. masc. *insult, grudge, anger.* acc. pl. **æfðoncan** 14/265.

æg. neut. es/os-stem. *egg.*

æghwǣr. adv. *everywhere.* J/88; 5/10, 20, 50; 7/80, etc.

æghwider. adv. *in all directions.* **æghweder** 4/4.

æghwonon. adv. *from everywhere, everywhere.* 7/65.

æghwylc. indef. pron. *every.* masc. acc. sg. **æghwylcne** 10/86; 14/50. masc. dat. sg. **æghwylcan, æghwylcum** 5/13; 14/166. fem. nom. sg. 10/120.

ægþer. indef. pron. *each.* neut. nom. sg. 5/25; 7/40.

ægþer ge. conj. *both* (in construction *ǣġðer ġe . . . ġe* 'both . . . and'. 1/5; 7/24.

ægylde. adj. *without compensation.* masc. nom. sg. 5/36.

Ǣgypta → Egypte.

ælc. A. adj. *each, every,* in pl. *all.* masc. nom. sg. 5/30; 7/9 (2x), 34. masc. gen. sg. **ælces** 7/3. neut. gen. sg. **ælces** 7/15, 70, 76. masc. dat. sg. **ælcum** 7/58. neut. dat. sg. **ælcum, ælcon** 1/1; 7/33 (2x). masc. inst. sg. **ælce.** gen. pl. **ælcra** 5/13.

B. indef. pron. *each, everyone.* masc. nom. sg. 5/23 (2x), 40. fem. nom. sg. 7/25.

ælda → ylde.

ælfscīne. adj. *of elven beauty.* fem. nom. sg. **ælfscīnu** 14/14.

ælmæsriht. neut. *right to receive alms, obligation to bestow alms.* nom. pl. 5/15.

ælmesse. fem. *alms, charity.* acc. pl. **ælmyssan** 2/30.

ælmihtig. adj. *almighty.* masc. nom. sg. 2/4; 6/13; 10/39, 93, 98, etc. masc. acc. sg. **ælmihtigne** c/1; 10/60. masc. dat.

sg. **ælmihtigum** 8/18. wk. masc. nom. sg. **ælmihtiga** 2/4, 8. wk. masc. dat. sg. **ælmihtigan** 14/7, 345.

ælmyssan → ælmesse.

ænde → ende.

ænig. A. adj. *any.* masc. nom. sg. c/11. neut. nom. sg. 5/46. masc. acc. sg. **ænigne** 2/27. fem. acc. sg. **ænige** 5/6, 12, 43. neut. acc. sg. 6/32. masc. dat. sg. **ænigum** 4/7; 5/52. dat. pl. **ænegum** 7/46.

B. indef. pron. *any.* masc. nom. sg. 5/21, 23; 7/73, 82; 10/110, etc. masc. dat. sg. **ængum** 7/72. neut. acc. sg. 5/11. neut. gen. sg. **ænges** 13/47.

ænne → ān.

ǣr. A. adv. *before, formerly, earlier.* B/7; H/4; K/1370; La/7; 2/8, etc. compar. **ǣrur** 10/108. superl. **ǣrest, ǣrost** G/6; J/82, 89; 2/11, 27, etc.

B. prep. *before* (in time). F/6; 5/3, 6, 17, 28, etc.

C. conj. *before.* K/1371; 3/4; 9/64, 69.

ǣr þām. conj. *before.* **ǣr þan** 10/88.

ǣr þām þe. conj. *before.* **ǣr þām þe, ǣr ðon ðe** 14/252.

ærcebiscop. masc. *archbishop.* nom. sg. **ærcebiscep.**

ǣrdæg. masc. *early day, former day.* dat. sg. **ǣrdæge.** dat. pl. **ǣrdagum** 13/16, 54.

ǣrest. adj. *first.* wk. fem. nom. sg. superl. **ǣreste** 6/24.

ǣrgewin. neut. *former strife.* acc. sg. 10/19.

ǣrgōd. adj. *old and good.*

ǣs. neut. *food, bait, carrion.* gen. sg. **ǣses.**

æsc. masc. *ash-tree, ash-wood, spear.* gen. pl. **asca** 9/99.

æscplega. masc. *play of spears, battle.* dat. sg. **æscplegan** 14/217.

æscrōf. adj. *spear-brave, brave in battle.* masc. nom. pl. **æscrōfe** 14/336.

ǣswice. masc. *violation of the law* (?), *adultery* (?). acc. pl. **ǣswicas** 5/48.

æt. A. adv. *near.* 6/7.
    B. prep. (with dat. or acc.). *at, from, by, with respect to.* 2/25; 3/2, 16 (2x); 4/5, etc.

ǣt. masc. *food, meal.* gen. sg. **ǣtes** 14/210. dat. sg. **ǣte.**

ǣt → (ge)etan.

geǣt → (ge)etan.

ætberan. st. 4. *carry* (to a place). past pl. **ætbǣron.**

ǣte → (ge)etan.

ætēowed → ætȳwan.

ætforan. prep. *before, in front of.*

ætgǣdere. adv. *together.* **ætgǣdere, ætgǣdre** 5/60; 6/32; 9/39; 10/48.

æthrīnan. st. 1. *touch.* past 3sg. **æthrān.**

ætlēapan. st. 7. *run away from, escape from.* subj. sg. **ætlēape** 5/36.

ǣton → (ge)etan.

ætsomne. adv. *together.* J/92; 6/29; 13/33, 50.

ǣtt → (ge)etan.

ætȳwan. wk. 1. *show, reveal to.* past 3sg. **ætȳwde.** inf. 14/174. past part. **ætēowed.**

æþel. adj. *noble.* fem. nom. sg. **æþelu** I/5. wk. masc. nom. sg. **æðela, æðele** 7/70. wk. fem. nom. sg. **æðele** 14/176, 256. wk. masc. gen. sg. **æðelan.**

æþeling. masc. *prince, nobleman.* nom. sg. 3/8. acc. sg. 3/3, 5, 10, 15. gen. sg. **æþelinges** I/1; 3/16. dat. sg. **æðelinge** 10/58. gen. pl. **æþelinga** J/89.

ǣwbryce. masc. *adultery.* acc. pl. **ǣwbrycas** 5/48.

æx. fem. *ax.* gen. sg. **æxe** 4/18.

bā → bāgen.

bacan. st. 6. *bake.*

gebād → (ge)bīdan.

baldor. masc. *lord.* nom. sg. 14/9, 49, 338.

bān. neut. *bone.* nom. pl. 7/71. acc. pl. 2/18, 20; 7/74. dat. pl. **bānum** 4/17.

bana. masc. *killer.* acc. sg. **banan** 3/12. gen. sg. **banan** 10/66. gen. pl. **banena.**

bānlēas. adj. *boneless.* wk. neut. acc. sg. **bānlēase** Lb/3.

bāt. masc. *boat.* gen. sg. **bātes** 13/6.

baþian. wk. 2. *bathe.* inf. 2/11 (3x); 9/47.

bæc. neut. *back.*

bæd → biddan.

gebæd → gebiddan.

bǣd- → biddan.

(ge)bǣdan. wk. 1. *impel.* past part. **gebǣded** 13/41.

bælc. masc. *arrogance.* nom. sg. 14/267.

bǣm → bēgen.

gebær → (ge)beran.

gebǣran. wk. 1. *behave.* subj. past sg. **gebǣrdon** 14/27.

gebǣre. neut. (indeclinable in sg.). *conduct, demeanor, gesture, cry.* acc. sg. **gebǣro** 12/44. inst. sg. **gebǣro** 12/21. dat. pl. **gebǣrum** 3/7.

gebǣre → (ge)beran.

bærnan. wk. 1. *burn.* pl. **bærnað** 5/46.

bǣron → (ge)beran.

be. prep. (with dat.). *by, along, about, with, according to.* **be, bi** B/3; F/3; La/1; 2/1, 11, etc.

be sūþan. prep. *to the south of.* 4/2.

be þām þe. conj. *as.* 1/6.

bēacen. neut. *sign.* nom. sg. 10/6. acc. sg. 10/21. dat. sg. **bēacne** 10/83. gen. pl. **bēacna** 10/118.

gebēad → (ge)bēodan.

beadolēoma. masc. *battle-light, sword.*

beadorinc. masc. *warrior.* gen. pl. **beadorinca** 14/276.

beadu. fem. *battle.* dat. sg. **beadowe, beaduwe** 14/175, 213.

beaducāf. adj. *battle-quick, battle-strong, battle-bold.* wk. masc. nom. sg. **beaducāfa** 11/11.

beaduweorc. neut. *work of battle.* gen. pl. **beaduweorca.**

bēag. masc. *ring.* acc. pl. **bēagas** 13/35. gen. pl. **bēaga** 14/340. dat. pl. **bēagum** J/82; 14/36.

bēahhroden. adj. *adorned with rings.* fem. nom. pl. **bēahhrodene** 14/138.

beald. adj. *bold.* masc. nom. pl. **bealde** 14/17.

bealofull. adj. *malicious, wicked.* masc. nom. sg. 14/63. wk. masc. nom. sg. **bealofulla** 14/48. wk. masc. acc. sg. **bealofullan** 14/100. wk. masc. gen. sg. **bealofullan** 14/248.

bealuwaru. fem. *dweller in evil, evil one.* gen. pl. **bealuwara** 10/79.

bēam. masc. *tree, beam, piece of wood, cross.* nom. sg. 10/97. acc. sg. 13/13. dat. sg. **bēame** 10/114, 122. gen. pl. **bēama** 10/6.

Bēamflēot. masc. *Benfleet.* dat. sg. **Bēamflēote.**

bearh → beorgan.

bearhtme → breahtm.

bearn. neut. *child.* nom. sg. м/11; 5/21, 32; 8/23; 10/83, etc. acc. sg. 5/32. dat. sg. **bearne** 5/21. nom. pl. 14/24. gen. pl. **bearna** к/1367; 14/51. dat. pl. **bearnum** 6/13; 14/33.

bearn → beirnan.

bearnmyrþre. fem. *murderer of children.* nom. pl. **bearnmyrðran** 5/56.

Bearrocscīr. fem. *Berkshire.* acc. sg. **Bearrocscīre** 4/2.

bearu. masc. *wood, grove.* dat. sg. **bearwe** ı/6; 12/27; 13/23. nom. pl. **bearwas** ғ/2; к/1363. dat. pl. **bearwum** ғ/3.

beæftan. A. adv. *behind.* 14/112.
  B. prep. (with dat.). *behind.* 3/9, 10.

bebēodan. st. 2. *command, commend.* past 1sg. **bebēad** 1/11, 17. past 3sg. **bebēad, bibēad** 1/3; 6/31; 14/38, 144. past pl. **bebudon** 6/18. pres. part. **bebēodende** 6/44. past part. **beboden** ɢ/9; 6/7, 19; 7/2, 8, etc.

bebod. neut. *command.* acc. sg. н/2.

beboden → bebēodan.

bebudon → bebēodan.

bebyrgan. wk. 1. *bury.* past 3sg. **bebyrgde, bebyrigde** c/5. past pl. **bebyrigdon** 4/19. past part. **bebyrged** 2/16.

bēc → bōc.

becuman. st. 4. *come.* past 3sg. **becōm, becwōm** 6/43; 14/310. past pl. **becōmon** 14/134.

becyrran. wk. 1. *turn, pass by, pervert, betray.* past 3sg. **becyrde** 4/5.

gebed. neut. *prayer.* acc. sg. в/6. acc. pl. **gebedu** 2/11. dat. pl. **gebedum** в/5.

bedǣlan. wk. 1. *deprive, separate, bereave.* past part. **bedǣled, bedǣlde, bidǣled** 5/11; 7/15; 9/20.

bedd. neut. *bed.* acc. sg. **bed** 14/48. gen. sg. **beddes** 14/63. dat. sg. **bedde** 14/72, 278.

gebedde. fem. *bedmate, wife.* acc. sg. **gebeddan** 2/7.

bedealf → bedelfan.

Bedefordscīr. fem. *Bedfordshire.* acc. sg. **Bedefordscīre** 4/2.

bedelfan. st. 3. *bury.* past 3sg. **bedealf** 10/75.

gebedman. masc. athematic. *praying man, cleric.* acc. pl. **gebedmen** 7/4.

bedrēosan. st. 2. *deprive.* past part. **bidrorene** 9/79.

bedrest. fem. *bed.* dat. sg. **bedreste** 14/36.

bedrīfan. st. 1. *drive, assail, cover.* past part. **bedrifen, bedrifenne** 10/62.

beēode → begān.

befæstan. wk. 1. *fasten, entrust.* past part. **befæst** 7/2.

befealdan. st. 7. *fold up, envelop.* past part. **bifealdne** 8/14.

befeallan. st. 7. *fall, befall, deprive of.* subj. sg. **befealle.**

befēran. wk. 1. *overtake.* past 3sg. **befērde.**

beflowen. adj. *surrounded by flowing something* (dat.). masc. nom. sg. **beflōwen** 12/49.

beforan. prep. (with dat. or acc.). *before, in front of.* **beforan, biforan** 9/46.

befrīnan. st. 1. *question.* past 3sg. **befrān.**

begān. anom. verb. *traverse, surround, cultivate, practice, worship.* past 3sg. **beēode** 3/4.

begeat → begytan.

begēaton → begytan.

bēgen. indef. pron. *both.* gen. pl. **bēgea, bēgra** 1/7; 14/128. dat. pl. **bǣm** ȷ/92.

masc. nom. pl. 14/207. fem. nom. pl.
bā 14/133. neut. nom. pl. **bū** J/82.

begēotan. st. 2. *pour over, infuse.* past part.
begoten 10/7, 49.

begytan. st. 5. *acquire, seize.* past 3sg.
begeat 12/32, 41. past pl. **begēaton.**

behātan. st. 7. *promise.* past 1sg. **behēt.**
past 3sg. **behēt** 2/8. past pl. **behēton,**
behētan 4/1, 21; 5/68. subj. past sg.
behēte 2/7. inf. 4/15.

behēafdian. wk. 2. *behead.* past part.
behēafdod 14/289.

behealdan. st. 7. *hold, keep, observe, behold.* past 1sg. **behēold** 10/25, 58. past
pl. **behēoldon** 10/9, 11, 64.

behēt- → behātan.

behofian. wk. 2. *require.* pl. **behofigen**
7/7.

behrēosan. st. 2. *fall upon, cover.* past part.
bihrorene 9/77.

behrīmed. adj. *frost-covered.* masc. nom.
sg. 12/48.

bēhþ. fem. *token, proof.* dat. sg. **bēhðe**
14/174.

behȳdan. wk. 1. *hide.* 1sg. **behȳde** 1/10.
past 3sg. **behȳdde** 1/8.

beirnan. st. 3. *run into, occur to.* past 3sg.
bearn.

belecgan. wk. 1. *surround, afflict.* past 3sg.
bilegde 11/11.

(ge)belgan. st. 3. *enrage.* past part.
gebolgen.

beliden. adj. *deprived* (lit. abandoned by).
masc. acc. sg. **belidenne** 14/280.

belimpan. st. 3. *regard, conduce, happen.*
past pl. **belumpon** 6/4. subj. past pl.
belumpen 6/1.

belūcan. st. 2. *lock.* past part. **belocen**
3/10.

belump- → belimpan.

benam → beniman.

benǣman. wk. 1. *deprive* someone (acc.)
of something (gen. or dat.). inf. 14/76.

benc. fem. *bench.* dat. pl. **bencum** 14/18.

bencsittend. masc. nd-stem. *bench-sitter.*
acc. pl. **bencsittende** 14/27.

beneah → benugan.

benemnan. wk. 1. *declare.* inf. 13/51.

beniman. st. 4. *take, deprive* someone
(acc.) of something (gen.). past 3sg.
benam 3/1. inf. 7/73.

benn. fem. *wound.* nom. pl. **benne** 9/49.

benugan. pret. pres. (with gen. object).
enjoy, have use of, possess. 3sg. **beneah**
13/48.

beodan → (ge)bīdan.

(ge)bēodan. st. 2. *command, proclaim,
offer.* 1sg. **bēode.** pl. **bēodaþ** 5/50.
past 3sg. **gebēad** 3/8, 11. past pl. **budon**
3/13. inf. **bēodon** 4/3. past part.
geboden 3/13.

bēodgenēat. masc. *table-retainer, retainer
who sits at his lord's table.* nom. pl.
bēodgenēatas.

bēon. anom. verb. *be.* 1sg. **eom, bēo** I/1;
1/10; 2/13; 6/37; 12/29, etc. 2sg. **eart,
bist** 1/9, 14, 16, 19; 6/33, etc. 3sg. **is,
bið, byð, ys** A/1, 2 (2x), 3 (2x), etc. pl.
**syndan, bēoð, sindon, synd, sint, syn,
bēo, sind, syndon, synt** A/4 (2x), 5;
E/1, 3, etc. past 1sg. **wæs** 10/62. past
2sg. **wǣre** 1/19; 8/8. past 3sg. **wæs, was**
B/5; F/1, 2, 4; H/1, etc. past pl. **wǣron,
wǣrun, wǣran** F/2 (2x), 3, 4, 6 (2x),
etc. subj. sg. **sīe, sȳ, sī, bēo, bīo** D/3;
I/5; M/1, 2, 7, etc. subj. pl. **sīen, sȳn**
7/14. subj. past sg. **wǣre** B/3; G/6; 1/11;
2/10, 11, etc. subj. past pl. **wǣren** 7/11.
imp. pl. **bēoð.** inf. **bēon, bīon** B/4; J/86;
M/13; 7/30, 34, etc. infl. inf. **tō bēonne.**
negated. 3sg. **nis** K/1361, 1372; 5/47;
6/40; 7/20, etc. past 3sg. **næs** H/4; 5/5;
14/257. subj. past sg. **nǣre** 3/12; 7/53.

bēor. neut. *beer.* gen. sg. **bēores.**

beorg. masc. *mountain, hill.* acc. sg. 10/32.
dat. sg. **beorge** 10/50. dat. pl. **beorgum.**

beorgan. st. 3. *save, spare, deliver, protect,
guard against.* past 3sg. **bearh** 5/21.
subj. sg. **beorgan, beorge** 5/16, 70. inf.
K/1372; 5/54, 60.

beorht. adj. *bright.* fem. nom. sg. 9/94.
masc. acc. pl. **beorhte.** gen. pl. **beorhtra**

14/340. wk. fem. nom. sg. **beorhte** 14/254. wk. fem. acc. sg. **beorhtan** 8/10; 14/58. wk. masc. dat. sg. **beorhtan** 10/66. wk. fem. dat. sg. **beorhtan** 14/326, 340. masc. nom. sg. superl. **beorhtast, beorhtost** 8/1; 10/6.

beorhtnes. fem. *brightness.*

beorn. masc. *man, warrior.* nom. sg. 9/70, 113; 10/42. nom. pl. **beornas** 10/32, 66; 14/213, 267. acc. pl. **beornas.** gen. pl. **beorna** 14/254.

gebēorscipe. masc. lit. *beer-company, banquet.* gen. sg. **gebēorscipes** 6/7. dat. sg. M/8; 6/6, 8.

(ge)bēot. neut. *vow, boast.* acc. sg. **bēot, gebēot** 9/70; 13/49.

bēotian. wk. 2. *vow, boast.* past pl. **bēotedan** 12/21.

bepǣcan. wk. 1. *deceive.* past 3sg. **bepǣhte** 1/13.

beprēwan. wk. 1. *wink.* inf. 7/40.

berād → berīdan.

(ge)beran. st. 4. *bear, carry, bring, give birth to.* 3sg. **bereð, bireð** 10/118; 11/17. past 3sg. **gebær** 8/20. past pl. **bǣron** 2/24; 10/32; 14/201. subj. past sg. **gebǣre** C/3. imp. pl. **berað** 6/34; 14/191. inf. **beran** 2/18. infl. inf. **berenne, tō berenne** G/7; 14/131. past part. **boren** 14/18.

Beranburg. fem. athematic. *Barbury Camp.* dat. sg. **Beranbyrg.**

berīdan. st. 1. *overtake, surround.* past 3sg. **berād** 3/4.

berstan. st. 3. *burst.* inf. 10/36.

berȳpan. wk. 1. *despoil, rob.* past part. **berȳpte** 5/11, 13.

besmītan. st. 1. *soil, defile.* subj. sg. **besmīte.** inf. 14/59.

bestēman. wk. 1. *drench.* past part. **bestēmed** 10/22, 48.

bestrȳpan. wk. 1. *strip.* past part. **bestrȳpte** 5/13.

beswīcan. st. 1. *deceive, betray.* 3sg. **beswīcð** 7/13. subj. sg. **beswīce** 5/25. past part. **beswicene** 5/14.

beswicen. adj. (past part. of *beswīcan*). *deceived.* masc. nom. pl. **beswicene.**

beswicene → beswīcan.

beswyllan. wk. 1. *drench.* past part. **beswyled** 10/23.

besyrwan. wk. 1. *ensnare.* past part. **besyrwde** 5/14.

bet → wel.

bētan. *amend, make amends, atone.*

(ge)bētan. wk. 1. *amend, make amends, atone, pay* (as a fine). past pl. **bēttan** 5/17. subj. sg. **gebēte, bēte** M/3, 5. subj. pl. **bētan** 5/54. inf. **bētan** 5/67.

betǣcan. wk. 1. *commend, deliver.* past 3sg. **betǣhte.** past part. **betǣht** 5/11.

(ge)betǣcan. *commend, deliver.*

beteran → gōd.

betere → gōd.

betonice. fem. *betony.* acc. sg. **betonican.**

betst → wel.

betst → gōd.

betstan → gōd.

betstum → gōd.

betwēonan. prep. *among, between.* 5/69.

betweox. prep. (with dat. or acc.). *among, between.* **betweox, betwux** F/4; 1/14, 15; 2/16; 4/5, etc.

betȳnan. wk. 1. *enclose, close, end, conclude.* past 3sg. **betȳnde** 6/27, 44.

beþeccan. wk. 1. *cover over, protect.* past part. **beþeahte** 8/13; 14/213.

beþencan. wk. 1. (sometimes with refl.). *consider, call to mind.* past pl. **beðōhton.** subj. pl. 5/66. inf. 5/58.

bewāwan. st. 7. *blow upon.* past part. **biwāune** 9/76.

beweaxen. adj. *overgrown.* masc. nom. pl. **beweaxne** 12/31.

beweorpan. st. 3. *surround.* past part. **biworpen** 11/5.

bewestan. prep. *to the west of.*

bewindan. st. 3. *wind about, wrap, grasp.* past pl. **bewundon** 2/24. past part. **bewunden** 2/23, 27; 10/5; 14/115.

bewrēon. st. 1. *cover, hide.* past 1sg.
biwrāh 9/23. past part. **bewrigen,**
bewrigene 10/17, 53.

bewunden → bewindan.

bewundon → bewindan.

bi → be.

bibēad → bebēodan.

gebicgan → (ge)bycgan.

bicgaծ → (ge)bycgan.

(ge)bīdan. st. 1. (with acc. or gen. object).
wait, wait for, experience, endure. 3sg.
gebīdeծ 9/1. past 1sg. **gebād** 10/125;
12/3. past pl. **beodan.** inf. **bīdan, ge-**
bīdan 5/6; 6/41; 9/70. past part. **gebid-**
en, gebidenne 5/6; 10/50, 79; 14/64.

bidǣled → bedǣlan.

biddan. st. 5. *ask, ask for* (with gen.), *pray.*
1sg. **bidde.** 3sg. **bideծ** 8/10. past 2sg.
bǣde D/1. past 3sg. **bæd** 2/9, 16; 6/30.
past pl. **bǣdon** B/5; 6/36. subj. past sg.
bǣde 6/31. inf. F/7; 7/65; 13/13; 14/84,
187, etc.

gebiddan. st. 5. *ask, entreat, pray* (often
with dat. or acc. refl.). pl. **gebiddaþ**
10/83. past 1sg. **gebæd** 10/122. past 3sg.
gebæd 6/42. subj. sg. **gebidde.**

gebiden → (ge)bīdan.

gebidenne → (ge)bīdan.

bideծ → biddan.

bidrorene → bedrēosan.

bīegan. wk. 1. *bend.*

bifealdne → befealdan.

bifian. wk. 2. *tremble, quake.* past 1sg.
bifode 10/42. inf. 10/36.

biforan → beforan.

bigspel → bīspell.

bihrorene → behrēosan.

bilegde → belecgan.

bilewit. adj. *innocent, pure, honest.* fem.
dat. sg. **bilwitre** 6/43.

gebind. neut. *binding, freezing.* acc. sg.
9/24, 57.

(ge)bindan. st. 3. *bind.* 3sg. **bindeծ** 9/102.
pl. **bindaծ, gebindaծ** 9/18, 40. subj.
sg. **binde** 9/13. inf. **bindan.** past part.
gebunden, gebundne F/3; 14/115.

binn. fem. *bin, crib, manger.* dat. sg.
binne.

binnan. prep. (with dat. or acc.). *within,*
in, into. 1/1; 14/64.

bīo → bēon.

bīon → bēon.

bireծ → (ge)beran.

bisceopscīre → biscopscīr.

biscepdōme → biscopdōm.

biscop. masc. *bishop.* nom. sg. **bisceop,**
biscep, biscop 2/7, 10. acc. sg. **bisceop**
4/6, 15, 17. gen. sg. **biscopes.** dat. sg.
bisceope, biscepe. nom. pl. **bisceopas**
4/19. gen. pl. **biscopa** 5/63.

biscopdōm. masc. *bishopric.* dat. sg. **biscep-**
dōme.

biscophād. masc. *bishopric.* dat. sg. **biscop-**
hāde.

biscopscīr. fem. *bishopric.* acc. sg. **bisceop-**
scīre.

bismrode → bysmerian.

bīspell. neut. *example, proverb, story,*
parable. acc. pl. **bigspel.**

bist → bēon.

bītan. st. 1. *bite.*

biter. adj. *bitter, cruel.* masc. gen. sg.
biteres 10/114. masc. nom. pl. **bitre**
12/31.

biծ → bēon.

biwāune → bewāwan.

bīwist. fem. *sustenance.* nom. sg. 7/7. acc.
sg. **bīwiste** 7/6.

biworpen → beweorpan.

biwrāh → bewrēon.

blāc. adj. *bright, pale.* masc. acc. sg. **blācne**
14/278.

blāchlēor. adj. *fair-faced.* fem. nom. sg.
14/128.

bladu → blæd.

blāwung. fem. *blowing.* acc. sg. **blāwunge.**

blǣcern. neut. *lantern.*

blæd. neut. *leaf, blade.* nom. pl. **bladu**
A/3.

blǣd. masc. *blowing, breath, spirit, life,*
glory, prosperity. nom. sg. 9/33. acc. sg.
14/63, 122. dat. pl. **blēdum** 10/149.

blēo. neut. *colour.* gen. sg. **blēos** 2/19. dat. pl. **blēom** 10/22.

(ge)bletsian. wk. 2. *bless.* past 3sg. **bletsode.** past part. **gebletsod.**

bletsung. fem. *blessing.* acc. sg. **bletsunge** B/6.

blīcan. st. 1. *shine.* inf. 14/137.

blind. adj. *blind.* gen. pl. **blindra.** wk. masc. acc. sg. **blindan.**

bliss. fem. *bliss, merriment.* nom. sg. **blis** 4/10; 10/139, 141. acc. sg. **blisse** 4/10. gen. sg. **blisse** 6/6. dat. sg. **blisse** 10/149, 153.

blissian. wk. 2. *rejoice.* inf. F/7. pres. part. **blyssigende** 2/24.

blīþe. A. adj. *happy, friendly.* masc. nom. sg. 6/36; 14/58, 154. neut. acc. sg. 12/44. neut. inst. sg. 10/122; 12/21. masc. nom. pl. 14/159. neut. acc. pl. 6/35. **B.** adv. *joyfully.*

blīþelice. adv. *joyfully.* **blȳðelice** 2/20. compar. **blīþelīcor.**

blīþemōd. adj. *happy, friendly.* masc. nom. sg. 6/37. masc. nom. pl. **blīðemōde** 6/36.

blōd. neut. *blood.* nom. sg. 4/18. dat. sg. **blōde** 10/48.

blōdgyte. masc. *bloodshed.* nom. sg. 5/18.

blōdig. adj. *bloody.* neut. acc. sg. 14/126, 174.

(ge)blondan. st. 7. *blend, corrupt.* past part. **geblonden** 14/34.

blondenfeax. adj. *with mixed hair, gray-haired.*

blyssigende → blissian.

blȳðelice → blīþelice.

bōc. fem. athematic. *book.* nom. sg. **booc** 6/24. acc. sg. 2/8. dat. sg. **bēc** 2/27; 7/16, 17. nom. pl. **bēc** D/3; 2/28, 30; 5/54, 57, etc. gen. pl. **bōca** 6/24; 7/29. dat. pl. **bōcum** 2/31; 7/17.

bōcere. masc. *writer, scholar.* gen. sg. **bōceres.** nom. pl. **bōceras.** acc. pl. **bōceras** 6/1.

boda. masc. *messenger.* nom. pl. **bodan** 5/50.

geboden → (ge)bēodan.

bodian. wk. 2. *announce, proclaim, preach.* 1sg. **bodie.** past 3sg. **bodode** 7/49. past pl. **bodedon** 14/244. inf. 14/251.

bōg. masc. *arm.* dat. pl. **bōgum** 11/11.

bogian. wk. 2. *dwell, inhabit.* inf. **bōgian.**

gebohte → (ge)bycgan.

bolca. masc. *gangway.* acc. sg. **bolcan.**

boldāgend. masc. *possessor of a hall.* dat. pl. **boldāgendum** J/92.

gebolgen → (ge)belgan.

bolla. masc. *bowl, cup.* nom. pl. **bollan** 14/17.

bolster. masc. *cushion.* dat. sg. **bolstre** 6/42.

booc → bōc.

bord. neut. *board, shield.* acc. pl. 14/192, 317. dat. pl. **bordum** 14/213.

boren → (ge)beran.

geboren. adj. *born.*

bōsm. masc. *bosom, breast.* dat. sg. **bōsme** I/6.

bōt. fem. *help, remedy, compensation, atonement, penance.* nom. sg. 5/8. acc. sg. **bōte** 5/5, 6, 7, 57; 9/113, etc. gen. sg. **bōte** 5/13.

brād. adj. *broad.* neut. dat. sg. **brādum** 7/16. fem. nom. pl. **brāde.**

brādswyrd. neut. *broadsword.* acc. pl. 14/317.

bræc → brecan.

brǣcan → brecan.

brǣd. fem. *breadth.*

(ge)brǣdan. 1. wk. 1. *roast.* past part. **gebrǣd. 2.** wk. 1. *spread.* inf. **brǣdan** 9/47. infl. inf. **tō brǣdanne, tō gebrǣdanne** 7/21, 30.

brǣdu. fem. *breadth.*

brēac → brūcan.

breahtm. masc. *noise, revelry.* dat. sg. **bearhtme** 14/39. gen. pl. **breahtma** 9/86.

brecan. st. 5. *break, torment* someone with curiosity (with *fyrwit* as subject), *transgress.* past 3sg. **bræc.** past pl. **brǣcan** 5/17, 67.

bred. neut. *surface, board.* dat. sg. **brede** 7/16.

bregdan. st. 3. *pull, shake, draw* (a sword). past pl. **brugdon** 14/229.

brego. masc. *ruler, lord.* nom. sg. 14/39, 254.

brēme. adj. *famous, glorious.* wk. masc. nom. sg. **brēma** 14/57.

brēmel. masc. *bramble, brier.* acc. pl. **brēmelas** 1/18.

(ge)brengan. wk. 1. *bring.* past 3sg. **brōhte, gebrōhte** 14/125. past pl. **brōhton, gebrōhton** 2/20; 14/54, 335. inf. **brengan, gebrengan** 7/80. past part. **brōht, gebrōht** 4/16; 5/11; 14/57.

brēost. neut. (often pl. with sg. sense). *breast.* dat. sg. **brēoste** 1/14. dat. pl. **brēostum** 9/113; 10/118; 14/192.

brēostcearu. fem. *sorrow in the breast.* acc. sg. **brēostceare** 12/44.

brēostcofa. masc. *breast-chamber.* dat. sg. **brēostcofan** 9/18.

brēr. fem. *briar.* dat. pl. **brērum** 12/31.

Bret. masc. *Briton.* acc. pl. **Brettas, Bryttas.** gen. pl. **Brytta** 5/61, 62. dat. pl. **Bryttan** 5/65.

Bretenlond. neut. *Britain.*

Brettisc. adj. *British.* masc. acc. sg. **Brettiscne.** masc. dat. sg. **Bryttiscum** 3/8.

Bretwēalas. masc. *the British.* dat. pl. **Bretwālum** 3/3.

brēðer → brōþor.

brimfugol. masc. *sea-bird.* acc. pl. **brimfuglas** 9/47.

(ge)bringan. st. 3. *bring, offer.* 3sg. **bringeð, gebringeð** 5/53; 9/54. subj. sg. **gebringe** 10/139. inf. **bringan** 7/10. past part. **brungen** 8/17.

gebrocod. adj. *afflicted.* masc. nom. pl. **gebrocode.**

brōga. masc. *terror.* gen. sg. **brōgan** 14/4.

brōht- → (ge)brengan.

gebrōht- → (ge)brengan.

brōþor. masc. r-stem. (sometimes with neut. ending in pl.). *brother.* nom. sg. **brōðor, brōþur, brōþer** D/1; 3/3; 5/21,

32; 6/1, etc. dat. sg. **brēðer.** nom. pl. **brōðor, brōðru** B/5; 6/37, 39.

gebrōþor. masc. r-stem. (pl., often with neut. ending). *brothers, monks.* nom. pl. **gebrōðra, gebrōðru** B/1; 2/20. acc. pl. **gebrōðra** 2/18.

brūcan. st. 2. (usually with gen. object, sometimes with acc.). *enjoy, use, benefit from, eat.* 2sg. **brȳcst** 1/19. past 2sg. **bruce.** past 3sg. **brēac** 9/44. past pl. **brucon.** subj. past sg. **bruce** 2/7. inf. 7/62; 10/144.

brugdon → bregdan.

brūn. adj. *brown, shiny.* masc. acc. pl. **brūne** 14/317.

brūnfāg. adj. *with shiny ornaments.* masc. acc. sg. **brūnfāgne.**

brungen → (ge)bringan.

bryce. masc. *breaking, violation.* dat. sg. 5/8.

brycg. fem. *bridge.* nom. pl. **brycga.**

brȳcst → brūcan.

brȳd. fem. *bride.* nom. sg. Lb/3.

brȳdbūr. neut. *bridal chamber.* dat. sg. **brȳdbūre.**

brȳdguma. masc. *bridegroom.* acc. sg. **brȳdguman.**

bryne. masc. *fire, burning.* nom. sg. 2/13; 5/18. acc. sg. 5/70; 10/149. dat. sg. 5/8; 14/116.

brytnian. wk. 2. *distribute.* inf. 13/34.

Brytt- → Bret.

brytta. masc. *giver.* nom. sg. 14/30, 93. acc. sg. **bryttan** 9/25; 14/90.

Bryttiscum → Brettisc.

bū → bēgen.

būan. anom. verb. (with strong pres. and past part. and weak past). *inhabit.* inf. **būgan** 13/18.

būc. masc. *vessel, container.* gen. pl. **būca.**

Buccingahāmscīr. fem. *Buckinghamshire.* acc. sg. **Buccingahāmscīre** 4/2.

budon → (ge)bēodan.

bufan. A. adv. *above.* 2/21.

B. prep. (with dat. or acc.). *above.* 2/19, 20.

būgan → būan.

(ge)būgan. st. 2. st. 2. *bow, bend, submit.* past pl. **bugon** 4/21. inf. **būgan, gebūgan** 5/67; 10/36, 42.

būgian. wk. 2. *inhabit, dwell.* pl. **būgiað** 7/21, 22, 24, 29. inf. **gebūgian** 7/18. infl. inf. **tō būgianne** 7/7, 20.

bugon → (ge)būgan.

gebunden → (ge)bindan.

gebundne → (ge)bindan.

bune. fem. *cup.* nom. sg. 9/94. nom. pl. **būnan** 14/18. dat. pl. **bunum** J/82.

būr. masc. *chamber, cottage.* acc. sg. 3/4.

gebūr. masc. *freeholder, farmer.* gen. sg. **gebūres** M/6. dat. sg. **gebūre** M/7.

burg. fem. athematic. *fortified place, fortress, town, city.* acc. sg. **buruh** 4/8. gen. sg. **burge, byrg, byrig** 7/26, 29, 31; 14/137. dat. sg. **byrig** 3/10; 4/7, 10; 14/149, 203, etc. acc. pl. **burga.** gen. pl. **burga** 14/58.

būrgeteld. neut. *tent used as a bedchamber.* acc. sg. 14/276. gen. sg. **būrgeteldes** 14/248. dat. sg. **būrgetelde** 14/57.

burglēoda → burhlēod.

burgtūn. masc. *fortified enclosure.* nom. pl. **burgtūnas** 12/31.

burgwaru. fem. (usually pl.; with collective sense in sg). *populace, town-dwellers.* nom. sg. **buruhwaru** 4/19. gen. pl. **burgwara** 9/86. dat. pl. **burgwarum** 7/75.

burhlēod. masc. *townsperson.* gen. pl. **burglēoda** 14/187. dat. pl. **burhlēodum** 14/175.

burhsittend. masc. nd-stem. *city-dweller.* nom. pl. **burhsittende** 14/159.

buruhwaru → burgwaru.

būtan. A. prep. (with dat. or acc.). *without, except for.* **būtan, būton** F/7; H/4; 2/30; 3/1, 8, etc.

    B. conj. *but, unless, except, except that.* **būton, būtan** D/3; 2/11 (2x); 5/16; 7/2, etc.

būtū. indef. pron. *both.* masc. nom. pl. **būta** 2/30. masc. acc. pl. 10/48.

(ge)bycgan. wk. 1. *buy, redeem.* pl. **bicgað** 5/30. past 3sg. **gebohte** 5/31. inf. **gebicgan, bycgan** J/81.

bydel. masc. *minister, beadle.* gen. pl. **bydela** 5/63.

gebyldan. wk. 1. *embolden, encourage.* past part. **gebylde** 14/268.

byldu. fem. *courage, confidence, arrogance, presumption.* acc. sg. **byldo** 8/10.

byre. masc. *son, young man.*

gebyrede → gebyrian.

byrg → burg.

byrgan. wk. 1. *taste.* past 3sg. **byrigde** 10/101.

byrgen. fem. *grave.* acc. sg. **byrgene** 2/20, 21. dat. sg. **byrgene** 2/18, 26. dat. pl. **byrgenum.**

gebyrian. wk. 2. *happen, pertain to.* pl. **gebyriað** 5/50. past 3sg. **gebyrede** 7/36.

byrig → burg.

byrigde → byrgan.

byrnan. st. 3. *burn.* pres. part. **byrnendum** C/11.

byrne. fem. *corslet.* acc. sg. **byrnan** 14/337. acc. pl. **byrnan** 14/327.

byrnham. masc. *corslet.* acc. pl. **byrnhomas** 14/192.

byrnwiga. masc. *warrior in mail.* nom. sg. 9/94. gen. pl. **byrnwigena** 14/39.

byrnwiggend. masc. nd-stem. *warrior in a mail coat.* nom. pl. **byrnwiggende** 14/17.

byrst. masc. *loss, injury.* nom. sg. 5/16. gen. pl. **byrsta** 5/6.

bysen. fem. *example.* nom. pl. **bysna** 2/31.

bysmer. masc. *disgrace, insult, reproach.* acc. sg. **bysmor** 5/16, 44. dat. sg. **bysmore** 5/40. gen. pl. **bysmara** 5/6.

bysmerian. wk. 2. *revile, mock, put to shame.* past 3sg. **bismrode** 7/49. past pl. **bysmeredon** 10/48.

bysmorlīce. adv. *shamefully, irreverently, contemptuously.* **bysmerlīce, bysmorlīce** 4/17; 14/100.

gebysnung. fem. *example.* dat. pl. **gebysnungum** 2/10.

byð → bēon.

cafertūn. masc. *vestibule, courtyard.* nom. sg. 7/20. acc. sg. 7/21.

cald. A. neut. *cold.* dat. sg. **calde. B.** adj. *cold.* dat. pl. **caldum.**

camb. masc. *comb.*

camp. masc. *battle.* dat. sg. **campe** 14/200.

campstede. masc. *battlefield.*

canōn. masc. *canon.* gen. sg. **canōnes** 6/24.

Cantwaraburh. fem. athematic. *Canterbury.* acc. sg. **Cantwareburuh** 4/5. dat. sg. **Cantwarebyrig** 2/17.

carcern. neut. *prison.* gen. sg. **carcernes.** dat. sg. **carcerne** 7/61.

carlēas. adj. *without cares, reckless.* wk. neut. nom. pl. **carlēasan.**

cāsere. masc. *Caesar, emperor.* nom. sg. н/1.

Caucaseas. masc. *Caucasus Mountains.* nom. pl. 7/29.

cǣg. fem. *key.*

ceaf. neut. *chaff.* dat. sg. **ceafe.**

ceafl. masc. *jaw.* dat. pl. **ceaflum** 5/63.

cealf. neut. es/os-stem. *calf.*

cēap. masc. *commerce, price, merchandise, purchase.* acc. sg. 5/31. dat. sg. **cēape** ɪ/81; 5/30.

cearful. adj. *full of care, miserable.* gen. pl. **cearfulra.**

cearu. fem. *care, sorrow.* nom. sg. **cearo** 9/55. acc. sg. **ceare** 9/9. nom. pl. **ceare.**

gecēas → gecēosan.

ceaster. fem. *fortress, town.* dat. sg. **ceastre.**

cempa. masc. *warrior, soldier.* nom. pl. **cempan.**

cende → cennan.

cēne. adj. *brave.* masc. nom. sg. 7/76. masc. nom. pl. 14/332. gen. pl. **cēnra** 14/200.

cennan. wk. 1. *conceive, give birth to, produce.* past 3sg. **cende.** past part. **cenned.**

Centingas. masc. *the people of Kent.* acc. pl. **Kentingas** 4/2.

cēolþel. neut. *ship-plank, the deck of a ship.* dat. sg. **cēolþele** 13/9.

ceorfan. st. 3. *carve.* past pl. **curfon** 10/66.

ceorl. masc. *peasant, freeman, husband.* gen. sg. **ceorles.** dat. sg. **ceorle** 5/14.

gecēosan. st. 2. *choose, decide.* past 3sg. **gecēas.** past part. **gecoren** 6/16.

cēpeman. masc. athematic. *merchant.* nom. pl. **cēpemen** 7/25.

(ge)cīdan. wk. 1. *quarrel, chide.* subj. pl. **gecīden** м/8. inf. **cīdan.**

gecierran → (ge)cyrran.

gecīgan. wk. 1. *call.* past part. **gecīged.**

cild. neut. *child.* dat. sg. **cilde.** acc. pl. 1/16. dat. pl. **cildum.**

cile. masc. *cold.* dat. sg. 7/18.

cirdon → (ge)cyrran.

cirm → cyrm.

cirman. wk. 1. *cry out.* inf. 14/270.

clāþ. masc. *cloth, clothes* (in pl.). nom. pl. **clāþas** 7/7.

clǣne. A. adj. *clean, chaste, innocent, open* (of land). neut. nom. sg. с/3; 6/22. dat. pl. **clǣnum. B.** adv. *entirely.* 5/11, 13.

clǣnness. fem. *cleanness, chastity.* acc. sg. **clǣnnysse, clǣnnesse** 2/28, 31. dat. sg. **clǣnnysse** 2/4, 29, 31.

clǣnsian. wk. 2. *cleanse.* inf. 5/69.

cleopedon → clipian.

cleopian → clipian.

clif. neut. *cliff.* dat. sg. **clife** ғ/3, 4 (2x).

clipian. wk. 2. *call, cry out.* 3sg. **clypað.** past 3sg. **clipode, clypode** 1/9. past pl. **cleopedon.** imp. sg. **clypa.** inf. **clypian, cleopian** 5/63.

clipiend. masc. *one who calls.* gen. sg. **clipiendes.**

clomm. masc. *bond, fetter.* dat. pl. **clommum.**

clumian. wk. 2. *mumble.* past pl. **clumedan** 5/63.

clyp- → clipian.

clyppan. wk. 1. *embrace, honor, cherish.* subj. sg. **clyppe** 9/42. inf. 6/20.

cnapa. masc. *youth, boy.*

gecnāwan. st. 7. *know, recognise, understand.* subj. sg. **gecnāwe** 5/16, 34. imp. pl. **gecnāwað** 5/1.

cnēoris. fem. *nation.* nom. sg. 14/323.

cnēow. neut. *knee.* dat. sg. **cnēo** La/5; 9/42.

cniht. masc. *young man, boy, warrior.* nom. sg. M/13.

cnyssan. wk. 1. *press, strike, crash against, beat, oppress.* pl. **cnyssað** 9/101.

cnyttan. wk. 1. *bind.* 3sg. **cnyt** 5/41.

cohhetan. wk. 1. *cough.* inf. 14/270.

cōlian. wk. 2. *cool.* past 3sg. **cōlode** 10/72.

collenferþ. adj. *proud, stout-hearted, bold.* masc. nom. sg. 9/71. fem. nom. pl. **collenferhðe** 14/134.

cōlode → cōlian.

cōm- → cuman.

compwīg. neut. *battle.* dat. sg. **compwīge** 14/332.

con → cunnan.

gecoren. adj. (past part. of *ġeċēosan*). *choice, elect, distinguished.* masc. nom. pl. **gecorene** 7/13. dat. pl. **gecorenum** 2/8.

gecoren- → gecēosan.

gecost. adj. *select, tested, excellent.* neut. acc. pl. **gecoste** 14/231.

cradolcild. neut. *child in the cradle, infant.* nom. pl. 5/15.

cræft. masc. *strength, skill, trade, virtue.* nom. sg. 7/9, 72. acc. sg. **cræft, cræftas, cræftes** 7/3 (2x), 5, 10, 47, etc. gen. sg. **cræftes** 7/3. dat. sg. **cræfte** 7/10. nom. pl. **cræftas** 7/9. gen. pl. **cræfta** 7/58. dat. pl. **cræftum** 7/50.

cræftig. adj. *strong, skillful, learned.* masc. nom. sg. 7/76.

crēopan. st. 2. *creep.*

gecringan. st. 3. *fall, die.* past 3sg. **gecrong** 9/79.

Cristen. adj. *Christian.* masc. nom. sg. 2/2. neut. gen. sg. **Cristenes** 5/29. nom. pl. **Cristene** 5/12. gen. pl. **Cristenra** 5/43, 50. wk. masc. nom. pl. **Cristenan** C/12.

Cristendōm. masc. *Christendom.* nom. sg. 4/10. gen. sg. **Cristendōmes** 4/9. dat. sg. **Cristendōme** 5/36.

gecrong → gecringan.

cuǣdon → cweþan.

cucene → cwic.

culfre. fem. *dove.* nom. sg. G/4.

cuman. st. 4. *come.* 3sg. **cymð, cymeð** A/3; C/9, 11; G/5 (2x), etc. pl. **cumað** A/6. past 3sg. **cōm, cwōm, cuōm** B/6; C/2; 1/8; 4/10, 12, etc. past pl. **cōmon, cwōman** 2/30; 4/5; 10/57; 14/11. subj. sg. **cyme** 8/11. subj. past sg. **cōme** B/5; 7/29. imp. sg. **cum.** inf. 7/26. past part. **cumen, cumene** 6/16; 7/13; 10/80; 13/8; 14/146, etc.

cumbol. neut. *standard, banner.* dat. pl. **cumblum** 14/332.

cumbolgehnāst. neut. *clash of banners.* gen. sg. **cumbolgehnāstes.**

cumbolwiga. masc. *warrior.* acc. sg. **cumbolwigan** 14/259. acc. pl. **cumbolwigan** 14/243.

cunnan. pret. pres. *know, know how to, be able to, can.* 1sg. **con** 6/8. past 1sg. **cūðe** 6/8. past pl. **cūþon** 5/43. subj. sg. **cunne** 5/16, 34, 38; 9/69, 71, etc. inf. 13/9. past part. **cūþ.**

(ge)cunnian. wk. 2. *find out, investigate, experience.* 3sg. **cunnað** 9/29. inf. **gecunnian** 14/259.

cuōm → cuman.

curfon → ceorfan.

cūþ. adj. (past part. of *cunnan*). *known, familiar.* neut. acc. sg. **cūþe** La/5. gen. pl. **cūðra** 9/55.

cūþ- → cunnan.

cwalu. fem. *killing.* nom. sg. 5/19.

cwǣd- → cweþan.

cwǣð → cweþan.

cweartern. neut. *prison.* dat. sg. **cwearterne.**

cweccan. wk. 1. *shake.*

gecweden → cweþan.

cwelan. st. 4. *die.* 3sg. cwelð. pl. cwelað.

cwellan. wk. 1. *kill.*

cwellere. masc. *executioner.* nom. pl. cwelleras.

gecwēman. wk. 1. (with gen. object). *please, be obedient to.* past pl. gecwēmdon c/12.

cwēn. fem. *queen.* nom. sg. ı/3; 2/17. acc. sg. cwēne ȷ/81. gen. sg. cwēne. dat. sg. cwēne.

cwene. fem. *woman, wife.* acc. sg. cwenan 5/30, 40.

cweþan. st. 5. *say, call.* 3sg. cwyð 10/111. past 1sg. cwæð 7/72. past 3sg. cwæð G/2; 1/1, 4, 9, 10, etc. past pl. cwǣdon, cuǣdon, cwǣdan 2/14; 3/12, 13, 14; 5/49, etc. imp. sg. cweð. inf. 7/54; 10/116. infl. inf. tō cweþenne 5/15, 56. pres. part. cweþende. past part. gecweden.

cwic. adj. *alive.* masc. acc. sg. cucene. gen. pl. cwicera, cwicra 9/9; 14/235, 311, 323.

cwiddung. fem. *saying, report.* dat. sg. cwiddunge 7/47.

cwide. masc. *saying.*

cwidegiedd. neut. *speech, song.* gen. pl. cwidegiedda 9/55.

cwīþan. st. 1. *lament, bewail.* past pl. cwīðdon 10/56. inf. 9/9.

cwōm → cuman.

cwōman → cuman.

cwyldrōf. adj. *slaughter-bold, bold in battle.*

cwyð → cweþan.

cȳdde → (ge)cȳþan.

cyme. masc. *coming, advent.* dat. sg. 6/24.

cyme → cuman.

cymeð → cuman.

cymð → cuman.

gecynd. neut. *origin, kind, species, nature, character.* gen. sg. gecyndes. dat. sg. gecynde 7/13.

cynerōf. adj. *noble and renowned.* masc. nom. pl. cynerōfe 14/200, 311.

cyning. masc. *king.* nom. sg. cyning, cynincg ȷ/81; 2/2, 7, 10; 3/5, etc. acc. sg. cyning, cynincg 2/9; 3/4, 6, 17; 10/44, etc. gen. sg. cyninges, cynges, cynincges ı/3; ᴍ/1, 2; 2/5; 3/7, etc. dat. sg. cyninge, cynge, cynincge, kyninge 2/5; 3/4, 13, 14; 4/21, etc. nom. pl. cyningas. gen. pl. cyninga 14/155.

cynn. neut. *kind, species, family, people, nation.* acc. sg. ᴅ/2, 3; 10/94. gen. sg. cynnes 14/52, 310. dat. sg. cynne 14/226. gen. pl. cynna 14/323.

cynnbān. neut. *chin bone, jawbone.* dat. sg. cynnbāne 2/12.

gecyrde → (ge)cyrran.

cyrice. fem. *church.* dat. sg. cyrcan 2/18, 24.

cyrichata. masc. *persecutor of the Church.* nom. pl. cyrichatan 5/50.

cyrm. masc. *uproar.* nom. sg. cirm, cyrm.

(ge)cyrran. wk. 1. *turn, change, return, turn back, go.* past 3sg. gecyrde. past pl. cirdon 14/311. inf. gecierran.

cyssan. wk. 1. *kiss.* subj. sg. cysse 9/42.

cyst. 1. fem. *chest, coffin.* nom. sg. 2/27. dat. sg. cyste 2/16, 22. 2. fem. *choicest, best.* acc. sg. 10/1.

(ge)cȳþan. wk. 1. *make known, perform, practise.* 3sg. cȳð G/1. pl. cȳðaþ 2/5. past 3sg. cȳðde, cȳdde 2/2; 6/15; 7/29, 50. past pl. cȳþdon 3/11. inf. cȳðan 7/3, 5; 14/56, 243. past part. gecȳðed 14/155.

cȳþþ. fem. *kinship, family, homeland.* acc. sg. cȳþþe. dat. sg. cȳððe 14/311.

gedafenian. wk. 2. *befit.* 3sg. gedafenað. past 3sg. gedeofanade 6/4.

dag- → dæg.

gedāl. neut. *separation.* dat. sg. gedāle 7/59.

datarum. masc. (Latin gen. pl. used as dat. sg.). *date.* dat. sg. 4/13.

dǣd. fem. *deed.* gen. sg. dǣde 5/23, 47. nom. pl. dǣda 5/32. acc. pl. dǣda 5/65; 7/36, 37. gen. pl. dǣda 6/26. dat. pl. dǣdum 3/1.

dæg. masc. *day.* acc. sg. A/5; C/9; 1/8; 2/26; 12/37, etc. gen. sg. **dæges.** dat. sg. **dæge** 1/5; 2/16; 6/24. inst. sg. **dæge** B/1. acc. pl. **dagas.** gen. pl. **daga** 3/18 (2x); 10/136. dat. pl. **dagum** 1/14, 17; 2/8 (2x); 6/28, etc.

dæges. adv. *by day.* A/2.

dægeweorc. neut. *day's work.* dat. sg. **dægeweorce** 14/266.

dæghwāmlīce. adv. *every day.* 5/5, 45.

dægrǽd. neut. *dawn.* acc. sg. **dægrǽd, dægrēd** 14/204.

dǽl. masc. *part, share.* nom. sg. 14/292, 308. acc. sg. 2/27; 7/18, 23; 9/65. gen. sg. **dǽles** 7/18. dat. sg. **dǽle** 5/52, 67; 7/19, 22.

gedǽlan. wk. 1. *divide, share, distribute, dispense, part.* pl. **gedǽlað.** past 3sg. **gedǽlde** 9/83. subj. past sg. **gedǽlde** 12/22.

dēad. adj. *dead.* masc. nom. sg. 14/107. masc. nom. pl. **dēade** C/10; 1/4.

dēaf. adj. *deaf.*

dear → durran.

dēaþ. masc. *death.* nom. sg. 7/70, 82 (2x); 12/22. acc. sg. 10/101. gen. sg. **dēaþes** 8/15; 10/113. dat. sg. **dēaðe** C/5, 7, 10; 7/57; 9/83, etc. inst. sg. **dēaðe** 6/43.

dēawigfeþere. adj. *dewy-feathered.*

dehter → dohtor.

dēma. masc. *judge.* nom. sg. 14/59, 94. gen. sg. **dēman** 14/4.

(ge)dēman. wk. 1. *judge, condemn.* inf. **dēman** 10/107. past part. **gedēmed** 6/6; 14/196.

Denisc. adj. *Danish.* neut. acc. sg. D/2. wk. masc. nom. pl. **Deniscan.**

denu. fem. *valley.* nom. pl. **dena** 12/30.

gedeofanade → gedafenian.

dēofol. masc. (often neut. in pl.). *devil, demon.* nom. sg. 5/4. gen. sg. **dēofles.** nom. pl. **dēoflu.** dat. pl. **dēoflum** C/11.

dēofulcund. adj. *diabolical.* wk. masc. nom. sg. **dēofulcunda** 14/61.

dēop. adj. *deep.* wk. masc. dat. sg. **dēopan** 10/75.

dēope. adv. *deeply.* 9/89.

dēor. neut. *animal.*

deorc. adj. *dark.* neut. acc. sg. **deorce** 9/89. neut. acc. pl. 8/15. dat. pl. **deorcan** 10/46.

dēore. adv. *dearly.* 5/31.

gedeorfan. st. 3. *labor, perish, be shipwrecked.* past pl. **gedurfon.**

derian. wk. 1. (with dat. object). *harm.* 3sg. **dereð** 5/33. past 3sg. **derede** 5/19, 23.

dēð → (ge)dōn.

gedēð → (ge)dōn.

dīacon. masc. *deacon.* nom. pl. **dīaconas.**

dimm. adj. *dark, gloomy.* fem. nom. pl. **dimme** 12/30.

dīore. adj. *beloved.* masc. nom. sg. 7/70.

dōgor. masc. *day.* inst. sg. **dōgore** 14/12. gen. pl. **dōgra** 9/63.

dogorrīm. neut. *count of days, lifetime.* dat. sg. **dogorrīme** 7/82.

dohte → dugan.

dohten → dugan.

dohtor. fem. r-stem. *daughter.* nom. sg. I/5; Lb/5; 13/48. acc. sg. 5/40. dat. sg. **dehter.** dat. pl. **dohtrum.**

dolg. *wound.* 1. masc. nom. sg. **dolh** 2/16. 2. neut. nom. pl. 10/46.

dolhwund. adj. *wounded.* masc. nom. sg. 14/107.

dōm. masc. *judgment, law, reputation, glory.* nom. sg. 14/266. acc. sg. C/10; 3/11; 5/70; 14/196. gen. sg. **dōmes** A/5; C/9; 6/24; 10/107. dat. sg. **dōme** C/9; M/2; 6/16; 7/16; 14/299, etc. dat. pl. **dōmum** 6/25.

dōmdæg. masc. *doomsday.* dat. sg. **dōmdæge** 10/105.

dōmgeorn. adj. *eager for glory.* masc. nom. pl. **dōmgeorne** 9/17.

dōmlīce. adv. *gloriously.* 14/318.

(ge)dōn. anom. verb. *do, take, put, bring about, cause to be.* 3sg. **dēð, gedēð** A/3; 5/12, 35, 53; 7/70, etc. pl. **dōð** D/1; 5/30. past 2sg. **dydest, dydestū** (contracted with *þū*) 1/13, 14. past 3sg. **dyde**

в/6; 1/8; 2/15; 6/7, 31, etc. past pl.
dydan, dydon, gedydon 5/6; 7/37;
11/14. subj. sg. **dō** 5/23. subj. pl. **dōn**
7/46. imp. sg. **dō** 7/19. inf. **dōn, gedōn**
2/4, 8, 18; 5/60, 65, etc. past part. **gedōn**
4/4; 7/10.

dorste → durran.

draca. masc. *dragon.* acc. sg. **dracan.** nom.
pl. **dracan.**

drāf. fem. *herd, company.* acc. sg. **drāfe**
5/43.

drāf → drīfan.

dranc → drincan.

gedreag. neut. *assembly, multitude.* acc. sg.
12/45.

drēam. masc. *joy, mirth, music.* nom. sg.
10/140. gen. sg. **drēames** 10/144. dat.
sg. **drēame** 9/79. acc. pl. **drēamas**
14/349. dat. pl. **drēamum** 10/133.

gedrēas → (ge)drēosan.

(ge)dreccan. wk. 1. *vex, afflict, oppress,*
ravage. past pl. **gedrehtan, drehton**
5/19.

(ge)drēfan. wk. 1. *agitate,* fig. *travel* (of
rowing in the sea), *afflict.* subj. past
sg. **drēfde** 13/21. past part. **gedrēfed**
10/20, 59; 14/88.

gedrehtan → (ge)dreccan.

drehton → (ge)dreccan.

drencan. wk. 1. *make drunk, submerge,*
drown. past 3sg. **drencte** 14/29.

drēogan. st. 2. *perform, commit, exper-*
ience, endure. 3sg. **drēogeð** 12/50. pl.
drēogað 5/30. past pl. **drugon** 14/158.
inf. 8/15; 12/26.

drēorig. adj. *bloody, cruel, sorrowful.* masc.
acc. sg. **drēorigne** 9/17.

drēorighlēor. adj. *sad-faced.* masc. nom.
sg. 9/83.

drēorsele. masc. *dreary hall.* dat. sg. 12/50.

(ge)drēosan. st. 2. *fall, perish, fail.* 3sg.
drēoseð 9/63. past 3sg. **gedrēas** 9/36.

drīfan. st. 1. *drive.* 1sg. **drīfe.** 2sg. **drīfst.**
3sg. **drīfð.** pl. **drīfað** 5/43. past 2sg.
drife. past 3sg. **drāf.** past pl. **drifon.**
subj. sg. **drīfe** 5/25.

Drihten. masc. *the Lord, Lord, God.* nom.
sg. **Drihten, Dryhten** 6/12, 13; 10/101;
14/21. acc. sg. **Dryhten, Drihten** 10/64,
144. gen. sg. **Dryhtnes, Drihtnes** 2/30;
7/82; 10/9, 35, 75, etc. dat. sg. **Drihtne,**
Dryhten, Dryhtne 6/17, 43; 10/105;
14/342, 346, etc.

drihtnē. masc. *corpse.* dat. pl. **drihtnēum.**

drincan. st. 3. *drink.* past 3sg. **dranc.** past
pl. **druncon.**

drīum → drȳge.

drohtnian. wk. 2. *pass life, live, behave.*
past 3sg. **drohtnode** 2/11. past pl.
drohtnodon 2/31.

drohtnung. fem. *way of life, condition.* dat.
sg. **drohtnunge** 2/9, 30.

drugon → drēogan.

druncen. adj. *drunk.* masc. nom. sg. 14/67,
107. masc. nom. pl. **druncene** 4/16.

druncon → drincan.

drȳge. adj. *dry.* dat. pl. **drīum.**

Dryhten → Drihten.

dryhtguma. masc. *warrior.* acc. pl.
dryhtguman 14/29.

Dryhtne → Drihten.

Dryhtnes → Drihten.

dugan. pret. pres. *do well, prosper, be good*
for anything. past 3sg. **dohte** 5/18, 39.
subj. past pl. **dohten** 7/37.

duguþ. fem. *body of experienced retainers,*
army, host. nom. sg. 9/79. acc. sg.
dugeþe, duguðe 5/62; 14/31. gen. sg.
duguþe 9/97. gen. pl. **dugeða** 14/61.
dat. pl. **duguðum** 7/70.

dumb. adj. *dumb.*

dūn. fem. *hill.* nom. pl. **dūna** 12/30.

dūnland. neut. *hilly land.* dat. pl.
dūnlandum.

gedurfon → gedeorfan.

durran. pret. pres. *dare.* 1sg. **dear** 13/11.
3sg. **dear** 5/10, 11, 12. past 1sg. **dorste**
10/35, 42, 45, 47. past 3sg. **dorste**
14/258. subj. sg. **durre** 9/10.

duru. fem. u-stem. *door.* acc. sg. 3/5.

dūst. neut. *dust.* nom. sg. 1/19. dat. sg.
dūste A/4; 1/19.

dwǣs. adj. *foolish.* dat. pl. **dwǣsan** 5/54.

dwelian. wk. 2. *lead astray.* past 3sg. **dwelode** 5/4.

dweorh. masc. *dwarf.*

gedwolgod. masc. *false god.* gen. pl. **gedwolgoda** 5/10, 12. dat. pl. **gedwolgodan** 5/11.

dyd- –> (ge)dōn.

gedydon –> (ge)dōn.

dȳgel. adj. *secret.* neut. acc. sg. κ/1357.

dynian. wk. 2. *resound.* past 3sg. **dynede** 14/23. past pl. **dynedan** 14/204.

dynt. masc. *blow.* dat. sg. **dynte** 4/18.

dȳre. adj. *dear, precious.* masc. acc. pl. 14/318.

dyrne. adj. *secret.* masc. acc. sg. 12/12.

gedȳrsian. wk. 2. *glorify.* past part. **gedȳrsod** 14/299.

dysig. A. neut. *folly.* acc. sg. 7/10. inst. sg. **dysige** 7/27.

 B. adj. *foolish.* masc. nom. pl. **dysige** 5/50.

ēa. fem. *river.* nom. pl. **ēan.**

ēac. A. adv. *also.* **ēac, eac** A/4; B/1, 4; D/1; 1/1, etc.

 B. prep. (with dat. or inst.). *in addition to.* 12/44.

geēacnung. fem. *child-bearing.* acc. pl. **geēacnunga** 1/16.

ēad. neut. *happiness, prosperity.* gen. sg. **ēades** 14/273.

ēadhrēþig. adj. *triumphantly blessed.* fem. nom. pl. **ēadhrēðige** 14/135.

ēadig. adj. *wealthy, prosperous, happy, blessed.* masc. nom. sg. A/1. masc. nom. pl. **ēadige.** wk. fem. nom. sg. **ēadige.** wk. fem. acc. sg. **ēadigan** 14/35.

ēage. neut. *eye.* acc. sg. 7/40. nom. pl. **ēagan** 1/5, 7. acc. pl. **ēagan.** dat. pl. **ēagum** D/2; 1/6.

eahta. card. num. as noun. *eight.* **eahta, ehta** E/1; 4/14.

eahtoþa. ord. num. *eighth.* neut. dat. sg. **eahteoðan** 2/12.

ēalā. interj. *oh, alas.* **ēalā, ēala** 5/58; 7/2, 13 (2x), 68, etc.

eald. adj. *old, ancient, senior.* masc. nom. sg. 12/29. neut. acc. sg. 13/49. neut. nom. pl. 9/87. gen. pl. **ealdra** 5/13. dat. pl. **ealdum** 2/8. wk. masc. nom. sg. **ealda** B/4. wk. masc. nom. pl. **ealdan, ealde** 14/166. wk. masc. acc. pl. **ealde** 14/265. wk. masc. nom. pl. superl. **yldestan** 4/12. wk. masc. acc. pl. superl. **yldestan** 14/10. wk. dat. pl. superl. **yldestan** 14/242.

ealdes. adv. (from adj. *eald*). *formerly.* 12/4.

ealdfēond. masc. nd-stem. *ancient enemy.* dat. pl. **ealdfēondum** 14/315.

ealdgenīþla. masc. *ancient enemy.* acc. pl. **ealdgenīðlan** 14/228.

ealdgewyrht. fem. *ancient deed.* dat. pl. **ealdgewyrhtum** 10/100.

ealdhettend. masc. nd-stem. *ancient adversary.* acc. pl. **ealdhettende** 14/320.

ealdor. 1. masc. *leader, lord.* nom. sg. **ealdor, aldor** 10/90; 14/32, 38, 58, 88, etc. **2.** neut. *life, eternity.* acc. sg. **aldor, ealdor** κ/1371; 14/185. dat. sg. **aldre, ealdre** 14/76, 120, 347.

ealdorduguþ. fem. *body of nobles.* gen. sg. **ealdorduguðe** 14/309.

ealdorman. masc. athematic. *ruler, chief, overseer, nobleman.* nom. sg. **ealdorman, aldormon, ealdormon** 2/5; 3/10; 4/12; 6/15. acc. sg. **aldormon** 3/1, 2. gen. sg. **aldormonnes, ealdormonnes** M/3; 3/15. dat. sg. **ealdormenn, ealdormen** 2/3.

ealdorþegn. masc. *chief thegn.* dat. pl. **ealdorþegnum** 14/242.

eall. A. adj. *all, each.* masc. nom. sg. **eal, eall** 2/2; 7/16. fem. nom. sg. **eal, eall** 7/66; 9/79, 115; 10/12, 55, etc. neut. nom. sg. **eall, eal** A/3; 4/14; 5/29, 32; 7/18, etc. masc. acc. sg. **ealne** 5/44; 14/28. fem. acc. sg. **ealle** 4/8; 5/5, 29, 58; 6/28, etc. neut. acc. sg. **eall, eal** C/6; 2/4; 5/53; 6/24; 7/13, etc. masc. gen. sg. **ealles** M/12; 7/17, 20; 12/41. fem. gen. sg. **ealre** 7/16; 9/74. neut. gen. sg. **ealles**

c/2; m/1; 7/31. masc. dat. sg. **eallum**
6/35. fem. dat. sg. **ealre, eallre** 4/19;
5/16, 36; 7/38. neut. dat. sg. **eallum**
4/4; 6/26. neut. inst. sg. **ealle** 5/53, 62;
7/22, 23. masc. nom. pl. **ealle, alle**
c/10 (2x); h/3; m/13; 2/21, etc. fem.
nom. pl. **ealle** 4/3. neut. nom. pl. **ealle**
f/1; 1/1; 7/18. masc. acc. pl. **ealle, alle**
2/11; 3/15; 4/2, 7; 6/16, etc. fem. acc.
pl. **ealle**. neut. acc. pl. **ealle, eal, eall**
c/1; 2/9; 6/14, 22; 7/19, etc. gen. pl.
ealra, eallra c/4; 5/25, 56; 6/16; 7/13,
etc. dat. pl. **eallum** 1/14 (2x), 17; 2/22;
5/17, etc.
  B. adv. *all, entirely*. **eal, eall** 2/19, 23;
5/39 (2x), 42, etc.
eall swā. conj. *as, just as*. e/3.
ealle. adv. *entirely, quite*. h/2.
ealles. adv. *all, entirely*. 5/5, 10, 13, 22, 27
(2x), etc.
eallgylden. adj. *entirely golden*. neut. nom.
sg. 14/46.
ealnig. adv. *always*. 7/69.
ealo. masc. dental stem. *ale*. nom. sg. **ealu**
7/7.
eard. masc. *country, land*. acc. sg. 4/21;
5/62, 64; 13/18. dat. sg. **earde** 5/14, 20,
24, 25, 29, etc.
eardgeard. masc. *habitation, world*. acc.
sg. 9/85.
eardian. wk. 2. *dwell*. past pl. **eardedon**
8/22.
eardstapa. masc. *land-traveler, wanderer*.
nom. sg. 9/6.
eardung. fem. *dwelling*. nom. sg. f/2.
ēare. neut. *ear*.
earendel. masc. *shining light, rising sun,
morning star*. nom. sg. 8/1.
earfoþe. neut. *hardship, labor*. gen. pl.
earfeþa, earfoþa 9/6; 12/39.
earfoþlic. adj. *difficult, full of hardship,
laborious*. neut. nom. sg. 9/106.
earfoþness. fem. *hardship, affliction, difficulty*. dat. sg. **earfoþnesse** b/5.
earg. adj. *wretched, vile, useless, cowardly*.
masc. acc. sg. **eargne** 11/16.

earhlīc. adj. *cowardly, disgraceful*. fem.
nom. pl. **earhlīce** 5/38.
earm. adj. *poor, wretched, miserable*. masc.
acc. sg. **earmne** 9/40. fem. dat. sg.
earman 5/57. masc. nom. pl. **earme**
5/14; 10/68. neut. acc. pl. **earme** 4/4.
gen. pl. **earmra** 10/19. wk. fem. dat. sg.
earman 4/10.
earmcearig. adj. *wretchedly sorrowful*.
masc. nom. sg. 9/20.
earmlīce. adv. *miserably*. 5/58.
earn. masc. *eagle*. nom. sg. 14/210. dat.
sg. **earne**.
earnian. wk. 2. (with gen.). *strive for,
deserve*. pl. **earniað** 7/47. past pl.
geearnedan 5/7. inf. 5/6.
geearnian. wk. 2. *earn, merit*. 3sg.
geearnaþ 10/109. past pl. **geearnedon**
a/6. inf. **geearnian, geearnigan** 5/70;
7/38.
earnung. fem. *labour, merit, desert*. dat.
pl. **earnungan** 5/7 (2x).
eart → bēon.
geearwodest → (ge)gearwian.
ēast. adv. *east*. 7/65.
ēastan. adv. *from the east*. 14/190.
Ēastengle. masc. *East Angles*. acc. pl. 4/2.
gen. pl. **Ēastengla** 2/2.
Ēasterdæg. masc. *Easter-day*. nom. sg.
4/13.
ēasteweard. adj. *east*. masc. dat. sg.
ēasteweardum 7/16.
Ēastre. fem. (always pl.). *Easter*. acc. pl.
Ēastron 4/14. dat. pl. **Ēastron** 4/12.
Ēastseaxe. masc. *East Saxons*. acc. pl.
Ēastsexe 4/2.
ēaþe. adv. *easily*. 2/8; 5/58; 7/66; 11/18.
compar. **ēð** 7/73. superl. **ēaðost** 14/75,
102.
ēaþmēdu. fem. *humility* (pl. has sg. sense).
dat. pl. **ēaðmēdum** 14/170.
ēaþmōd. adj. *humble*. masc. nom. sg.
10/60.
ēaþmōdlīce. adv. *humbly*. 6/26.
eaxl. fem. *shoulder*. dat. pl. **eaxlum**
10/32.

eaxlegespann. neut. *shoulder-span, cross-beam.* dat. sg. **eaxlegespanne** 10/9.

eaxlgestealla. masc. *person who is by one's shoulder, companion.* nom. sg. I/1.

Ebrēas. masc. *the Hebrews.* nom. pl. 14/218. gen. pl. **Ebrēa** 14/253, 262, 298.

Ebrēisc. adj. *Hebrew.* masc. nom. pl. **Ebrisce** 14/241, 305. wk. neut. dat. sg. **Ebrēiscan.**

ēce. adj. *eternal.* masc. nom. sg. 6/12, 13. fem. acc. sg. 7/38. neut. acc. sg. 7/41. wk. masc. nom. sg. **ēca** 7/82. wk. neut. gen. sg. **ēcean.** wk. fem. dat. sg. **ēcan** C/11.

ecg. fem. *edge.* acc. sg. **ecge.** dat. pl. **ecgum** 14/231.

ecgplega. masc. *edge-play, battle.* acc. sg. **ecgplegan** 14/246.

ēcness. fem. *eternity.* dat. sg. **ēcnesse, ēcnysse** C/12; F/7; 2/31.

(ge)edcennan. wk. 1. *bear again.* past part. **geedcenned.**

ederas → eodor.

edwenden. fem. *turning back, change.*

edwit. neut. *disgrace, blame, scorn.* acc. sg. 14/215.

efenēce. adj. *co-eternal.* masc. nom. sg. 8/19.

efenlang. adj. *just as long.* neut. acc. sg. La/7.

efne. A. adv. *indeed, only, just, once* (in calculation). B/3; E/1; 6/4.
   B. interj. *indeed.*

efnmǣre. adj. *equally glorious.* masc. acc. sg. **efnmǣrne** 7/70.

efstan. wk. 1. *hurry.* inf. 10/34. pres. part. **efstende.**

eft. adv. *again, afterwards, thereupon, back.* 1/4, 8; 2/10, 30; 5/36, etc.

ege. masc. *fear, terror.* acc. sg. 5/52.

egeful. adj. *awe-inspiring, terrible.* masc. nom. sg. **egeful, egefulle, egesful, egesfull** 7/29; 14/21, 257.

egesa. masc. *awe, fear.* nom. sg. 10/86; 14/252.

egesful → egeful.

egesfull → egeful.

egeslic. adj. *terrible.* fem. nom. sg. 10/74. neut. nom. sg. 5/3, 30. fem. nom. pl. **egeslīce** 5/32. wk. fem. dat. sg. **egeslican.** wk. masc. nom. pl. **egeslice.**

eglan. wk. 1. *trouble, molest.* inf. 14/185.

ēglond. neut. *island.* nom. sg. 11/5.

Egypte. masc. *Egyptians.* gen. pl. **Egypta, Ægypta** 6/24.

Egyptisc. adj. *Egyptian.* wk. fem. acc. sg. **Egyptiscan.**

ehta → eahta.

ehtan. wk. 1. *attack.* past pl. **ēhton** 14/237.

Eligmynster. neut. *the monastery of Ely.* dat. sg. **Eligmynstre** 2/10.

ellen. neut. *zeal, strength, courage.* dat. sg. **elne** 9/114; 14/95. inst. sg. **elne** 10/34, 60, 123.

ellendǣd. fem. *deed of valour.* gen. pl. **ellendǣda** 14/273.

ellenmǣrþu. fem. *reputation for valour.* dat. pl. **ellenmǣrðum.**

ellenrōf. adj. *courageous.* fem. nom. sg. 14/109, 146.

ellenþrīste. adj. *valorous.* fem. nom. pl. 14/133.

ellenwōdness. fem. *zeal.* gen. sg. **ellenwōdnisse** 6/27.

elles. adv. *else.* 12/23.

ellor. adv. *elsewhere.* 13/4; 14/112.

elne → ellen.

elþēod. fem. *foreign nation, foreigners* (in pl.). gen. sg. **elþēode** 13/37. acc. pl. **elðēoda** 14/237.

elþēodig. adj. *foreign.* gen. pl. **elðēodigra** 14/215.

embe → ymb.

geendade → geendian.

geendað → geendian.

ende. masc. *end, edge, front edge.* nom. sg. C/11; 7/42. acc. sg. 7/40, 44 (2x); 14/64. dat. sg. F/6, 7; I/8; 5/2, 13, etc. inst. sg. **ænde** 6/27.

endebyrdness. fem. *order, series, degree, rank.* nom. sg. **endebyrdnes** 6/11. acc. sg. **endebyrdnesse** 6/6.

geendian. wk. 2. *end.* 3sg. **geendað** 7/45. past 3sg. **geendade** 6/27, 42.

geendodlīc. adj. *finite.* wk. neut. acc. sg. **geendodlīce** 7/43.

geendung. fem. *ending, death.* acc. sg. **geendunge.** dat. sg. **geendunge** 2/17.

engel. masc. *angel.* acc. sg. 10/9. nom. pl. **englas** 2/30; 10/106. gen. pl. **engla** 8/1. dat. pl. **englum** c/12; 1/5; 10/153.

Engle. masc. *the English.* nom. pl. 5/39, 42. gen. pl. **Engla** 5/62. dat. pl. **Englum** 5/65.

Englisc. adj. *English.* wk. neut. dat. sg. **Engliscan** 2/1. wk. masc. acc. pl. **Engliscan** D/1.

Engliscgereord. neut. *English language.* dat. sg. **Engliscgereorde** 6/1.

ent. masc. *giant.* acc. pl. **entas.** gen. pl. **enta** 9/87.

ēod- → gān.

geēodon → gegān.

eodor. masc. *boundary, enclosure, dwelling,* fig. *lord.* acc. sg. J/89. nom. pl. **ederas** 9/77.

eodorcan. wk. 1. *chew, ruminate.* pres. part. **eodorcende** 6/22.

eom → bēon.

eorl. masc. *warrior, nobleman.* nom. sg. 9/84, 114. gen. sg. **eorles** I/5. dat. sg. **eorle** J/83; 9/12. nom. pl. **eorlas** 14/273, 336. acc. pl. **eorlas** 9/99. gen. pl. **eorla** 9/60; 14/21, 257.

eorlgebyrd. fem. (pl. with sg. meaning). *noble birth.* dat. pl. **eorlgebyrdum** 7/70.

eorlgestrēon. neut. *acquisition of men.* gen. pl. **eorlgestrēona** 13/47.

eornost. neut. *earnestness.* acc. sg. 5/43.

eornoste. adv. *resolutely.* 14/108, 231.

eornostlīce. adv. *truly, indeed.*

eorþbūend. masc. nd-stem. *earth-dweller.* nom. pl. **eorðbūende** 7/70. gen. pl. **eorðbūendra** 7/72.

eorþe. fem. *earth.* nom. sg. 1/17; 7/66. acc. sg. **eorþan** G/2; 1/14; 4/18; 7/27, 32, etc. gen. sg. **eorðan** 1/18; 6/13; 7/16, 18, 67,

etc. dat. sg. **eorðan** B/3; c/5; G/7; 1/1, 17, etc.

eorþlic. adj. *earthly.* wk. masc. gen. sg. **eorðlican** 7/2. wk. neut. gen. sg. **eorð-lican** 7/2. wk. neut. dat. sg. **eorðlican** 7/62. wk. neut. acc. pl. **eorðlican** 7/62.

eorþscræf. neut. *earthen cave.* dat. sg. **eorðscræfe** 9/84; 12/28. acc. pl. **eorðscrafu** 12/36.

eorþsele. masc. *earthen hall.* nom. sg. 12/29.

eorþweg. masc. *earthly region.* dat. sg. **eorðwege** 10/120.

ēow → þū, gē.

ēowan. wk. 1. *display.* past pl. **ēowdon** 14/240.

ēower. adj. *your.* masc. nom. sg. 7/22, 30. masc. acc. sg. **ēowerne** 7/21, 23, 24, 27. fem. acc. sg. **ēowre** 7/21. neut. acc. sg. D/2. fem. gen. sg. **ēowre** 7/47. neut. gen. sg. **ēoweres, ēowres** 7/47 (2x). masc. dat. sg. **ēowrum** 7/68. fem. dat. sg. **ēowerre** 7/38. masc. nom. pl. **ēowre, ēowere** D/1; 3/14; 14/195. neut. nom. pl. **ēowre, ēowru** 1/5. masc. acc. pl. **ēowre** D/2. gen. pl. **ēowerra** 7/47. dat. pl. **ēowrum** 7/38.

ermðe → yrmþu.

esne. masc. *slave, servant, young man.* nom. sg. LA/4.

(ge)etan. st. 5. *eat.* 2sg. **etst, ytst** 1/14, 17, 18. pl. **etað** 1/2, 5. past 1sg. **æt, ætt** 1/12, 13. past 2sg. **æte** 1/17. past 3sg. **æt, geæt** 1/6 (2x). past pl. **æton.** subj. pl. **eton, ete** 1/4. subj. past sg. **æte** 1/11 (2x), 17. subj. past pl. **æton** 1/1, 3. inf. **etan.** infl. inf. **tō etanne, tō etenne** 1/6.

ēð → ēaþe.

ēþel. masc. *homeland.* nom. sg. 10/156. acc. sg. 13/26, 37. dat. sg. **ēðle** 9/20; 14/169.

ēþelweard. masc. *guardian of the homeland.* nom. pl. **ēðelweardas** 14/320.

fācenful. adj. *deceitful.*

fadian. wk. 2. *arrange, order.* past 3sg. **fadode** 5/21. inf. 5/69.

fāg. adj. *variegated, adorned.* masc. nom. sg. **fāh** 9/98. masc. dat. sg. **fāgum** 14/104. dat. pl. **fāgum** 14/194, 264, 301.

fāh. adj. *guilty* of something (dat.), *outlawed.* masc. nom. sg. 10/13; 12/46.

fāh → fāg.

fandian. wk. 2. (usually with gen. object). *try, test, examine.* inf. 7/49, 51.

gefara → gefēra.

faran. st. 6. *travel, go.* 3sg. **færð** 7/61. past 3sg. **fōr** H/4; 14/297. past pl. **fōron** 14/202. inf. c/11, 12; 13/43.

gefaran. st. 6. *go, traverse, die, come about, happen.* pl. **gefarað** 7/25. inf. 7/18. past part. **gefaren** 5/58.

fatu → fæt.

fæc. neut. *space, time.* acc. sg. 6/42. dat. sg. **fæce** 6/1.

fæder. masc. r-stem. *father.* nom. sg. 2/2; 5/21, 32; 14/5. gen. sg. 8/7. dat. sg. 5/21; 8/18; 9/115. nom. pl. **fæderas** D/1.

fǣge. adj. *about to die, doomed.* masc. nom. pl. 14/19. masc. acc. pl. 14/195. dat. pl. **fǣgum** 14/209.

fægen. adj. *glad, joyful, rejoicing.* masc. nom. sg. 9/68.

fæger. adj. *fair, beautiful, pleasant.* neut. nom. sg. 10/73; 14/47. fem. acc. sg. **fægre** 13/38. masc. inst. sg. **fægre** 6/27. masc. nom. pl. **fægere** 10/8, 10. wk. fem. dat. sg. **fægran** 10/21.

fægnian. wk. 2. *rejoice.* 3sg. **fægnað** 7/62.

gefægnian. wk. 2. *rejoice.* past 3sg. **fægnode** 2/24.

fægre. adv. *fairly, well.* 14/300.

fǣhþo. fem. *feud, enmity.* nom. sg. 13/19. acc. sg. **fǣhðe** 12/26.

fǣmne. fem. *woman.* nom. sg. 8/20. acc. sg. **fǣmnan, fēmnan** 2/27. gen. sg. **fǣmnan.** dat. sg. **fǣmnan.** nom. pl. **fǣmnan.**

fænne → fenn.

fǣrlīce. adv. *suddenly, precipitously.* 9/61.

fǣrspel. neut. *story of an attack.* acc. sg. 14/244.

færð → faran.

fæst. adj. *fixed, secure, enclosed.* masc. nom. sg. B/3; K/1364. neut. nom. sg. 11/5.

fæstan. wk. 1. *fast.* subj. sg. **fæste.** pres. part. **fæstende** 2/11.

fæste. adv. *firmly, securely.* 5/41; 6/14; 9/13, 18; 10/38, etc.

fæsten. neut. *stronghold.* dat. sg. **fæstenne** 14/143.

fæstenbryce. masc. *failure to fast.* nom. pl. **fæstenbrycas** 5/49.

fæstengeat. neut. *gate to the stronghold.* gen. sg. **fæstengeates** 14/162.

(ge)fæstnian. wk. 2. *fasten.* past pl. **gefæstnodon** 10/33. inf. **fæstnian.**

fæstnung. fem. *stability, security, safety, protection.* nom. sg. 9/115.

fæstrǣd. adj. *steadfast.* wk. masc. nom. sg. **fæstrǣda** 7/76.

fæt. neut. *container, cup.* nom. pl. **fatu.**

fǣted. adj. *ornamented.* wk. neut. gen. sg. **fǣttan** 13/36.

fǣtels. masc. *pouch.* dat. sg. **fǣtelse** 14/127.

fēa. A. adj. *few.* dat. pl. **fēawum.**
B. indef. pron. *few.* neut. nom. pl. **fēawa** 2/18. neut. acc. pl. **fēawa.**
C. adv. *little.* 10/115.

gefēa. masc. *joy.* acc. sg. **gefēan** F/7.

gefeah → gefēon.

feaht → (ge)feohtan.

gefeaht → (ge)feohtan.

feala → fela.

(ge)feallan. st. 7. *fall.* 3sg. **fealleþ** 9/63. past 3sg. **gefēoll, fēol, gefēol** 4/18; 14/67, 280, 307. inf. **feallan** 10/43. pres. part. **feallende.**

fealu. adj. *yellow, tawny, dark.* masc. acc. pl. **fealwe** 9/46.

fealwian. wk. 2. *become yellow, wither.* pl. **fealwiað** A/3.

feax. neut. *hair.* acc. sg. 14/281. dat. sg. **feaxe** 14/99.

fēdan. wk. 1. *feed.* inf. 4/21.

gefēgan. wk. 1. *join, fix, attach.* past part. **gefēged** 2/19.

fela. A. adj. (indeclinable). *many.* **fela,
feala** 2/27, 30; 5/20, 47; 10/50, etc. neut.
acc. 9/54.

    B. indef. pron. *many, much.* 5/4 (2x),
5, 6, 17, etc.

    C. adv. *much.*

felalēof. adj. *much-loved.* wk. masc. gen.
sg. **felalēofan** 12/26.

feld. masc. u-stem. *field.* dat. sg. **felda**
ᴍ/7.

fēmnan → **fǣmne.**

fēng- → **fōn.**

gefēng → **gefōn.**

fengelād. neut. *fen-path.* acc. pl. ᴋ/1359.

fenland. neut. *fenland.* dat. sg. **fenlande**
2/18.

fenn. masc. *fen.* dat. sg. **fænne, fenne**
7/22, 23; 11/5. nom. pl. **fennas** 7/19.
dat. pl. **fennum** 7/25.

feoh. neut. *cattle, property, wealth, money.*
nom. sg. 9/108. acc. sg. 3/8; 4/15. gen.
sg. **fēos** 3/11. dat. sg. **fēo** 2/7.

feohgestrēon. neut. *acquired treasure.* gen.
pl. **feohgestrēona** 13/36.

feohgīfre. adj. *greedy for wealth.* masc.
nom. sg. 9/68.

gefeoht. neut. *battle.* dat. sg. **gefeohte**
5/39; 14/189, 202. dat. pl. **gefeohtum**
3/3.

(ge)feohtan. st. 3. *fight, obtain by fighting*
(with *ġe-* prefix). past 3sg. **feaht,
gefeaht** 3/3; 14/291. past pl. **fuhton,
gefuhton** 14/262. subj. sg. **gefeohte**
ᴍ/1, 3, 4, 6. inf. **gefeohtan** 4/3. pres.
part. **feohtende** 3/6, 8, 15. past part.
gefohten ᴍ/7; 14/122.

fēol → **(ge)feallan.**

gefēol → **(ge)feallan.**

fēolan. st. 3. *enter, penetrate.* past pl.
fulgon 3/15.

gefēoll → **(ge)feallan.**

gefēon. st. 5. *rejoice* about something
(gen.). past 3sg. **gefeah** 14/205. pres.
part. **gefēonde** 6/32.

fēond. masc. nd-stem. *enemy.* nom. sg.
ʙ/4. acc. sg. ʙ/5. nom. pl. **fēondas, fȳnd**

ꜰ/3; 10/30, 33; 14/195. acc. pl. **fēondas,
fȳnd** 10/38; 14/319. gen. pl. **fēonda.** dat.
pl. **fēondum** 5/31.

fēondrǣden. fem. *enmity.* acc. sg. **fēondrǣdenne** 1/15.

fēondsceaþa. masc. *enemy who does harm.*
acc. sg. **fēondsceaðan** 14/104.

feor. A. adj. *far, distant.* masc. nom. sg.
9/21. neut. nom. sg. 6/40. neut. gen. sg.
feorres 12/47.

    B. adv. *far, long ago.* ᴋ/1361; 9/26,
90; 12/25.

feorgbold. neut. *life-dwelling, body.* nom.
sg. 10/73.

feorh. masc. *life.* acc. sg. ᴋ/1370; 3/8, 15.

feorhhord. neut. *treasure of life, life.*

feorhsweng. masc. *blow that takes a life,
death-blow.*

feorran. adv. *from afar.* ᴋ/1370; 10/57;
14/24.

fēorþa. ord. num. *fourth.* fem. nom. sg.
fēorðe. masc. gen. sg. **fēorðan** 7/18.
masc. dat. sg. **fēorðan** 7/19. masc. inst.
sg. **fēorðan** 14/12.

fēos → **feoh.**

fēower. A. card. num. as noun. *four.* ᴇ/1.

    B. as adj. *four.* neut. acc. pl. ʜ/1.

fēowertig. card. num. as noun. *forty.* ᴇ/1;
4/14, 21.

fēowertȳne. A. card. num. as noun. *fourteen.* ᴇ/1.

    B. as adj. *fourteen.* dat. pl. **fēower-
tȳnum** 6/28.

gefēra. masc. *companion.* nom. sg. **gefara**
ɪ/2. dat. sg. **gefēran** 1/12; 9/30. nom.
pl. **gefēran** 3/14. dat. pl. **gefērum**
3/13.

fēran. wk. 1. *go, journey.* past 3sg. **fērde**
ᴄ/6; 2/30. past pl. **fērdon** 4/4. inf. 12/9;
14/12.

ferdman. masc. athematic. *man of the
army, warrior.* acc. pl. **ferdmen** 7/4.

fered- → **ferian.**

ferhþ. masc. *mind, intellect, spirit, life,
being.* nom. sg. **ferð** 9/54. dat. sg. **ferðe**
9/90.

ferhþglēaw. adj. *wise in mind.* wk. fem. acc. sg. **ferhðglēawe** 14/41.

ferian. *carry.* 1. wk. 1. past 3sg. **ferede** 9/81. past pl. **feredon** 2/30. 2. wk. 2. past 3sg. **ferode** 4/19.

fers. neut. *verse.* acc. pl. 6/11.

gefērscipe. masc. *society.* nom. pl. **gefērscipas** 7/7. dat. pl. **gefērscipum** 7/6.

ferþloca. masc. *life-enclosure.* nom. sg. 9/33. acc. sg. **ferðlocan** 9/13.

fēseð → **fȳsan.**

fēt → **fōt.**

gefetian. wk. 2. *fetch.* subj. sg. **gefetige** 10/138. inf. **fetigan** 14/35.

fetor. fem. *fetter.* dat. pl. **feterum** 9/21.

fettian. wk. 2. *contend.* past 3sg. **fettode** G/1.

fēþelāst. masc. *foot-path.* dat. sg. **fēðelāste** 14/139.

feþer. fem. *feather, wing.* acc. pl. **feþra** 9/47. dat. pl. **feðerum** G/2.

fīclēaf. neut. *figleaf.* nom. pl. 1/7.

fielle → **fyll.**

fierd- → **fyrd.**

fīf. A. card. num. as noun. *five.* E/1; 4/21. **B.** as adj. *five.* neut. nom. pl. **fife** 10/8.

fīfta. ord. num. *fifth.* masc. dat. sg. **fīftan** 7/22.

fīftig. card. num. as noun. *fifty.* E/1.

fīftȳne. card. num. as noun. *fifteen.* E/3.

findan. st. 3. *find.* 2sg. **findest, findst** 7/42; 13/12, 28. past 1sg. **funde** 12/18. past 3sg. **funde** 14/2, 278. past pl. **fundon** 14/41. inf. H/4; 9/26.

finger. masc. *finger.*

Finnas. masc. *Lapps.*

fīras. masc. *people.* gen. pl. **fīra** 14/24, 33. dat. pl. **fīrum** 6/13.

firen. fem. *crime, sin.* gen. pl. **firena** 8/20.

(ge)firenian. wk. 2. *commit a crime, sin, make sinful.* past part. **gefirenode** F/6.

firenlust. masc. *criminal desire.* dat. pl. **firenlustum** H/2.

firenum. adv. *criminally, sinfully.*

fisc. masc. *fish.* nom. pl. **fixas.** gen. pl. **fisca.**

flān. masc. *arrow.* gen. pl. **flāna** 14/221.

flǣsc. neut. *flesh.* acc. sg. 8/20. dat. sg. **flǣsce.**

flēah → **flēogan.**

flēam. masc. *flight.* acc. sg. 14/291.

flēogan. st. 2. *fly, flee.* past 3sg. **flēah** 14/209. past pl. **flugon** 14/296. inf. 14/221.

flēohnet. neut. *fly-net, curtain.* nom. sg. 14/47.

flēotan. st. 2. *float.* pres. part. **flēotendra** 9/54.

flēow → **flōwan.**

flet. neut. *floor, dwelling, hall.* acc. sg. 9/61.

fletsittend. masc. nd-stem. *sitter in the hall, courtier.* dat. pl. **fletsittendum** 14/19, 33.

flocc. masc. *company, band of men, flock.* dat. sg. **flocce.**

flocmǣlum. adv. *in troops.* 4/4.

flōd. masc. *water, sea, tide.* nom. sg. K/1361. dat. sg. **flōde** K/1366.

flōr. fem. *floor.* acc. sg. **flōre** 14/111.

flotman. masc. athematic. *seaman, viking.* nom. pl. **flotmen** 5/39.

flotweg. masc. *sea-way.* acc. sg. 13/43.

flōwan. st. 7. *flow.* past 3sg. **flēow.**

flugon → **flēogan.**

geflȳman. wk. 1. *drive, drive out, exile.* past part. **geflȳmdum, geflȳmed** K/1370.

foca. masc. *cake.* acc. sg. **focan.**

fōda. masc. *food.*

gefohten → (ge)feohtan.

folc. neut. *people.* nom. sg. 10/140; 14/162, 262, 292. acc. sg. 7/13. gen. sg. **folces** 4/7; 5/3, 29, 64; 6/24, etc. dat. sg. **folce, folc** 7/29; 14/143, 176. acc. pl. 4/4. gen. pl. **folca.**

folclagu. fem. *secular law.* nom. pl. **folclaga** 5/13.

folclond. neut. *nation.* gen. sg. **folclondes** 12/47.

folcstede. masc. *place for people, dwelling-place, battlefield.* dat. sg. 14/319.

folctoga. masc. *leader of the people.* gen. sg. **folctogan** 14/47. acc. pl. **folctogan** 14/194.

folde. fem. *earth.* acc. sg. **foldan** κ/1361; 6/13; 13/38. gen. sg. **foldan** 9/33; 10/8, 43. dat. sg. **foldan** 10/132; 14/281.

folgaþ. masc. *service, office, authority.* acc. sg. 12/9.

folgian. wk. 2. *follow.* inf. 3/12.

folm. fem. *hand.* dat. sg. **folme** 14/80. dat. pl. **folmum** 14/99.

fōn. st. 7. *take, catch, begin,* with prep. *on undertake* something (acc.), *succeed.* past 3sg. **fēng** 3/17, 18; 14/299. past pl. **fēngon.**

gefōn. st. 7. *seize.* past 3sg. **gefēng.**

for. prep. (with dat., sometimes with acc.). *for, because of, instead of, in spite of, with respect to, before* (of location), *in the presence of.* B/5; C/2, 4; G/8; J/88, etc.

fōr → faran.

for þām. A. adv. *therefore, and so.* **for ðon, for ðām, for þan, for ðǣm** 5/6, 17, 20, 24; 6/4, etc.

  B. conj. *because.* **for þām, for þon, for ðan** A/6; G/8, 9; 4/5, 16, etc. **for þām þe.** conj. *because.* **for þām þe, for ðan ðe, for ðǣm þe, for ðān ðe, for þon ðe** G/3; H/2; 1/10, 14, 17, etc.

for þȳ. A. adv. *therefore.* 7/9, 34, 36, 72.

  B. conj. *because.* 7/72.

foran. adv. *in front.* La/2.

forbærnan. wk. 1. *burn.* past 3sg. **forbærnde** 5/26.

forbærst → forberstan.

forbēodan. st. 2. *forbid.* past 3sg. **forbēad** 1/1; 4/15.

forberan. st. 4. *forbear, endure, tolerate.* subj. sg. **forbere** M/9.

forberstan. st. 3. *burst, collapse.* past 3sg. **forbærst** 7/56. past pl. **forburston** F/5.

forbīgan. wk. 1. *bend down, abase.* past part. **forbīged** 14/267.

forburston → forberstan.

forceorfan. st. 3. *cut out, cut through.* past 3sg. **forcearf** 14/105. past pl. **forcurfon.** inf. H/3.

forcūþ. adj. *infamous.* wk. masc. nom. sg. superl. **forcūþesta** 7/14.

ford. masc. *ford.*

fordōn. anom. verb. *ruin, destroy.* 1sg. **fordō.** past pl. **fordydon.** inf. 5/62.

fordrīfan. st. 1. *compel.* past 3sg. **fordrāf** 14/277.

fordyslic. adj. *very foolish.* neut. nom. sg. 7/21.

forealdian. wk. 2. *decay.* past pl. **forealdodon** 7/37. past part. **forealdod** 7/9.

foregenga. masc. *predecessor, ancestor, servant.* nom. sg. 14/127.

foremǣre. adj. *outstanding.* masc. acc. sg. **foremǣrne** 14/122. masc. acc. pl. 7/80. masc. gen. pl. **formǣrra** 7/45. masc. nom. pl. superl. **formǣroste** 7/36.

forescēawung. fem. *providence.* acc. sg. **forescēawunge** 2/25.

forespreca. masc. *advocate, sponsor.* nom. pl. **forespecan, foresprecan** 5/68.

forfaran. st. 6. *perish, destroy.* past 3sg. **forfor** 5/27.

forgeaf → forgifan.

forgēafe → forgifan.

forgieldan. wk. 1. *pay for.* past part. **forgolden** 14/217.

forgietan. st. 5. *forget.* past part. **forgitene** 7/9, 80.

forgifan. st. 5. *give, grant.* past 2sg. **forgēafe** 1/12. past 3sg. **forgeaf** 10/147. imp. sg. **forgif** 14/88. past part. **forgifen** 2/3, 5; 6/17.

forgolden → forgieldan.

forhæfdness. fem. *abstinence, moderation.* dat. sg. **forhæfdnesse.**

forhealdan. st. 7. *withhold.* pl. **forhealdað** 5/10. inf. 5/10.

forhelan. st. 4. *conceal.* past part. **forholene** 7/9.

forhogdness. fem. *contempt.* dat. sg. **forhogdnisse** 6/2.

forholene → forhelan.

forht. adj. *afraid, fearful, timid.* masc. nom. sg. 9/68; 10/21.

forhtian. wk. 2. *be afraid.* pl. **forhtiað** 10/115.

forhtlīce. adv. *fearfully.* 14/244.

forlǣtan. st. 7. *leave, leave alone, abandon, allow, permit, release.* 3sg. **forlǣt** 7/70. pl. **forlǣtað** D/1. past 3sg. **forlēt** 6/7; 7/82. past pl. **forlēton** 7/36; 10/61; 14/170. subj. 1sg. **forlǣte.** imp. sg. **forlǣt.** inf. 2/9; 5/67; 14/150. pres. part. **forlǣtende** 6/43.

forlegen. adj. (past part. of *forlicgan*). *adulterous.* masc. nom. pl. **forlegene** 5/56.

forlēogan. st. 2. *lie, perjure, falsely accuse.* past part. **forlogen, forlogene** 5/34, 49.

forlēosan. st. 2. (with dat. object). *lose.* past 3sg. **forlēas.** inf. 14/63. past part. **forloren** 5/49.

forlēt- → forlǣtan.

forliger. neut. *fornication.* acc. pl. **forligru** 5/48.

forlogen- → forlēogan.

forloren → forlēosan.

forma. ord. num. *first.* masc. acc. sg. **forman.** neut. dat. sg. **forman** J/90.

formǣroste → foremǣre.

formǣrra → foremǣre.

formolsnian. wk. 2. *decay.* inf. 2/26. past part. **formolsnodan** 2/26.

forniman. st. 4. *take away.* past 3sg. **fornom** 9/80. past pl. **fornōman** 9/99. past part. **fornumene** 5/15.

fornȳdan. wk. 1. *compel.* past part. **fornȳdde** 5/14.

foroft. adv. *very often.* 5/19, 21, 47.

fōron → faran.

forrǣdan. wk. 1. *plot against, betray.* past 3sg. **forrǣdde** 5/26. subj. sg. **forrǣde** 5/25.

forscomu. fem. *shame, modesty.* dat. sg. **forscome** 6/6.

forsēon. st. 5. *neglect, despise, scorn, reject.* 3sg. **forsihð** 7/62. pl. **forsēoð, forsīoð**

D/2; 7/47. past pl. **forsāwon** H/2. past part. **forsāwene** 5/15.

forsīþian. wk. 2. *fare amiss.* past part. **forsīðod.**

forspillan. wk. 1. *destroy, waste.* past 3sg. **forspilde** 5/27.

forst. masc. *frost.* dat. sg. **forste.**

forstandan. st. 6. *avail, benefit.* 3sg. **forstent** 7/57. past 3sg. **forstōd** 7/57.

forsugod → forswigian.

forswerian. st. 6. *swear falsely.* past part. **forsworene** 5/34.

forswigian. wk. 2. *keep silent about, ignore, suppress.* past part. **forsugod** 7/9.

forswīþe. adv. *very much.* 7/2.

forsworene → forswerian.

forsyngian. wk. 2. *burden by sin.* past part. **forsyngod, forsyngodon** 5/47, 57.

forþ. adv. *forwards, forth, greatly* (in phrase *tō forþ* 'too greatly'). 5/53; 7/80; 10/132.

forþbringan. wk. 1. *bring forth, bring about.* past 3sg. **forþbrōhte** 6/1. inf. 7/32, 35.

forþfēran. wk. 1. *die.* past 3sg. **forþfērde.** pres. part. **forðfērendum.**

forþfōr. fem. *departure, death.* nom. sg. 6/31. gen. sg. **forðfōre** 6/28, 45. dat. sg. **forðfōre** 6/29, 33.

forþgān. anom. verb. *go forth.* past 3sg. **forðēode** 10/54.

forþgesceaft. fem. *the future, eternity.* acc. sg. 10/10.

forþgewītan. st. 1. *depart, die.* past part. **forðgewitene** 7/77.

forþolian. wk. 2. (with dat.). *do without.* inf. 9/38.

forþsīþ. masc. *journey forth, passing, death.* gen. sg. **forðsīþes** 13/43. dat. sg. **forðsīðe** 2/30.

forþweg. masc. *the way forward, departure, death.* dat. sg. **forðwege** 9/81; 10/125.

forþylman. wk. 1. *enclose, cover.* past part. **forðylmed** 14/118.

forwel. adv. *very, very well.* 7/2.

forweorþan. st. 3. *perish.* past pl. forwurdan 5/28, 64. subj. pl. 5/60. inf.
14/288.

forworhtan → forwyrcan.

forwundian. wk. 2. *wound severely.* past
part. forwunded, forwundod 10/14,
62.

forwurdan → forweorþan.

forwyrcan. wk. 1. *destroy.* past pl.
forworhtan 5/64. subj. pl. 5/53.

forwyrd. fem. *destruction, ruin.* nom. sg.
14/285. dat. sg. forwyrde c/11.

foryrman. wk. 1. *reduce to poverty.* past
part. foryrmde 5/14.

fōt. masc. athematic. *foot.* nom. pl. fēt.
acc. pl. fēt. dat. pl. fōtum.

fracod. adj. *wicked, criminal.* masc. gen.
sg. fracodes 10/10.

fram. A. adv. *from there.* from 3/13.
B. prep. (with dat.). *from, by.* fram,
from G/5 (2x); 1/8; 3/11; 5/43, etc.

gefrægen → (ge)frignan.

frægn → (ge)frignan.

gefrægn → (ge)frignan.

(ge)frætwian. wk. 2. *adorn.* past 3sg.
frætwode 2/13. past part. gefrætewod
14/171, 328.

frēa. masc. *lord, the Lord.* nom. sg. 6/13;
14/300. acc. sg. frēan 10/33. gen. sg.
frēan J/90; La/2; 12/33; 13/10. dat. sg.
frēan 1/2.

frēcne. adj. *daring, dangerous.* neut. acc.
pl. K/1359.

frēfran. wk. 1. *console.* inf. 9/28.

fremde. adj. *foreign.* masc. dat. sg.
fremdan 5/21. gen. pl. fremdra 7/47.
dat. pl. fremdum 5/14, 32.

fremian. wk. 2. *benefit, aid.* past 3sg.
fremode 2/27.

(ge)fremman. wk. 1. *do, bring about,
make, aid, provide, support, perpetrate.*
past 3sg. gefremede 14/6, 181. past pl.
fremedon 14/37. inf. gefremman,
fremman 9/16, 114; 13/19.

fremsumness. fem. *benefit, kindness.* dat.
pl. fremsumnessum 6/25.

frēogan. wk. 2. *set free.*

frēolic. adj. *free-born, noble.* neut. nom.
pl. frēolicu.

frēolsbryce. masc. *failure to observe a
festival.* nom. pl. frēolsbricas 5/49.

frēolsdæg. masc. *feast day.* nom. sg. 2/11.

frēomǣg. masc. *free kinsman, noble kinsman.* dat. pl. frēomǣgum 9/21.

frēond. masc. nd-stem. *friend, loved one.*
nom. sg. 9/108; 10/144; 12/47. nom. pl.
frēondas, frīend, frȳnd 10/76; 12/33.
gen. pl. frēonda 10/132; 12/17.

frēondlēas. adj. *friendless.* masc. acc. sg.
frēondlēasne 9/28.

frēondscipe. masc. *friendship, love.* nom.
sg. 12/25. acc. sg. frēondscype 13/19.

frēorig. adj. *frozen,* fig. *unhappy.* masc.
nom. sg. 9/33; 14/281.

frēoriht. neut. *rights of freemen.* nom. pl.
5/15.

frīend → frēond.

(ge)frignan. st. 3. *ask, hear of.* 3sg. frīneð
10/112. past 1sg. gefrægn, gefrægen
Lb/1; 14/7, 246. past 3sg. frægn 6/32,
35, 39. past pl. gefrūnon 10/76.

frīolīce. adv. *freely.* 7/61.

friþ. masc. *peace.* acc. sg. 4/4. gen. sg.
friðes 4/1.

friþþāþ. masc. *oath of peace.* nom. pl.
friðāþas 4/20.

(ge)friþian. wk. 2. *make peace with, protect, defend.* past 3sg. gefriðode 14/5.

frōd. adj. *old, mature, wise.* masc. nom.
sg. K/1366; 9/90.

frōfor. fem. *consolation, help, benefit.* acc.
sg. frōfre 9/115. gen. sg. frōfre 14/83.
dat. sg. frōfre 14/296.

from → fram.

fromlīce. adv. *boldly.* 14/41, 220, 301.

fromsīþ. masc. *journey away, departure.*
nom. sg. 12/33.

fruma. masc. *beginning, origin.* dat. sg.
fruman 6/24; 7/44.

frumbearn. neut. *first-born child.*

frumcenned. adj. *first-born.* masc. acc. sg.
frumcennedan.

frumgār. masc. *lead-spear, leader.* acc. pl. **frumgāras** 14/195.

frumsceaft. masc. *first creation.* acc. sg. 6/10.

gefrūnon → (ge)frignan.

frymþ. fem. *beginning, origin, creation.* dat. sg. **frymðe** 8/18. gen. pl. **frymða** 14/5, 83, 189.

frȳnd → frēond.

fugel. masc. *bird.* nom. sg. G/4; 9/81; 14/207. dat. pl. **fuglum** 14/296.

fugolcynn. neut. *species of bird.* dat. sg. **fugolcynne.**

fuhton → (ge)feohtan.

gefuhton → (ge)feohtan.

ful. adv. *very, fully.* **ful, full** 5/8, 25, 38, 47, 51, etc.

fūl. adj. *foul.* masc. acc. sg. **fūlne** 5/64. masc. nom. pl. **fūle** 5/56. wk. masc. nom. sg. **fūla** 14/111.

fulfremed. adj. *perfect.* gen. pl. **fulfremedra** 7/13.

fulgon → fēolan.

full. A. neut. *cup.* dat. sg. **fulle** J/90.
   B. adj. *full.* masc. nom. pl. **fulle** 14/19. fem. acc. pl. **fulle.**

fullǣstan. wk. 1. *assist.*

fullīce. adv. *fully, completely.* 5/36, 37.

fūllīce. adv. *foully.*

fulluht- → fulwiht.

fultum. masc. *help, support, protection.* acc. sg. 14/300. dat. sg. **fultum, fultume** 14/186.

gefultuman. wk. 1. *aid.* past part. **gefultumed** 6/3.

gefulwian. wk. 2. *baptize.* past part. **gefulwad.**

fulwiht. neut. *baptism.* acc. sg. **fulluht, fulwiht** 5/68. dat. sg. **fulluhte** 5/68.

funde → findan.

fundian. wk. 2. *come, hasten, strive.* 3sg. **fundaþ** 10/103.

fundon → findan.

furþum. adv. *even.* 7/14, 18, 25, 26, 27, etc.

fūs. adj. *in a hurry, ready to go, eager, brave.* wk. neut. acc. sg. **fūse** 10/21. wk. masc. nom. pl. **fūse** 10/57.

fūslic. adj. *ready.* neut. acc. pl. **fūslicu.**

gefylde → gefyllan.

fylgan. wk. 1. (with dat. or acc. object). *follow, serve.* past 3sg. **fyligde.** inf. **fylgan, fylgean** 5/68; 14/33.

fyll. masc. *fall, death.* acc. sg. **fyl, fyll** 10/56. dat. sg. **fielle.**

gefyllan. 1. wk. 1. *fill, feed.* past 3sg. **gefylde** La/7. past part. **gefylde, gefylled** H/2. 2. wk. 1. *fell, kill.* imp. pl. **fyllað** 14/194. inf. **fyllan, gefyllan** 10/38, 73.

fyllu. fem. *fullness, feast.* gen. sg. **fylle** 14/209.

fȳlþ. fem. *filth, immorality.* acc. sg. **fȳlþe** 5/30. dat. sg. **fȳlþe** 5/30.

fȳnd → fēond.

fȳr. neut. *fire.* acc. sg. K/1366; 5/8. dat. sg. **fȳre** C/11.

fyrd. fem. *army.* acc. sg. **fierd.** dat. sg. **fierde.**

fyrding. fem. *expedition, army.* dat. sg. **fyrdinge.**

fyrdrinc. masc. *man of an army, warrior.* gen. sg. **fyrdrinces** I/2.

fyrdsearu. neut. *army-trappings, armour.*

fyrdwīc. neut. *military encampment.* dat. pl. **fyrdwīcum** 14/220.

fyrgenstrēam. masc. *mountain stream.* nom. sg. K/1359.

fyrhtu. fem. *fear.* dat. sg. 6/24.

gefyrn. adv. *formerly, long ago.* 2/27; 7/77.

fyrngeflit. neut. *ancient quarrel.* acc. pl. **fyrngeflitu** 14/264.

fyrst. masc. *period, space of time.* acc. sg. 14/324.

fyrwit. neut. *curiosity.* nom. sg. **fyrwyt.**

fȳsan. wk. 1. *hasten* (often with refl. pron.), *incite, drive off, put to flight.* 3sg. **fēseð** 5/39. subj. pl. 14/189.

gād. neut. *lack.* nom. sg. 13/45.

(ge)gaderian. wk. 2. *gather.* past 3sg. **gegaderode.** subj. pl. **gaderian.** inf. **gaderian** 2/20. past part. **gegaderod** 4/20.

gafol. neut. *tribute.* nom. sg. 4/14, 20. acc. sg. 4/1, 3. dat. sg. **gafole** 4/4.

gafolgelda. masc. *rent-payer, tenant.* gen. sg. **gafolgeldan** M/5.

gāl. adj. *lustful.*

galan. st. 6. *sing.* inf. 10/67; 13/23.

gālferhþ. adj. *lascivious.* masc. nom. sg. 14/62.

gālmōd. adj. *lascivious.* wk. masc. nom. sg. **gālmōda** 14/256.

gamol. adj. *old.* wk. masc. nom. sg. **gamela.**

gān. anom. verb. *go, walk.* 1sg. **gā.** 2sg. **gǣst** 1/14. 3sg. **gǣþ** A/1; 3/16. pl. **gāð.** past 1sg. **ēode** 6/8. past 3sg. **ēode** 1/8; 3/5; 6/6, 19, 32, etc. past pl. **ēodon** B/3; 3/10, 13; 14/15, 55, etc. imp. sg. **gā.** imp. pl. **gāð.** inf. 14/149.

gegān. anom. verb. *arrive, obtain.* past pl. **geēodon** 14/331. past part. 14/140, 219.

gang. masc. *going, passage, flow.* dat. sg. **gange** 10/23.

(ge)gangan. st. 7. *go, walk.* 1sg. **gange, gonge** 12/35. subj. pl. **gongen** M/13. imp. sg. **gang.** inf. **gangan, gegangan, gongan** 6/28; 14/54. pres. part. **gongende** 6/7, 30.

gār. masc. *spear.* acc. pl. **gāras** 14/224.

gārgewinn. neut. *battle with spears.* gen. sg. **gārgewinnes** 14/307.

gārmitting. fem. *meeting of spears.* gen. sg. **gārmittinge.**

gārsecg. masc. *ocean, sea.*

gāst. masc. *spirit.* nom. sg. **gǣst** 14/83, 112. acc. sg. G/4; 6/44; 10/49. gen. sg. **gāstes, gǣstes** 6/24; 14/279. dat. sg. **gāste.** nom. pl. **gāstas** 10/11. gen. pl. **gāsta** 10/152.

gāstlic. adj. *spiritual, religious.* wk. neut. dat. sg. **gāstlican** 2/10.

gatu → **geat.**

gāð → **gān.**

gǣlsa. masc. *lust.* acc. sg. **gǣlsan** 5/64.

gǣrs. neut. *grass.*

gǣst → **gān.**

gǣst → **gāst.**

gǣstes → **gāst.**

gǣstlic. adj. *spiritual.* neut. nom. sg. 9/73.

gǣþ → **gān.**

ge. conj. *and, both.* 1/5; 6/28 (2x); 7/14, 24 (2x), etc.

gē → **þū, gē.**

gēa. adv. *yes.*

gēac. masc. *cuckoo.* acc. sg. 13/23.

geador. adv. *together.* 11/19; 13/50.

gēafon → **gifan.**

gealga. masc. *gallows.* nom. sg. 10/10. acc. sg. **gealgan** 10/40.

gealgtrēow. neut. *gallows tree.* dat. sg. **gealgtrēowe** 10/146.

gēap. adj. *deceitful.* fem. nom. sg. compar. **gēapre** 1/1.

gēar. neut. *year.* dat. sg. **gēare** 2/12; 4/1, 5, 12. inst. sg. **gēare** 3/17, 18. acc. pl. H/1; 2/5; 7/44. gen. pl. **gēara** 2/29, 30; 5/4, 20, 47, etc. dat. pl. **gēarum** 2/18.

geāra. adv. *formerly.* 9/22; 10/28.

gearcian. wk. 2. *prepare, procure, supply.* past 3sg. **gearcode.**

geārdæg. masc. *day of yore.* dat. pl. **geārdagum** 9/44.

geare. adv. *thoroughly, well.* 2/13.

gegearewod → **(ge)gearwian.**

gearo. adj. *ready, complete.* masc. nom. sg. 3/7; 8/6.

gearwe. adv. *readily, well, sufficiently, thoroughly.* **gearwe, geare** 9/69, 71; 14/2.

(ge)gearwian. wk. 2. *prepare.* past 2sg. **geearwodest.** past 3sg. **gegearwode** 6/38. subj. past sg. **gegearwode** 6/30. past part. **gegearewod, gegearwod** 5/70; 14/199.

geat. neut. *gate.* acc. sg. 14/151. acc. pl. **gatu** 3/10, 15.

Gēat. masc. *Geat, member of the Geatish nation.* gen. pl. **Gēata.**

gēat → **gēotan.**

gegnum. adv. *straight, directly.* 14/132.

gelp- → **gielp.**

gēmde → **gȳman.**

geō. adv. *long ago.* **iū, geō** 7/71; 9/22; 10/28, 87.

geoc. neut. *yoke.* acc. sg. **gioc** 7/68.

gēoc. fem. *help, consolation.* dat. sg. **gēoce** 8/21.

geocian. wk. 2. *yoke.*

geoguþ. fem. *youth.* dat. sg. **iugoðe, geoguðe** 2/13; 9/35.

Geōl. neut. *Yule, Christmas, December.*

geōmor. adj. *sad.* masc. nom. sg. 12/17; 14/87. masc. acc. sg. **geōmorne** 13/23. fem. dat. sg. **geōmorre** 12/1. dat. pl. **geōmrum** 8/21.

geōmormōd. adj. *sad in spirit.* masc. nom. sg. 12/42. neut. dat. sg. **geōmormōdum** 14/144.

geōmrung. fem. *groaning, lamentation.*

geond. prep. (with acc., sometimes with dat.). *throughout, through, over.* **geond, gynd** 5/5, 15, 27, 58; 7/27, etc.

geondhweorfan. st. 3. *pass through, review.* 3sg. **geondhweorfeð** 9/51.

geondscēawian. wk. 2. *survey, examine.* 3sg. **geondscēawað** 9/52.

geondscīnan. st. 1. *shine over, illuminate.* inf. G/9.

geondþencan. wk. 1. *think through, ponder.* 1sg. **geondþence** 9/60. 3sg. **geondþenceð** 9/89.

geong. adj. *young.* masc. nom. sg. 10/39; 12/42. fem. dat. sg. **geongre.** masc. nom. pl. **geonge** 14/166.

georn. adj. *eager.* masc. nom. sg. 9/69; 13/43; 14/210.

georne. adv. *eagerly, earnestly, thoroughly.* C/2, 9; 2/9, 22; 5/4, etc. superl. **geornost** 5/60.

geornfulness. fem. *zeal, desire, diligence.* dat. sg. **geornfulnesse** 6/26.

geornlīce. adv. *zealously, diligently, earnestly.* F/7; 6/26; 7/15, 16.

gēotan. st. 2. *pour.* past 3sg. **gēat.**

gēsne. adj. *barren, lacking something* (gen.), *lifeless.* masc. nom. sg. 14/112. masc. acc. sg. 14/279.

gēt → **gīt.**

giedd. neut. *song, poem, tale.* acc. sg. 11/19; 12/1. dat. sg. **giedde** I/10.

giefstōl. masc. *gift-seat, throne.* acc. pl. **giefstōlas** 9/44.

gielp. masc. *boast, boasting, fame.* nom. sg. **gelp, gilp** 7/22, 67. acc. sg. **gelp** 7/65. gen. sg. **gelpes, gielpes, gilpes** 7/13, 57, 67; 9/69. dat. sg. **gilpe, gelpe** 7/50, 82.

gielpan. st. 3. *boast.* past pl. **gulpon.**

gierde → **gyrd.**

gīese. adv. *yes.*

giestrandæg. masc. *yesterday.*

gīet → **gīt.**

gif. conj. *if.* **gif, gyf** M/1, 3 (2x), 5, 8, etc.

gifan. st. 5. *give.* 3sg. **gyfð.** past 3sg. **geaf** 14/342. past pl. **gēafon.** subj. sg. **gife** 11/1. imp. sg. **gif.**

gīferness. fem. *greed, greedy deed.* acc. pl. **gīfernessa** 5/48.

gifeþe. adj. *given, granted.* masc. nom. sg. 14/157.

gifu. fem. *gift, grace.* nom. sg. 6/17. acc. sg. **gife** 6/3, 15, 20. dat. sg. **gife** 6/1. nom. pl. **gifa** 7/7. gen. pl. **gifena** 14/2. dat. pl. **geofum** J/83.

gilp- → **gielp.**

gīmelēst. fem. *carelessness.* dat. sg. **gīmelēste** 7/36.

gimm. masc. *gem.* nom. pl. **gimmas** 10/7, 16.

gimstān. masc. *gemstone.* dat. pl. **gymstānum** 2/13.

gingre. fem. *maidservant.* dat. sg. **gingran** 14/132.

ginn. adj. *wide, spacious.* masc. acc. sg. **gynne.** wk. fem. dat. sg. **ginnan** 14/149. wk. masc. inst. sg. **ginnan** 14/2.

gioc → **geoc.**

giōdagum. adv. *in days of old.* 7/49.

girn- → **gyrnan.**

girwan → **(ge)gyrwan.**

gīsl. masc. *hostage.* dat. sg. **gīsle** 3/8.

gist. masc. *guest, stranger.*

git → **þū, gē.**

gīt. adv. *still, yet.* **gȳt, gīt, gēt, gīet, gȳta** E/3; 2/26; 5/33, 58; 6/39, etc.

gitsung. fem. *avarice, avaricious deed.* acc. sg. **gītsunge** 5/63. gen. sg. **gitsunge** 7/67. nom. pl. **gītsung** 7/2. acc. pl. **gitsunga** 5/48.

glæd. adj. *bright, cheerful, glad.*

glædlīce. adv. *joyfully.* 6/33.

glædmōd. adj. *happy-minded.* fem. nom. pl. glædmōde 14/140.

geglængde → geglengan.

glēaw. adj. *wise.* masc. nom. sg. 9/73. fem. nom. sg. 14/13. fem. acc. sg. glēawe 14/333. wk. fem. nom. sg. glēawe 14/171.

glēawhydig. adj. *wise in thought.* neut. nom. sg. 14/148.

geglengan. wk. 1. *adorn.* past 3sg. geglængde 6/1. past part. geglenged 6/19.

glīwian. wk. 2. *make merry, sing.* pres. part. glēowiende 6/32.

glīwstæf. masc. *melody, joy.* dat. pl. glīwstafum 9/52.

gnæt. masc. *gnat.*

God. masc. (often neut. in pl.). *God, god.* nom. sg. God, Godd A/6; G/2; 1/1 (2x), 3, etc. acc. sg. 2/2, 8; 5/53, 62, 66, etc. gen. sg. Godes A/2; B/5, 6; 1/8; 2/6, etc. dat. sg. Gode 2/12, 16, 20; 4/10; 5/6, etc. nom. pl. godas, godu. acc. pl. godas. dat. pl. godum.

gōd. A. neut. *good, goods, property.* acc. sg. 1/5. gen. sg. gōdes 7/15. dat. sg. gōde A/3; 7/46; 14/271. gen. pl. gōda 14/32. dat. pl. gōdum 6/21.

B. adj. *good.* masc. nom. sg. J/83. fem. nom. sg. good 1/10. neut. nom. sg. 1/6. masc. acc. sg. gōdne La/3; 5/40; 7/14, 38. fem. acc. sg. gōde 10/70. masc. gen. sg. gōdes 7/36. gen. pl. gōdra 6/26; 7/13, 58. dat. pl. gōdum 2/10; 7/11. wk. masc. nom. sg. gōda. wk. masc. nom. pl. gōdan c/12. wk. gen. pl. gōdena 7/47. neut. nom. sg. compar. betere. masc. nom. pl. compar. beteran. masc. nom. sg. superl. sēlost G/4. fem. nom. sg. superl. sēlost, betst G/3 (2x), 4. neut. nom. sg. superl. betst. neut. acc. sg. superl. sēlest 10/118. dat. pl. superl. betstum 7/57. wk. masc. nom. sg. superl. sēlesta 10/27. wk. neut. inst. sg. superl. betstan 6/19.

godbearn. neut. *godchild.* acc. pl. 5/27.

godcund. adj. *divine.* fem. gen. sg. godcundre 6/18. fem. dat. sg. godcundre 6/1. gen. pl. godcundra 5/50. dat. pl. godcundum 6/1. wk. dat. pl. godcundan 6/25.

godcundlīce. adv. *divinely.* 6/3.

gōddǣd. fem. *good deed.* acc. pl. gōddǣda 5/51. dat. pl. gōddǣdan 5/51.

godfyrht. adj. *God-fearing.* masc. acc. pl. godfyrhte 5/51.

gōdian. wk. 2. *improve.* pres. part. gōdiende 5/7.

godsibb. masc. *baptismal sponsor.* acc. pl. godsibbas 5/27.

godsunu. masc. u-stem. *godson.* nom. sg. 3/15.

gold. neut. *gold.* nom. sg. 9/32. acc. sg. 10/18. gen. sg. goldes 13/36. dat. sg. golde 2/13; 10/7, 16, 77; 14/171, etc.

goldgifa. masc. *gold-giver, lord.* acc. sg. goldgifan 14/279.

goldhladen. adj. *gold-laden, wearing gold ornaments.*

goldhord. neut. *hoard of gold, treasure.*

goldsmiþ. masc. *goldsmith.* gen. sg. goldsmiðes 7/71.

goldwine. masc. *gold-friend, gold-lord, generous lord.* nom. sg. 9/35; 14/22. acc. sg. 9/22.

gong- → (ge)gangan.

good → gōd.

gram. adj. *angry, fierce.* masc. nom. pl. grame 14/224, 238.

Grantabricscīr. fem. *Cambridgeshire.* acc. sg. Grantabricscīre 4/2.

Grantanceaster. fem. *Grantchester.* dat. sg. Grantanceastre 2/19.

grāpian. wk. 2. *seize.* past 3sg. grāpode Lb/3.

grǣdig. adj. (with gen.). *greedy.* masc. nom. sg. F/3. masc. nom. pl. grǣdige.

(ge)gremian. wk. 2. *anger.* past pl. gegræmedan 5/62. past part. gegremede 14/305.

grēot. neut. *earth.* acc. sg. 14/307.

grēotan. st. 2. *weep.* pres. part. **grēotende** 10/70.

(ge)grētan. wk. 1. *greet.* 3sg. **grēteð, gegrēteð** 5/52; 9/52. past 3sg. **grētte** 6/7. inf. **grētan, gegrētan** J/89; La/6.

grimlic. adj. *fierce, cruel, terrible.* neut. nom. sg. 5/3.

grimm. adj. *savage.* masc. nom. pl. **grimme** 5/50.

grimness. fem. *cruelty, severity.* acc. sg. **grimnysse.**

(ge)grīpan. st. 1. (with acc. or gen. object). *seize, attack.* inf. **gegrīpan** 7/82. pres. part. **grīpende** F/3.

gristbitian. wk. 2. *gnash the teeth.* inf. 14/271.

griþ. neut. *truce, protection, sanctuary.* acc. sg. 4/4. dat. sg. **griðe** 4/4; 5/28.

griþian. wk. 2. *make peace, protect.* inf. 5/12.

griþlēas. adj. *without protection.* fem. nom. pl. **griðlēase** 5/13.

grund. masc. *bottom, country, earth, land.* acc. sg. K/1367. inst. sg. **grunde** 14/2. acc. pl. **grundas** 14/348.

grundwong. masc. *ground-plain, bottom.*

guldon → gyldan.

gulpon → gielpan.

guma. masc. *man, mankind.* nom. sg. 7/82; 9/45. gen. sg. **guman** 10/49, 146. nom. pl. **guman** 14/305. gen. pl. **gumena** K/1367; 14/9, 22, 32, 62, etc. dat. pl. **gumum.**

gūþ. fem. *war, battle.* nom. sg. J/83. dat. sg. **gūþe** 14/123, 305.

gūþcræft. masc. *war-craft, skill in fighting.*

gūþfana. masc. *battle-standard.* dat. pl. **gūðfanum** 14/219.

gūþfreca. masc. *warrior.* nom. pl. **gūðfrecan** 14/224.

gūþsceorp. neut. *battle-ornament, battle-equipment.* acc. pl. 14/328.

gyddian. wk. 2. *speak formally, sing.* inf. 7/64.

gyf → gif.

gyfð → gifan.

gyldan. st. 3. *pay, repay.* pl. **gyldað** 5/44, 45. past pl. **guldon** 14/263. subj. sg. **gylde** 5/37.

gylden. adj. *golden.* masc. acc. sg. **gyldenne.**

gyllan. wk. 1. *yell.* past 3sg. **gylede** 14/25.

gylt. masc. *guilt, sin.* acc. sg. 2/13.

gȳman. wk. 1. *care for, take care, take heed of, obey.* past 3sg. **gēmde** 6/26. subj. sg. **gȳme** 5/9.

gymstānum → gimstān.

gynd → geond.

gynne → ginn.

gyrd. fem. *rod, staff.* acc. sg. **gyrde, gierde.**

gyrde → (ge)gyrwan.

gegyred → (ge)gyrwan.

gyredon → (ge)gyrwan.

gyrnan. wk. 1. (with gen.). *yearn for, desire, ask for.* pl. **girnað** 7/27. past 3sg. **girnde, gyrnde** 7/2; 14/346. past pl. **gyrndon** 4/1.

(ge)gyrwan. wk. 1. *prepare, equip* somebody (acc.) with something (dat.), *dress, adorn, serve* (with *up*, 'serve up'). past 3sg. **gyrde.** inf. **girwan** 14/9. past part. **gegyred, gyredon, gegyrwed** 10/16, 23, 77.

gystern. neut. *guest-house.* dat. sg. **gysterne** 14/40.

gyt → þū, gē.

gȳt → gīt.

gȳta → gīt.

gytesæl. masc. *joy at pouring* (of drinking). dat. pl. **gytesālum** 14/22.

habban. wk. 3. *have, hold.* 1sg. **hæbbe, hafu** I/6; 10/50, 79. 2sg. **hæfst.** 3sg. **hæfð, hafað** La/3; 5/70; 7/18, 19 (2x), etc. pl. **habbað, hæbbe** 5/6, 11, 16, 42, 52, etc. past 1sg. **hæfde** 12/7. past 3sg. **hæfde** 2/8; 3/1, 3; 6/14, 19, etc. past pl. **hæfdon** 3/6, 10; 4/2, 4, 8, etc. subj. sg. **hæbbe** 7/4, 82. subj. pl. **hæbben** 7/38 (2x). subj. past pl. **hæfden** H/3; 7/37. inf. C/12; 5/69; 7/4, 6, 14, etc. past part. **hæfd** B/3.

negated. 3sg. **næfð** 7/44. pl. **nabbað**. subj. past 3sg. **næfde** B/7.

hādbryce. masc. *crime against persons in orders.* acc. pl. **hādbrycas** 5/48.

gehādian. wk. 2. *ordain, consecrate.* past 3sg. **gehādode** 2/10. past part. **gehādod, gehādode, gehādodan** 2/10, 17; 4/7, 12; 5/21, etc.

hafað → habban.

hafela. masc. *head.* acc. sg. **hafelan** K/1372.

hafoc. masc. *hawk.*

hafu → habban.

hafu → hæf.

hagol. masc. *hail.* dat. sg. **hagle** 9/48.

hagolfaru. fem. *hailstorm.* acc. sg. **hæglfare** 9/105.

hāl. adj. *healthy, whole, sound.* fem. nom. sg. 2/22. neut. acc. sg. 2/26. masc. nom. pl. **hāle** 2/27.

hālettan. wk. 1. *salute.* past 3sg. **hālette** 6/7.

hālga. masc. *saint.* dat. pl. **hālgum** 2/8; 10/143, 154.

gehālgian. wk. 2. *consecrate.* past 3sg. **gehālgode.**

hālig. adj. *holy, saintly.* masc. nom. sg. 6/13. fem. nom. sg. **hālige** 14/160. neut. acc. sg. 6/18. fem. dat. sg. **hāligre** 14/98. masc. nom. pl. **hālige** 10/11. fem. nom. pl. **hālige** 5/28. wk. masc. nom. sg. **hālga** 2/8. wk. fem. nom. sg. **hālige** 14/56. wk. neut. nom. sg. **hālige** 4/18. wk. masc. acc. sg. **hālgan** G/4. wk. fem. acc. sg. **hālgan, hāligan** 2/27; 4/18; 14/260. wk. masc. gen. sg. **hālgan** 4/19; 6/24. wk. fem. gen. sg. **hālgan.** wk. neut. gen. sg. **hālgan** 2/25; 6/21, 24. wk. fem. dat. sg. **hālgan, hāligan** 2/1; 14/203.

hāligdōm. masc. *holiness, chapel, relic, sacrament.*

hāligness. fem. *holiness, sanctuary.* nom. pl. **hālignessa** 5/13.

hālwende. adj. *healing, salutary.* neut. acc. sg. 6/44.

hām. A. masc. *home.* acc. sg. 6/6, 19; 10/148. dat. sg. 14/121.

B. adv. *homewards, home.* 14/131.

hāmfæst. adj. *resident.* masc. nom. sg. 7/26, 36.

Hamtūnscīr. fem. *Hampshire.* dat. sg. **Hamtūnscīre** 3/1; 4/2 (2x).

hand. fem. u-stem. *hand.* acc. sg. **hand, hond** I/4; J/90; 14/130, 198. dat. sg. **handa, honda** 6/35; 10/59. nom. pl. **handa** B/4. acc. pl. **honda, handa** 6/44; 9/43. dat. pl. **handum, hondum, handon** F/3; Lb/4; 9/4.

hangelle. fem. *hanging thing.* gen. sg. **hangellan** La/6.

hangian. wk. 2. *hang.* 3sg. **hongað** La/1. pl. **hongiað** K/1363. past pl. **hangodon** F/3, 5.

hār. adj. *hoary, gray, old.* fem. acc. pl. **hāre** 14/327. wk. masc. nom. sg. **hāra** 9/82. wk. masc. acc. sg. **hārne** F/1.

hāt. A. neut. *heat.*

B. adj. *hot.* wk. masc. nom. sg. **hāta** 2/13.

(ge)hātan. st. 7. *command, call, name, be called, promise.* 1sg. **hāte** 10/95. pl. **hātað** 7/29. past 3sg. **hēt, heht** 2/16, 20; 6/16 (2x), 21, etc. past pl. **hēton** 10/31. subj. past sg. **hēte** 14/53. imp. sg. **hāt.** inf. **gehātan** 13/11. past part. **gehāten, hāten** 2/14; 3/3; 7/28, 75.

passive. 1sg. **hātte** I/11. 3sg. **hātte** G/3; 7/16. past 3sg. **hātte** 2/2; 5/61.

hāte. adv. *hotly.* 14/94.

hātheort. adj. *hot-hearted, angry.* masc. nom. sg. 9/66.

gehātland. neut. *promised land.* gen. sg. **gehātlandes** 6/24.

hæbb- → habban.

hæf. neut. *sea.* acc. pl. **hafu** 13/8.

hæfd- → habban.

hæfen → hebban.

hæfst → habban.

hæft. neut. *hilt.* dat. sg. **hæfte** 14/263.

(ge)hæftan. wk. 1. *bind, imprison.* past part. **gehæfted** 14/116.

hæfð → habban.

hæglfare → hagolfaru.

hǣlan. wk. 1. *heal.* inf. 10/85.

gehǣlan. wk. 1. *heal.* 1sg. **gehǣle.** past part. **gehǣled, gehǣlede** 2/23, 27.

hǣle. masc. dental stem. *warrior, man.* nom. sg. **hǣleð, hǣle** 9/73; 10/39, 78, 95. nom. pl. **hǣleð** 14/56, 177, 203, 225, 302, etc. acc. pl. **hǣleð** 14/247. gen. pl. **hǣleða** 7/65, 82; 13/39; 14/51. dat. pl. **hǣleþum** 9/105.

Hǣlend. masc. nd-stem. *Savior.* nom. sg. 2/31. acc. sg. 2/6. gen. sg. **Hǣlendes** 10/25. dat. sg. **Hǣlende** 2/31.

hǣlþ. fem. *health, salvation.* dat. sg. **hǣlðe.**

hǣlu. fem. *health, prosperity, salvation.* acc. sg. **hǣle, hǣlo** 8/16.

hǣmed. neut. *sexual intercourse.* dat. sg. **hǣmede** 2/4, 30.

hǣmedþing. neut. *sexual intercourse, marriage.*

Hǣstingas. masc. *Hastings.* acc. pl. 4/2.

hǣto. fem. *heat.* dat. sg. **hǣte** 7/18.

hǣþen. adj. *heathen, pagan.* masc. gen. sg. **hǣðenes** 14/179. masc. acc. pl. **hǣþene** 5/48. gen. pl. **hǣðenra** D/1, 3; 14/216. dat. pl. **hǣþenum** 5/10, 11, 12. wk. fem. nom. sg. **hǣðene.** wk. masc. acc. sg. **hǣðenan** 14/98, 110. wk. masc. nom. pl. **hǣþenan.** wk. gen. pl. **hǣðenra.**

hǣþenscipe. masc. *paganism, idolatry.*

hǣþstapa. masc. *heath-walker.* nom. sg. K/1368.

hē. pron. **1.** pers. *he, it.* masc. nom. sg. A/2, 3 (2x); B/3 (2x), etc. masc. acc. sg. **hine, hiene, hyne** B/2; C/3, 5 (3x), etc. masc. gen. sg. **his, hys** A/2 (2x), 3 (3x), etc. masc. dat. sg. **him** A/3; B/7; H/3; 2/7, 16, etc. **2.** refl. *he, himself.* masc. acc. sg. **hine** 1/8; 3/5; 5/40, 59; 6/38, etc. masc. gen. sg. **his** 12/46. masc. dat. sg. **him** 6/38, 42; 9/1, 31, 111, etc.

hēafod. neut. (occasionally pl. with sg. meaning). *head.* nom. sg. 4/9; 14/110. acc. sg. 1/15; 4/18; 6/42; 9/43; 14/126, etc. dat. sg. **hēafde** La/6; 2/25 (2x).

acc. pl. **hēafdu.** dat. pl. **hēafdum** 4/17; 10/63.

hēafodgerīm. neut. *number of heads, number of men.* gen. sg. **hēafodgerīmes** 14/308.

hēafodweard. masc. *chief guardian.* nom. pl. **hēafodweardas** 14/239.

hēah. adj. *high, deep, great.* masc. nom. sg. 9/98. masc. acc. sg. **hēanne** 9/82; 10/40. masc. nom. pl. **hēa.** neut. acc. pl. 13/8. dat. pl. **hēaum.** wk. masc. acc. sg. **hēanne** 14/161. wk. neut. dat. sg. **hēan** 14/43. wk. masc. nom. sg. superl. **hēhsta, hȳhsta** 14/94, 308. wk. masc. gen. sg. superl. **hēhstan** 14/4 (2x).

hēahfæder. masc. r-stem. *high father, patriarch, God.* dat. sg. **hēahfædere** 10/134.

hēahtīd. fem. *holy day.* dat. pl. **hēahtīdum** 2/11.

(ge)healdan. st. 7. *hold, keep, observe, preserve, maintain, govern, satisfy.* 3sg. **hylt, gehealdeþ** D/3; 9/112. past 3sg. **hēold, gehēold** 2/4, 6, 10, 26; 3/17, etc. past pl. **hēoldon, hēoldan** D/1; 2/28; 5/22; 14/142. subj. sg. **healde** 9/14; 13/37. subj. past sg. **hēolde.** inf. **healdan, gehealdan** J/86; 4/21; 5/12, 69; 7/8, etc. pres. part. **healdende.** past part. **gehealden** 7/34.

healdend. masc. nd-stem. (pres. part. of *healdan* 'hold'). *possessor, lord.* nom. sg. 14/289.

healf. **A.** fem. *half, side.* acc. sg. **healfe** 7/29; 10/20.

B. adj. *half.* fem. acc. sg. **healfe** 4/2. neut. acc. sg. **healfne** 14/105. neut. dat. sg. **healfum** 7/22.

hēalic. adj. *high, exalted, noble, fine.* dat. pl. **hēalicum** 2/13.

healm. masc. *straw.*

healreced. neut. *hall.*

healsbēag. masc. *necklace.*

healt. adj. *lame.* gen. pl. **healtra.**

hēan. adj. *lowly, poor, wretched.* masc. nom. sg. 9/23. masc. acc. sg. **hēanne** 14/234.

hēanne → hēah.

hēap. masc. *company*. dat. sg. **hēape** 2/14. dat. pl. **hēapum** 14/163.

heard. adj. *hard, stern, cruel*. masc. nom. sg. 12/43. fem. nom. sg. ı/8. neut. nom. sg. Lа/3. masc. acc. sg. **heardne** 14/79. gen. pl. **heardra** 14/225. dat. pl. **heardum** 14/263. masc. nom. sg. compar. **heardra**. neut. nom. sg. superl. **heardost** 10/87.

hearde. adv. *hard, firmly, painfully*. 14/116, 216. superl. **heardost** 7/67.

heardsǣlig. adj. *unfortunate*. masc. acc. sg. **heardsǣligne** 12/19.

heardsǣlþ. fem. *misfortune, misdeed*. acc. pl. **heardsǣlþa** 7/36.

hearmcwidian. wk. 2. *slander*. inf. 7/52.

hearpe. fem. *harp*. acc. sg. **hearpan** 6/6. gen. sg. **hearpan**. dat. sg. **hearpan** 6/6.

hēarra. masc. *lord*. dat. sg. **hēarran** 14/56.

heaþobyrne. fem. *battle-corslet*.

heaþorinc. masc. *warrior*. gen. sg. **heaðorinces** 14/179. nom. pl. **heaðorincas** 14/212.

heaþufȳr. neut. *war-fire*. gen. sg. **heaðufȳres**.

(ge)hēawan. st. 7. *cut, hack*, fig. *kill*. 3sg. **hēaweþ** 5/23. inf. **gehēawan** 14/90. past part. **gehēawen, hēowon** 14/288, 294, 303.

hebban. st. 6. *lift*. 3sg. **hefeð** Lа/5. inf. в/2; Lb/2; 10/31. past part. **hæfen**.

hefgad → hefigian.

hefig. adj. *heavy, grievous*. neut. dat. sg. **hefian** 10/61. fem. nom. pl. compar. **hefigran** 9/49. neut. nom. sg. superl. **hefegost** G/7.

hefigian. wk. 2. *make heavy, oppress, afflict*. past part. **hefgad** 6/28.

hefiglīce. adv. *heavily, severely*. 7/13.

hefigness. fem. *heaviness, weight*. acc. sg. **hefignesse** в/7.

hefonum → heofon.

hēhst- → hēah.

heht → (ge)hātan.

hell. fem. *hell*. acc. sg. **helle** G/8. gen. sg. **helle** 14/116. dat. sg. **helle** c/6, 11.

hellewīte. neut. *hellish punishment*. gen. sg. **hellewītes** 5/70.

helm. masc. *helmet, protector*. acc. sg. 14/337. acc. pl. **helmas** 14/193, 317, 327. dat. pl. **helmum** 14/203.

help. fem. *help*. acc. sg. **helpe** 9/16. dat. sg. **helpe** 10/102; 14/96.

helpan. st. 3. (with gen. object). *help*. subj. sg. **helpe** 5/71.

hēo. pron. 1. pers. *she, it*. fem. nom. sg. **hēo, hīo** G/3, 4, 5, 8, 9 (2x), etc. fem. acc. sg. **hī, hīe, hȳ** 2/4, 6, 10, 22, 24, etc. fem. gen. sg. **hire, hyre** ı/85; 1/6, 15 (2x); 2/2, etc. fem. dat. sg. **hire, hyre** G/9 (2x); 1/6; 2/9, 10, etc. 2. refl. *she, herself*. fem. acc. sg. **hī** 2/11. fem. dat. sg. **hyre** 2/25.

hēo → hīe.

heofon. masc. *heaven*. acc. sg. 6/13; 7/16. gen. sg. **heofenes, heofones** 7/65; 10/64. dat. sg. **heofene**. acc. pl. **heofonas, heofenas** G/2; 6/24; 10/103. gen. pl. **heofona** 10/45. dat. pl. **heofonum, heofenum, hefonum** c/8, 12; 2/30; 7/61; 9/107, etc.

heofone. fem. *heaven*. dat. sg. **heofonan**. dat. pl. **heofonum**.

heofonlic. adj. *heavenly*. fem. nom. sg. 6/17. masc. acc. sg. **heofonlicne** 10/148. neut. gen. sg. **heofonlican** 7/62. wk. neut. gen. sg. **heofonlecan, heofonlican** 6/2, 24. wk. neut. inst. sg. **heofonlecan** 6/38.

heofonrīce. neut. *kingdom of heaven*. gen. sg. **heofonrices, heofonrīces** 6/12; 10/91.

hēold- → (ge)healdan.

gehēold → (ge)healdan.

heolfrig. adj. *bloody*. neut. acc. sg. 14/130, 316.

heolstor. A. masc. *darkness, concealment*. dat. sg. **heolstre** 9/23.

B. adj. *dark*. wk. masc. dat. sg. **heolstran** 14/121.

heonan. adv. *hence.* heonan, heonon
к/1361; 10/132; 12/6; 13/27.

heonanforþ. adv. *henceforth.* 5/7, 9.

heora → hīe.

heord. fem. *herd, keeping, care.* nom. sg.
6/7. acc. pl. heorda.

heorde → hyrde.

hēore. adj. *safe, pleasant.* fem. nom. sg.
hēoru к/1372.

heorot. masc. *hart, stag.* nom. sg. к/1369.

heorte. fem. *heart.* nom. sg. 14/87. acc. sg.
heortan. gen. sg. heortan 9/49; 12/43.
dat. sg. heortan. dat. pl. heortum.

Heortfordscīr. fem. *Hertfordshire.* acc. sg.
Heortfordscīre 4/2.

heoruwǣpen. neut. *sword-weapon.* dat. pl.
heoruwǣpnum 14/263.

hēowon → (ge)hēawan.

hēr. adv. *here.* c/12; ғ/6; ɢ/1; 3/1; 4/1, etc.

gehēran → (ge)hȳran.

hērbūend. masc. nd-stem. *one who dwells
here.* gen. pl. hērbūendra 14/96.

gehērd- → (ge)hȳran.

here. masc. *army, viking army, glory* (?).
nom. sg. 4/15, 20; 5/18, 39; 7/78, etc.
acc. sg. 5/62. gen. sg. herges, heriges
ı/8; 14/293. dat. sg. here, herige 4/1,
21; 14/135. nom. pl. hergas.

gehēred → (ge)hȳran.

herefolc. neut. *army.* gen. sg. herefolces
14/234, 239.

herefugol. masc. *war-bird.* nom. pl.
herefugolas.

heregodon → (ge)hergian.

herehȳþ. fem. *booty, plunder.*

hereness. fem. *praise.* acc. sg. herenisse
6/44. dat. sg. herenesse 6/11.

hererēaf. neut. *plunder from an army.* acc.
sg. 14/316.

heretoga. masc. *commander.* nom. sg.
7/75. gen. sg. heretogan 7/28.

herewǣþa. masc. *warrior.* gen. sg.
herewǣðan 14/126, 173.

(ge)hergian. wk. 2. *plunder, harry, seize,
capture.* pl. hergiað 5/46. past 3sg.
gehergode c/6. past pl. heregodon 4/4.

hergung. fem. *harrying.* acc. sg. hergunge
4/1.

herheard. masc. *residence in a pagan
shrine.* acc. sg. 12/15.

herian. wk. 1. *praise.* subj. pl. herien
7/70. inf. herian, herigean 5/53; 6/12.

herpaþ. masc. *path for an army.* acc. sg.
14/302.

hērtōēacan. adv. *in addition.* 5/58.

gehērð → (ge)hȳran.

hēt- → (ge)hātan.

hete. masc. *hate, enmity, hostile act.* nom.
sg. 5/19, 39.

hetelīce. adv. *with enmity, violently.*
5/34.

heteþoncol. adj. *hostile-minded.* masc. acc.
sg. heteþoncolne 14/105.

hetol. adj. *hostile.* masc. nom. pl. hetole
5/50.

hī → hēo.

hicgan. wk. 3. *think, intend.* past 1sg.
hogode 11/9. past 3sg. hogode. past
pl. hogedon 14/250, 273. subj. sg. hycge
9/14; 13/11. inf. hycgan 12/11. pres.
part. hycgendne 12/20.

hider. adv. *hither, to this place.* 6/8;
10/103.

hīe. pron. 1. pers. *they, themselves.* nom.
pl. hīe, hī, hȳ, hēo, hig ᴀ/4; ʙ/2, 5; ғ/7;
ʜ/2, etc. acc. pl. hī, hīe, hȳ, hig 2/10,
19; 4/4 (2x), 5, etc. gen. pl. heora, hiera,
hiora, hira, hyra ᴀ/1; ғ/3 (2x), 6; ɢ/1,
etc. dat. pl. him ᴀ/4; ᴅ/2; ғ/5; ʜ/3; ᴊ/91,
etc. 2. refl. *themselves.* acc. pl. hīe, hȳ
3/14; 5/53. dat. pl. him 1/7 (2x); 4/8;
10/31, 63, etc.

hīe → hēo.

hiene → hē.

hīer- → (ge)hȳran.

hīerd- → (ge)hȳran.

gehīerdun → (ge)hȳran.

hige → hyge.

higerōf. adj. *brave-hearted.* masc. nom.
pl. higerōfe 14/302.

higesnotor. adj. *wise in mind.* dat. pl.
higesnotrum 7/66.

higeþoncol. adj. *thoughtful.* fem. dat. sg. **higeðoncolre** 14/131.

hiht → hyht.

hild. fem. *battle.* acc. sg. **hilde** 14/251. gen. sg. **hilde.** dat. sg. **hilde** 14/293.

hildedēor. adj. *brave in battle.*

hildelēoþ. neut. *war-song.* acc. sg. 14/211.

hildenædre. fem. *battle-serpent, arrow.* acc. pl. **hildenædran** 14/222.

hilderinc. masc. *warrior.* nom. pl. **hilderincas** 10/61. gen. pl. **hilderinca** 10/72.

him → hē.

him → hīe.

hine → hē.

hingrigendne → hyngrian.

hingrode → hyngrian.

hinsīþ. masc. *departure, death.* dat. sg. **hinsīðe** 14/117.

hīo → hēo.

hiora → hīe.

hira → hīe.

hire → hēo.

gehīre → (ge)hȳran.

hīred. masc. *household, family, company.* gen. sg. **hīredes** M/12.

his → hē.

hisping. fem. *scorn, mockery.* acc. sg. **hispinge** 7/53.

hit. pers. pron. *it.* neut. nom. sg. B/1, 4; M/7, 9; 2/1, etc. neut. acc. sg. A/4; H/2, 3; 2/4, 5, etc.

hīw. neut. *appearance, form, kind, color.* gen. sg. **hīwes.**

hīwcūþ. adj. *familiar.* masc. acc. pl. **hīwcūðe** 7/80.

hlāf. masc. *bread, loaf.* gen. sg. **hlāfes** 1/19. acc. pl. **hlāfas.** gen. pl. **hlāfa.** dat. pl. **hlāfum.**

hlāford. masc. *lord, the Lord.* nom. sg. 3/12; 5/41; 12/6, 15. acc. sg. 5/25; 10/45. gen. sg. **hlāfordes** G/7; 5/25. dat. sg. **hlāforde** 5/36; 14/251. acc. pl. **hlāfordas.**

hlāfordswica. masc. *traitor to one's lord.* nom. pl. **hlāfordswican** 5/24.

hlāfordswice. masc. *betrayal of one's lord.* nom. sg. 5/25 (2x).

hlagol. adj. *inclined to laugh.*

hlanc. adj. *lank, lean.* wk. masc. nom. sg. **hlanca** 14/205.

hlǣfdige. fem. *lady.* acc. sg. **hlǣfdigan.**

gehlǣstan. wk. 1. *load.* past part. **gehlǣste** 14/36.

hlǣw. masc. *burial mound.* gen. pl. **hlǣwa** 7/74.

hlehhan. st. 6. *laugh.* past 3sg. **hlōh** 14/23.

hlēoþrian. wk. 2. *speak.* past 3sg. **hlēoðrode** 10/26.

hlid. neut. *covering, lid, roof.* acc. sg. **hlyd** 2/19.

hlīfian. wk. 2. *rise high, tower.* 1sg. **hlīfige** 10/85.

hlimman. st. 3. *resound.* past pl. **hlummon** 14/205.

hlīsa. masc. *fame, approbation.* nom. sg. 7/30, 31, 45, 55, 78, etc. acc. sg. **hlīsan** 7/14, 21, 31, 32, 38, etc. gen. sg. **hlīsan** 7/13, 57, 58, 65, 67, etc. dat. sg. **hlīsan** 7/15, 46, 59.

hliþ. neut. *cliff, hill, slope.* gen. sg. **hliþes** 13/22.

hlōh → hlehhan.

hlūde. adv. *loudly.* 14/205, 223, 270.

hlummon → hlimman.

hlūtor. adj. *pure, clear, bright, sincere.* neut. inst. sg. **hlūttre** 6/43.

hlyd → hlid.

hlȳdan. st. 1. *make a loud noise, shout.* past 3sg. **hlȳdde** 14/23.

hlynnan. wk. 1. *make noise, shout.* past 3sg. **hlynede** 14/23.

hlystan. wk. 1. *listen.* imp. sg. **hlyst.**

hnāg → hnīgan.

hnecca. masc. *neck.* dat. sg. **hneccan** D/2.

hnīgan. st. 1. *bend, bow.* past 1sg. **hnāg** 10/59.

hnutu. fem. athematic. *nut.* nom. pl. **hnyte.**

hocor. masc. *derision.* dat. sg. **hocere** 5/51.

hocorwyrde. adj. *derisive.* masc. nom. pl. 5/50.

hogedon → hicgan.

hogode → hicgan.

hōh. masc. *heel.* dat. sg. **hō** 1/15.

hol. neut. *hole.* acc. sg. Lа/5.

hōl. neut. *slander.* nom. sg. 5/19.

gehola. masc. *confidant.* gen. pl. **geholena** 9/31.

hold. adj. *friendly, gracious, loyal.* gen. pl. **holdra** 12/17.

holm. masc. *sea.* acc. sg. 9/82.

holmclif. neut. *sea-cliff.* acc. pl. **holmclifu.**

holt. neut. *forest.* gen. sg. **holtes** 10/29.

holtwudu. masc. *wood of the forest.* acc. sg. к/1369; 10/91.

hōn. st. 7. *hang.*

hond- → hand.

hongað → hangian.

hongiað → hangian.

hopian. wk. 2. *hope, expect.* 1sg. **hopie.** 2sg. **hopast.** 3sg. **hopað.** pl. **hopiað.** past 2sg. **hopodest.** past 3sg. **hopode.** past pl. **hopodon.** inf. 14/117.

hordcofa. masc. *hoard-chamber, breast, thought.* acc. sg. **hordcofan** 9/14.

hordwela. masc. *hoarded wealth.* acc. sg. **hordwelan.**

hōring. masc. *fornicator.* nom. pl. **hōringas** 5/56.

horn. masc. *horn.* dat. pl. **hornum** к/1369.

hornboga. masc. *bow* (tipped with horn or curved like a horn). dat. sg. **hornbogan** 14/222.

hors. neut. *horse.*

hosp. masc. *reproach, contempt.* acc. sg. 14/216.

gehradian. wk. 2. *hasten, further, prosper.* past 3sg. **gehradode** 2/19.

hraþe, raþe, rade. adv. *quickly.* **hraðe, hræðe** 7/15; 14/37. superl. **radost, raþost** н/3; 3/7.

hræd. adj. *quick, brief.* neut. nom. sg. superl. **hrædest, hraðost** 5/15, 56; 7/11.

hræding. fem. *haste, brevity.* acc. sg. **hrædinge** 5/58.

hrædlīce. adv. *quickly.*

hrædness. fem. *quickness, speed.* dat. sg. **hrædnesse** в/7.

hrædwyrde. adj. *hasty of speech.* masc. nom. sg. 9/66.

hræfen → hrefn.

hrægl. neut. *cloth, sheet, clothing, garment, sail.* acc. sg. Lа/4; 14/282. dat. sg. **hrægle** Lb/4. dat. pl. **hreglum.**

hræðe → hraþe, raþe, rade.

hræw. neut. *body.* nom. sg. 10/72. acc. sg. 10/53. acc. pl. 14/313.

hrēam. masc. *outcry, tumult.*

hrēaw. adj. *raw.* neut. gen. sg. **hrēawes.**

hrefn. masc. *raven.* nom. sg. **hrefn, hræfen** 14/206. nom. pl. **hremmas.**

hreglum → hrægl.

hrēoh. adj. *rough, fierce, disturbed, troubled.* masc. nom. sg. 14/282. fem. acc. sg. **hrēo** 9/105. wk. masc. nom. sg. **hrēo** 9/16.

Hrēopadūn. fem. *Repton, Derbyshire.* dat. sg. **Hrēopadūne** 3/17.

hrēopon → hrōpan.

hrēosan. st. 2. *fall.* inf. 9/48. pres. part. **hrēosende** 9/102.

hrēowcearig. adj. *sorrowful.* masc. nom. sg. 10/25.

hrēowigmōd. adj. *regretful, sorrowful.* masc. nom. pl. **hrēowigmōde** 14/289.

hrēowlīce. adv. *sadly.* 5/14.

hrepian. wk. 2. *touch.* past pl. **hrepodon** 2/27. subj. past pl. **hrepodon** 1/3.

hrēran. wk. 1. *move, stir.* inf. 9/4.

hreþer. masc. *breast, heart, mind.* dat. sg. **hreðre** 14/94. gen. pl. **hreþra** 9/72.

hrīm. masc. *frost.* acc. sg. 9/48. dat. sg. **hrīme** 9/77.

hrīmceald. adj. *frost-cold.* fem. acc. sg. **hrīmcealde** 9/4.

hrīmig. adj. *frosty.* masc. nom. pl. **hrīmige** F/2.

hrind. adj. *frost-covered.* masc. nom. pl. **hrinde** к/1363.

hring. masc. *ring.* dat. pl. **hringum** 14/37.

hringed. adj. *made of rings.* fem. acc. sg. **hringde.**

hringedstefna. masc. *ring-prow, ship with ringed prow.*

hrīþ. masc. *frost.* nom. sg. 9/102.

hrīþig. adj. *snow-swept.* masc. nom. pl. **hrȳðge** 9/77.

(ge)hroden. adj. *adorned.* fem. acc. sg. **gehrodene** 14/37.

hrōf. masc. *roof, summit.* dat. sg. **hrōfe** 6/13; 7/13; 14/67.

hrōpan. st. 7. *shout, cry out, scream.* past pl. **hrēopon.**

hrūse. fem. *earth* (sometimes pl. with sg. sense). acc. sg. **hrūsan** 9/102. gen. sg. **hrūsan** 9/23. nom. pl. **hrūsan** 7/74.

hrycg. masc. *ridge, back.*

hryre. masc. *fall, death.* gen. pl. 9/7.

hrȳþer. neut. *cow.* gen. pl. **hrȳþera** 4/17.

hrȳþge → hrīþig.

hū. A. adv. *how.* 5/35, 58, 62; 6/39; 7/15 (4x), etc.
B. conj. *how.* G/1; 2/31; 4/7; 9/30, 35, etc.

hund. A. 1. card. num. as noun. *hundred.* E/2. **2.** masc. *dog.* acc. sg. G/6; 14/110. dat. pl. **hundum** K/1368; 5/30.
B. as adj. *hundred.* masc. acc. pl. **hunde** H/1.

hundeahtatig. card. num. as noun. *eighty.* E/2.

hundnigontig. card. num. as adj. *ninety.* masc. acc. pl. H/1.

hundred. card. num. as noun. *hundred.* E/2.

hundseofontig. card. num. as noun. *seventy.* E/1; 7/25.

hundtwelftig. card. num. as noun. *one hundred and twenty.*

hungor. masc. *hunger, famine.* nom. sg. **hunger** 5/18.

hunig. neut. *honey.*

Huntadūnscīr. fem. *Huntingdonshire.* acc. sg. **Huntadūnscīre** 4/2.

hupseax. neut. *sword worn on the hip, short-sword.* acc. pl. 14/327.

hūru. adv. *indeed, certainly.* 5/3, 23, 59; 10/10; 14/345, etc.

hūs. neut. *house.* nom. sg. 6/29. acc. sg. B/1; 6/7. gen. sg. **hūses** B/2. dat. sg. **hūse** M/1, 4, 6; 6/6, 19, etc. nom. pl. 5/13. acc. pl. 5/11.

hūsl. neut. *eucharist.* acc. sg. 6/32, 34. gen. sg. **hūsles** 6/33.

hūsting. neut. *court.* dat. sg. **hūstinge** 4/17.

hwā. pron. **1.** interrog. *who, what.* masc. nom. sg. 1/11; 7/74. neut. nom. sg. **hwæt** G/7; I/11; 5/46; 6/16; 7/22, etc. neut. acc. sg. **hwæt** 5/47; 6/10; 7/31, 82; 10/116, etc. neut. inst. sg. **hwan, hwon** G/8; 6/31; 7/23; 9/59. **2.** indef. *what, any, anyone, anything.* masc. nom. sg. M/1, 3 (2x), 11; 7/70, etc. masc. acc. sg. **hwæne, hwone** 7/65; 14/52. neut. nom. sg. **hwæt** 7/10, 35. neut. acc. sg. **hwæt** 6/1.

gehwā. indef. pron. *every, everyone, everything.* masc. nom. sg. 5/59. masc. dat. sg. **gehwām** 9/63. fem. acc. sg. **gehwane, gehwæne** 8/4; 14/186. fem. dat. sg. **gehwǣre.** neut. nom. sg. **gehwæt** 7/7. neut. gen. sg. **gehwæs** 6/12. neut. dat. sg. **gehwǣm** K/1365.

hwan → hwā.

hwanon. adv. *whence.* **hwanon, hwonon** G/5; 6/16.

hwæl. masc. *whale.*

gehwǣm → gehwā.

hwæne → hwā.

gehwæne → gehwā.

hwænne → hwonne.

hwǣr. A. adv. *where.* 1/9; 7/71, 75, 76, 77, etc.
B. conj. *where.* G/2; 5/32; 9/26; 10/112; 12/8, etc.

gehwǣre → gehwā.

gehwæs → gehwā.

hwæt. A. adj. *vigorous.*
B. interj. *lo, behold.* 5/8; 7/2, 3, 5, 28, etc.

hwæt → hwā.

gehwæt → gehwā.

hwæthwugu. indef. pron. *something.* neut. acc. sg. 6/7; 7/40.

hwæþer. A. interrog. pron. *which of two.* B. conj. *whether.* **hwæðer, hweðer** G/9; M/2; 6/32, 35; 7/46, etc.

gehwæþer. indef. pron. *both.*

hwæþre. adv. *however, nevertheless, yet.* **hwæðre, hwæðere** 6/3, 9, 28, 31; 10/18, etc.

hwealf. A. fem. *vault.* nom. pl. **hwealfe** 7/65. B. adj. *concave.* dat. pl. **hwealfum** 14/214.

hwearf. masc. *crowd.* dat. pl. **hwearfum** 14/249.

hwearf → hweorfan.

hwelc. pron. 1. interrog. *which, what, what kind of.* masc. nom. sg. G/4, 6. masc. acc. sg. **hwelcne** A/6. fem. nom. sg. **hwelc, hwylc** G/3; 6/33. fem. acc. sg. **hwylce** 6/15. neut. inst. sg. **hwelce** 7/27. dat. pl. **hwelcum.** 2. indef. *which, whatever, whoever, any.* masc. nom. sg. **hwelc, hwylc** 3/7; 5/36; 7/32. masc. dat. sg. **hwelcum, hwylcum** 1/5; 7/74. masc. nom. pl. **hwylce.**

gehwelc. indef. pron. *each, every.* masc. acc. sg. **gehwylcne** 14/95. masc. dat. sg. **gehwelcum, gehwilcum, gehwylcum** 3/8; 5/9; 10/108. masc. inst. sg. **gehwylce** 9/8; 10/136. neut. gen. sg. **gehwylces** 14/32.

hwelp. masc. *cub, young of an animal.* acc. sg. 11/16.

hweorfan. st. 3. *turn, change, go.* past 3sg. **hwearf** 14/112. inf. 9/72.

gehwerfde → gehwyrfan.

hwettan. wk. 1. *urge.*

hweðer → hwæþer.

hwī → hwȳ.

hwider. conj. *to where, whither.* 9/72.

hwīl. fem. *time, space of time.* acc. sg. **hwīle** 2/21; 3/17; 5/29, 58; 7/11, etc. gen. sg. **hwīle** 7/40. nom. pl. **hwīla** 7/40. acc. pl. **hwīla** 7/39 (2x).

gehwilcum → gehwelc.

hwīle. adv. *for a while.* 10/64, 84; 14/214.

hwīlendlic. adj. *transitory.* wk. neut. gen. sg. **hwīlendlican** 7/39.

hwīlum. adv. *sometimes, at times.* **hwīlum, hwīlon** 1/3, 7; 2/8; 5/21, 39 (2x), etc.

hwīt. adj. *white.* neut. gen. sg. **hwītes** 2/19. masc. dat. sg. **hwītum** 2/19.

hwītlocced. adj. *fair-haired.* fem. nom. sg. **hwītloccedu** 1/4.

hwomm. masc. *corner.* dat. sg. **hwomme.**

hwon → hwā.

hwōn. adv. *little.* 7/80.

hwone → hwā.

hwonne. adv. *when.* **hwænne** 10/136.

hwonon → hwanon.

hwȳ. adv. (inst. of *hwā*). *why.* **hwī, hwȳ** G/9; 1/1, 13; 7/68, 69, etc.

hwylc- → hwelc.

gehwylc- → gehwelc.

gehwyrfan. wk. 1. *turn, convert, move.* past 3sg. **gehwerfde, gehwyrfde** 6/18, 22.

hȳ → hēo.

hȳ → hīe.

hycg- → hicgan.

gehȳdan. wk. 1. *hide.* past 3sg. **gehȳdde** 9/84.

gehygd. fem. *mind, thought, intention.* nom. sg. 9/72.

hyge. masc. *thought, mind, heart.* nom. sg. **hyge, hige** 9/16; 12/17; 14/87. dat. sg. 13/11.

hygegeōmor. adj. *sad in mind.* masc. acc. sg. **hygegeōmorne** 12/19.

hygewlonc. adj. *proud in mind.* fem. nom. sg. Lb/4.

hȳhsta → hēah.

hyht. masc. *hope.* nom. sg. **hyht, hiht** 10/126, 148; 14/98.

hyhtful. adj. *hopeful.* masc. nom. pl. **hyhtfulle** 8/16.

hyhtwynn. fem. *the joy of hope.* gen. pl. **hyhtwynna** 14/121.

hyldan. wk. 1. *lean, bend* (transitive). inf. 10/45.

hyldo. fem. *favour, grace, protection.* acc. sg. 14/4.

hylt → (ge)healdan.

(ge)hȳnan. wk. 1. *humiliate, oppress, condemn.* pl. **hȳnað** 5/45. past part. **gehȳnede** 5/14.

hyne → hē.

hyngrian. wk. 2. (impersonal). *be hungry.* past 3sg. **hingrode.** pres. part. sg. **hingrigendne.**

hyra → hīe.

(ge)hȳran. wk. 1. *hear, listen to, hear of, obey* (with dat.). 1sg. **hīere, gehīre, gehȳre** 1/10; 13/50. 2sg. **hīerst, gehȳrest, gehȳrst** 11/16. 3sg. **gehērð, hīerð** 7/26. pl. **hīerað, gehȳrað.** past 1sg. **gehȳrde** 10/26. past 2sg. **gehērdest, hīerdest, gehȳrdest** 1/17; 7/49. past 3sg. **gehērde, hīerde, gehȳrde** 6/11; 7/31, 53. past pl. **gehȳrdon, gehērdon, hīerdon, gehīerdun, gehȳrdan, hȳrdon** 1/8; 2/27; 3/9; 5/65; 6/45, etc. subj. past sg. **gehȳrde** 13/22. imp. pl. **gehȳrað.** inf. **gehȳran, gehēran, hȳran** 10/78; 14/24. infl. inf. **tō gehȳranne, tō gehȳrenne** 2/28; 6/23. past part. **gehēred** 7/53.

hyrde. masc. *shepherd, guide, guardian.* nom. sg. 7/76; 14/60. dat. sg. **heorde.** nom. pl. **hyrdas.**

hyre → hēo.

hyrnednebb. adj. *horny-beaked.* wk. masc. nom. sg. **hyrnednebba** 14/212.

gehȳrness. fem. *hearing.* dat. sg. **gehȳrnesse** 6/22.

hyrst. fem. *ornament, trappings.* acc. pl. **hyrsta** 14/316.

hyrwan. wk. 1. *deride, slander.* 3sg. **hyrweð** 5/51, 53.

hys → hē.

hyspan. wk. 1. *scorn, revile, mock.* past pl. **hyspton** H/2. inf. 7/52.

hȳþ. fem. *harbour.* dat. sg. **hȳðe.**

ic, wē. pron. 1. pers. *I, myself.* nom. sg. **ic** D/1, 3; G/2, 3, 4, etc. acc. sg. **mē, mec** I/3; 1/13; 9/28; 10/30, 32 (2x), etc. gen. sg. **mīn** 7/11. dat. sg. **mē** D/1; G/2, 3, 4,

5, etc. nom. pl. **wē** C/1, 2, 3, 4, 5, etc. acc. pl. **ūs** 5/19, 44, 45, 57 (2x), etc. gen. pl. **ūre** C/4; 5/21, 71. dat. pl. **ūs, unc** D/3; 1/3; 2/28, 30; 4/3, etc. nom. dual **wit** 12/13, 21. acc. dual **unc** 10/48; 12/12, 22. **2.** refl. *I, myself.* acc. sg. **mē** 1/10; 10/45. dat. sg. **mē** 10/122; 12/9. acc. pl. **ūs** 5/65, 66, 70. dat. pl. **ūs** 5/60, 70.

īcan. wk. 1. *increase, augment.* past 3sg. **īhte** 5/5. inf. **īecan, ȳcan** 14/183.

īdel. adj. *void, empty, idle, vain.* neut. nom. sg. 9/110. masc. gen. sg. **īdelan** 7/57. neut. gen. sg. **īdles** 6/4. neut. nom. pl. **īdlu** 9/87. dat. pl. **īdelan** 5/54.

ides. fem. *woman, lady.* nom. sg. 14/14, 109, 128, 146. acc. sg. **idese** 14/55, 58. dat. sg. **idese** 14/340. nom. pl. **idesa** 14/133.

īdles → īdel.

īdlu → īdel.

īecan → īcan.

īeg. fem. *island.* dat. sg. **īege, īge** 11/4, 6.

ierfe. neut. *property, inheritance.* gen. sg. **ierfes** M/2.

iermða → yrmþu.

īge → īeg.

īhte → īcan.

ilca. indef. pron. *same.* masc. acc. sg. **ylcan** 2/8. fem. dat. sg. **ilcan** 7/36. neut. nom. sg. **ilce** 3/13. neut. acc. sg. **ilce** 6/14. neut. gen. sg. **ilcan** 7/14. neut. dat. sg. **ylcan.** neut. inst. sg. **ilcan** 3/17, 18.

in. A. adv. *in.* K/1371; 14/170.
B. prep. (with dat. or acc.). *in, into.* B/3; J/83; 6/1 (3x), etc.

inbryrdness. fem. *inspiration, ardor.* acc. sg. **inbryrdnisse** 6/1.

inc → þū, gē.

inca. masc. *question, grievance.* acc. sg. **incan** 6/36. dat. sg. **incan** 6/35.

incer → þū, gē.

indryhten. adj. *noble, excellent.* masc. nom. sg. 9/12.

ingeþanc. neut. *thought, conscience.* acc. sg. 5/69. gen. sg. **ingeðonces** 7/47.

ingong. masc. *entrance, entering.* acc. sg. 6/38. dat. sg. **ingonge** 6/24.

inlædan. wk. 1. *lead in.* inf. **inlædon** 6/29.

inlīhtan. wk. 1. *illuminate.* 2sg. **inlīhtes** 8/5. subj. sg. **inlēohte** 8/12.

inn. neut. *dwelling.* dat. sg. **inne** 14/70.

innan. A. adv. *from within, within.* 5/13. **B.** prep. (with dat. or acc.). *in, into.* 5/13.

inne. adv. *inside, within.* 4/7; 5/11 (2x), 18, 39, etc.

innoþ. masc. *womb.* dat. sg. **innoðe.**

intinga. masc. *cause.* nom. sg. 6/6.

intō. A. adv. *into the place.* 4/5. **B.** prep. (usually with dat., sometimes with acc.). *into.* c/12; 2/18, 24.

inwidda. masc. *wicked one.* nom. sg. 14/28.

inwidhlemm. masc. *hostile wound.* nom. pl. **inwidhlemmas** 10/47.

īow → þū, gē.

irnan. st. 3. *run, flow.* pl. **irnað.** past pl. **urnon** 3/7; 14/164. pres. part. **irnende.**

is → bēon.

īs. neut. *ice.*

īsen. adj. *iron.* dat. pl. **īsenum.**

īsig. adj. *icy.* wk. dat. pl. **īsigean** F/3.

Israhēla. masc. *of the Israelites.* gen. pl. 6/24.

Israhēlisc. adj. *Israelite.* wk. neut. acc. sg. **Israhēlisce.**

iū → geō.

Iūdēisc. adj. *Jewish.* wk. masc. nom. pl. **Iūdēiscan.**

iugoðe → geoguþ.

lā. interj. *O, Oh.* 5/8, 35, 42 (2x), 46, etc.

lāc. neut. *offering, sacrifice, gift.* acc. sg. 11/1. dat. pl. **lācum** 5/11.

gelāc. neut. *motion, commotion, tossing* (of waves), *play.* acc. sg. 12/7.

lād. fem. *course, way, journey.* gen. sg. **lāde** 13/25.

lāf. fem. *remainder, widow.* acc. sg. **lāfe.** dat. sg. **lāfe** E/3, 4.

gelagian. wk. 2. *decree by law.* past part. **gelagod** 5/10.

lāgon → licgan.

lagu. 1. masc. u-stem. *water, sea.* acc. sg. 13/21. **2.** fem. *law.* acc. sg. **lage** 5/9, 12, 22. dat. sg. **lage** 5/22, 50. nom. pl. **laga** 5/15, 38. dat. pl. **lagum** 5/68.

gelagu. fem. of the sea, *expanse.* acc. sg. 13/42.

lagulād. fem. *sea-way.* acc. sg. **lagulāde** 9/3.

lahbryce. masc. *violation of the law.* acc. pl. **lahbrycas** 5/48.

lahlīce. adv. *according to law.* 5/21.

lamb. neut. *lamb.*

gelamp → (ge)limpan.

land. neut. *land, nation.* nom. sg. 7/7. acc. sg. **land, lond** K/1357; 7/4; 13/18. gen. sg. **londes** 3/11; 7/22; 12/8; 13/4. dat. sg. **lande, londe** 2/7; 5/4, 24, 25, 31, etc. acc. pl. **lond** H/4. dat. pl. **londum** 7/25.

landbūend. masc. nd-stem. *inhabitant.* nom. pl. **landbūende** 14/226. dat. pl. **londbūendum** 14/314.

lang. adj. *long.* masc. nom. sg. 7/45. fem. acc. sg. **lange** 7/81; 10/24. neut. nom. sg. 7/42, 82. neut. acc. sg. 2/10. nom. pl. **lange.** neut. gen. sg. compar. **lengran** 14/184.

lange. adv. *long.* **lange, longe** 4/7, 11, 14; 5/13, 18, etc. compar. **leng** 5/2; 14/153. superl. **lengest** 3/1.

langian. wk. 2. (impersonal, with acc.). *long, yearn.* past 3sg. **langian, longade** 12/14.

langoþ. masc. *longing.* gen. sg. **longaþes** 12/41. dat. sg. **langoþe** 12/53.

langsum. adj. *long-lasting, tedioius.* masc. nom. sg. 7/55.

langunghwīl. fem. *time of longing.* gen. pl. **langunghwīla** 10/126.

lār. fem. *learning, doctrine, teaching.* acc. sg. **lāre** 5/22; 14/333. gen. sg. **lāre** 6/18. dat. sg. **lāre** 6/24. nom. pl. **lāra** 5/15. acc. pl. **lāra.**

lārcwide. masc. *lore-speech, teaching.* dat. pl. **lārcwidum** 9/38.

lārēow. masc. *teacher.* nom. sg. 2/27. nom.
pl. lārēowas 6/23. gen. pl. lārīowa
7/79. dat. pl. lārēowum.

lārlic. adj. *instructive, doctrinal.* wk. neut.
acc. sg. lārlican.

lāst. masc. *track.* acc. sg. 14/209, 291. dat.
sg. lāste 9/97; 14/297.

late. adv. *late.* 14/275.

latian. wk. 2. *tarry, delay* (with gen.
object). subj. sg. latige 5/59.

lāþ. **A.** neut. *pain, harm, injury, misfortune.* nom. sg. 11/12.
B. adj. *hateful, hated, hostile.* masc.
nom. sg. 14/45. neut. nom. sg. 5/29.
masc. acc. sg. lāðne 14/72, 101. neut.
dat. sg. lāðum 14/226. nom. pl. lāðe
H/3. fem. nom. pl. lāðe 5/15. gen. pl.
lāðra 14/297, 303. wk. neut. gen. sg.
lāðan 14/310. neut. acc. sg. compar.
lāþre. masc. gen. sg. superl. lāðestan
14/178. masc. nom. pl. superl. lāðost
14/322. neut. nom. sg. superl. lāðost
10/88. wk. masc. dat. sg. superl.
lāðestan 14/314.

lāþettan. wk. 1. *hate.* 3sg. lāðet 5/53.

lāþlice. adv. *wretchedly.* superl. lāðlicost
12/14.

gelāþung. fem. *congregation, church.* dat.
sg. gelāþunge.

gelæccan. wk. 1. *seize.* past pl. gelæhton.

læce. masc. *physician.* nom. sg. 2/14 (2x),
22, 23.

(ge)lædan. wk. 1. *lead, bring.* 1sg. gelæde.
pl. lædað 5/46. past 3sg. lædde, gelædde
6/15; 14/129. past pl. læddon, gelæd-
don 4/8, 17; 14/72, 325. subj. sg. gelæde
F/7. inf. lædan, gelædan 10/5; 14/42.

Læden. neut. *Latin.* acc. sg. Lýden.

læfan. wk. 1. *leave.* past 3sg. læfde 3/10.
infl. inf. tō læfanne 7/11. past part.
læfed 7/20.

læg → licgan.

læg- → licgan.

gelæhton → gelæccan.

lændagas. masc. *transitory days.* gen. pl.
lændaga.

læne. adj. *transitory.* masc. nom. sg. 7/15;
9/108, 109 (2x). neut. nom. sg. 9/108.
neut. dat. sg. lænum 10/109. wk. neut.
dat. sg. lænan 10/138.

(ge)læran. wk. 1. *teach, advise, persuade.*
past 3sg. lærde 6/20. inf. læran 2/7;
6/21; 13/21. pres. part. lærende. past
part. gelæred 6/3.

gelæred. adj. (past part. of *læran*). *learned.*
wk. masc. acc. pl. superl. gelæredestan
6/16.

læs. neut. (indeclinable). *less.* 5/39.

(ge)læstan. wk. 1. *follow, perform, abide
by, endure, pay.* subj. sg. gelæste 5/9.
subj. pl. gelæstan 5/68. inf. læstan
13/53. past part. gelæst 4/14, 20.

lætan. st. 7. *let, leave, allow, pretend, consider.* past 3sg. lēt, læt 5/40, 62. past pl.
lēton 4/6; 14/221. imp. sg. læt 13/24.

gelæte. neut. *meeting.* dat. pl. gelætum.

læþþ. fem. *injury, malice.* gen. pl. læðða
14/158. dat. pl. læððum 14/184.

læwede. adj. *lay, unlearned.* masc. nom.
pl. 4/12; 5/21. wk. neut. dat. sg.
læwedum.

lēaf. **1.** fem. *leave, permission.* acc. sg. lēafe
7/82. **2.** neut. *leaf.* nom. pl. A/3.

gelēafa. masc. *faith.* acc. sg. gelēafan
14/6, 89, 344. inst. sg. gelēafan 14/97.

gelēafful. adj. *faithful.* wk. masc. dat. sg.
gelēaffullum 2/14.

lēah. masc. *pasture, meadow.*

lēan. neut. *reward, gift, loan.* gen. sg.
lēanes 14/346.

lēap. masc. *basket,* fig. *body.* nom. sg.
14/111.

lēas. adj. *lacking, false.* masc. nom. sg.
14/121. neut. nom. sg. 12/32. neut. acc.
sg. 8/20. masc. gen. sg. lēases 7/13, 58.
masc. dat. sg. lēasum 7/50. neut. nom.
pl. lēas, lēase 9/86.

lēasbregdness. fem. *deception, falsehood.*
acc. pl. lēasbregdnessa.

lēasung. fem. *falsehood.* gen. sg. lēasunge
6/4. acc. pl. lēasunga 5/49. dat. pl.
lēasungum 7/55.

lecgan. wk. 1. *lay.* 3sg. **legeð** 1/4. past pl. **lēdon** 2/24. subj. sg. **lecge** 9/42.

leger. neut. *bed.* acc. pl. 12/34.

legeð → lecgan.

lehtrian. wk. 2. *accuse, revile.* 3sg. **lehtreð** 5/51.

lenctenfæsten. neut. *Lenten fast.*

leng. fem. *length.*

leng → lange.

lengest → lange.

lengran → lang.

lengþu. fem. *length.*

lengu. fem. *length.* acc. sg. **lenge** 7/40.

lēo. masc. *lion.* nom. pl. **lēon.**

lēod. 1. masc. *person.* gen. pl. **lēoda** 14/178. dat. pl. **lēodum** J/85; 10/88; 11/1; 12/6; 14/147, etc. **2.** fem. *nation.* gen. sg. **lēode** 5/63. dat. pl. **lēodum** 5/12.

lēodfruma. masc. *leader of the people, lord.* nom. sg. 12/8.

lēodhata. masc. *tyrant.* acc. sg. **lēodhatan** 14/72. nom. pl. **lēodhatan** 5/50.

lēodmægen. neut. *might of a people, army.* gen. sg. **lēodmægnes.**

lēof. A. masc. *sir.* nom. sg. 1/10.
  B. adj. *beloved, dear, pleasant, agreeable.* masc. nom. sg. 1/2. fem. nom. sg. J/85; 14/147. masc. acc. sg. **lēofne.** masc. gen. sg. **lēofes** 9/38; 12/53. fem. gen. sg. **lēofre** 9/97. masc. nom. pl. **lēofe** 12/34. gen. pl. **lēofra** 9/31; 12/16. wk. masc. nom. sg. **lēofa** 10/78, 95. wk. masc. dat. sg. **lēofan** 14/346. wk. masc. nom. pl. **lēofan** 5/1; 6/37. masc. nom. sg. compar. **lēofra** 3/12.

leofað → libban.

lēoflic. adj. *beloved.*

lēoflīce. adv. *lovingly.*

lēoht. A. neut. *light.* dat. sg. **lēohte** 10/5.
  B. adj. *bright.* masc. acc. sg. **lēohtne** 14/191.

lēohte. adv. *brightly.*

leohtmōd. adj. *lighthearted, easygoing.* fem. nom. sg. J/85.

lēoma. masc. *light, radiance.* nom. sg. 8/3. acc. sg. **lēoman** 14/191.

leomu → lim.

leornere. masc. *scholar.* acc. pl. **leorneras** 6/16.

(ge)leornian. wk. 2. *learn.* past 2sg. **leornodest, liornodest** 7/16, 17. past 3sg. **leornade, geleornade, geleornode** 6/1, 3, 5. past pl. **leornodon** 6/23. inf. **geleornian** 6/22.

leorningcniht. masc. *disciple.* nom. pl. **leorningcnihtas.** acc. pl. **leorningcnihtas.** dat. pl. **leorningcnihtum.**

leornung. fem. *learning.*

lēoþ. neut. *song.* nom. sg. 6/23. acc. sg. 6/5, 16, 22, 24; 7/1, etc. gen. sg. **lēoþes** 6/4. inst. sg. **lēoðe** 6/19. acc. pl. 6/1, 3.

lēoþcræft. masc. *art of poetry, art of song.* acc. sg. 6/3.

lēoþsang. masc. *song, poem, poetry.* gen. sg. **lēoþsonges** 6/18. dat. pl. **lēoþsongum** 6/2.

lēt- → lǣtan.

gelettan. wk. 1. *hinder, prevent* someone from going on a journey (gen.). inf. 13/25.

lēw. fem. *injury.* acc. sg. **lēwe** 5/54.

gelēwian. wk. 2. *injure.* past part. **gelēwede** 5/55.

libban. wk. 3. *live.* 3sg. **leofað, lifað** K/1366. pl. **lifiaþ** 10/134. past 1sg. **lifde** 7/11. past 3sg. **lifode.** past pl. **lifdon, lifodon, lyfdon** 12/14; 14/296. inf. 7/81. infl. inf. **tō libbanne** 7/11. pres. part. **libbende, libbendum, lifgende, lifgendne, lifgendum, lifiendne, lifigendan, lifigendum** 5/25; 7/60; 12/34; 13/25, 53, etc.

gelic → gelīc.

līc. neut. *body, corpse.* nom. sg. 3/16, 17. acc. sg. 2/11, 26. gen. sg. **līces** 10/63.

gelīc. adj. *like, similar, equal.* neut. acc. sg. **gelic** 7/33. masc. nom. pl. **gelīce** 1/5. masc. acc. pl. **gelīce** 7/70. wk. masc. nom. pl. **gelīcan** 7/80. masc. nom. pl. compar. **gelīcran** A/4.

līcað → līcian.

gelīce. adv. *similarly, equally, like.* 5/54; 6/3. superl. gelīccast 5/30.

līcettan. wk. 1. *pretend.* subj. past sg. līcette 7/53.

licgan. st. 5. *lie, be situated, be arranged.* 3sg. līð, ligeð 2/24; 3/16, 17; 7/19; 14/288, etc. pl. licgað 9/78. past 3sg. læg B/2; 2/22, 27; 3/10; 14/106, etc. past pl. lāgon, lǣgon 3/8; 14/30. subj. sg. licge 5/36. subj. past sg. lǣge 2/22. inf. 14/278. pres. part. licgende 10/24.

līchama. masc. *body, corpse.* nom. sg. 2/26. acc. sg. līchaman 2/24; 4/19. gen. sg. līchoman 7/59, 61. nom. pl. līchaman. acc. pl. līchaman 2/26.

līchamlic. adj. *bodily.* fem. dat. sg. līchomlicre 6/28.

līchomlīce. adv. *in the flesh.* 7/60.

līchomlicre → līchamlic.

līcian. wk. 2. *please.* 3sg. līcað 7/33 (2x). past 3sg. līcode 7/2, 32, 34. subj. sg. licige 7/35.

līcsang. masc. *dirge.* acc. sg. 2/21.

lif- → libban.

līf. neut. *life.* acc. sg. M/2; 5/21; 6/27, 42; 7/37, etc. gen. sg. līfes D/1; F/6; 1/14, 17; 6/2, etc. dat. sg. līfe D/3; 2/10; 4/5; 5/25; 7/11, etc. acc. pl. 9/60.

ligetu. fem. *lightning.* nom. sg. līgetu G/5.

ligeð → licgan.

līhting. fem. *shining, illumination.* dat. sg. līhtinge.

lilige. fem. *lily.* nom. sg. G/3.

lim. neut. *limb.* acc. pl. leomu 6/7. dat. pl. limum 2/22.

gelimp. neut. *event, good fortune, misfortune.* dat. sg. gelimpe. dat. pl. gelimpum 5/46.

(ge)limpan. st. 3. *happen, befall.* 3sg. limpð, gelimpð A/4; 5/38. past 3sg. gelamp, gelomp B/1; 7/49. past pl. gelumpon 4/3. inf. gelimpan 5/35; 13/30.

gelimplic. adj. *suitable.* fem. acc. sg. gelimplice 6/7.

gelimplīce. adv. *fittingly, suitably.* 2/19.

limwērig. adj. *weary in limb.* masc. acc. sg. limwērigne 10/63.

lind. fem. *linden, shield.* acc. pl. linde 14/191, 303. dat. pl. lindum 14/214.

lindwerod. neut. *shield-bearing army.* nom. sg. 14/297.

lindwiggend. masc. nd-stem. *warrior bearing a linden shield.* nom. pl. lindwiggende 14/42.

liornodest → (ge)leornian.

listum. adv. *skillfully.* 14/101.

līð → licgan.

lōcian. wk. 2. *look.* 3sg. lōcað G/8; 5/40. past 3sg. lōcude 3/5. imp. sg. lōca.

lof. neut. *praise.* nom. sg. 7/36. acc. sg. 6/39, 44; 7/33. dat. sg. lofe 7/46.

gelōgian. wk. 2. *place, lodge.* past 3sg. gelōgode 5/28.

gelōme. adv. *often.* 2/1, 5; 5/10, 16, 18, etc.

gelōmlīce. adv. *often, frequently, repeatedly.*

gelomp → (ge)limpan.

lond- → land.

londbūendum → landbūend.

londstede. masc. *place in the land, country.* dat. sg. 12/16.

gelong. adj. *dependent on* (with æt). fem. nom. sg. 12/45.

longade → langian.

longaþes → langoþ.

longe → lange.

lor. neut. *loss.*

losian. wk. 2. *be lost, perish.* past pl. losodon 7/37. inf. 7/72; 14/287.

lūcan. st. 2. *lock.*

lufian. wk. 2. *love.* 3sg. lufað. pl. lufiað D/1; 5/52. past 3sg. lufode 2/6, 7, 11. subj. pl. lufie. inf. lufian, lufigean 5/53, 68; 6/20.

lufu. fem. *love.* dat. sg. lufan, lufe 2/28; 6/26 (2x).

gelumpon → (ge)limpan.

Lunden. noun. *London.* dat. sg. Lundene 4/19.

Lundenburg. fem. athematic. *London.* dat. sg. Lundenbyrig 4/12.

lungre. adv. *quickly.* 14/147, 280.

lūs. fem. athematic. *louse.*

lust. masc. *desire, lust, pleasure.* acc. sg. 5/22. dat. pl. **lustum** 14/161.

lustbǣre. adj. *desirable, pleasant.* neut. nom. sg. 1/6.

lustum. adv. *with pleasure.* 13/21.

Lȳden → Lǣden.

lȳfan. wk. 1. *allow, grant* something (gen.). past 3sg. **lȳfde** 2/10.

gelȳfan. wk. 1. *believe.* 3sg. **gelȳfð.** pl. **gelȳfað** c/1; 8/16. subj. sg. **gelȳfe** 5/29.

lyfdon → libban.

gelȳfed. adj. (past part.). *advanced.* fem. gen. sg. **gelȳfdre** 6/5.

lyft. fem. *air.* acc. sg. **lyft, lyfte** 10/5; 14/347. dat. sg. **lyfte.**

lȳsan. wk. 1. *release, liberate, redeem.* inf. 10/41.

gelystan. wk. 1. (impersonal). *desire* something (gen.), with acc. of person. 3sg. **lysteð** 7/67. past 3sg. **gelyste** 14/306. subj. sg. **lyste** 7/65, 68.

lȳt. adj. *little, few.* neut. acc. sg. 9/31; 12/16.

lȳtel. A. adj. *little, small.* masc. nom. sg. 7/15, 20, 79. fem. nom. sg. **lȳtel, lȳtlu** 7/16, 66. neut. nom. sg. 7/40. fem. acc. sg. **lȳtle** 3/17. fem. dat. sg. **lȳtelre** 5/15. neut. dat. sg. **lȳtlan** 7/46. masc. inst. sg. **lȳtle** 3/4. fem. nom. pl. **lȳtle** 5/4. wk. masc. dat. sg. **lȳtlan** 7/24.

B. indef. pron. *little.* neut. acc. sg. 5/10.

lȳthwōn. adv. *a little,* as pron *few.* 14/310.

lȳtle. adv. *a little.*

lȳþre. adj. *wicked.* fem. acc. sg. 5/63.

mā. neut. *more.* b/3; 5/39, 49.

mā → micle.

macian. wk. 2. *make.* past 3sg. **macode** 2/19. past pl. **macodon.**

mādma → māþum.

mādmas → māþum.

māga → mǣg.

magan. pret. pres. *be able to, can, may.* 1sg. **mæg** 9/58; 10/85; 12/2, 38, 39, etc.

2sg. **meaht, miht** 6/9; 7/16, 18, 20; 10/78, etc. 3sg. **mæg, mag** g/9 (2x); к/1365; м/13; 2/4, etc. pl. **magon, magan, māgon** 5/54, 58, 60; 7/18 (2x), etc. past 1sg. **meahte, mihte** 9/26; 10/18, 37. past 3sg. **meahte, mihte, mehte** в/4; н/4; 2/7, 8, 16, etc. past pl. **mihton** в/2, 4; 2/28. subj. sg. **mæge, mǣge** 5/23; 14/330. subj. 3sg. **mæge** 7/31, 40. subj. pl. **mægen** 7/38. subj. past sg. **meahte** н/3; 7/54. subj. past pl. **mihten** в/5; 14/24, 136.

māgas → mǣg.

mago. masc. *kinsman, young man, warrior.* nom. sg. 9/92.

māgon → magan.

magorinc. masc. *man.* nom. pl. **magorincas** 7/79.

maguþegn. masc. *noble kinsman.* nom. pl. **magoþegnas, maguþegnas** 9/62; 14/236.

man. A. masc. athematic. *man, person, husband.* nom. sg. **mon, man, mann** g/6; 2/2; 5/58; 6/5, 7, etc. acc. sg. **mon, monn** 6/3; 13/25. gen. sg. **monnes, mannes** g/7; 7/26, 36, 53; 8/23, etc. dat. sg. **men** 4/7; 6/20; 7/58, 66. nom. pl. **men, menn** в/2; c/10; 2/27; 3/4, 10, etc. acc. pl. **men, menn** 3/15; 4/7; 5/28, 51; 6/16, etc. gen. pl. **manna, monna** в/3; d/1, 3; 5/5, 9, etc. dat. pl. **mannum, monnum** c/2; 2/24; 5/4, 20, 35, etc.

B. indef. pron. *one, someone.* masc. nom. sg. **man, mon** c/5; 2/21; 3/17; 4/3, 4, etc.

geman → gemunan.

mān. neut. *evil deed, crime, sin.* gen. pl. **māna** 5/56.

gemāna. masc. *company, companionship, intercourse.* acc. sg. **gemānan** c/3.

mancynn. neut. *mankind.* nom. sg. **moncynn** 7/18. acc. sg. **mancyn, mancynn** 10/41, 104. gen. sg. **mancynnes, moncynnes, monncynnes** c/2; 6/13, 24; 10/33, 99, etc.

māndæd. fem. *evil deed.* acc. pl. māndæda
5/48. gen. pl. māndæda 6/26.

mānfordǣdla. masc. *evil-doer.* nom. pl.
mānfordǣdlan.

mānful. adj. *wicked, evil.* wk. masc. nom.
pl. mānfullan.

gemang → gemong.

manig. adj. *many, much.* masc. nom. sg.
mænig, monig. neut. nom. sg. mænig.
neut. acc. sg. monig 6/24, 25, 44. neut.
dat. sg. manegum 7/29. masc. nom. pl.
manege, manige, mænege, mænige,
monige 5/14, 24, 30, 34, 50, etc. fem.
nom. pl. manega, manege, manige
F/3; 2/31; 5/28; 7/24. masc. acc. pl.
manege 5/53. fem. acc. pl. manega,
manege 2/10; 5/5; 7/25. neut. acc. pl.
monig 6/14; 7/70. gen. pl. manigra,
monigra B/4; 6/2; 10/41. dat. pl.
manegum, monegum, manegan 2/4,
27; 5/27; 6/24; 7/25, etc.

manigeo → menigu.

manigfeald. adj. *manifold, various,*
numerous. fem. acc. pl. mænigfealde
5/47, 64. dat. pl. mænigfealdum 2/13.
neut. nom. sg. compar. mænigfealdre
5/33.

manna. masc. *man.* acc. sg. mannan,
monnan 12/18; 13/28; 14/98, 101.

mannslaga. masc. *killer.* nom. pl. mannslagan 5/56.

mannsylen. fem. *sale of men.* acc. pl.
mannsylena 5/48.

manode → monian.

manslyht. masc. *manslaughter.* acc. pl.
manslyhtas 5/48.

mānswora. masc. *swearer of false oaths.*
nom. pl. mānsworan 5/56.

mār- → micel.

māra. indef. pron. *more.* neut. nom. sg.
māre 5/33; 7/20, 23. neut. acc. sg.
māran, māre 5/23; 7/35. neut. gen.
sg. māran 7/79.

marmstān. masc. *marble.* dat. sg.
marmstāne 2/19 (2x).

gemartiredon → gemartyrian.

martyr. masc. *martyr.* gen. sg. martires
4/19.

gemartyrian. wk. 2. *martyr.* past pl.
gemartiredon 4/11. past part.
gemartyrode.

maþelian. wk. 2. *speak* (formally). past
3sg. maþelode.

māþþumgyfa. masc. *treasure-giver.* nom.
sg. 9/92.

māþum. masc. *treasure.* acc. pl. mādmas
14/318. gen. pl. māðma, mādma
13/46; 14/329, 340. dat. pl. māþmum
J/87.

gemæc. adj. *equal, similar, suitable.* masc.
acc. sg. gemæcne 12/18.

mæd. fem. *meadow.* nom. pl. mædwa. dat.
pl. mædum.

mæden- → mægden.

mæg → magan.

mæg. masc. *kinsman.* nom. sg. 3/12;
9/109. dat. sg. mæge. nom. pl. māgas,
mægas 3/11; 12/11. gen. pl. māga 9/51.
dat. pl. mægum 3/13.

mægden. neut. *maiden, virgin.* nom. sg.
mæden c/3; 2/1, 5, 8, 26, etc. acc. sg.
mæden, mægden. gen. sg. mædenes
2/25. dat. sg. mædene 2/1. gen. pl.
mægdena.

mæge → magan.

mæge → magan.

mægen. neut. *might, army, virtue.* nom.
sg. 14/253, 261. gen. pl. mægena 7/13.

mægen → magan.

mægenēacen. adj. *mighty.* neut. nom. sg.
14/292.

mægræs. masc. *attack on relatives.* acc. pl.
mægræsas 5/48.

mægslaga. masc. *killer of a kinsman.* nom.
pl. mægslagan 5/56.

mægþ. fem. dental stem. *maiden.* nom.
sg. 14/78, 125, 145, 254. acc. sg. 14/35,
43, 165, 260. gen. sg. 14/334. nom. pl.
14/135.

mægþ. fem. *family, tribe, nation.* dat. sg.
mægðe 5/36. gen. pl. mægþa 14/324.
dat. pl. mægþum.

gemǣgþ. fem. *longing* for something (gen.). nom. sg. 7/2.

mægþhād. masc. *virginity.* nom. sg. 2/4. acc. sg. 2/5.

mǣl. neut. *occasion, season, meal.* dat. sg. **mǣle** 2/11.

mǣnan. wk. 1. *tell, intend, complain, grieve.* past 3sg. **mǣnde** H/4.

gemǣne. adj. *common, joint, universal.* masc. nom. sg. 5/16. neut. nom. sg. 5/36. fem. acc. sg. 5/30. masc. dat. sg. **gemǣnum** 5/30. neut. nom. pl. 5/38.

mænege → manig.

mænig- → manig.

mænig- → menigu.

mænigfeald- → manigfeald.

gemænigfyldan. wk. 1. *multiply, increase.* 1sg. **gemænifylde** 1/16. past part. **gemenifylde.**

gemǣran. wk. 1. *glorify.* past part. **gemǣred** 6/1.

mǣre. adj. *great, famous, glorious.* fem. acc. sg. 2/19. wk. fem. nom. sg. 9/100; 10/12, 82. wk. masc. dat. sg. **mǣran** 10/69; 14/3. wk. neut. dat. sg. **mǣran.** gen. pl. compar. **mærra** 14/329. masc. nom. sg. superl. **mǣrost** 7/71. wk. fem. nom. sg. superl. **mǣrost** 14/324.

mǣrþ. fem. *fame, glory.* acc. sg. **mǣrðe** 14/343. acc. pl. **mǣrða** 2/5; 5/70.

mæsse. fem. *mass.* dat. sg. **mæssan** 4/5.

mæssedæg. masc. *mass-day, feast.*

mæsseprēost. masc. *mass-priest.*

mæsserbana. masc. *killer of a priest.* nom. pl. **mæsserbanan** 5/56.

mǣst. indef. pron. *most.* neut. acc. sg. 4/4.

mǣst- → micel.

mǣst- → micle.

(ge)mǣtan. wk. 1. *dream* (impersonal). past 3sg. **mǣtte, gemǣtte** 10/2.

mǣte. adj. *poor, inferior, small.* neut. inst. sg. 10/69, 124.

gemǣte. A. adj. *suitable.* masc. nom. sg. 2/25.

    B. adv. *suitably.* 2/25.

mǣþ. fem. *honour.* acc. sg. **mǣþe** 5/28. dat. sg. **mǣþe** 5/11.

mǣw. masc. *mew, sea-gull.* gen. sg. **mǣwes** 13/26.

mē → ic, wē.

meaht- → magan.

meaht- → miht.

mēara → mearh.

mearcweard. masc. *border-warden.* nom. pl. **mearcweardas.**

mearh. masc. *horse.* nom. sg. **mearg** 9/92. gen. pl. **mēara** 13/46. dat. pl. **mēarum** J/87.

mearu. adj. *tender, delicate.* masc. acc. sg. **mearune.**

mēarum → mearh.

mec → ic, wē.

mēce. masc. *sword.* acc. sg. 14/78. dat. sg. 14/104.

mēd. fem. *reward, payment.* acc. sg. **mēde** 7/47; 14/343. gen. sg. **mēde** 7/48. dat. sg. **mēde** 14/334.

medmicel. adj. *moderate, short.* neut. acc. sg. 6/42. neut. dat. sg. **medmiclum** 6/1.

medoærn. neut. *mead-hall.*

medobyrig → meoduburg.

medowērig. adj. *weary from drinking mead, hung over.* masc. acc. pl. **medowērige** 14/229. dat. pl. **medowērigum** 14/245.

medu. masc. *mead.*

medudrēam. masc. *mead-joy, joy in the mead-hall.* gen. pl. **meododrēama** 13/46.

medugāl. adj. *drunk with mead.* masc. nom. sg. 14/26.

meduheall. fem. *mead-hall.* dat. sg. **meoduhealle** 9/27.

mehte → magan.

men → man.

(ge)mengan. wk. 1. *mix, mingle, stir up.* inf. **mengan** 13/44. past part. **gemenged** 9/48.

gemenifylde → gemænigfyldan.

menigu. fem. *multitude.* dat. sg. **manigeo, mænige** 10/112, 151.

menn → man.

menniscness. fem. *humanity, incarnation.* dat. sg. **menniscnesse** 6/24.

meododrēama → medudrēam.

meodorǣden. fem. *mead-drinking,* fig. *assembly.* dat. sg. **meodorǣdenne** J/87.

meodosetl. neut. *mead-seat, seat in a mead-hall.* gen. pl. **meodosetla.**

meoduburg. fem. athematic. *mead-town, happy town.* dat. sg. **medobyrig** 14/167. dat. pl. **meoduburgum** 13/17.

meoduhealle → meduheall.

Meotodes → Metod.

Meotudes → Metod.

mēowle. fem. *woman.* nom. sg. 14/56. acc. sg. **mēowlan** 14/261.

Merantūn. masc. *Merton.* dat. sg. **Merantūne** 3/4.

mere. masc. *sea, lake.* nom. sg. K/1362. acc. sg. 13/26.

merelād. fem. *sea-way.* acc. sg. **merelāde** 13/28.

merestrēam. masc. *sea-stream.* acc. pl. **merestrēamas** 13/44.

mergen → morgen.

gemet. neut. *measure, measurement, boundary, ability, meter.* acc. sg. 6/14; 7/17.

metan. st. 5. *measure.* subj. sg. **mete** 7/44. infl. inf. **tō metanne** 7/16, 43, 45.

(ge)mētan. wk. 1. *meet, encounter, find.* pl. **gemētað.** past pl. **gemētton, mētton** 2/19; 3/10.

mete. masc. *food.* nom. sg. 7/7.

metelēas. adj. *without food.*

metelīst. fem. *lack of food.* dat. sg. **metelīeste.** nom. pl. **metelīste** 11/15.

gemetgung. fem. *temperance, moderation.*

gemetlīce. adv. *moderately.* 6/28.

Metod. masc. *God, Creator.* nom. sg. 14/154. gen. sg. **Meotodes, Meotudes, Metodes, Metudes** 6/12; 8/23; 9/2; 14/261.

metsung. fem. *provision.* acc. sg. **metsunge** 4/1.

mēþe. adj. *weary, dejected.* masc. nom. sg. 10/65. masc. nom. pl. 10/69.

micclum → miclum.

micel. A. adj. *much, large, big, great, vast.* masc. nom. sg. **micel, mycel** 5/25; 10/130. fem. nom. sg. **micel, mycel** 5/8, 9, 66; 10/139. neut. nom. sg. **micel, mycel** 2/12; 7/28. masc. acc. sg. **micelne, miclan, mycelne** 5/70; 7/31 (2x). fem. acc. sg. **micle** 12/51. fem. gen. sg. **micelre** 6/27. neut. gen. sg. **micles** 7/32. masc. dat. sg. **miclan, mycelum** 5/8 (2x). fem. dat. sg. **micelre, miclan, mycelre** B/7; 2/24; 10/102. neut. inst. sg. **mycle** 10/34, 60, 123. fem. nom. pl. **micle** 5/24, 32. dat. pl. **micelan, miclan, miclum** 3/3; 5/7 (2x). wk. masc. nom. sg. **micla.** wk. neut. nom. sg. **mycele.** wk. masc. acc. sg. **miclan** C/10. wk. fem. acc. sg. **miclan.** wk. masc. dat. sg. **miclan** C/9. wk. neut. dat. sg. **miclan** 10/65. masc. nom. sg. compar. **māra** 13/31. fem. acc. sg. compar. **māran** 14/92. fem. nom. sg. compar. **māre** 5/35; 7/58. masc. acc. sg. compar. **māran.** neut. acc. sg. compar. **māre** D/3. masc. nom. sg. superl. **mǣst, mǣsta** 5/25; 14/292. neut. nom. sg. superl. **mǣst** 14/181. masc. acc. sg. superl. **mǣste** 14/3. fem. acc. sg. superl. **mǣstan** 6/1. wk. masc. acc. sg. superl. **mǣstan** 7/18.

B. indef. pron. *a great deal.* neut. nom. sg. 4/7. neut. acc. sg. **micel, mycel** C/4; 2/7; 4/2 (2x); 5/10, etc.

micellic. adj. *great, magnificent.* neut. gen. sg. **micellices** 7/22.

micle. adv. *much, almost* (superl. *mǣst* only). compar. **mā** 3/14; 5/21; 7/41, 69; 12/4, etc. superl. **mǣst** 5/23 (2x).

miclum. adv. *greatly, very.* **miclum, micclum, mycclum** 2/20, 27; 3/5; 7/70; 14/10, etc.

mid. A. adv. *with.* 2/23, 27; 10/106.

B. prep. (usually with dat., sometimes with acc.). *with, among.* B/5, 7; c/11, 12 (2x), etc.

midd. adj. *middle.* masc. acc. sg. **midne**
1/8. fem. acc. sg. **midde** 6/32. masc. dat.
sg. **middum** m/7. fem. dat. sg. **midre**
10/2. dat. pl. **middum.** wk. fem. dat.
sg. **middan** 14/68.

middaneard. masc. *world.* acc. sg. g/9.

middangeard. masc. *world.* nom. sg.
9/62. acc. sg. f/1; 6/13, 43; 8/2; 9/75,
etc. gen. sg. **middangeardes** 6/24; 7/16,
17, 44. dat. sg. **middanearde.**

Middelseaxe. masc. *Middle Saxons.* acc.
pl. **Middelsexe** 4/2.

Mierce. masc. *the Mercians.* gen. pl.
Miercna 3/17.

miht. fem. athematic. *might.* nom. sg.
2/26. acc. sg. **meahte, mihte** 2/4; 6/12.
dat. sg. **mihte** 10/102. acc. pl. **mihta**
4/19.

miht- → magan.

mihtig. adj. *mighty.* masc. nom. sg. 8/23;
10/151; 14/92, 198. masc. nom. pl.
mihtige.

mīl. fem. *mile.* gen. pl. **mīla** f/4.

milde. adj. *mild, kind.*

mildheort. adj. *merciful, compassionate.*
masc. nom. pl. **mildheorte.**

mīlgemearc. neut. *distance in miles.* gen.
sg. **mīlgemearces** k/1362.

milts. fem. *compassion, mercy.* acc. sg.
miltse 14/349. gen. sg. **miltse** 9/2;
14/85, 92.

gemiltsian. wk. 2. *have mercy on.* imp. sg.
gemiltsa.

mīn. adj. *my, mine.* masc. nom. sg. 2/13;
9/59; 10/78, 95; 11/13, etc. fem. nom.
sg. i/8, 10; 10/130. masc. acc. sg. **mīnne**
2/13; 9/10, 19, 22. fem. acc. sg. **mīne**
9/9. masc. gen. sg. **mīnes** 11/9; 12/26;
13/10. fem. gen. sg. **mīnre** 12/2, 10, 40.
masc. dat. sg. **mīnum** i/2; 10/30; 14/94.
neut. dat. sg. **mīnum** 7/11. masc. nom.
pl. **mīne** 6/37 (2x); 7/9. neut. nom. pl.
mīne. masc. acc. pl. **mīne** 9/27; 12/38.
gen. pl. **mīnra** 12/5; 14/90. dat. pl.
mīnum 11/1.

mīn → ic, wē.

misbēodan. st. 2. (with dat. object). *mis-treat.* inf. 5/12.

misdǣd. fem. *misdeed.* acc. pl. **misdǣda**
5/47, 54. gen. pl. **misdǣda** 5/56. dat.
pl. **misdǣdan, misdǣdum** 5/51, 62.

mislic. adj. *various, diverse.* fem. nom. pl.
mislica 7/24, 32. masc. acc. pl. **mislice.**
fem. acc. pl. **mistlice** 5/24, 49. neut. acc.
pl. **mistlice** 5/48. dat. pl. **mislicum**
7/25.

mislīce. adv. *variously.*

mislimpan. st. 3. *turn out badly.* subj. sg.
mislimpe 5/47.

missenlic. adj. *various, manifold, diverse.*
neut. gen. sg. **missenlices.** gen. pl.
myssenlicra.

missenlīce. adv. *variously, here and there.*
9/75.

mistlice → mislic.

mīþan. st. 1. *conceal, be concealed, refrain
from.* pres. part. **mīþendne** 12/20.

mōd. neut. *heart, mind, spirit, courage.*
nom. sg. 2/9; 7/1, 12, 13, 63, etc. acc.
sg. 12/20. dat. sg. **mōde** 7/19; 9/41, 111;
10/130; 14/57, etc. inst. sg. **mōde** 6/32,
43; 10/122. nom. pl. 6/2. acc. pl. 6/35;
7/13.

mōdcearig. adj. *sorrowful at heart.* masc.
nom. sg. 9/2.

mōdcearu. fem. *sorrow of mind.* acc. sg.
mōdceare 12/51. gen. sg. **mōdceare**
12/40.

mōdgehygd. fem. *mind's thought.* dat. pl.
mōdgehygdum.

mōdgeþanc. masc. *thought, conception,
purpose.* acc. sg. 6/12.

mōdig. adj. *spirited, brave, proud.* masc.
nom. sg. 10/41; 14/26. fem. gen. sg.
mōdigre 14/334. masc. nom. pl. **mōdge**
9/62. gen. pl. **mōdigra.** wk. masc. nom.
sg. **mōdiga** 14/52.

mōdlufu. fem. *heart's love.* acc. sg.
mōdlufun 13/10.

mōdor. fem. *mother.* acc. sg. 5/32; 10/92.

mōdorlīce. adv. *in motherly fashion.*
2/10.

mōdsefa. masc. *mind, spirit, soul.* nom. sg. 9/59; 10/124. acc. sg. **mōdsefan** 9/10, 19.

molde. fem. *earth.* acc. sg. **moldan** 10/12, 82. gen. sg. **moldan** 14/343.

moldern. neut. *earthen house, sepulchre.* acc. sg. 10/65.

mon → man.

gemon → gemunan.

mōna. masc. *moon.* dat. sg. **mōnan.**

monade → monian.

Mōnandæg. masc. *Monday.*

mōnaþ. masc. *month.* gen. sg. **mōnðes** 14/324. acc. pl. 2/10.

moncynn → mancynn.

moncynnes → mancynn.

mondryhten. masc. *lord of men.* nom. sg. 13/7. acc. sg. 9/41.

monegum → manig.

gemong. neut. *multitude, assembly.* acc. sg. **gemong, gemang** 14/193, 225, 303.

monian. wk. 1. *admonish, exort, advise.* past 3sg. **manode, monade** 6/20; 14/26.

monig- → manig.

monn- → man.

monn- → manna.

monncynnes → mancynn.

monnian. wk. 2. *man.* past part. **monnad** 7/4.

mōr. masc. *moor.* dat. sg. **mōre.** nom. pl. **mōras** 7/19.

morgen. masc. *morning.* dat. sg. **morgenne, mergen, morgene** G/9; 3/9; 4/19; 6/15, 19, etc.

morgenceald. adj. *morning-cold.*

morgencollen. masc. (attested only here). *morning terror* (?). acc. sg. **morgencollan** 14/245.

morgenswēg. masc. *morning-sound.*

morgentīd. fem. *morning.* acc. sg. 14/236.

morþdǣd. fem. *murderous deed.* acc. pl. **morðdǣda** 5/48.

morþor. neut. *murder.* acc. sg. 12/20. gen. sg. **morðres** 14/90. gen. pl. **morðra** 14/181.

morþorwyrhta. masc. *one who causes death.* nom. pl. **morþorwyrhtan** 5/56.

mōst- → mōtan.

gemōt. neut. *assembly.* gen. sg. **gemōtes.**

mōtan. pret. pres. *may, can, must.* 1sg. **mōt** 10/142; 12/37. 3sg. **mōt** 7/62, 82. pl. **mōtan, mōte, mōton** F/7; 5/6, 7. past sg. **mōste** 4/15. past 3sg. **mōste** 14/185. past pl. **mōston** 13/17. subj. sg. **mōte** 10/127; 14/89, 118. subj. pl. **mōtan, mōten** 7/81; 13/33. subj. past sg. **mōste** 2/9.

gemunan. pret. pres. *think of, remember.* 1sg. **geman** 10/28. 3sg. **gemon** 9/34, 90; 12/51. subj. past sg. **gemunde** 13/14.

mund. fem. u-stem. *hand, protection.* dat. sg. **munde** 5/11. dat. pl. **mundum** 14/229.

mundbyrd. fem. *protection.* nom. sg. 10/130. acc. sg. 14/3.

munt. masc. *mountain.* dat. sg. **munte.** acc. pl. **muntas** 7/29. gen. pl. **munta** 7/29. dat. pl. **muntum** 7/25.

munuchād. masc. *monastic orders.* acc. sg. 6/20.

munuclic. adj. *monastic.* fem. dat. sg. **munuclicere** 2/30.

murnan. st. 3. *be anxious, be fearful.* inf. 14/154. pres. part. **murnende** 11/15.

mūþ. masc. *mouth.* dat. sg. **mūðe** 6/23.

mycclum → miclum.

mycel- → micel.

mycl- → micel.

myltestre. fem. *prostitute.* nom. pl. **myltestran** 5/56.

gemynd. fem. *memory, thought, mind.* acc. sg. 9/51. dat. sg. **gemynde** 6/14. dat. pl. **gemyndum** 13/31.

gemyndgian. wk. 2. *remember.* past 3sg. **gemyndgade** 6/22.

gemyndig. adj. *mindful, remembering.* masc. nom; sg. 9/6. fem. nom. sg. 14/74. masc. nom. pl. 7/11.

mynecen. fem. *nun.* dat. sg. **mynecene** 2/10. acc. pl. **mynecena** 2/10.

mynster. neut. *monastery.* acc. sg. м/3; 6/21. gen. sg. **mynstres** в/1. dat. sg. **mynstre** 2/10, 11, 20; 4/19; 6/1, etc.

mynsterhata. masc. *persecutor of monasteries.* nom. pl. **mynsterhatan** 5/56.

mynsterlic. adj. *monastic.* fem. dat. sg. **mynsterlicre** 2/9.

myntan. wk. 1. *intend, suppose.* past pl. **mynton** в/2; 14/253.

myrhþa. fem. *joy.* acc. pl. 5/70.

myrran. wk. 1. *mar, disturb, squander, hinder.* pl. **myrrað.**

myssenlicra → missenlic.

nā. adv. *no, not at all, never.* **nā, nō** a/4; d/3; к/1366; 5/28, 47, etc.

nabbað → habban.

naca. masc. *ship.* acc. sg. **nacan** 13/41. gen. sg. **nacan.**

nacod. adj. *naked.* masc. nom. sg. 1/10, 11. masc. nom. pl. **nacode** 1/7.

nāge → āgan.

nāh → āgan.

nāht. indef. pron. *nothing.* neut. nom. sg. **nāuht** 7/44. neut. acc. sg. **nōht, nāht, nāuht** 6/4, 8 (2x); 7/42.

nāhte → āgan.

nāhwǣr. adv. *nowhere, not at all.* **nāwer** 7/18, 27.

nales. adv. *not at all, emphatically not.* **nales, nalæs, nalles** 6/3; 9/32, 33; 11/15.

nam → (ge)niman.

genam → (ge)niman.

genām- → (ge)niman.

nama. masc. *name.* nom. sg. 7/26, 29, 76. acc. sg. **naman** 7/23, 24, 26, 27, 29, etc. dat. sg. **naman, noman** 5/60; 6/7; 10/113; 14/81. inst. sg. **naman** 7/28. acc. pl. **naman.**

nāman → (ge)niman.

namian. wk. 2. *name, appoint.* subj. sg. **namige.**

nān. A. adj. *no.* masc. nom. sg. **nān, nōn** 7/3, 5, 10, 33. neut. nom. sg. 5/47. masc. acc. sg. **nǣnne** 7/3 (2x), 10, 44. neut. acc. sg. 4/15 (2x). dat. pl. **nǣnum** 7/50.

B. indef. pron. *no, none.* masc. sg. 7/42. masc. nom. sg. 9/9; 14/257. masc. acc. sg. **nānne, nǣnne** 14/68, 233. neut. acc. sg. 7/8. masc. acc. pl. **nāne** 7/82.

nāp → (ge)nīpan.

genāp → (ge)nīpan.

nāt → witan.

nāteshwōn. adv. *not at all.* 1/4.

nāthwā. indef. pron. *something.* neut. acc. sg. **nāthwæt** lb/1.

nāthwelc. indef. pron. *I don't know which, one or another.* masc. gen. sg. **nāthwylces.**

naþelǣs. adv. *nevertheless.* 4/4.

nāþor. conj. *neither.* 5/22.

nāuht → nāht.

nāwer → nāhwǣr.

nǣdre. fem. *snake, serpent.* nom. sg. **nǣddre, nǣdre** 1/1 (2x), 4, 13. dat. sg. **nǣddran** 1/14. nom. pl. **nǣdran.**

næfde → habban.

nǣfre. adv. *never.* c/3; 3/12; 6/4, 5, 11, etc.

næfð → habban.

nǣgan. wk. 1. *approach, attack.*

nægl. masc. *nail.* dat. pl. **næglum** 10/46.

næglian. wk. 2. *nail.* past part. **næglede** 13/35.

nǣnig. indef. pron. *none, no one, no.* masc. nom. sg. 3/8, 12; 6/3; 7/77; 14/51, etc. masc. acc. sg. **nǣnigne** 6/36. masc. dat. sg. **nǣnigum** 10/47. fem. acc. sg. **nǣnige** в/7. neut. acc. sg. 6/5. neut. inst. sg. **nǣnige** 7/67.

nǣnne → nān.

nǣnum → nān.

nǣre → bēon.

næs. A. masc. *headland, ground.* acc. sg. 14/113. acc. pl. **næssas** к/1358. gen. pl. **næssa** к/1360.

B. adv. *not at all.*

næs → bēon.

ne. A. adv. *not.* a/1 (2x), 4 (2x), 5 (3x), etc.

B. conj. *neither, nor.* a/1 (3x), 3, 4, etc.

ne ne. conj. *nor*. A/3.

nēah. A. adj. *near, last* (in superl.). fem. nom. sg. 6/31. neut. nom. sg. 6/33, 39. neut. dat. sg. superl. nȳhstan 5/62. wk. masc. dat. sg. superl. nēhstan 14/73.
   B. adv. *near*. A/3; 7/18, 21, 27; 9/26, etc. compar. nēar 14/53.
   C. prep. *near*.

geneahhe. adv. *sufficiently, abundantly, often*. 9/56; 14/26.

neaht- → niht.

(ge)nēalǣcan. wk. 1. *approach*. 3sg. nēalǣcð 5/2. past 3sg. nēalǣhte, nēalǣcte, genēalǣhte 6/28; 14/34, 261. inf. genēalǣcan, nēalēcan 6/6.

nearo. adj. *narrow, limited*. masc. nom. sg. 7/30. masc. acc. pl. nearowan 7/67.

nēat. neut. *animal, cattle*. gen. pl. nēata 6/7.

nēawest. fem. *neighborhood*. dat. sg. nēaweste 6/29.

nēhstan → nēah.

nellað → willan.

nelle → willan.

nemnan. wk. 1. *name, call*. 3sg. nemneð. past 3sg. nemnde 6/7. inf. 14/81. past part. nemned 7/75.

nemne. A. prep. *except for*. 12/22.
   B. conj. *unless*.

nemþe. conj. *unless*. nemþe, nymðe 9/113; 14/52.

nēod. fem. *necessity, business, difficulty*. nom. sg. nēod, nȳd 5/60; 14/277. dat. sg. nēode, nȳde C/4; 2/18; 13/41.

nēode. adv. *necessarily*.

neorxnawang. masc. *Paradise*. gen. sg. neorxnawonges 1/8. dat. sg. neorxna-wange 1/3, 8, 10.

nēosan. wk. 1. (with gen. object). *seek, go to*. inf. 14/63.

neoþan. adv. *from beneath, below*. neoðan, nēoðan F/4.

neowol. adj. *prostrate, deep*. masc. acc. sg. neowelne 14/113.

Nergend- → Neriend.

(ge)nerian. wk. 1. *save, rescue, defend*. 3sg. genereþ. past 1sg. nerede. past 2sg. neredest. past 3sg. generede 3/15; 4/5. past pl. neredon.

Neriend. masc. nd-stem. *Saviour*. acc. sg. Nergend 14/81. gen. sg. Nergendes 14/73. dat. sg. Nergende 14/45.

generwed → genyrwan.

nese. adv. *no*.

nest. neut. *provisions*. acc. sg. 14/128.

nēten- → nȳten.

nēþan. wk. 1. *dare, risk*. past 3sg. nēðde 14/277.

nēxta. masc. *neighbour*. acc. pl. nēxtan.

nicor. masc. *water-monster*. nom. pl. nicras F/5. gen. pl. nicra F/2, 3.

nīetenum → nȳten.

nigon. card. num. as noun. *nine*. E/1.

niht. fem. athematic. *night*. nom. sg. 14/34. acc. sg. neaht 6/32. gen. sg. neahte 6/30. dat. sg. nihte, neahte 6/7; 10/2; 14/64. gen. pl. nihta K/1365. dat. pl. nihtum.

nihtes. adv. *by night*. A/2; 14/45.

nihthelm. masc. *cover of night*. acc. sg. 9/96.

nihtscūa. masc. *night-shadow*. nom. sg. 9/104.

nihtwæcce. noun. *night-watch*.

(ge)niman. st. 4. *take, seize, capture*. past 3sg. genam, nam 1/6; 4/4; 14/77, 98. past pl. genāmon, genāman, nāman 2/20; 4/6, 7, 17; 10/30, etc. imp. sg. nim, nym. inf. niman 12/15. infl. inf. tō nimanne 14/313. past part. genumen 1/19; 7/19 (2x).

genip. neut. *mist, darkness*. nom. pl. genipu F/2. acc. pl. genipu K/1360.

(ge)nīpan. st. 1. *grow dark*. 3sg. nīpeð 9/104. past 3sg. nāp, genāp 9/96.

nis → bēon.

nīþ. masc. *strife, enmity, evil*. dat. sg. nīðe 14/53. gen. pl. nīða 14/34. dat. pl. nīðum 14/287.

niþer. adv. *down, downwards*. niðer, nyþer F/1, 5; K/1360; 4/18.

nīþheard. adj. *fierce in strife.* masc. nom. sg. 14/277.

nīþhycgende. adj. *intending malice.* masc. nom. pl. 14/233.

nīþwundor. neut. *evil wonder.* acc. sg. ĸ/1365.

genīwad → genīwian.

nīwe. adj. *new, recent.* masc. nom. sg. 7/29. fem. nom. pl. 2/23. dat. pl. **nīwum** 2/24.

nīwes. adv. (from adj. *nīwe*). *recently.* 12/4.

genīwian. wk. 2. *renew, restore.* past part. **genīwad, genīwod** 9/50, 55; 10/148; 14/98.

nō → nā.

genōg. adj. *enough, many.* neut. acc. sg. **genōh** 13/35. masc. nom. pl. **genōge** 10/33.

genōh. adv. *sufficiently, very.* 5/40.

genōh → genōg.

nōht → nāht.

nold- → willan.

noman → nama.

nōn → nān.

norþ. adv. *north.* ꜰ/2; 7/70.

norþan. adv. *from the north.* 9/104.

norþanweard. adj. *northern part of.* masc. acc. sg. **norðanweardne** ꜰ/1.

norþdæl. masc. *northern region.* dat. sg. **norþdæle.**

norþeweard. adj. *north.* masc. acc. sg. **norðeweardne** 7/16.

notian. wk. 2. *make use of* something (gen.). pl. **notigað** 7/18.

nū. A. adv. *now.* ᴇ/4; ꜰ/7; 2/1, 8 (2x), etc. **B.** conj. *now that, since.* ᴅ/1; 6/33; 7/23.

genumen → (ge)niman.

nȳd → nēod.

nȳde. adv. *necessarily.* 5/3, 8; 14/287.

nȳde → nēod.

nȳdgyld. neut. *forced payment.* nom. pl. 5/38.

nȳdmāge. fem. *near kinswoman, female cousin.* acc. sg. **nȳdmāgan** 5/40.

nȳdþearf. fem. *necessity.* nom. sg. 5/9.

nȳhstan → nēah.

nylle → willan.

nym → (ge)niman.

nymðe → nemþe.

genyrwan. wk. 1. *narrow, restrict.* past part. **generwed, genyrwde** 5/15; 7/22.

nyste → witan.

nyte → witan.

nȳten. neut. *beast, animal.* nom. sg. **nēten** 6/22. nom. pl. **nȳtenu, nētenu** 1/1; 7/18. dat. pl. **nīetenum, nȳtenum** 1/14.

nyþer → niþer.

(ge)nyþerian. wk. 2. *bring low.* past part. **genyðerad** 14/113.

of. prep. (with dat.). *from, of.* ᴄ/7, 10; ꜰ/2; 1/1, 2, etc.

ofdūne. adv. *down.* 14/290.

ofer. prep. (with dat. or acc.). *over, beyond, upon, concerning, after, against.* ʙ/4; ꜰ/1; ɢ/2; ĸ/1363; ʟa/5, etc.

ōfer. masc. *bank, shore.* dat. sg. **ōfre** ĸ/1371.

ofercuman. st. 4. *overcome, overtake.* inf. 14/235.

oferdrencan. wk. 1. *give too much to drink.* past 3sg. **oferdrencte** 14/31.

oferfyll. fem. *overeating.* acc. pl. **oferfylla** 5/64.

ofergān. anom. verb. *go across, traverse, conquer, overtake.* past part. 4/2.

oferhelmian. wk. 2. *cover over.* 3sg. **oferhelmað** ĸ/1364.

oferhoga. masc. *despiser* (with gen. of what one despises). nom. pl. **oferhogan** 5/50.

oferlīce. adv. *excessively.* 5/62.

ofermōd. adj. *proud.* wk. masc. nom. pl. **ofermōdan** 7/68.

ofermōdlic. adj. *proud.* masc. dat. sg. **ofermōdlicum** 7/50.

ofersēon. st. 5. *observe.* past pl. **ofersēgon.**

ofersittan. st. 5. *occupy.* past part. **oferseten, ofseten** 7/18, 19.

oferswīþan. wk. 1. *overpower.* past part. **oferswīðed.**

oferwinnan. st. 3. *overcome.* past part. oferwunnen 13/45; 14/319.

offrian. wk. 2. *offer.* past pl. offrodon.

ofgifan. st. 5. *give up, leave.* past pl. ofgēafon 9/61.

ofhrēowan. st. 2. *cause pity* for someone (gen.). 3sg. ofhrīewð.

oflongad. adj. (past part. of *-longian*). *seized with longing.* fem. nom. sg. 12/29.

ofost. fem. *haste.* dat. sg. ofste 5/2.

ofostlīce. adv. *quickly.* 14/150, 169.

ōfre → ōfer.

ofseten → ofersittan.

ofslēan. st. 6. *kill, slay.* 1sg. ofslēa. past 3sg. ofslōg 3/1, 17. past pl. ofslōgon 3/15. past part. ofslægen, ofslægene, ofslægenne, ofslegen 3/6, 9, 10, 14.

ofspring. masc. *offspring.* dat. sg. ofspringe 1/15 (2x).

ofste → ofost.

ofstingan. st. 3. *stab to death.* past 3sg. ofstang 3/2.

ofstum. adv. *hastily.* 14/10, 35, 70.

oft. adv. *often.* H/3, 4 (2x); I/9; La/7, etc. compar. oftor 5/17; 10/128. superl. oftost 5/50.

oftēon. st. 2. *deprive* someone (dat.) of something (gen.), *withhold.* past 3sg. oftēah.

oftorfian. wk. 2. *pelt to death.* past pl. oftorfedon 4/17.

ofþyncan. wk. 1. *seem displeasing, be a matter of regret.* past 3sg. ofðūhte.

geofum → gifu.

oll. neut. *scorn.* dat. sg. olle 5/52.

ombeht. masc. *officer, retainer.*

on. A. adv. *on, in.* I/4; 7/18; 10/34, 98.

B. prep. (with dat. or acc.). *on, in, to, into, onto, at, at the time of, during, against, from.* on, a, an A/1 (3x), 2, 5 (2x), etc.

ōn → ān.

on ān. adv. *continuously, at once.* C/11, 12.

onbærnan. wk. 1. *kindle, inspire.* past part. onbærnde, onbærned 6/2, 27.

onbryrdan. wk. 1. *inspire.* past 3sg. onbryrde 14/95.

onbyrigan. wk. 1. (with gen. or dat. object). *taste.* inf. 10/114.

oncerran. wk. 1. *divert.* inf. 7/73.

oncnāwan. st. 7. *recognize, perceive, acknowledge, disclose.* past pl. oncnēowon 1/7.

ond → and.

ondrǣdan. st. 7. *be afraid, dread.* 1sg. ondrǣde 1/10. past 1sg. ondrēd.

ondswarian. wk. 2. *answer.* past 3sg. andswarode, ondswarade, ondswarede 6/8, 37; 7/1, 54. past pl. ondswaredon, ondswarodon 6/33, 36, 40.

ondweardum → andweard.

ondweorc → andweorc.

ōnettan. wk. 1. *hasten.* past 3sg. ōnette 14/162. past pl. 14/139.

onfindan. st. 3. *find out, discover.* past 3sg. onfand. past pl. onfundon 3/7. subj. past pl. onfunden 3/4.

onfōn. st. 7. (with acc., gen. or dat. object). *receive, succeed to, take.* past 3sg. onfēng 6/3, 11, 15, 21. past pl. onfēngon F/5. subj. past sg. onfēnge 6/20. past part. onfongne 6/19.

onfund- → onfindan.

ongan → onginnan.

ongēan. A. adv. *back, again, in opposition.* 7/53.

B. prep. (with dat. or acc.). *against, towards, opposite.* ongēan, angēan 1/15; 4/15; 14/165.

ongeat → ongietan.

ongēaton → ongietan.

Ongelþēod. fem. *English people, England.* dat. sg. Ongelþēode 6/3.

ongietan. st. 5. *understand, perceive.* 3sg. ongit 7/15. pl. ongite 7/30. past 3sg. ongeat 3/5. past pl. ongēaton 14/168, 238. inf. ongetan, ongietan, ongitan, ongytan 7/16, 20; 9/73; 10/18. past part. ongieten B/4.

onginnan. st. 3. *begin, endeavour, undertake.* past 3sg. ongan, ongon 6/11, 20;

7/12, 49, 52, etc. past pl. **ongunnon**
6/3; 10/65, 67; 12/11; 14/42, etc. subj.
pl. **āginnan, onginnen** 5/57; 10/116.
subj. past sg. **ongunne**. imp. sg. **ongin**
13/26.

ongit → ongietan.

ongitan → ongietan.

ongite → ongietan.

ongyrwan. wk. 1. *undress.* past 3sg.
ongyrede 10/39.

ongytan → ongietan.

onhǣtan. wk. 1. *heat, inflame.* past part.
onhǣted 14/87.

onhrēran. wk. 1. *arouse.* past part. **on-hrēred.**

onhweorfan. st. 3. *change.* past part. **on-hworfen** 12/23.

onhyldan. wk. 1. *bend down, lower.* past
3sg. **onhylde** 6/42.

oninnan. prep. *within, in the middle of, in
the midst of.* 14/312.

onlǣnan. wk. 1. *lend, grant.* 3sg. **onlǣnð**
7/72.

onlēon. st. 2. *lend* something (gen.) to
someone (dat.), *give* something (gen.)
to someone (dat.). past 3sg. **onlēah**
14/124.

onlēsed → onlȳsan.

onlīc. adj. *similar.* neut. gen. sg. **anlīces,
onlīces** 7/40, 42, 44.

onlīcness. fem. *likeness.* dat. sg. **onlīcnesse**
F/3.

onlȳsan. wk. 1. *release, redeem.* past 3sg.
onlȳsde 10/147. past part. **onlēsed**
7/61.

onmiddan. prep. (with dat.). *in the middle of.* 1/3, 8.

onmunan. pret. pres. *consider worthy
of* something (gen.). subj. past pl.
onmunden 3/14.

onsǣge. adj. *falling upon, attacking.* neut.
nom. sg. 5/17.

onsǣgedness. fem. *offering, sacrifice.* acc.
pl. **onsǣgednessa.**

onscyte. masc. *attack, calumny.* dat. pl.
onscytan 5/23, 54.

onsendan. wk. 1. *send.* 3sg. **onsendeð**
9/104. past 3sg. **onsende** 13/7. subj.
sg. **onsende** 8/11. past part. **onsended**
10/49.

onsittan. st. 5. *occupy, oppress, fear* (with
refl.). 3sg. **onsit** 5/34. pl. **onsittað** 5/7.
imp. sg. **onsite** 13/27.

onslēpan. wk. 1. *go to sleep, sleep.* past
3sg. **onslēpte** 6/7, 42.

onstellan. wk. 1. *institute, establish.* past
3sg. **onstealde** 6/12.

onstyrian. wk. 2. *move, budge, rouse, disturb.* inf. B/2, 4.

onsundran. adv. *singly, apart, privately.*
13/1.

onswīfan. st. 1. *turn, turn aside.* inf.
7/73.

ontīgan. wk. 1. *untie.* past part. **ontīged**
7/61.

onufan. prep. (with dat.). *upon.* 14/252.

onwacan. st. 6. *awake.* subj. past sg.
onwōce 14/77.

onwæcnan. wk. 1. *awake.* 3sg. **onwæcneð**
9/45.

onweald. masc. *authority, power, territory.*
nom. sg. **anweald** 7/9. acc. sg. **anweald,
anwald** 7/2, 3, 9 (2x). gen. sg.
anwealdes 7/2, 13, 14. dat. sg. **anwealde**
1/16.

onweg. adv. *away.* **āweg, onweg** B/5; 4/6.

onwendan. wk. 1. *change, overturn.* 3sg.
onwendeð 9/107.

onwōce → onwacan.

onwrēon. st. 1. *uncover, reveal.* imp. sg.
onwrēoh 10/97.

onwrīþan. st. 1. *unwrap.* inf. 14/173.

open. adj. *open.* masc. nom. pl. **opene**
10/47. wk. masc. nom. sg. **opena.**

geopenian. wk. 2. *open.* past 3sg. **geopenode** 2/21, 22. past part. **geopenode,
geopenod** 1/5, 7; 2/16.

openlīce. adv. *openly, plainly.* B/4; 7/80.

ōr. neut. *beginning, origin.* acc. sg. 6/12.

ōra. masc. *border, edge, shore.* dat. sg. **ōran**
13/22.

orc. masc. *cup.* nom. pl. **orcas** 14/18.

ōretmæcg. masc. *combatant.* acc. pl. ōretmæcgas 14/232.

orfcwealm. masc. *murrain, pestilence of cattle.* nom. sg. 5/19.

orfeorme. adj. *destitute of, lacking.* masc. nom. pl. 14/271.

orgellīce. adv. *proudly, arrogantly.* 7/49.

orsāwle. adj. *without a soul, dead.* masc. nom. sg. 14/108.

geortrūwian. wk. 2. *despair.*

orþung. fem. *breath.* gen. sg. orðunge.

oþ. A. prep. (usually with acc., sometimes with dat.). *until, as far as, to.* 2/24, 26; 4/11; 6/5; 7/16 (2x), etc.
  B. conj. *until.* 3/1, 5, 8; 4/14; 14/140, etc.

oþ þæt. conj. *until.* 1/19; 2/30; 3/2, 6, 15, etc.

oþberan. st. 4. *bear away.* past 3sg. oþbær 9/81.

ōþer. A. adj. and ord. num. *other, second.* masc. acc. sg. ōðerne. fem. acc. sg. ōðre 6/27; 7/29. neut. acc. sg. oþer M/5. masc. gen. sg. ōðres M/4. neut. gen. sg. ōðres 6/38. masc. dat. sg. ōðrum 5/21. fem. dat. sg. ōþerre 11/4. neut. dat. sg. ōðrum 7/32 (2x). masc. inst. sg. ōðre 7/28; 14/109. neut. nom. pl. ōðre 1/1. masc. acc. pl. ōðre. neut. acc. pl. ōþra H/4. dat. pl. ōðrum 6/24; 7/46.
  B. indef. pron. *other, another.* masc. acc. sg. ōþerne 5/23 (2x), 32. neut. nom. sg. 5/46. neut. acc. sg. 6/25; 7/21, 66. neut. gen. sg. ōðres 7/42. neut. dat. sg. ōðrum 5/5, 23, 30, 40. dat. pl. ōðran, ōðrum 5/27; 7/33. masc. nom. pl. ōðer, ōðre M/9 (2x); 6/3. neut. acc. pl. ōðre E/3.

oþþe. conj. *or.* G/9; M/4, 6; 4/3; 5/40 (2x), etc.

oþþon. conj. *or.* 5/25, 68.

oþþringan. st. 3. *force out.* past 1sg. oðþrong 14/185.

ōwiht. neut. *anything.* nom. sg. 12/23.

oxa. masc. *ox.* gen. sg. oxan. acc. pl. oxan.

Oxenafordscīr. fem. *Oxfordshire.* acc. sg. Oxenafordscīre 4/2.

pāpa. masc. *pope.* dat. sg. pāpan.

Paradīsus. noun. *Paradise.* dat. sg. Paradīsum 1/1, 2.

Parþas. masc. *Parthians.* dat. pl. Parðum 7/29.

pearroc. masc. *enclosure.* dat. sg. pearroce 7/24.

portic. masc. *vestibule.* dat. sg. porticum.

prēost. masc. *priest.* nom. pl. prēostas.

price. fem. *point.* nom. sg. 7/16, 21.

Pryfetesflōde. fem. *Privett, Hampshire.* dat. sg. Pryfetesflōdan 3/2.

prȳte. fem. *pride.* dat. sg. prȳtan 5/54.

pund. neut. *pound.* gen. pl. punda 4/14.

gerād. adj. *conditioned, circumstanced, wise.*

radost → hraþe, raþe, rade.

ranc. adj. *proud, haughty, arrogant.* masc. acc. sg. rancne 5/40.

rand. masc. *edge,* (metonymically) *shield.* acc. pl. randas.

randwiggendra → rondwiggend.

raþost → hraþe, raþe, rade.

gerǣcan. wk. 1. *reach, obtain, present.* inf. J/91; 5/7.

rǣd. masc. *advice, sense, reason.* acc. sg. J/91. gen. sg. rǣdes. dat. sg. rǣde 14/97. gen. pl. rǣda 14/68.

rǣdan. wk. 1. *read, advise, rule.* imp. sg. rǣd.

rǣdend. masc. (pres. part. of *rǣdan*). *ruler.*

ræfnan. wk. 1. *perform.* past pl. ræfndon 14/11.

ræpling. masc. *prisoner.* nom. sg. 4/9.

rǣran. wk. 1. *raise, offer up, promote, commit.* past 3sg. rǣrde 5/5. inf. 6/39.

rǣsan. wk. 1. *rush.* past 3sg. rǣsde 3/5.

rǣswa. masc. *leader, ruler.* dat. sg. rǣswan 14/12. nom. pl. rǣswan 14/178.

rēad. adj. *red.* neut. dat. sg. rēadum 14/338. wk. fem. nom. G/8. wk. fem. dat. sg. Rēadan.

rēade. adv. *redly.* G/9.

Rēadingas. masc. *people of Reading, Reading.* dat. pl. **Rēadingum.**

rēaf. neut. *garment.* gen. sg. **rēafes** 2/27.

rēaferas → rēfere.

rēafian. wk. 2. *plunder.* pl. **rēafiað** 5/46. past 3sg. **rēafode.**

rēaflāc. neut. *plundering.* nom. sg. 5/19. acc. sg. 5/63.

rēcan, reccan. wk. 1. *care, care for.* pl. **reccað** 7/46. past pl. **rōhtan, rōhton** 2/28; 5/47. subj. sg. **recce.** inf. **reccan** 7/2, 3. infl. inf. **tō reccenne** 7/9.

(ge)reccan. wk. 1. *tell, reckon, count as.* past pl. **rehton** 6/18. inf. **reccan, gerēccan** 2/28; 7/10.

reccað → rēcan, reccan.

recce → rēcan, reccan.

reccelēst. fem. *negligence.* dat. sg. **reccelēste** 7/36.

reced. neut. *hall.*

recene → rycene.

gerēfa. masc. *reeve, sheriff.* acc. sg. **gerēfan** 4/6. dat. sg. **gerēfan.**

rēfere. masc. *plunderer.* nom. pl. **rēaferas** 5/56.

regollic. adj. *regular.* dat. pl. **regollecum** 6/26.

regollīce. adv. *according to rule.* 5/21.

rehton → (ge)reccan.

reliquias. masc. *relics.*

gerēnian. wk. 2. *arrange, ornament.* past part. **gerēnode** 14/338.

rēnig. adj. *rainy.* neut. nom. sg. 11/10.

gerēnode → gerēnian.

rēnscūr. masc. *rain shower.*

rēocan. st. 2. *reek, steam.* pres. part. **rēocende** 14/313.

gereord. neut. *meal, feast, banquet.* dat. sg. **gereorde.**

reordberend. masc. nd-stem. *speech-bearer, person.* nom. pl. 10/3. dat. pl. **reordberendum** 10/89.

reordian. wk. 2. *speak.*

gereordian. wk. 2. *feed, eat* (with refl.). past pl. **gereordodon.**

rēotig. adj. *wailing, lamenting.* fem. nom. sg. **rēotugu** 11/10.

rēowan → rōwan.

rest. fem. *rest, bed.* acc. sg. **reste** 6/32; 10/3; 14/54. dat. sg. **reste** 6/7; 14/68.

restan. wk. 1. *rest.* past 3sg. **reste** 10/64, 69; 14/44. past pl. **reston** 14/321.

gerestan. wk. 1. *rest.* inf. 6/30; 12/40.

rēþe. adj. *fierce, cruel, raging, severe.* masc. acc. pl. 14/348. masc. nom. sg. superl. **rēðost.**

rīce. A. neut. *rule, authority, kingdom, empire.* nom. sg. 7/28; 9/106. acc. sg. 3/3; 10/119, 152. gen. sg. **rīces** 3/1, 11; 6/24; 7/2. dat. sg. 3/17, 18; 4/18; 14/343.

  B. adj. *powerful, noble, wealthy.* masc. nom. sg. 7/49. masc. acc. sg. **rīcne** 5/40; 10/44; 14/234. masc. gen. sg. **rīces** 7/26. gen. pl. **rīcra** 5/63; 10/131. wk. masc. nom. sg. **rīca** 7/75; 14/20, 44, 68. wk. masc. dat. sg. **rīcan** 14/11.

ricene → rycene.

rīcsian. wk. 2. *rule, prevail.* past 3sg. **rīcsode** 3/16; 5/4. infl. inf. **tō rīcsianne** 7/4.

rīdan. st. 1. *ride.* 1sg. **rīde** I/7. past pl. **ridon** 3/10.

riht. adj. *correct.* masc. acc. sg. **rihtne, ryhtne** 10/89. fem. dat. sg. **rihtre** A/3. masc. inst. sg. **rihte** 14/97.

(ge)riht. neut. *straight line, law, justice, obligation, dues* (always pl.), *privilege.* acc. sg. **riht** 5/52. dat. sg. **rihte, gerihte** 5/9, 50, 67; 14/202. nom. pl. **gerihta** 5/13. acc. pl. **gerihta** 5/9, 10. gen. pl. **gerihta** 5/13.

(ge)rihtan. wk. 1. *make straight, correct, guide, direct.* past part. **geriht** 10/131.

rihte. adv. *correctly, justly.* 5/23.

rihtfæderencyn. neut. *direct paternal ancestry.* nom. sg. **ryhtfæderencyn** 3/16.

rihtlagu. fem. *law.* gen. pl. **rihtlaga** 5/50.

gerihtlǣcan. wk. 1. *correct, amend.*

rihtlīce. adv. *rightly, justly, correctly.* 5/69.

rihtryne. masc. *correct course.* dat. sg. 7/73.

rihtwīs. adj. *righteous.* wk. masc. nom. pl. **rihtwīs** A/6. wk. gen. pl. **rihtwīsena** A/5.

rihtwīsness. fem. *righteousness.* nom. sg. **rihtwīsnys.**

rīnan. st. 1. *rain.* subj. pl. **rīnon.**

rinc. masc. *man, warrior.* gen. pl. **rinca** 7/73; 14/54, 338.

rīsan. st. 1. *rise.*

gerisene. neut. *what is fitting, dignity.* gen. pl. **gerisena** 5/13.

gerisenlic. adj. *suitable, becoming.* neut. acc. pl. **gerisenlice** 6/1.

gerisenlīce. adv. *fittingly.* 7/2.

rōd. fem. *cross, crucifix.* nom. sg. 10/44, 136. acc. sg. **rōde** 10/119. dat. sg. **rōde** c/5; 10/56, 131.

rōdetācn. neut. *sign of the cross.* dat. sg. **rōdetācne** 6/42.

rodor. masc. *sky, heaven.* acc. sg. 7/73. acc. pl. **roderas** 14/348. gen. pl. **rodora** 7/70. dat. pl. **roderum** 14/5.

rōf. adj. *brave, renowned.* masc. nom. pl. **rōfe** 14/20. gen. pl. **rōfra** 14/53.

rōht- → rēcan, reccan.

Rōmāne. masc. *Romans.* nom. pl. H/2, 3. gen. pl. **Rōmāna** 7/28, 29, 75.

Rōmānisc. adj. *Roman.* masc. nom. sg. 7/31.

Rōmeburg. fem. athematic. *Rome.* nom. sg. H/1.

Rōmweg. masc. *road to Rome.* dat. sg. **Rōmwege.**

rondbēag. masc. *boss.* nom. sg. 7/16.

rondwiggend. masc. nd-stem. *warrior armed with a shield.* nom. pl. **rond-wiggende** 14/11, 20. gen. pl. **rand-wiggendra** 14/188.

rōtlīce. adv. *cheerfully.* 6/33.

rōwan. st. 7. *row.* past pl. **rēowan** 2/19.

rūm. A. masc. *space, opportunity.* nom. sg. 14/313. acc. sg. 7/70.

  B. adj. *spacious.* masc. acc. pl. **rūme** 14/348.

rūme. adv. *abundantly.* 14/97.

rūmedlic. adj. *generous.* neut. gen. sg. **rūmedlices** 7/22.

rūmheort. adj. *generous-hearted.* fem. nom. sg. J/86.

rūn. fem. *mystery, counsel, secret, rune.* acc. sg. **rūne** J/86. dat. sg. **rūne** 9/111; 14/54.

rycene. adv. *quickly, hastily.* **ricene, recene, rycene** J/91; 9/112; 14/188.

ryht- → riht.

ryhtfæderencyn → rihtfæderencyn.

(ge)rȳman. wk. 1. *make room, clear a way, yield.* past 1sg. **gerȳmde** 10/89. past part. **gerȳmed.**

ryne. masc. *course, flow, stream, period of time.* dat. pl. **rynum** A/3.

rȳpan. wk. 1. *plunder, rob.* pl. **rȳpaþ** 5/46. past pl. **rȳpton** 4/4.

rȳpere. masc. *robber.* nom. pl. **rȳperas** 5/56. gen. pl. **rȳpera** 5/19.

sācerd. masc. *priest.* nom. pl. **sācerdas.**

sacu. fem. *strife, dispute, battle, lawsuit.* nom. sg. H/4. dat. sg. **sæcce** 14/288.

sadol. masc. *saddle.*

saga → secgan.

sāh → sīgan.

salo. adj. *dark, sallow.* masc. nom. sg. J/11.

salowigpād. adj. *dark-coated.* wk. masc. nom. sg. **salowigpāda** 14/211.

same. adv. in phrase **swā same swā**, *just as.* **some** 7/37.

gesamnode → gesomnian.

sanctus. A. *saint.* 1. masc. gen. sg. **sanctes.** 2. fem. dat. sg. **sancte** 2/1.

  B. adj. *saint.* masc. nom. sg. F/1; G/6. masc. acc. sg. F/7. masc. gen. sg. **sancte** 4/5, 19.

sang. masc. *song.* nom. sg. **song** 6/23. gen. sg. **songes** 6/14. dat. sg. **sange** 2/30. dat. pl. **sangum** 2/24.

sang → singan.

sangcræft. masc. *art of song.* acc. sg. **songcræft** 6/3.

sār. adj. *sore, painful, grievous, sorrowful.* fem. nom. pl. **sāre** 9/50. gen. pl. **sārra** 10/80; 14/182.

sāre. adv. *painfully, grievously.* 5/14, 55; 10/59.

sārlīce. adv. *painfully, grievously.* 7/36.

sārness. fem. *pain.* dat. sg. sārnysse 1/16.

sāul- → sāwol.

gesāwe → (ge)sēon.

sāwllēas. adj. *soulless, lifeless.* wk. masc. acc. sg. sāwllēasan 2/24.

sāwol. fem. *soul.* nom. sg. sāwl 7/60, 61; 10/120. acc. sg. sāwle, sāule 2/30; 4/18; 5/25. gen. sg. sāwle 7/59. nom. pl. sāwla F/3, 5, 6. acc. pl. sāwla F/7. dat. pl. sāwlum.

gesāwon → (ge)sēon.

sǣ. fem. *sea.* nom. sg. 7/18, 19. acc. sg. 9/4. dat. sg. 5/43 (2x); 7/22, 23, 25, etc. dat. pl. sǣm.

sǣcce → sacu.

sǣd- → secgan.

gesǣd → secgan.

sǣfæreld. neut. *sea-journey.* dat. sg. sǣfærelde.

sǣflōd. neut. *flood.*

(ge)sǣgan. wk. 1. *lay low, destroy.* past part. gesǣged 14/293.

sǣgd- → secgan.

sǣgrund. masc. *sea-floor.* dat. sg. sǣgrunde.

sǣl. masc. *time, occasion.* nom. sg. 10/80.

(ge)sǣlan. 1. wk. 1. *happen.* subj. sg. gesǣle 7/70. 2. wk. 1. *fasten, bind, confine.* inf. sǣlan 9/21. past part. gesǣled 14/114.

sǣlida. masc. *seafarer.*

sǣman. masc. athematic. *seaman, viking.* nom. pl. sǣmen 5/43.

sǣnaca. masc. *sea-going ship.* acc. sg. sǣnacan 13/27.

gesǣne → gesȳne.

sǣt → (ge)sittan.

gesǣt → (ge)sittan.

sǣte → (ge)sittan.

Sǣternesdæg. masc. *Saturday.* acc. sg. 4/15.

sǣton → (ge)sittan.

sǣtt → (ge)sittan.

scamian. wk. 2. (impersonal, with acc. of person). *shame, be ashamed* of something (gen.). 3sg. scamað 5/51, 53, 54, 57 (2x), etc. inf. 7/67.

scamu. fem. *shame, disgrace.* nom. sg. 5/35.

scandlic. adj. *shameful.* neut. nom. sg. 5/30. neut. nom. pl. scandlīce 5/38. dat. pl. sceandlican 5/23. wk. fem. acc. sg. sceandlican D/3.

scǣron → scyran.

sceacan. st. 6. *shake, brandish, hasten, depart.* inf. 14/291.

scead. neut. *shadow.* acc. pl. sceadu 8/15.

sceadu. fem. *shadow.* nom. sg. 10/54.

gesceādwīsnes. fem. *reason.* nom. sg. 7/2, 12. gen. sg. gesceādwīsnesse 7/47.

gesceaft. fem. *creature, creation, origin, destiny, nature.* nom. sg. 9/107; 10/12, 55, 82. acc. sg. gesceafte 5/31.

sceal → sculan.

scealc. masc. *servant, retainer, warrior, man.* gen. sg. scealces. nom. pl. scealcas 14/230. gen. pl. scealca.

sceall → sculan.

scealt → sculan.

sceandlican → scandlic.

gesceap. neut. *form, creature, creation.* dat. sg. gesceape 6/24.

gesceapen → (ge)scyppan.

sceard. neut. *shard, gap.* acc. pl. 7/19.

scearp. adj. *sharp.* masc. acc. sg. scearpne 14/78.

scēat. masc. *corner, region, surface, garment.* dat. sg. scēate La/2. acc. pl. scēatas 7/67; 10/37. dat. pl. scēatum 10/8, 43.

scēaþ. fem. *sheath.* dat. sg. scēaðe 14/79. dat. pl. sceaðum 14/230.

sceaþa. masc. *criminal, enemy.* gen. pl. sceaðena 14/193.

sceaðum → scēaþ.

scēawian. wk. 2. *look, see, examine.* past 1sg. scēawode 10/137. past 3sg. scēawode 2/22.

scel → sculan.

scelde → scild.

scendan. wk. 1. *injure, disgrace*. pl. scendað 5/40, 44.

sceol- → sculan.

sceold- → sculan.

sceōp → (ge)scyppan.

gesceōp → (ge)scyppan.

scēotan. st. 2. *shoot, rush, contribute*. pl. scēotað 5/30.

scēotend. masc. nd-stem. *archer, warrior*. nom. pl. 14/304.

sceþþan. wk. 1. (with dat. object). *injure*. pl. sceþþað. inf. 10/47.

sciell. fem. *shell*. acc. sg. scielle.

scild. masc. *shield*. dat. sg. scelde 7/16. nom. pl. scildas 14/204.

scildburh. fem. athematic. *shield-fortification, shield-wall*. acc. sg. 14/304.

Scildinga → Scylding.

scilling. masc. *shilling*. nom. pl. scillingas. acc. pl. scillingas M/3, 5, 6, 7, 8, etc.

scīma. masc. *brightness, splendour*. acc. sg. scīman 10/54.

scīnan. st. 1. *shine*. 3sg. scīnð, scȳnð G/9; 2/13. pl. scīnað. past pl. scinon. inf. 10/15.

scip. neut. *ship*. dat. sg. scipe 5/46. nom. pl. scipu. acc. pl. scipu. gen. pl. scypa 4/21. dat. pl. scypan 4/8.

scipen. fem. *stall, shed*. dat. sg. scipene 6/7.

scīr. adj. *shining, resplendent*. masc. acc. sg. scīrne 10/54. masc. acc. pl. scīre 14/193.

scīrmǣled. adj. *brightly adorned*. neut. acc. pl. 14/230.

Sciþþeas. masc. *Scythians* (inhabiting much of eastern Europe and Russia in ancient times). nom. pl. 7/29.

scold- → sculan.

scopgereord. neut. *poetic language*. dat. sg. scopgereorde 6/1.

scort. adj. *short*. masc. nom. sg. 7/45. wk. masc. dat. sg. scortan 7/46.

scrīfan. st. 1. *decree, judge, shrive, care*. pl. scrīfað, scrīfeð 5/30; 7/70.

scrift. masc. *penance, confessor*. dat. sg. scrifte.

scrīn. neut. *shrine, reliquary*.

scrȳdan. wk. 1. *clothe*. inf. 4/21.

sculan. pret. pres. *be obliged, must, have to, ought to, shall, should*. 1sg. sceal, sculon 5/70; 6/10; 12/25; 13/3. 2sg. scealt 13/9. 3sg. sceal, sceall, scel J/81, 83; 5/3, 7, 8 (2x), etc. pl. sculon, sceolon C/10, 11, 12; J/82; 6/12, etc. past 1sg. sceolde 9/8, 19; 10/43. past 3sg. scolde, sceolde 2/14; 4/21; 5/5, 21, 23, etc. past pl. sceoldon, scoldan, sceoldan 5/12, 22, 63; 6/6, 29, etc. subj. sg. scyle, scule 7/32; 12/42. subj. pl. scylan, scylen 5/6; 7/24. subj. past pl. sceolden, scolden 6/39; 7/48.

scūr. masc. *shower, storm*, fig. *battle*. acc. pl. scūras 14/221. dat. pl. scūrum 14/79.

scyl- → sculan.

scyldan. wk. 1. *shield, defend*. past 3sg. scylde 7/53.

gescyldan. wk. 1. *shield, protect*. subj. sg. gescylde.

scyldig. adj. *guilty, liable*. masc. nom. sg. M/1.

Scylding. masc. *descendant of Scyld, Dane*. gen. pl. Scildinga, Scyldinga.

scȳne. adj. *beautiful*. fem. acc. sg. 14/316.

scynscaþa. masc. *demonic foe*.

scȳnð → scīnan.

scyp- → scip.

(ge)scyppan. st. 6. *make*. past 3sg. gesceōp, sceōp C/1; 6/13; 14/347. past part. gesceapen 2/25.

Scyppend. masc. nd-stem. *Creator*. nom. sg. 6/13; 9/85. gen. sg. Scyppendes 6/11, 44; 14/78.

scyran. st. 4. *cut*. past pl. scǣron 14/304.

scytta. masc. *archer*. gen. pl. scyttena.

se. pron. 1. demonst. *the, that one, that, this, the aforementioned, he*. masc. nom. sg. A/1; B/4, 6, 7; D/3, etc. masc. acc. sg. þone, þæne B/5 (2x); C/10; G/4; K/1367, etc. masc. gen. sg. ðæs 2/5; 3/3, 7, 9,

15, etc. masc. dat. sg. þām, þǣm A/1;
B/4, 5; C/9; F/2 (2x), etc. masc. inst. sg.
þȳ 14/12. fem. nom. sg. sēo, sīo G/3,
8; 1/1 (2x), 4, etc. fem. acc. sg. þā D/3;
1/14; 2/20 (2x), 21 (2x), etc. fem. gen.
sg. þǣre 1/18; 5/13; 6/41; 12/40. fem.
dat. sg. þǣre B/3, 5; 1/14, 17; 2/1, etc.
neut. nom. sg. þæt, tæt A/3; F/4; K/1361,
1372; 1/2, etc. neut. acc. sg. þæt La/5;
Lb/3; 1/3, 13; 2/14, etc. neut. gen. sg.
þæs B/1, 2; C/11; D/1; F/6, etc. neut. dat.
sg. þām, þǣm, þan A/3; C/8; D/2; F/1,
3, etc. neut. inst. sg. þȳ, þon, þe 3/14,
17, 18; 5/21; 6/19, etc. nom. pl. þā A/4,
5 (2x), 6 (2x), etc. acc. pl. þā D/1; E/3
(2x); 2/11, 18, etc. gen. pl. þāra, þǣra
A/5; F/3; 1/2; 2/7; 5/11, etc. dat. pl. þām,
þǣm D/2, 3; F/3, 5; 4/12, etc. **2.** rel. *who,
which, that which, that.* masc. nom.
sg. 2/29; 3/3, 15; 7/17, 28, etc. masc.
acc. sg. þone B/2, 4. masc. dat. sg. þām
2/31. fem. acc. sg. ðā. neut. nom. sg.
þæt A/3 (2x); 1/6; 5/13, 30 (2x), etc.
neut. acc. sg. þæt La/7; 2/4; 5/1, 53 (2x),
etc. neut. dat. sg. þǣm 6/29, 45. acc. pl.
þā 6/22. gen. pl. þāra 6/7, 11.

se þe. rel. pron. *that, which, who, he
who, whoever.* masc. nom. sg. 2/26; 4/9;
5/16, 29, 32, etc. masc. acc. sg. ðone þe
7/45; 9/27. masc. gen. sg. ðæs þe 7/18.
masc. dat. sg. þām þe 9/31, 56, 114.
fem. nom. sg. sēo ðe 2/17; 10/121. fem.
dat. sg. ðǣre ðe 1/19. neut. gen. sg. þæs
þe 5/58; 7/7. nom. pl. þā þe F/5, 6;
2/27; 3/11; 6/1, etc. acc. pl. þā þe 6/14.
gen. pl. þāra þe 10/86. dat. pl. þām þe,
þǣm þe 7/57; 10/149, 154.

geseah → (ge)sēon.

sealde → (ge)sellan.

gesealde → (ge)sellan.

sealdon → (ge)sellan.

sealm. masc. *psalm.* acc. pl. **sealmas**
2/21.

sealobrūn. adj. *deep brown.*

sealt. adj. *salt.* masc. acc. pl. **sealte**
13/5.

searacræftas → searocræft.

sēarian. wk. 2. *become sere, wither.* pl.
sēariað A/3.

searocræft. masc. *art, artifice, wile.* acc.
pl. **searacræftas** 5/48.

searoþoncol. adj. *shrewd, wise.* fem.
nom. sg. 14/145. gen. pl. **searoþoncelra**
14/330.

searowrenc. masc. *trick.* acc. pl.
syruwrencas 4/5.

sēaþ. masc. *pit.* dat. sg. **sēaþe** 10/75.

(ge)sēcan. wk. 1. *seek.* 3sg. **sēceð** 9/114;
14/96. past 1sg. **sōhte, gesōhte** 9/25;
13/6. past 3sg. **gesōhte** 14/14. past pl.
sōhton 10/133. subj. sg. **sēce** K/1369.
inf. **sēcan, gesēcan** C/10; 10/104, 119,
127; 12/9, etc. infl. inf. **tō sēcenne**
2/18.

Seccandūn. fem. *Seckington, Warwickshire.*
dat. sg. **Seccandūne** 3/17.

secg. masc. *man.* nom. pl. **secgas** 14/201.
gen. pl. **secga** 9/53. dat. pl. **secgum**
10/59; 13/34.

secgan. wk. 3. *say, tell.* 1sg. **secge** D/1, 3;
G/2, 3, 4, etc. 3sg. **segeð, segð.** pl. **secgað**
D/3; 2/28, 29, 30. past 3sg. **sǣde, sǣgde**
1/11; 2/7, 27; 5/63; 6/15 (2x), etc. past
pl. **sǣdon, sǣgdon** 6/18. subj. sg. **secge**
10/96. imp. sg. **saga, sege** G/2, 3, 4, 5, 6,
etc. inf. 6/16, 45; 8/25; 10/1; 12/2, etc.
infl. inf. **tō secganne** 7/11. past part.
gesǣd.

sefa. masc. *mind, spirit.* acc. sg. **sefan**
9/57.

sege → secgan.

segen. masc. *banner, standard.*

gesegen → (ge)sēon.

segeð → secgan.

segl. masc. *sail.*

seglian. wk. 2. *sail.*

(ge)segnian. wk. 2. *sign, cross.* past 3sg.
gesegnode 6/42. pres. part. **segniende**
6/44.

segð → secgan.

geselda. masc. *hall-companion.* nom. sg.
1/3. acc. pl. **geseldan** 9/53.

seldcyme. masc. *seldom coming.* nom. pl. seldcymas 11/14.

seldhwænne. adv. *seldom.* seldhwænne, seldhwonne 2/11; 7/35.

seledrēam. masc. *hall-joy, hall-revelry.* nom. pl. seledrēamas 9/93.

seledrēorig. adj. *hall-sorrowful, sorrowful at separation from the hall.* masc. nom. sg. 9/25.

selesecg. masc. *man of the hall, retainer.* acc. pl. selesecgas 9/34.

sēlest → gōd.

sēlesta → gōd.

seleð → (ge)sellan.

self. pron. 1. adding emphasis to a pron. or noun. *self, himself, herself, itself, myself, yourself.* dat. sg. sylfum 8/5. masc. nom. sg. sylf, sylfa, self H/4; I/11; 2/8; 7/51; 8/11, etc. masc. acc. sg. sylfne 5/53, 66. masc. gen. sg. seolfes 6/45. masc. dat. sg. sylfum, selfum C/12; 6/17; 12/45. fem. nom. sg. sylf 2/16; 13/14. fem. acc. sg. sylfe 10/92. fem. gen. sg. sylfre 12/2. fem. dat. sg. sylfre 14/335. neut. dat. sg. selfum 7/63. gen. pl. selfra, sylfra 7/68; 14/285. masc. nom. pl. seolfan, sylf 6/23. 2. refl. *self, himself, herself.* masc. nom. sg. sylfa. masc. acc. sg. sylfne, selfne, seolfne 5/40, 59; 6/44; 8/26. fem. acc. sg. sylfe 2/11. fem. dat. sg. sylfre 2/25. dat. pl. sylfum 5/60. masc. nom. pl. selfe 5/64.

(ge)sellan. wk. 1. *give, sell, yield (of crops).* 3sg. seleð, selð A/3; K/1370. pl. syllað 5/31. past 3sg. sealde, gesealde 1/6, 12; 5/29, 32 (2x), etc. past pl. sealdon. subj. sg. geselle M/5, 6, 9, 11. imp. pl. sille. inf. syllan 4/15. past part. gesealde 5/14.

sēlost → gōd.

sencan. wk. 1. *submerge.*

(ge)sendan. wk. 1. *send.* 3sg. sendeð. past 3sg. sende 2/18; 4/1. past pl. sendon 14/224. subj. sg. sende 14/190. imp. sg. gesend. inf. sendan 8/26; 9/56. past part. sended B/5; 8/2.

gesēne → gesȳne.

sengan. wk. 1. *singe.*

sēo → se.

sēo ðe → se þe.

sēoc. adj. *sick.* fem. acc. sg. sēoce 11/14.

seofian. wk. 2. *sigh.* past pl. seofedun.

seofon. A. card. num. as noun. *seven.* E/1 (2x).
    B. as adj. *seven.* masc. acc. pl. H/1.

geseoh → (ge)sēon.

seolf- → self.

seolfor. neut. *silver.* dat. sg. seolfre 10/77.

(ge)sēon. st. 5. *see, look.* 1sg. gesēo. 2sg. gesihst. 3sg. gesihð 9/46. past 1sg. geseah 10/14, 21, 33, 36, 51, etc. past 3sg. geseah F/1, 3; 1/6; 4/10; 6/6, etc. past pl. gesāwe, gesāwon. subj. past sg. gesāwe 10/4. imp. sg. geseoh. inf. gesēon, sēon K/1365; 4/10; 7/18; 14/136. pres. part. gesēonde F/1. past part. gesegen, gesewen 6/17, 45; 8/22.

sēoþan. st. 2. *boil.*

geset. neut. *seat, habitation.* nom. pl. gesetu 9/93.

geseted → (ge)settan.

geseteness. fem. *institution, law.* nom. pl. gesetenessa 7/32.

setl. masc. *seat, throne, see.* dat. sg. setle A/1.

(ge)settan. wk. 1. *set, put, establish, institute, compose.* 1sg. sette 1/15. past 1sg. gesette. past 3sg. gesette 2/8, 27; 6/7, 44. past pl. setton, gesetton 10/67. inf. settan 13/4. past part. geseted, geset 6/5; 10/141.

gesewen → (ge)sēon.

sī → bēon.

sibb. fem. *relationship, love, friendship, peace.* dat. sg. sibbe H/4.

gesibb. adj. *related.* masc. nom. sg. gesib 5/21. masc. dat. sg. gesibban 5/21.

sibliger. neut. *incest.* acc. pl. siblegeru 5/48.

sīd. adj. *broad.* fem. acc. sg. sīde 14/337.

sīde. A. fem. *side.* dat. sg. sīdan 10/49.
    B. adv. *amply, widely.* 5/51; 10/81.

sidu. masc. u-stem. *manners, morality.* dat. pl. **sidum** 7/24.

sīe → bēon.

sīen → bēon.

gesīene → gesȳne.

sīgan. st. 1. *descend, issue.* past 3sg. **sāh** 2/15.

sigebēam. masc. *tree of victory.* nom. sg. 10/13. acc. sg. 10/127.

sigedryhten. masc. *lord of victory.* dat. sg. **sigedryhtne** 8/25.

sigefolc. neut. *victorious people.* dat. sg. **sigefolce** 14/152.

sigelēas. adj. *without victory.* masc. nom. pl. **sigelēase** 5/39.

sigerōf. adj. *renowned in victory.* masc. nom. pl. **sigerōfe** 14/177.

sigeþēod. fem. *victorious people.* dat. sg. **sigeþēode** 13/20.

sigeþūf. masc. *victory-banner.* acc. pl. **sigeþūfas** 14/201.

sigewong. masc. *field of victory.* dat. sg. **sigewonge** 14/294.

sigor. masc. *victory.* acc. sg. 14/89. gen. sg. **sigores** 14/124. dat. sg. **sigore** 14/298. gen. pl. **sigora** 10/67.

sigorfæst. adj. *secure in victory.* masc. nom. sg. 10/150.

sigorlēan. neut. *reward of victory.* acc. sg. 14/344.

gesihst → (ge)sēon.

gesihþ. fem. *sight.* acc. sg. **gesyhðe** 10/96. dat. sg. **gesyhðe, gesihðe** 1/6, 8; 6/43; 10/21, 41, etc.

gesihð → (ge)sēon.

sille → (ge)sellan.

simle → symble.

sīn. adj. *his, her, its, their.* fem. dat. sg. **sīnre** 14/132. neut. dat. sg. **sīnum** 14/99. masc. acc. pl. **sīne** 14/29.

sinc. neut. *treasure.* acc. sg. 13/34. gen. sg. **sinces** 9/25; 14/30, 339. dat. sg. **since** 10/23.

sinchroden. adj. *adorned with treasure.* fem. nom. sg. 13/14.

sincþegu. fem. *receiving of treasure.* acc. sg. **sincþege** 9/34.

sind → bēon.

sindon → bēon.

singal. adj. *everlasting.* fem. nom. sg. 10/141.

singallīce. adv. *constantly.* 5/45; 7/13.

singan. st. 3. *sing.* past 3sg. **song, sang** 6/14, 24; 14/211. past pl. **sungon** 2/21. imp. sg. **sing** 6/7, 10. inf. 6/4, 6, 8 (2x), 9, etc. pres. part. **singende** 7/64.

sinneahtes. adv. *in perpetual night.* 8/14.

sinsorg. fem. *everlasting sorrow, huge sorrow.* gen. pl. **sinsorgna** 12/45.

sint → bēon.

sīo → se.

(ge)sittan. st. 5. *sit.* 3sg. **siteð, sitt** A/1; 12/47. past 1sg. **sæt** 11/10. past 3sg. **sæt, gesæt, sætt** B/4; G/2; 9/111. past pl. **sæton** 8/14; 14/141. subj. past sg. **sæte** G/2; 14/252. inf. **sittan** 12/37; 14/15.

sīþ. A. masc. *journey, undertaking,* fig. *plight, time* i.e. occasion. acc. sg. 12/2; 14/145. gen. sg. **sīþes** 13/24. dat. sg. **sīðe** 14/73. inst. sg. **sīðe** 14/109.
  B. adv. *late.* 14/275.

gesīþ. masc. *companion, retainer.* nom. pl. **gesīðas** 14/201. dat. pl. **gesīþum** 13/34.

sīþfæt. masc. (often with neut. ending in pl.). *journey.* dat. sg. **sīðfate** 10/150; 14/335.

sīþian. wk. 2. *travel, journey.* inf. 10/68.

gesīþmægen. neut. *band of retainers.* acc. sg. J/88.

siþþan. A. adv. *afterwards.* **syððan, siððan** C/5, 7, 11, 12; 2/10 (2x), etc.
  B. conj. *after, since.* **siððan, syððan** 2/12, 16; 7/53, 61, 62, etc.

sīþum. adv. (dat. pl. of *sīð*). *times.* **sīðon** E/1.

slǣp. masc. *sleep.* nom. sg. 9/39. dat. sg. **slǣpe** 2/22; 6/14; 14/247.

slǣpan. st. 7. *sleep.* pres. part. **slǣpende** 6/14.

slǣwþ. fem. *sloth, laziness.* dat. sg. **slǣwðe** 7/36.

(ge)slēan. st. 6. *strike, kill, pitch.* past 3sg. **slōh** 4/18; 14/103, 108. past pl. **slōgon**

4/4; 14/231. inf. **slēan** 2/20. past part.
geslegene 14/31.

slegefǣge. adj. *doomed to death*. masc. acc.
pl. 14/247.

geslegene → (ge)slēan.

slīþen. adj. *cruel*. fem. nom. sg. 9/30.

slōgon → (ge)slēan.

slōh → (ge)slēan.

smēagan. wk. 2. *ponder, meditate*. past 3sg.
smēade 5/5. subj. sg. **smēage** 5/59. inf.
7/16. pres. part. **smēagende** A/2.

smolt. adj. *peaceful, gentle*. neut. acc. pl.
6/35.

smylte. adj. *mild, peaceable, calm, cheerful*. fem. dat. sg. **smyltre** 6/43. masc.
inst. sg. 6/43.

snāw. masc. *snow*. acc. sg. 9/48.

snell. adj. *quick, bold*. gen. pl. **snelra**
14/199.

snīwan. wk. 1. *snow*. past 3sg. **snīwde**.

Snotengahām. masc. *Nottingham*.

snoternys → snotorness.

snotor. adj. *wise*. masc. nom. sg. **snottor**
9/111. wk. masc. nom. sg. **snotera**. wk.
fem. nom. sg. **snotere** 14/125. wk. fem.
acc. sg. **snoteran** 14/55.

snotorness. fem. *wisdom*. nom. sg.
snoternys. acc. sg. **snotornesse**.

snūde. adv. *quickly*. 14/55, 125, 199.

gesoden. adj. *boiled*.

sōfte. adv. *softly*.

sōht- → (ge)sēcan.

gesōhte → (ge)sēcan.

some → same.

gesomnian. wk. 2. *assemble, unite, gather*.
inf. 6/16. past part. **gesamnode, ge-
somnad** 11/18.

gesomnung. fem. *assembly, company*. dat.
sg. **gesomnunge** 6/21.

somod. adv. *simultaneously, together, also*.
8/22; 9/39; 14/163, 269, 282, etc.

sōna. adv. *soon, immediately*. B/6; 2/15,
19, 27; 6/11, etc.

song → sang.

song → singan.

songcræft → sangcræft.

songes → sang.

sorg. fem. *sorrow, pain*. nom. sg. 9/30,
39, 50. acc. sg. **sorge**. gen. pl. **sorga**
10/80; 14/182. dat. pl. **sorgum** 10/20,
59; 14/88.

sorhlēoþ. neut. *sorrowful song, dirge*. acc.
sg. 10/67.

sōþ. **A**. neut. *truth*. gen. sg. **sōþes** 5/63.
dat. sg. **sōþe** 9/11.

   B. adj. *true*. neut. nom. sg. 5/1, 13,
65. masc. acc. sg. **sōðne** 14/89, 344. wk.
masc. gen. sg. **sōþan** 8/7. wk. masc. dat.
sg. **sōðan**.

sōþfæst. adj. *true, righteous, truthful*. wk.
masc. nom. sg. **sōðfæsta** 8/3.

sōþlīce. adv. *truly*. 1/5; 2/26.

spanan. st. 7. *urge*. past 3sg. **spēon** 2/9.

sparian. wk. 2. *spare*. past pl. **sparedon**
14/233.

spǣcan → (ge)sprecan.

spēdig. adj. *successful, prosperous*. masc.
nom. sg. 10/151.

spell. neut. *story, narrative, homily*. acc.
sg. **spel, spell** 6/18; 7/64. gen. sg. **spelles**
6/21. dat. pl. **spellum** 6/24.

spēon → spanan.

spēow → (ge)spōwan.

gespēow → (ge)spōwan.

spere. neut. *spear*.

(ge)spōwan. st. 7. (impersonal). *succeed*.
past 3sg. **spēow, gespēow** 14/175, 274.

spræc → (ge)sprecan.

sprǣc. fem. *speech, statement, saying*. nom.
sg. 7/25. acc. sg. **sprǣce**. dat. sg. **sprǣce**
7/24. gen. pl. **sprǣca** 7/25.

(ge)sprecan. st. 5. *speak, say*. 3sg. **spriceð**
9/70. pl. **sprecað** 7/75. past 3sg. **spræc**
14/160, 176. past pl. **sprǣcon, spǣcan,
gesprǣcon, gesprǣconn** 5/4; 7/24, 46;
13/16, 54, etc. inf. **sprecan** 6/28; 7/12;
10/27. infl. inf. **tō specenne** 5/30. pres.
part. **sprecende** G/6; 6/9, 32, 33. past
part. **gesprecen** 7/12.

spyrian. wk. 2. *track, enquire, strive to
attain*. inf. 7/15.

spyrte. fem. *basket*. acc. pl. **spyrtan**.

stafum → stæf.

gestāh → (ge)stīgan.

stalian. wk. 2. *steal.* subj. sg. stalie M/11, 12.

stalu. fem. *theft, stealing.* nom. sg. 5/19. acc. pl. stala 5/48.

stān. masc. *stone.* nom. sg. B/2, 7; 2/25. acc. sg. B/5; F/1; 2/18. dat. sg. stāne B/4; F/2 (2x); 10/66.

(ge)standan. st. 6. *stand, exist.* 3sg. stondeð, standeð, stent A/1; K/1362; 9/74, 97, 115, etc. pl. stondaþ 9/76. past 1sg. stōd 10/38. past 3sg. stōd 6/7. past pl. stōdon, gestōdon 9/87; 10/7, 63, 71; 14/267, etc. imp. sg. stand. inf. standan 10/43, 62. pres. part. standende 2/19.

stānhliþ. neut. *stony cliff, stony slope.* dat. sg. stānhliþe 12/48. acc. pl. stānhleoþu 9/101.

starian. wk. 2. *gaze.* inf. 14/179.

staþol. masc. *foundation, place, condition.* dat. sg. staðole 10/71.

stæf. masc. *staff, letter, writing.* dat. pl. stafum 6/1.

stæppan. st. 6. *go.* past pl. stōpon 14/39, 69, 200, 212, 227, etc.

stǣr. neut. *story, history.* acc. sg. 6/24. gen. sg. stǣres 6/21.

steall. masc. *place, position.*

gesteall. neut. *foundation.* nom. sg. gesteal 9/110.

stēam. masc. *steam, moisture, blood.* dat. sg. stēame 10/62.

stēap. adj. *deep, tall.* masc. nom. pl. stēape 14/17.

stede. masc. *place, position, stability.* acc. sg. LA/3. dat. sg. 7/66.

stedeheard. adj. *of enduring hardness.* masc. acc. pl. stedehearde 14/223.

stefn. 1. masc. *root.* dat. sg. stefne 10/30. 2. fem. *voice.* nom. sg. 10/71. acc. sg. stemne 1/8, 10, 17.

stenc. masc. *odor, fragrance.* dat. sg. stence.

stent → (ge)standan.

stēoran → (ge)stȳran.

steorfa. masc. *pestilence.* nom. sg. 5/19.

stēorlēas. adj. *without guidance.* masc. dat. sg. stēorlēasum 7/66.

steorra. masc. *star.* nom. pl. steorran.

stercedferhþ. adj. *courageous, cruel-minded.* masc. nom. pl. stercedferhðe 14/55, 227.

(ge)stīgan. st. 1. *ascend, climb.* past 3sg. gestāh 10/40. inf. gestīgan 10/34.

stilness. fem. *stillness, quiet, peace.* dat. sg. stilnesse 6/42.

stincan. st. 3. *stink.* 3sg. stincð.

stīoran → (ge)stȳran.

stīþ. adj. *stiff, firm.* neut. nom. sg. LA/3.

stīþlīce. adv. *firmly, severely.* C/4.

stīþmōd. adj. *resolute, courageous.* masc. nom. sg. 10/40. wk. masc. nom. sg. stīðmōda 14/25.

stōd → (ge)standan.

stōdon → (ge)standan.

gestōdon → (ge)standan.

stond- → (ge)standan.

stōpon → stæppan.

storm. masc. *storm.* dat. sg. storme 12/48. nom. pl. stormas 9/101.

stōw. fem. *place.* nom. sg. K/1372. acc. sg. stōwe 6/30. dat. sg. stōwe. nom. pl. stōwa 5/28. dat. pl. stōwum.

strang. adj. *strong.* masc. nom. sg. 10/40. masc. nom. pl. strange 5/39; 10/30.

strǣl. masc. *arrow,* fig. *nail.* acc. pl. strǣlas 14/223. dat. pl. strǣlum 10/62.

strēam. masc. *stream, current,* in plur. *sea.* acc. pl. strēamas 13/5; 14/348.

strengþ. fem. *strength.*

strīc. neut. *sedition* (?), *pestilence* (?). nom. sg. 5/19.

stronglic. adj. *strong, stable.* fem. sg. 7/66.

strūdung. fem. *robbery.* acc. pl. strūdunga 5/48.

gestrȳnan. wk. 1. *acquire, gain, produce, beget.* past 3sg. gestrȳnde 2/30.

styccemǣlum. adv. *here and there.*

stȳpel. masc. *steeple.* nom. pl. stȳplas.

(ge)stȳran. wk. 1. *steer, guide, restrain* from something (gen.), *punish.* past 3sg.

gestȳrde 14/60. inf. **stēoran, stīoran** 7/2, 3.

styrman. wk. 1. *storm, rage.* past 3sg. **styrmde** 14/25. past pl. **styrmdon** 14/223.

styrnmōd. adj. *stern-minded.* masc. nom. pl. **styrnmōde** 14/227.

gesūgian → (ge)swīgian.

gesūgode → (ge)swīgian.

sulh. fem. athematic. *plough.* dat. sg. **sylh.**

sum. indef. pron. *a certain, one, some, about.* masc. nom. sg. 2/14; 6/1, 7; 7/18 (2x), etc. masc. acc. sg. **sumne** F/1; 2/18; 9/81, 82, 83, etc. masc. dat. sg. **suman, sumum** 2/29; 5/67. masc. inst. sg. **sume** B/1. fem. acc. sg. **sume** 7/53. fem. dat. sg. **sumre** 6/7; 7/29. neut. acc. sg. I/9; 2/12; 6/18. masc. nom. pl. **sume** 2/14; 7/80. masc. acc. pl. **sume** 2/10; 5/28; 9/80. fem. acc. pl. **sume** 5/69. neut. acc. pl. **sumu** 6/32.

sumorlang. adj. *summer-long* (i.e. extra long as in summer). masc. acc. sg. **sumorlangne** 12/37.

gesund. adj. *sound, whole, healthy.* masc. nom. pl. **gesunde** 3/13.

sundor. adv. *apart.* 9/111.

sundoryrfe. neut. *private inheritance* (presumably as opposed to the public treasury). gen. sg. **sundoryrfes** 14/339.

sungon → singan.

Sunnanǣfen. masc. *Sunday eve, Saturday evening.* acc. sg. 4/17.

Sunnandæg. masc. *Sunday.*

sunne. fem. *sun.* nom. sg. G/8. acc. sg. **sunnan** 7/73; 8/11. gen. sg. **sunnan** 8/3. dat. sg. **sunnan.**

sunu. masc. u-stem. *son.* nom. sg. C/2; 3/18; 8/7, 23; 10/150, etc. nom. pl. **suna, suno.** acc. pl. **suna** 2/30.

sūsl. neut. *torment.* dat. sg. **sūsle** 14/114.

sutelað → (ge)swutelian.

sūþ. adv. *south.* 7/65, 70; 13/27.

sūþan. adv. *from the south.* 4/16.

sūþeweard. adj. *south.* masc. dat. sg. **sūðeweardum** 7/16.

Sūþrīge. noun. *Surrey.* acc. sg. 4/2.

Sūþsexe. masc. *the South Saxons.* acc. pl. 4/2.

swā. A. adv. *so, thus, in such a way, as.* A/4; B/4, 7; F/1; G/9, etc.

   B. conj. *as, as if, so that.* A/3; B/6; G/9; M/11; 1/5, etc.

swā swā. conj. *as, just as.* F/3; 2/1, 2, 5, 8 (2x), etc.

swā þēah. adv. *nevertheless.* B/3; 2/1, 29.

swān. masc. *swineherd.* nom. sg. 3/2.

swāse → swǣs.

swāt. neut. *sweat, blood.* gen. sg. **swātes** 10/23. dat. sg. **swāte** 1/19.

swātig. adj. *sweaty, bloody.* masc. acc. sg. **swātigne** 14/337.

swaþu. fem. *path.* dat. sg. **swaðe** 14/321.

swæc. masc. *flavor, taste, fragrance.* gen. sg. **swæcces.**

swǣr. adj. *heavy, oppressive.* wk. neut. acc. sg. **swǣre** 7/68.

swǣs. adj. *intimate, beloved, gentle, sweet.* masc. acc. sg. **swǣsne** 9/50. fem. nom. pl. **swāse.**

swǣsende. neut. nd-stem. (often pl. with singular sense). *food, meal, banquet.* acc. pl. **swǣsendo** 14/9.

swǣtan. wk. 1. *sweat, bleed.* inf. 10/20.

swealt → sweltan.

sweart. adj. *black, dark.* neut. nom. sg. F/4. fem. nom. pl. **swearte** F/3. wk. masc. dat. sg. **sweartan.**

swebban. wk. 1. *put to sleep, kill.*

swefn. neut. *dream.* acc. sg. 6/7, 16. gen. pl. **swefna** 10/1.

sweg. masc. *sound.* nom. sg. **swēg.** acc. sg. **swēg.** dat. sg. **swege.**

swegl. neut. *sky, heaven.* gen. sg. **swegles** 8/7; 14/80, 88, 124, 344, etc.

geswel. neut. *tumor.* nom. sg. 2/12, 13. acc. sg. **geswell** 2/14, 22.

swelc. pron. **1.** indef. *such, the same.* masc. acc. sg. **swelcne** 7/21. fem. nom. sg. H/4. fem. dat. sg. **swilcere, swylcere** 2/13, 18. neut. dat. sg. **swilcan** 5/65. gen. pl. **swelcra** 7/79. dat. pl. **swylcum**

2/31. masc. nom. pl. **swelce** A/4. **2.** rel. *as, such as.* masc. acc. sg. **swylcne** 14/65. fem. nom. sg. H/4. masc. nom. pl. **swelce** H/2.

swelce. A. adv. *likewise, also, as it were, approximately.* **swylce, swelce, swilce** F/4; 1/1, 16; 2/23; 6/3, etc. **B.** conj. *as if, as, like.* **swelce, swilce, swylce** B/3, 7; 2/16, 22, 23, etc.

sweltan. st. 3. *die, perish.* pl. **sweltað** 7/60. past 3sg. **swealt.** subj. pl. **swelton** 1/3.

geswencan. wk. 1. *trouble, torment, afflict, pursue.* past part. **geswenct, geswenced** κ/1368; 2/13.

swēoran → swūra.

gesweorcan. st. 3. *become dark.* subj. sg. **gesweorce** 9/59.

sweorcendferhþ. adj. *dark in mind, gloomy.* masc. nom. pl. **sweorcendferhðe** 14/269.

sweord. neut. *sword.* nom. sg. **sweord, swurd.** acc. sg. 14/337. gen. sg. **sweordes.** dat. sg. **sweorde, swurde** 14/288. inst. sg. **sweorde** 14/89. acc. pl. **swyrd** 14/230. gen. pl. **sweorda.** dat. pl. **swyrdum, sweordum** 14/194, 264, 294, 301, 321, etc.

sweostor. fem. r-stem. *sister.* nom. sg. **sweostor, swuster, swustor** 2/17, 24. acc. sg. **swustor.** gen. sg. **swustor** 2/18.

gesweostor. fem. (pl. only). *sisters.* dat. pl. **geswustrum** 2/16.

swēot. neut. *army.* nom. sg. 14/298.

sweotole → swutole.

sweotollīce. adv. *clearly.* 14/136.

sweotule → swutole.

swer. masc. *column.* nom. pl. **sweras.**

geswētan. wk. 1. *sweeten.* past 3sg. **geswētte.**

swēte. adj. *sweet.* wk. neut. acc. sg. superl. **swēteste** 6/22.

swētness. fem. *sweetness.* acc. sg. **swētnisse** 6/1. dat. sg. **swētnesse** 6/24.

swica. masc. *deceiver, traitor.*

geswīcan. st. 1. *depart, cease* (with gen. or

dat. object), *betray.* past pl. **geswicon** 4/1. inf. F/6.

swicdōm. masc. *deception, betrayal.* acc. pl. **swicdōmas** 5/48.

swician. wk. 2. *wander, deceive.* past 3sg. **swicode** 5/23.

swicol. adj. *cunning, false, deceitful.*

geswicon → geswīcan.

swift. adj. *swift.* wk. masc. acc. sg. **swiftan** 7/73.

(ge)swīgian. wk. 2. *fall silent, be silent about something* (gen.). past 3sg. **gesūgode** 7/1, 12. past pl. **geswugedan** 5/63. inf. **gesūgian, swīgian** 7/54.

swilc- → swelc.

swilc- → swelce.

swīma. masc. *swoon.* dat. sg. **swīman** 14/30, 106.

swimman. st. 3. *swim.* pl. **swimmað** 9/53.

geswinc. neut. *toil, hardship.* nom. sg. 7/21. acc. sg. 2/12. dat. pl. **geswyncum** 1/17.

swincan. st. 3. *labour* (with *ymb*, for something). pl. **swincað** 7/30. subj. pl. **swincen** 7/69.

swingan. st. 3. *beat, flog.* past pl. **swungon.**

swinsung. fem. *sound, melody.* acc. sg. **swinsunge** 6/18.

swīran → swūra.

swīþ. adj. *strong,* in comparative *right* (hand, side). fem. acc. sg. compar. **swīðran** 10/20. fem. dat. sg. compar. **swīðran** 14/80.

swīþe. adv. *very, very much, severely.* **swȳðe, swīðe** F/2; H/2, 3; 2/2, 11, etc. compar. **swȳþor, swīðor** 5/51; 14/182. superl. **swȳðost** 2/7; 5/50, 52.

swīþlic. adj. *very great, violent, intense.* neut. acc. sg. 14/240.

swīþmōd. adj. *stout-hearted, arrogant.* masc. nom. sg. 14/30, 339.

geswiþrian. wk. 2. *decrease, end.* past part. **geswiðrod** 14/266.

swōt. adj. *sweet.* dat. pl. **swōtum.**

geswugedan → (ge)swīgian.

swungon → swingan.

swūra. masc. *neck.* nom. sg. 2/13. acc. sg.
swēoran, swūran H/3; 2/13; 14/106. dat.
sg. swūran, swīran 2/12 (2x); 7/68.

swūrbēag. masc. *torque, necklace.* dat. pl.
swūrbēagum 2/13.

swurd- → sweord.

swuster → sweostor.

swustor → sweostor.

geswustrum → gesweostor.

(ge)swutelian. wk. 2. *reveal, prove.* 3sg.
sutelað, geswutelað 2/4; 4/19. pl.
geswuteliað D/2; 2/1. past part. ge-
swutelod 2/26; 14/285.

swutol. adj. *evident, manifest.* neut. nom.
sg. 2/26; 5/17, 46. neut. nom. pl.
swutele 2/5.

swutole. adv. *clearly, plainly, openly.*
sweotole, sweotule 7/65; 9/11; 14/177.

swylc- → swelc.

swylc- → swelce.

geswyncum → geswinc.

swyrd → sweord.

swyrdgeswing. neut. *striking with swords.*
acc. sg. 14/240.

swyrdum → sweord.

swȳþ- → swīþe.

sȳ → bēon.

gesyhðe → gesihþ.

sylf- → self.

sylh → sulh.

syll- → (ge)sellan.

syllic. adj. *rare, wonderful.* masc. nom. sg.
10/13. neut. acc. sg. compar. syllicre
10/4.

symbel. A. neut. *feast, banquet.* dat. sg.
symle, symble 6/6; 10/141; 14/15. gen.
pl. symbla 9/93.
   B. adj. *continuous.* neut. acc. sg.
14/44.

symble. adv. *always, continuously.* symle,
simle, symble J/88; 3/8; 7/68; 8/5, 25,
etc.

symle → symbel.

symle → symble.

syn. fem. *sin.* nom. pl. synna G/7. acc. pl.
synna 5/47, 64. gen. pl. synna 6/26. dat.

pl. synnum, synnan 5/3, 39, 62; 8/14,
22, etc.

syn → bēon.

sȳn → bēon.

synd- → bēon.

synderlīce → syndriglīce.

syndrig. adj. *separate, special, various, private.* neut. acc. pl. syndrige 2/11.

syndriglīce. adv. *specially.* synderlīce,
syndriglīce 6/1; 7/26.

gesȳne. adj. *visible, evident.* neut. nom. sg.
gesȳne, gesǣne, gesēne 5/17, 34, 46, 57.
neut. nom. pl. gesīene 10/46.

synfull. adj. *sinful.* masc. nom. sg. synful.
gen. pl. synfulra A/1. wk. masc. nom.
pl. synfullan A/5; C/11.

syngian. wk. 2. *sin.* subj. pl. 5/53.

synlēaw. fem. *injury of sin.* acc. pl.
synlēawa 5/55.

synscipe. masc. *marriage, sexual intercourse.* gen. sg. synscipes 2/7. dat. sg.
synscipe, synscype 2/5, 28.

synt → bēon.

gesynto. fem. (sometimes pl. with sg.
sense). *health, salvation, grace.* gen. pl.
gesynta 14/90.

syruwrencas → searowrenc.

syrwan. wk. 1. *contrive, plot.* 2sg. syrwst
1/15.

siððan → syþþan.

sȳwian. wk. 2. *sew.* past pl. sȳwodon 1/7.

syx. card. num. as noun. *six.* E/1.

syxtig. card. num. as noun. *sixty.* E/1.

syxtȳne. card. num. as adj. *sixteen.* 2/18.

tācen. neut. *sign.*

getācnian. wk. 2. *betoken, represent, show,
signal.* 3sg. getācnað G/3, 4. past 3sg.
getācnode. past part. getācnod 14/197,
286.

taltrigan → tealtrian.

tǣcan. wk. 1. *teach, instruct.* 3sg. tǣcð.
subj. sg. tǣce. subj. pl. 5/54, 57.

getæl. neut. *number, account.* acc. sg.
getæl, getæll 6/21.

tǣlan. wk. 1. *scold, slander, despise, deride.*
3sg. tǣleð 5/52.

tǽlwyrþlic. adj. *blameworthy*. neut. nom. sg. superl. **tǽlwyrðlicosð** 7/32.

tæt → se.

tēah → tēon.

teala → tela.

tealt. adj. *unsteady, wavering*. fem. nom. pl. **tealte** 5/20.

tealtrian. wk. 2. *stumble, become unstable*. inf. **taltrigan**.

tēam. masc. *family*. nom. sg. 2/2.

tēdre. adj. *weak, infirm*. masc. nom. sg. 7/15.

tela. interj. *good!*. **teala** 6/41.

geteld. neut. *tent*. acc. sg. 2/20.

(ge)tellan. wk. 1. *count, consider, relate*. 2sg. **getelest** 7/39. subj. sg. **telle** 7/44. imp. sg. **tele** 7/40, 41. inf. **tellan**.

Temes. noun. *Thames*. dat. sg. **Temese** 4/2.

tempel. neut. *temple*. dat. sg. **temple**.

tēn → tȳn.

tēon. 1. st. 1. *accuse*. 2. st. 2. *draw, pull*. past 3sg. **tēah** 14/99. 3. wk. 1. *prepare, furnish, adorn, create*. past 3sg. **tēode** 6/13.

tēona. masc. *injury, insult, anger*. acc. sg. **tēonan** D/2.

tēoþa. ord. num. *tenth*. masc. acc. sg. **tēoðan** 7/23.

teran. st. 4. *tear*. inf. 14/281.

tīd. fem. *time, hour, season*. acc. sg. **tīd**, **tīde** 6/5, 7, 28; 7/81; 14/306, etc. gen. sg. **tīde** 6/41. dat. sg. **tīde** A/3; 6/7, 28, 39; 14/286, etc. nom. pl. **tīda**. gen. pl. **tīda** 8/4. dat. pl. **tīdum** 5/61.

tīenwintre. adj. *ten-year-old*. masc. nom. sg. M/13.

tigolgeweorc. neut. *brick-making*. dat. sg. **tigolgeweorce**.

tihte → tyhtan.

til. adj. *good*. masc. nom. sg. 9/112.

tilian. wk. 2. *endeavour, procure, provide something* (gen.) *for someone* (dat.). pl. **tiliað, tioliað** 7/30, 69. inf. 14/208.

tīma. masc. *time*. acc. sg. **tīman** 4/11. dat. sg. **tīman** 4/3.

getimbran. wk. 1. *build*. past part. **getimbred** H/1.

timbrian. wk. 2. *build*. past pl. **timbredon** B/1.

timbrung. fem. *building, construction*. dat. sg. **timbrunge** B/2.

getīmian. wk. 2. *happen*. past 3sg. **getīmode** 2/8.

tintreglic. adj. *full of torment, infernal*. wk. neut. gen. sg. **tintreglican** 6/24.

tioliað → tilian.

tīr. masc. *glory, fame*. nom. sg. 14/157. acc. sg. 14/197. gen. sg. **tīres** 14/93, 272.

tīrfæst. adj. *glorious*. fem. acc. sg. **tīrfæste** 13/12.

tīþ. fem. *permission, grant, favour*. acc. sg. **tīðe** 14/6.

tō. A. adv. *too, in addition, to that place*. B/3; 2/9; 5/4 (2x), 5, etc.

  B. prep. (usually with dat.). *to, towards, into, as, on, at* (of time), *for, from, against*. **tō, to** A/3 (2x), 6; B/5; C/2, etc.

tōblāwan. st. 7. *blow apart, scatter*. 3sg. **tōblǽwð** A/4.

tōbræc → tōbrecan.

tōbrǽdan. wk. 1. *spread out*. subj. pl. **tōbrǽden** 7/23. inf. **tōbrǽdan, tō-brēdan** 7/24, 27, 32, 67.

tōbrecan. st. 4. *break*. past 3sg. **tōbræc**. past part. **tōbrocene** 5/34.

tōbrēdan. st. 3. *tear apart, awaken* from. inf. 14/247.

tōbrēdan → tōbrǽdan.

tōbrocene → tōbrecan.

tōbrȳtan. wk. 1. *crush*. 3sg. **tōbrȳtt** 1/15.

tōcyme. masc. *arrival, advent*. dat. sg. 5/3.

tōdæg. adv. *today*.

tōdǽlan. wk. 1. *divide*. subj. past pl. **tōdǽlden** 12/12. imp. pl. **tōdǽlað** E/3. past part. **tōdǽled, tōdǽlda** 7/25 (3x).

tōēacan. prep. *in addition to*. 5/27.

tōfēran. wk. 1. *disperse*. past 3sg. **tōfērde** 4/20.

tōforan. prep. (with dat.). *before*. 4/12.

tōgædere. adv. *together*. tōgædere,
tōgædre 5/30, 43.

tōgēanes. prep. *towards*. 14/149.

tōgeþēodan. wk. 1. *add*. past 3sg.
tōgeþēodde 6/14.

tohte. fem. *battle*. dat. sg. tohtan 14/197.

tōl. neut. *tool*. nom. sg. 7/4. acc. pl. 7/8.
gen. pl. tōla 7/2. dat. pl. tōlum 7/3, 5,
6, 8.

tōlicgan. st. 5. *divide, separate*. past part.
tōlegena 7/25.

tōmiddes. adv. *in the middle*. в/2.

tōmorgen. adv. *tomorrow*.

tōniman. st. 4. *divide*. past part. tōnumen.

torht. adj. *bright, beautiful*. masc. nom.
sg. 8/4. wk. fem. acc. sg. torhtan 14/43.

torhtlic. adj. *bright, beautiful*. masc. nom.
sg. 14/157.

torhtmōd. adj. *noble-minded, glorious*.
masc. nom. sg. 14/6, 93.

torn. neut. *anger, grief, suffering*. acc. sg.
9/112; 14/272.

torne. adv. *grievously*. 14/93.

tōslītan. st. 1. *tear apart*. 3sg. tōslīteð
11/18.

tōþ. masc. athematic. *tooth*. gen. pl. tōða.
dat. pl. tōðon 14/272.

tōweard. adj. *future, impending, heading*.
masc. nom. sg. 14/157. fem. nom. sg.
14/286. wk. masc. gen. sg. tōweardan
6/24.

tōwrītan. st. 1. *describe*. past 3sg. tōwrāt
7/17.

træf. neut. *tent*. acc. sg. 14/268. dat. sg.
træfe 14/43, 255.

trēocyn. neut. *kind of tree*. nom. sg. 13/2.

trēow. 1. fem. *faith, promise, trust*. acc.
sg. trēowe 9/112; 13/12. 2. neut. *tree*.
nom. sg. 1/6. acc. sg. 1/3; 10/4, 14, 17,
25, etc. gen. sg. trēowes 1/3, 6. dat. sg.
trēowe A/3; 1/1, 4, 5, 8, etc. gen. pl.
trēowa 1/2.

getrēowe. adj. *true, faithful*. wk. masc.
nom. sg. getrēowa.

trēowen. adj. *wooden*. fem. dat. sg.
trēowenre 2/16.

getrēowþ. fem. (often pl. with sg.
sense). *truth, honour, loyalty*. nom. pl.
getrēowþa, getrȳwða 5/4, 20. acc. pl.
getrȳwða 5/69.

trēowwyrhta. masc. *carpenter*.

trum. adj. *firm, strong*. masc. nom. sg.
к/1369. masc. acc. sg. trumne 14/6.

getrymman. wk. 1. *strengthen*. pres. part.
getrymmende 6/38.

getrȳwlīce. adv. *loyally*. 5/23.

getrȳwða → getrēowþ.

tū → twēgen.

tūdor. neut. *offspring, fruit*. dat. sg. tūdre
13/2.

tūn. masc. *enclosure, dwelling, village,
town*. gen. pl. tūna.

tunge. fem. *tongue*. nom. sg. 1/8; 6/44. acc.
sg. tungan 6/4.

tūngerēfa. masc. *town reeve*. dat. sg.
tūngerēfan 6/15.

tungol. neut. *star*. gen. sg. tungles. acc.
pl. tunglas 8/4.

tūsc. masc. *tusk*.

twā. card. num. as noun. *two*. E/1.

twā → twēgen.

twām → twēgen.

getwǣfan. wk. 1. (with gen.). *separate
from, deprive of, hinder*. inf. 13/24.

twēgen. card. num. as adj. *two*. masc.
nom. pl. в/2; 5/43. fem. nom. pl. twā.
fem. acc. pl. tū. neut. acc. pl. twā 7/25.
gen. pl. twēga 13/49. dat. pl. twām
2/1.

twelf. A. card. num. as noun. *twelve*. twelf,
twelfe F/4; 5/40.

B. as adj. *twelve*. masc. acc. sg. 2/10.
neut. acc. pl. 2/5.

twēntig. A. card. num. as noun. *twenty*.
E/1.

B. as adj. *twenty*.

twēogan. wk. 2. (with gen.). *doubt*. past
3sg. twēode 14/1, 345.

twēone. card. num. as adj. (only in construction *be* + noun + *twēonum* =
between two of a thing). *two*. dat. pl.
twēonum.

twēonian. wk. 2. *be doubtful.* 3sg. **twēonað** G/9.

twīa. adv. *twice.* E/1.

twig. neut. *twig, branch.* nom. pl. **twigu** F/5. dat. pl. **twigum** F/5.

tyhtan. wk. 1. *stretch, incite, persuade.* past 3sg. **tihte.**

tȳman. wk. 1. *have children.* past 3sg. **tȳmde.**

tȳn. card. num. as noun. *ten.* **tēn, tȳne, tȳn** E/1; 5/39, 40; 7/40, 41, etc.

tyslian. wk. 2. *dress.* pl. **tysliað** D/2.

tyslung. fem. *fashion* (in clothing). acc. sg. **tyslunge** D/3.

þā. A. adv. *then.* B/2, 3, 5, 6, 7, etc.
  B. conj. *when.* G/2; 4/8, 20; 5/68; 6/7 (2x), etc.

þā → se.

þā hwīle þe. conj. *while.*

þā þā. conj. *when.* 1/8; 2/5.

þā þe → se þe.

(ge)þāfian. wk. 2. *allow, consent to.* past 3sg. **þāfode** 6/20. inf. **geðafian** 14/60.

þafung. fem. *consent.* acc. sg. **þafunge** 5/39.

ðāh → (ge)þēon.

þām → se.

þām þe → se þe.

þan → se.

geþanc. masc. *thought, purpose, design, mind.* dat. sg. **geþance, geðonce** 5/53; 14/13.

þancian. wk. 2. (with dat. of person and gen. of thing). *thank.* past 3sg. **þancode** 2/12. pres. part. **ðancigende** 2/20.

þancolmōd. adj. *thoughtful.* fem. acc. sg. **þancolmōde** 14/172.

þanon. A. adv. *thence.* **þonan, þanon** C/11; 9/23; 14/118.
  B. conj. *from which, whence.* 4/10.

þanonne. adv. *thence.* 14/132.

þāra → se.

þāra þe → se þe.

þās → þes.

þǣm → se.

þǣm þe → se þe.

þæne → se.

þænne → þonne.

þǣr. A. adv. *there.* B/2, 3, 6; C/11, 12, etc.
  B. conj. *where.* F/1, 7; K/1359; 1/8; 3/10, etc.

þǣr þǣr. conj. *where.* 2/24.

þǣra → se.

þǣre → se.

ðǣre ðe → se þe.

þǣrinne. adv. *therein, inside.* 3/15; 14/50.

þǣrof. adv. *from there.* C/6.

þǣron. adv. *therein.* 10/67.

þǣrrihte. adv. *instantly.* 7/56.

þǣrtō. adv. *thereto, to it, belonging to, from there.* 2/19; 3/10; 7/48.

þǣrymbūtan. adv. *thereabouts.* 7/29.

þæs. adv. *afterwards, accordingly, therefore, to that extent, so.* K/1366; 7/49.

þæs → se.

þæs þe. conj. *after, because, as.* 3/3; 5/63; 8/26; 13/31, etc.

þæs þe → se þe.

þæt. conj. *that, so that.* B/1, 4, 5 (2x); C/2, etc.

þæt → se.

þætte. A. rel. pron. *that, which.* neut. nom. sg. 7/13; 11/18.
  B. conj. *that, when.* 6/1, 23, 39, 43; 7/5, etc.

þe. A. rel. pron. *that, which, who, when.* A/1, 3; C/1, 3, 12, etc.
  B. conj. *when, where, than, or.* M/2; 3/14; 4/11; 5/21; 7/53, etc.

þe → se.

þē → þū, gē.

þē → þȳ.

þe lǣs → þȳ lǣs.

þēah. A. adv. *though, nevertheless.* 3/15; 7/2, 13, 29, 37, etc.
  B. conj. *though, although.* **þēah, þēh** I/5; M/7; 5/4, 16, 36, etc.

þēah þe. conj. *although, though.* K/1368; 1/4; 2/1, 8, 10, etc.

geþeaht. neut. *counsel, advice.* acc. sg. A/1. dat. sg. **geþeahte** A/5.

þeahte → þeccan.

þearf. fem. *need* for something (gen.), *benefit, distress.* nom. sg. 5/13, 65, 66, 67; 6/33, etc. acc. sg. **þearfe** 14/3, 92. dat. sg. **ðearfe** c/2. dat. pl. **þearfum** 8/9.

þearf → þurfan.

þearfende. adj. (past part. of *þearfan* 'be in need'). *needy.* fem. dat. sg. **þearfendre** 14/85.

þearle. adv. *severely, exceedingly, vigorously.* 5/19; 10/52; 14/74, 86, 262, etc.

þearlmōd. adj. *severe.* masc. nom. sg. 14/66, 91.

þēaw. masc. *custom, habit, morals.* nom. sg. 6/29; 9/12. nom. pl. **þēawas** 7/32. acc. pl. **ðēawas** d/1 (2x), 3; 7/36. gen. pl. **þēawa** 5/50. dat. pl. **þēawum** 7/24; 14/129.

þec → þū, gē.

þeccan. wk. 1. *cover.* past 3sg. **þeahte** Lb/4. subj. pl. **þeccen** 7/74.

þecen. fem. *roof.* acc. sg. **þecene** Lb/2.

þegengylde. neut. *wergild for a thegn.* acc. sg. 5/37.

þegn. masc. *servant, retainer, nobleman, master.* nom. sg. **þegn, þegen** 3/10; 5/37; 6/31. acc. sg. **þegen, þegn** 5/36, 41; 6/30. gen. sg. **þegenes** 5/40. dat. sg. **þegne, þegene** 2/29; 5/36. nom. pl. **þegnas** 3/7, 9; 10/75. acc. pl. **ðegnas** 14/10, 306. dat. pl. **þēnan, þēnum** 5/12.

þegnian. wk. 2. *serve.* inf. 6/29.

þēgon → (ge)þicgan.

þēh → þēah.

þēnan → þegn.

(ge)þencan. wk. 1. *think of, imagine, remember, intend.* 3sg. **þenceð** 10/121. pl. **þencaþ** 10/115. past 3sg. **þōhte** 5/23; 14/58. past pl. **þōhton** 14/208. imp. pl. **geðencað** 7/24. inf. **geþencan** 9/58.

þenden. conj. *while.* 13/17; 14/66.

þenian. wk. 2. *stretch out.* inf. 10/52.

þēnian. wk. 2. *serve.* inf. 2/11.

þēnum → þegn.

þēod. fem. *nation, people, country.* acc. sg. **ðēode** 5/4, 5, 15, 27, 43, etc. gen. sg.

þēode 7/26. dat. sg. **þēode** 5/13, 16, 17, 34, 38, etc. nom. pl. **þēoda** 7/24. acc. pl. **þīoda** 7/25, 69. gen. pl. **þēoda** 7/24, 32. dat. pl. **þēodum, þēode, þīodum** 5/10, 11, 33; 7/19.

geþēodan. wk. 1. *join.* past 3sg. **geþēodde** 6/21.

þēode → þēowan.

þēoden. masc. *king, ruler.* nom. sg. 13/29; 14/66, 91. gen. sg. **þēodnes** 9/95; 13/48; 14/165, 268. dat. sg. **þēodne, þēodnes** Lb/5; 10/69; 14/3, 11.

þēodguma. masc. *man of a nation.* nom. pl. **þēodguman** 14/208, 331.

geþēodness. fem. *joining, association.* dat. sg. **geþēodnisse** 6/2.

þēodscipe. masc. *association, nation, discipline, instruction, erudition.* nom. sg. 5/47. dat. pl. **þēodscipum** 6/26.

þēodwita. masc. *scholar.* nom. sg. 5/61.

þēoh. neut. *thigh.* dat. sg. **þēo** La/1.

(ge)þēon. st. 1. *prosper, benefit* someone (dat.). past 3sg. **ðāh.** subj. sg. **ðīo** 7/70. inf. **geþēon** j/84.

þēos → þes.

ðeosse → þes.

þeossum → þes.

þēostrum → þīestru.

þēow. masc. *servant, slave.* nom. pl. **þēowas, þēowum** 5/11, 12. acc. pl. **ðēowas** 2/6; 5/12. gen. pl. **þēowa** 6/21.

þēowa. masc. *servant, slave.*

þēowan. wk. 1. *serve.* past 3sg. **þēode** 6/43.

þēowen. fem. *female servant, handmaiden.* nom. sg. 14/74.

(ge)þēowian. wk. 2. *serve, enslave.* past 3sg. **þēowode.** inf. **þēowian** 2/9. past part. **geþēowede** 5/15.

þēowot. neut. *servitude, slavery.* acc. sg. m/13.

þes. demonst. pron. *this.* masc. nom. sg. 2/13; 5/47; 9/62; 12/29. masc. acc. sg. **þisne, ðysne** F/1; G/9; 2/26; 4/21; 7/73, etc. masc. gen. sg. **þises, þisses** 7/2, 16, 17, 44. masc. dat. sg. **þysan, ðisum,**

þeossum, þissum 5/14, 20, 25, 29; 6/8, etc. masc. inst. sg. **ðȳs** 14/2. fem. nom. sg. **þēos** 5/2; 7/66; 10/12, 82. fem. acc. sg. **þās** 2/8; 5/4, 5, 15, 27, etc. fem. gen. sg. **þisse, ðeosse, þisere** 6/1; 7/16, 18, 21; 9/74, etc. fem. dat. sg. **þysse** 5/13, 16, 17, 33, 34, etc. neut. nom. sg. **þis** F/6; 2/13; 6/11; 7/12; 9/110, etc. neut. acc. sg. **þis** 1/14; 2/24; 7/1, 64; 9/89, etc. neut. gen. sg. **þisses** D/1; 7/2, 39 (2x). neut. dat. sg. **þissum, þysan, þyssum, þysum, ðisum, þysson** 2/27; 4/1, 4, 5, 12, etc. neut. inst. sg. **þȳs** 14/89. nom. pl. **þās** 4/3. acc. pl. **þās** 7/8, 62, 67; 9/91, 101, etc. gen. pl. **þyssa** 14/187. dat. pl. **þisum, þissum** 7/5, 8 (2x).

ðī lǣs ðe → þȳ lǣs þe.

(ge)þicgan. st. 5. *accept, receive, consume, eat.* past pl. **þēgon** 14/19. inf. **geþicgean** 3/8.

þider. adv. *thither, to that place.* **þider, þyder** B/6; 3/7, 10; 14/129.

þider þe. conj. *whither, towards the place where.*

þiefþ. fem. *theft.* dat. sg. **ðīefðe, þȳfþe** M/13; 5/15.

þīestre. adj. *dark.* neut. nom. pl. **þīestru** F/2. wk. fem. nom. sg. **þȳstre** 14/34.

þīestru. fem. (often pl. with sg. sense). *darkness.* nom. pl. **þȳstro** 10/52. dat. pl. **þēostrum, þȳstrum** 8/13; 14/118.

þīn. adj. *your, of you.* neut. nom. sg. 8/9. masc. acc. sg. **þīnne.** fem. acc. sg. **þīne** 1/10. neut. acc. sg. 1/15; 7/40. masc. gen. sg. **þīnes** 1/19 (2x). fem. gen. sg. **þīnre** 14/85, 91. neut. gen. sg. **ðīnes** 1/14, 17 (2x). masc. dat. sg. **þīnum** 1/15. fem. dat. sg. **þīnre** 6/33. neut. dat. sg. **þīnum** 1/14, 17; 7/19. masc. nom. pl. **þīne** 11/14. fem. nom. pl. **þīne** 11/13. fem. acc. pl. **ðīne** 1/16 (2x). dat. pl. **þīnum.**

þīn → þū, gē.

þinc- → þyncan.

þindan. st. 3. *swell.* inf. Lb/2.

þīnen. fem. *maid-servant, handmaid.* acc. sg. **þīnene, ðīnenne** 14/172. dat. pl. **þīnenum** 2/11.

þing. neut. *thing, motive, reason, means.* acc. sg. Lb/5; 4/15; 14/153. gen. sg. **þinges** 7/70, 76; 14/60. acc. pl. C/1; 5/50 (2x); 6/32; 7/62, etc. gen. pl. **þinga** 5/11; 7/8, 67. dat. pl. **þingum** 7/46.

geþinge. neut. *agreement, result.*

þingian. wk. 2. *settle.* subj. pl. 5/66.

ðīo → (ge)þēon.

þīoda → þēod.

þīodisc. neut. *language.* acc. pl. 7/70.

þīodum → þēod.

þis- → þes.

þōht- → (ge)þencan.

geþōht. masc. *thought.* nom. sg. 12/43. acc. sg. 12/12. inst. sg. **geþōhte** 9/88. nom. pl. **geþōhtas.**

(ge)þolian. wk. 2. *suffer, endure, remain, lose.* pl. **þoliað** 5/44. past 3sg. **þolode, geðolode** C/4; 2/12. past pl. **þoledon, þolodan** 10/149; 14/215. pres. part. **þoligende** 14/272.

þon → se.

þonan → þanon.

þonc. masc. *thought, thanks* (with gen. of what one is grateful for). acc. sg. 8/24.

geðonce → geþanc.

þoncwyrþe. adj. *deserving of thanks, acceptable, memorable.* neut. acc. sg. 14/153.

þone → se.

ðone þe → se þe.

þonēcan þe. conj. *whenever, as soon as.* 7/37.

þonne. A. adv. *then.* **þonne, þænne** C/10, 12; F/5, 6; M/5, etc.
   B. conj. *when, whenever, than.* A/4; D/2; F/5; La/4; 1/1, etc.

þorftun → þurfan.

þorn. masc. *thorn.* acc. pl. **ðornas** 1/18.

þracu. fem. *power, violence, attack.* acc. sg. **þræce.**

þrāg. fem. *time, period.* nom. sg. 9/95. acc. sg. **þrāge** 14/237.

þrang → (ge)þringan.

þræce → þracu.

þræl. masc. *slave*. nom. sg. 5/36, 41. acc. sg. 5/37. dat. sg. þræle 5/36, 41. gen. pl. þræla 5/36.

þrælriht. neut. *rights of slaves*. nom. pl. 5/15.

þrē → þrīe.

þrēagan. wk. 2. *chastise*.

þrēat. masc. *band of men, army, violence, cruelty*. acc. sg. 11/2, 7. dat. sg. ðrēate 14/62. dat. pl. ðrēatum 14/164.

þrēo. card. num. as noun. *three*. E/1.

þrēo → þrīe.

þridda. ord. num. *third*. fem. nom. sg. þridde. masc. dat. sg. ðriddan 2/16. masc. inst. sg. þriddan 7/28.

þrīe. card. num. as adj. *three*. masc. nom. pl. þrīe, þrē, þrȳ B/2; 5/43; 7/7. masc. acc. pl. þrȳ 2/30. fem. acc. pl. þrēo. neut. acc. pl. þrēo. dat. pl. ðrim 7/6.

þrindan. st. 3. *swell*. pres. part. þrindende Lb/5.

(ge)þringan. st. 3. *crowd, press, oppress*. past 3sg. þrang. past pl. þrungon 14/164. inf. þringan 14/249. past part. geþrungen 14/287.

þrīttig. card. num. as noun. *thirty*. þrīttig, þrȳttig E/1; 2/29, 30.

þrīwa. adv. *thrice*. E/1.

þrosm. masc. *smoke, darkness*. dat. sg. þrosme 8/13.

þrōwian. wk. 2. *suffer*. past 3sg. þrōwode c/4; 10/84, 98, 145. subj. past sg. þrōwade.

þrōwung. fem. *passion*. dat. sg. þrōwunge 6/24.

þrūh. fem. athematic. *coffin*. nom. sg. 2/25. acc. sg. 2/19, 20. dat. sg. þrȳh 2/24.

geþrungen → (ge)þringan.

þrungon → (ge)þringan.

þrȳ → þrīe.

þryccan. wk. 1. *oppress, afflict*. past part. þrycced 6/28.

þrȳh → þrūh.

þrym. masc. *army, might, splendor*. nom. sg. 9/95; 14/86. gen. sg. þrymmes 14/60. dat. sg. þrymme 14/331. dat. pl. ðrymmum 14/164.

þrymfæst. adj. *glorious*. masc. nom. sg. 10/84.

þrymful. adj. *filled with glory*. fem. nom. sg. 14/74.

þrymlic. adj. *glorious*. neut. acc. pl. 14/8.

Þrȳness. fem. *Trinity*. gen. sg. Ðrȳnesse 14/86.

þrȳttig → þrīttig.

þrȳþ. fem. *might, splendor, multitude, host*. nom. pl. þrȳþe 9/99.

þū, gē. pron. 1. pers. *you, yourself*. nom. sg. þū D/1; 1/9, 11 (3x), etc. acc. sg. þē, þec 8/9; 10/95; 13/13, 24. gen. sg. þīn 13/29, 48. dat. sg. þē D/1; G/2, 3, 4, 6, etc. nom. pl. gē D/1 (2x), 2 (2x); 1/1, etc. acc. pl. ēow D/2; 7/68, 70. dat. pl. ēow, īow D/1; 1/1; 6/37; 7/38, 69, etc. nom. dual git, gyt 13/16, 17, 33, 54. gen. dual incer 13/49. dat. dual inc 13/32. 2. refl. *you*. dat. sg. þē 8/11.

geþūht → þyncan.

þūhte → þyncan.

geþungen. adj. *accomplished, senior, noble*. fem. nom. sg. 14/129. masc. gen. sg. geðungenes M/4.

þunian. wk. 2. *stand out, be prominent*. inf. Lb/2.

þunorrād. fem. *peal of thunder*. nom. pl. ðunorrāda.

þurfan. pret. pres. *have need, have occasion*. 3sg. þearf 10/117; 14/117. past pl. þorftun. subj. pl. þyrfen 14/153.

þurh. prep. (usually with acc., sometimes with dat. or gen.). *through, by, by means of, because of*. þurh, þuruh 2/2, 8, 25, 26, 27, etc.

þurhdrīfan. st. 1. *drive through*. past pl. þurhdrifan 10/46.

þurhfaran. st. 6. *pass through, penetrate, pierce*. 3sg. þurhfærð.

þurhwunian. wk. 2. *remain, persevere.* 3sg.
þurhwunað 2/8. past 3sg. þurhwunode
2/8. subj. sg. þurhwunige 7/45.

þus. adv. *thus, so.* þus, þuss 6/33 (2x);
7/1.

þūsend. card. num. as noun. *thousand.*
4/14; 7/40, 41, 42. nom. pl. þūsenda,
ðūsend, þūsendu.

þūsendmǣlum. adv. *by thousands.* 14/165.

geþwǣre. adj. *harmonious.* masc. nom. pl.
8/24.

þwēan. st. 6. *wash.* past pl. þwōgon 2/24.

þȳ. A. adv. *therefore.* ʌ/5; 5/2, 17, 51, 66,
etc.

    B. conj. *because.* þē 7/14.

þȳ → se.

þȳ lǣs. conj. *lest.* þe lǣs, þȳ lǣs 5/60.

þȳ lǣs þe. conj. *lest.* ðī lǣs ðe 1/3.

þyder → þider.

þȳfþe → þīefþ.

geþyld. neut. *patience.* dat. sg. geðylde
ᴍ/9.

geþyldelīce. adv. *patiently.* 7/53.

geþyldig. adj. *patient.* masc. nom. sg.
7/54; 9/65.

þyncan. wk. 1. *seem* to someone (dat.).
3sg. þinceð, þincð 7/38; 9/41. past 3sg.
þūhte 1/6; 6/31; 10/4. subj. sg. ðince
7/42, 66, 81, 82. subj. past sg. þūhte
7/53. inf. þincan 5/20, 47, 55; 7/66. past
part. geþūht 2/13, 16.

geþyncþ. fem. *dignity, rank.* dat. pl.
geþyncðum.

þyrel. adj. *pierced.* neut. nom. sg. ʟʌ/2.

þyrfen → þurfan.

þyrstan. wk. 1. (impersonal). *be thirsty.*
past 3sg. þyrste. pres. part. sg.
þyrstendne.

þys- → þes.

ðȳs → þes.

þȳstre → þīestre.

þȳstro → þīestru.

þȳstrum → þīestru.

ufan. adv. *from above.*

ūhtcearu. fem. *dawn-care, sorrow at dawn.*
acc. sg. ūhtceare 12/7.

ūhte. fem. *dawn.* dat. sg. ūhtan 12/35. gen.
pl. ūhtna 9/8.

ūhtsang. masc. *lauds, nocturns.* acc. sg.
ūhtsong 6/39.

unārīmedlic. adj. *innumerable.*

unāsecgendlic. adj. *inexpressible.* neut.
nom. sg. 4/7.

unc → ic, wē.

uncer. adj. *our, of us two.* masc. nom. sg.
12/25. masc. acc. sg. uncerne 11/16.
neut. acc. sg. 11/19.

unclǣne. adj. *unclean.* masc. dat. sg.
unclǣnum.

uncoþu. fem. *disease.* nom. sg. 5/19.

uncrǣft. masc. *evil practice.* dat. pl.
uncrǣftan 5/69.

undǣd. fem. *misdeed.* dat. sg. undǣde 5/53.

under. prep. (with dat. or acc.). *under.*
ꜰ/2, 4; ᴋ/1360, 1361; ʟʌ/2, etc.

underfōn. st. 7. *receive.* 2sg. underfēhst.
past pl. underfēngan, underfēngon
4/19; 5/68.

underlūtan. st. 2. *bow under.* inf. 7/68.

underniman. st. 4. *receive.* past 3sg.
undernam.

understandan. st. 6. *understand.* subj. sg.
understande 5/32, 38. imp. pl. understandað 5/4. inf. 5/43, 70.

underþēodan. wk. 1. *add, subjugate, subject.* past part. underþēoded 6/26.

undyrne. adj. *not secret, manifest.*

unearg. adj. *not cowardly.* masc. acc. sg.
uneargne.

unforht. adj. *unafraid.* masc. nom. sg.
10/110.

unforworht. adj. *innocent.* masc. nom. pl.
unforworhte 5/14.

unfracoþlīce. adv. *not ignominiously,
honourably.* 7/2.

unfriþ. masc. *strife.*

ungedafenlīce. adv. *improperly.* 7/32.

ungeendod. adj. *unending.* wk. neut. acc.
sg. ungeendode 7/41. wk. neut. gen. sg.
ungeendodan 7/39.

ungeendodlic. adj. *eternal.* wk. neut. acc.
sg. ungeendodlīce 7/43.

ungefēalīce. adv. *unhappily.* 3/17.

ungefēre. adj. *impassable.* dat. pl. ungefērum 7/25.

ungelīc. adj. *different.* neut. nom. sg. 11/3. masc. nom. pl. ungelīce 7/32. fem. nom. pl. ungelica 7/24.

ungelīce. adv. *differently.* 11/8.

ungelimp. neut. *misfortune.* gen. pl. ungelimpa 5/38.

ungemet. A. neut. *lack of moderation.* dat. sg. ungemete H/4.
B. adv. *immeasurably.* unigmet 7/66.

ungemetlic. adj. *immeasurable.* masc. gen. sg. ungemetlices 7/13.

ungemetlīce. adv. *immeasurably.* 7/21, 23, 24, 32.

ungerīm. neut. *a countless number.* nom. sg. 5/56.

ungesǣlþ. fem. *misfortune.* nom. pl. ungesǣlða 4/3.

ungetrȳwþ. fem. *treachery, disloyalty.* nom. pl. ungetrȳwþa 5/24.

ungeþyldelīce. adv. *impatiently.* 7/53.

ungewemmed. adj. (past part.). *undefiled, pure.* fem. nom. sg. 2/5, 8, 26.

ungylde. neut. *excessive tax.* nom. pl. ungylda 5/19.

unhēanlīce. adv. *not ignobly.* 3/5.

unigmet → ungemet.

unlagu. fem. *illegal act, crime.* acc. pl. unlaga 5/5, 15, 63.

unlǣd. adj. *wretched, evil.* wk. masc. gen. sg. unlǣdan 14/102.

unlond. neut. *not-land, useless land.* gen. sg. unlondes 7/22.

unlyfigende. adj. *not living.* masc. gen. sg. unlyfigendes 14/180. dat. pl. unlyfigendum 14/315.

unlȳtel. adj. *not a little.* neut. nom. sg. 5/8.

(ge)unnan. pret. pres. (with gen. object). *grant, give, allow.* pl. unnon D/1. past 3sg. ūðe 14/123, 183. past pl. ūþon 3/11. subj. sg. geunne 13/32. imp. sg. geunne 14/90.

unnyt. adj. *useless.* masc. nom. sg. unnet 7/67. masc. acc. sg. unnytne 7/65. neut. acc. sg. unnet 7/69.

unrǣd. masc. *folly, crime, treachery.* acc. pl. unrǣdas 4/3.

unriht. A. neut. *injustice, vice, sin.* acc. sg. 5/5, 67. dat. sg. unrihte F/6. nom. pl. 5/20. gen. pl. unrihta 5/4.
B. adj. *illegal, unjust, wicked, sinful.* neut. acc. sg. 5/14. masc. gen. sg. unryhtes 7/13. dat. pl. unryhtum 3/1.

unrihtlīce. adv. *wrongly, unjustly.* D/1; 5/23; 7/30.

unrihtwīs. adj. *unrighteous.* gen. pl. unrihtwīsra A/1. wk. masc. nom. pl. unrihtwīs A/4, 5, 6.

unrōt. adj. *dejected.* masc. nom. pl. unrōte 14/284.

unryhtes → unriht.

unryhtum → unriht.

unscyldig. adj. *innocent.* masc. acc. pl. unscyldige 5/27.

unsidu. masc. u-stem. *bad custom.* acc. pl. unsida 5/48.

unsōfte. adv. *ungently.* 14/228.

unstilness. fem. *lack of quiet, tumult.* acc. sg. unstilnesse 3/7.

unswǣslic. adj. *ungentle, cruel.* masc. acc. sg. unswǣslicne 14/65.

unsȳfre. adj. *unclean.* wk. masc. nom. sg. unsȳfra 14/76.

untrum. adj. *unwell, sick.* gen. pl. untrumra 6/29. masc. acc. pl. compar. untrumran 6/29.

untrumness. fem. *illness.* dat. sg. untrumnysse, untrymnesse 2/13; 6/28.

geuntrumod. adj. (past part.). *sick.* fem. nom. sg. 2/12.

untrymnesse → untrumness.

unþanc. masc. *displeasure.*

unþances. adv. *unwillingly.*

unþēaw. masc. *vice, sin.* dat. pl. unþēawum D/2; H/2.

unwæstm. masc. *failure of crops.* gen. pl. unwæstma 5/19.

unweder. neut. *bad weather* (pl. with sg. sense). nom. pl. **unwedera** 5/19.

unwemme. adj. *undefiled, pure.* fem. acc. sg. 2/6.

unwendedlic. adj. *unchangeable.* masc. nom. sg. в/3.

unweorþian. wk. 2. *dishonour.* 3sg. **unwurþað** ᴅ/3.

unwīs. adj. *unwise.* dat. pl. **unwīsum** 7/66.

unwriten. adj. *unwritten.* masc. acc. pl. 7/36.

unwurþað → unweorþian.

unwyrþe. adj. *unworthy* of something (gen.). masc. nom. pl. 7/14.

ūp. adv. *up.* в/2, 5, 7; 2/18; 7/49, etc.

ūpāstīgness. fem. *ascension.* dat. sg. **ūpāstīgnesse** 6/24.

ūphēah. adj. *high, lofty.* fem. nom. pl. **ūphēa** 12/30.

ūplic. adj. *high, lofty, supreme.* dat. pl. **ūplicum.**

uppan. prep. *upon.*

uppe. adv. *up.* 10/9.

ūre. adj. *our, ours.* neut. acc. sg. 5/69. masc. nom. pl. 5/68. masc. nom. sg. 2/31; 14/289. fem. nom. sg. 14/285. masc. acc. sg. **ūrne.** masc. gen. sg. **ūres.** fem. acc. pl. ꜰ/7. neut. acc. pl. 4/4. dat. pl. **ūrum** 2/8; 5/39.

ūre → ic, wē.

ūrigfeþere. adj. *dewy-winged.* wk. masc. nom. sg. **ūrigfeðera** 14/210.

ūrne → ūre.

urnon → irnan.

ūrum → ūre.

ūs → ic, wē.

ūt. adv. *out.* 2/15; 3/5; 5/14, 29, 43, etc.

utan → uton.

ūtan. adv. *from outside, outside.* 3/4; 7/65.

ūte. adv. *outside, without.* 5/11 (2x), 18, 39; 14/284, etc.

ūtgān. anom. verb. *go out.*

ūtgang. masc. *departure.* dat. sg. **ūtgonge** 6/24.

uton. *let us.* subj. pl. **utan, uton, wutan, wuton** ꜰ/7; 5/60, 65, 67, 68, etc.

ūðe → (ge)unnan.

ūþon → (ge)unnan.

ūþwita. masc. *philosopher.* nom. sg. 7/49, 53 (3x), 54, etc. gen. sg. **ūðwitan** 7/49.

uuiþ → wiþ.

wā. A. masc. *woe.* nom. sg. 12/52. **B.** interj. *alas.* 5/42 (2x).

wāc. adj. *weak, cowardly.* masc. nom. sg. 9/67.

wacian. wk. 2. *be awake, keep watch.* pres. part. **waciende.**

wadan. st. 6. *go, advance, travel.* past 1sg. **wōd** 9/24. inf. 9/5.

wald. masc. *forest.* dat. sg. **walde** 14/206.

waldend → wealdend.

wand → windan.

wandrian. wk. 2. *wander.* past 3sg. **wandrode.**

wanedan → (ge)wanian.

wange. neut. *cheek.*

wanhȳdig. adj. *careless, rash, reckless.* masc. nom. sg. 9/67.

(ge)wanian. wk. 2. *diminish* (transitive), *lessen, dwindle.* past pl. **wanedan** 5/13. inf. **gewanian** 5/11. past part. **gewanode** 5/15.

wann. adj. *dark.* masc. nom. sg. **won, wonn** 9/103. fem. nom. sg. 10/55. wk. masc. nom. sg. **wanna, wonna** 14/206.

gewanode → (ge)wanian.

warian. wk. 2. *beware, guard, defend, hold, possess.* 3sg. **warað** 9/32. pl. **warigeað** ᴋ/1358.

warnian. wk. 2. (sometimes with refl. pron.). *warn, take warning.* inf. 5/65.

was → bēon.

wāst → witan.

wāt → witan.

gewāt → gewītan.

waþum. masc. *wave.* gen. pl. **waþema** 9/24, 57.

wæccan. wk. 1. *watch, wake.* pres. part. **wæccende** 14/142.

wǣd. fem. *clothing.* dat. pl. **wǣdum** 10/15, 22.

gewǣd. fem. *clothing, garment.* nom. pl. **gewǣda** 2/23. dat. pl. **gewǣdum** 2/24.

wǣdbrēc. fem. athematic. (always pl.). *breeches.* acc. pl. 1/7.

wǣdla. adj. *poor.* dat. pl. **wǣdlum** 7/70.

wǣfersȳn. fem. *spectacle.* dat. sg. **wǣfersȳne** 10/31.

wægn. masc. *waggon, cart, carriage.*

wǣgon → wregan.

wæl. neut. *slaughter,* collectively *the slain.*

wælcēasega. masc. *chooser of the slain, corpse-picker.*

wælcyrie. fem. *sorceress.* nom. pl. **wælcyrian** 5/56.

wælgīfre. adj. *greedy for slaughter.* masc. nom. sg. 14/207. neut. nom. pl. **wælgīfru** 9/100. dat. pl. **wælgīfrum** 14/295.

wælhrēow. adj. *slaughter-cruel, bloodthirsty, savage.* masc. nom. pl. **wælrēowe** 11/6. fem. acc. pl. **wælhrēowe** 5/15.

wælscel. masc. *company of the slain* (?). acc. sg. 14/312.

wælsliht. masc. *slaughter.* gen. pl. **wælsleahta** 9/7, 91.

wælstōw. fem. *place of slaughter, battlefield* (*wealdan wælstōwe* = win the battle). gen. sg. **wælstōwe.**

wǣpen. neut. *weapon.* nom. pl. **wǣpen, wǣpnu** 7/7; 9/100. acc. pl. 14/290.

wǣpengewrixl. neut. *exchange of weapons, battle.* nom. sg. **wǣpngewrixl** 5/36. gen. sg. **wǣpengewrixles.**

wǣr. fem. *faith, agreement, protection.* acc. sg. **wǣre** 13/52.

wǣr- → bēon.

wǣrlīce. adv. *carefully.* 5/69.

wǣrloga. masc. *breaker of pledges, treacherous person.* acc. sg. **wǣrlogan** 14/71.

wǣs → bēon.

wæstm. masc. *fruit.* dat. sg. **wæstme** 1/2, 3, 6. acc. pl. **wæstmas** A/3.

wǣta. masc. *moisture.* dat. sg. **wǣtan** 10/22.

wæter. neut. *water.* nom. sg. F/4; 5/8. acc. sg. K/1364. gen. sg. **wæteres.** dat. sg. **wætere, wætre** F/1, 4; G/5; 12/49. nom. pl. **wæteru** F/1. acc. pl. **wæteru.** gen. pl. **wætera** A/3.

wæterǣdre. fem. *vein of water, artery of water, spring.* nom. pl. **wæterǣdran.**

wē → ic, wē.

wēa. masc. *misfortune, misery.* acc. pl. **wēan** 13/45.

wēagesīþ. masc. *companion in woe, companion in crime.* nom. pl. **wēagesīðas** 14/16.

geweald. neut. *power.* acc. sg. 10/107. dat. sg. **gewealde** 5/14, 31, 32.

(ge)wealdan. st. 7. (with gen. or dat. object). *rule, control, have, bring about.* 3sg. **gewylt** 1/16. past pl. **wēoldan, wēoldon** 5/19. inf. **gewealdan** 14/103.

wealdend. masc. nd-stem. *ruler, the Lord.* nom. sg. **waldend, wealdend** 7/70; 10/111, 155; 14/5, 61, etc. acc. sg. 10/67. gen. sg. **wealdendes** 10/17, 53. dat. sg. **wealdende** 10/121. nom. pl. **waldend** 9/78.

wealgeat. neut. *wall-gate* (i.e. city gate). dat. sg. **wealgate** 14/141.

weall. masc. *wall.* nom. sg. **weal** 9/98. acc. sg. 2/19; 14/161. gen. sg. **wealles** 14/151. dat. sg. **wealle** 9/80. nom. pl. **weallas** 9/76. acc. pl. **weallas** 14/137.

weallan. st. 7. *boil, well.* pres. part. **weallendan** 5/70.

wealsteal. masc. *wall-place, foundation?.* acc. sg. 9/88.

weard. A. masc. *guard, guardian, guardianship.* nom. sg. 6/13. acc. sg. 6/12; 10/91; 14/80. dat. sg. **wearde** 14/142.

   B. adv. (with prep. *tō* or *wið*). *towards.* 14/99.

weardian. wk. 2. *guard, occupy, inhabit.* pl. **weardiað** 12/34. inf. **weardigan** 13/18.

wearg. masc. *criminal, monster, evil spirit.*
acc. pl. **wergas** 10/31. gen. pl. **wearga**
F/2.

wearm. adj. *warm.*

wearme. adv. *warmly.*

wearð → (ge)weorþan.

gewearð → (ge)weorþan.

wēaþearf. fem. *woeful need.* dat. sg.
wēaþearfe 12/10.

(ge)weaxan. st. 7. *grow, increase.* past 1sg.
wēox 12/3. past 3sg. **wēox, gewēox** I/6;
2/12. imp. pl. **weaxað.** inf. **weaxan,**
geweaxan J/84; Lb/1.

weccan. wk. 1. *wake.* inf. **weccean.**

wedbryce. masc. *violation of an agreement.*
acc. pl. **wedbrycas** 5/49.

wedd. neut. *agreement, covenant.* acc.
sg. **wed** 5/69. gen. sg. **weddes.** nom. pl.
wed 5/34.

weder. neut. *weather.* nom. sg. 11/10.

weg. masc. *road, way.* acc. sg. A/6; 9/53;
10/88. dat. sg. **wege** A/1. gen. pl. **wega.**

wēg. masc. *wave.* acc. pl. **wēgas** 9/46.

wegan. st. 5. *carry, bring, weigh.* past pl.
wǣgon 14/325.

wegnest. neut. *journey-food.* inst. sg.
wegneste 6/38.

wel. adv. *well, indeed, fully.* **wel, well** C/12
(2x); 2/11, 13; 5/4, etc. compar. **bet**
5/6; 7/81. superl. **betst** 7/32.

wela. masc. *wealth, prosperity.* nom. sg.
9/74. acc. sg. **welan.** dat. pl. **welum**
7/70.

weldōnd. masc. *performer of good deeds,*
benefactor. dat. pl. **weldōndum.**

gewelede → gewelian.

gewelhwǣr. adv. *everywhere.* 5/11.

gewelhwelc. indef. pron. *every.* masc. dat.
sg. **gewelhwilcan, gewelhwylcan** 5/18,
39.

gewelian. wk. 2. *bind.* past part. **gewelede**
5/43.

welig. adj. *wealthy.* wk. masc. acc. sg.
welegan 7/70.

welm. masc. *boiling, burning, fervor.* dat.
sg. **welme** 6/27.

wēn. fem. *hope, expectation* (with gen.
of what is expected). nom. pl. **wēna**
11/13. dat. pl. **wēnum** 11/9; 13/29.

wēna. masc. *idea, opinion, hope, expecta-*
tion. dat. sg. **wēnan.**

wēnan. wk. 1. (with gen.). *expect, suspect,*
believe, think. 1sg. **wēne** 10/135. 2sg.
wēnstū (contracted with *þū*) 7/31.
past 3sg. **wēnde** 7/51; 14/20. past pl.
wēndon. subj. sg. **wēne** 5/16. subj. pl.
wēnen 7/81.

(ge)wendan. wk. 1. (frequently with refl.
pron.). *turn, change, go, return.* past 3sg.
wende. past pl. **wendon** 4/8. subj. sg.
gewende 1/19. inf. **wendan** 10/22.

Wendle. masc. *Wendels* (an unidentified
nation). gen. pl. **Wendla.**

wenian. wk. 2. *accustom, entertain.* past
3sg. **wenede** 9/36. inf. 9/29.

wēold- → (ge)wealdan.

wēop → wēpan.

weorc. neut. *work, labor, deed.* acc. sg.
6/12. dat. sg. **weorce** 1/17; 7/2. acc. pl.
5/69; 10/79. gen. pl. **weorca** 7/13, 47.
dat. pl. **weorcum** 2/2; 7/11.

geweorc. neut. *work, construction, fort-*
ification. nom. sg. 8/9. nom. pl. 9/87.

weorcgerēfa. masc. *overseer.* dat. pl.
weorcgerēfum.

weorcman. masc. athematic. *working man.*
acc. pl. **weorcmen** 7/4.

weorcstān. masc. *hewn stone.* gen. pl.
weorcstāna 2/18.

weorode → werian.

weorode → werod.

weorodum → werod.

weorpan. st. 3. *throw, cast.* past pl.
wurpon 14/290. imp. sg. **wurp.**

weorþ. neut. *value, price, money.* dat. sg.
weorðe 5/31, 32.

(ge)weorþan. st. 3. *become, turn, change,*
convert, happen, turn out, be (frequent
with past part. in passive constructions).
2sg. **gewyrst** 1/19. 3sg. **wyrð, weorþeð**
5/3, 16; 7/36; 9/110. past 3sg. **wearð,**
gewearð B/7; H/1; 2/2, 3, 5, etc. past pl.

wurdon, wurdun 1/7; 2/27; 14/159. subj. sg. weorþe, geweorþe 5/36 (3x). subj. past sg. wurde, gewurde 2/4; 5/40. subj. past pl. wurden 7/9. inf. weorðan 5/7; 9/64. past part. geworden 5/25, 30, 51, 63; 6/43, etc.

weorþfullic. adj. *worthy.* neut. gen. sg. weorðfullices 7/22.

weorþfullīce. adv. *worthily.* 7/11.

weorþgeorn. adj. *desirous of honour, ambitious.* wk. masc. nom. sg. weorðgeorna 7/76. masc. nom. pl. superl. weorðgeornuste 7/36.

(ge)weorþian. wk. 2. *honor, worship, exalt.* pl. weorðiað 10/81. past 3sg. geweorðode, wurðode 2/6; 10/90, 94. past pl. wurþodon. imp. pl. weorða. inf. weorþian 10/129. infl. inf. tō weorðianne. past part. geweorðad, geweorðod, geweorðode, gewurðod 2/2; 6/1; 7/70; 10/15; 14/298, etc.

weorþlīce. adv. *worthily, splendidly.* 10/17.

weorþmynt. fem. *honor, glory.* nom. sg. wurðmynt 2/31. acc. sg. weorðmynde 14/342.

weorþscipe. masc. *honour, respect.* acc. sg. 7/31. dat. sg. 5/44.

weorþung. fem. *honour, veneration, worship.* dat. sg. weorðunge 5/10.

weoruld → woruld.

weoruldhāde → woruldhād.

wēox → (ge)weaxan.

gewēox → (ge)weaxan.

wēpan. st. 7. *weep.* past 3sg. wēop 10/55. inf. 12/38.

wer. masc. *man, husband.* nom. sg. A/1; B/6; 2/30; 9/64. acc. sg. 2/8. gen. sg. weres C/3; La/1; 1/16. dat. sg. were B/5; 1/6. nom. pl. weras 2/31; 11/6; 14/71, 142, 163, etc. acc. pl. weras 4/7; 7/80. gen. pl. wera B/4. dat. pl. werum 2/1.

wergas → wearg.

werian. 1. wk. 1. *defend.* 3sg. wereð. past 3sg. werede 3/5. 2. wk. 2. *wear.* past 3sg. weorode 2/11.

wērig. adj. *weary.* neut. nom. sg. 9/15. masc. acc. sg. wērigne 9/57.

wērigferhþ. adj. *weary in spirit.* masc. nom. pl. wērigferhðe 14/290. masc. acc. pl. wērigferhðe 14/249.

wērigmōd. adj. *weary in spirit.* masc. nom. sg. 12/49.

werod. neut. *army, host, troop, multitude.* nom. sg. 14/199. dat. sg. weorode 10/152. inst. sg. weorode, werede, werode 3/4; 10/69, 124. gen. pl. weroda, weruda 10/51; 14/342. dat. pl. weorodum 8/17.

wesan. anom. verb. *be.* 2sg. wes. inf. J/83, 85; 10/110, 117; 12/42, etc.

west. adv. *west.* 7/65.

wēste. adj. *waste, uncultivated, barren, ruined.* masc. nom. sg. 9/74. neut. gen. sg. wēstes 7/19.

wēsten. neut. *wilderness, desert.* dat. sg. wēstene, wēstenne. dat. pl. wēstenum 7/25.

westeweard. adj. *west.* masc. acc. sg. westeweardne 7/16.

Westseaxe, Westseaxan. masc. *West Saxons.* gen. pl. Westseaxna 3/1.

wīc. neut. *habitation.* nom. sg. 12/32. dat. sg. wīce. acc. pl. 12/52.

wicca. masc. *witch.* nom. pl. wiccan 5/56.

wicg. neut. *horse.* dat. sg. wicge 1/7.

wīcian. wk. 2. *camp, dwell, live.* pl. wīciað. past part. gewīcode.

wīcing. masc. *viking.* dat. sg. wīcinge 5/36.

gewīcode → wīcian.

wīd. adj. *wide, long* (of time). wk. neut. dat. sg. wīdan 14/347.

wīde. adv. *widely.* 4/20; 5/3, 5, 12, 13, etc.

gewīde. adv. *far apart.* superl. gewīdost 12/13.

wīdgil. adj. *broad, extensive.* fem. nom. sg. wīdgel 7/66. fem. nom. pl. 7/65.

wīdl. masc. *filth.* dat. sg. wīdle 14/59.

wīdlāst. masc. *long journey.* dat. pl. wīdlāstum 11/9.

wīf. neut. *woman, wife.* nom. sg. J/84; M/11; 1/2, 6, 8, etc. gen. sg. **wīfes** 1/17; 3/7. dat. sg. **wīfe** 1/1, 4, 13, 15, 16, etc. nom. pl. 2/31; 14/163. acc. pl. 4/7. gen. pl. **wīfa** 10/94. dat. pl. **wīfum.**

wīfcȳþþu. fem. *company of a woman.* dat. sg. **wīfcȳþþe** 3/4.

gewīfian. wk. 2. *marry.* past 3sg. **gewīfode.**

wīfman. masc. *woman.*

gewīfode → gewīfian.

wīg. neut. *war, battle.* nom. sg. J/84; 9/80.

wiga. masc. *warrior.* nom. sg. 9/67. gen. pl. **wigena** 14/49.

wīgend. A. masc. nd-stem. *warrior.* acc. sg. **wiggend** 14/258. nom. pl. **wiggend** 14/69, 141, 312. dat. pl. **wiggendum** 14/283.

B. adj. *fighting.* gen. pl. **wīgendra.**

wiht. adv. *at all.* 14/274.

wiites → wīte.

wilddēor. neut. *wild beast, wild animal.* dat. pl. **wildēorum** 1/14.

wile → willan.

will. neut. *desire.* gen. sg. **willes.**

willa. masc. *will, purpose, desire, pleasure, consent.* nom. sg. A/2; 10/129; 13/30. acc. sg. **willan** 5/70. gen. sg. **willan** 7/63. dat. sg. **willan** 14/295. gen. pl. **wilna** 13/45. dat. pl. **willum** 7/68.

willan. anom. verb. *wish, be willing, desire, will.* 1sg. **wylle, wille** 10/1; 13/1; 14/84, 187. 2sg. **wilt, wylt** 7/16 (2x). 3sg. **wile** La/5; 2/4; 7/15, 30; 10/107, etc. pl. **willað, wyllað** 2/1; 11/2, 7. past 1sg. **wolde** 7/54, 65. past 3sg. **wolde** c/6; H/4; 2/5, 9, 11 (3x), etc. past pl. **woldon** 4/7, 21; 6/27; 7/14, 27, etc. subj. sg. **wille** K/1371; 5/29, 32; 7/41, 65, etc. subj. pl. 5/54.

negated. 1sg. **nelle, nylle.** pl. **nellað** 5/54. past 3sg. **nolde** 2/4; 3/8; 4/3, 15. past pl. **noldon** F/6; 3/11, 12.

wilnian. wk. 2. *desire* something (gen.), *seek* something (gen.) from (*tō*) some source. 3sg. **wilnað** 7/14. pl. **wilniað, wilnigað, wilnige** 7/14, 21, 23, 24, 48,

etc. past 1sg. **wilnode** 7/2, 9, 11. past 3sg. **wilnode** 7/55, 58. past pl. **wilnodon** 7/57. subj. sg. **wilnige** 7/32, 35. subj. pl. **wilnigen** 7/81.

gewilnian. wk. 2. *wish, ask.* past 3sg. **gewilnode** 2/10.

wilnung. fem. *desire* for something (gen.). nom. sg. 7/13.

wilsumness. fem. *devotion.* dat. sg. **wilsumnesse** 6/43.

wilt → willan.

Wiltūnscīr. fem. *Wiltshire.* dat. sg. **Wiltūnscīre** 4/2.

wīn. neut. *wine.* nom. sg. 4/16. dat. sg. **wīne** 14/29, 67.

Winceasterlēode. fem. *the people of Winchester.*

wincel. masc. *corner.* dat. sg. **wincle** Lb/1.

wind. masc. *wind.* nom. sg. A/4. acc. sg. 14/347. dat. sg. **winde** G/5; 9/76. gen. pl. **winda** G/2.

windan. st. 3. *wind, twist, fly in a circle, roll.* past 3sg. **wand** 14/110. past pl. **wundon.** past part. **wunden** 9/32.

windig. adj. *windy.* masc. acc. pl. **windige** K/1358.

wine. masc. *friend, lord, husband.* nom. sg. 12/49, 50; 13/39.

winedryhten. masc. *friend and lord.* acc. sg. 14/274. gen. sg. **winedryhtnes** 9/37.

winelēas. adj. *friendless.* masc. nom. sg. 9/45; 12/10.

winemǣg. masc. *dear kinsman.* gen. pl. **winemǣga** 9/7.

winetrēow. fem. *conjugal fidelity, conjugal agreement.* acc. sg. **winetrēowe** 13/52.

wīngeard. masc. *vineyard.* dat. sg. **wīngearde.**

wīngedrinc. neut. *wine-drinking.* dat. sg. **wīngedrince** 14/16.

wīnhāte. fem. *invitation to wine.* acc. sg. **wīnhātan** 14/8.

gewinn. neut. *labor, profit, strife, battle.* acc. sg. **gewin** H/4. dat. sg. **gewinne** 10/65.

winnan. st. 3. *labor, struggle, contend, suffer.* pl. **winnað** 7/21. past 1sg. **wonn** 12/5. subj. past sg. **wunne.**

gewinnan. st. 3. *win, conquer.* inf. 5/62.

wīnsæd. adj. *satiated with wine.* masc. nom. pl. **wīnsade** 14/71.

wīnsæl. neut. *wine-hall.* nom. pl. **wīnsalo** 9/78.

Wintanceaster. fem. *Winchester.* acc. sg. **Wintanceastre** 3/16.

winter. masc. u-stem. *winter, year.* gen. sg. **wintres** 9/103. gen. pl. **wintra** H/1; 3/3, 16, 18; 7/40, etc.

wintercearig. adj. *sorrowful as winter.* masc. nom. sg. 9/24.

wiotan → wita.

gewis. adj. *certain, aware.* masc. nom. sg. 6/45.

wīs. adj. *wise.* masc. nom. sg. 7/49, 51; 9/64. masc. inst. sg. **wīse** 9/88. gen. pl. **wīsra** 7/16. dat. pl. **wīsum.** wk. masc. nom. sg. **wīsa** 7/51, 54, 76. wk. masc. acc. sg. **wīsan** 7/67. wk. masc. gen. sg. **wīsan** 7/53, 71, 74. masc. nom. sg. compar. **wīsra.**

wīsdōm. masc. *wisdom.* nom. sg. 7/1, 64. acc. sg. G/1. dat. sg. **wīsdōme** 7/9, 10.

wīse. fem. *manner, way, subject matter.* nom. sg. I/10. acc. sg. **wīsan** 5/12; 6/19, 27. acc. pl. **wīsan** 5/24. dat. pl. **wīsum** 2/4.

wīslīce. adv. *wisely.* 7/15.

wisse → witan.

wist. fem. *abundance, nourishment, feast.* dat. sg. **wiste** 9/36.

wiston → witan.

wit → ic, wē.

wita. masc. *wise man, counselor,* (Roman) *senator.* nom. sg. 7/75; 9/65. gen. sg. **witan** M/4. nom. pl. **witan, wiotan** 3/1; 4/1, 12.

gewita. masc. *witness, one with knowledge of something* (gen.), *accomplice.* nom. sg. M/13; 7/63.

witan. pret. pres. *know, understand.* 1sg. **wāt** 2/13; 9/11. 2sg. **wāst** 7/2, 3, 5, 17,

28, etc. 3sg. **wāt** A/6; 1/5; 7/74; 9/29, 37, etc. pl. **witan, witon** C/2, 9; 5/8, 32, 47, etc. past 3sg. **wisse** 9/27. past pl. **wiston** 6/36; 14/207. subj. sg. **wite** K/1367. inf. J/91; 5/28; 7/16. infl. inf. **tō witanne** 5/30. pres. part. **witende** 1/5. negated. 1sg. **nāt** 7/27. 3sg. **nāt** 7/77. past 3sg. **nyste** 14/68. subj. sg. **nyte** M/11.

gewītan. st. 1. (sometimes with refl. pron.). *depart.* 3sg. **gewīteð** K/1360. pl. **gewītað** F/1. past **gewiton.** past 1sg. **gewāt** 6/8; 12/9. past 3sg. **gewāt** 2/5, 16; 9/95; 10/71; 12/6, etc. past pl. **gewiton, gewitan** F/5; 10/133; 14/290. imp. sg. **gewīt.**

wīte. neut. *punishment, perdition, torment.* acc. sg. 12/5. gen. sg. **wiites, wītes** 6/24; 7/32. dat. sg. M/5, 6, 8, 10, 12, etc. gen. pl. **wīta** 10/87. dat. pl. **wītum** A/6; 14/115.

wītega. masc. *prophet.*

wītegian. wk. 2. *prophesy, predict.* past 3sg. **wītegode** 2/12.

gewīteness. fem. *departure.* gen. sg. **gewītenesse** 6/28.

gewitloca. masc. *container of intellect, mind.* dat. sg. **gewitlocan** 7/67; 13/15; 14/69.

gewitness. fem. *knowledge* (*on gewitnesse* = with the knowledge of), *witness.* dat. sg. **gewitnesse** M/12.

witod. adj. *decreed.*

witodlīce. adv. *truly, indeed.*

gewiton → gewītan.

wiþ. A. adv. *towards, against.* 4/3.

   B. prep. (with acc., dat. or gen.). *towards, against, in exchange for, with* (of conversation or negotiation), *near.* **wiþ, uuiþ** G/6; 2/19; 3/3; 4/4, 15, etc.

wiþ þām þe. conj. *on condition that, provided that.* 4/1.

wiþertrod. neut. *the way back.* acc. sg. 14/312.

wiþstondan. st. 6. *withstand.* inf. 9/15.

wlanc → wlonc.

wlance → wlonc.

wlenco. fem. (pl. with sg. sense). *pride, splendour.* dat. pl. **wlencum** 7/70.

wlītan. st. 1. *look.* inf. 14/49.

wlitig. adj. *beautiful.* neut. nom. sg. 1/6. wk. fem. gen. sg. **wlitegan** 14/137. wk. neut. dat. sg. **wlitegan** 14/255.

wlonc. adj. *splendid, lofty, proud, arrogant.* fem. nom. sg. **wlanc, wlonc** 9/80; 14/325. neut. dat. sg. **wloncum** ɪ/7. fem. nom. pl. **wlance** 14/16.

wōd → wadan.

wōdlīce. adv. *madly.*

wōh. adj. *crooked, depraved, evil, unjust.* wk. masc. nom. sg. **wō.**

wōhdōm. masc. *wrongful judgement.* acc. pl. **wōhdōmas** 5/63.

wōhgestrēon. neut. *ill-gotten gains.* gen. pl. **wōhgestrēona** 5/63.

wōlberend. adj. *pestilential.* neut. dat. sg. **wōlbærendum** A/1.

wolcen. neut. *cloud, sky, heaven.* dat. sg. **wolcne.** gen. pl. **wolcna** 14/67. dat. pl. **wolcnum** 7/65; 10/53, 55.

wold- → willan.

wōma. masc. *noise, tumult.* nom. sg. 9/103.

womful. adj. *impure, criminal, sinful.* masc. nom. sg. **womfull** 14/77.

womm. masc. *stain, defilement, sin.* dat. sg. **womme** 14/59. dat. pl. **wommum** 10/14.

won → wann.

wonn → wann.

wonn → winnan.

wonna → wann.

wōp. masc. *weeping, lamentation.*

word. neut. *word.* acc. sg. 6/44; 8/17; 10/35; 14/82, 151, etc. gen. sg. **wordes** 5/23, 47. dat. sg. **worde** 10/111. acc. pl. 5/69; 6/11, 14, 18, 44, etc. dat. pl. **wordum** 6/14; 7/65; 10/97; 14/241.

wordbēotung. fem. *promise in words.* acc. pl. **wordbēotunga** 13/15.

geworden → (ge)weorþan.

wordlēan. neut. *reward for words.* gen. pl. **wordlēana** ɪ/9.

worht- → (ge)wyrcan.

geworht- → (ge)wyrcan.

wōrian. wk. 2. *wander, decay.* pl. **wōriað** 9/78.

worn. masc. *multitude.* acc. sg. 9/91. dat. pl. **wornum** 14/163.

woroldscame → woruldscamu.

woroldstrūderas → woruldstrūdere.

woruld. fem. *world.* nom. sg. **worold** 5/2. acc. sg. **woruld, weoruld, worulde** 7/21; 9/58, 107; 14/156. gen. sg. **worulde** 6/2; 7/21; 9/74; 10/133; 12/46, etc. dat. sg. **worulde, worolde** c/11, 12; ꜰ/6; 2/16; 4/10, etc.

woruldbūend. masc. nd-stem. *dweller in the world.* gen. pl. **woruldbūendra** 14/82.

woruldhād. masc. *secular life.* acc. sg. 6/20. dat. sg. **weoruldhāde** 6/5.

woruldlic. adj. *worldly.* dat. pl. **woruldlicum.**

woruldman. masc. athematic. *layman.* nom. pl. **woruldmen, woruldmenn** 2/28; 7/14.

woruldrīce. neut. *kingdom of the world.* dat. sg. 9/65; 12/13.

woruldscamu. fem. *worldly shame, public disgrace.* dat. sg. **woroldscame** 5/42, 43.

woruldstrūdere. masc. *robber of worldly goods.* nom. pl. **woroldstrūderas** 5/56.

woruldþing. neut. *worldly thing, worldly affair.* acc. pl. **woruldþincg** 2/9.

wōþ. fem. *noise, speech, song.*

wōþbora. masc. *orator, singer, poet.* dat. sg. **wōðboran** ɪ/9.

wrāþ. adj. *angry, hostile, terrible, grievous, cruel.* gen. pl. **wrāþra** 9/7; 10/51.

wrāþe. adv. *fiercely, cruelly.* 12/32.

wræc → (ge)wrecan.

wræcca. masc. *exile, wretch.* nom. sg. 12/10. acc. sg. **wræccan** 7/73.

wræclāst. masc. *path of exile.* nom. sg. 9/32. acc. pl. **wræclāstas** 9/5.

wræcmæcg. masc. *exile, outcast, wretch, devil.* nom. sg. **wræcmæcgas.**

wræcsīþ. masc. *journey of exile.* acc. pl. **wræcsīþas** 12/38. gen. pl. **wræcsīþa** 12/5.

wrǣtlic. adj. *ornamental, curious, wondrous.* neut. nom. sg. ʟa/1.

(ge)wrecan. st. 5. *drive, push, avenge, take revenge, tell, relate.* 1sg. **wrece** 12/1. past 3sg. **wræc** ʜ/3; 3/2. imp. sg. **gewrec** 14/92.

wreccan. wk. 1. *awaken.* past pl. **wrehton** 14/228, 243.

wreoton → wrītan.

gewrit. neut. *writing, scripture.* gen. sg. **gewrites** 6/24. nom. pl. **gewritu** 7/37.

wrītan. st. 1. *write.* past pl. **wreoton, writon** 6/23; 7/37.

wrītere. masc. *writer.* nom. pl. **wrīteras** 7/37. gen. pl. **wrītera** 7/36.

writon → wrītan.

wrīþan. st. 1. *twist, bind, torture.*

wrixendlīce. adv. *in turn.* 6/36.

wudu. masc. u-stem. *wood, forest.* nom. sg. ᴋ/1364; 10/27. gen. sg. **wuda** 12/27. dat. sg. **wuda** 11/17. dat. pl. **wudum** 7/25.

wuldor. neut. *glory.* nom. sg. 2/26, 31; 14/155, 347. acc. sg. 14/342. gen. sg. **wuldres** 10/14, 90, 97, 133; 14/59, etc. dat. sg. **wuldre** 2/16, 31; 8/7; 10/135, 143, etc.

wuldorblǣd. masc. *glorious success.* nom. sg. 14/156.

wuldorfæder. masc. *Father of glory.* gen. sg. 6/12.

wulf. masc. *wolf.* nom. sg. ꜰ/3; 9/82; 11/17; 14/206. nom. pl. **wulfas.** dat. pl. **wulfum** 14/295.

wulfhliþ. neut. *wolf-slope, wild land.* acc. pl. **wulfhleoþu** ᴋ/1358.

gewuna. masc. *custom, habit.* dat. sg. **gewunan.** dat. pl. **gewunan** 5/51.

wunade → (ge)wunian.

gewunade → (ge)wunian.

wund. fem. *wound.* nom. sg. 2/23.

wunden → windan.

wundenlocc. adj. *wavy-haired.* fem. nom. sg. 14/77, 103, 325.

gewundian. wk. 2. *wound.* past 3sg. **gewundode** 3/5. past part. **gewundad** 3/8, 15.

wundon → windan.

wundor. neut. *wonder, miracle.* nom. sg. 5/47. nom. pl. **wundra** 2/1, 5. gen. pl. **wundra** 6/12.

wundorlic. adj. *wonderful, strange.* neut. nom. sg. 2/1, 25.

wundorlīce. adv. *wonderfully, miraculously.* 2/31.

wundrian. wk. 2. *wonder, be astonished.* past 3sg. **wundrode** 6/31.

wundrum. adv. *wondrously.* 9/98; 14/8.

wundrung. fem. *wonder, spectacle.* dat. sg. **wundrunge** 2/24.

(ge)wunian. wk. 2. *live* (in a place), *dwell, remain, be accustomed.* pl. **wuniaþ** 10/135. past 3sg. **wunode, wunade, gewunade** ʙ/3; 2/1, 5, 10; 3/1, etc. past pl. **wunedon, wunodon** 2/31; 10/3, 155. inf. **wunian** c/11; 10/121, 143; 12/27; 14/119, etc. pres. part. **wunigende** 2/30.

wunne → winnan.

wunung. fem. *dwelling.* acc. sg. **wununge** c/12.

wurd- → (ge)weorþan.

gewurde → (ge)weorþan.

wurp → weorpan.

gewurpan. wk. 1. *recover.* inf. 2/16.

wurpon → weorpan.

wurðmynt → weorþmynt.

wurþod- → (ge)weorþian.

gewurþod- → (ge)weorþian.

wutan → uton.

wuton → uton.

wydewe. fem. *widow.* nom. pl. **wydewan** 5/14.

wyllað → willan.

wylle → willan.

wyllen. adj. *woollen.* neut. acc. sg. 2/11.

wylspring. masc. *spring.* nom. pl. **wylspringas.**

wylt → willan.

gewylt → (ge)wealdan.

wynlic. adj. *joyful.* neut. acc. pl. compar. **wynlicran** 12/52.

wynn. fem. *joy, pleasure.* nom. sg. **wyn** 9/36; 11/12; 12/46. gen. pl. **wynna** 12/32. dat. pl. **wynnum** 9/29; 10/15.

wynsum. adj. *pleasant, delightful, joyful.* masc. gen. sg. **wynsumes.** neut. nom. pl. **wynsumu** 6/23. wk. fem. acc. sg. **wynsuman.**

(ge)wyrcan. wk. 1. *work, make, create, build, perform, bring about.* 3sg. **wyrcð** 2/1; 5/41. pl. **gewyrcað** 5/70. past 3sg. **geworhte, worhte** C/1; G/2; 1/1; 2/23; 6/24, etc. past pl. **worhton, worhtan, geworhton** 1/7; 2/30; 5/22, 47; 10/31, etc. imp. sg. **wyrc.** inf. **wyrcan, wyrcean** 6/1, 3, 4; 7/3, 8, etc. infl. inf. **tō wyrcanne, tō wyrcenne** 7/2, 8. past part. **geworht, geworhte** 2/19, 25; 5/49; 6/1.

wyrd. fem. *event, fate, fortune, destiny.* nom. sg. 9/5, 100; 10/74. gen. sg. **wyrde.** dat. sg. **wyrde** 9/15. gen. pl. **wyrda** 9/107; 10/51.

gewyrht. fem. *deed, merit.* dat. pl. **gewyrhtum** 5/35; 8/25.

wyrm. masc. *serpent, snake, dragon, worm.* nom. pl. **wyrmas.** dat. pl. **wyrmum** 14/115.

wyrmlīc. neut. *likeness of a serpent.* dat. pl. **wyrmlīcum** 9/98.

wyrms. neut. *pus.* nom. sg. 2/15.

wyrmsele. masc. *hall of serpents* (i.e. hell). dat. sg. 14/119.

wyrsan → yfel.

wyrse → yfel.

wyrse → yfle.

wyrsian. wk. 2. *worsen.* past pl. **wyrsedan** 5/13.

gewyrst → (ge)weorþan.

wyrt. fem. *plant, herb, vegetable, root.* nom. sg. G/3 (2x). nom. pl. **wyrta.** acc. pl. **wyrta** 1/18. dat. pl. **wyrtum** K/1364.

wyrtwala. masc. *root.* dat. sg. **wyrtwalan** B/3.

wyrð → (ge)weorþan.

wyrþe. adj. *worth, valued, precious, worthy, deserving.* fem. nom. sg. 2/13. neut. nom. sg. 7/32. masc. gen. sg. **wyrðes** 6/14. masc. nom. pl. H/2; 7/79.

wȳscan. wk. 1. *wish.* 1sg. **wȳsce.** past 3sg. **wȳscte** H/3.

ȳcan → īcan.

yfel. A. neut. *evil, harm.* nom. sg. 7/13. acc. sg. 1/5; 5/5. gen. sg. **yfeles.** dat. sg. **yfele** 4/4. gen. pl. **yfela.**

B. adj. *bad, evil, wretched, sick.* masc. dat. sg. **yfelum.** dat. pl. **yfelan** 5/51, 53. wk. masc. nom. pl. **yfelan.** neut. nom. sg. compar. **wyrse** 7/80. fem. acc. pl. compar. **wyrsan** 5/65.

yfelian. wk. 2. *become worse.* inf. 5/3.

yfelness. fem. *evilness.* nom. sg. **yfelnes.**

yfle. adv. *badly.* compar. **wyrse** 5/2.

ylcan → ilca.

ylde. masc. (pl. only). *men.* gen. pl. **ælda, yldo** 9/85; 13/3. dat. pl. **yldum.**

yldestan → eald.

yldo. fem. *age.* gen. sg. **ylde** 6/5.

yldra. masc. (compar. of *eald*). *elder.* acc. pl. **yldran** D/2.

ymb. prep. (usually with acc., sometimes with dat.). *around, near, about, concerning, after.* **ymb, embe, ymbe** A/2; D/3; G/1; 2/10; 3/3, etc.

ymbclyppan. wk. 1. *embrace.* past 3sg. **ymbclypte** 10/42.

ymbescīnan. st. 1. *shine about.* past 3sg. **ymbescān.**

ymbesittan. st. 5. *sit around, surround, besiege.* past pl. **ymbsǣton** 4/5.

ymbeþencan. wk. 1. *consider, ponder.* subj. past sg. **ymbeþōhte** 7/65.

ymbhwyrft. masc. *circle, extent.* acc. sg. 7/16.

ymbsǣton → ymbesittan.

ymbsēon. st. 5. *look about.* subj. past sg. **ymbsāwe** 7/65.

ymbsprǣce. adj. *spoken of.* masc. nom. pl. 7/80.

ymbstandan. st. 6. *stand around.* past pl. **ymbstōdan.**

ymbūtan. prep. *about, around.* 7/65.

ȳr. noun. *back* (?). dat. sg. **ȳre** 4/18.

yrfenuma. masc. *heir.*

yrfeweardness. fem. *inheritance.* nom. sg. **yrfweardnyss.**

geyrgan. wk. 1. *intimidate.* past part. **geyrigde** 5/39.

yrgþo. fem. *cowardice.* acc. sg. **yrhðe** 5/63.

geyrigde → geyrgan.

yrmþu. fem. *misery, poverty, crime.* nom. sg. **yrmð** 5/32. acc. sg. **yrmðe, ermðe** 4/10; 5/30. dat. sg. **yrmðe** 5/42. acc. pl.

yrmða, iermða 1/16; 5/7. gen. pl. **yrmþa** 12/3.

yrre. A. neut. *anger.* nom. sg. G/7; 5/34. acc. sg. 5/16, 35, 38, 39, 41, etc. dat. sg. 5/46.

   B. adj. *angry.* masc. nom. pl. 14/225.

ys → bēon.

ȳtmæst. adj. *uttermost, last.* wk. masc. nom. pl. **ȳtmestan** 7/70. wk. neut. acc. pl. superl. **ȳtmæstan** 6/44.

ytst → (ge)etan.

ȳþ. fem. *wave.* gen. pl. **ȳþa** 12/7; 13/42.

ȳþan. wk. 1. *lay waste, devastate.* past 3sg. **ȳþde** 9/85.

References

[1]   Alexander, J. J. G. *Insular Manuscripts, 6th to the 9th Century*. Volume 1 of Survey of Manuscripts Illuminated in the British Isles. London: Harvey Miller, 1978.

[2]   Alexander, Michael. *Old English Literature*. History of Literature Series. New York: Schocken Books, 1983.

[3]   Assmann, Bruno, editor. *Angelsächsische Homilien und Heiligenleben*. Reprint with supplementary introduction by Peter Clemoes. Volume 3 of Bibliothek der angelsächsischen Prosa. Darmstadt: Wissenschaftliche Buchgesellschaft, 1964.

[4]   Baker, Peter S., editor. *The Beowulf Reader*. First published in 1995 as *Beowulf: Basic Readings*. Volume 1 of Basic Readings in Anglo-Saxon England. New York: Garland Press, 2000.

[5]   Baker, Peter S. and Michael Lapidge, editors. *Byrhtferth's Enchiridion*. Volume 15 of Early English Text Society, Supplementary Series. Oxford: Oxford University Press, 1995.

[6]   Bately, Janet, editor. *The Old English Orosius*. Volume 6 of Early English Text Society, Supplementary Series. London: Oxford University Press, 1980.

[7]   Bately, Janet, editor. *The Anglo-Saxon Chronicle: A Collaborative Edition. Vol. 3, MS A*. Cambridge: D. S. Brewer, 1986.

[8]   Bessinger, Jess B. *A Concordance to the Anglo-Saxon Poetic Records*. Programmed by Philip H. Smith, Jr. The Cornell Concordances. Ithaca, NY: Cornell University Press, 1978.

[9]   Bethurum, Dorothy, editor. *The Homilies of Wulfstan*. Oxford: Clarendon Press, 1957.

[10] Bjork, Robert E., editor. *Cynewulf: Basic Readings*. Volume 4 of Basic Readings in Anglo-Saxon England. New York: Garland Press, 1996.

[11] Bjork, Robert E. and John D. Niles, editors. *A Beowulf Handbook*. Exeter: University of Exeter Press, 1997.

[12] Bliss, A. J. *The Metre of Beowulf*. 2nd edition. Oxford: Blackwell, 1967.

[13] Bosworth, Joseph, T. Northcote Toller, and Alistair Campbell. *An Anglo-Saxon Dictionary*. Vol. 2: Supplement by T. N. Toller; Vol. 3: Enlarged Addenda and Corrigenda by A. Campell to the Supplement by T. N. Toller. Oxford: Oxford University Press, 1882–98, 1908–21, 1972.

[14] Bradley, S. A. J. *Anglo-Saxon Poetry*. Everyman's Library. London: Dent, 1982.

[15] Bright, James W. and Robert L. Ramsay, editors. *Liber Psalmorum: The West-Saxon Psalms, Being the Prose Portion, or the 'First Fifty', of the so-called Paris Psalter*. D. C. Heath, 1907.

[16] Brunner, Karl. *Altenglische Grammatik nach der angelsächsischen Grammatik von Eduard Sievers*. 3rd edition. Tübingen: Max Niemeyer Verlag, 1964.

[17] Cable, Thomas. *The English Alliterative Tradition*. Middle Ages Series. Philadelphia: University of Pennsylvania Press, 1991.

[18] Calder, Daniel G. and Michael J. Allen, editors. *Sources and Analogues of Old English Poetry: The Major Latin Texts in Translation*. Cambridge: D. S. Brewer, 1976.

[19] Calder, Daniel G. et al., editors. *Sources and Analogues of Old English Poetry II: The Major Germanic and Celtic Texts in Translation*. Cambridge: D. S. Brewer, 1983.

[20] Cameron, Angus, Ashley Crandell Amos, Sharon Butler, Christine Franzen, Antonette diPaolo Healey, Joan Holland, Ian McDougall, David McDougall, Nancy Porter, Nancy Speirs, and Pauline Thompson. *Dictionary of Old English*. Not yet complete. Toronto: Pontifical Institute of Medieval Studies, from 1986.

[21] Cameron, Angus, Allison Kingsmill, and Ashley Crandell Amos. *Old English Word Studies: A Preliminary Author and Word Index*. Volume 8 of Toronto Old English Series. Toronto: University of Toronto Press, 1983.

[22] Campbell, A. *Old English Grammar*. Oxford: Clarendon Press, 1959.

[23] Campbell, Jackson J., editor. *The Advent Lyrics of the Exeter Book*. Princeton, NJ: Princeton University Press, 1959.

[24] Campbell, James, Eric John, and Patrick Wormald. *The Anglo-Saxons*. Oxford: Phaidon, 1982.

[25] Chambers, R. W., Max Förster, and Robin Flower, editors. *The Exeter Book of Old English Poetry*. London: P. Lund, 1933.

[26] Clark Hall, John R. *A Concise Anglo-Saxon Dictionary*. With a supplement by Herbert D. Meritt. 4th edition. Cambridge: Cambridge University Press, 1960.

[27] Crawford, Samuel J., editor. *The Old English Version of the Heptateuch, Ælfric's Treatise on the Old and New Testament, and His Preface to Genesis*. Reprint of 1922 edn. with additional material by N. R. Ker. Volume 160 of Early English Text Society. London: Oxford University Press, 1969.

[28] Cross, James E. and Thomas D. Hill, editors. *The Prose Solomon and Saturn and Adrian and Ritheus*. Volume 1 of McMaster Old English Texts and Studies. Toronto: University of Toronto Press, 1982.

[29] Colgrave, Bertram, editor. *The Life of Bishop Wilfrid by Eddius Stephanus*. Cambridge: Cambridge University Press, 1927.

[30] Dodwell, D. R. and P. A. M. Clemoes, editors. *The Old English Illustrated Hexateuch*. Volume 18 of Early English Manuscripts in Facsimile. Copenhagen: Rosenkilde and Bagger, 1974.

[31] Donoghue, Daniel. *Style in Old English Poetry: The Test of the Auxiliary*. Volume 196 of Yale Studies in English. New Haven, CT: Yale University Press, 1987.

[32] Dunning, T. P. and A. J. Bliss, editors. *The Wanderer*. New York: Appleton-Century-Crofts, 1969.

[33] Fell, Christine E. *Women in Anglo-Saxon England*. London: British Museum Publications, 1984.

[34] Flower, Robin and Hugh Smith, editors. *The Parker Chronicle and Laws*. Volume 208 of Early English Text Society. London: Oxford University Press, 1941.

[35] Fulk, R. D., editor. *Interpretations of Beowulf: A Critical Anthology*. Bloomington: Indiana University Press, 1991.

[36] Fulk, R. D. *A History of Old English Meter*. Middle Ages Series. Philadelphia: University of Pennsylvania Press, 1992.

[37] Garmonsway, G. N. and Jacqueline Simpson, editors. *Beowulf and Its Analogues*. London: Dent, 1969.

[38] Godden, Malcolm and Michael Lapidge, editors. *The Cambridge Companion to Old English Literature*. Cambridge: Cambridge University Press, 1991.

[39] Gollancz, Israel, editor. *The Cædmon Manuscript of Anglo-Saxon Biblical Poetry*. Oxford: Oxford University Press, 1927.

[40] Gordon, R. K. *Anglo-Saxon Poetry*. Everyman's Library. London: Dent, 1954.

[41] Greenfield, Stanley B. and Daniel G. Calder. *A New Critical History of Old English Literature*. Includes a survey of the Anglo-Latin background by Michael Lapidge. New York: New York University Press, 1986.

[42] Greenfield, Stanley B. and Fred C. Robinson. *A Bibliography of Publications on Old English Literature to the End of 1972*. Toronto: University of Toronto Press, 1980.

[43] Griffith, Mark, editor. *Judith*. Exeter Medieval English Texts and Studies. Exeter: University of Exeter Press, 1997.

[44] Griffiths, Bill, editor. *Alfred's Metres of Boethius*. 2nd edition. Pinner, Middlesex: Anglo-Saxon Books, 1994.

[45] Hasenfratz, Robert J. *Beowulf Scholarship: An Annotated Bibliography, 1979–1990*. Volume 14 of Garland medieval bibliographies. New York: Garland Press, 1993.

[46] Healey, Antonette diPaolo and Richard L. Venezky. *A Microfiche Concordance to Old English*. Toronto: Dictionary of Old English Project, 1980.

[47] Hecht, Hans, editor. *Bischof Wærferths von Worcester Übersetzung der Dialoge Gregors des grossen*. 2nd edition. Volume 5 of Bibliothek der angelsächsischen Prosa. Darmstadt: Wissenschaftliche Buchgesellschaft, 1965.

[48] Henel, Heinrich, editor. *Aelfric's De Temporibus Anric*. Volume 2 of Early English Text Society. London: Oxford University Press, 1942.

[49] Hogg, Richard M. *A Grammar of Old English*. Oxford: Blackwell, 1992.

[50] Holthausen, F. *Altenglisches etymologisches Wörterbuch*. 2nd edition. Heidelberg: Carl Winter, 1963.

[51] Hunter Blair, Peter. *An Introduction to Anglo-Saxon England*. 2nd edition. Cambridge: Cambridge University Press, 1977.

[52]   Karkov, Catherine E., editor. *The Archaeology of Anglo-Saxon England: Basic Readings*. Volume 7 of Basic Readings in Anglo-Saxon England. New York: Garland Press, 1999.

[53]   Ker, N. R. *Catalogue of Manuscripts Containing Anglo-Saxon*. Oxford: Clarendon Press, 1957. See also Ker 1976.

[54]   Ker, N. R. 'Supplement to *"Catalogue of Manuscripts Containing Anglo-Saxon."*' *Anglo-Saxon England* 5 (1976): 121–31.

[55]   Keynes, Simon. *Anglo-Saxon History: A Select Bibliography*. A more current version is on line at http://www.wmich.edu/medieval/rawl/keynes1/home.htm. Volume 13 of Old English Newsletter Subsidia. Binghamton, NY: Center for Medieval and Early Renaissance Studies, 1987.

[56]   Kiernan, Kevin S., editor. *The Electronic Beowulf*. Ann Arbor: University of Michigan Press, 2000.

[57]   Klaeber, F., editor. *Beowulf and the Fight at Finnsburg*. Includes two supplements. 3rd edition. Boston, MA: D. C. Heath, 1950.

[58]   Klinck, Anne L., editor. *The Old English Elegies: A Critical Edition and Genre Study*. Montreal: McGill-Queen's University Press, 1992.

[59]   Kluge, F. 'Fragment eines angelsächsischen Briefes.' *Englische Studien* 8 (1885): 62–3.

[60]   Krapp, George Philip and Elliott Van Kirk Dobbie, editors. *The Anglo-Saxon Poetic Records*. New York: Columbia University Press, 1931–53.

[61]   Lapidge, Michael, John Blair, Simon Keynes, and Donald Scragg, editors. *The Blackwell Encyclopaedia of Anglo-Saxon England*. Oxford: Blackwell, 1999.

[62]   Lapidge, Michael and Michael Herren. *Aldhelm: The Prose Works*. Ipswich: D. S. Brewer, 1979.

[63]   Lapidge, Michael and James L. Rosier. *Aldhelm: The Poetic Works*. Cambridge: D. S. Brewer, 1985.

[64]   Lass, Roger. *Old English: A Historical Linguistic Companion*. Cambridge: Cambridge University Press, 1994.

[65]   Leslie, R. F., editor. *Three Old English Elegies*. 2nd edition. Exeter Medieval English Texts and Studies. Exeter: University of Exeter Press, 1988.

[66]   Magoun, Francis P. 'The Oral-Formulaic Character of Anglo-Saxon Narrative Poetry.' *Speculum* 28 (1953): 446–67.

[67]   Miller, Thomas, editor. *The Old English Version of Bede's Ecclesiastical History of the English People*. Volumes 95, 96, 110, 111 of Early English Text Society. London: Oxford University Press, 1890–8.

[68]   Mitchell, Bruce. *Old English Syntax*. Oxford: Clarendon Press, 1985.

[69]   Mitchell, Bruce and Fred C. Robinson. *A Guide to Old English*. 5th edition. Oxford: Blackwell, 1992.

[70]   Mitchell, Bruce and Fred C. Robinson, editors. *Beowulf: An Edition with Relevant Shorter Texts*. Includes 'Archaeology and *Beowulf*' by Leslie Webster. Oxford: Blackwell, 1998.

[71]   Morrell, Minnie Cate. *A Manual of Old English Biblical Materials*. Knoxville: University of Tennessee Press, 1965.

[72]   Morris, R., editor. *The Blickling Homilies*. First published 1874–80. Volumes 58, 63, 73 of Early English Text Society. London: Oxford University Press, 1967.

[73] Muir, Bernard J., editor. *The Exeter Anthology of Old English Poetry*. Exeter Medieval English Texts and Studies. Exeter: University of Exeter Press, 1994.

[74] O'Keeffe, Katherine O'Brien, editor. *Old English Shorter Poems: Basic Readings*. Volume 3 of Basic Readings in Anglo-Saxon England. New York: Garland Press, 1994.

[75] O'Keeffe, Katherine O'Brien, editor. *Reading Old English Texts*. Cambridge: Cambridge University Press, 1997.

[76] O'Keeffe, Katherine O'Brien, editor. *The Anglo-Saxon Chronicle: A Collaborative Edition. Vol. 5, MS C*. Cambridge: D. S. Brewer, 2001.

[77] Pelteret, David A. E. *Slavery in Early Medieval England*. Volume 7 of Studies in Anglo-Saxon History. Woodbridge, Suffolk: Boydell Press, 1995.

[78] Pope, John C. and R. D. Fulk, editors. *Eight Old English Poems*. 3rd edition. New York: W. W. Norton, 2000.

[79] Pulsiano, Phillip, A. N. Doane, and Ronald Buckalew, editors. *Anglo-Saxon Manuscripts in Microfiche Facsimile*. In progress. Tempe, AZ: Medieval and Renaissance Texts and Studies, from 1994.

[80] Richards, Mary P., editor. *Anglo-Saxon Manuscripts: Basic Readings*. Volume 2 of Basic Readings in Anglo-Saxon England. New York: Garland Press, 1994.

[81] Robinson, Orrin W. *Old English and Its Closest Relatives: A Survey of the Earliest Germanic Languages*. Stanford, CA: Stanford University Press, 1992.

[82] Russom, Geoffrey. *Old English Meter and Linguistic Theory*. Cambridge: Cambridge University Press, 1987.

[83] Sedgefield, Walter John, editor. *King Alfred's Old English Version of Boethius De Consolatione Philosophiae*. Oxford: Clarendon Press, 1899.

[84] Sherley-Price, Leo. *Bede: Ecclesiastical History of the English People*. Revised edition. London: Penguin Books, 1990.

[85] Short, Douglas D. *Beowulf Scholarship: An Annotated Bibliography*. Volume 193 of Garland reference library of the humanities. New York: Garland Press, 1980.

[86] Skeat, Walter W., editor. *Ælfric's Lives of Saints*. Volumes 76, 82, 94, 114 of Early English Text Society. London: Oxford University Press, 1881–1900.

[87] Stenton, F. M. *Anglo-Saxon England*. 3rd edition. Volume 2 of the Oxford History of England. Oxford: Clarendon Press, 1971.

[88] Swanton, Michael, editor. *The Dream of the Rood*. 2nd edition. Exeter Medieval English Texts and Studies. Exeter: University of Exeter Press, 1987.

[89] Swanton, Michael. *Anglo-Saxon Prose*. 2nd edition. London: Dent, 1993.

[90] Temple, E. *Anglo-Saxon Manuscripts, 900–1066*. Volume 2 of Survey of Manuscripts Illuminated in the British Isles. London: Harvey Miller, 1976.

[91] Whitelock, Dorothy, editor. *Sermo Lupi ad Anglos*. 3rd edition. Methuen's Old English Texts. London: Methuen, 1963.

[92] Whitelock, Dorothy, editor. *Sweet's Anglo-Saxon Reader in Prose and Verse*. 15th edition. Oxford: Oxford University Press, 1975.

[93] Williamson, Craig, editor. *The Old English Riddles of the Exeter Book*. Chapel Hill: University of North Carolina Press, 1977.

[94] Wilson, David M., editor. *The Archaeology of Anglo-Saxon England*. Cambridge: Cambridge University Press, 1981.

[95] Wilson, David M. *Anglo-Saxon Art from the Seventh Century to the Norman Conquest*. Woodstock, NY: Overlook Press, 1984.

[96] Zupitza, Julius and Norman Davis, editors. *Beowulf. Reproduced in Facsimile from the Unique Manuscript, British Museum Ms. Cotton Vitellius A. XV.* 2nd edition. Volume 245 of Early English Text Society. London: Oxford University Press, 1967.

Further Reading

1 General works

For a well-illustrated general account of the Anglo-Saxons, consult Campbell, John and Wormald [24]. If you have a specific query, consult Lapidge et al. [61], which is also good for browsing.

2 Grammars

Several scholarly grammars will give you far more information about Old English than this book does. Campbell [22] is the standard grammar for English speakers; although a bit dated, it is still a mine of information, especially on the pre-history of the language. For those who know German, Brunner [16] is also invaluable, especially for its information on Old English dialects. A more recent grammar than either of these, Hogg [49] is informed by recent linguistic theory; only vol. 1 (Phonology) has appeared so far. For Old English syntax, the standard reference is Mitchell [68].

Lass [64] is a well-written tour of the history of Old English for students who know at least a little about linguistics. For a survey of the other Germanic languages, see Robinson [81].

3 Dictionaries and concordances

The standard dictionary of Old English is Bosworth, Toller and Campbell [13]. Its quality is uneven, largely because Bosworth, who was responsible for the letters A–G, was not quite up to the job of compiling an Old English dictionary. However, Toller was an excellent lexicographer, and if one remembers always to check his *Supplement* for words beginning A–G, the dictionary is still quite serviceable (Campbell's contribution is a thin supplement published about fifty years afer the dictionary was complete). This venerable dictionary is being superseded by Cameron et al. [20], now complete through E; it has so far been issued on microfiche, but will soon be issued on CD-ROM instead. Clark Hall [26] is an excellent compact dictionary for students. The standard etymological dictionary is Holthausen [50].

The entire corpus of Old English was concorded by the Dictionary of Old English Project at the University of Toronto; the result is Healey and Venezky [46], published on microfiche. Those whose libraries subscribe to the Old English Corpus on-line (for information, see http://www.press.umich.edu/), however, should generally prefer that as a much more flexible tool for researching the language. If you want a concordance of the poetry only, consult Bessinger [8].

4   Bibliographies

Greenfield and Robinson [42] is a comprehensive bibliography of publications on Old English literature up to 1972. For annotated bibliographies of *Beowulf* scholarship, see Short [85] and Hasenfratz [45]. For a bibliography of Anglo-Saxon history, see Keynes [55]. The home page of the Richard Rawlinson Center for Anglo-Saxon Studies and Manuscript Research (http://www.wmich.edu/medieval/rawl/index.html) has several useful bibliographies, including an on-line version of Keynes and 'A Bibliography of *The Battle of Maldon*' by Wendy E. J. Collier.

Comprehensive annual bibliographies are published in two journals, *Old English Newsletter* and *Anglo-Saxon England*. The poetry section of the bibliography in *Old English Newsletter* is classified by work and therefore very useful for literary research.

5   Old English texts and translations

Several published collections contain texts for students of Old English. Especially good ones are Mitchell and Robinson [69], Whitelock [91] and Pope and Fulk [78]. Methuen's Old English Library, which published student-oriented editions of prose and poetry, has been discontinued, but its editions have been reissued (with additional bibliography) in the series Exeter Medieval English Texts, which has also published several Old English editions of its own. Mitchell and Robinson [70] is a good edition of *Beowulf* for students. *Old English Aerobics* includes a growing collection of on-line texts of Old English prose and poetry with complete glossaries and full grammatical information about each word and clause.

To locate scholarly editions of Old English texts, see Greenfield and Robinson [42]. For editions published after 1972, consult the annual bibliographies listed under Bibliographies, above. The standard edition of almost all the Old English poetry is Krapp and Dobbie [60]. For the poems of the Exeter Book, see also Muir [73], and for *Beowulf* see Klaeber [57] (the standard scholarly edition, now showing its age).

Several series have published significant numbers of Old English texts. The Early English Text Society has been publishing Old English and Middle English texts since

1864; most Old English editions published up to around 1900 are accompanied by translations. A German series, Bibliothek der angelsächsischen Prosa, published editions of Old English prose in the late nineteenth and early twentieth centuries; several of these are still useful.

In addition to the translations included with some of the editions mentioned above, the student should know of two important collections, Bradley [14] for poetry (supersedes Gordon [40], which is nevertheless still useful) and Swanton [89] for prose.

6   Literary criticism; sources and analogues; metre

To get started reading about Old English literature, you may wish to begin with a general work such as Greenfield and Calder [41] or Alexander [2]. Godden and Lapidge [38] and O'Keeffe [75] are collections of essays usefully broken down by topic. All of these books contain bibliographies.

The series Basic Readings in Anglo-Saxon England collects useful essays on individual topics, authors and works: see Baker [4], O'Keeffe [74], Bjork [10]. Fulk [35] is a good collection of criticism on *Beowulf*, and Bjork and Niles [11] surveys the history of *Beowulf* scholarship.

Sources and analogues of Old English poetry have been conveniently collected in Calder and Allen [18] and Calder et al. [19]; for analogues of *Beowulf*, see Garmonsway and Simpson [37].

If you are interested in reading about metre, consult these books: Bliss [12], Russom [82], Cable [17] and Fulk [36].

7   History and culture

Readers interested in Anglo-Saxon history should consult Keynes [55]. Here we list a few works of general interest. The standard history of Anglo-Saxon England (if there is such a thing) is Stenton [87]. Two good general introductions to the history and culture are Hunter Blair [51] and Campbell, John and Wormald [24]. See Fell [33] for an account of women in Anglo-Saxon England.

8   Manuscripts, art and archeology

The indispensable guide to the manuscripts containing Old English is Ker [53]; see also Ker [54], the supplement to his *Catalogue*. For a survey of illuminated manuscripts, see Alexander [1] and Temple [90], and for a collection of useful essays, Richards [80].

The series Early English Manuscripts in Facsimile has published twenty-six volumes of high-quality facsimiles of Anglo-Saxon manuscripts. Pulsiano, Doane and Buckalew [79] aims to produce descriptions and microfiche facsimiles of all manuscripts containing Old English. Important facsimiles of individual manuscripts and works include Zupitza and Davis [96] for *Beowulf*, Chambers, Förster and Flower [25] for the

Exeter Book, Gollancz [39] for the Junius Manuscript and Flower and Smith [34] for the oldest manuscript of the *Anglo-Saxon Chronicle*.

A good (and copiously illustrated) introduction to the art of Anglo-Saxon England is Wilson [95]. For the archeology, see Wilson [94], and the essays in Karkov [52].

Kiernan [56] is especially notable as a pioneering electronic edition and facsimile containing not only the *Beowulf* manuscript, but also the 'Thorkelin Transcripts' of *Beowulf*, from which editors restore damaged passages in that poem, and the collations of early nineteenth-century scholars.

9   On-line aids

For World Wide Web browsing, you should add several pages to your list of bookmarks:

www.georgetown.edu/cball/oe/old_english.html Cathy Ball's 'Old English Pages' offers a wide-ranging collection of links to Anglo-Saxon sites.

info.ox.ac.uk/departments/humanities/toebi/www.html 'Teachers of Old English in Britain and Ireland' is similar, and may load faster for European users.

www.trin.cam.ac.uk/sdk13/sdk13home.html Simon Keynes's homepage contains a comprehensive collection of links for historians.

www.ucalgary.ca/UofC/eduweb/engl401/ Murray McGillivray of the University of Calgary offers an on-line course in Old English; the site for the course contains a good bit of publicly available material.

www.georgetown.edu/cball/hwaet/hwaet_toc.html Cathy Ball's 'Hwæt' is a basic vocabulary drill.

labyrinth.georgetown.edu/ 'The Labyrinth' is a collection of links and materials for medievalists; it offers a good collection of Old English electronic texts.

www.wmich.edu/medieval/rawl/index.html The Richard Rawlinson Center for Anglo-Saxon Studies and Manuscript Research at Western Michigan University has published several original on-line editions of Old English texts on its site and is the home of or has links to a number of other scholarly projects.

Index

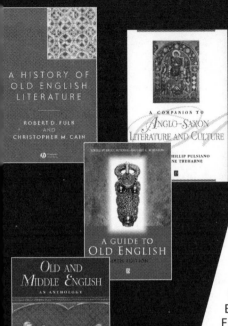